Jesse Liberty
David B. Horvath, CCP

816 3036
Parllev

SAMS
Teach Yourself
C++ for Linux
in 21 Days

SAMS

A Division of Macmillan USA
201 West 103rd St., Indianapolis, Indiana, 46290

Sams Teach Yourself C++ for Linux in 21 Days

Copyright © 2000 by Sams Publishing

International Standard Book Number: 0-672-31895-4

Library of Congress Catalog Card Number: 99-068205

Printed in the United States of America

First Printing: April, 2000

03   02   01   00   4   3   2   1

Trademarks

Warning and Disclaimer

ASSOCIATE PUBLISHER
Michael Stephens

ACQUISITIONS EDITOR
Carol Ackerman

DEVELOPMENT EDITOR
Robyn Thomas

MANAGING EDITOR
Charlotte Clapp

PROJECT EDITOR
Christina Smith

COPY EDITOR
Margaret Berson

INDEXER
Eric Schroeder

PROOFREADER
Candice Hightower

TECHNICAL EDITORS
Javad Abdollahi
Sean Coughlin
Rory Bray

TEAM COORDINATOR
Pamalee Nelson

MEDIA DEVELOPER
Jason Haines

INTERIOR DESIGNER
Gary Adair

COVER DESIGNER
Aren Howell

COPYWRITER
Eric Borgert

PRODUCTION
Brandon Allen
Cheryl Lynch

Contents at a Glance

Contents

About the Authors

Lead Authors

Jesse Liberty is the author of *C++ From Scratch*, as well as a dozen other books on C++ and Web applications development and object-oriented programming. Jesse is the president of Liberty Associates, Inc., where he provides custom programming, training, mentoring, and consulting. He is a former Vice President of electronic delivery for Citibank and a Distinguished Software Engineer at AT&T. Jesse also serves as the series editor of Que's *Programming From Scratch* books. He supports his books at `http://www.LibertyAssociates.com`.

David B. Horvath, CCP, is a Senior Consultant in the Philadelphia Pennsylvania area. He has been a consultant for over 14 years and is also a part-time Adjunct Professor at local colleges teaching topics that include C/C++ Programming, UNIX, and Database Techniques. He has an M.S. degree in Organizational Dynamics from the University of Pennsylvania (and is taking more classes as this book is being published). He has provided seminars and workshops to professional societies and corporations on an international basis.

David is the author of *UNIX for the Mainframer* (Prentice-Hall/PTR), contributing author to *UNIX Unleashed* Second Edition (with cover credit), *Red Hat Linux* Second Edition, *Using UNIX* Second Edition (Que), *UNIX Unleashed* Third Edition, *Learn Shell Programming in 24 Hours*, *Red Hat Linux 6 Unleashed*, *Linux Unleashed* Fourth Edition, and has written numerous magazine articles.

When not at the keyboard, he can be found working in the garden, soaking in the hot tub, or engaging in various activities that upset people. He has been married for over 12 years to his wife and has several dogs and cats (the number of which seems to keep going up).

David can be reached at `cpplinux@cobs.com` for questions related to this book, and his Web page is `http://www.cobs.com/`. No spam please!

Contributing Authors

Paul Cevoli is a software engineer living in Boston, MA, where he has been a software engineer for the past 11 years. He specializes in system software, device drivers, and operating system internals. Paul is currently employed in the system software group of an internet appliance company in the metro Boston area.

Jonathan Parry-McCulloch is a technical consultant for a major financial institution in the city of London, where he provides cryptographic expertise for automated trading systems for trading financial futures. He also writes cross-platform C++ GUI applications, largely for fun, and is a confirmed Linux freak. He has a First Class degree in Electronic Engineering and is pleased that it bears no relevance to his job.

You can reach Jonathan at jm@antipope.org, if you have questions about his portions of this book, or anything else that crosses your mind. One word of warning: he really hates spammers. So don't do it.

Hal Moroff has been designing embedded systems for 20 years. From the East Coast originally, he worked for several years in Europe and Japan, and is now programming full-time in California's Silicon Valley. He writes a regular column in *Linux Magazine*, and reads the source whenever he can.

Dedication

This book is dedicated to the living memory of David Levine.

—Jesse

I would like to dedicate this book to all the good teachers I have had through the years. Those that taught that questions are not stupid, even if they may seem to be simple; that there is more to learn than exactly what is written in the book; that the best way to learn anything that requires thinking is to try it—what some people call playing is often learning. Those teachers already know who they are!

I also want to dedicate this book to my students. They've asked some amazing questions. I thought I knew computing and programming before I started teaching; in having to answer their questions, they've forced me to learn even more about my topics!

—David

Acknowledgments

I would like to thank and acknowledge the many people who made this and the previous editions of this book possible. First among them are Stacey, Robin, and Rachel Liberty. I must also thank the editors at SAMS, including Carol Ackerman, Tracy Dunkelberger, Holly Allender, Sean Dixon, Chris Denny, Brad Jones, Robyn Thomas, Christina Smith, and Margaret Berson.

Many readers contributed suggestions and improvements to this book and I thank you all. Finally, and again, I thank Mrs. Kalish, who taught my sixth-grade class how to do binary arithmetic in 1965, when neither she nor we knew why.

—Jesse

I want to acknowledge all the good folks at Sams (Macmillan Computer Publishing) who helped this book along its path. Carol Ackerman (Acquisitions Editor) came to me with the idea of writing this book, Christina Smith was the Project Editor riding herd over the editing process, Margaret Berson performed the copy edit (checking grammar, syntax, clarity, and so on), Robyn Thomas was the development editor (content and structure), and Javad Abdollahi and Sean Coughlin performed most of the technical edit along with Rory Bray. Without them, this book would not be nearly as good as it is now.

I absolutely must thank my co-author, Jesse Liberty. When Carol and I were first discussing this project, I asked for a sample of a *Sams Teach Yourself in 21 Days* book. She sent me a copy of *Sams Teach Yourself C in 21 Days*. After reviewing the book, I commented to Carol that this book would be much easier if there already existed a C++ book similar to the C book. It turned out that there already was—Jesse's. So creating this book was much easier because of the base C++ information already written. After all, there are just so many ways to explain a `while` loop or polymorphism.

The contributing authors, Hal, Paul, and Jon have been a huge help covering some of the very specific Linux topics that go well beyond the C++ language itself. Deserving special attention is Jon Parry-McCulloch, who took on the GUI chapter on short notice and had to contend with the time zone differences (he lives in England). Jon is a fellow contributor to the Cult of Father Darwin Internet email discussion group (which discusses the manifestation of Darwinian theories in the daily actions and mistakes of various people). I'm not going to tell you how to find the group because we try to keep the Signal-to-Noise ratio high (if you're interested, you'll have to find it yourself). I had the chance to meet Jon and another group member when I was attending a class in London in 1999. There is a big difference between talking via email and talking in person.

As with any large project, someone has to make a sacrifice. In my case the one who suffers most from the time commitments a book like this takes is my wife Mary. The amazing thing is that she doesn't even complain (or at least not too much).

Last, and certainly not least, are the folks at DCANet (`www.dca.net`) who provide virtual Web site hosting for my Web page, handle my domain, POP my email, and have a large modem pool that are local calls for me. These people are very responsive; I never get busy signals, and Andrew White is a System Administrator without peer! They are in the Greater Philadelphia Metropolitan Area, and I've directed a number of organizations to their services. No, I'm not getting paid for this plug (but they do take good care of me).

I'm sure I've forgotten someone along the way. I assure you it was not intentional!

—*David*

Tell Us What You Think!

As the reader of this book, *you* are our most important critic and commentator. We value your opinion and want to know what we're doing right, what we could do better, what areas you'd like to see us publish in, and any other words of wisdom you're willing to pass our way.

As an Associate Publisher for Sams Publishing, I welcome your comments. You can fax, email, or write me directly to let me know what you did or didn't like about this book— as well as what we can do to make our books stronger.

Please note that I cannot help you with technical problems related to the topic of this book, and that due to the high volume of mail I receive, I might not be able to reply to every message.

When you write, please be sure to include this book's title and author as well as your name and phone or fax number. I will carefully review your comments and share them with the author and editors who worked on the book.

Fax: 317-581-4770
Email: michael.stephens@macmillanusa.com
Mail: Michael Stephens
Associate Publisher
Sams Publishing
201 West 103rd Street
Indianapolis, IN 46290 USA

Introduction

This book is designed to help you teach yourself how to program with C++ under the Linux operating system. In just 21 days, you will learn about such fundamentals as managing I/O, loops and arrays, object-oriented programming, templates, and creating C++ applications—all in well-structured and easy-to-follow lessons. Lessons provide sample listings—complete with sample output and an analysis of the code—to illustrate the topics of the day. Syntax examples are clearly marked for handy reference.

To get you up to speed with the features, tools, and environment specific to Linux, there is a bonus week! You can learn C++ without that week, but it does build your Linux-specific skills.

To help you become more proficient, each lesson ends with a set of common questions and answers, exercises, and a quiz. You can check your progress by examining the quiz and exercise answers provided in Appendix D, "Answers to Exercises and Quizzes."

Who Should Read This Book

You do not need any previous experience in programming to learn C++ with this book. This book starts you from the beginning and teaches you both the language and the concepts involved with programming C++. You'll find the numerous examples of syntax and detailed analysis of code an excellent guide as you begin your journey into this rewarding environment. Whether you are just beginning or already have some experience programming, you will find that this book's clear organization makes learning C++ fast and easy.

This book does not teach you how to use or install Linux, although a copy is included on the CD-ROM. There are plenty of other good books for that purpose (like the Sams *Linux Unleashed* series).

C++ (like the C language before it) is a standard language, so it is the same core language under Linux as on other platforms. In other words, the C++ you learn from this book applies to many different systems and compilers.

Two different compilers are available under Linux—gcc (GNU C/C++ Compiler) and egcs (Experimental GNU Compiler System). The CD-ROM contains egcs, whereas older distributions of Linux (and the current MS-DOS version) use gcc. From the command line, it is hard to tell the difference. However, egcs has the more advanced and current C++ features.

Versions of the GNU compilers are available for most platforms and operating systems. So the skills you learn in this book are useful for more than just Linux.

You must be running Linux to use the included compiler.

Conventions

Note   These boxes highlight information that can make your C++ programming more efficient and effective.

Frequently Asked Questions

FAQ: What do FAQs do?

Answer: These Frequently Asked Questions provide greater insight into the use of the language and clarify potential areas of confusion.

Caution   The cautions focus your attention on problems or side effects that can occur in specific situations.

These boxes provide clear definitions of essential terms.

Do	**Don't**
DO use the "Do/Don't" boxes to find a quick summary of a fundamental principle in a lesson.	**DON'T** overlook the useful information offered in these boxes.

This book uses various typefaces to help you distinguish C++ code from regular English. Actual C++ code is typeset in a special monospace font. Placeholders—words or characters temporarily used to represent the real words or characters you would type in code— are typeset in *italic monospace*. New or important terms are typeset in *italic*.

In the listings in this book, each real code line is numbered. If you see an unnumbered line in a listing, you'll know that the unnumbered line is really a continuation of the preceding numbered code line (some code lines are too long for the width of the book). You will also see a line continuation character like this ➡. In this case, you should type the two lines as one; do not divide them.

The listings are also included on the CD-ROM with filenames that begin with 1st, followed by the 2-digit lesson number, a dash, and then the 2-digit listing number within that lesson. For example, the first example in Day 1 is 1st01-01.cxx.

WEEK 1

At a Glance

As you prepare for your first week of learning how to program in C++, you will need a few things: a compiler, an editor, and this book. If you don't have a C++ compiler and an editor, you can still use this book, but you won't get as much out of it as you would if you did the exercises.

The best way to learn to program is by writing programs! At the end of each day you will find a workshop containing a quiz and some exercises. Be sure to take the time to answer all the questions, and to evaluate your work as objectively as you can. The later lessons build on what you've learned in the earlier lessons, so be sure you fully understand the material before moving on.

A Note to C Programmers

The material in the first five days will be familiar to you. Be sure to skim the material and to do the exercises to make sure you are fully up to speed before going on to Day 6, "Basic Classes." If you know C but have not used it under Linux, you should closely read the introduction to the GNU compilers in the first couple of lessons.

Where You Are Going

The first week covers the material you need to get started with programming in general, and with C++ in particular. On Day 1, "Getting Started," and Day 2, "The Parts of a C++ Program," you will be introduced to the basic concepts of programming and program flow. On Day 3, "Variables and Constants," you will learn about variables and constants and how to use data in your programs. On Day 4, "Expressions and Statements," you will learn how programs branch based on the data provided and the conditions encountered when the program is running. On Day 5, "Functions," you will learn what functions are and how to use them, and on Day 6, "Basic Classes," you will learn about classes and objects. Day 7, "More Program Flow," teaches more about program flow, and by the end of the first week you will be writing real object-oriented programs.

DAY 1

Getting Started

Welcome to *Sams Teach Yourself C++ for Linux in 21 Days*! Today you will get started on your way to becoming a proficient C++ programmer. You will learn:

- What the GNU compilers are and how GNU and Linux are related
- Why C++ is the emerging standard in software development
- The steps to develop a C++ program
- The basics on how to use the GNU compilers
- How to enter, compile, and link your first working C++ program

What Is GNU?

The acronym GNU stands for "GNU is Not UNIX." It is the name of a series useful software packages commonly found in UNIX environments that are being distributed by the GNU project at MIT. The packages are generally free and available at various locations on the Internet (you are charged if you want a copy on a physical medium like floppy or tape). The development of the packages is a cooperative process with the work being done by many volunteers. This effort is largely led by Richard M. Stallman (one of the developers of the EMACS editor).

Linux is an operating system that is very similar to UNIX (without infringing on the trademarks and copyrights of commercial versions of UNIX). But it is primarily just a kernel (the core of the operating system).

Most of the commands that you use under Linux are actually part of the GNU project sponsored by the Free Software Foundation. Twenty-eight percent of a typical Linux distribution is GNU, and only 3% is truly Linux.

Note

> Yes, the GNU acronym is self-referencing, but it was created that way on purpose. This type of naming has a history in products related to, but not covered by the trademark of, UNIX. A non-commercial operating system similar to UNIX was known as XINU: "XINU is Not UNIX."

So, in reality, you are using GNU utilities when you think you are issuing Linux commands. The folks who work on Linux saw no reason to duplicate the work done by the GNU folks. That is part of the whole philosophy of UNIX: reuse, do not recreate.

If you look closely at the documentation included with your Linux system, you should see mention of GNU.

The GNU project also includes C and C++ compilers (along with many other tools, languages, and utilities). The C compiler is known as gcc, and the C++ compiler is known as g++ (under Linux) or gxx (under another operating system such as DOS that does not allow the plus sign in filenames).

The nice thing about the GNU tools is that they exist for many platforms, not just Linux. So you can get a GNU compiler for Linux, or for DOS, or for DEC (Compaq) Alpha, or for a number of other systems.

This means that you can learn one compiler and use it many places. You can also have a personal C++ project under Linux that you work on in your own time and work on it when you are supposed to being doing "real work" at your employer—even if you only have access to a Microsoft Windows/DOS-based machine. Of course, you would never do anything like that!

Getting GNU Tools

The easiest way to get the GNU compiler and other tools is to install the copy of Linux contained on the CD-ROM included with this book. For installation details, you will have to review the instructions on the CD-ROM as this book focuses on C++, not Linux.

1

SAMS publishes some good Linux books also (this is more than a boldfaced plug for SAMS as I have contributed chapters to several of those books).

As mentioned before, you can also get the compiler for other platforms and operating systems.

If you already have Linux installed, there is a good chance that you already have the GNU compilers (but you may have an older version).

The best place to go (besides the CD-ROM) is http://www.gnu.org. Here you can download the GNU tools and compilers for various platforms for free. You can also get information on purchasing the GNU software on CD-ROM. Either way, you should consider sending them a donation. After all, it costs money to maintain Web pages and print documentation. Personally, I ordered a full set of the binaries and tools for all platforms so that I would have them for comparison purposes. (I do not get any money when you purchase from or donate to the Free Software Foundation; I just believe in what they are doing.)

Developing code takes time. And it takes time to get CD-ROM disks cut, duplicated, and delivered. As a result, there are different versions for different platforms and different versions between distribution media. You can download the latest version or purchase a slightly older version.

The CD-ROM included with this book includes version 2.9.5 of the GNU compilers (the latest at the time this book was written). The current version on the CD-ROM available from the Free Software Foundation is 2.7.2. In general, the newer compiler is better.

Examples in this book will compile under both versions unless otherwise noted.

The newer versions of the compiler are part of the EGCS (Experimental GNU Compiler System)—pronounced "eggs". Much of the work of creating the new compiler was done by the folks at Cygnus (http://www.cygnus.com). Cygnus has been named as the official maintainer of the GNU compilers (under the oversight of a steering committee).

A Brief History of C++

Computer languages have undergone dramatic evolution since the first electronic computers were built to assist in artillery trajectory calculations during World War II. Early on, programmers worked with the most primitive computer instructions: machine language. These instructions were represented by long strings of ones and zeroes. Soon, assemblers were invented to map machine instructions to human-readable and -manageable mnemonics, such as ADD and MOV.

In time, higher-level languages evolved, such as BASIC and COBOL. These languages let people work with something approximating words and sentences, such as Let I = 100. These instructions were translated back into machine language by interpreters and compilers. An *interpreter* translates a program as it reads it, turning the program instructions, or code, directly into actions. A *compiler* translates the code into an intermediary form. This step is called compiling, and it produces an object file. The compiler then invokes a *linker*, which turns the object file into an executable program.

Because interpreters read the code as it is written and execute the code on the spot, interpreters are easy for the programmer to work with. Compilers introduce the extra steps of compiling and linking the code, which is inconvenient. However, compilers produce a program that is very fast each time it is run because the time-consuming task of translating the source code into machine language has already been accomplished.

Another advantage of many compiled languages such as C++ is that you can distribute the executable program to people who do not have the compiler. With an interpretive language, you must have the interpreter to run the program.

Some languages, such as Visual Basic, call the interpreter the runtime library. Java calls its runtime interpreter a Virtual Machine (VM), but in this case the VM is provided by the browser (such as Internet Explorer or Netscape).

For many years, the principal goal of computer programmers was to write short pieces of code that would execute quickly. The program needed to be small, because memory was expensive, and it also needed to be fast, because processing power was expensive. As computers have become smaller, cheaper, and faster, and as the cost of memory has fallen, these priorities have changed. Today the cost of a programmer's time far outweighs the cost of most of the computers in use by businesses. Well-written, easy-to-maintain code is at a premium. "Easy to maintain" means that as business requirements change, the program can be extended and enhanced without great expense.

Programs

The word *program* is used in two ways: to describe individual instructions (or source code) created by the programmer, and to describe an entire piece of executable software. This distinction can cause enormous confusion, so we will try to distinguish between the source code on one hand, and the executable on the other.

A program can be defined as either a set of written instructions created by a programmer or an executable piece of software.

Source code can be turned into an executable program in two ways: Interpreters translate the source code into computer instructions, and the computer acts on those instructions immediately. Alternatively, compilers translate source code into a program, which you can run at a later time. Although interpreters are easier to work with, most serious programming is done with compilers because compiled code runs much faster. C++ is a compiled language.

Solving Problems

The problems programmers are asked to solve have been changing. Twenty years ago, programs were created to manage large amounts of raw data. The people writing the code and the people using the program were all computer professionals. Today, computers are in use by far more people, and most know very little about how computers and programs work. Computers are tools used by people who are more interested in solving their business problems than in struggling with the computer.

Ironically, to become easier to use for this new audience, programs have become far more sophisticated. Gone are the days when users typed cryptic commands at esoteric prompts, only to see a stream of raw data. Today's programs use sophisticated "user-friendly interfaces" involving multiple windows, menus, dialog boxes, and the myriad of metaphors with which we have become familiar. The programs written to support this new approach are far more complex than those written only ten years ago.

With the development of the Web, computers have entered a new era of market penetration; more people are using computers than ever before and their expectations are very high. In the last few years, programs have become larger and more complex, and the need for object-oriented programming techniques to manage this complexity has become manifest.

As programming requirements have changed, both languages and the techniques used for writing programs have evolved. Although the complete history is fascinating, this book focuses on the transformation from procedural programming to object-oriented programming.

Procedural, Structured, and Object-Oriented Programming

Until recently, programs were thought of as a series of procedures that acted upon data. A *procedure*, or function, is a set of specific instructions executed one after the other. The data was quite separate from the procedures, and the trick in programming was to keep track of which functions called which other functions, and what data was changed. To make sense of this potentially confusing situation, structured programming was created.

The principal idea behind structured programming is as simple as the idea of divide and conquer. A computer program can be thought of as consisting of a set of tasks. Any task that is too complex to be described simply would be broken down into a set of smaller component tasks, until the tasks were sufficiently small and self-contained that they were easily understood.

As an example, computing the average salary of every employee of a company is a rather complex task. You can, however, break it down into the following subtasks:

1. Find out what each person earns.
2. Count how many people you have.
3. Total all the salaries.
4. Divide the total by the number of people you have.

Totaling the salaries can be broken down into the following steps:

1. Get each employee's record.
2. Access the salary.
3. Add the salary to the running total.
4. Get the next employee's record.

In turn, obtaining each employee's record can be broken down into the following:

1. Open the file of employees.
2. Go to the correct record.
3. Read the data from disk.

Structured programming remains an enormously successful approach for dealing with complex problems. By the late 1980s, however, some of the deficiencies of structured programming had become all too clear.

First, a natural desire is to think of data (employee records, for example) and what you can do with data (sort, edit, and so on) as a single idea. Procedural programming worked against this, separating data structures from functions that manipulated that data.

Second, programmers found themselves constantly reinventing new solutions to old problems. This is often called "reinventing the wheel," which is the opposite of reusability. The idea behind reusability is to build components that have known properties, and then to be able to plug them into your program as you need them. This is modeled after the hardware world—when an engineer needs a new transistor, she usually does not invent a new one; she goes to the big bin of transistors and finds one that works the way she needs it to, or perhaps modifies it. No similar option existed for a software engineer.

NEW TERM The way we are now using computers—with menus, buttons, and windows— fosters a more interactive, event-driven approach to computer programming. *Event-driven* means that an event happens—the user clicks a button or chooses from a menu—and the program must respond. Programs are becoming increasingly interactive, and it has became important to design for that kind of functionality.

Old-fashioned programs forced the user to proceed step by step through a series of screens. Modern event-driven programs present all the choices at once and respond to the user's actions.

NEW TERM *Object-oriented* programming attempts to respond to these needs, providing techniques for managing enormous complexity, achieving reuse of software components, and coupling data with the tasks that manipulate that data.

The essence of object-oriented programming is to treat data and the procedures that act upon the data as a single object—a self-contained entity with an identity and certain characteristics of its own.

C++ and Object-Oriented Programming

C++ fully supports object-oriented programming, including the three pillars of object-oriented development: encapsulation, inheritance, and polymorphism.

Encapsulation

When an engineer needs to add a resistor to the device she is creating, she typically does not build a new one from scratch. She walks over to a bin of resistors, examines the colored bands that indicate the properties, and picks the one she needs. The resistor is a "black box" as far as the engineer is concerned—she does not care much about how it does its work as long as it conforms to her specifications; she does not need to look inside the box to use it in her design.

The property of being a self-contained unit is called *encapsulation*. With encapsulation, we can accomplish data hiding. *Data hiding* is the highly valued characteristic that an object can be used without the user knowing or caring how it works internally. Just as you can use a refrigerator without knowing how the compressor works, you can use a well-designed object without knowing about its internal data members.

Similarly, when the engineer uses the resistor, she does not need to know anything about the internal state of the resistor. All the properties of the resistor are encapsulated in the resistor object; they are not spread out through the circuitry. It is not necessary to understand how the resistor works to use it effectively. Its data is hidden inside the resistor's casing.

C++ supports the properties of encapsulation through the creation of user-defined types, called classes. You will see how to create classes on Day 6, "Basic Classes." After you create a well-defined class, it acts as a fully encapsulated entity—it is used as a whole unit. The actual inner workings of the class should be hidden. Users of a well-defined class do not need to know how the class works; they just need to know how to use it.

Inheritance and Reuse

When the engineers at Acme Motors want to build a new car, they have two choices: They can start from scratch, or they can modify an existing model. Perhaps their Star model is nearly perfect, but they want to add a turbocharger and a six-speed transmission. The chief engineer would prefer not to start from the ground up, but would rather say, "Let's build another Star, but let's add these additional capabilities. We'll call the new model a Quasar." A Quasar is a kind of Star, but a specialized one with new features.

C++ supports inheritance. A new type, which is an extension of an existing type, can be declared. This new subclass is said to derive from the existing type and is sometimes called a derived type. The Quasar is derived from the Star and thus inherits all its qualities but can add to them as needed. Inheritance and its application in C++ are discussed on Day 11, "Inheritance," and Day 15, "Advanced Inheritance."

Polymorphism

The new Quasar might respond differently than a Star does when you press down on the accelerator. The Quasar might engage fuel injection and a turbocharger, whereas the Star would simply let gasoline into its carburetor. A user, however, does not have to know about these differences. She can just "floor it," and the right thing will happen, depending on which car she is driving.

C++ supports the idea that different objects do "the right thing" through what is called *function polymorphism* and class polymorphism. Poly means many, and morph means form. Polymorphism refers to the same name taking many forms, and it is discussed on Day 10, "Advanced Functions," and Day 13, "Polymorphism."

How C++ Evolved

As object-oriented analysis, design, and programming began to catch on, Bjarne Stroustrup took the most popular language for commercial software development, C, and extended it to provide the features needed to facilitate object-oriented programming.

Although it is true that C++ is a superset of C and that virtually any legal C program is a legal C++ program, the leap from C to C++ is very significant. C++ benefited from its relationship to C for many years because C programmers could ease into their use of C++. To really get the full benefit of C++, however, many programmers found they had to unlearn much of what they knew and learn a new way of conceptualizing and solving programming problems.

Should I Learn C First?

The question inevitably arises: "Because C++ is a superset of C, should you learn C first?" Stroustrup and most other C++ programmers agree that not only is it unnecessary to learn C first, it may be advantageous not to do so.

This book does not assume you have any prior programming experience. If you are a C programmer, however, the first five chapters of this book will largely be review. But it will tell you how to use the GNU compilers. Starting in Day 6 we begin the real work of object-oriented software development.

C++ and Java

C++ is now the overwhelmingly predominant language for the development of commercial software. In recent years, Java has challenged that dominance, but the pendulum swings back, and many of the programmers who left C++ for Java have recently begun to return. In any case, the two languages are so similar that to learn one is to learn 90 percent of the other.

The ANSI Standard

The Accredited Standards Committee, operating under the procedures of the American National Standards Institute (ANSI), has created an international standard for C++.

The C++ Standard is now also referred to as ISO (International Standards Organization) Standard, the NCITS (National Committee for Information Technology Standards) Standard, the X3 (the old name for NCITS) Standard, and the ANSI/ISO Standard. This book will continue to refer to ANSI standard code because that is the more commonly used term.

Note ANSI is usually pronounced "antsy" with a silent "t."

The ANSI standard is an attempt to ensure that C++ is portable—ensuring, for example, that ANSI-standard compliant code you write for the GNU compilers will compile without errors, using a compiler from any other vendor (like Microsoft). Further, because the code in this book is ANSI compliant, it should compile without errors on a Mac, a Windows box, or an Alpha.

For most students of C++, the ANSI standard will be invisible. The standard has been stable for a while, and all the major manufacturers support the ANSI standard. We have endeavored to ensure that all the code in this edition of this book is ANSI compliant.

Preparing to Program

C++, perhaps more than other languages, demands that the programmer design the program before writing it. Trivial problems, such as the ones discussed in the first few chapters of this book, do not require much design. Complex problems, however, such as the ones professional programmers are challenged with every day, do require design, and the more thorough the design, the more likely it is that the program will solve the problems it is designed to solve, on time and within budget. A good design also makes for a program that is relatively bug-free and easy to maintain. It has been estimated that 90 percent of the cost of software is the combined cost of debugging and maintenance. To the extent that good design can reduce those costs, it can have a significant impact on the bottom-line cost of the project.

The first question you need to ask when preparing to design any program is, "What is the problem I'm trying to solve?" Every program should have a clear, well-articulated goal, and you will find that even the simplest programs in this book do so.

The second question every good programmer asks is, "Can this be accomplished without resorting to writing custom software?" Reusing an old program, using pen and paper (the old, original, manual, stand-by way of doing work), or buying software off the shelf is often a better solution to a problem than writing something new. The programmer who can offer these alternatives will never suffer from lack of work; finding less expensive solutions to today's problems will always generate new opportunities later.

Assuming you understand the problem and that it requires writing a new program, you are ready to begin your design.

The process of fully understanding the problem (analysis) and creating a solution (design) is the necessary foundation for writing a world-class commercial application. Although these steps logically come before coding—that is, you must understand the problem and design the solution before you implement it—you are, in fact, better off learning the fundamental syntax and semantics of C++ before learning formal analysis and design techniques.

The GNU/Linux Development Environment

This book makes the assumption that you are using the GNU compilers in a text environment or similar combination. That is, your compiler has a mode in which you can write directly to the screen, without worrying about a graphical environment, such as the ones in Windows or on the Macintosh. This is known as a *console* mode and is standard for the GNU compilers. If you are working under a different environment, you will have to look for an option such as *console* or *easy window* or check your compiler's documentation. If you are using one of the graphical environments under Linux, your best bet is to open a terminal emulation window (like KDT) so that you can work in pure text mode.

With GNU, you can use EMACS, vi, or any other text editor that you prefer. If you are using a different compiler, you will have different choices—your compiler may have its own built-in text editor, or you can use a commercial text editor to produce text files. The important thing is that whatever you write your program in, it must save simple, plain-text files, with no word processing commands embedded in the text. Examples of safe editors include Windows Notepad, the DOS `edit` command, Brief, Epsilon, EMACS, and vi. Many commercial word processors, such as WordPerfect, Word, and dozens of others, embed special characters but also offer a method for saving simple text files—so be sure how you are saving your file.

The files you create with your editor are called source files, and for C++ they typically are named with the extension .cpp, .cp, or .c. In this book, we named all the source code files with the .cxx extension because the GNU compilers accept this as C++ source code on different platforms. If you are using something different, check your compiler for what it needs.

Note

The GNU compilers treat the file extension as being significant. You should use .cxx or .c++.

Many other C++ compilers do not treat the extension as significant. If you don't specify otherwise, many will use .cpp by default. Be careful, however; some compilers treat .c files as C code and .cpp files as C++ code. Again, please check your documentation.

Do	Don't
DO use a simple text editor (like vi, EMACS, or even the DOS `edit` command) to create your source code, or use the built-in editor that comes with your compiler.	**DON'T** use a word processor that saves special formatting characters. If you do use a word processor, save the file as ASCII text.
DO save your files with the .cxx or .c++ extension.	
DO check the man pages for the GNU compiler for specifics about how it and the linker work to ensure that you know how to compile and link your programs.	

Compiling the Source Code

Although the source code in your file is somewhat cryptic, and anyone who does not know C++ will struggle to understand what it is for, it is still in what we call human-readable form. Your source code file is not a program, and it cannot be executed, or run, as a program can.

To turn your source code into a program, you use a compiler. The simplest way to invoke the g++ compiler looks like this:

```
g++ file.c++ -o file
```

Or if you are on a platform that does not support the plus sign (+) in a filename, like MS-DOS, you would use the following:

```
gxx file.cxx -o file.exe
```

In both cases, you replace *file* in the command with the name you selected. It will produce an executable with the name `file` or `file.exe`. If you leave off the `-o` option, it will produce a file called `a.out` (Linux) or `a.exe` (MS-DOS) respectively.

If you are using a different compiler, you will have to check its documentation to determine how to invoke it and how to tell it where to find your source code—this varies from compiler to compiler.

After your source code is compiled, an object file is produced. This file is often named with the extension .o (Linux) or .obj (MS-DOS). However, this is still not an executable program. To turn this into an executable program, you must run your linker.

Creating an Executable File with the Linker

C++ programs are typically created by linking one or more object files with one or more libraries. A *library* is a collection of linkable files that were supplied with your compiler, that you purchased separately, or that you created and compiled. All C++ compilers come with a library of useful functions (or procedures) and classes that you can include in your program. A *function* is a block of code that performs a service, such as adding two numbers or printing to the screen. A *class* is a collection of data and related functions; we will talk about classes a lot, starting on Day 5, "Functions."

The steps to create an executable file are

1. Create a source code file, with a .c++ or .cxx extension.
2. Compile the source code into a file in the object format.
3. Link your object file with any needed libraries to produce an executable program.

The GNU compilers automatically invoke the linker (known as ld) to produce the executable file.

The Development Cycle

If every program worked the first time you tried it, that would be the complete development cycle: Write the program, compile the source code, link the program, and run it. Unfortunately, almost every program, no matter how trivial, can and will have errors, or bugs. Some bugs will cause the compile to fail, some will cause the link to fail, and some will show up only when you run the program.

Whatever type of bug you find, you must fix it, and that involves editing your source code, recompiling and relinking, and then rerunning the program. This cycle is represented in Figure 1.1, which diagrams the steps in the development cycle.

Figure 1.1

The steps in the development of a C++ program.

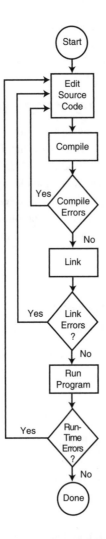

`hello.cxx`—Your First C++ Program

Traditional programming books begin by teaching you how to write the words "Hello World" to the screen, or a variation on that statement. This time-honored tradition is carried on here.

Type the first program directly into your editor, exactly as shown in Listing 1.1. After you are certain it is correct, save the file, compile it, link it, and run it. It will print the words Hello World to your screen. Do not worry too much about how it works; this example is really just to get you comfortable with the development cycle. Every aspect of this program will be covered over the next couple of days.

Note

All the listings contained in this book are stored on the CD-ROM to make your life easier. They have filenames in the format `lstCC-NN.cxx`. *CC* stands for day number (01, 02, and so on) and *NN* stands for listing number (01 for the first in a day, 02 for the second, and so on).

The first listing of the book (Listing 1.1) is the file `lst01-01.cxx`.

Not all listing files will compile. When this is the case, it is so noted in the text.

Caution

The following listing, like the rest of the listings in this book, contains line numbers on the left. These numbers are only for reference within the book. You should not type them into your editor. For example, in line 1 of Listing 1.1, you should enter:

`#include <iostream.h>`

INPUT **LISTING 1.1** `hello.cxx`, The Hello World Program

```
1: #include <iostream.h>
2:
3: int main()
4: {
5:     cout << "Hello World!\n";
6:     return 0;
7: }
```

Use the listing file from the CD-ROM; if you choose to enter this program yourself, make certain you enter this exactly as shown. Pay careful attention to the punctuation. The << in line 5 is the redirection symbol, produced on most keyboards by holding the Shift key and pressing the comma key twice. Line 5 ends with a semicolon (;). Do not leave this off!

To compile and link this program using the GNU compiler under Linux, you would enter

`g++ lst01-01.cxx -o lst01-01`

If you choose to use a different compiler, check to make sure you are following your compiler directions properly. Most compilers will link automatically, but check your documentation.

If you get errors, look over your code carefully and determine how it is different from Listing 1.1. If you see an error on line 1, such as `cannot find file iostream.h`, check your compiler documentation for directions on setting up your include path or environment variables.

If you receive an error that there is no prototype for `main` (from a non-GNU compiler), add the line `int main();` just before line 3. You will need to add this line before the beginning of the `main` function in every program in this book. Most compilers do not require this line, but a few do.

Your finished program will look like this:

```
1: #include <iostream.h>
2: int main(); // most compilers don't need this line
3: int main()
4: {
5:     cout <<"Hello World!\n";
6:     return 0;
7: }
```

Note

It is difficult to read a program to yourself if you do not know how to pronounce the special characters and keywords. You read the first line "Pound include (some say hash-include) eye-oh-stream dot h." You read line 5 "see-out 'Hello World'."

Try running the executable for `1st01-01`; it should write

Hello World!

directly to your screen. If so, congratulations! You just entered, compiled, and ran your first C++ program. It may not look like much, but almost every professional C++ programmer started out with this exact same program.

Using the Standard Libraries

To ensure that readers who are using older compilers will not have trouble with the code in this book, we are using the older style include files

```
#include <iostream.h>
```

rather than the new standard library headers:

```
#include <iostream>
```

This should work on all compilers and has few disadvantages. If you prefer to use the new standard libraries, however, simply change your code to

```
#include <iostream>
```

and add the line

```
using namespace std;
```

just below your list of included files. The advanced topic of the use of namespace is explained in detail in Day 17, "Namespaces."

Whether or not you use standard header files, the code in this book should run without modification. The principal difference between the older libraries and the new standard library is in the iostream library (described in Day 16, "Streams"). Even these changes will not affect the code in this book; the changes are subtle, esoteric, and beyond the scope of an introductory primer.

Using the g++ Compiler

All the programs in this book were tested with the GNU g++ compiler version 2.9.5; many of them were also tested with version 2.7.2. In theory, because this is ANSI-compliant code, all the programs in this book should run well on any ANSI-compliant compiler from any vendor.

In theory, theory and practice are the same. In practice, they never are.

To get you started, this section briefly introduces how to edit, compile, link, and run a program using the GNU compiler. If you are using a different compiler, the details of each step may be somewhat different. Even if you are using the GNU version 2.7.2 or 2.9.5 compiler, please check your documentation for details on how to proceed from here.

Building the Hello World Project

To create and test the Hello World program, follow these steps:

1. Pick an editor and create a file.
2. Enter the code as shown in Listing 1.1 (or you can use the editor to open the lst01-01.cxx file).
3. Save the file and exit your editor.
4. Enter the `compile` command.
5. Enter the executable name to run the program.

Compile Errors

Compile-time errors can occur for any number of reasons. Usually they are a result of a typo or other inadvertent minor error. Good compilers (like GNU) not only tell you what you did wrong, they point you to the exact place in your code where you made the mistake. The great ones will even suggest a remedy!

You can see this by intentionally putting an error into your program. If the Hello World program ran smoothly, edit it now and remove the closing brace on line 7. Your program will now look like Listing 1.2.

INPUT   **LISTING 1.2**   Demonstration of Compiler Error

```
1: #include <iostream.h>
2:
3: int main()
4: {
5:    cout << "Hello World!\n";
6:    return 0;
```

Recompile your program and GNU will show you the following error:

```
./lst01-02.cxx: In function `int main()':
./lst01-02.cxx:7: parse error at end of input
```

Other compilers will give you an error message like:

```
Hello.cpp, line 7: Compound statement missing terminating; in
➥function main().
```

or an error, which looks like this:

```
F:\Mcp\Tycpp21d\Testing\List0101.cpp(8) : fatal error C1004:
unexpected end of file found
Error executing cl.exe.
 }
```

This error tells you the file and line number of the problem and what the problem is (although I admit it is somewhat cryptic). Note that the error message points you to line 7. The compiler was not sure if you intended to put the closing brace before or after the cout statement on line 6. Sometimes the errors just get you to the general vicinity of the problem. If a compiler could perfectly identify every problem, it would fix the code itself.

Summary

After completing this day, you should have a good understanding of how C++ evolved and what problems it was designed to solve. You should feel confident that learning C++ is the right choice for anyone interested in programming in the next decade. C++ provides the tools of object-oriented programming and the performance of a systems-level language, which makes C++ the development language of choice.

Today you learned how to enter, compile, link, and run your first C++ program, and what the normal development cycle is. You also learned a little of what object-oriented programming is all about. You will return to these topics during the next three weeks. During the bonus week, you will learn advanced topics of working with the GNU tool set and Linux programming.

Q&A

Q What is the difference between a text editor and a word processor?

A A text editor produces files with plain text in them. No formatting commands or other special symbols are required by a particular word processor. Text files do not have automatic word wrapping, bold or italic formatting, and so forth.

Q If my compiler has a built-in editor, must I use it?

A The GNU compilers do not come with built-in text editors. Linux comes with vi and EMACS. Almost all other compilers will compile code produced by any text editor. The advantages of using the built-in text editor, however, might include the capability to quickly move back and forth between the edit and compile steps of the development cycle. Sophisticated compilers include a fully integrated development environment, enabling the programmer to access help files, edit and compile the code in place, and to resolve compile and link errors without ever leaving the environment.

Q Can I ignore warning messages from my compiler?

A Many books hedge on this one, but I'll stake myself to this position: No! Get into the habit, from day one, of treating warning messages as errors. C++ uses the compiler to warn you when you are doing something you may not intend. Heed those warnings and do what is required to make them go away.

Warnings mean that the compiler is able to create an executable from your source code but doesn't believe you really want to do what you coded!

Q What is compile time?

A Compile time is the time when you run your compiler, in contrast to *link time* (when you run the linker) or *runtime* (when running the program). This is just programmer shorthand to identify the three times when errors usually surface. Because the GNU compiler invokes the linker if the compilation is successful, the link time is easy to miss (but believe me, it is there).

Workshop

The Workshop provides quiz questions to help you solidify your understanding of the material covered and exercises to provide you with experience in using what you learned. Try to answer the quiz and exercise questions before checking the answers in Appendix D, "Answers to Exercises and Quizzes," and make sure you understand the answers before continuing to the next day.

Quiz

1. What is the difference between an interpreter and a compiler?

2. How do you compile the source code with your compiler?

3. What does the linker do?

4. What are the steps in the normal development cycle?

Exercises

1. Look at the following program and try to guess what it does without running it.

```
1: #include <iostream.h>
2: int main()
3: {
4:    int x = 5;
5:    int y = 7;
6:    cout << "\n";
7:    cout << x + y << " " << x * y;
8:    cout << "\n";
9:    return 0;
10:}
```

2. Type the program from Exercise 1, and then compile and link it. What does it do? Does it do what you guessed?

3. Type the following program and compile it. What error do you receive?

```
1: include <iostream.h>
2: int main()
3: {
4:     cout << "Hello World\n";
5:     return 0;
6: }
```

4. Fix the error in the program in Exercise 3 and recompile, link, and run it. What does it do?

1

DAY **2**

The Parts of a C++ Program

C++ programs consist of objects, functions, variables, and other component parts. Most of this book is devoted to explaining these parts in depth, but to get a sense of how a program fits together, you must see a complete working program. Today you will learn:

- The parts of a C++ program
- How the parts work together
- What a function is and what it does
- The options for use with the g++ compiler

A Simple Program

Even thesimple program HELLO.cpp from Day 1, "Getting Started," had many interesting parts. This section reviews this program in more detail. Listing 2.1 reproduces the original version of HELLO.cpp for your convenience.

LISTING 2.1   HELLO.cpp Demonstrates the Parts of a C++ Program

```
1: #include <iostream.h>
2:
3:  int main()
4: {
5:    cout << "Hello World!\n";
6:    return 0;
7: }
```

Hello World!

On line 1, the file iostream.h is included into the current file.

Here is how the preprocessor works: the first character is the # (pound) symbol, which is a signal to the preprocessor. Another name for the pound sign or symbol is *octothorpe*, which has its history in the darkest ages of the telephone company. Each time you start your compiler, the preprocessor is run. The preprocessor reads through your source code, looking for lines that begin with the pound symbol (#), and acts on those lines before the compiler runs. The preprocessor is discussed in detail on Day 21, "What's Next."

Include is a preprocessor instruction that says, "What follows is a filename. Find that file and read it in right here." The angle brackets around the filename tell the preprocessor to look in all the usual places for this file. If your compiler is set up correctly, the angle brackets will cause the preprocessor to look for the file iostream.h in the directory that holds all the .h files for your compiler. The file iostream.h (input-output-stream) is used by cout, which assists with writing to the screen. The effect of line 1 is to include the file iostream.h into this program as if you had typed it in yourself. The preprocessorruns before your compiler each time the compiler is invoked. The preprocessor translates any line that begins with a pound symbol (#) into a special command, getting your code file ready for the compiler.

Line 3 begins the actual program with a function named main(). Every C++ program has a main() function. A *function* is a block of code that performs one or more actions. Usually functions are invoked or called by other functions, but main() is special. When your program starts, main() is called automatically (by the operating system).

main(), like all functions, must state what kind of value it will return. The return value type for main() in HELLO.cpp is int, which means that this function will return an integer to the operating system when it completes. In this case, it returns the integer value 0, as shown on line 6. Returning a value to the operating system is a relatively unimportant and little-used feature, but the C++ standard does require that main() be declared as shown.

Note

GNU and some other compilers will let you declare main() to return void. This is no longer legal C++, and you should not get into bad habits. Have main() return int, and simply return 0 as the last line in main().

2

Note

Some operating systems (like Linux) enable you to test the value returned by a program. The convention is to return 0 to indicate that the program ended normally. If you are using the bash or pdksh shell, the $? environment variable contains this return value.

All functions begin with an opening brace ({) and end with a closing brace (}). The braces for the main() function are on lines 4 and 7. Everything between the opening and closing braces is considered a part of the function.

The main processing of this program is on line 5.

The object cout is used to print a message to the screen. This book covers objects in general on Day 6, "Basic Classes," and cout and its related object cin in detail on Day 16, "Streams." These two objects, cin and cout, are used in C++ to handle input (for example, from the keyboard) and output (for example, to the screen), respectively.

cout is used this way: Type the word **cout**, followed by the output redirection operator (<<). Whatever follows the output redirection operator is written to the screen. If you want a string of characters written, be sure to enclose them in a pair of double quotes ("), as shown on line 5.

A text string is a series of printable characters.

The final two characters, \n, tell cout to put a new line after the words "Hello World!" This special code is explained in detail when cout is discussed on Day 17, "Namespaces."

The main() function ends on line 7 with the closing brace.

A Brief Look at cout

On Day 16, you will see how to use cout to print data to the screen. For now, you can use cout without fully understanding how it works. To print a value to the screen, write the word cout, followed by the insertion operator (<<), which you create by typing the less-than character (<) twice. Even though these are two characters, C++ treats them as one.

Follow the insertion character with your data. Listing 2.2 illustrates how this is used. Enter the example exactly as written, but substitute your own name where you see "Jesse Liberty."

INPUT   **LISTING 2.2**   Using cout

```
1: // Listing 2.2 using cout
2: #include <iostream.h>
3: int main()
4: {
5:     cout << "Hello there.\n";
6:     cout << "Here is 5: " << 5 << "\n";
7:     cout << "The manipulator endl writes a new line to the screen.";
8:     cout <<
9:         endl;
10:     cout << "Here is a very big number:\t" << 70000 << endl;
11:     cout << "Here is the sum of 8 and 5:\t" << 8+5 << endl;
12:     cout << "Here's a fraction:\t\t" << (float) 5/8 << endl;
13:     cout << "And a very very big number:\t";
14:     cout << (double) 7000 * 7000 <<
15:         endl;
16:     cout << "Don't forget to replace Jesse Liberty
[ic:ccc]with your name...\n";
17:     cout << "Jesse Liberty is a C++ programmer!\n";
18:     return 0;
19:     }
```

OUTPUT
```
Hello there.
Here is 5: 5
The manipulator endl writes a new line to the screen.
Here is a very big number:      70000
Here is the sum of 8 and 5:     13
Here's a fraction:              0.625
And a very very big number:     4.9e+07
Don't forget to replace Jesse Liberty with your name...
Jesse Liberty is a C++ programmer!
```

Note

Some compilers (other than g++) have a bug that requires that you put parentheses around the addition before passing it to cout. Thus, line 10 would change to

```
10:        cout << "Here is the sum of 8 and 5:\t" << (8+5) << endl;
```

ANALYSIS On line 2, the statement #include <iostream.h> causes the iostream.h file to be added to your source code. This is required if you use cout and its related functions.

On line 5 is the simplest use of cout, printing a string or series of characters. Thesymbol \n is a special formatting character. It tells cout to print a newline character to the screen; it is pronounced "backslash-n" or "new line."

Three values are passed to cout on line 6, and each value is separated by the insertion operator. The first value is the string "Here is 5: ". Note the space after the colon. The space is part of the string. Next, the value 5 is passed to the insertion operator and the newline character (always in double quotes or single quotes). This causes the line

```
Here is 5: 5
```

to be printed to the screen. Because no newline character is present after the first string, the next value is printed immediately afterward. This is called *concatenating* the two values.

On line 7, an informative message is printed, and then the manipulator endl is used. The purpose of endl is to write a new line to the screen. (Other uses for endl are discussed on Day 16.)

Note

endl stands for *end l*ine and is end-ell rather than end-one. It is commonly pronounced "end-ell."

On line 10, a new formatting character, \t, is introduced. This inserts a tab character and is used on lines 10 to 13 to line up the output. Line 9 shows that not only integers, but long integers as well, can be printed. Line 11 demonstrates that cout will do simple addition. The value of 8+5 is passed to cout, but 13 is printed.

On line 12, the value $5/8$ is inserted into cout. The term (float) tells cout that you want this value evaluated as a decimal equivalent, and so a fraction is printed. On line 14, the value `7000` `*` `7000` is given to `cout`, and the term `(double)` is used to tell `cout` that you want this to be printed using scientific notation. All this will be explained on Day 3, "Variables and Constants," when data types are discussed.

On line 16, you substituted your name, and the output confirmed that you are indeed a C++ programmer. It must be true, because the computer said so!

Comments

When you are writing a program, it is always clear and self-evident what you are trying to do. Funny thing, though—a month later, when you return to the program, it can be quite confusing and unclear. I really am not sure how that confusion creeps into your program, but it always does.

To fight the onset of bafflement, and to help others understand your code, you should use comments. *Comments* are text that is ignored by the compiler, but that may inform the reader of what you are doing at any particular point in your program.

Types of Comments

C++ comments come in two flavors: the double-slash (`//`) comment, and the slash-star (`/*`) comment. The double-slash comment, which is referred to as a C++-style comment, tells the compiler to ignore everything that follows this comment until the end of the line.

The slash-star comment tells the compiler to ignore everything that follows until it finds a star-slash (`*/`) comment mark. These marks are referred to as C-style comments. Every `/*` must be matched with a closing `*/`.

As you might guess, C-style comments are used in the C language as well, but C++-style comments are not part of the official definition of C.

Many C++ programmers use the C++-style comment most of the time and reserve C-style comments for blocking out large blocks of a program. You can include C++-style comments within a block "commented out" by C-style comments; everything, including the C++-style comments, is ignored between the C-style comment marks.

Using Comments

As a general rule, the overall program should have comments at the beginning, telling you what the program does. Each function should also have comments explaining what the function does and what values it returns. And these should be updated when the program is changed. At the very least, a change history should be maintained here.

Functions should be named so that little ambiguity exists about what they do, and confusing and obscure bits of code should be redesigned and rewritten so as to be self-evident. As often as not, comments are a lazy programmer's excuse for obscurity.

This is not to suggest that comments ought never be used—only that they should not be relied upon to clarify obscure code; instead, fix the code. In short, write your code well, and use comments to supplement understanding.

Listing 2.3 demonstrates the use of comments, showing that they do not affect the processing of the program or its output.

INPUT **LISTING 2.3** HELP.cpp Demonstrates Comments

```
1: #include <iostream.h>
2:
3: int main()
4: {
5:     /* this is a comment
6:     and it extends until the closing
7:     star-slash comment mark */
8:     cout << "Hello World!\n";
9:     // this comment ends at the end of the line
10:     cout << "That comment ended!\n";
11:
12:     // double slash comments can be alone on a line
13:     /* as can slash-star comments */
14:     return 0;
15: }
```

OUTPUT
```
Hello World!
That comment ended!
```

ANALYSIS The comments on lines 5 through 7 are completely ignored by the compiler, as are the comments on lines 9, 12, and 13. The comment on line 9 ended with the end of the line, however, but the comments on lines 5 and 13 required a closing comment mark.

A Final Word of Caution About Comments

Comments that state the obvious are less than useful. In fact, they can be counterproductive because the code may change and the programmer may neglect to update the comment. What is obvious to one person may be obscure to another so judgment is required.

The bottom line is that comments should not say *what* is happening; they should say *why* it is happening.

Functions

Although main() is a function, it is an unusual one. To be useful, a function must be called, or invoked, during the course of your program. main() is invoked by the operating system.

A program is executed line by line in the order it appears in your source code until a function is reached. Then the program branches off to execute the function. When the function finishes, it returns control to the line of code immediately following the call to the function.

A good analogy for this is sharpening your pencil. If you are drawing a picture and your pencil point breaks, you might stop drawing, go sharpen the pencil, and then return to what you were doing. When a program needs a service performed, it can call a function to perform the service and then pick up where it left off when the function is finished running. Listing 2.4 demonstrates this idea.

INPUT   **LISTING 2.4**   Demonstrating a Call to a Function

```
1:     #include <iostream.h>
2:
3:     // function Demonstration Function
4:     // prints out a useful message
5:     void DemonstrationFunction()
6:     {
7:         cout << "In Demonstration Function\n";
8:     }
9:
10:    // function main - prints out a message, then
11:    // calls DemonstrationFunction, then prints out
12:    // a second message.
13:    int main()
14:    {
15:        cout << "In main\n" ;
16:        DemonstrationFunction();
17:        cout << "Back in main\n";
18:        return 0;
19:    }
```

OUTPUT
```
In main
In Demonstration Function
Back in main
```

ANALYSIS   The function DemonstrationFunction() is defined on lines 5 to 8. When it is called, it prints a message to the screen and then returns.

Line 13 is the beginning of the actual program. On line 15, `main()` prints out a message saying it is in `main()`. After printing the message, line 16 calls `DemonstrationFunction()`. This call causes the commands in `DemonstrationFunction()` to execute. In this case, the entire function consists of the code on line 7, which prints another message. When `DemonstrationFunction()` completes (line 8), it returns back to where it was called from. In this case, the program returns to line 17, where `main()` prints its final line.

Using Functions

Functions either return a value or they return void, meaning they return nothing. A function that adds two integers might return the sum, and thus would be defined to return an integer value. A function that just prints a message has nothing to return and would be declared to return `void`.

Functions consist of a header and a body. The header consists of the return type, the function name, and the parameters to that function. The parameters to a function enable values to be passed into the function. Thus, if the function were to add two numbers, the numbers would be the parameters to the function. A typical function header looks like:

```
int Sum(int a, int b)
```

A parameter is a declaration of what type of value will be passed in; the actual value passed in by the calling function is called the argument. Many programmers use these two terms, parameters and arguments, as synonyms. Others are careful about the technical distinction. This book uses the terms interchangeably.

The body of a function consists of an opening brace, zero or more statements, and a closing brace. The statements constitute the work of the function. A function may return a value, using a `return` statement. This statement will also cause the function to exit. If you do not put a `return` statement into your function, it will automatically return void (no value) at the end of the function. The value returned must be of the type declared in the function header.

Note

Functions are covered in more detail on Day 5, "Functions." The types that can be returned from a function are covered in more detail on Day 3. The information provided today is to present you with an overview because functions will be used in almost all your C++ programs.

Listing 2.5 demonstrates a function that takes two integer parameters and returns an integer value. Do not worry about the syntax or the specifics of how to work with integer values (for example, int x) for now; that is covered in detail on Day 3.

LISTING 2.5   FUNC.cpp Demonstrates a Simple Function

```
1:      #include <iostream.h>
2:      int Add (int x, int y)
3:      {
4:
5:          cout << "In Add(), received " << x << " and " << y << "\n";
6:          return (x+y);
7:      }
8:
9:      int main()
10:     {
11:         cout << "I'm in main()!\n";
12:         int a, b, c;
13:         cout << "Enter two numbers: ";
14:         cin >> a;
15:         cin >> b;
16:         cout << "\nCalling Add()\n";
17:         c=Add(a,b);
18:         cout << "\nBack in main().\n";
19:         cout << "c was set to " << c;
20:         cout << "\nExiting...\n\n";
21:         return 0;
22:     }
```

OUTPUT
```
I'm in main()!
Enter two numbers: 3 5

Calling Add()
In Add(), received 3 and 5

Back in main().
c was set to 8
Exiting...
```

ANALYSIS   The function Add() is defined on line 2. It takes two integer parameters and returns an integer value. The program itself begins on line 9 and on line 11, where it prints a message. The program prompts the user for two numbers (lines 13 to 15). The user types each number, separated by a space, and then presses the Enter key. main() passes the two numbers entered by the user as arguments to the Add() function on line 17.

Processing branches to the Add() function, which starts on line 2. The parameters a and b are printed and then added. The result is returned on line 6, and the function returns.

In lines 14 and 15, the cin object is used to obtain a number for the variables a and b, and cout is used to write the values to the screen. Variables and other aspects of this program are explored in depth in the next few days.

More About the GNU Compiler

Whenever you are in doubt about how to do something, you should check the documentation for your compiler. The GNU compiler g++ is no exception. Included with the distribution are manual pages and info files.

You can access the man page by entering the following:

```
man g++
```

Or under MS-DOS

```
man gxx
```

And you can review the larger manual page for gcc and g++ with the following command:

```
man gcc
```

You can also review the combined info file for gcc and g++ with the following command:

```
info gcc
```

If you request info for g++, you will only get the manual page (so don't waste your time).

Note

info is the primary online documentation for Linux and the GNU tools. It is hypertext-based and can be output to various forms. You can get quick information about it with this command:

```
man info
```

or

```
info
```

The next two sections provide information about the more common command-line options and some quick tips about using the compiler.

GCC Compiler Options

Compiler options are specified using command-line switches or arguments. The most commonly used compiler options are shown in Table 2.1.

TABLE 2.1 Compiler Options

Option	Meaning
(no options used)	Compile and link program on command line and produce executable with default name (a.out for Linux, a.exe for MS-DOS).
-c	Compile but do not link; create file with .o extension.
-Dmacro=value	Define *macro* inside program as *value*.
-E	Preprocess, do not compile or link; output is sent to the screen.
-g	Include debugging information in executable.
-Idir	Include *dir* as directory to search for include files (where the name is within <>); multiple directories are separated by semicolons (;)
-Ldir	Include *dir* as directory to search for library files (used by linker to resolve external references); multiple directories are separated by semicolons (;).
-llibrary	Include *library* when linking.
-O	Optimize.
-ofile	Save the executable as *file*.
-Wall	Enable warnings for all code that should be avoided.
-w	Disable all warning messages

You can use multiple options on each compilation command line. You should insert a space before the beginning of each option (the minus sign). You should not have a space between the option and any arguments (such as -o and *file*).

GCC Compiler Tips

It is a good idea when creating an executable to use the -o option so you can specify the executable name (otherwise, the next compilation will overlay it with the default name).

By default, any error messages goes to your screen. You may want to redirect them to a file so you can review them at length using a text editor. This is especially handy when you have a lot of errors. You redirect the output to a file:

```
g++ lst02-01.g++ -olst02-01 > lst02-01.lst
```

Of course, the selection of filename is entirely up to you. I like to use a suffix of `.1st`.

As you build function libraries (more about functions in Day 5), you can compile them once and reuse them. If you do not change the source, there is no need to recompile. The `-c` option will create the intermediate compiled formatted object file. When you want to use the compiled code, you merely include its name on the command line.

As always, the biggest tip with any compiler or Linux tool is to check the manual page (or info file). Review the options, try them out, and see how they behave. They might help you!

Summary

The difficulty in learning a complex subject, such as programming, is that so much of what you learn depends on everything else there is to learn. This chapter introduced the basic parts of a simple C++ program. It also introduced the development cycle and a number of important new terms.

Q&A

Q What does `#include` do?

A This is a directive to the preprocessor, which runs when you call your compiler. This specific directive causes the file named after the word `include` to be read, as if it were typed in at that location in your source code.

Q What is the difference between `//` comments and `/*` style comments?

A The double-slash comments (`//`) "expire" at the end of the line. Slash-star (`/*`) comments are in effect until a closing comment (`*/`). Remember, not even the end of the function terminates a slash-star comment; you must put in the closing comment mark, or you will get a compile-time error.

Q What differentiates a good comment from a bad comment?

A A good comment tells the reader why this particular code is doing whatever it is doing or explains what a section of code is about to do. A bad comment restates what a particular line of code is doing. Lines of code should be written so that they speak for themselves. Reading the line of code should tell you what it is doing without needing a comment.

Workshop

The Workshop provides quiz questions to help you solidify your understanding of the material covered and exercises to provide you with experience in using what you learned today. Try to answer the quiz and exercise questions before checking the answers in Appendix D, "Answers to Exercises and Quizzes," and make sure you understand the answers before continuing to the next day.

Quiz

1. What is the difference between the compiler and the preprocessor?
2. Why is the function `main()` special?
3. What are the two types of comments, and how do they differ?
4. Can comments be nested?
5. Can comments be longer than one line?

Exercises

1. Write a program that writes "I love C++" to the screen.
2. Write the smallest program that can be compiled, linked, and run.
3. **BUG BUSTER:** Enter this program and compile it. Why does it fail? How can you fix it?

```
1: #include <iostream.h>
2: int main()
3: {
4:    cout << Is there a bug here?";
5:    return 0;
6: }
```

4. Fix the bug in Exercise 3 and recompile, link, and run it.

DAY **3**

Variables and Constants

Programs need a way to store the data they use. Variables and constants offer various ways to represent and manipulate that data.

Today you will learn:

- How to declare and define variables and constants
- How to assign values to variables and manipulate those values
- How to write the value of a variable to the screen

What Is a Variable?

In C++, a *variable* is a place to store information. A variable is a location in your computer's memory in which you can store a value and from which you can later retrieve that value.

Your computer's memory can be viewed as a series of cubbyholes. Each cubbyhole is one of many, many such holes all lined up. Each cubbyhole—or memory location—is numbered sequentially. These numbers are known as memory addresses. A variable reserves one or more cubbyholes in which you may store a value.

Your variable's name (for example, myVariable) is a label on one of these cubbyholes so that you can find it easily without knowing its actual memory address. Figure 3.1 is a schematic representation of this idea. As you can see from the figure, myVariable starts at memory address 103. Depending on the size of myVariable, it can take up one or more memory addresses.

FIGURE 3.1

A schematic representation of memory.

Variable Name

RAM

Address

> **Note**
>
> RAM is random access memory. When you run your program, it is loaded into RAM from the disk file. All variables are also created in RAM. When programmers talk about memory, it is usually RAM to which they are referring.

Variables are also known as *lvalues* because they can be used on the left side of an assignment operator. The assignment operator is the equal sign (more about the assignment operator in today's lesson, in the section "Assigning Values to Your Variables," and in Day 4, "Expressions and Statements," in the "Expressions" section). Variables can also be used on the right side of the assignment operator.

Setting Aside Memory

When you define a variable in C++, you must tell the compiler what kind of variable it is: an integer, a character, and so forth. This information tells the compiler how much room to set aside and what kind of value you want to store in your variable.

Each cubbyhole is 1 byte large. If the type of variable you create is 4 bytes in size, it needs 4 bytes of memory, or four cubbyholes. The type of the variable (for example, integer) tells the compiler how much memory (how many cubbyholes) to set aside for the variable.

Because computers use bits and bytes to represent values, and because memory is measured in bytes, it is important that you understand and are comfortable with these concepts. For a full review of this topic, please read Appendix C, "Binary, Octal, and Hexadecimal Numbers and an ASCII Chart."

Determining the Size of Integers and Other Data Types

On any one computer, each variable type takes up a single, unchanging amount of room. That is, an integer might be 2 bytes on one machine and four on another, but on either computer it is always the same, day in and day out.

A `char` variable (used to hold characters) is most often 1 byte long.

Note

There is endless debate about how to pronounce char. Some say it as "car," some say it as char as in charcoal, and others say it as "care." Feel free to say it however you like, but some people do make an issue about it—as if there were one true way.

3

A short integer is 2 bytes on most computers, a long integer is usually 4 bytes, and an integer (without the keyword `short` or `long`) can be 2 or 4 bytes. The size of an integer is determined by the computer (16-bit or 32-bit) and the compiler you use. On modern 32-bit (Pentium) computers using modern compilers (for example, gcc version 2 or newer), integers are 4 bytes. This book assumes a 4-byte integer, although your mileage may vary. Listing 3.1 should help you determine the exact size of these types on your computer.

A character is a single letter, number, or symbol that takes up 1 byte of memory.

INPUT **LISTING 3.1** Determining the Size of Variable Types on Your Computer

```
1:   #include <iostream.h>
2:
3:   int main()
4:   {
5:      cout << "The size of an int is:\t\t"    << sizeof(int)
        << " bytes.\n";
6:      cout << "The size of a short int is:\t" << sizeof(short)
        << " bytes.\n";
7:      cout << "The size of a long int is:\t"  << sizeof(long)
        << " bytes.\n";
8:      cout << "The size of a char is:\t\t"    << sizeof(char)
        << " bytes.\n";
9:      cout << "The size of a float is:\t\t"   << sizeof(float)
        << " bytes.\n";
```

continues

LISTING 3.1   CONTINUED

```
10:    cout << "The size of a double is:\t"    << sizeof(double)
➡ << " bytes.\n";
11:    cout << "The size of a bool is:\t"     << sizeof(bool)
➡   << " bytes.\n";
12:
13:    return 0;
14: }
```

OUTPUT

```
The size of an int is:        4 bytes.
The size of a short int is:   2 bytes.
The size of a long int is:    4 bytes.
The size of a char is:        1 bytes.
The size of a float is:       4 bytes.
The size of a double is:      8 bytes.
The size of a bool is:        1 bytes.
```

Note | On your computer, the number of bytes presented might be different.

ANALYSIS Most of Listing 3.1 should be pretty familiar. The one new feature is the use of the sizeof() operator in lines 5 through 11. sizeof() is provided by your compiler, and it tells you the size of the object you pass in as a parameter. On line 5, for example, the keyword int is passed into sizeof(). Using sizeof(), I was able to determine that on my computer an int is equal in size to a long int, which is 4 bytes.

Using Signed and Unsigned Integers

In addition, all integer types come in two varieties: signed and unsigned. The idea here is that sometimes you need negative numbers and sometimes you don't. Integers (short and long) without the word "unsigned" are assumed to be signed. Signed integers are either negative or positive. Unsigned integers are always positive.

Because you have the same number of bytes for both signed and unsigned integers, the largest number you can store in an unsigned integer is twice as big as the largest positive number you can store in a signed integer. An unsigned short integer can handle numbers from 0 to 65,535. Half the numbers represented by a signed short are negative, thus a signed short can only represent numbers from –32,768 to 32,767. If this is confusing, be sure to read Appendix C.

Understanding Fundamental Variable Types

Several other variable types are built into C++. They can be conveniently divided into integer variables (the type discussed so far), floating-point variables, and character variables.

Floating-point variables have values that can be expressed as fractions—that is, they are real numbers. Character variables hold a single byte and are used for holding the 256 characters and symbols of the ASCII and extended ASCII character sets.

The ASCII character set is the set of characters standardized for use on computers. ASCII is an acronym for American Standard Code for Information Interchange. Nearly every computer operating system supports ASCII, although many support other international character sets as well.

The types of variables used in C++ programs are described in Table 3.1. This table shows the variable type, how much room this book assumes it takes in memory, and what kinds of values can be stored in these variables. The values that can be stored are determined by the size of the variable types, so check your output against what you see in Listing 3.1.

TABLE 3.1 Variable Types

Type	Size	Values
bool	1 byte	True or false
unsigned short int	2 bytes	0 to 65,535
short int	2 bytes	–32,768 to 32,767
unsigned long int	4 bytes	0 to 4,294,967,295
long int	4 bytes	–2,147,483,648 to 2,147,483,647
int (16-bit)	2 bytes	–32,768 to 32,767
int (32-bit)	4 bytes	–2,147,483,648 to 2,147,483,647
unsigned int (16-bit)	2 bytes	0 to 65,535
unsigned int (32-bit)	4 bytes	0 to 4,294,967,295
char	1 byte	256 character values, if signed, then –128 to 127; if unsigned, then 0 to 255
float	4 bytes	–1.2e–38 to 3.4e38
double	8 bytes	–2.2e–308 to 1.8e308

Note

The sizes of variables might be different from those shown in Table 3.1, depending on the compiler and the computer you are using. If your computer had the same output as presented in Listing 3.1, Table 3.1 should apply to your compiler. If your output was different from that shown in Listing 3.1, you should consult the manual pages for the values that your variable types can hold on your system.

Another place you can look is in the header file limits.h.

Defining a Variable

You create or define a variable by stating its type, followed by one or more spaces, followed by the variable name and a semicolon. The variable name must begin with a letter or an underscore and can contain virtually any combination of letters, numbers, and underscores, but it cannot contain spaces. Legal variable names include x, J23qrsnf, my_Age, and myAge. Good variable names tell you what the variables are for; using good names makes it easier to understand the flow of your program. The following statement defines an integer variable called myAge:

```
int myAge;
```

Note

When you define or declare a variable, memory is allocated (set aside) for that variable. The *value* of the variable will be whatever happened to be in that memory at that time. You will see in a moment how to assign a new value to that memory.

Structures and object classes behave a little differently than regular variables. You will learn that difference when you get to that day's lesson. You can define or declare an object class but not use any memory. It is when you actually create the object that space is allocated.

As a general programming practice, avoid such horrific names as J23qrsnf, and restrict single-letter variable names (such as x or i) to variables that are used only very briefly. Try to use expressive names such as myAge or howMany. Such names are easier to understand three weeks later when you are scratching your head trying to figure out what you meant when you wrote that line of code.

Try this experiment. Guess what these pieces of programs do, based on the first few lines of code:

Example 1

```
int main()
{
    unsigned short x;
    unsigned short y;
    unsigned short z;
    z = x * y;
    return 0;
}
```

Example 2

```
int main ()
{
    unsigned short Width;
    unsigned short Length;
    unsigned short Area;
    Area = Width * Length;
    return 0;
}
```

Note If you compile this program, your compiler will warn you that these values are not initialized. You'll see how to solve this problem shortly.

Clearly, the purpose of the second program is easier to guess, and the inconvenience of having to type the longer variable names is more than made up for by how much easier it is to maintain the second program.

Case Sensitivity

C++ is case sensitive. In other words, uppercase and lowercase letters are considered to be different. A variable named age is different from Age, which is different from AGE.

Note Some compilers allow you to turn case sensitivity off. The GNU compilers do not, so do not be tempted to do this.

Various conventions exist for naming variables, and although it does not matter much which method you adopt, it is important to be consistent throughout your program.

Many programmers prefer to use all lowercase letters for their variable names. If the name requires two words (for example, my car), two popular conventions are used: my_car or myCar. The latter form is called *camel notation* because the capitalization looks something like a camel's hump.

Some people find the underscore character (my_car) to be easier to read, but others prefer to avoid the underscore because it is more difficult to type. This book uses camel notation, in which the second and all subsequent words are capitalized: myCar, theQuickBrownFox, and so forth.

> **Note**
>
> Many advanced programmers employ a notation style that is often referred to as *Hungarian notation*. The idea behind Hungarian notation is to prefix every variable with a set of characters that describes its type. Integer variables might begin with a lowercase letter i, and longs might begin with a lowercase l. Other notations indicate constants, globals, pointers, and so forth. Most of this is much more important in C programming because C++ supports the creation of user-defined types (see Day 6, "Basic Classes") and because C++ is strongly typed.

Keywords

Some words are reserved by C++, and you may not use them as variable names. Another name for keywords is *reserved words*. These are keywords used by the compiler to control your program. Keywords include if, while, for, and main. Your compiler manual should provide a complete list, but generally, any reasonable name for a variable is almost certainly not a keyword. A list of C++ keywords is available in Appendix B, "C++ Keywords."

Do	Don't
DO define a variable by writing the type, then the variable name.	**DON'T** use C++ keywords as variable names.
DO use meaningful variable names.	**DON'T** use unsigned variables for negative numbers.
DO remember that C++ is case sensitive.	
DO understand the number of bytes each variable type consumes in memory and what values can be stored in variables of that type.	

> **Note**
>
> Variable names can contain keywords but cannot be solely that keyword.
> `return_value` is a valid variable name, but `return` is not.

Creating More Than One Variable at a Time

You can create more than one variable of the same type in one statement by writing the type and then the variable names, separated by commas. For example:

```
unsigned int myAge, myWeight;   // two unsigned int variables
long int area, width, length;    // three long integers
```

As you can see, `myAge` and `myWeight` are each declared as unsigned integer variables. The second line declares three individual long variables named `area`, `width`, and `length`. The type (`long`) is assigned to all the variables, so you cannot mix types in one definition statement.

Assigning Values to Your Variables

You assign a value to a variable by using the assignment operator (`=`). Thus, you would assign 5 to `Width` by writing

```
unsigned short Width;
Width = 5;
```

> **Note**
>
> `long` is a shorthand version of `long int`, and `short` is a shorthand version of `short int`.

You can combine these steps and initialize `Width` when you declare it by writing

```
unsigned short Width = 5;
```

Initialization looks very much like assignment, and with integer variables, the difference is minor. Later, when constants are covered, you will see that some values must be initialized because they cannot be assigned to. The essential difference is that initialization takes place at the moment you create the variable.

Just as you can define more than one variable at a time, you can initialize more than one variable at the same time. For example:

```
// create two long variables and initialize them
long width = 5, length = 7;
```

This example initializes the long integer variable width to the value 5 and the long integer variable length to the value 7. You can even mix definitions and initializations:

```
int myAge = 39, yourAge, hisAge = 40;
```

This example creates three type int variables, and it initializes the first and third.

Listing 3.2 shows a complete program, ready to compile, that computes the area of a rectangle and writes the answer to the screen.

INPUT   **LISTING 3.2**   A Demonstration of the Use of Variables

```
1:   // Demonstration of variables
2:   #include <iostream.h>
3:
4:   int main()
5:   {
6:       unsigned short int Width = 5, Length;
7:       Length = 10;
8:
9:       // create an unsigned short and initialize with result
10:      // of multiplying Width by Length
11:      unsigned short int Area  = (Width * Length);
12:
13:      cout << "Width:" << Width << "\n";
14:      cout << "Length: "  << Length << endl;
15:      cout << "Area: " << Area << endl;
16:      return 0;
17:  }
```

OUTPUT
```
Width:5
Length: 10
Area: 50
```

ANALYSIS Line 2 includes the required include statement for the iostream's library so that cout will work. Line 4 begins the program.

On line 6, Width is defined as an unsigned short integer, and its value is initialized to 5. Another unsigned short integer, Length, is also defined, but it is not initialized. On line 7, the value 10 is assigned to Length.

On line 11, an unsigned short integer, Area, is defined, and it is initialized with the value obtained by multiplying Width times Length. On lines 13 to 15, the values of the variables are printed to the screen. Note that the special word endl creates a new line.

Using `typedef`

It can become tedious, repetitious, and, most important, error-prone to keep writing `unsigned short int`. C++ enables you to create an alias for this phrase by using the keyword `typedef`, which stands for type definition.

In effect, you are creating a synonym, and it is important to distinguish this from creating a new type (which you will do on Day 6) because `typedef` does not create a new data type.

`typedef` is used by writing the keyword `typedef`, followed by the existing type, then the new name, and ending with a semicolon. For example,

```
typedef unsigned short int USHORT;
```

creates the new name `USHORT` that you can use anywhere you might have written `unsigned short int`. Listing 3.3 is a replay of Listing 3.2, using the type definition `USHORT` rather than `unsigned short int`.

INPUT   **LISTING 3.3**   A Demonstration of `typedef`

```
1:   // ******************
2:   // Demonstrates typedef keyword
3:   #include <iostream.h>
4:
5:   typedef unsigned short int USHORT;       //typedef defined
6:
7:   int main()
8:   {
9:      USHORT  Width = 5;
10:     USHORT Length;
11:     Length = 10;
12:     USHORT Area  = Width * Length;
13:     cout << "Width:" << Width << "\n";
14:     cout << "Length: "  << Length << endl;
15:     cout << "Area: " << Area <<endl;
16:     return 0;
17: }
```

OUTPUT
```
Width:5
Length: 10
Area: 50
```

ANALYSIS   On line 5, `USHORT` is typedefined as a synonym for `unsigned short int`. The program is very much like Listing 3.2, and the output is the same.

When to Use short and When to Use long

One source of confusion for new C++ programmers is when to declare a variable to be type long and when to declare it to be type short. The rule, when understood, is fairly straightforward: If any chance exists that the value you will want to put into your variable will be too big for its type, use a larger type.

As shown in Table 3.1, unsigned short integers, assuming that they are 2 bytes, can hold a value only up to 65,535. Signed short integers split their values between positive and negative numbers, and thus their maximum value is only half that of the unsigned.

Although unsigned long integers can hold an extremely large number (4,294,967,295), that is still quite finite. If you need a larger number, you'll have to go to float or double, and then you lose some precision. Floats and doubles can hold extremely large numbers, but only the first 7 or 19 digits are significant on most computers. That means that the number is rounded off after that many digits.

Shorter variables use up less memory. These days, memory is cheap and life is short. Feel free to use int, which will probably be 4 bytes on your machine.

Wrapping Around an unsigned Integer

The fact that unsigned long integers have a limit to the values they can hold is only rarely a problem, but what happens if you do run out of room?

When an unsigned integer reaches its maximum value, it wraps around and starts over, much as a car odometer might. Listing 3.4 shows what happens if you try to put too large a value into a short integer.

INPUT | **LISTING 3.4** A Demonstration of Putting Too Large a Value in an unsigned Integer

```
1: #include <iostream.h>
2: int main()
3: {
4:     unsigned short int smallNumber;
5:     smallNumber = 65535;
6:     cout << "small number:" << smallNumber << endl;
7:     smallNumber++;
8:     cout << "small number:" << smallNumber << endl;
9:     smallNumber++;
10:    cout << "small number:" << smallNumber << endl;
11:    return 0;
12: }
```

OUTPUT
```
small number:65535
small number:0
small number:1
```

ANALYSIS On line 4, smallNumber is declared to be an unsigned short int, which on my computer is a 2-byte variable, able to hold a value between 0 and 65,535. On line 5, the maximum value is assigned to smallNumber, and it is printed on line 6.

On line 7, smallNumber is incremented; that is, 1 is added to it. The symbol for incrementing is ++ (as in the name C++—an incremental increase from C). Thus, the value in smallNumber would be 65,536. However, unsigned short integers can't hold a number larger than 65,535, so the value is wrapped around to 0, which is printed on line 8.

On line 9, smallNumber is incremented again, and then its new value, 1, is printed.

Wrapping Around a signed Integer

A signed integer is different from an unsigned integer, in that half of the values you can represent are negative. Instead of picturing a traditional car odometer, you might picture one that rotates up for positive numbers and down for negative numbers. One mile from 0 is either 1 or –1. When you run out of positive numbers, you run right into the most negative numbers (largest absolute value) and then count back down to 0. Listing 3.5 shows what happens when you add 1 to the maximum positive number in a short integer.

INPUT **LISTING 3.5** A Demonstration of Adding Too Large a Number to a signed Integer

```
1:  #include <iostream.h>
2:  int main()
3:  {
4:      short int smallNumber;
5:      smallNumber = 32767;
6:      cout << "small number:" << smallNumber << endl;
7:      smallNumber++;
8:      cout << "small number:" << smallNumber << endl;
9:      smallNumber++;
10:     cout << "small number:" << smallNumber << endl;
11:     return 0;
12: }
```

OUTPUT
```
small number:32767
small number:-32768
small number:-32767
```

ANALYSIS On line 4, `smallNumber` is declared this time to be a signed short integer (if you do not explicitly say that it is unsigned, it is assumed to be signed). The program proceeds much as the preceding one, but the output is quite different. To fully understand this output, you must be comfortable with how signed numbers are represented as bits in a 2-byte integer.

The bottom line, however, is that just like an unsigned integer, the signed integer wraps around from its highest positive value to its most negative value (highest absolute value).

Using Character Variables

Character variables (type `char`) are typically 1 byte, enough to hold 256 values (see Appendix C). A `char` can be interpreted as a small number (–128 to 127 or if unsigned, 0 to 255) or as a member of the ASCII set. ASCII stands for the American Standard Code for Information Interchange. The ASCII character set and its ISO (International Standards Organization) equivalent are a way to encode all the letters, numerals, and punctuation marks.

Note
> Computers do not know about letters, punctuation, or sentences. All they understand is numbers. In fact, all they really know about is whether a sufficient amount of electricity is at a particular junction of wires. If so, it is represented internally as a 1; if not, it is represented as a 0. By grouping ones and zeros, the computer is able to generate patterns that can be interpreted as numbers, and these, in turn, can be assigned to letters and punctuation.
>
> Your program is stored in memory as a bunch of ones and zeros also; the computer knows how to interpret them properly.

In the ASCII code, the lowercase letter "a" is assigned the value 97. All the lower- and uppercase letters, all the numerals, and all the punctuation marks are assigned values between 0 and 127. An additional 128 marks and symbols are reserved for use by the computer maker, although the IBM extended character set has become something of a standard.

Note
> ASCII is usually pronounced "Ask-ee."

> **Note**
>
> Linux is ASCII-based; older operating systems (IBM mainframe and some others) use the EBCDIC character set. EBCDIC stands for Extended Binary Coded Decimal Interchange Code and is related to the way holes are punched in Hollerith cards (a data entry method I hope you never get to see, except in a museum).

Characters as Numbers

When you put a character, for example, "a," into a char variable, what really is there is a number between −128 and 127. Some systems use unsigned characters, which are numbers between 0 and 255. The compiler knows, however, how to translate back and forth between characters (represented by a single quotation mark and then a letter, numeral, or punctuation mark, followed by a closing single quotation mark) and one of the ASCII values.

The value/letter relationship is arbitrary; there is no particular reason that the lowercase "a" is assigned the value 97. As long as everyone (your keyboard, compiler, and screen) agrees, no problem occurs. It is important to realize, however, that a big difference exists between the value 5 and the character '5'. The latter is actually valued at 53, much as the letter "a" is valued at 97.

Listing 3.6 shows that characters are stored as numbers in memory.

INPUT   **LISTING 3.6**   Printing Characters Based on Numbers

```
1:   #include <iostream.h>
2:   int main()
3:   {
4:       for (int i = 32; i<128; i++)
5:           cout << (char) i;
6:       return 0;
7:   }
```

OUTPUT
```
 !"#$%'()*+,./0123456789:;<>?@ABCDEFGHIJKLMNOP
_QRSTUVWXYZ[\]^'abcdefghijklmnopqrstuvwxyz{|}~
```

ANALYSIS   This simple program prints the character values for the integers 32 through 127.

Day 12, "Arrays, C Strings, and Linked Lists," provides more information on combining characters together in arrays and strings to build things like words.

Special Printing Characters

The C++ compiler recognizes some special characters for formatting. Table 3.2 shows the most common ones. You put these into your code by typing the backslash (called the escape character), followed by the character. Thus, to put a tab character into your code, you would enter a single quotation mark, a backslash, the letter t, and then a closing single quotation mark:

```
char tabCharacter = '\t';
```

This example declares a char variable (`tabCharacter`) and initializes it with the character value \t, which is recognized as a tab. The special printing characters are used when printing either to the screen or to a file or other output device.

An escape character changes the meaning of the character that follows it. For example, normally the character n means the letter n, but when it is preceded by the escape character (\), it means new line.

TABLE 3.2   The Escape Characters

Character	What It Means
\n	New line
\t	Tab
\b	Backspace
\"	Double quote
\'	Single quote
\?	Question mark
\\	Backslash

Using Constants

Like variables, constants are data storage locations. Unlike variables, and as the name implies, constants don't change. You must initialize a constant when you create it, and you cannot assign a new value later.

Literal Constants

C++ has two types of constants: literal and symbolic.

A literal constant is a value typed directly into your program wherever it is needed, for example:

```
int myAge = 39;
```

`myAge` is a variable of type `int`; 39 is a literal constant. You are not allowed to assign a value to 39, and its value can't be changed. It is an *rvalue* because it can only appear on the right side of an assignment statement.

Symbolic Constants

A symbolic constant is a constant that is represented by a name, just as a variable is represented. Unlike a variable, however, after a constant is initialized, its value can't be changed.

If your program has one integer variable named `students` and another named `classes`, you could compute how many students you have, given a known number of classes, if you knew each class consisted of 15 students:

```
students = classes * 15;
```

Note	* indicates multiplication.

In this example, 15 is a literal constant. Your code would be easier to read, and easier to maintain, if you substituted a symbolic constant for this value:

```
students = classes * studentsPerClass
```

If you later decided to change the number of students in each class, you could do so where you define the constant `studentsPerClass` without having to make a change every place you used that value.

Two ways exist to declare a symbolic constant in C++. The old, traditional, and now obsolete way is with a preprocessor directive, `#define` and the `const` keyword.

Defining Constants with `#define`

To define a constant the traditional way, you would enter this:

```
#define studentsPerClass 15
```

Note that `studentsPerClass` is of no particular type (`int`, `char`, and so on). `#define` does a simple text substitution. Every time the preprocessor sees the word `studentsPerClass`, it puts in the number 15.

Because the preprocessor runs before the compiler, your compiler never sees your constant; it sees the number 15.

Just because it is old and obsolete does not mean you don't have to understand it—many programmers grew up with this directive, and there are many lines of code that use it.

Defining Constants with `const`

Although `#define` works, a new, much better way exists to define constants in C++:

```
const unsigned short int studentsPerClass = 15;
```

This example also declares a symbolic constant named `studentsPerClass`, but this time `studentsPerClass` is typed as an `unsigned short int`. This method has several advantages in making your code easier to maintain and in preventing bugs. The biggest difference is that this constant has a type, and the compiler can enforce that it is used according to its type.

Note

Constants cannot be changed while the program is running. If you need to change `studentsPerClass`, for example, you need to change the code and recompile.

Do	Don't
DO watch for numbers overrunning the size of the integer and wrapping around incorrect values.	**DON'T** use the term `int`. Use `short` and `long` to make it clear which size number you intended.
DO give your variables meaningful names that reflect their use.	**DON'T** use keywords as variable names.

Using Enumerated Constants

Enumerated constants enable you to create new types and then to define variables of those types whose values are restricted to a set of possible values. For example, you can declare COLOR to be an enumeration, and you can define five values for COLOR: RED, BLUE, GREEN, WHITE, and BLACK.

The syntax for enumerated constants is to write the keyword enum, followed by the type name, an open brace, each of the legal values separated by a comma, and finally, a closing brace and a semicolon. Here's an example:

```
enum COLOR { RED, BLUE, GREEN, WHITE, BLACK };
```

This statement performs two tasks:

   1. It makes COLOR the name of an enumeration, that is, a new type.

2. It makes RED a symbolic constant with the value 0, BLUE a symbolic constant with the value 1, GREEN a symbolic constant with the value 2, and so forth.

Every enumerated constant has an integer value. If you don't specify otherwise, the first constant will have the value 0, and the rest will count up from there. Any one of the constants can be initialized with a particular value, however, and those that are not initialized will count upward from the ones before them. Thus, if you write

```
enum Color { RED=100, BLUE, GREEN=500, WHITE, BLACK=700 };
```

then RED will have the value 100; BLUE, the value 101; GREEN, the value 500; WHITE, the value 501; and BLACK, the value 700.

You can define variables of type COLOR, but they can be assigned only one of the enumerated values (in this case, RED, BLUE, GREEN, WHITE, or BLACK, or else 100, 101, 500, 501, or 700). You can assign any color value to your COLOR variable. In fact, you can assign any integer value, even if it is not a legal color, although a good compiler will issue a warning if you do. It is important to realize that enumerator variables actually are of type unsigned int, and that the enumerated constants equate to integer variables. It is, however, very convenient to be able to name these values when working with colors, days of the week, or similar sets of values.

With enumerated variables, you do not create a new data type—you just hide the implementation details. As a programmer, you use words like RED or BLUE, but the compiler substitutes numbers behind the scenes. This process makes creating and understanding the program a lot easier.

Listing 3.7 presents a program that uses an enumerated type.

INPUT   **LISTING 3.7**   A Demonstration of Enumerated Constants

```
1: #include <iostream.h>
2: int main()
3: {
4:    enum Days { Sunday, Monday, Tuesday,
5:       Wednesday, Thursday, Friday, Saturday };
6:    int choice;
7:    cout << "Enter a day (0-6): ";
8:    cin >> choice;
9:    if (choice == Sunday || choice == Saturday)
10:      cout << "\nYou're already off on weekends!\n";
11:   else
12:      cout << "\nOkay, I'll put in the vacation day.\n";
13:   return 0;
14: }
```

OUTPUT
```
Enter a day (0-6): 6
You're already off on weekends!
```

ANALYSIS
On line 4, the enumerated constant DAYS is defined, with seven values. Each of these evaluates to an integer, counting upward from 0; thus, Tuesday's value is 2.

The user is prompted for a value between 0 and 6. The user cannot type the word "Sunday" when prompted for a day; the program does not know how to translate the characters in Sunday into one of the enumerated values. You can, however, test the value the user enters against one or more of the enumerated constants, as shown in line 9. Here the use of enumerated constants makes the intent of the comparison more explicit. This same effect could have been accomplished by using constant integers, as shown in Listing 3.8, but with a little more programming effort.

Note

For this and all the small programs in this book, all the code you would normally write to deal with what happens when the user types inappropriate data has been left out. For example, this program does not check, as it would in a real program, to make sure that the user types a number between 0 and 6. This detail has been left out to keep these programs small and simple, and to focus on the issue at hand.

In real programs, this data validation should be included. You never know what a user (or some cracker trying to break into your system) is going to do. The generic term for this is *defensive programming* because you defend the consistency and proper behavior of your code and data.

INPUT   **LISTING 3.8**   Same Program Using Constant Integers

```
1: #include <iostream.h>
2: int main()
3: {
4:     const int Sunday = 0;
5:     const int Monday = 1;
6:     const int Tuesday = 2;
7:     const int Wednesday = 3;
8:     const int Thursday = 4;
9:     const int Friday = 5;
10:    const int Saturday = 6;
11:
12:    int choice;
13:    cout << "Enter a day (0-6): ";
14:    cin >> choice;
15:
16:    if (choice == Sunday || choice == Saturday)
17:        cout << "\nYou're already off on weekends!\n";
```

```
18:    else
19:       cout << "\nOkay, I'll put in the vacation day.\n";
20:
21:    return 0;
22:}
```

OUTPUT
```
Enter a day (0-6): 6
You're already off on weekends!
```

ANALYSIS The output of this listing is identical to that shown in Listing 3.7. Here, each of the constants (Sunday, Monday, and so on) was explicitly defined, and no enumerated Days type exists. Enumerated constants have the advantage of being self-documenting—the intent of the Days enumerated type is immediately clear.

Summary

Today's lesson has discussed numeric and character variables and constants, which are used by C++ to store data during the execution of your program. Numeric variables are either integral (char, int, short int, and long int) or they are floating point (float and double). Numeric variables can also be signed or unsigned. Although all the types can be of various sizes among different computers, the type specifies an exact size on any given computer.

You must declare a variable before it can be used, and then you must store the type of data that you've declared as correct for that variable. If you put too large a number into an integral variable, it wraps around and produces an incorrect result.

This lesson also reviewed literal and symbolic constants as well as enumerated constants, and it showed two ways to declare a symbolic constant: using #define and using the keyword const.

Q&A

Q If a short int can run out of room and wrap around, why not always use long integers?

A Both short integers and long integers will run out of room and wrap around, but a long integer will do so with a much larger number. For example, an unsigned short int will wrap around after 65,535, whereas an unsigned long int will not wrap around until 4,294,967,295. However, on most machines, a long integer takes up twice as much memory every time you declare one (4 bytes versus 2 bytes), and a program with 100 such variables will consume an extra 200 bytes of RAM. Frankly, this is less of a problem than it used to be because most personal computers now come with many thousands (if not millions) of bytes of memory.

Q What happens if I assign a number with a decimal point to an integer rather than to a float? Consider the following line of code:

```
int aNumber = 5.4;
```

A A good compiler will issue a warning, but the assignment is completely legal. The number you've assigned will be truncated into an integer. Thus, if you assign 5.4 to an integer variable, that variable will have the value 5. Information will be lost, however, and if you then try to assign the value in that integer variable to a float variable, the float variable will have only 5.

Q Why not use literal constants; why go to the bother of using symbolic constants?

A If you use the value in many places throughout your program, a symbolic constant allows all the values to change just by changing the one definition of the constant. Symbolic constants also speak for themselves. It might be hard to understand why a number is being multiplied by 360, but it's much easier to understand what's going on if the number is being multiplied by `degreesInACircle`.

Q What happens if I assign a negative number to an unsigned variable? Consider the following line of code:

```
unsigned int aPositiveNumber = -1;
```

A A good compiler will warn, but the assignment is legal. The negative number will be assessed as a bit pattern and assigned to the variable. The value of that variable will then be interpreted as an unsigned number. Thus, 1, whose bit pattern is 11111111 11111111 (0xFF in hex), will be assessed as the unsigned value 65,535. If this information confuses you, refer to Appendix C.

Q Can I work with C++ without understanding bit patterns, binary arithmetic, and hexadecimal?

A Yes, but not as effectively as if you do understand these topics. C++ does not do as good a job as some languages at "protecting" you from what the computer is really doing. This is actually a benefit because it provides you with tremendous power that other languages don't. As with any power tool, however, to get the most out of C++, you must understand how it works. Programmers who try to program in C++ without understanding the fundamentals of the binary system often are confused by their results.

Workshop

The Workshop provides quiz questions to help you solidify your understanding of the material covered and exercises to provide you with experience in using what you've learned. Try to answer the quiz and exercise questions before checking the answers in Appendix D, "Answers to Exercises and Quizzes," and make sure that you understand the answers before continuing to the next day.

Quiz

1. What is the difference between an integer variable and a floating-point variable?

2. What are the differences between an `unsigned short int` and a `long int`?

3. What are the advantages of using a symbolic constant rather than a literal constant?

4. What are the advantages of using the `const` keyword rather than `#define`?

5. What makes for a good or bad variable name?

6. Given this enum, what is the value of `BLUE`?

   ```
   enum COLOR { WHITE, BLACK = 100, RED, BLUE, GREEN = 300 };
   ```

7. Which of the following variable names are good, which are bad, and which are invalid?

   a. `Age`

   b. `!ex`

   c. `R79J`

   d. `TotalIncome`

   e. `__Invalid`

Exercises

1. What would be the correct variable type in which to store the following information?

   a. Your age.

   b. The area of your back yard.

   c. The number of stars in the galaxy.

   d. The average rainfall for the month of January.

2. Create good variable names for the information in question 1.

3. Declare a constant for *pi* as 3.14159.

4. Declare a float variable and initialize it using your *pi* constant.

DAY 4

Expressions and Statements

At its heart, a program is a set of commands executed in sequence. The power in a program comes from its capability to execute one or another set of commands, based on whether a particular condition is true or false. Today you will learn:

- What statements are
- What blocks are
- What expressions are
- How to branch your code based on conditions
- What truth is, and how to act on it

Statements

In C++, a *statement* controls the sequence of execution, evaluates an expression, or does nothing (the null statement). All C++ statements end with a semicolon, even the `null` statement, which is just the semicolon and nothing else. One of the most common statements is the following assignment statement:

```
x = a + b;
```

Unlike in algebra, this statement does not mean that x equals a+b. This is read, "Assign the value of the sum of a and b to x," or "Assign to x: a+b." Even though this statement is doing two things, it is one statement and thus has one semicolon. The assignment operator assigns whatever is on the right side of the equal sign to whatever is on the left side.

Whitespace

Whitespace (which you create by using tabs, spaces, and newline characters) is generally ignored in statements. The assignment statement previously discussed could be written as

```
x=a+b;
```

or as

```
x                           =a
+              b            ;
```

Although this last variation is perfectly legal, it is also perfectly foolish. Whitespace can be used to make your programs more readable and easier to maintain, or it can be used to create horrific and indecipherable code. In this, as in all things, C++ provides the power; you supply the judgment.

Whitespace characters (spaces, tabs, and newline characters) cannot be seen. If these characters are printed, you see only the white of the paper.

Blocks and Compound Statements

Any place you can put a single statement, you can put a compound statement, also called a block. A block begins with an opening brace ({) and ends with a closing brace (}). Although every statement in the block must end with a semicolon, the block itself does not end with a semicolon, as shown in the following example:

```
{
    temp = a;
    a = b;
    b = temp;
}
```

This block of code acts as one statement and swaps the values in the variables a and b.

Do	Don't
DO use a closing brace any time you have an opening brace.	
DO end your statements with a semicolon.	
DO use whitespace judiciously to make your code clearer.	

Compound statements are very important, as you will find when you get to the sections about if/else, for, while, and do/while statements. Those statements can only have one statement after them (as part of the true or false results of the if/else or loop body of the for, while, and do/while). In order to put more than one statement after any of those, you have to use a compound statement (which counts as the one statement) to contain as many statements as you need. You will learn more about this in the section "The if Statement" in this lesson.

Expressions

Anything that evaluates to a value is an *expression* in C++. An expression is said to return a value. Thus the statement 3+2; returns the value 5, so it is an expression. All expressions are statements.

The myriad pieces of code that qualify as expressions might surprise you. Here are three examples:

```
3.2                     // returns the value 3.2

PI                      // float const that returns the value 3.14

SecondsPerMinute        // int const that returns 60
```

Assuming that PI is a constant equal to 3.14 and SecondsPerMinute is a constant equal to 60, all three of these statements are expressions.

The complex expression

```
x = a + b;
```

not only adds a and b and assigns the result to x, but returns the value of that assignment (the value of x) as well. Thus this statement is also an expression. Because it is an expression, it can be on the right side of an assignment operator:

```
y = x = a + b;
```

This line is evaluated in the following order:

Add a to b.

Assign the result of the expression a + b to x.

Assign the result of the assignment expression x = a + b to y.

If a, b, x, and y are all integers, and if a has the value 2 and b has the value 5, both x and y will be assigned the value 7.

Listing 4.1 shows how C++ evaluates complex expressions.

INPUT   **LISTING 4.1**   Evaluating Complex Expressions

```
1:     #include <iostream.h>
2:     int main()
3:     {
4:         int a=0, b=0, x=0, y=35;
5:         cout << "a: " << a << " b: " << b;
6:         cout << " x: " << x << " y: " << y << endl;
7:         a = 9;
8:         b = 7;
9:         y = x = a+b;
10:        cout << "a: " << a << " b: " << b;
11:        cout << " x: " << x << " y: " << y << endl;
12:        return 0;
13:    }
```

OUTPUT   a: 0 b: 0 x: 0 y: 35
              a: 9 b: 7 x: 16 y: 16

ANALYSIS   On line 4, the four variables are declared and initialized. Their values are printed on lines 5 and 6. On line 7, a is assigned the value 9. On line 8, b is assigned the value 7. On line 9, the values of a and b are summed and the result is assigned to x. This expression (x = a+b) evaluates to a value (the sum of a + b), and that value is, in turn, assigned to y.

Operators

An *operator* is a symbol that causes the compiler to take an action. Operators act on operands, and in C++ all operands are expressions. In C++ several categories of operators exist. Two of these categories are

- Assignment operators
- Mathematical operators

Assignment Operator

The assignment operator (=) causes the operand on the left side of the assignment operator to have its value changed to the value on the right side of the assignment operator. The following expression

```
x = a + b;
```

assigns the value that is the result of adding a and b to the operand x.

An operand that can legally be on the left side of an assignment operator is called an *l-value* (lvalue). That which can be on the right side is called (you guessed it) an *r-value* (rvalue).

Constants are r-values. They cannot be l-values. Thus you can write

```
x = 35;          // ok
```

but you cannot legally write

```
35 = x;          // error, not an l-value!
```

This is important for you to remember, so it gets repeated: An l-value is an operand that can be on the left side of an expression. An r-value is an operand that can be on the right side of an expression. Note that all l-values are r-values, but not all r-values are l-values. An example of an r-value that is not an l-value is a literal. Thus you can write x = 5;, but you cannot write 5 = x; (x can be an l-value or an r-value, 5 can only be an r-value)

Mathematical Operators

The five primary mathematical operators are addition (+), subtraction (-), multiplication (*), division (/), and modulus (%).

Addition and subtraction work as you would expect, although subtraction with unsigned integers can lead to surprising results if the result is a negative number. You saw

4

something much like this yesterday, when variable overflow was described. Listing 4.2 shows what happens when you subtract a large unsigned number from a small unsigned number.

INPUT **LISTING 4.2** A Demonstration of Subtraction and Integer Overflow

```
1: // Listing 4.2 - demonstrates subtraction and
2: // integer overflow
3: #include <iostream.h>
4:
5: int main()
6: {
7:     unsigned int difference;
8:     unsigned int bigNumber = 100;
9:     unsigned int smallNumber = 50;
10:     difference = bigNumber - smallNumber;
11:     cout << "Difference is: " << difference;
12:     difference = smallNumber - bigNumber;
13:     cout << "\nNow difference is: " << difference <<endl;
14:     return 0;
15: }
```

OUTPUT
```
Difference is: 50
Now difference is: 4294967246
```

ANALYSIS The subtraction operator is invoked on line 10, and the result is printed on line 11, much as you might expect. The subtraction operator is called again on line 12, but this time a large unsigned number is subtracted from a small unsigned number. The result would be negative, but because it is evaluated (and printed) as an unsigned number, the result is an overflow, as described yesterday. This topic is reviewed in detail in Appendix A, "Operator Precedence."

Integer Division and Modulus

Integer division is somewhat different from everyday division. In fact, integer division is *the same as* division you learned when you were in second grade. When you divide 21 by 4 (21 / 4), and you are doing integer division (or you are seven years old), the answer is 5 remainder 1.

To get the remainder, you take 21 modulus 4 (21 % 4), and the result is 1. The modulus operator tells you the remainder after an integer division.

Finding the modulus can be very useful. For example, you might want to print a statement on every tenth action. Any number whose value is 0 when you modulus 10 with that number is an exact multiple of 10. Thus 1 % 10 is 1, 2 % 10 is 2, and so forth, until

10 % 10, whose result is 0. 11 % 10 is back to 1, and this pattern continues until the next multiple of 10, which is 20. You will see this technique when looping is discussed on Day 7, "More Program Flow."

Frequently Asked Questions

FAQ: When I divide 5/3, I get 1. What is going wrong?

Answer: If you divide one integer by another, you get an integer as a result.

Thus 5/3 will be 1.

To get a fractional (with decimal) return value, you must use floats.

5.0 / 3.0 will give you a fractional (with decimal) answer: 1.66667.

If your method takes integers as parameters, you have to cast them to type float.

When you cast a variable, you force a change in its type. Essentially, you are saying to the compiler, "I know what I am doing." And you had better, because the compiler will say "Okay, boss, you're on your own."

In this particular case, you want to say to the compiler, "I know you think this is an integer, but I know what I am doing: This is really a float."

Two ways exist to do this cast: You can use the old C-style cast or use the new ANSI-approved static_cast operator. Listing 4.3 illustrates casting to a float.

INPUT   **LISTING 4.3**   Casting to a Float

```
1: #include <iostream.h>
2:
3: void intDiv(int x, int y)
4: {
5:      int z = x / y;
6:      cout << "z: " << z << endl;
7: }
8:
9: void floatDiv(int x, int y)
10:{
11:     float a = (float)x;                    // old style
12:     float b = static_cast<float>(y);    // preferred style
13:     float c = a / b;
14:
15:     cout << "c: " << c << endl;
16:}
17:
18: int main()
19: {
```

4

continues

LISTING 4.3 CONTINUED

```
20:        int x = 5, y = 3;
21:        intDiv(x,y);
22:        floatDiv(x,y);
23:        return 0;
24: }
```

OUTPUT

```
z: 1
c: 1.66667
```

ANALYSIS On line 20, a pair of integer variables are declared. They are passed as parameters to `intDiv` on line 21 and as parameters to `floatDiv` on line 22. This second method is shown beginning on line 9. On lines 11 and 12, the integers are cast to float and assigned to float variables. The result of the division is assigned to a third float on line 13 and printed on line 15.

Combining the Assignment and Mathematical Operators

It is not uncommon to want to add a value to a variable and then to assign the result back into the variable. If you have a variable `myAge` and you want to increase the value by two, you can write

```
int myAge = 5;
int temp;
temp = myAge + 2;   // add 5 + 2 and put it in temp
myAge = temp;              // put it back in myAge
```

This method, however, is terribly convoluted and wasteful. In C++, you can put the same variable on both sides of the assignment operator; thus the preceding becomes

```
myAge = myAge + 2;
```

which is much better. In algebra, this expression would be meaningless, but in C++ it is read as "add two to the value in `myAge` and assign the result to `myAge`."

Even simpler to write, but perhaps a bit harder to read is

```
myAge += 2;
```

The self-assigned addition operator (+=) adds the r-value to the l-value and then reassigns the result into the l-value. This operator is pronounced "plus-equals." The statement would be read "`myAge` plus-equals two." If `myAge` had the value 4 to start, it would have 6 after this statement.

Self-assigned subtraction (−=), division (/=), multiplication (*=), and modulus (%=) operators exist as well.

Increment and Decrement

The most common value to add (or subtract) and then reassign into a variable is 1. In C++, increasing a value by 1 is called *incrementing*, and decreasing by 1 is called *decrementing*. Because this operation is so common, most computers have operators built into the hardware to perform these actions. C++ has special operators to perform these actions.

The increment operator (++) increases the value of the variable by 1, and the decrement operator (−) decreases it by 1. Thus, if you have a variable named C, and you want to increment it, you would use the following statement:

```
C++;                // Start with C and increment it.
```

This statement is equivalent to the more verbose statement

```
C = C + 1;
```

that you learned is also equivalent to the moderately verbose statement

```
C += 1;
```

4

 Note

> You may notice that the name of this language ("C++") looks like an increment operator applied to the variable C. This is not by accident. The C++ language was developed as an incremental improvement over the existing C language—not as a completely new language. Hence the name mimics that philosophy.

Prefix and Postfix

Both the increment operator (++) and the decrement operator(—) come in two varieties: prefix and postfix. The prefix variety is written before the variable name (++myAge); the postfix variety is written after (myAge++).

In a simple statement, it does not much matter which you use, but in a complex statement when you are incrementing (or decrementing) a variable and then assigning the result to another variable, it matters very much. The prefix operator is evaluated before the assignment; the postfix is evaluated after.

The semantics of prefix are this: Increment the value and then fetch it. The semantics of postfix are different: Fetch the value and then increment the original.

This can be confusing at first, but if x is an integer whose value is 5 and you write

```
int a = ++x;
```

you have told the compiler to increment x (making it 6) and then fetch that value and assign it to a. Thus a is now 6 and x is now 6.

If, after doing this, you write

```
int b = x++;
```

you have now told the compiler to fetch the value in x (6) and assign it to b, and then go back and increment x. Thus, b is now 6, but x is now 7. Listing 4.4 shows the use and implications of both types.

INPUT   **LISTING 4.4**   A Demonstration of Prefix and Postfix Operators

```
1:  // Listing 4.4 - demonstrates use of
2:  // prefix and postfix increment and
3:  // decrement operators
4:  #include <iostream.h>
5:  int main()
6:  {
7:      int myAge = 39;        // initialize two integers
8:      int yourAge = 39;
9:      cout << "I am: " << myAge << " years old.\n";
10:     cout << "You are: " << yourAge << " years old\n";
11:     myAge++;           // postfix increment
12:     ++yourAge;         // prefix increment
13:     cout << "One year passes...\n";
14:     cout << "I am: " << myAge << " years old.\n";
15:     cout << "You are: " << yourAge << " years old\n";
16:     cout << "Another year passes\n";
17:     cout << "I am: " << myAge++ << " years old.\n";
18:     cout << "You are: " << ++yourAge << " years old\n";
19:     cout << "Let's print it again.\n";
20:     cout << "I am: " << myAge << " years old.\n";
21:     cout << "You are: " << yourAge << " years old\n";
22:     return 0;
23: }
```

OUTPUT

```
I am: 39 years old.
You are: 39 years old
One year passes...
I am: 40 years old.
You are: 40 years old
Another year passes
I am: 40 years old.
You are: 41 years old
Let's print it again.
I am: 41 years old.
You are: 41 years old
```

ANALYSIS On lines 7 and 8, two integer variables are declared, and each is initialized with the value 39. Their values are printed on lines 9 and 10.

On line 11, myAge is incremented using the postfix increment operator, and on line 12, yourAge is incremented using the prefix increment operator. The results are printed on lines 14 and 15, and they are identical (both 40).

On line 17, myAge is incremented as part of the printing statement, using the postfix increment operator. Because it is postfix, the increment happens after the print, and so the value 40 is printed again. In contrast, on line 18, yourAge is incremented using the prefix increment operator. Thus it is incremented before being printed, and the value displays as 41.

Finally, on lines 20 and 21, the values are printed again. Because the increment statement has completed, the value in myAge is now 41, as is the value in yourAge.

Operator Precedence

In the following complex statement

```
x = 5 + 3 * 8;
```

which is performed first, the addition or the multiplication? If the addition is performed first, the answer is 8 * 8, or 64. If the multiplication is performed first, the answer is 5 + 24, or 29.

Every operator has a precedence value, and the complete list is shown in Appendix A. Multiplication has higher precedence than addition; thus the value of the expression is 29.

When two mathematical operators have the same precedence, they are performed in left-to-right order. Thus

```
x = 5 + 3 + 8 * 9 + 6 * 4;
```

is evaluated multiplication first, left to right. Thus 8*9 = 72, and 6*4 = 24. Now the expression is essentially

```
x = 5 + 3 + 72 + 24;
```

Now the addition, left to right, is 5 + 3 = 8; 8 + 72 = 80; 80 + 24 = 104.

Be careful with this. Some operators, such as assignment, are evaluated in right-to-left order! In any case, what if the precedence order does not meet your needs? Consider the expression

```
TotalSeconds = NumMinutesToThink + NumMinutesToType * 60
```

In this expression, you do not want to multiply the `NumMinutesToType` variable by 60 and then add it to `NumMinutesToThink`. You want to add the two variables to get the total number of minutes, and then you want to multiply that number by 60 to get the total seconds.

In this case, you use parentheses to change the precedence order. Items in parentheses are evaluated at a higher precedence than any of the mathematical operators. Thus

```
TotalSeconds = (NumMinutesToThink + NumMinutesToType) * 60
```

will accomplish what you want.

Nesting Parentheses

For complex expressions, you might need to nest parentheses one within another. For example, you might need to compute the total seconds and then compute the total number of people who are involved before multiplying seconds times people:

```
TotalPersonSeconds = ( ( (NumMinutesToThink + NumMinutesToType) * 60) *
(PeopleInTheOffice + PeopleOnVacation) )
```

This complicated expression is read from the inside out. First, `NumMinutesToThink` is added to `NumMinutesToType` because these are in the innermost parentheses. Then this sum is multiplied by 60. Next, `PeopleInTheOffice` is added to `PeopleOnVacation`. Finally, the total number of people found is multiplied by the total number of seconds.

This example raises an important related issue. This expression is easy for a computer to understand, but very difficult for a human to read, understand, or modify. Here is the same expression rewritten, using some temporary integer variables:

```
TotalMinutes = NumMinutesToThink + NumMinutesToType;
TotalSeconds = TotalMinutes * 60;
TotalPeople = PeopleInTheOffice + PeopleOnVacation;
TotalPersonSeconds = TotalPeople * TotalSeconds;
```

This example takes longer to write and uses more temporary variables than the preceding example, but it is far easier to understand. Add a comment at the top to explain what this code does and change the 60 to a symbolic constant. You then will have code that is easy to understand and maintain.

Do	Don't
DO remember that expressions have a value. **DO** use the prefix operator (++variable) to increment or decrement the variable before it is used in the expression. **DO** use the postfix operator (variable++) to increment or decrement the variable after it is used. **DO** use parentheses to change the order of precedence.	**DON'T** nest too deeply because the expression becomes hard to understand and maintain.

The Nature of Truth

In previous versions of C++, all truth and falsity were represented by integers, but the new ANSI standard has introduced a new type: bool. This new type has two possible values: false or true.

Every expression can be evaluated for its truth or falsity. Expressions that evaluate mathematically to zero will return false; all others will return true.

Note

Many compilers previously offered a bool type, which was represented internally as an int and typically had a size of 4 bytes. Now ANSI-compliant compilers often provide a 1-byte bool.

The GNU compilers are ANSI-compliant; their bool occupies 1 byte. I made sure. How, you might ask? By writing a quick sample program that used the sizeof() operator like the examples in Day 3, "Variables and Constants."

4

Relational Operators

The relational operators are used to determine whether two numbers are equal or one is greater or less than the other. Every relational statement evaluates to either true or false. The relational operators are presented in Table 4.1.

Note

> The new ANSI standard has introduced the new bool type, and all relational operators now return a value of type bool: either true or false. In previous versions of C++, these operators returned either 0 for false or a non-zero value (usually 1) for true.

If the integer variable myAge has the value 39, and the integer variable yourAge has the value 40, you can determine whether they are equal by using the relational "equals" operator:

```
myAge == yourAge;   // is the value in myAge the same as in yourAge?
```

This expression evaluates to 0, or false, because the variables are not equal. The expression

```
myAge > yourAge;   // is myAge greater than yourAge?
```

evaluates to 0 or false.

Caution

> Many novice C++ programmers confuse the assignment operator (=) with the equals (equality) operator (==). This can create a nasty bug in your program.

The six relational operators are equals (==), less than (<), greater than (>), less than or equal to (<=), greater than or equal to (>=), and not equals (!=). Table 4.1 shows each relational operator, its use, and a sample code use.

TABLE 4.1 The Relational Operators

Name	Operator	Sample	Evaluates
Equals	==	100 == 50;	false
		50 == 50;	true
Not Equals	!=	100 != 50;	true
		50 != 50;	false

Name	Operator	Sample	Evaluates
Greater Than	>	100 > 50;	true
		50 > 50;	false
Greater Than or Equals	>=	100 >= 50;	true
		50 >= 50;	true
Less Than	<	100 < 50;	false
		50 < 50;	false
Less Than or Equals	<=	100 <= 50;	false
		50 <= 50;	true

Do	Don't
DO remember that relational operators return the value true or false.	**DON'T** confuse the assignment operator (=) with the equals relational operator (==). This is one of the most common C++ programming mistakes—be on guard for it.

4

The if Statement

Normally, your program flows along line by line in the order in which it appears in your source code. The if statement enables you to test for a condition (such as whether two variables are equal) and branch to different parts of your code, depending on the result.

The simplest form of an if statement is the following:

```
if (expression)
    statement;
```

The expression in the parentheses can be any expression at all, but it usually contains one of the relational expressions. If the expression has the value false, the statement is skipped. If it evaluates true, the statement is executed. Consider the following example:

```
if (bigNumber > smallNumber)
    bigNumber = smallNumber;
```

This code compares bigNumber and smallNumber. If bigNumber is larger, the second line sets its value to the value of smallNumber.

Because a block of statements surrounded by braces is equivalent to a single statement, the following type of branch can be quite large and powerful:

```
if (expression)
{
```

```
    statement1;
    statement2;
    statement3;
}
```

A simple example of this usage looks like this:

```
if (bigNumber > smallNumber)
{
    bigNumber = smallNumber;
    cout << "bigNumber: " << bigNumber << "\n";
    cout << "smallNumber: " << smallNumber << "\n";
}
```

This time, if bigNumber is larger than smallNumber, not only is it set to the value of smallNumber, but an informational message is printed. Listing 4.5 shows a more detailed example of branching based on relational operators.

INPUT   LISTING 4.5   A Demonstration of Branching Based on Relational Operators

```
1:  // Listing 4.5 - demonstrates if statement
2:  // used with relational operators
3:  #include <iostream.h>
4:  int main()
5:  {
6:       int RedSoxScore, YankeesScore;
7:       cout << "Enter the score for the Red Sox: ";
8:       cin >> RedSoxScore;
9:
10:      cout << "\nEnter the score for the Yankees: ";
11:      cin >> YankeesScore;
12:
13:      cout << "\n";
14:
15:      if (RedSoxScore > YankeesScore)
16:          cout << "Go Sox!\n";
17:
18:      if (RedSoxScore < YankeesScore)
19:      {
20:          cout << "Go Yankees!\n";
21:          cout << "Happy days in New York!\n";
22:      }
23:
24:      if (RedSoxScore == YankeesScore)
25:      {
```

```
26:             cout << "A tie? Naah, can't be.\n";
27:             cout << "Give me the real score for the Yanks: ";
28:             cin >> YankeesScore;
29:
30:             if (RedSoxScore > YankeesScore)
31:                 cout << "Knew it! Go Sox!";
32:
33:             if (YankeesScore > RedSoxScore)
34:                 cout << "Knew it! Go Yanks!";
35:
36:             if (YankeesScore == RedSoxScore)
37:                 cout << "Wow, it really was a tie!";
38:         }
39:
40:     cout << "\nThanks for telling me.\n";
41:      return 0;
42:  }
```

OUTPUT

```
Enter the score for the Red Sox: 10

Enter the score for the Yankees: 10

A tie? Naah, can't be
Give me the real score for the Yanks: 8
Knew it! Go Sox!
Thanks for telling me.
```

ANALYSIS This program asks for user input of scores for two baseball teams; the scores are stored in integer variables. The variables are compared in the if statement on lines 15, 18, and 24.

If one score is higher than the other, an informational message is printed. If the scores are equal, the block of code that begins on line 25 and ends on line 38 is entered. The second score is requested again, and then the scores are compared again.

Note that if the initial Yankees' score was higher than the Red Sox score, the if statement on line 15 would evaluate as false, and line 16 would not be invoked. The test on line 18 would evaluate as true, and the statements on lines 20 and 21 would be invoked. Then the if statement on line 24 would be tested and this would be false (if line 18 was true). Thus, the program would skip the entire block, falling through to line 39.

In this example, getting a true result in one if statement does not stop other if statements from being tested.

4

Caution   Many novice C++ programmers inadvertently put a semicolon after their `if` statements:

```
if(SomeValue < 10);
    SomeValue = 10;
```

What was intended here was to test whether `SomeValue` is less than 10, and if so, to set it to 10, making 10 the minimum value for `SomeValue`. Running this code snippet will show that `SomeValue` is always set to 10! Why? The `if` statement terminates with the semicolon (the do-nothing operator).

Remember that indentation has no meaning to the compiler. This snippet could more accurately have been written as

```
if (SomeValue < 10)   // test
;   // do nothing
SomeValue = 10;   // assign
```

Removing the semicolon will make the final line part of the `if` statement and will make this code do what was intended.

Indentation Styles

Listing 4.5 shows one style of indenting `if` statements. Nothing is more likely to create a religious war, however, than to ask a group of programmers what is the best style for brace alignment. Although dozens of variations are possible, the following appear to be the favorite three:

- Putting the initial brace after the condition and aligning the closing brace under the `if` to close the statement block:

```
if (expression){
    statements
}
```

- Aligning the braces under the `if` and indenting the statements:

```
if (expression)
{
    statements
}
```

- Indenting the braces and statements:

```
if (expression)
    {
    statements
    }
```

This book uses the middle alternative because both authors find it easier to understand where blocks of statements begin and end if the braces line up with each other and with the condition being tested. Again, it does not matter much which style you choose, so long as you are consistent with it. It does not matter to the compiler at all.

else

Often your program will want to take one branch if your condition is true, and another if it is false. In Listing 4.5, you wanted to print one message (Go Sox!) if the first test (RedSoxScore > Yankees) evaluated true, and another message (Go Yanks!) if it evaluated false.

The method shown so far—testing first one condition and then the other—works fine but is a bit cumbersome. The keyword else can make for far more readable code:

```
if (expression)
    statement;
else
    statement;
```

Listing 4.6 demonstrates the use of the keyword else.

INPUT **LISTING 4.6** Demonstrating the else Keyword

```
1:   // Listing 4.6 - demonstrates if statement
2:   // with else clause
3:   #include <iostream.h>
4:   int main()
5:   {
6:       int firstNumber, secondNumber;
7:       cout << "Please enter a big number: ";
8:       cin >> firstNumber;
9:       cout << "\nPlease enter a smaller number: ";
10:      cin >> secondNumber;
11:      if (firstNumber > secondNumber)
12:          cout << "\nThanks!\n";
13:      else
14:          cout << "\nOops. The second is bigger!\n";
15:
16:      return 0;
17:  }
```

OUTPUT
```
Please enter a big number: 10

Please enter a smaller number: 12
Oops. The second is bigger!
```

ANALYSIS The if statement on line 11 is evaluated. If the condition is true, the statement on line 12 is run; if it is false, the statement on line 14 is run. If the else clause on line 13 was removed, the statement on line 14 would run whether or not the if statement was true. Remember, the if statement ends after line 12. If the else was not there, line 14 would just be the next line in the program.

Remember that either or both of these statements could be replaced with a block of code in braces.

The if Statement

The syntax for the if statement is as follows:

Form 1

```
if (expression)
statement;
next statement;
```

If the expression is evaluated as true, the statement is executed and the program continues with the next statement. If the expression is not true, the statement is ignored and the program jumps to the next statement.

Remember that the statement can be a single statement ending with a semicolon or a block enclosed in braces.

Form 2

```
if (expression)
    statement1;
else
    statement2;
next statement;
```

If the expression evaluates true, statement1 is executed; otherwise, statement2 is executed. Afterward, the program continues with the next statement.

Example 1

```
if (SomeValue < 10)
  cout << "SomeValue is less than 10");
else
  cout << "SomeValue is not less than 10!");
cout << "Done." << endl;
```

Advanced if Statements

It is worth noting that any statement can be used in an if or else clause, even another if or else statement. Thus, you might see complex if statements in the following form:

```
if (expression1)
{
```

```
    if (expression2)
        statement1;
    else
    {
        if (expression3)
            statement2;
        else
            statement3;
    }
}
else
    statement4;
```

This cumbersome if statement says, "If expression1 is true and expression2 is true, execute statement1. If expression1 is true but expression2 is not true, then if expression3 is true execute statement2. If expression1 is true but expression2 and expression3 are false, execute statement3. Finally, if expression1 is not true, execute statement4." As you can see, complex if statements can be confusing!

Listing 4.7 gives an example of one such complex if statement.

INPUT **LISTING 4.7** A Complex, Nested if Statement

4

```
1:  // Listing 4.7 - a complex nested
2:  // if statement
3:  #include <iostream.h>
4:  int main()
5:  {
6:      // Ask for two numbers
7:      // Assign the numbers to bigNumber and littleNumber
8:      // If bigNumber is bigger than littleNumber,
9:      // see if they are evenly divisible
10:     // If they are, see if they are the same number
11:
12:     int firstNumber, secondNumber;
13:     cout << "Enter two numbers.\nFirst: ";
14:     cin >> firstNumber;
15:     cout << "\nSecond: ";
16:     cin >> secondNumber;
17:     cout << "\n\n";
18:
19:     if (firstNumber >= secondNumber)
20:     {
21:       if ( (firstNumber % secondNumber) == 0) // evenly divisible?
22:       {
23:           if (firstNumber == secondNumber)
24:               cout << "They are the same!\n";
```

continues

LISTING 4.7 CONTINUED

```
25:            else
26:                cout << "They are evenly divisible!\n";
27:        }
28:        else
29:            cout << "They are not evenly divisible!\n";
30:     }
31:     else
32:         cout << "Hey! The second one is larger!\n";
33:     return 0;
34: }
```

OUTPUT

```
Enter two numbers.
First: 10

Second: 2

They are evenly divisible!
```

ANALYSIS Two numbers are prompted for one at a time, and then compared. The first `if` statement, on line 19, checks to ensure that the first number is greater than or equal to the second. If not, the `else` clause on line 31 is executed.

If the first `if` is true, the block of code beginning on line 20 is executed, and the second `if` statement is tested on line 21. This checks to see whether the first number modulus the second number yields no remainder. If so, the numbers are either evenly divisible or equal. The `if` statement on line 23 checks for equality and displays the appropriate message either way.

If the `if` statement on line 21 fails, the `else` statement on line 28 is executed.

Braces in Nested `if` Statements

Although it is legal to leave out the braces on `if` statements that are only a single statement, and it is legal to nest `if` statements, such as

```
if (x > y)          // if x is bigger than y
    if (x < z)      // and if x is smaller than z
        x = y;      // then set x to the value in y
```

when you are writing large nested statements, this can cause enormous confusion. Remember, whitespace and indentation are a convenience for the programmer; they make no difference to the compiler. It is easy to confuse the logic and inadvertently assign an `else` statement to the wrong `if` statement. Listing 4.8 illustrates this problem.

INPUT

LISTING 4.8 A Demonstration of Why Braces Help Clarify Which `else` Statement Goes with Which `if` Statement

```
1:   // Listing 4.8 - demonstrates why braces
2:   // are important in nested if statements
3:   #include <iostream.h>
4:   int main()
5:   {
6:     int x;
7:     cout << "Enter a number less than 10 or greater than 100: ";
8:     cin >> x;
9:     cout << "\n";
10:
11:    if (x >= 10)
12:       if (x > 100)
13:          cout << "More than 100, Thanks!\n";
14:    else                              // not the else intended!
15:       cout << "Less than 10, Thanks!\n";
16:
17:    return 0;
18:  }
```

OUTPUT

```
Enter a number less than 10 or greater than 100: 20

Less than 10, Thanks!
```

4

ANALYSIS The programmer intended to ask for a number less than 10 or greater than 100, check for the correct value, and then print a thank-you note.

If the `if` statement on line 11 evaluates `true`, the following statement (line 12) is executed. In this case, line 12 executes when the number entered is greater than 10. Line 12 contains an `if` statement also. This `if` statement evaluates `true` if the number entered is greater than 100. If the number is greater than 100, the statement on line 13 is executed.

If the number entered is less than 10, the `if` statement on line 11 evaluates `false`. Program control goes to the next line following the `if` statement, in this case line 16. If you enter a number less than 10, the output is as follows:

```
Enter a number less than 10 or greater than 100: 9
```

The `else` clause on line 14 was clearly intended to be attached to the `if` statement on line 11, and thus is indented accordingly. Unfortunately, the `else` statement is really attached to the `if` statement on line 12, and thus this program has a subtle bug.

The bug is a subtle because the compiler will not complain. This is a legal C++ program, but it does not provide the intended result. Furthermore, most of the time the programmer tests this program, it will appear to work. As long as a number that is greater than

100 is entered, the program will seem to work just fine. This is a good example of a logic error!

Listing 4.9 fixes the problem by putting in the necessary braces.

INPUT

LISTING 4.9   A Demonstration of the Proper Use of Braces with an `if` Statement

```
1:     // Listing 4.9 - demonstrates proper use of braces
2:     // in nested if statements
3:     #include <iostream.h>
4:     int main()
5:     {
6:       int x;
7:       cout << "Enter a number less than 10 or greater than 100: ";
8:       cin >> x;
9:       cout << "\n";
10:
11:      if (x >= 10)
12:      {
13:         if (x > 100)
14:             cout << "More than 100, Thanks!\n";
15:      }
16:      else                          // fixed!
17:         cout << "Less than 10, Thanks!\n";
18:      return 0;
19:    }
```

OUTPUT   Enter a number less than 10 or greater than 100: 20

ANALYSIS   The braces on lines 12 and 15 make everything between them into one statement, and now the `else` on line 16 applies to the `if` on line 11, as intended.

The user typed 20, so the `if` statement on line 11 is true; however, the `if` statement on line 13 is `false`, so nothing is printed. It would be better if the programmer put another `else` clause after line 14 so that errors would be caught and a message printed.

Note

The programs shown in this book are written to demonstrate the particular issues being discussed. They are kept intentionally simple; no attempt is made to "bulletproof" the code to protect against user error. Ideally, in professional-quality code, every possible user error is anticipated and handled gracefully.

Remember to program defensively!

Logical Operators

Often you want to ask more than one relational question at a time. "Is it true that x is greater than y, and also true that y is greater than z?" A program might need to determine that both of these conditions are true—or that some other condition is true—in order to take an action.

Imagine a sophisticated alarm system that has this logic: "If the door alarm sounds AND it is after 6 p.m. AND it is NOT a holiday, OR if it is a weekend, then call the police." C++'s three logical operators are used to make this kind of evaluation. These operators are listed in Table 4.2.

TABLE 4.2 The Logical Operators

Operator	Symbol	Example
AND	&&	expression1 && expression2
OR	||	expression1 || expression2
NOT	!	!expression

Logical AND

A logical AND statement evaluates two expressions, and if both expressions are true, the logical AND statement is true as well. If it is true that you are hungry, and it is true that you have money, then it is true that you can buy lunch. Thus

```
if ( (x == 5) && (y == 5) )
```

would evaluate true if both x and y are equal to 5, and it would evaluate false if either one is not equal to 5. Note that both sides must be true for the entire expression to be true.

Note that the logical AND is two && symbols. A single & symbol is a different operator, which is discussed on Day 21, "What's Next."

Logical OR

A logical OR statement evaluates two expressions. If either one is true, the expression is true. If you have money or you have a credit card, you can pay the bill. You do not need both money and a credit card; you need only one, although having both would be fine as well. Thus,

```
if ( (x == 5) || (y == 5) )
```

evaluates true if either x or y is equal to 5, or if both are equal to 5.

Note that the logical OR is two || symbols. A single | symbol is a different operator, which is discussed on Day 21.

Logical NOT

A logical NOT statement evaluates true if the expression being tested is false. Again, if the expression being tested is false, the value of the test is true! Thus

```
if ( !(x == 5) )
```

is true only if x is not equal to 5. This is the same as writing

```
if (x != 5)
```

Short Circuit Evaluation

When the compiler is evaluating an AND statement, such as

```
if ( (x == 5) && (y == 5) )
```

the compiler will evaluate the truth of the first statement (x==5), and if this fails (that is, if x is not equal to 5), the compiler will NOT go on to evaluate the truth or falsity of the second statement (y == 5) because AND requires both to be true.

Similarly, if the compiler is evaluating an OR statement, such as

```
if ( (x == 5) || (y == 5) )
```

if the first statement is true (x == 5), the compiler will never evaluate the second statement (y == 5) because the truth of *either* is sufficient in an OR statement.

This matters if there are side effects—for example, if you had used the increment or decrement operators on x or y. If the second statement is not evaluated, the increment or decrement would not occur.

Relational Precedence

Relational operators and logical operators, because they are C++ expressions, each return a value: true or false. Like all expressions, they have a precedence order (see Appendix A) that determines which relations are evaluated first. This fact is important when determining the value of the statement, for example:

```
if ( x > 5 && y > 5  || z > 5)
```

It might be that the programmer wanted this expression to evaluate true if both x and y are greater than 5 or if z is greater than 5. On the other hand, the programmer might have wanted this expression to evaluate true only if x is greater than 5 and if it is also true that either y is greater than 5 or z is greater than 5.

If x is 3, and y and z are both 10, the first interpretation will be true (z is greater than 5, so ignore x and y), but the second will be false (it is not true that x is greater than 5 and thus it does not matter what is on the right side of the (&&) symbol because both sides must be true).

Although precedence will determine which relation is evaluated first, parentheses can both change the order and make the statement clearer:

```
if (  (x > 5)  && (y > 5 ||  z > 5) )
```

Using the values from earlier, this statement is false. Because it is not true that x is greater than 5, the left side of the AND statement fails, and thus the entire statement is false. Remember that an AND statement requires that both sides be true—something is not both "good tasting" AND "good for you" if it is not good tasting.

Note

> It is often a good idea to use extra parentheses to clarify what you want to group. Remember, the goal is to write programs that work and that are easy to read and to understand.
>
> Whenever you are in doubt about the order of operations, put the parentheses in. It will cause the compiler to use some small number of milliseconds and probably result in the same execution time.

4

More About Truth and Falsehood

In C++, zero evaluates false, and all other values evaluate true. Because an expression always has a value, many C++ programmers take advantage of this feature in their if statements. A statement such as

```
if (x)           // if x is true (nonzero)
    x = 0;
```

can be read as "If x has a nonzero value, set it to 0." This is a bit of a cheat; it would be clearer if written

```
if (x != 0)      // if x is nonzero
    x = 0;
```

Both statements are legal, but the latter is clearer. It is good programming practice to reserve the former method for true tests of logic, rather than for testing for nonzero values.

These two statements also are equivalent:

```
if (!x)          // if x is false (zero)

if (x == 0)      // if x is zero
```

The second statement, however, is somewhat easier to understand and is more explicit if you are testing for the mathematical value of x rather than for its logical state.

Do	Don't
DO put parentheses around your logical tests to make them clearer and to make the precedence explicit. **DO** use braces in nested `if` statements to make the `else` statements clearer and to avoid bugs.	**DON'T** use `if(x)` as a synonym for `if(x != 0)`; the latter is clearer. **DON'T** use `if(!x)` as a synonym for `if(x == 0)`; the latter is clearer.

Conditional (Ternary) Operator

The conditional operator (`?:`) is C++'s only ternary operator; that is, it is the only operator to take three terms.

The conditional operator takes three expressions and returns a value:

```
(expression1) ? (expression2) : (expression3)
```

This line is read as "If `expression1` is true, return the value of `expression2`; otherwise, return the value of `expression3`." Typically, this value would be assigned to a variable.

Listing 4.10 shows an `if` statement rewritten using the conditional operator.

INPUT   **LISTING 4.10**   A Demonstration of the Conditional Operator

```
1:   // Listing 4.10 - demonstrates the conditional operator
2:   //
3:   #include <iostream.h>
4:   int main()
5:   {
6:       int x, y, z;
7:       cout << "Enter two numbers.\n";
8:       cout << "First: ";
9:       cin >> x;
10:      cout << "\nSecond: ";
11:      cin >> y;
12:      cout << "\n";
```

```
13:
14:     if (x > y)
15:        z = x;
16:     else
17:        z = y;
18:
19:     cout << "z: " << z;
20:     cout << "\n";
21:
22:     z =  (x > y) ? x : y;
23:
24:     cout << "z: " << z;
25:     cout << "\n";
26:     return 0;
27:  }
```

OUTPUT
```
Enter two numbers.
First: 5

Second: 8

z: 8
z: 8
```

4

ANALYSIS Three integer variables are created: x, y, and z. The first two are given values by the user. The if statement on line 14 tests to see which is larger and assigns the larger value to z. This value is printed on line 19.

The conditional operator on line 22 makes the same test and assigns z the larger value. It is read like this: "If x is greater than y, return the value of x; otherwise, return the value of y." The value returned is assigned to z. That value is printed on line 24. As you can see, the conditional statement is a shorter equivalent to the if...else statement.

Summary

This lesson has covered a lot of material. You have learned what C++ statements and expressions are, what C++ operators do, and how C++ if statements work.

You have seen that a block of statements enclosed by a pair of braces can be used anywhere a single statement can be used.

You have learned that every expression evaluates to a value, and that value can be tested in an if statement or by using the conditional operator. You have also seen how to evaluate multiple statements using the logical operator, how to compare values using the relational operators, and how to assign values using the assignment operator.

You have also explored operator precedence. And you have seen how parentheses can be used to change the precedence and to make precedence explicit and thus easier to manage.

Q&A

Q Why use unnecessary parentheses when precedence will determine which operators are acted on first?

A Although it is true that the compiler will know the precedence and that a programmer can look up the precedence order, code that is easy to understand is easier to maintain.

Q If the relational operators always return `true` or `false`, why is any nonzero value considered true?

A The relational operators return `true` or `false`, but every expression returns a value, and those values can also be evaluated in an `if` statement. Here is an example:

```
if ( (x = a + b) == 35 )
```

This is a perfectly legal C++ statement. It evaluates to a value even if the sum of a and b is not equal to 35. Also note that x is assigned the value that is the sum of a and b in any case.

Q What effect do tabs, spaces, and newline characters have on the program?

A Tabs, spaces, and newline characters (known as whitespace) have no effect on the program, although judicious use of whitespace can make the program easier to read.

Q Are negative numbers true or false?

A All nonzero numbers, positive and negative, are true.

Workshop

The Workshop provides quiz questions to help you solidify your understanding of the material covered and exercises to provide you with experience in using what you have learned. Try to answer the quiz and exercise questions before checking the answers in Appendix D, "Answers to Exercises and Quizzes," and make sure that you understand the answers before continuing to the next day.

Quiz

1. What is an expression?

2. Is x = 5 + 7 an expression? What is its value?

3. What is the value of 201 / 4?

4. What is the value of 201 % 4?

5. If myAge, a, and b are all `int` variables, what are their values after
```
myAge = 39;
a = myAge++;
b = ++myAge;
```

6. What is the value of 8+2*3?

7. What is the difference between x = 3 and x == 3?

8. Do the following values evaluate true or false?

   a. 0

   b. 1

   c. -1

   d. x = 0

   e. x == 0 // assume that x has the value of 0

Exercises

1. Write a single `if` statement that examines two integer variables and changes the larger to the smaller, using only one `else` clause.

2. Examine the following program. Imagine entering three numbers, and write what output you expect.
```
1: #include <iostream.h>
2: int main()
3: {
4:     int a, b, c;
5:     cout << "Please enter three numbers\n";
6:     cout << "a:    ";
7:     cin >> a;
8:     cout << "\nb:    ";
9:     cin >> b;
10:    cout << "\nc:    ";
11:    cin >> c;
12:
13:    if (c = (a-b))
14:    {cout << "a:    ";
15:    cout << a;
16:    cout << "minus b:    ";
17:    cout << b;
18:    cout << "equals c:    ";
19:    cout << c << endl;}
20:    else
21:    cout << "a-b does not equal c:    " << endl;
22:    return 0;
23: }
```

4

3. Enter the program from Exercise 2; compile, link, and run it. Enter the numbers 20, 10, and 50. Did you get the output you expected? Why not?

4. Examine this program and anticipate the output:

```
1: #include <iostream.h>
2: int main()
3: {
4:     int a = 1, b = 1, c;
5:     if (c = (a-b))
6:         cout << "The value of c is: " << c;
7:     return 0;
8: }
```

5. Enter, compile, link, and run the program from Exercise 4. What was the output? Why?

DAY 5

Functions

Although object-oriented programming has shifted attention from functions and toward objects, functions nonetheless remain a central component of any program. Today you will learn:

- What a function is and what its parts are
- How to declare and define functions
- How to pass parameters into functions
- How to return a value from a function
- How to build and use function libraries
- What the standard libraries are and contain

What Is a Function?

A `function` is, in effect, a subprogram that can act on data and return a value. Every C++ program has at least one function— `main()`. When your program starts, `main()` is called automatically. `main()` might call other functions, some of which might call still others.

Each function has its own name, and when that name is encountered, the execution of the program branches to the body of that function. This is called *calling* the function. When the function returns, execution resumes on the next line of the calling function. This flow is illustrated in Figure 5.1.

FIGURE 5.1

When a program calls a function, execution switches to the function and then resumes at the line after the function call.

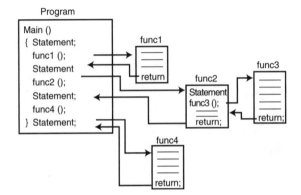

Well-designed functions perform a specific and easily understood task. Complicated tasks should be broken down into multiple functions, and then each can be called in turn.

Functions come in two varieties: user-defined and built-in. *Built-in* functions are part of your compiler package—they are supplied by the manufacturer for your use. *User-defined* functions are the functions you write yourself.

Return Values, Parameters, and Arguments

Functions can *return* a value. When you call a function, it can do work and then send back a value as a result of that work. This is called its *return value*, and the type of that return value must be declared. Thus if you write

```
int myFunction();
```

you are declaring that myFunction will return an integer value.

You can also send values *into* the function. The description of the values you send is called a *parameter list*.

```
int myFunction(int someValue, float someFloat);
```

This declaration indicates that myFunction will not only return an integer, it will take an integer value and a float as parameters.

A parameter describes the *type* of the value that will be passed into and the variable name used in the function when the function is called. The actual values you pass into the function are called the *arguments*.

```
int theValueReturned = myFunction(5,6.7);
```

Here you see that an integer variable *theValueReturned* is initialized with the value returned by myFunction, and that the values 5 and 6.7 are passed in as arguments. The type of the arguments must match the declared parameter types.

Declaring and Defining Functions

Using functions in your program requires that you first declare the function and that you then define the function. The declaration tells the compiler the name, return type, and parameters of the function. The definition tells the compiler how the function works. No function should be called from any other function if it has not first been declared. A declaration of a function is called a *prototype*.

Declaring the Function

Three ways exist to declare a function:

- Write your prototype into a file, and then use the #include directive to include it in your program.
- Write the prototype into the file in which your function is used.
- Define the function before it is called by any other function. When you do this, the definition acts as its own declaration.

Although you can define the function before using it and thus avoid the necessity of creating a function prototype, this is not good programming practice for three reasons.

First, it is a bad idea to require that functions appear in a file in a particular order. Doing so makes it hard to maintain the program as requirements change.

Second, it is possible that function A() needs to be able to call function B(), but function B() also needs to be able to call function A() under some circumstances. It is not possible to define function A() before you define function B() and also to define function B() before you define function A(), so at least one of them must be declared in any case.

Third, function prototypes are a good and powerful debugging technique. If your prototype declares that your function takes a particular set of parameters or that it returns a particular type of value, and then your function does not match the prototype, the compiler can flag your error instead of waiting for it to show itself when you run the program.

5

Using Function Prototypes

Many of the built-in functions you use will have their function prototypes already written in the files you include in your program by using #include. For functions you write yourself, you must include the prototype.

The function prototype is a statement, which means it ends with a semicolon. It consists of the function's return type and signature. A function signature is its name and parameter list.

The parameter list is a list of all the parameters and their types, separated by commas. Figure 5.2 illustrates the parts of the function prototype.

FIGURE 5.2

Parts of a function prototype.

The function prototype and the function definition must agree exactly about the return type and signature. If they do not agree, you will get a compile-time error. Note, however, that the function prototype does not need to contain the names of the parameters—just their types. A prototype that looks like this is perfectly legal:

```
long Area(int, int);
```

This prototype declares a function named Area() that returns a long and that has two parameters, both integers. Although this is legal, it is not a good idea. Adding parameter names makes your prototype clearer. The same function with named parameters might be

```
long Area(int length, int width);
```

It is now obvious what this function does and what the parameters are.

The compiler does not require the variable names and essentially ignores them in the prototype. They are there for us humans.

Note that all functions have a return type. If none is explicitly stated, the return type defaults to int. Your programs will be easier to understand, however, if you explicitly declare the return type of every function, including main(). Listing 5.1 demonstrates a program that includes a function prototype for the Area() function.

LISTING 5.1 A Function Declaration and the Definition and Use of That Function

```
1:   // Listing 5.1 - demonstrates the use of function prototypes
2:   //
3:   #include <iostream.h>
4:   int Area(int length, int width); //function prototype
5:
6:   int main()
7:   {
8:      int lengthOfYard;
9:     int widthOfYard;
10:     int areaOfYard;
11:
12:     cout << "\nHow wide is your yard? ";
13:     cin >> widthOfYard;
14:     cout << "\nHow long is your yard? ";
15:     cin >> lengthOfYard;
16:
17:     areaOfYard= Area(lengthOfYard,widthOfYard);
18:
19:     cout << "\nYour yard is ";
20:     cout << areaOfYard;
21:     cout << " square feet\n\n";
22:          return 0;
23:  }
24:
25:  int Area(int yardLength, int yardWidth)
26:  {
27:       return yardLength * yardWidth;
28:  }
```

5

How wide is your yard? 100

How long is your yard? 200

Your yard is 20000 square feet

The prototype for the Area() function is on line 4. Compare the prototype with the definition of the function on line 25. Note that the name, the return type, and the parameter types are the same. If they were different, a compiler error would have been generated. In fact, the only required difference is that the function prototype ends with a semicolon and has no body.

Also note that the parameter names in the prototype are length and width, but the parameter names in the definition are yardLength and yardWidth. As discussed, the names in the prototype are not used; they are there as information for the programmer. It is good programming practice to match the prototype parameter names to the implementation parameter names, but this is not required.

The arguments are passed into the function in the order in which the parameters are declared and defined, but no matching of the names occurs. Had you passed in widthOfYard, followed by lengthOfYard, the FindArea() function would have used the value in widthOfYard for yardLength and lengthOfYard for yardWidth. The body of the function is always enclosed in braces, even when it consists of only one statement, as in this case.

Defining the Function

The definition of a function consists of the function header and its body. The header is like the function prototype except that the parameters must be named, and no terminating semicolon is used.

The body of the function is a set of statements enclosed in braces. Figure 5.3 shows the header and body of a function.

FIGURE 5.3

The header and body of a function.

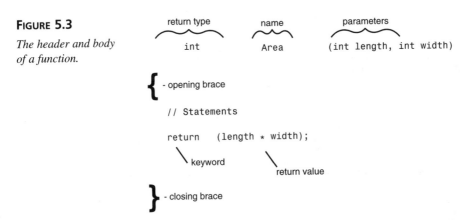

```
Functions
Function Prototype Syntax:

        return_type function_name ( [type [parameterName]]...);

Function Definition Syntax:

        return_type function_name ( [type parameterName]...)
        {
            statements;
        }
```

A function prototype tells the compiler the return type, name, and parameter list. Functions are not required to have parameters, and if they do, the prototype is not required to list their names, only their types. A prototype always ends with a semicolon (;).

A function definition must agree in return type and parameter list with its prototype. It must provide names for all the parameters, and the body of the function definition must be surrounded by braces. All statements within the body of the function must be terminated with semicolons, but the function itself is not ended with a semicolon (;). It ends with a closing brace.

If the function returns a value, it should end with a return statement, although return statements can legally appear anywhere in the body of the function.

Every function has a return type. If one is not explicitly designated, the return type will be int. Be sure to give every function an explicit return type. If a function does not return a value, its return type will be void.

Function Prototype Examples:

```
long FindArea(long length, long width);
➥// returns long, has two parameters
void PrintMessage(int messageNumber);
➥// returns void, has one parameter
int GetChoice();
➥// returns int, has no parameters
BadFunction();                              // returns int, has no
parameters
```

Function Definition Examples:

```
long FindArea(long l, long w)
{
     return l * w;
}


void PrintMessage(int whichMsg)
{
     if (whichMsg == 0)
          cout << "Hello.\n";
     if (whichMsg == 1)
          cout << "Goodbye.\n";
     if (whichMsg > 1)
          cout << "I'm confused.\n";
}
```

5

Execution of Functions

When you call a function, execution begins with the first statement after the opening brace ({). Branching can be accomplished by using the if statement (and related statements that will be discussed on Day 7, "More Program Flow"). Functions can also call other functions and can even call themselves (see the "Recursion" section later in this day).

Local Variables

Not only can you pass in variables to the function, but you also can declare variables within the body of the function. This is done using local variables, so named because they exist only locally within the function itself. When the function returns, the local variables are no longer available.

Local variables are defined the same as any other variables. The parameters passed into the function are also considered local variables and can be used exactly as if they had been defined within the body of the function. Listing 5.2 is an example of using parameters and locally defined variables within a function.

INPUT   **LISTING 5.2**   The Use of Local Variables and Parameters

```
1:      #include <iostream.h>
2:
3:      float Convert(float);
4:      int main()
5:      {
6:          float TempFer;
7:          float TempCel;
8:
9:          cout << "Please enter the temperature in Fahrenheit: ";
10:         cin >> TempFer;
11:         TempCel = Convert(TempFer);
12:         cout << "\nHere's the temperature in Celsius: ";
13:         cout << TempCel << endl;
14:                 return 0;
15:     }
16:
17:     float Convert(float TempFer)
18:     {
19:         float TempCel;
20:         TempCel = ((TempFer - 32) * 5) / 9;
21:         return TempCel;
22:     }
```

OUTPUT

```
Please enter the temperature in Fahrenheit: 212

Here's the temperature in Celsius: 100

Please enter the temperature in Fahrenheit: 32

Here's the temperature in Celsius: 0

Please enter the temperature in Fahrenheit: 85

Here's the temperature in Celsius: 29.4444
```

ANALYSIS On lines 6 and 7, two float variables are declared, one to hold the temperature in Fahrenheit and one to hold the temperature in degrees Celsius. The user is prompted to enter a Fahrenheit temperature on line 9, and that value is passed to the function Convert().

Execution jumps to the first line of the function Convert() on line 19, where a local variable, also named TempCel, is declared. Note that this local variable is not the same as the variable TempCel on line 7. This variable exists only within the function Convert(). The value passed as a parameter, TempFer, is also just a local copy of the variable passed in by main().

This function could have named the parameter FerTemp and the local variable CelTemp, and the program would work equally well. You can enter these names again and recompile the program to see this work.

The local function variable TempCel is assigned the value that results from subtracting 32 from the parameter TempFer, multiplying by 5, and then dividing by 9. This value is then returned as the return value of the function, and on line 11 it is assigned to the variable TempCel in the main() function. The value is printed on line 13.

The program is run three different times. The first time, the value 212 is passed in to ensure that the boiling point of water in degrees Fahrenheit (212) generates the correct answer in degrees Celsius (100). The second test is the freezing point of water. The third test is a random number chosen to generate a fractional result.

As an exercise, try entering the program again with other variable names as illustrated here:

5

```
1:      #include <iostream.h>
2:
3:      float Convert(float);
4:      int main()
5:      {
6:          float TempFer;
7:          float TempCel;
8:
9:          cout << "Please enter the temperature in Fahrenheit: ";
10:         cin >> TempFer;
11:         TempCel = Convert(TempFer);
12:         cout << "\nHere's the temperature in Celsius: ";
13:         cout << TempCel << endl;
14:         return 0;
15:     }
16:
17:     float Convert(float Fer)
18:     {
19:         float Cel;
```

```
20:          Cel = ((Fer - 32) * 5) / 9;
21:          return Cel;
22:      }
```

You should get the same results.

A variable has scope, which determines how long it is available to your program and where it can be accessed. Variables declared within a block are scoped to that block; they can be accessed only within that block and "go out of existence" when that block ends. Global variables have global scope and are available anywhere within your program.

Normally scope is obvious, but some tricky exceptions exist. You will see more about this when we discuss for loops on Day 7.

None of this matters very much if you are careful not to reuse your variable names within any given function.

Global Variables

Variables defined outside of any function have global scope and thus are available from any function in the program, including main().

Local variables with the same name as global variables do not change the global variables. A local variable with the same name as a global variable *hides* the global variable, however. If a function has a variable with the same name as a global variable, the name refers to the local variable—not the global—when used within the function. Listing 5.3 illustrates these points.

INPUT   **LISTING 5.3**   Demonstrating Global and Local Variables

```
1:    #include <iostream.h>
2:    void myFunction();              // prototype
3:
4:    int x = 5, y = 7;              // global variables
5:    int main()
6:    {
7:
8:        cout << "x from main: " << x << "\n";
9:        cout << "y from main: " << y << "\n\n";
10:       myFunction();
11:       cout << "Back from myFunction!\n\n";
12:       cout << "x from main: " << x << "\n";
13:       cout << "y from main: " << y << "\n";
14:       return 0;
15:   }
16:
```

```
17:  void myFunction()
18:  {
19:      int y = 10;
20:
21:      cout << "x from myFunction: " << x << "\n";
22:      cout << "y from myFunction: " << y << "\n\n";
23:  }
```

OUTPUT

```
x from main: 5
y from main: 7

x from myFunction: 5
y from myFunction: 10

Back from myFunction!

x from main: 5
y from main: 7
```

ANALYSIS This simple program illustrates a few key, and potentially confusing, points about local and global variables. On line 4, two global variables, x and y, are declared. The global variable x is initialized with the value 5, and the global variable y is initialized with the value 7.

On lines 8 and 9 in the function main(), these values are printed to the screen. Note that the function main() defines neither variable; because they are global, they are already available to main().

When myFunction() is called on line 10, program execution passes to line 18, and a local variable, y, is defined and initialized with the value 10. On line 21, myFunction() prints the value of the variable x, and the global variable x is used, just as it was in main(). On line 22, however, when the variable name y is used, the local variable y is used, hiding the global variable with the same name.

The function call ends, and control returns to main(), which again prints the values in the global variables. Note that the global variable y was totally unaffected by the value assigned to myFunction()'s local y variable.

Global Variables: A Word of Caution

In C++, global variables are legal, but they are almost never used. C++ grew out of C, and in C global variables are a dangerous but necessary tool. They are necessary because there are times when the programmer needs to make data available to many functions, and he does not want to pass that data as a parameter from function to function.

Globals are dangerous because they are shared data, and one function can change a global variable in a way that is invisible to another function. This can and does create bugs that are very difficult to find.

On Day 14, "Special Classes and Functions," you will see a powerful alternative to global variables that C++ offers, but that is unavailable in C.

More on Local Variables

Variables declared within the function are said to have *local scope*. That means, as discussed, that they are visible and usable only within the function in which they are defined. In fact, in C++ you can define variables anywhere within the function, not just at its top. The scope of the variable is the block in which it is defined. Thus, if you define a variable inside a set of braces within the function, that variable is available only within that block. Listing 5.4 illustrates this idea.

INPUT   **LISTING 5.4**   Variables Scoped Within a Block

```
1:    // Listing 5.4 - demonstrates variables
2:    // scoped within a block
3:
4:    #include <iostream.h>
5:
6:    void myFunc();
7:
8:    int main()
9:    {
10:      int x = 5;
11:      cout << "\nIn main x is: " << x;
12:
13:      myFunc();
14:
15:      cout << "\nBack in main, x is: " << x << endl;
16:        return 0;
17:    }
18:
19:    void myFunc()
20:    {
21:
22:      int x = 8;
23:      cout << "\nIn myFunc, local x: " << x << endl;
24:
25:      {
26:        cout << "\nIn block in myFunc, x is: " << x;
27:
28:        int x = 9;
```

```
29:
30:        cout << "\nVery local x: " << x;
31:    }
32:
33:    cout << "\nOut of block, in myFunc, x: " << x << endl;
34: }
```

OUTPUT

```
In main x is: 5
In myFunc, local x: 8

In block in myFunc, x is: 8
Very local x: 9
Out of block, in myFunc, x: 8
Back in main, x is: 5
```

ANALYSIS This program begins with the initialization of a local variable, x, on line 10, in main(). The printout on line 11 verifies that x was initialized with the value 5.

MyFunc() is called, and a local variable, also named x, is initialized with the value 8 on line 22. Its value is printed on line 23.

A block is started on line 25, and the variable x from the function is printed again on line 26. A new variable also named x, but local to the block, is created on line 28 and initialized with the value 9.

The value of the newest variable x is printed on line 30. The local block ends on line 31, and the variable created on line 28 goes "out of scope" and is no longer visible.

When x is printed on line 33, it is the x that was declared on line 22. This x was unaffected by the x that was defined on line 28; its value is still 8.

On line 34, MyFunc() goes out of scope, and its local variable x becomes unavailable. Execution returns to line 15, and the value of the local variable x, which was created on line 10, is printed. It was unaffected by either of the variables defined in MyFunc().

Needless to say, this program would be far less confusing if these three variables were given unique names!

Function Statements

Virtually no limit exists to the number or types of statements that can be placed in the body of a function. Although you cannot define another function from within a function, you can *call* a function, and of course, main() does just that in nearly every C++ program. Functions can even call themselves, which is discussed in the section on recursion.

5

Although no limit exists to the size of a function in C++, well-designed functions tend to be small. Many programmers advise keeping your functions short enough to fit on a single screen so that you can see the entire function at one time. This is a rule of thumb, often broken by very good programmers, but a smaller function is easier to understand and maintain.

Each function should carry out a single, easily understood task. If your functions start getting large, look for places where you can divide them into component tasks.

More About Function Arguments

Function arguments do not all have to be of the same type. It is perfectly reasonable to write a function that takes an integer, two longs, and a character as its arguments.

Any valid C++ expression can be a function argument, including constants, mathematical and logical expressions, and other functions that return a value.

Using Functions as Parameters to Functions

Although it is legal for one function to take as a parameter a second function that returns a value, it can make for code that is hard to read and hard to debug.

As an example, suppose you have the functions double(), triple(), square(), and cube(), each of which returns a value. You could write

```
Answer = (double(triple(square(cube(myValue)))));
```

This statement takes a variable, myValue, and passes it as an argument to the function cube(), whose return value is passed as an argument to the function square(), whose return value is in turn passed to triple(), and that return value is passed to double(). The return value of this doubled, tripled, squared, and cubed number is now passed to Answer.

It is difficult to be certain what this code does (was the value tripled before or after it was squared?), and if the answer is wrong, it will be hard to figure out which function failed.

An alternative is to assign each step to its own intermediate variable:

```
unsigned long myValue = 2;
unsigned long cubed   =  cube(myValue);      // cubed = 8
unsigned long squared = square(cubed);       // squared = 64
unsigned long tripled = triple(squared);     // tripled = 192
unsigned long Answer =  double(tripled);     // Answer = 384
```

Now each intermediate result can be examined, and the order of execution is explicit.

Parameters Are Local Variables

The arguments passed into the function are local to the function. Changes made to the arguments do not affect the values in the calling function. This is known as passing *by value*, which means a local copy of each argument is made in the function. These local copies are treated the same as any other local variables. Listing 5.5 illustrates this point.

INPUT   **LISTING 5.5**   A Demonstration of Passing by Value

```
1:      // Listing 5.5 - demonstrates passing by value
2:
3:      #include <iostream.h>
4:
5:      void swap(int x, int y);
6:
7:      int main()
8:      {
9:        int x = 5, y = 10;
10:
11:         cout << "Main. Before swap, x: " << x << " y: " << y << "\n";
12:         swap(x,y);
13:         cout << "Main. After swap, x: " << x << " y: " << y << "\n";
14:           return 0;
15:      }
16:
17:      void swap (int x, int y)
18:      {
19:        int temp;
20:
21:         cout << "Swap. Before swap, x: " << x << " y: " << y << "\n";
22:
23:        temp = x;
24:        x = y;
25:        y = temp;
26:
27:         cout << "Swap. After swap, x: " << x << " y: " << y << "\n";
28:
29:      }
```

OUTPUT
```
Main. Before swap, x: 5 y: 10
Swap. Before swap, x: 5 y: 10
Swap. After swap, x: 10 y: 5
```
Main. After swap, x: 5 y: 10

ANALYSIS   This program initializes two variables in main() and then passes them to the swap() function, which appears to swap them. When they are examined again in main(), however, they are unchanged!

5

The variables are initialized on line 9, and their values are displayed on line 11. swap() is called, and the variables are passed in.

Execution of the program switches to the swap() function, where on line 21 the values are printed again. They are in the same order as they were in main(), as expected. On lines 23–25 the values are swapped, and this action is confirmed by the printout on line 27. Indeed, while in the swap() function, the values are swapped.

Execution then returns to line 13, back in main(), where the values are no longer swapped.

As you may have figured out, the values passed into the swap() function are passed by value, meaning that copies of the values are made that are local to swap(). These local variables are swapped in lines 23–25, but the variables back in main() are unaffected.

On Day 8, "Pointers," and Day 10, "Advanced Functions," you will see alternatives to passing variables that will allow the values in main() to be changed.

More About Return Values

Functions return a value or return void. Void is a signal to the compiler that no value will be returned.

To return a value from a function, write the keyword return followed by the value you want to return. The value might itself be an expression that returns a value. For example:

```
return 5;
return (x > 5);
return (MyFunction());
```

These are all legal return statements, assuming that the function MyFunction() itself returns a value. The value in the second statement, returns (x > 5), will be false if x is not greater than 5, or it will be true. What is returned is the value of the expression, false or true, not the value of x.

When the return keyword is encountered, the expression following return is returned as the value of the function. Program execution returns immediately to the calling function, and any statements following the return are not executed.

It is legal to have more than one return statement in a single function. But a single return statement can only return one value. Listing 5.6 illustrates the idea of multiple return statements.

```
1:     // Listing 5.6 - demonstrates multiple return
2:     // statements
3:
4:     #include <iostream.h>
5:
6:     int Doubler(int AmountToDouble);
7:
8:     int main()
9:     {
10:
11:         int result = 0;
12:         int input;
13:
14:         cout << "Enter a number between 0 and 10,000 to double: ";
15:         cin >> input;
16:
17:         cout << "\nBefore doubler is called... ";
18:         cout << "\ninput: " << input << " doubled: " << result
➥<< "\n";
19:
20:         result = Doubler(input);
21:
22:         cout << "\nBack from Doubler...\n";
23:         cout << "\ninput: " << input << "    doubled: " << result
➥<< "\n";
24:
25:
26:         return 0;
27:     }
28:
29:     int Doubler(int original)
30:     {
31:         if (original <= 10000)
32:             return original * 2;
33:         else
34:             return -1;
35:         cout << "You can't get here!\n";
36:     }
```

OUTPUT

```
Enter a number between 0 and 10,000 to double: 9000

Before doubler is called...
input: 9000 doubled: 0

Back from doubler...

input: 9000    doubled: 18000
```

```
Enter a number between 0 and 10,000 to double: 11000

Before doubler is called...
input: 11000 doubled: 0

Back from doubler...
input: 11000  doubled: -1
```

ANALYSIS A number is requested on lines 14 and 15 and printed on line 18, along with the local variable result. The function `Doubler()` is called on line 20, and the input value is passed as a parameter. The result will be assigned to the local variable `result`, and the values will be reprinted on line 23.

On line 31, in the function `Doubler()`, the parameter is tested to see whether it is greater than 10,000. If it is not, the function returns twice the original number. If it is greater than 10,000, the function returns -1 as an error value.

The statement on line 35 is never reached because whether or not the value is greater than 10,000, the function returns on either line 32 or line 34—before it gets to line 35. A good compiler will warn that this statement cannot be executed, and a good programmer will take it out!

Frequently Asked Questions

FAQ: What is the difference between int main() and void main(); which one should I use? I have used both and they both worked fine, so why do I need to use int main(){ return 0;}?

Answer: Both will work on GNU and most other compilers, but only int main() is ANSI compliant, and thus only int main() is guaranteed to continue working in the future.

The difference is that int main() returns a value to the operating system. When your program completes, that value can be captured, for example, by batch programs.

We will not be using the return value from main in our examples (you could check it in one of your shell scripts if you want to), but the ANSI standard requires it.

Default Parameters

For every parameter you declare in a function prototype and definition, the calling function must pass in a value. The value passed in must be of the declared type. Thus if you have a function declared as

```
long myFunction(int);
```

the function must in fact take an integer variable. If the function definition differs, or if you fail to pass in an integer, you will get a compiler error.

The one exception to this rule is if the function prototype declares a default value for the parameter. A default value is a value to use if none is supplied. The preceding declaration could be rewritten as

```
long myFunction (int x = 50);
```

This prototype says, "myFunction() returns a long and takes an integer parameter. If an argument is not supplied, use the default value of 50." Because parameter names are not required in function prototypes, this declaration could have been written as

```
long myFunction (int = 50);
```

The function definition is not changed by declaring a default parameter. The function definition header for this function would be

```
long myFunction (int x)
```

If the calling function did not include a argument, the compiler would fill x with the default value of 50. The name of the default parameter in the prototype need not be the same as the name in the function header; the default value is assigned by position, not name.

Any or all of the function's parameters can be assigned default values. The one restriction is this: If any of the parameters does not have a default value, no previous parameter may have a default value.

If the function prototype looks like

```
long myFunction (int Param1, int Param2, int Param3);
```

you can assign a default value to Param2 only if you have assigned a default value to Param3. You can assign a default value to Param1 only if you assigned default values to both Param2 and Param3. Listing 5.7 demonstrates the use of default values.

INPUT **LISTING 5.7** A Demonstration of Default Parameter Values

```
1:    // Listing 5.7 - demonstrates use
2:    // of default parameter values
3:
4:    #include <iostream.h>
5:
6:    int VolumeCube(int length, int width = 25, int height = 1);
```

continues

LISTING 5.7 CONTINUED

```
7:
8:    int main()
9:    {
10:        int length = 100;
11:        int width = 50;
12:        int height = 2;
13:        int volume;
14:
15:        volume = VolumeCube(length, width, height);
16:        cout << "First volume equals: " << volume << "\n";
17:
18:        volume = VolumeCube(length, width);
19:        cout << "Second time volume equals: " << volume << "\n";
20:
21:        volume = VolumeCube(length);
22:        cout << "Third time volume equals: " << volume << "\n";
23:         return 0;
24:    }
25:
26:    VolumeCube(int length, int width, int height)
27:    {
28:
29:        return (length * width * height);
30:     }
```

OUTPUT

```
First volume equals: 10000
Second time volume equals: 5000
Third time volume equals: 2500
```

ANALYSIS On line 6, the VolumeCube() prototype specifies that the VolumeCube() function takes three integer parameters. The last two have default values.

This function computes the volume of the cube whose dimensions are passed in. If no width is passed in, a width of 25 is used and a height of 1 is used. If the width but not the height is passed in, a height of 1 is used. It is not possible to pass in the height without passing in a width.

On lines 10 to 12, the dimensions length, height, and width are initialized, and they are passed to the VolumeCube() function on line 15. The values are computed, and the result is printed on line 16.

Execution returns to line 18, where VolumeCube() is called again, but with no value for height. The default value is used, and again the dimensions are computed and printed.

Execution returns to line 21, and this time neither the width nor the height is passed in. Execution branches for a third time to line 27. The default values are used. The volume is computed and then printed.

Do	**Don't**
DO remember that function parameters act as local variables within the function.	**DON'T** try to create a default value for a first parameter if no default value exists for the second. This also applies to the second and other additional parameters: Do not give a parameter a default value if the parameter to the right does not have one.
	DON'T forget that arguments passed by value cannot affect the variables in the calling function.
	DON'T forget that changes to a global variable in one function change that variable for all functions.

Overloading Functions

C++ enables you to create more than one function with the same name. This is called *function overloading*. The functions must differ in their parameter list with a different type of parameter, a different number of parameters, or both. Here is one example:

```
int myFunction (int, int);
int myFunction (long, long);
int myFunction (long);
```

myFunction() is overloaded with three parameter lists. The first and second versions differ in the types of the parameters, and the third differs in the number of parameters.

The return types can be the same or different on overloaded functions. You should note that two functions with the same name and parameter list, but different return types, generate a compiler error.

Function overloading is also called *function polymorphism. Poly* means many, and *morph* means form: a polymorphic function is many-formed.

Function polymorphism refers to the capability to "overload" a function with more than one meaning. By changing the number or type of the parameters, you can give two or more functions the same function name, and the right one will be called by matching the parameters used. This enables you to create a function that can average integers, doubles, and other values without having to create individual names for each function, such as AverageInts(), AverageDoubles(), and so on.

5

Suppose you write a function that doubles whatever input you give it. You would like to be able to pass in an `int`, a `long`, a `float`, or a `double`. Without function overloading, you would have to create four function names:

```
int DoubleInt(int);
long DoubleLong(long);
float DoubleFloat(float);
double DoubleDouble(double);
```

With function overloading, you make this declaration:

```
int Double(int);
long Double(long);
float Double(float);
double Double(double);
```

This is easier to read and easier to use. You do not have to worry about which one to call; you just pass in a variable, and the right function is called automatically. Listing 5.8 illustrates the use of function overloading.

INPUT   **LISTING 5.8**   A Demonstration of Function Polymorphism

```
1:     // Listing 5.8 - demonstrates
2:     // function polymorphism
3:
4:     #include <iostream.h>
5:
6:     int Double(int);
7:     long Double(long);
8:     float Double(float);
9:     double Double(double);
10:
11:    int main()
12:    {
13:        int       myInt = 6500;
14:        long      myLong = 65000;
15:        float     myFloat = 6.5F;
16:        double    myDouble = 6.5e20;
17:
18:        int       doubledInt;
19:        long      doubledLong;
20:        float     doubledFloat;
21:        double    doubledDouble;
22:
23:        cout << "myInt: " << myInt << "\n";
24:        cout << "myLong: " << myLong << "\n";
25:        cout << "myFloat: " << myFloat << "\n";
26:        cout << "myDouble: " << myDouble << "\n";
27:
```

```
28:         doubledInt = Double(myInt);
29:         doubledLong = Double(myLong);
30:         doubledFloat = Double(myFloat);
31:         doubledDouble = Double(myDouble);
32:
33:         cout << "doubledInt: " << doubledInt << "\n";
34:         cout << "doubledLong: " << doubledLong << "\n";
35:         cout << "doubledFloat: " << doubledFloat << "\n";
36:         cout << "doubledDouble: " << doubledDouble << "\n";
37:
38:          return 0;
39:    }
40:
41: int Double(int original)
42: {
43:   cout << "In Double(int)\n";
44:   return 2 * original;
45: }
46:
47: long Double(long original)
48: {
49:   cout << "In Double(long)\n";
50:   return 2 * original;
51: }
52:
53: float Double(float original)
54: {
55:   cout << "In Double(float)\n";
56:   return 2 * original;
57: }
58:
59: double Double(double original)
60: {
61:   cout << "In Double(double)\n";
62:   return 2 * original;
63: }
```

5

OUTPUT
```
myInt: 6500
myLong: 65000
myFloat: 6.5
myDouble: 6.5e+20
In Double(int)
In Double(long)
In Double(float)
In Double(double)
DoubledInt: 13000
DoubledLong: 130000
DoubledFloat: 13
DoubledDouble: 1.3e+21
```

The `Double()` function is overloaded with `int`, `long`, `float`, and `double`. The prototypes are on lines 6 to 9, and the definitions are on lines 41 to 63.

In the body of the main program, eight local variables are declared. On lines 13 to 16, four of the values are initialized, and on lines 28 to 31, the other four are assigned the results of passing the first four to the `Double()` function. Note that when `Double()` is called, the calling function does not distinguish which one to call; it just passes in an argument, and the correct one is invoked.

The compiler examines the arguments and chooses which of the four `Double()` functions to call. The output reveals that each of the four was called in turn, as you would expect.

Special Topics About Functions

Because functions are so central to programming, a few special topics arise that might be of interest when you confront unusual problems. Used wisely, inline functions can help you squeak out that last bit of performance. Function recursion is one of those wonderful, esoteric bits of programming, which, every once in a while, can cut through a thorny problem not easily solved otherwise.

Inline Functions

When you define a function, normally the compiler creates just one set of instructions in memory. When you call the function, execution of the program jumps to those instructions, and when the function returns, execution jumps back to the next line in the calling function. If you call the function 10 times, your program jumps to the same set of instructions each time. This means only one copy of the function exists, not 10.

Some performance overhead occurs in jumping in and out of functions. It turns out that some functions are very small, just a line or two of code, and some efficiency can be gained if the program can avoid making these jumps just to execute one or two instructions. When programmers speak of efficiency, they usually mean speed; the program runs faster if the function call can be avoided.

If a function is declared with the keyword inline, the compiler does not create a real function; it copies the code from the inline function directly into the calling function. No jump is made; it is just as if you had written the statements of the function right into the calling function.

Note that inline functions can bring a heavy cost. If the function is called 10 times, the inline code is copied into the calling functions each of those 10 times. The tiny improvement in speed you might achieve is more than swamped by the increase in size of the executable program. Even the speed increase might be illusory. First, today's optimizing compilers do a terrific job on their own, and declaring a function inline almost never results in a big gain. More important, the increased size brings its own performance cost.

What is the rule of thumb? If you have a small function—one or two statements—it is a candidate for inline. When in doubt, though, leave it out. Listing 5.9 demonstrates an inline function.

INPUT   **LISTING 5.9**   Demonstrates an Inline Function

```cpp
1:   // Listing 5.9 - demonstrates inline functions
2:
3:   #include <iostream.h>
4:
5:   inline int Double(int);
6:
7:   int main()
8:   {
9:     int target;
10:
11:    cout << "Enter a number to work with: ";
12:    cin >> target;
13:    cout << "\n";
14:
15:    target = Double(target);
16:    cout << "Target: " << target << endl;
17:
18:    target = Double(target);
19:    cout << "Target: " << target << endl;
20:
21:
22:    target = Double(target);
23:    cout << "Target: " << target << endl;
24:       return 0;
25:  }
26:
27:  int Double(int target)
28:  {
29:    return 2*target;
30:  }
```

OUTPUT
```
Enter a number to work with: 20

Target: 40
Target: 80
Target: 160
```

5

On line 5, `Double()` is declared to be an inline function taking an `int` parameter and returning an `int`. The declaration is just like any other prototype except that the keyword `inline` is prepended just before the return value.

This compiles into code that is the same as if you had written the following:

```
target = 2 * target;
```

everywhere you entered

```
target = Double(target);
```

By the time your program executes, the instructions are already in place, compiled into the executable file. This saves a jump in the execution of the code at the cost of a larger program.

> **Note**   Inline is a hint to the compiler that you would like the function to be inlined. The compiler is free to ignore the hint and make a real function call.

Recursion

A function can call itself. This is called *recursion*, and recursion can be direct or indirect. Recursion is direct when a function calls itself; it is indirect when a function calls another function that then calls the first function.

Some problems are most easily solved by recursion, usually those in which you act on data and then act in the same way on the result. Both types of recursion, direct and indirect, come in two varieties: those that eventually end and produce an answer, and those that never end and produce a runtime failure. Programmers think that the latter is quite funny (when it happens to someone else).

It is important to note that when a function calls itself, a new copy of that function is run. The local variables in the second version are independent of the local variables in the first, and they cannot affect one another directly any more than the local variables in `main()` can affect the local variables in any function it calls, as was illustrated in Listing 5.4.

To illustrate solving a problem using recursion, consider the Fibonacci series:

1,1,2,3,5,8,13,21,34…

Each number, after the second, is the sum of the two numbers before it. A Fibonacci problem might be to determine what the twelfth number in the series is.

One way to solve this problem is to examine the series carefully. The first two numbers are 1. Each subsequent number is the sum of the previous two numbers. Thus the seventh number is the sum of the sixth and fifth numbers. More generally, the nth number is the sum of n-2 and n -1, as long as n > 2.

Recursive functions need a stop condition. Something must happen to cause the program to stop recursing, or it will never end. In the Fibonacci series, n < 3 is a stop condition.

The algorithm to use is the following:

1. Ask the user for a position in the series.
2. Call the fib() function with that position, passing in the value the user entered.
3. The fib() function examines the argument (n). If n < 3, it returns 1; otherwise, fib() calls itself (recursively) passing in n-2, calls itself again passing in n-1, and returns the sum.

If you call fib(1), it returns 1. If you call fib(2), it returns 1. If you call fib(3), it returns the sum of calling fib(2) and fib(1). Because fib(2) returns 1 and fib(1) returns 1, fib(3) will return 2.

If you call fib(4), it returns the sum of calling fib(3) and fib(2). We already established that fib(3) returns 2 (by calling fib(2) and fib(1)) and that fib(2) returns 1, so fib(4) will sum these numbers and return 3, which is the fourth number in the series.

Taking this one more step, if you call fib(5), it will return the sum of fib(4) and fib(3). We established that fib(4) returns 3 and fib(3) returns 2, so the sum returned will be 5.

This method is not the most efficient way to solve this problem (in fib(20) the fib() function is called 13,529 times!), but it does work. Be careful—if you feed in too large a number, you will run out of memory. Every time fib() is called, memory is set aside. When it returns, memory is freed. With recursion, memory continues to be set aside before it is freed, and this system can eat memory very quickly. Listing 5.10 implements the fib() function.

Caution When you run Listing 5.10, use a small number (less than 15). Because this uses recursion and cout for each call of the function, it produces a lot of output and can consume a lot of memory.

INPUT   **LISTING 5.10**   Demonstrates Recursion Using the Fibonacci Series

```
1: #include <iostream.h>
2:
3: int fib (int n);
4:
5:    int main()
6:    {
7:
8:      int n, answer;
9:     cout << "Enter number to find: ";
10:     cin >> n;
11:      cout << "\n\n";
12:
13:      answer = fib(n);
14:
15:      cout << answer << " is the " << n << "th Fibonacci number\n";
16:        return 0;
17:    }
18:    int fib (int n)
19:    {
20:      cout << "Processing fib(" << n << ")... ";
21:      if (n < 3 )
22:      {
23:        cout << "Return 1!\n";
24:        return (1);
25:      }
26:      else
27:      {
28:        cout << "Call fib(" << n-2 << ") and fib(" << n-1 << ").\n";
29:        return( fib(n-2) + fib(n-1));
30:      }
31:    }
```

OUTPUT   Enter number to find: 6

```
Processing fib(6)... Call fib(4) and fib(5).
Processing fib(4)... Call fib(2) and fib(3).
Processing fib(2)... Return 1!
Processing fib(3)... Call fib(1) and fib(2).
Processing fib(1)... Return 1!
Processing fib(2)... Return 1!
Processing fib(5)... Call fib(3) and fib(4).
Processing fib(3)... Call fib(1) and fib(2).
Processing fib(1)... Return 1!
Processing fib(2)... Return 1!
Processing fib(4)... Call fib(2) and fib(3).
Processing fib(2)... Return 1!
Processing fib(3)... Call fib(1) and fib(2).
```

```
Processing fib(1)... Return 1!
Processing fib(2)... Return 1!
8 is the 6th Fibonacci number
```

Note

Some compilers (other than GNU) have difficulty with the use of operators in a cout statement. If you receive a warning on line 28, place parentheses around the subtraction operation so that line 28 becomes

```
28:        cout << "Call fib(" << (n-2) << ") and
➥fib(" << (n-1) << ").\n";
```

The program asks for a number to find on line 9 and assigns that number to n. It then calls fib() with n. Execution branches to the fib() function, where, on line 20, it prints its argument.

The argument n is tested to see whether it is less than 3 on line 21; if so, fib() returns the value 1. Otherwise, it returns the sum of the values returned by calling fib() on n-2 and n-1.

It cannot return these values until the call (to fib()) is resolved. Thus, you can picture the program diving into fib repeatedly until it hits a call to fib, which returns a value. The only calls that return a value immediately are the calls to fib(2) and fib(1). These are then passed up to the waiting callers, which, in turn, add the return value to their own, and then they return. Figures 5.4 and 5.5 illustrate this recursion into fib().

FIGURE 5.4

Using recursion.

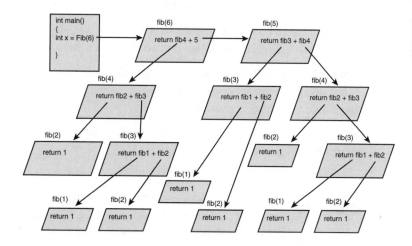

FIGURE 5.5

Returning from recursion.

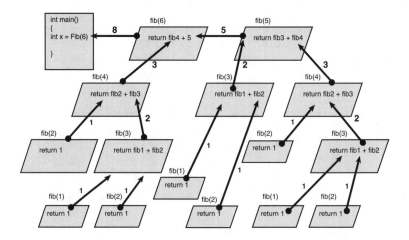

In the example, n is 6 so fib(6) is called from main(). Execution jumps to the fib() function, and n is tested for a value less than 3 on line 21. The test fails, so fib(6) returns the sum of the values returned by fib(4) and fib(5).

```
29:        return( fib(n-2) + fib(n-1));
```

That means that a call is made to fib(4) [because n == 6, fib(n-2) is the same as fib(4)] and another call is made to fib(5) [fib(n-1)], and then the function you are in [fib(6)] *waits* until these calls return a value. When these return a value, this function can return the result of summing those two values.

Because fib(5) passes in an argument that is not less than 3, fib() will be called again, this time with 4 and 3. fib(4) will in turn call fib(3) and fib(2).

The output traces these calls and the return values. Compile, link, and run this program, entering first 1, then 2, then 3, building up to 6, and watch the output carefully.

This would be a great time to start experimenting with your debugger. Put a break point on line 20 and then trace *into* each call to fib, keeping track of the value of *n* as you work your way into each recursive call to fib.

Recursion is not used often in C++ programming, but it can be a powerful and elegant tool for certain needs.

Note

Recursion is a tricky part of advanced programming. It is presented here because it can be useful to understand the fundamentals of how it works, but do not worry too much if you do not fully understand all the details.

How Functions Work—A Look Under the Hood

When you call a function, the code branches to the called function, parameters are passed in, and the body of the function is executed. When the function completes, a value is returned (unless the function returns void), and control returns to the calling function.

How is this task accomplished? How does the code know where to branch? Where are the variables kept when they are passed in? What happens to variables that are declared in the body of the function? How is the return value passed back out? How does the code know where to resume?

Most introductory books do not try to answer these questions, but without understanding this information, you will find that programming remains a fuzzy mystery. The explanation requires a brief tangent into a discussion of computer memory.

Levels of Abstraction

One of the principal hurdles for new programmers is grappling with the many layers of intellectual abstraction. Computers, of course, are only electronic machines. They do not know about windows and menus, they do not know about programs or instructions, and they do not even know about ones and zeros. All that is really going on is that voltage is being measured at various places on an integrated circuit. Even this is an abstraction: Electricity itself is just an intellectual concept representing the behavior of subatomic particles.

Few programmers bother with any level of detail below the idea of values in RAM. After all, you do not need to understand particle physics to drive a car, make toast, or hit a baseball, and you do not need to understand the electronics of a computer to program one.

You do need to understand how memory is organized, however. Without a reasonably strong mental picture of where your variables are when they are created and how values are passed among functions, it will all remain an unmanageable mystery.

Partitioning RAM

When you begin your program, Linux sets up various areas of memory based on the requirements of the compiled program. As a C++ programmer, you will often be concerned with the global name space, the free store, the registers, the code space, and the stack.

5

Global variables are in global name space. We will talk more about global name space and the free store in coming days, but for now we will focus on the registers, code space, and stack.

Registers are a special area of memory built right into the Central Processing Unit (or CPU). They take care of internal housekeeping. A lot of what goes on in the registers is beyond the scope of this book, but what we are concerned with is the set of registers responsible for pointing, at any given moment, to the next line of code. We call these registers, together, the instruction pointer. It is the job of the instruction pointer to keep track of which line of code is to be executed next.

The code itself is in *code space*, which is that part of memory set aside to hold the binary form of the instructions you created in your program. Each line of source code is translated into a series of instructions, and each of these instructions is at a particular address in memory. The instruction pointer has the address of the next instruction to execute. Figure 5.6 illustrates this idea.

FIGURE 5.6

The instruction pointer.

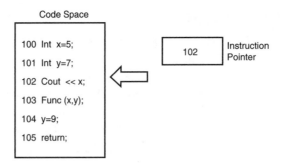

Code Space

```
100  Int  x=5;
101  Int  y=7;
102  Cout << x;
103  Func (x,y);
104  y=9;
105  return;
```

| 102 | Instruction Pointer |

The *stack* is a special area of memory allocated for your program to hold the data required by each of the functions in your program. It is called a stack because it is a last-in, first-out queue, much like a stack of dishes at a cafeteria, as shown in Figure 5.7.

FIGURE 5.7

A stack.

Last-in, first-out means that whatever is added to the stack last will be the first thing taken off. Most queues are like a line at a theater: The first one in line is the first one off. A stack is more like a stack of coins: If you stack 10 pennies on a tabletop and then take some back, the last three you put on will be the first three you take off.

When data is *pushed* onto the stack, the stack grows; as data is *popped* off the stack, the stack shrinks. It is not possible to pop a dish off the stack without first popping off all the dishes placed on after that dish.

A stack of dishes is the common analogy. It is fine as far as it goes, but it is wrong in a fundamental way. A more accurate mental picture is of a series of cubbyholes aligned top to bottom. The top of the stack is whatever cubby the stack pointer (which is another register) happens to be pointing to.

Each of the cubbies has a sequential address, and one of those addresses is kept in the stack pointer register. Everything below that magic address, known as the top of the stack, is considered to be on the stack. Everything above the top of the stack is considered to be off the stack and invalid. Figure 5.8 illustrates this idea.

FIGURE 5.8

The stack pointer.

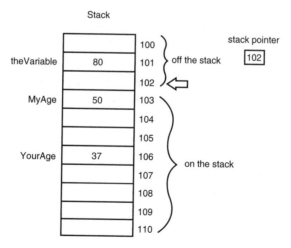

When data is put on the stack, it is placed into a cubby above the stack pointer, and then the stack pointer is moved to the new data. When data is popped off the stack, all that really happens is that the address of the stack pointer is changed by moving it down the stack. Figure 5.9 makes this rule clear.

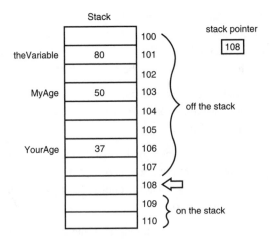

FIGURE 5.9

Moving the stack pointer.

The Stack and Functions

The following is what happens when a program, running on most systems, branches to a function:

1. The address in the instruction pointer is incremented to the next instruction past the function call. That address is then placed on the stack, and it will be the return address when the function returns.

2. Room is made on the stack for the return type you declared. On a system with 2-byte integers, if the return type is declared to be int, another 2 bytes are added to the stack, but no value is placed in these bytes.

3. The address of the called function, which is kept in a special area of memory set aside for that purpose, is loaded into the instruction pointer, so the next instruction executed will be in the called function.

4. The current top of the stack is now noted and is held in a special pointer called the stack frame. Everything added to the stack from now until the function returns will be considered "local" to the function.

5. All the arguments to the function are placed on the stack.

6. The instruction now in the instruction pointer is executed, thus executing the first instruction in the function.

7. Local variables are pushed onto the stack as they are defined.

When a function is ready to return, the following occurs:

1. The return value is placed in the area of the stack reserved at step 2 above.

2. The stack is then popped all the way up to the stack frame pointer, which effectively throws away all the local variables and the arguments to the function.

3. The return value is popped off the stack and assigned as the value of the function call itself

4. The current top of the stack is now noted and is held in a special pointer called the stack frame. Everything added to the stack from now until the function returns will be considered "local" to the function.

5. The address stashed away in step 1 of the call is retrieved and put into the instruction pointer. The program thus resumes immediately after the function call, with the value of the function retrieved.

Some of the details of this process change from compiler to compiler, or between computers, but the essential ideas are consistent across environments. In general, when you call a function, the return address and the parameters are put on the stack. During the life of the function, local variables are added to the stack. When the function returns, these are all removed by popping the stack.

In the coming days, we will look at other places in memory that are used to hold data that must persist beyond the life of the function.

Multiple Source File Programs (Programmer-Created Function Libraries)

One of the greatest strengths of C and C++ is the ability to reuse code. Now all languages support this ability. However, for many of them, the mechanism is one of cut and paste (also known as cloning): when you want to use existing code, you copy the source into the new program and go from there. The problem with this approach is the maintenance nightmares. When the business rule embodied in the code changes (and they all will at some time), all copies of the code have to change. But each version is a little different and has to be carefully reviewed before it can be changed.

C and C++ provide a better mechanism for code reuse: function and object libraries. These are collections of code that is already compiled into the object file form (.o or .obj). With proper discipline, there is one version only that all programmers use. Only that version of the source is changed, and any affected programs are recompiled or relinked.

In addition to the object file, you should create a header file that contains the prototypes for those functions.

Linux also supports a "library" file in the form of an archive file. An archive file contains multiple object files. The linker knows how to read files in plain object format or extract them from an archive file. The ar command is used to manipulate archives. Check the manual page or info file for more information.

In addition, you can create project files (known as make files, after the command that uses them—make). These project files control compilation and linking based on rules that you create. In the simplest form, your program will recompile and link if any of its parts change—main source, header files, and libraries.

The next section shows you how to create and use simple libraries of functions; the section after that introduces the GNU make command (gmake).

How to Create and Use Function Libraries with g++

A simple function library consists of three parts: function source (the functions themselves), function prototypes in a header file, and the compiled functions.

You can break the function out of the Fibonacci series program shown in Listing 5.10. Listing 5.11 contains the header file and should be saved as fib.h.

INPUT   **LISTING 5.11**   Heading file (fib.h) to Demonstrate Function Libraries

```
1: // fib.h header file
2:#ifndef __FIB_H
3:#define __FIB_H
4: int fib (int n);
5:#endif
```

Listing 5.12 contains the fib() function. This will be compiled separately from the main program and linked in later.

INPUT   **LISTING 5.12**   Function Library

```
1: #include <iostream.h>
2: #include "fib.h"
3: // Listing 5.12
4:    int fib (int n)
5:    {
6:      cout << "Processing fib(" << n << ")... "; 23:
7:      if (n < 3 )
8:      {
9:         cout << "Return 1!\n";
10:         return (1);
11:      }
12:      else
13:      {
14:         cout << "Call fib(" << n-2 << ") and fib(" << n-1 << ").\n";
15:         return( fib(n-2) + fib(n-1));
16:      }
17:    }
```

Listing 5.13 contains the main program that calls the fib() function. This is the same as the program in Listing 5.10 except that the function has been removed and the function prototype is in a header file (instead of in the same file as main()).

LISTING 5.13 Demonstrates Recursion Using the Fibonacci Series—Using
INPUT   Libraries

```
 1: #include <iostream.h>
 2: #include "fib.h"
 3: // Listing 5.13 - multiple source files (using libraries)
 4:
 5:    int main()
 6:    {
 7:
 8:       int n, answer;
 9:      cout << "Enter number to find: ";
10:      cin >> n;
11:       cout << "\n\n";
12:
13:       answer = fib(n);
14:
15:       cout << answer << " is the " << n << "th Fibonacci number\n";
16:          return 0;
17:    }
```

There are two ways you can compile the fib() function and main() together, the first being at the same time:

```
g++ lst05-13.c++ lst05-12.c++ -o lst05-13
```

Or you can use two separate commands:

```
g++ -c lst05-12.c++
g++ lst05-13.c++ lst05-12.o -o lst05-13
```

The advantage of the second method is that you can compile lst05-12.c++ into an object file once and provide the object and header file to other programmers. That allows the programmers to use your function without being able to change it (because they do not have the source code).s

Creating Project Files (for make)

In the simplest form, the make command under Linux allows you to set up a project and let those rules control what gets compiled when. Only when needed (when something changes) will code actually be changed.

5

These rules are stored in a file known as a *makefile* (which is also the default name for the file), although you can give it any name you want.

The general format of a makefile consists of two different kinds of lines. The first is the target/dependency, which defines the target to be made along with any files that it depends on. The other lines are the commands required to produce that target. The makefile for Listings 5.11 through 5.13 is shown in Listing 5.14.

INPUT

LISTING 5.14 Makefile for Use with Listings 5.11 through 5.13 (lst05-14.mak)

```
1: lst05-12.o: lst05-12.c++ fib.h
2:        g++ -c lst05-12.c++
3: #
4: lst05-13: lst05-13.c++ lst05-12.o fib.h
5:        g++ lst05-13.c++ lst05-12.o -o lst05-13
```

The first line shows that lst05-12.o (the function library, our target) depends on lst05-12.c++ and fib.h. Line 2 is the command to produce that target. Line 3 is a comment.

The line 4 shows that lst05-13 (the executable, our target of this step) depends on lst05-13.c++, lib05-12.o, and fib.h. Line 5 is the command to produce that target.

Note

Lines 2 and 5 have a tab character before the g++ command. This must be a tab character. if you use any other character here (including spaces), you will get the following error message from make:

```
yourfile.mak:2: *** missing separator.  Stop.
```

When fib.h changes and you try to make the executable using the following command, it builds all the parts needed:

```
make -f lst05-14.mak lst05-13
```

OUTPUT

```
g++ -c lst05-12.c++
gcc: -lgpp: linker input file unused since linking not done
gcc: -lstdcx: linker input file unused since linking not done
gcc: -lm: linker input file unused since linking not done
g++ lst05-13.c++ lst05-12.o -o lst05-13
```

ANALYSIS The specified target is lst05-13. It needs lst05-12.o and fib.h. lst05-12.o needs fib.h. I changed fib.h (I added an extra space at the end of a line) before issuing the make command. This command is smart enough to analyze the rules you give it to determine whether there are any other dependencies. It determined that because `lst05-13` needs `lst05-12.o` and `fib.h` changed since the last time `lst05-12.o` was created, `lst05-12.c++` needed to be recompiled before `lst05-13.c++`.

The `make` command is much more sophisticated than this simple example shows. Take a look at the info page for more information; `make` supports a programming language of its own.

You can create simple project files like this one for your programs. Then you do not need to remember what the dependencies are.

Standard C++ Library Functions (libg++)

All compilers that subscribe to the ANSI standard come with a series of functions for you to use. These functions are said to be *built-in* because they come with the compiler; you do not write them yourself. The GNU compiler is no exception. There is a standard library of functions for C programs and a superset library of functions and objects for C++ programmers.

You will learn about many of the standard objects in later days. You can always use the `info` command to get more information:

```
info libg++
```

You can get details on the C standard functions through the `info` command:

```
info libc
```

The standard functions for C and C++ are very important. You can use them instead of writing your own. This makes program creation easier (less to do) and greatly simplifies maintenance because the compiler vendors (GNU Project contributors/Free Software Foundation) worry about maintaining those functions. They are categorized in the following sections by Math, Character, and General functions.

Math Functions

The standard library math functions allow you to perform common (and some not-so-common) mathematical operations. This allows you to worry about how to use the results instead of worrying about how to calculate the results. For example, there is a function to calculate the square root of a positive number. As a programmer, you do not need to know how to code this—another programmer has done so. You just need to know what to do with the results (or why you would want to get the square root of a number).

Some of the most commonly used math functions are shown in Table 5.1.

TABLE 5.1 Common Mathematical Functions

Function	Usage
ceil(f)	Rounds f to the smallest integer not less than f: ceil(3.3) is 4, ceil(-3.3) is -3.
cos(f)	Calculates the cosine of f (where f is in radians): cos(0.0) is 1, cos(3.1415926) is -1.
exp(f)	Exponential function in the form of e^f: exp(0.0) is 1, exp(1.0) is 2.718 (e).
fabs(f)	Floating absolute value of f: fabs(-1.0) is 1, fabs(0.0) is 0, fabs(1.0) is 1.
floor(f)	Rounds f to the largest integer that is not greater than f: floor(3.3) is 3, floor(-3.3) is -4; compare with the ceil() function.
fmod (f, g)	Calculates the remainder of f/g as a float.
log (f)	Natural logarithm of f using base e: log(1.0) is 0.0, log(2.718) is 1.0.
log10 (f)	Base 10 logarithm of f: log10 (0.0) is undefined, log10 (1.0) is 0.0, log10(10.0) 1, log10(1000.0) is 3.
pow (f, g)	Raises f to the g power (f^g): pow(2.0, 3.0) is 8.0, pow (3.0, 2.0) is 9.0.
sin (f)	Calculates the sine of f (where f is in radians): sin (0.0) is 0, and sin (3.1415926 / 2.0) is 1.
sqrt (f)	Square root of f: sqrt (4.0) is 2, sqrt (9.0) is 3.0.
tan (f)	Calculates the tangent of f (where f is in radians): tan (0.0) is 0, and tan (3.1415926 / 4.0) is 1.
acos, asin, atan	Arc (anti or inverse) cosine, sine, and tangent.
acosh, asinh, atanh	Arc (anti or inverse) hyperbolic cosine, sine, and tangent.
cosh, sinh, tanh	Hyperbolic cosine, sine, and tangent.

For all these functions, you must include the math.h header file (in order to get the functional prototypes).

Character and String Functions

Character and string manipulation is a common task in most programs. As a result, a large library of functions has built up over time and have become part of the standard.

As with the math functions, these functions exist to make your life easier!

Some of the most commonly used string and character functions are shown in Table 5.2.

TABLE 5.2 Common String and Character Functions

Function	Usage
strcpy (s1, s2)	Copies s2 into s1 character by character until the null terminator is copied.
strncpy (s1, s2, n)	Copies s2 into s1 character by character until the null terminator is copied or n characters are moved; s1 is not null terminated if the count terminated the copy.
strcat (s1, s2)	Copies s2 onto the end of s1.
strncat (s1, s2, n)	Copies, at most, n characters of s2 onto the end of s1.
strcmp (s1, s2)	Compares s1 with s2 character by character and returns the difference. If the strings are the same, 0 is returned; otherwise, a positive or negative value shows the difference between the two.
strncmp (s1, s2, n)	Compares, at most, n characters of s1 with s2 character by character and returns the difference. If the strings are the same, 0 is returned; otherwise, a positive or negative value shows the difference between the two.
strlen (s1)	Returns the length (in characters, not counting the null terminator) of s1.
strlwr (s1)	Converts s1 to lowercase.
strtok (s1, s2)	Breaks s1 into tokens based on values in s2. This parses s1 into pieces delimited by characters in s2. The first time strtok is called, s2 is provided; each subsequent time, use NULL instead of s2.
strtod (s1), strtol(s1)	Converts s1 into an integer or long numeric value.
strupr(s1)	Converts s1 to uppercase.

5

For all these functions, you must include the string.h header file (in order to get the functional prototypes).

General Functions

There are many other functions that are part of the standard library. Some of the more common functions that are not math- or character-based are shown in Table 5.3.

TABLE 5.3 Other Commonly Used Functions

Function	Usage
system (s1)	Issues s1 as a command to the operating system or command shell.
malloc (n)	Allocates n bytes of memory and returns a pointer to that address. Returns NULL on failure.
free (ptr)	Frees memory allocated via malloc or realloc.
realloc(ptr, n)	Allocates n bytes growing or shrinking space previously allocated (malloc or realloc). Allows implementation of "dynamic" arrays.
abs (n)	Returns integer absolute value of n. abs (-1) is 1, abs (0) is 0, and abs (1) is 1.
asctime (t)	Converts internal format time t to printable time.
bsearch ()	Performs binary search on sorted data structure.
qsort ()	Sorts data structure.
isalpha (c)	Returns true if character c is alphabetic.
isdigit (c)	Returns true if character c is numeric digit.
islower (c)	Returns true if character c is lowercase alphabetic.
isupper (c)	Returns true if character c is uppercase alphabetic.

There are many, many, many more functions available in the standard library. Check the info or manual pages for more information about these and other functions. Some of the functions are very complex (such as bsearch and qsort) and require much more explanation, which can be best found in the documentation.

Much More

Remember, code reuse is one of the basics of C and C++. It is also one of the basics of software engineering. Any code that you can reuse is code that does not have to be written new or maintained. It can be much more robust and tested more strenuously than that written by individual programmers. And if changes are required, they can be changed one place (in the library) instead of having to track down all the code.

Check the standard libraries (C and C++) before writing functions of your own—one that solves your problem may already exist. It may take several standard library functions to perform your desired task, but it will save you time and effort.

I remember one project during which I was out of town attending a conference. There was a junior consultant on the project. He was a good coder and understood C well, but he was not all that familiar with the library. He needed to sort some data within his program (not a lot, so the sort algorithm was not important). Because very few people memorize how to write sort routines, he had to dig up his notes from college, code, test, and tweak the code. This took him several hours over a couple of days. I returned from the conference, and on hearing about his coding, pulled down the volume with the standard library, turned to the qsort page, and showed it to him.

In an hour or two, in the same day, using one standard function (and a special function to determine data order), he could have had his sort. Instead he took longer, had to work harder, and created more code to maintain. I used the masculine gender in this description because the person I worked with was male. The same mistake can be made no matter what your gender.

Remember this lesson!

Summary

This chapter introduced functions. A function is, in effect, a subprogram into which you can pass parameters and from which you can return a value. Every C++ program starts in the main() function, and main(), in turn, can call other functions.

A function is declared with a function prototype, which describes the return value, the function name, and its parameter types. A function can optionally be declared inline. A function prototype can also declare default variables for one or more of the parameters.

The function definition must match the function prototype in return type, name, and parameter list. Function names can be overloaded by changing the number or type of parameters; the compiler finds the right function based on the argument list.

Local function variables, and the arguments passed into the function, are local to the block in which they are declared. Parameters passed by value are copies and cannot affect the value of variables in the calling function.

Q&A

Q Why not make all variables global?

A At one time, this was exactly how programming was done. As programs became more complex, however, it became very difficult to find bugs in programs because data could be corrupted by any of the functions—global data can be changed anywhere in the program. Years of experience have convinced programmers that data should be kept as local as possible, and access to changing that data should be narrowly defined.

5

Q **When should the keyword `inline` be used in a function prototype?**

A If the function is very small, no more than a line or two, and won't be called from many places in your program, it is a candidate for inlining.

Q **Why aren't changes to the value of function arguments reflected in the calling function?**

A Arguments passed to a function are passed by value. That means that the argument in the function is actually a copy of the original value. This concept is explained in depth in the section "How Functions Work—A Look Under the Hood."

Q **If arguments are passed by value, what do I do if I need to reflect the changes back in the calling function?**

A On Day 8, pointers will be discussed. Use of pointers will solve this problem, as well as provide a way around the limitation of returning only a single value from a function.

Q **What happens if I have the following two functions:**

```
int Area (int width, int length = 1); int Area (int size);
```

Will these overload? A different number of parameters exist, but the first one has a default value.

A The declarations will compile, but if you invoke `Area` with one parameter, you will receive a compile-time error: ambiguity between `Area(int, int)` and `Area(int)`.

Workshop

The Workshop provides quiz questions to help you solidify your understanding of the material covered and exercises to provide you with experience in using what you learned today. Try to answer the quiz and exercise questions before checking the answers in Appendix D, "Answers to Exercises and Quizzes," and make sure that you understand the answers before continuing to the next day.

Quiz

1. What are the differences between the function prototype and the function definition?

2. Do the names of parameters have to agree in the prototype, definition, and call to the function?

3. If a function does not return a value, how do you declare the function?

4. If you do not declare a return value, what type of return value is assumed?

5. What is a local variable?

6. What is scope?

7. What is recursion?

8. When should you use global variables?

9. What is function overloading?

10. What is polymorphism?

Exercises

1. Write the prototype for a function named `Perimeter()`, which returns an unsigned long int and takes two parameters, both unsigned short ints.

2. Write the definition of the function `Perimeter()` as described in Exercise 1. The two parameters represent the length and width of a rectangle. Have the function return the perimeter (twice the length plus twice the width).

3. **BUG BUSTER:** What is wrong with the function in the following code?

```
#include <iostream.h>
void myFunc(unsigned short int x);
int main()
{
unsigned short int x, y;
y = myFunc(int);
cout << "x: " << x << " y: " << y << "\n";
}

void myFunc(unsigned short int x)
{
return (4*x);
}
```

4. **BUG BUSTER:** What is wrong with the function in the following code?

```
#include <iostream.h>
int myFunc(unsigned short int x);
int main()
{
unsigned short int x, y;
y = myFunc(x);
cout << "x: " << x << " y: " << y << "\n";
}

int myFunc(unsigned short int x);
{
return (4*x);
}
```

5. Write a function that takes two unsigned short integer arguments and returns the result of dividing the first by the second. Do not do the division if the second number is zero, but do return -1.

5

6. Write a program that asks the user for two numbers and calls the function you wrote in Exercise 5. Print the answer, or print an error message if you get -1.

7. Write a program that asks for a number and a power. Write a recursive function that takes the number to the power. Thus, if the number is 2 and the power is 4, the function will return 16.

DAY 6

Basic Classes

Classes extend the built-in capabilities of C++ to assist you in representing and solving complex, real-world problems. Today you will learn:

- What classes and objects are
- How to define a new class and create objects of that class
- What member functions and member data are
- What constructors are and how to use them

Creating New Types

You have already learned about a number of variable types, including unsigned integers and characters. The type of a variable tells you quite a bit about it. For example, if you declare Height and Width to be unsigned short integers, you know that each one can hold a number between 0 and 65,535, assuming an unsigned short integer is 2 bytes. That is the meaning of saying they are unsigned integers; trying to hold anything else in these variables causes an error. You cannot store your name in an unsigned short integer, and you should not even try.

Just by declaring these variables to be unsigned short integers, you know that it is possible to add `Height` to `Width` and to assign that number to another variable.

The type of these variables tells you

- Their size in memory
- What information they can hold
- What actions can be performed on them

More generally, a type is a category. Familiar types include car, house, person, fruit, and shape. In C++, the programmer can create any type needed, and each of these new types can have all the functionality and power of the built-in types.

Why Create a New Type?

Programs are usually written to solve real-world problems, such as keeping track of employee records or simulating the workings of a heating system. Although it is possible to solve complex problems by using programs written with only integers and characters, it is far easier to grapple with large complex problems if you can create representations of the objects that you are talking about.

In other words, simulating the workings of a heating system is easier if you can create variables that represent rooms, heat sensors, thermostats, and boilers. The more closely these variables correspond to reality, the easier it is to write the program.

Introducing Classes and Members

You make a new type by declaring a class. A class is just a collection of variables—often of different types—combined with a set of related functions.

One way to think about a car is as a collection of wheels, doors, seats, windows, and so forth. Another way is to think about what a car can do: It can move, speed up, slow down, stop, park, and so on. A class enables you to encapsulate, or bundle, these various parts and various functions into one collection, which is called an object.

Encapsulating everything you know about a car into one class has a number of advantages for a programmer. Everything is in one place, which makes it easy to refer to, copy, and manipulate the data. Likewise, clients of your class—that is, the parts of the program that use your class—can use your object without worrying about what is in it or how it works.

A class can consist of any combination of the variable types and also other class types. The variables in the class are referred to as the *member variables* or *data members*. A

Car class might have member variables representing the seats, radio type, tires, and so forth.

Member variables, also known as data members, are the variables in your class. Member variables are part of your class, just as the wheels and engine are part of your car.

The functions in the class typically manipulate the member variables. They are referred to as *member functions* or *methods* of the class. Methods of the Car class might include Start() and Brake(). A Cat class might have data members that represent age and weight; its methods might include Sleep(), Meow(), and ChaseMice().

Member functions, also known as methods, are the functions in your class. Member functions are as much a part of your class as the member variables. They determine what your class can do.

Declaring a Class

To declare a class, use the class keyword followed by an opening brace, and then list the data members and methods of that class. End the declaration with a closing brace and a semicolon. The declaration of a class called Cat looks like this:

```
class Cat
{
    unsigned int  itsAge;
    unsigned int  itsWeight;
    void Meow();
};
```

Declaring this class does not allocate memory for a Cat. It just tells the compiler what a Cat is, what data it contains (itsAge and itsWeight), and what it can do (Meow()). It also tells the compiler how big a Cat is—that is, how much room the compiler must set aside for each Cat that you create. In this example, if an integer is 4 bytes, a Cat is 8 bytes big: itsAge is 4 bytes, and itsWeight is another 4 bytes. Meow() takes up no room because no storage space is set aside for member functions (methods).

A Word on Naming Conventions

As a programmer, you must name all your member variables, member functions, and classes. As you learned on Day 3, "Variables and Constants," these should be easily understood and meaningful names. Cat, Rectangle, and Employee are good class names. Meow(), ChaseMice(), and StopEngine() are good function names because they tell you what the functions do. Many programmers name the member variables with the prefix its, as in itsAge, itsWeight, and itsSpeed. This helps to distinguish member variables from nonmember variables.

6

C++ is case sensitive, and all class names should follow the same pattern. That way, you never have to check how to spell your class name; was it Rectangle, rectangle, or RECTANGLE? Some programmers like to prefix every class name with a particular letter—for example, cCat or cPerson—whereas others put the name in all uppercase or all lowercase. The convention used in this book is to name all classes with initial capitalization, as in Cat and Person.

Similarly, many programmers begin all functions with capital letters and all variables with lowercase. Words are usually separated with an underscore—as in Chase_Mice—or by capitalizing each word—for example, ChaseMice or DrawCircle.

As mentioned a few days ago when you learned about variables, the important idea is that you should pick one style and stay with it through each program. Over time, your style will evolve to include not only naming conventions, but also indentation, alignment of braces, and commenting style.

 Note

It is very common for development companies to have house standards for many style issues. This ensures that all developers can easily read one another's code.

Even where there are not formal standards, groups develop their preferred methods.

Defining an Object

You define an object of your new type the same as you define an integer variable:

```
unsigned int GrossWeight;       // define an unsigned integer
Cat Frisky;                     // define a Cat
```

This code defines a variable called GrossWeight, whose type is an unsigned integer. It also defines Frisky, which is an object whose class (or type) is Cat.

Comparing Classes and Objects

You never pet the definition of a cat; you pet individual cats. You draw a distinction between the idea of a cat and the particular cat who right now is shedding all over your living room. In the same way, C++ differentiates between the class Cat, which is the idea of a cat, and each individual Cat object. Thus Frisky is an object of type Cat in the same way in which GrossWeight is a variable of type unsigned int.

An *object* is an individual instance of a class. The technical term for creating an object is *instantiation*.

Note

Sometimes terminology gets reused and misused. The meaning of individual terms or which term should be used where is often a matter of discussion and convention. As a result, the correct word today can be the incorrect word tomorrow.

In this book, the words *declare* and *define* are used interchangably to mean you are specifying or defining something. When you describe the members (data and functions) in an object class, you are declaring that class.

When working with normal variables (like int or float), there is no difference between the process of describing and creating. With object classes there is.

You describe the object class (define or declare) at one place in the program (often in a .hpp file) and then create a specific object later on.

With object classes, when you actually allocate memory, you are *creating* a specific object. Some authors use the word *specify* for this purpose.

Accessing Class Members

After you define an actual Cat object—for example, Frisky—you use the dot operator (.) to access the members of that object. Therefore, to assign 50 to Frisky's Weight member variable, you would write

```
Frisky.itsWeight = 50;
```

In the same way, to call the Meow() function, you would write

```
Frisky.Meow();
```

When you use a class method, you call the method. In this example, you are calling Meow() on Frisky.

Assign to Objects, Not to Classes

In C++ you do not assign values to types; you assign values to variables. For example, you would never write

```
int = 5;            // wrong
```

The compiler would flag this as an error because you cannot assign 5 to an integer. Rather, you must define an integer variable and assign 5 to that variable. For example,

```
int  x;            // define x to be an int
x = 5;             // set x's value to 5
```

6

This is a shorthand way of saying, "Assign 5 to the variable x, which is of type int." In the same way, you would not write

```
Cat.itsAge=5;            // wrong
```

The compiler would flag this as an error because you cannot assign 5 to the age part of a Cat. Rather, you must define a Cat object and assign 5 to that object, for example:

```
Cat Frisky;              // just like  int x;
Frisky.itsAge = 5;       // just like  x = 5;
```

If You Don't Declare It, Your Class Won't Have It

Try this experiment: Walk up to a three-year-old and show her a cat. Then say, "This is Frisky. Frisky knows a trick. Frisky, bark." The child will giggle and say, "No, silly, cats can't bark."

If you wrote

```
Cat  Frisky;             // make a Cat named Frisky
Frisky.Bark()            // tell Frisky to bark
```

the compiler would say, "No, silly, Cats can't bark." Actually, the GNU compiler will tell you:

```
example.cxx: In function `int main()':
example.cxx:25: no member function `Cat::Bark()' defined
```

The compiler knows that Frisky cannot bark because the Cat class does not have a Bark() function. The compiler would not even let Frisky meow if you did not define a Meow() function.

Do	Don't
DO use the keyword class to declare a class. **DO** use the dot operator (.) to access class members and functions.	**DON'T** confuse a declaration with a definition. A declaration says what a class is. A definition sets aside memory for an object. **DON'T** confuse a class with an object. **DON'T** assign values to a class. Assign values to the data members of an object.

Defining Scope as Private Versus Public

Other keywords are used in the declaration of a class. Two of the most important are `public` and `private`.

All members of a class—data and methods—are private by default. Private members can be accessed only within methods of the class itself. Public members can be accessed through any object of the class. This distinction is both important and confusing. To make it a bit clearer, consider an example from earlier in this chapter:

```
class Cat
{
  unsigned int  itsAge;
  unsigned int  itsWeight;
  void Meow();
};
```

In this declaration, `itsAge`, `itsWeight`, and `Meow()` are all private because all members of a class are private by default. This means that unless you specify otherwise, they are private.

However, if you write the following in `main()` (for example):

```
Cat  Boots;
Boots.itsAge=5;          // error! can't access private data!
```

the compiler flags this as an error. In effect, you told the compiler, "I'll access `itsAge`, `itsWeight`, and `Meow()` only from within member functions of the `Cat` class." Yet here you accessed the `itsAge` member variable of the `Boots` object from outside a `Cat` method. The fact that `Boots` is an object of class `Cat` does not mean that you can access the parts of `Boots` that are private.

This is a source of endless confusion to new C++ programmers. I can almost hear you yelling, "Hey! I just said Boots is a cat. Why can't Boots access his own age?" The answer is that `Boots` can, but you cannot. `Boots`, in his own methods, can access all his parts—public and private. Even though you created a `Cat`, that does not mean that you can see or change the parts of it that are private.

6

The way to use Cat so that you can access the data members is

```
class Cat
{
public:
    unsigned int  itsAge;
    unsigned int  itsWeight;
    void Meow();
};
```

Now itsAge, itsWeight, and Meow() are all public. Boots.itsAge=5 compiles without problems.

Listing 6.1 shows the declaration of a Cat class with public member variables.

INPUT   **LISTING 6.1**   Accessing the Public Members of a Simple Class

```
1:   // Demonstrates declaration of a class and
2:   // definition of an object of the class,
3:
4:   #include <iostream.h>    // for cout
5:
6:   class Cat                // declare the class object
7:   {
8:    public:                 // members that follow are public

9:       int itsAge;
10:      int itsWeight;
11:  };
12:
13:
14:  int main()
15:  {
16:     Cat Frisky;
17:     Frisky.itsAge = 5;    // assign to the member variable
18:     cout << "Frisky is a cat who is ";
19:     cout << Frisky.itsAge << " years old.\n";
20:     return 0;
21:  }
```

OUTPUT   Frisky is a cat who is 5 years old.

ANALYSIS   Line 6 contains the keyword class. This tells the compiler that what follows is a declaration. The name of the new class comes after the keyword class. In this case, it is Cat.

The body of the declaration begins with the opening brace in line 7 and ends with a closing brace and a semicolon in line 11. Line 8 contains the keyword public, which indicates that everything that follows is public until the keyword `private` or the end of the class declaration.

Lines 9 and 10 contain the declarations of the class members `itsAge` and `itsWeight`.

Line 14 begins the main function of the program. `Frisky` is defined in line 16 as an instance of a `Cat`—that is, as a `Cat` object. In line 17, `Frisky`'s age is set to 5. In lines 18 and 19, the `itsAge` member variable is used to print out a message about `Frisky`.

Note

Try commenting out line 8 and try to recompile. You will receive an error on lines 17 and 19 because `itsAge` will no longer have public access. The default for classes is private access. The GNU compiler will tell you this as follows:

```
lst06-01.cxx: In function `int main()':
lst06-01.cxx:17: member `itsAge' is a private member of class `Cat'
lst06-01.cxx:19: member `itsAge' is a private member of class `Cat'
```

Make Member Data Private

As a general rule of design, you should keep the member data of a class private. Therefore, you must create public functions known as accessor methods to set and get the private member variables. These *accessor methods* are the member functions that other parts of your program call to get and set your private member variables.

A *public accessor method* is a class member function used either to read the value of a private class member variable or to set its value.

Why bother with this extra level of indirect access? After all, it is simpler and easier to use the data instead of working through accessor functions.

Accessor functions enable you to separate the details of how the data is stored from how it is used. This enables you to change how the data is stored without having to rewrite functions that use the data.

If a function that needs to know a `Cat`'s age accesses `itsAge` directly, that function would need to be rewritten if you, as the author of the `Cat` class, decided to change how that data is stored. By having the function call `GetAge()`, your `Cat` class can easily return the right value no matter how you arrive at the age. The calling function does not need to know whether you are storing it as an unsigned integer or a long, or whether you are computing it as needed.

6

This technique makes your program easier to maintain. It gives your code a longer life because design changes do not make your program obsolete. It is good software engineering and defensive programming because it hides the details from the caller.

Listing 6.2 shows the Cat class modified to include private member data and public accessor methods. Note that this is not an executable listing.

INPUT **LISTING 6.2** A Class with Accessor Methods

```
1:      // Cat class declaration
2:      // Data members are private, public accessor methods
3:      // mediate setting and getting the values of the private data
4:
5:  class Cat
6:  {
7:  public:
8:      // public accessors
9:      unsigned int GetAge();
10:     void SetAge(unsigned int Age);
11:
12:     unsigned int GetWeight();
13:     void SetWeight(unsigned int Weight);
14:
15:      // public member functions
16:     void Meow();
17:
18:      // private member data
19: private:
20:     unsigned int  itsAge;
21:     unsigned int  itsWeight;
22:
23: };
```

ANALYSIS This class has five public methods. Lines 9 and 10 contain the accessor methods for itsAge. Lines 12 and 13 contain the accessor methods for itsWeight. These accessor functions set the member variables and return their values.

The public member function Meow() is declared in line 16. Meow() is not an accessor function. It does not get or set a member variable; it performs another service for the class, printing the word Meow.

The member variables themselves are declared in lines 20 and 21.

To set Frisky's age, you would pass the value to the SetAge() method, as in the following example:

```
Cat  Frisky;
Frisky.SetAge(5);     // set Frisky's age using the public accessor
```

Distinguishing Privacy and Security

Declaring methods or data private enables the compiler to find programming mistakes before they become bugs. Any programmer worth his consulting fees can find a way around privacy if he wants to. Stroustrup, the inventor of C++, said, "The C++ access control mechanisms provide protection against accident—not against fraud." (ARM, 1990)

The `class` Keyword

Syntax for the `class` keyword is as follows:

```
class class_name
{
// access control keywords here
// class variables and methods declared here
};
```

You use the `class` keyword to declare new types. A *class* is a collection of class member data, which are variables of various types, including other classes. The class also contains class functions—or methods—which are functions used to manipulate the data in the class and to perform other services for the class.

You define objects of the new type in much the same way in which you define any variable. State the type (`class`) and then the variable name (the object). You access the class members and functions by using the dot (.) operator.

You use access control keywords to declare sections of the class as public or private. The default for access control is private. Each keyword changes the access control from that point on to the end of the class or until the next access control keyword. Class declarations end with a closing brace and a semicolon.

Example 1

```
class Cat
{
      public:
      unsigned int Age;
      unsigned int Weight;
      void Meow();
};

Cat  Frisky;
Frisky.Age = 8;
Frisky.Weight = 18;
Frisky.Meow();
```

6

```
Example 2
    class Car
    {
    public:                              // the next five are public

        void Start();
        void Accelerate();
        void Brake();
        void SetYear(int year);
        int GetYear();

    private:                             // the rest is private

        int Year;
        Char Model [255];
    };                                   // end of class declaration

    Car OldFaithful;                     // make an instance of car
    int bought;                          // a local variable of type int
    OldFaithful.SetYear(84) ;            // assign 84 to the year
    bought = OldFaithful.GetYear();      // set bought to 84
    OldFaithful.Start();                 // call the start method
```

Do	Don't
DO declare member variables private. **DO** use public accessor methods. **DO** access private member variables from within class member functions.	**DON'T** try to use private member variables from outside the class.

Implementing Class Methods

As you have seen, an accessor function provides a public interface to the private member data of the class. Each accessor function, along with any other class methods that you declare, must have an implementation. The implementation is called the *function definition*.

A member function definition begins with the name of the class, followed by two colons, the name of the function, and its parameters. Listing 6.3 shows the complete declaration of a simple Cat class and the implementation of its accessor function and one general class member function.

```
1:   // Demonstrates declaration of a class and
2:   // definition of class methods,
3:
4:   #include <iostream.h>       // for cout
5:
6:   class Cat                    // begin declaration of the class
7:   {
8:     public:                    // begin public section
9:        int GetAge();           // accessor function
10:       void SetAge (int age);  // accessor function
11:       void Meow();            // general function
12:    private:                   // begin private section
13:       int itsAge;             // member variable
14:   };
15:
16:   // GetAge, Public accessor function
17:   // returns value of itsAge member
18:   int Cat::GetAge()
19:   {
20:      return itsAge;
21:   }
22:
23:   // definition of SetAge, public
24:   // accessor function
25:   // sets itsAge member
26:   void Cat::SetAge(int age)
27:   {
28:      // set member variable itsAge to
29:      // value passed in by parameter age
30:      itsAge = age;
31:   }
32:
33:   // definition of Meow method
34:   // returns: void
35:   // parameters: None
36:   // action: Prints "meow" to screen
37:   void Cat::Meow()
38:   {
39:      cout << "Meow.\n";
40:   }
41:
42:   // create a cat, set its age, have it
43:   // meow, tell us its age, then meow again.
44:   int main()
45:   {
```

6

continues

LISTING 6.3   CONTINUED

```
46:     Cat Frisky;
47:     Frisky.SetAge(5);
48:     Frisky.Meow();
49:     cout << "Frisky is a cat who is ";
50:     cout << Frisky.GetAge() << " years old.\n";
51:     Frisky.Meow();
52:      return 0;
53:  }
```

OUTPUT
```
Meow.
Frisky is a cat who is 5 years old.
Meow.
```

ANALYSIS
Lines 6–14 contain the definition of the Cat class. Line 8 contains the keyword public, which tells the compiler that what follows is a set of public members. Line 9 has the declaration of the public accessor method GetAge(). GetAge() provides access to the private member variable itsAge, which is declared in line 13. Line 10 has the public accessor function SetAge(). SetAge() takes an integer as an argument and sets itsAge to the value of that argument.

Line 11 has the declaration of the class method Meow(). Meow() is not an accessor function. Here it is a general method that prints the word Meow to the screen.

Line 12 begins the private section, which includes only the declaration in line 13 of the private member variable itsAge. The class declaration ends with a closing brace and semicolon in line 14.

Lines 18–21 contain the definition of the member function GetAge(). This method takes no parameters; it returns an integer. Note that class methods include the class name followed by two colons and the function name (Line 18). This syntax tells the compiler that the GetAge() function that you are defining here is the one that you declared in the Cat class. With the exception of this header line, the GetAge() function is created the same as any other function.

The GetAge() function takes only one line; it returns the value in itsAge. Note that the main() function cannot access itsAge because itsAge is private to the Cat class. The main() function has access to the public method GetAge(). Because GetAge() is a member function of the Cat class, it has full access to the itsAge variable. This access enables GetAge() to return the value of itsAge to main().

Line 26 contains the definition of the SetAge() member function. It takes an integer parameter and sets the value of itsAge to the value of that parameter in line 30. Because it is a member of the `Cat` class, `SetAge()` has direct access to the member variable `itsAge`.

Line 37 begins the definition, or implementation, of the `Meow()` method of the `Cat` class. It is a one-line function that prints the word `Meow` to the screen, followed by a new line. Remember that the `\n` character prints a new line to the screen.

Line 44 begins the body of the program with the familiar `main()` function. In this case, it takes no arguments. In line 46, `main()` declares a `Cat` named `Frisky`. In line 47, the value 5 is assigned to the `itsAge` member variable by way of the `SetAge()` accessor method. Note that the method is called by using the object name (`Frisky`) followed by the member operator (`.`) and the method name (`SetAge()`). In this same way, you can call any of the other methods in a class.

Line 48 calls the `Meow()` member function, lines 49 and 50 print a message using the `GetAge()` accessor. Line 51 calls `Meow()` again.

Understanding Constructors and Destructors

Two ways exist to define an integer variable. You can define the variable and then assign a value to it later in the program, for example:

```
int Weight;          // define a variable
...                  // other code here
Weight = 7;          // assign it a value
```

Or you can define the integer and immediately initialize it. For example,

```
int Weight = 7;      // define and initialize to 7
```

Initialization combines the definition of the variable with its initial assignment. Nothing stops you from changing that value later. Initialization ensures that your variable is never without a meaningful value.

Classes have a special member function called a *constructor*, which initializes the member data of that class. The constructor can take parameters as needed, but it cannot have a return value—not even void. The constructor is a class method with the same name as the class itself.

Whenever you declare a constructor, you should also declare a destructor. Just as constructors create and initialize objects of your class, destructors clean up after your object and free any memory you might have allocated. A destructor always has the name of the class, preceded by a tilde (~). Destructors take no arguments and have no return value. Therefore, the `Cat` declaration includes

```
~Cat();
```

6

Note

> You can have multiple constructors using function overloading. The compiler selects which constructor function to use by the parameters you provide in the call or creation. But be very careful when combining multiple constructors and default arguments—the compiler needs to be able to pick the constructor you want.

Default Constructors and Destructors

If you do not declare a constructor or a destructor, the compiler makes one for you. The default constructor and destructor take no arguments and do nothing.

> **Frequently Asked Questions**
>
> **FAQ:** Is it called the default constructor because it has no arguments or because it is the constructor provided by the compiler if I don't declare one?
>
> **Answer:** A constructor that takes no arguments is called a default constructor—whether the compiler creates it for you, or you create it yourself! You receive a default constructor *by default*.

Confusingly, the default destructor is the destructor provided by the compiler. Because all destructors take no parameters, what distinguishes the default destructor is that it takes no action—it has an empty function body.

Using the Default Constructor

What good is a constructor that does nothing? In part, it is a matter of form. All objects must be constructed and destructed, and these do-nothing functions are called at the right time. However, to declare an object without passing in parameters, such as

```
Cat Rags;          // Rags gets no parameters
```

you must have a constructor in the following form:

```
Cat();
```

When you define an object of a class, the constructor is called. If the `Cat` constructor took two parameters, you might define a `Cat` object by writing

```
Cat Frisky (5,7);
```

If the constructor took one parameter, you would write

```
Cat Frisky (3);
```

In the event that the constructor takes no parameters at all (that is, that it is a *default* constructor), you leave off the parentheses and write

```
Cat Frisky;
```

This is an exception to the rule that states all functions require parentheses, even if they take no parameters. This is why you are able to write

```
Cat Frisky;
```

This is interpreted as a call to the default constructor. It provides no parameters, and it leaves off the parentheses.

Note that you do not have to use the compiler-provided default constructor. You are always free to write your own default constructor—that is, a constructor with no parameters. You are free to give your default constructor a function body in which you might initialize the class.

As a matter of form, if you declare a constructor, be sure to declare a destructor, even if your destructor does nothing. Although it is true that the default destructor would work correctly, it never hurts to declare your own. It makes your code clearer.

Listing 6.4 rewrites the Cat class to use a constructor to initialize the Cat object, setting its age to whatever initial age you provide, and it demonstrates where the destructor is called.

INPUT   **LISTING 6.4**   Using Constructors and Destructors

```
1:    // Demonstrates declaration of a constructor and
2:    // destructor for the Cat class
3:
4:    #include <iostream.h>        // for cout
5:
6:    class Cat                    // begin declaration of the class
7:    {
8:      public:                    // begin public section
9:        Cat(int initialAge);     // constructor
10:       ~Cat();                  // destructor
11:       int GetAge();            // accessor function
12:       void SetAge(int age);    // accessor function
13:       void Meow();
14:     private:                   // begin private section
15:       int itsAge;              // member variable
16:    };
17:
18:    // constructor of Cat,
```

6

continues

LISTING 6.4   CONTINUED

```
19:   Cat::Cat(int initialAge)
20:   {
21:      itsAge = initialAge;
22:   }
23:
24:   Cat::~Cat()                        // destructor, takes no action
25:   {
26:   }
27:
28:   // GetAge, Public accessor function
29:   // returns value of itsAge member
30:   int Cat::GetAge()
31:   {
32:      return itsAge;
33:   }
34:
35:   // Definition of SetAge, public
36:   // accessor function
37:
38:   void Cat::SetAge(int age)
39:   {
40:      // set member variable itsAge to
41:      // value passed in by parameter age
42:      itsAge = age;
43:   }
44:
45:   // definition of Meow method
46:   // returns: void
47:   // parameters: None
48:   // action: Prints "meow" to screen
49:   void Cat::Meow()
50:   {
51:      cout << "Meow.\n";
52:   }
53:
54:   // create a cat, set its age, have it
55:    // meow, tell us its age, then meow again.
56:   int main()
57:   {
58:     Cat Frisky(5);
59:     Frisky.Meow();
60:     cout << "Frisky is a cat who is " ;
61:     cout << Frisky.GetAge() << " years old.\n";
62:     Frisky.Meow();
63:     Frisky.SetAge(7);
64:     cout << "Now Frisky is " ;
65:     cout << Frisky.GetAge() << " years old.\n";
66:      return 0;
67: }
```

OUTPUT
```
Meow.
Frisky is a cat who is 5 years old.
Meow.
Now Frisky is 7 years old.
```

ANALYSIS Listing 6.4 is similar to 6.3, except that line 9 adds a constructor that takes an integer. Line 10 declares the destructor, which takes no parameters. Destructors never take parameters, and neither constructors nor destructors return a value—not even void.

Lines 19 to 22 show the implementation of the constructor. It is similar to the implementation of the SetAge() accessor function. There is no return value.

Lines 24 to 26 show the implementation of the destructor ~Cat(). This function does nothing, but you must include the definition of the function if you declare it in the class declaration.

Line 58 contains the definition of a Cat object, Frisky. The value 5 is passed in to Frisky's constructor. No need exists to call SetAge() because Frisky was created with the value 5 in its member variable itsAge, as shown in line 61. In line 63, Frisky's itsAge variable is reassigned to 7. Line 65 prints the new value.

Do	**Don't**
DO use constructors to initialize your objects.	DON'T give constructors or destructors a return value.
	DON'T give destructors parameters.

Using const Member Functions

If you declare a class method const, you are promising that the method will not change the value of any of the members of the class. To declare a class method constant, put the keyword const after the parentheses but before the semicolon. The declaration of the constant member function SomeFunction() takes no arguments and returns void. It looks like this:

```
void SomeFunction() const;
```

Accessor functions are often declared as constant functions by using the const modifier. The Cat class has two accessor functions:

```
void SetAge(int anAge);
int GetAge();
```

6

`SetAge()` cannot be const because it changes the member variable `itsAge`. `GetAge()`, on the other hand, can and should be const because it does not change the class at all. `GetAge()` simply returns the current value of the member variable `itsAge`. Therefore, the declaration of these functions should be written like this:

```
void SetAge(int anAge);
int GetAge() const;
```

If you declare a function to be const, and the implementation of that function changes the object by changing the value of any of its members, the compiler flags it as an error. For example, if you wrote `GetAge()` in such a way that it kept count of the number of times that the `Cat` was asked its age, it would generate a compiler error. This is because you would be changing the `Cat` object by calling this method.

 Note   Use const whenever possible. Declare member functions to be const whenever they should not change the object. This enables the compiler to help you find errors; it is faster and less expensive than doing it yourself.

Distinguishing Interface from Implementation

As you have learned, clients are the parts of the program that create and use objects of your class. You can think of the public interface to your class—the class declaration—as a contract with these clients. The contract tells how your class will behave.

In the `Cat` class declaration, for example, you create a contract that every `Cat`'s age can be initialized in its constructor, assigned to by its `SetAge()` accessor function, and read by its `GetAge()` accessor. You also promise that every `Cat` will know how to `Meow()`. Note that you say nothing in the public interface about the member variable `itsAge`; that is an implementation detail that is not part of your contract. You will provide an age (`GetAge()`) and you will set an age (`SetAge()`), but the mechanism (`itsAge`) is invisible.

If you make `GetAge()` a const function—as you should—the contract also promises that `GetAge()` will not change the `Cat` on which it is called.

C++ is strongly typed, which means that the compiler enforces these contracts by giving you a compiler error when you violate them. Listing 6.5 demonstrates a program that will not compile because of violations of these contracts.

> **Caution**   Listing 6.5 does not compile!

```
1:    // Demonstrates compiler errors
2:    // this will not compile!!!
3:
4:    #include <iostream.h>            // for cout
5:
6:    class Cat
7:    {
8:    public:
9:       Cat(int initialAge);
10:      ~Cat();
11:      int GetAge() const;           // const accessor function
12:      void SetAge (int age);
13:      void Meow();
14:   private:
15:      int itsAge;
16:  };
17:
18:      // constructor of Cat,
19:      Cat::Cat(int initialAge)
20:      {
21:         itsAge = initialAge;
21:         cout << "Cat Constructor\n";
22:      }
23:
24:      Cat::~Cat()                    // destructor, takes no action
25:      {
26:         cout << "Cat Destructor\n";
27:      }
28:   // GetAge, const function
29:   // but we violate const!
30:   int Cat::GetAge() const
31:   {
32:      return (itsAge++);            // violates const!
33:   }
34:
35:   // definition of SetAge, public
36:   // accessor function
37:
38:   void Cat::SetAge(int age)
39:   {
40:      // set member variable itsAge to
```

continues

6

LISTING 6.5 CONTINUED

```
41:        // value passed in by parameter age
42:        itsAge = age;
43:    }
44:
45:    // definition of Meow method
46:    // returns: void
47:    // parameters: None
48:    // action: Prints "meow" to screen
49:    void Cat::Meow()
50:    {
51:        cout << "Meow.\n";
52:    }
53:
54:    // demonstrate various violations of the
55     // interface, and resulting compiler errors
56:    int main()
57:    {
58:        Cat Frisky;                 // doesn't match declaration
59:        Frisky.Meow();
60:        Frisky.Bark();              // No, silly, cats can't bark.
61:        Frisky.itsAge = 7;          // itsAge is private
62:        return 0;
63:    }
```

ANALYSIS As it is written, this program will not compile. Therefore, there is no output.

Line 11 declares GetAge() to be a const accessor function—as it should be. In the body of GetAge(), however, in line 32, the member variable itsAge is incremented. Because this method is declared to be const, it must not change the value of itsAge. Therefore, it is flagged as an error when the program is compiled.

In line 13, Meow() is not declared const. Although this is not an error, it is bad programming practice. A better design takes into account that this method does not change the member variables of Cat. Therefore, Meow() should be const.

Line 58 shows the definition of a Cat object, Frisky. Cat now has a constructor, which takes an integer as a parameter. This means that you must pass in a parameter. Because no parameter exists in line 58, it is flagged as an error.

Tip

> If you provide *any* constructor, the compiler will not provide one at all. Thus, if you create a constructor that takes a parameter, you will then have no default constructor unless you write your own.

Line 60 shows a call to a class method, `Bark()`. `Bark()` was never declared. Therefore, it is illegal.

Line 61 shows `itsAge` being assigned the value `7`. Because `itsAge` is a private data member, it is flagged as an error when the program is compiled.

Why Use the Compiler to Catch Errors?

Although it would be wonderful to write 100 percent bug-free code, few programmers have been able to do so. However, many programmers have developed a system to help minimize bugs by catching and fixing them early in the process.

Although compiler errors are infuriating and are the bane of a programmer's existence, they are far better than the alternative. A weakly typed language enables you to violate your contracts without a peep from the compiler, but your program will crash at run-time—when, for example, your boss is watching.

Compile-time errors—that is, errors found while you are compiling—are far better than runtime errors—that is, errors found while you are executing the program. This is because compile-time errors can be found much more reliably. It is possible to run a program many times without going down every possible code path. Thus, a runtime error can hide for quite a while. Compile-time errors are found every time you compile. Thus, they are easier to identify and fix. It is the goal of quality programming to ensure that the code has no runtime bugs. One tried-and-true technique to accomplish this is to use the compiler to catch your mistakes early in the development process.

Where to Put Class Declarations and Method Definitions

Each function that you declare for your class must have a definition. The definition is also called the *function implementation*. Like other functions, the definition of a class method has a function header and a function body.

The definition must be in a file that the compiler can find. Most C++ compilers want that file to end with .c or .cpp. GNU compilers will handle extensions of .C, .cpp, .cxx, or .c++. The listing files use .cxx so that you can use them under Linux or a Microsoft Windows/DOS FAT file system. If you are using a different compiler, you will have to determine which it prefers. Be careful with case sensitivity under Linux—.CXX is not the same as .cxx.

6

You are free to put the declaration in this file as well, but that is not good programming
practice. The convention that most programmers adopt is to put the declaration into what
is called a header file, usually with the same name but ending in .h, .hp, or .hpp. This
book names the header files with .hpp, but check your compiler to see what it prefers.

For example, you put the declaration of the Cat class into a file named cat.hpp, and you
put the definition of the class methods into a file called cat.cxx. You then attach the
header file to the C++ source file by putting the following code at the top of cat.cxx:

```
#include "Cat.hpp"
```

This tells the compiler to read cat.hpp into the file, the same as if you had typed in its
contents at this point. Note: Some compilers insist that the capitalization agree between
your #include statement and your file system.

Why bother separating the contents of your .hpp file and your .cxx file if you are just
going to read the .hpp file back into the .cxx file? Most of the time, clients of your class
do not care about the implementation specifics. Reading the header file tells them everything they need to know; they can ignore the implementation files. In addition, you might
very well end up including the .hpp file into more than one .cpp file.

Using include (header) files is just good software engineering—it is easier to reuse your
code.

Applying Inline Implementation

Just as you can ask the compiler to make a regular function inline, you can make class methods inline. The keyword `inline` appears before the return type. The inline implementation of the `GetWeight()` function, for example, looks like this:

```
inline int Cat::GetWeight()
{
return itsWeight;        // return the Weight data member
}
```

You can also put the definition of a function into the declaration of the class, which automatically makes that function inline, for example:

```
class Cat
{
public:
int GetWeight() { return itsWeight; }    // inline
void SetWeight(int aWeight);
};
```

Note the syntax of the `GetWeight()` definition. The body of the inline function begins immediately after the declaration of the class method; no semicolon is used after the parentheses. Like any function, the definition begins with an opening brace and ends with a closing brace. As usual, whitespace does not matter; you could have written the declaration as

```
class Cat
{
public:
int GetWeight() const
{
return itsWeight;
}                              // inline
void SetWeight(int aWeight);
};
```

Listings 6.6 and 6.7 re-create the `Cat` class, but they put the declaration in `cat.hpp` and the implementation of the functions in `cat.cxx`. Listing 6.7 also changes the accessor functions and the `Meow()` function to inline.

6

INPUT   **LISTING 6.6**   Cat Class Declaration in `cat.hpp`

```
1:   #include <iostream.h>
2:   class Cat
3:   {
```

continues

LISTING 6.6 CONTINUED

```
4:   public:
5:         Cat (int initialAge);
6:         ~Cat();
7:         int GetAge() const { return itsAge;}              // inline!
8:         void SetAge (int age) { itsAge = age;}     // inline!
9:         void Meow() const  { cout << "Meow.\n";}          // inline!
10:  private:
11:        int itsAge;
12:  };
```

INPUT   **LISTING 6.7**   Cat Implementation in `cat.cpp`

```
1:   // Demonstrates inline functions
2:   // and inclusion of header files
3:
4:   #include "cat.hpp"  // be sure to include the header files!
5:
6:
7:   Cat::Cat(int initialAge)    //constructor
8:   {
9:       itsAge = initialAge;
10:  }
11:
12:  Cat::~Cat()                 //destructor, takes no action
13:  {
14:  }
15:
16:  // Create a cat, set its age, have it
17:  // meow, tell us its age, then meow again.
18:  int main()
19:  {
20:     Cat Frisky(5);
21:     Frisky.Meow();
22:     cout << "Frisky is a cat who is " ;
23:     cout << Frisky.GetAge() << " years old.\n";
24:     Frisky.Meow();
25:     Frisky.SetAge(7);
26:     cout << "Now Frisky is " ;
27:     cout << Frisky.GetAge() << " years old.\n";
28:      return 0;
29:  }
```

```
Meow.
Frisky is a cat who is 5 years old.
Meow.
Now Frisky is 7 years old.
```

ANALYSIS The code presented in Listing 6.6 and Listing 6.7 is similar to the code in Listing 6.4, except that three of the methods are written inline in the declaration file and the declaration has been separated into cat.hpp.

GetAge() is declared in line 7, and its inline implementation is provided. Lines 8 and 9 provide more inline functions, but the functionality of these functions is unchanged from the previous "outline" implementations.

Line 4 of Listing 6.7 shows #include "cat.hpp", which brings in the listings from cat.hpp. By including cat.hpp, you have told the precompiler to read cat.hpp into the file as if it had been typed there, starting on line 5.

This technique enables you to put your declarations into a different file from your implementation, yet have that declaration available when the compiler needs it. This is a very common technique in C++ programming. Typically, class declarations are in an .hpp file that is then #included into the associated .cpp file.

Lines 18 to 29 repeat the main function from Listing 6.4. This shows that making these functions inline does not change their performance.

Using Classes with Other Classes as Member Data

It is not uncommon to build up a complex class by declaring simpler classes and including them in the declaration of the more complicated class. For example, you might declare a wheel class, a motor class, a transmission class, and so forth, and then combine them into a car class. This declares a relationship. A car has a motor, it has wheels, and it has a transmission.

Consider a second example. A rectangle is composed of lines. A line is defined by two points. A point is defined by an x coordinate and a y coordinate. Listing 6.8 shows a complete declaration of a Rectangle class, as might appear in rect.hpp (short for rectangle.hpp). Because a rectangle is defined as four lines connecting four points, and each point refers to a coordinate on a graph, you first declare a Point class to hold the x,y coordinates of each point. Listing 6.8 shows a complete declaration of both classes.

6

LISTING 6.8 Declaring a Complete Class

```
1:   // Begin rect.hpp
2:   #include <iostream.h>
3:   class Point      // holds x,y coordinates
4:   {
5:       // no constructor, use default
6:       public:
7:           void SetX(int x) { itsX = x; }
8:           void SetY(int y) { itsY = y; }
9:           int GetX()const { return itsX;}
10:          int GetY()const { return itsY;}
11:      private:
12:          int itsX;
13:          int itsY;
14:  };   // end of Point class declaration
15:
16:
17:  class  Rectangle
18:  {
19:      public:
20:          Rectangle (int top, int left, int bottom, int right);
21:          ~Rectangle () {}
22:
23:          int GetTop() const { return itsTop; }
24:          int GetLeft() const { return itsLeft; }
25:          int GetBottom() const { return itsBottom; }
26:          int GetRight() const { return itsRight; }
27:
28:          Point  GetUpperLeft() const { return itsUpperLeft; }
29:          Point  GetLowerLeft() const { return itsLowerLeft; }
30:          Point  GetUpperRight() const { return itsUpperRight; }
31:          Point  GetLowerRight() const { return itsLowerRight; }
32:
33:          void SetUpperLeft(Point Location)   {itsUpperLeft = Location;}
34:          void SetLowerLeft(Point Location)   {itsLowerLeft = Location;}
35:          void SetUpperRight(Point Location)  {itsUpperRight = Location;}
36:          void SetLowerRight(Point Location)  {itsLowerRight = Location;}
37:
38:          void SetTop(int top) { itsTop = top; }
39:          void SetLeft (int left) { itsLeft = left; }
40:          void SetBottom (int bottom) { itsBottom = bottom; }
41:          void SetRight (int right) { itsRight = right; }
42:
43:          int GetArea() const;
44:
45:      private:
46:          Point  itsUpperLeft;
47:          Point  itsUpperRight;
48:          Point  itsLowerLeft;
```

```
49:         Point   itsLowerRight;
50:         int     itsTop;
51:         int     itsLeft;
52:         int     itsBottom;
53:         int     itsRight;
54:     };
55:     // end rect.hpp
```

LISTING 6.9 rect.cpp

```
1:    // Begin rect.cpp
2:    #include "rect.hpp"
3:    Rectangle::Rectangle(int top, int left, int bottom, int right)
4:    {
5:          itsTop = top;
6:          itsLeft = left;
7:          itsBottom = bottom;
8:          itsRight = right;
9:
10:         itsUpperLeft.SetX(left);
11:         itsUpperLeft.SetY(top);
12:
13:         itsUpperRight.SetX(right);
14:         itsUpperRight.SetY(top);
15:
16:         itsLowerLeft.SetX(left);
17:         itsLowerLeft.SetY(bottom);
18:
19:         itsLowerRight.SetX(right);
20:         itsLowerRight.SetY(bottom);
21:    }
22:
23:
24:    // compute area of the rectangle by finding sides,
25:    // establish width and height and then multiply
26:    int Rectangle::GetArea() const
27:    {
28:         int Width = itsRight-itsLeft;
29:         int Height = itsTop - itsBottom;
30:         return (Width * Height);
31:    }
32:
33:    int main()
34:    {
35:         //initialize a local Rectangle variable
36:         Rectangle MyRectangle (100, 20, 50, 80 );
```

6

continues

LISTING 6.9   CONTINUED

```
37:
38:          int Area = MyRectangle.GetArea();
39:
40:          cout << "Area: "<< Area << "\n";
41:          cout << "Upper Left X Coordinate:";
42:          cout << MyRectangle.GetUpperLeft().GetX() << endl;
43:        return 0;
44:   }
```

OUTPUT

```
Area: 3000
Upper Left X Coordinate: 20
```

ANALYSIS   Lines 3 to 14 in Listing 6.8 declare the class Point, which is used to hold a specific x,y coordinate on a graph. As written, this program does not use Points much. However, other drawing methods require Points.

Within the declaration of the class Point, you declare two member variables (itsX and itsY) on lines 12 and 13. These variables hold the values of the coordinates. As the x coordinate increases, you move to the right on the graph. As the y coordinate increases, you move upward on the graph. Other graphs use different systems. Some windowing programs, for example, increase the y coordinate as you move down in the window.

The Point class uses inline accessor functions to get and set the X and Y points declared on lines 7 to 10. Points use the default constructor and destructor. Therefore you must set their coordinates explicitly.

Line 17 begins the declaration of a Rectangle class. A Rectangle consists of four points that represent the corners of the Rectangle.

The constructor for the Rectangle (line 20) takes four integers, known as top, left, bottom, and right. The four parameters to the constructor are copied into four member variables (Listing 6.9), and then the four Points are established.

In addition to the usual accessor functions, Rectangle has a function GetArea() declared in line 43. Instead of storing the area as a variable, the GetArea() function computes the area on lines 28 through 30 of Listing 6.9. To do this, it computes the width and the height of the rectangle, and then it multiplies these two values.

Getting the x coordinate of the upper-left corner of the rectangle requires that you access the UpperLeft point and ask that point for its X value. Because GetUpperLeft() is a method of Rectangle, it can directly access the private data of Rectangle, including itsUpperLeft. Because itsUpperLeft is a Point and Point's itsX value is private, GetUpperLeft() cannot directly access this data. Rather, it must use the public accessor function GetX() to obtain that value.

Line 33 of Listing 6.9 is the beginning of the body of the actual program. Until line 36, no memory has been allocated, and nothing has really happened. The only thing you did is tell the compiler how to make a point and how to make a rectangle, in case one is ever needed.

In line 36, you define a Rectangle by passing in values for Top, Left, Bottom, and Right.

In line 38, you make a local variable, Area, of type int. This variable holds the area of the Rectangle that you created. You initialize Area with the value returned by Rectangle's GetArea() function.

A client of Rectangle could create a Rectangle object and get its area without ever looking at the implementation of GetArea().

rect.hpp is shown in Listing 6.8. Just by looking at the header file, which contains the declaration of the Rectangle class, the programmer knows that GetArea() returns an int. How GetArea() does its magic is not of concern to the user of class Rectangle. In fact, the author of Rectangle could change GetArea() without affecting the programs that use the Rectangle class.

> **Frequently Asked Questions**
>
> **FAQ:** What is the difference between declaring and defining?
>
> **Answer:** A declaration introduces a name of something but does not allocate memory. A definition allocates memory.

With a few exceptions, all declarations are also definitions. The most important exceptions are the declaration of a global function (a prototype) and the declaration of a class (usually in a header file).

Using Structures

A very close cousin to the class keyword is the keyword struct, which is used to declare a structure. In C++, a structure is the same as a class, except that its members are public by default. You can declare a structure exactly as you declare a class, and you can give it the same data members and functions. In fact, if you follow the good programming practice of always explicitly declaring the private and public sections of your class, no difference will exist whatsoever.

6

Try re-entering Listing 6.8 with these changes:

- In line 3, change class `Point` to struct `Point`.
- In line 17, change class `Rectangle` to struct `Rectangle`.

Now run the program again and compare the output. No change should have occurred.

Why Two Keywords Do the Same Thing

You probably are wondering why two keywords do the same thing. This is an accident of history. When C++ was developed, it was built as an extension of the C language. C has structures, although C structures do not have class methods. Bjarne Stroustrup, the creator of C++, built upon structs, but he changed the name to class to represent the new expanded functionality.

Do	Don't
DO put your class declaration in an .hpp file and your member functions in a .cpp file.	
DO use const whenever you can.	
DO understand classes before you move on.	

Summary

Today you learned how to create new data types called classes. You learned how to define variables of these new types, which are called objects.

A class has data members, which are variables of various types, including other classes. A class also includes member functions—also known as methods. You use these member functions to manipulate the member data and to perform other services.

Class members, both data and functions, can be public or private. Public members are accessible to any part of your program. Private members are accessible only to the member functions of the class.

It is good programming practice to isolate the interface, or declaration, of the class in a header file. You usually do this in a file with an .hpp extension. The implementation of the class methods is written in a file with a .cpp extension.

Class constructors initialize objects. Class destructors destroy objects and are often used to free memory allocated by methods of the class.

Q&A

Q **How big is a class object?**

A A class object's size in memory is determined by the sum of the sizes of its member variables. Class methods don't take up room as part of the memory set aside for the object.

Some compilers align variables in memory in such a way that 2-byte variables actually consume somewhat more than 2 bytes. Check your compiler manual to be sure, but at this point you do not need to be concerned with these details.

Q **If I declare a class `Cat` with a private member `itsAge` and then define two `Cat` objects, `Frisky` and `Boots`, can `Boots` access `Frisky`'s `itsAge` member variable?**

A Yes. Private data is available to the member functions of a class, and different instances of the class can access each other's data. In other words, if `Frisky` and `Boots` are both instances of `Cat`, `Frisky`'s member functions can access `Frisky`'s data and also `Boots`'s data.

Q **Why shouldn't I make all the member data public?**

A Making member data private enables the client of the class to use the data without worrying about how it is stored or computed. For example, if the `Cat` class has a method `GetAge()`, clients of the `Cat` class can ask for the cat's age without knowing or caring whether the cat stores its age in a member variable or computes its age on-the-fly.

Q **If using a `const` function to change the class causes a compiler error, why shouldn't I just leave out the word `const` and be sure to avoid errors?**

A If your member function logically shouldn't change the class, using the keyword `const` is a good way to enlist the compiler in helping you find silly mistakes. For example, `GetAge()` might have no reason to change the `Cat` class, but your implementation might have this line:

```
if (itsAge = 100) cout << "Hey! You're 100 years old\n";
```

Declaring `GetAge()` to be const causes this code to be flagged as an error. You meant to check whether `itsAge` is equal to 100, but instead you inadvertently assigned 100 to `itsAge`. Because this assignment changes the class—and you said this method would not change the class—the compiler is able to find the error.

This kind of mistake can be hard to find just by scanning the code. The eye often sees only what it expects to see. More importantly, the program might appear to run correctly, but `itsAge` has now been set to a bogus number. This will cause problems sooner or later.

6

Q Is there ever a reason to use a structure in a C++ program?

A Many C++ programmers reserve the `struct` keyword for classes that have no functions. This is a throwback to the old C structures, which could not have functions. Frankly, I find it confusing and poor programming practice. Today's methodless structure might need methods tomorrow. Then you'll be forced either to change the type to class or to break your rule and end up with a structure with methods.

Workshop

The Workshop provides quiz questions to help you solidify your understanding of the material covered and exercises to provide you with experience in using what you learned. Try to answer the quiz and exercise questions before checking the answers in Appendix D, "Answers to Exercises and Quizzes," and make sure you understand the answers before continuing to the next day's lesson.

Quiz

1. What is the dot operator, and what is it used for?
2. Which sets aside memory—declaration or creation?
3. Is the declaration of a class its interface or its implementation?
4. What is the difference between public and private data members?
5. Can member functions be private?
6. Can member data be public?
7. If you declare two `Cat` objects, can they have different values in their `itsAge` member data?
8. Do class declarations end with a semicolon? Do class method definitions?
9. What would the header be for a `Cat` function, `Meow`, that takes no parameters and returns void?
10. What function is called to initialize a class?

Exercises

1. Write the code that declares a class called `Employee` with these data members: `age`, `yearsOfService`, and `Salary`.
2. Rewrite the `Employee` class to make the data members private, and provide public accessor methods to get and set each of the data members.
3. Write a program with the `Employee` class that makes two `Employees`; sets their `age`, `YearsOfService`, and `Salary`; and prints their values.

4. Continuing from Exercise 3, provide a method of `Employee` that reports how many thousands of dollars the employee earns, rounded to the nearest 1,000.

5. Change the `Employee` class so that you can initialize `age`, `YearsOfService`, and `Salary` when you create the employee.

6. **BUG BUSTER:** What is wrong with the following declaration?

```
 class Square
{
public:
    int Side;
}
```

7. **BUG BUSTER:** Why isn't the following class declaration very useful?

```
class Cat
{
    int GetAge()const;
private:
    int itsAge;
};
```

8. **BUG BUSTER:** What three bugs in this code will the compiler find?

```
class  TV
{
public:
    void SetStation(int Station);
    int GetStation() const;
private:
    int itsStation;
};
int main()
{
    TV myTV;
    myTV.itsStation = 9;
    TV.SetStation(10);
    TV myOtherTv(2);
    return 0;
}
```

6

DAY 7

More Program Flow

Programs accomplish most of their work by branching and looping. On Day 4, "Expressions and Statements," you learned how to branch your program using the `if` statement. Today you will learn:

- What loops are and how they are used
- How to build various loops
- An alternative to deeply nested `if`/`else` statements

Looping

Many programming problems are solved by repeatedly acting on the same data. Two ways to do this are recursion (discussed on Day 5, "Functions") and iteration. Iteration means doing the same thing again and again. The principal method of iteration is the loop.

The Roots of Looping: The `goto` Statement

In the primitive days of early computer science, programs were nasty, brutish, and short. Loops consisted of a label, some statements, and a jump.

In C++, a label is just a name followed by a colon (`:`). The label is placed to the left of a legal C++ statement or its own line, and a jump is accomplished by writing `goto` followed by the label name. Listing 7.1 illustrates this.

> **Caution**
>
> It is a bad practice to use the `goto` statement. It is only included here for completeness and for historical reasons.
>
> Good programmers limit their use of this statement!

INPUT   **LISTING 7.1**   Looping with the Keyword `goto`

```
1:    // Listing 7.1
2:    // Looping with goto
3:
4:    #include <iostream.h>
5:
6:    int main()
7:    {
8:          int counter = 0;       // initialize counter
9:    loop: counter ++;            // top of the loop
10:         cout << "counter: " << counter << "\n";
11:         if (counter < 5)            // test the value
12:           goto loop;               // jump to the top
13:
14:         cout << "Complete. Counter: " << counter << ".\n";
15:         return 0;
16:   }
```

OUTPUT
```
counter: 1
counter: 2
counter: 3
counter: 4
counter: 5
Complete. Counter: 5.
```

ANALYSIS   On line 8, `counter` is initialized to 0. The label `loop` is on line 9, marking the top of the loop. `counter` is incremented and its new value is printed. The value of `counter` is tested on line 11. If it is less than 5, the `if` statement is `true` and the `goto` statement is executed. This causes program execution to jump back to line 9. The program continues looping until `counter` is equal to 5, at which time it "falls through" the loop and the final output is printed.

Why goto Is Shunned

goto has received some rotten press lately, which is well deserved. goto statements can cause a jump to any location in your source code, backward or forward. The indiscriminate use of goto statements has caused tangled, miserable, and impossible-to-read programs known as "spaghetti code." Because of this, computer science teachers have spent the past 20 years drumming one lesson into the heads of their students: "Never, ever use goto!"

One of the biggest debugging problems with the goto is that you do not know how you got to that label. You have to search through the code looking for goto's with that label and then you have to figure out which one of them got you there. This is a lot of work!

To avoid the use of goto, more sophisticated, tightly controlled looping commands have been introduced: for, while, and do...while. Using these commands makes programs that are more easily understood, and goto is generally avoided, but one might argue that the case has been a bit overstated. Like any tool carefully used and in the right hands, goto can be a useful construct, and the ANSI committee decided to keep it in the language because it has its legitimate uses. But as they say, "Kids, don't try this at home."

The goto Statement

To use the goto statement, you write goto followed by a label name. This causes an unconditioned jump to the label.

Example:

```
if (value > 10)      goto end;if (value < 10)
➥goto end;cout << "value is
➥10!";end:cout << "done";
```

 Caution   Use of goto is almost always a sign of bad design. The best advice is to avoid using it. In our combined 20 or so years of programming, we have used it only a few times.

while Loops

A while loop causes your program to repeat a sequence of statements as long as the starting condition remains true. In the example of goto in Listing 7.1, counter was incremented until it was equal to 5. Listing 7.2 shows the same program rewritten to take advantage of a while loop.

INPUT   **LISTING 7.2**   while Loops

```
1:      // Listing 7.2
2:      // Looping with while
3:
4:      #include <iostream.h>
5:
6:      int main()
7:      {
8:        int counter = 0;                  // initialize the condition
9:
10:       while(counter < 5)      // test condition still true
11:         {
12:            counter++;                 // body of the loop
13:            cout << "counter: " << counter << "\n";
14:         }
15:
16:       cout << "Complete. Counter: " << counter << ".\n";
17:        return 0;
18:      }
```

OUTPUT
```
counter: 1
counter: 2
counter: 3
counter: 4
counter: 5
Complete. Counter: 5.
```

ANALYSIS This simple program demonstrates the fundamentals of the while loop. A condition is tested, and if it is true, the body of the while loop is executed. In this case, the condition tested on line 10 is whether counter is less than 5. If the condition is true, the body of the loop is executed; on line 12 the counter is incremented, and on line 13 the value is printed. When the conditional statement on line 10 fails (when counter is no longer less than 5), the entire body of the while loop (lines 11 to 14) is skipped. Program execution falls through to line 15.

The while Statement

The syntax for the while statement is as follows:

```
while ( condition )
statement;
```

condition is any C++ expression, and statement is any valid C++ statement or block of statements. When condition evaluates true (1), statement is executed, and then condition is tested again. This continues until condition tests false, at which time the while loop terminates and execution continues on the first line below statement.

Example

```
// count to 10
int x = 0;
while (x < 10)
cout << "X: " << x++;
```

More Complicated while Statements

The condition tested by a while loop can be as complex as any legal C++ expression. This can include expressions produced using the logical && (AND), || (OR), and ! (NOT) operators. Listing 7.3 is a somewhat more complicated while statement.

INPUT   **LISTING 7.3**   Complex while Loops

```
1:     // Listing 7.3
2:     // Complex while statements
3:
4:     #include <iostream.h>
5:
6:     int main()
7:     {
8:       unsigned short small;
9:       unsigned long  large;
10:      const unsigned short MAXSMALL=65535;
11:
12:        cout << "Enter a small number: ";
13:        cin >> small;
14:        cout << "Enter a large number: ";
15:        cin >> large;
16:
17:        cout << "small: " << small << "...";
18:
19:      // for each iteration, test three conditions
20:      while (small < large && large > 0 && small < MAXSMALL)
22:      {
23:         if (small % 5000 == 0)  // write a dot every 5k lines
24:            cout << ".";
25:
26:         small++;
27:
28:         large-=2;
29:      }
```

continues

7

LISTING 7.3   CONTINUED

```
30:
31:      cout << "\nSmall: " << small << " Large: " << large << endl;
32:      return 0;
33:    }
```

OUTPUT

```
Enter a small number: 2
Enter a large number: 100000
small: 2.........
Small: 33335 Large: 33334
```

ANALYSIS   This program is a game. Enter two numbers, one small and one large. The smaller number will count up by ones, and the larger number will count down by
twos. The goal of the game is to guess when the two will meet.

On lines 12 to 15, the numbers are entered. Line 20 sets up a while loop, which will
continue only as long as three conditions are met:

1. Small is not bigger than large.

2. Large is not negative or zero.

3. Small does not overrun the size of a small integer (MAXSMALL).

On line 23, the value in small is calculated modulus 5,000. This does not change the
value in small; however, it only returns the value 0 when small is an exact multiple of
5,000. Each time it is, a dot (.) is printed to the screen to show progress. On line 26,
small is incremented, and on line 28, large is decremented by 2.

When any of the three conditions in the while loop fails, the loop ends, and execution of
the program continues after the while loop's closing brace on line 29.

Note   The modulus operator (%) and compound conditions are covered on Day 4.

Using continue and break in Loops

At times, you want to return to the top of a while loop before the entire set of statements
in the while loop is executed. The continue statement jumps back to the top of the loop.

At other times, you may want to exit the loop before the exit conditions are met. The
break statement immediately exits the while loop, and program execution resumes after
the closing brace.

Listing 7.4 demonstrates the use of these statements. This time the game has become more complicated. The user is invited to enter a small number and a large number, a skip number, and a target number. The small number will be incremented by one, and the large number will be decremented by 2. The decrement will be skipped each time the small number is a multiple of the skip. The game ends if small becomes larger than large. If the large number reaches the target exactly, a statement is printed and the game stops.

The user's goal is to put in a target number for the large number that will stop the game.

INPUT   **LISTING 7.4**   break and continue

```
1:    // Listing 7.4
2:    // Demonstrates break and continue
3:
4:    #include <iostream.h>
5:
6:    int main()
7:    {
8:      unsigned short small;
9:      unsigned long  large;
10:     unsigned long  skip;
11:     unsigned long target;
12:     const unsigned short MAXSMALL=65535;
13:
14:     cout << "Enter a small number: ";
15:     cin >> small;
16:     cout << "Enter a large number: ";
17:     cin >> large;
18:     cout << "Enter a skip number: ";
19:     cin >> skip;
20:     cout << "Enter a target number: ";
21:     cin >> target;
22:
23:   cout << "\n";
24:
25:     // set up 3 stop conditions for the loop
26:     while (small < large && large > 0 && small < MAXSMALL)
27:
28:     {
29:
30:        small++;
31:
32:        if (small % skip == 0)  // skip the decrement?
33:        {
34:          cout << "skipping on " << small << endl;
```

continues

7

LISTING 7.4 CONTINUED

```
35:            continue;
36:         }
37:
38:         if (large == target)     // exact match for the target?
39:         {
40:           cout << "Target reached!";
41:           break;
42:         }
43:
44:         large-=2;
45:     }                        // end of while loop
46:
47:     cout << "\nSmall: " << small << " Large: " << large << endl;
48:     return 0;
49:     }
```

OUTPUT

```
Enter a small number: 2
Enter a large number: 20
Enter a skip number: 4
Enter a target number: 6

skipping on 4
skipping on 8

Small: 10 Large: 8
```

ANALYSIS In this play, the user lost; small became larger than large before the target number of six was reached.

On line 26, the while conditions are tested. If small continues to be smaller than large, large is larger than 0, and small has not overrun the maximum value for a small int, the body of the while loop is entered.

On line 32, the small value is taken modulus the skip value. If small is a multiple of skip, the continue statement is reached and program execution jumps to the top of the loop at line 26. This effectively skips over the test for the target and the decrement of large.

On line 38, target is tested against the value for large. If they are the same, the user has won. A message is printed and the break statement is reached. This causes an immediate break out of the while loop, and program execution resumes on line 46.

Note

Both `continue` and `break` should be used with caution. They are the next most dangerous commands after `goto`, for much the same reason. Programs that suddenly change direction are harder to understand, and liberal use of `continue` and `break` can render even a small `while` loop unreadable.

The `continue` Statement

`continue;` causes a `while` or `for` loop to begin again at the top of the loop.

See Listing 7.4 for an example of using `continue`.

The `break` Statement

`break;` causes the immediate end of a `while` or `for` loop. Execution jumps to the closing brace.

Example
```
while (condition)
{
    if (condition2)
        break;
    // statements;
}
```

while (true) Loops

The condition tested in a `while` loop can be any valid C++ expression. As long as that condition remains true, the `while` loop will continue. You can create a loop that will never end by using the value `true` for the condition to be tested. Listing 7.5 demonstrates counting to 10 using this construct.

INPUT **LISTING 7.5**   `while` Loops

```
1:    // Listing 7.5
2:    // Demonstrates a while true loop
3:
4:    #include <iostream.h>
```

continues

7

LISTING 7.5 CONTINUED

```
5:
6:    int main()
7:    {
8:      int counter = 0;
9:
10:     while (true)
11:     {
12:        counter ++;
13:        if (counter > 10)
14:            break;
15:     }
16:     cout << "Counter: " << counter << "\n";
17:      return 0;
18:   }
```

OUTPUT

```
Counter: 11
```

ANALYSIS On line 10, a while loop is set up with a condition that can never be false. The loop increments the counter variable on line 12, and then on line 13 it tests to see whether counter has gone past 10. If it has not, the while loop iterates. If counter is greater than 10, the break on line 14 ends the while loop, and program execution falls through to line 16, where the results are printed.

This program works, but it is not very pretty. This is a good example of using the wrong tool for the job. The same thing can be accomplished by putting the test of counter's value where it belongs—in the while condition.

Another name for this is "While forever" or "endless loop."

Caution

Eternal loops such as while (true) can cause your computer to hang if the exit condition is never reached. Use these with caution and test them thoroughly.

C++ gives you many ways to accomplish the same task. The real trick is picking the right tool for a particular job.

Do	**Don't**
DO use while loops to iterate while a condition is true.	**DON'T** use the goto statement.
DO exercise caution when using continue and break statements.	
DO make sure your loop will eventually end.	

while Loop Limitations

It is possible that the body of a while loop will never execute. The while statement checks its condition before executing any of its statements, and if the condition evaluates false, the entire body of the while loop is skipped. Listing 7.6 illustrates this.

INPUT   **LISTING 7.6**   Skipping the Body of the while Loop

```
1:    // Listing 7.6
2:    // Demonstrates skipping the body of
3:    // the while loop when the condition is false.
4:
5:    #include <iostream.h>
6:
7:    int main()
8:    {
9:        int counter;
10:       cout << "How many hellos?: ";
11:       cin >> counter;
12:       while (counter > 0)
13:       {
14:          cout << "Hello!\n";
15:          counter--;
16:       }
17:       cout << "Counter is OutPut: " << counter << endl;
18:        return 0;
19:     }
```

OUTPUT
```
How many hellos?: 2
Hello!
Hello!
Counter is OutPut: 0
```

Running the program a second time:

```
How many hellos?: 0
Counter is OutPut: 0>
```

7

ANALYSIS The user is prompted for a starting value on line 10. This starting value is stored in the integer variable counter. The value of counter is tested on line 12 and decremented in the body of the while loop. The first time through, counter was set to 2, and so the body of the while loop ran twice. The second time through, however, the user typed in 0. The value of counter was tested on line 12 and the condition was false; counter was not greater than 0. The entire body of the while loop was skipped, and Hello was never printed.

What if you want to ensure that Hello is always printed at least once? The while loop cannot accomplish this because the condition is tested before any printing is done. You can force the issue with an if statement just before entering the while, like this:

```
if (counter < 1)  // force a minimum value
counter = 1;
```

but that is what programmers call a "kludge," an ugly and inelegant solution. There is a better solution: the do...while loop in the next section.

do...while Loops

The do...while loop executes the body of the loop before its condition is tested and ensures that the body always executes at least one time. Listing 7.7 rewrites Listing 7.6, this time using a do...while loop.

INPUT   **LISTING 7.7**   Demonstrates do...while Loop

```
1:       // Listing 7.7
2:       // Demonstrates do while
3:
4:       #include <iostream.h>
5:
6:       int main()
7:       {
8:          int counter;
9:          cout << "How many hellos? ";
10:         cin >> counter;
11:         do
12:         {
13:            cout << "Hello\n";
14:            counter--;
15:         } while (counter >0 );
16:         cout << "Counter is: " << counter << endl;
17:           return 0;
18:       }
```

OUTPUT
```
How many hellos? 2
Hello
Hello
Counter is: 0
```

ANALYSIS The user is prompted for a starting value on line 9, which is stored in the integer variable counter. In the do...while loop, the body of the loop is entered before the condition is tested, and therefore, the body of the loop is guaranteed to run at least once. On line 13 the message is printed, on line 14 the counter is decremented, and on line 15 the condition is tested. If the condition evaluates true, execution jumps to the top of the loop on line 13; otherwise, it falls through to line 16.

The continue and break statements work in the do...while loop exactly as they do in the while loop. The only difference between a while loop and a do...while loop is when the condition is tested.

The do...while Statement

The syntax for the do...while statement is as follows:

```
do
statement
while (condition);
```

statement is executed, and then condition is evaluated. If condition is true, the loop is repeated; otherwise, the loop ends. The statements and conditions are otherwise identical to the while loop.

Example 1

```
// count to 10
int x = 0;
do
cout << "X: " << x++;
while (x < 10)
```

Example 2

```
// print lowercase alphabet.
char ch = 'a';
do
{
cout << ch << ' ';
ch++;
} while ( ch <= 'z' );
```

7

Do	Don't
DO use do...while when you want to ensure the loop is executed at least once. **DO** use while loops when you want to skip the loop if the condition is false. **DO** test all loops to make sure they do what you expect.	

for Loops

When programming while loops, you will often find yourself setting up a starting condition, testing to see if the condition is true, and incrementing or otherwise changing a variable each time through the loop. Listing 7.8 demonstrates this.

INPUT   **LISTING 7.8**   while Reexamined

```
1:    // Listing 7.8
2:    // Looping with while
3:
4:    #include <iostream.h>
5:
6:    int main()
7:    {
8:      int counter = 0;
9:
10:       while(counter < 5)
11:       {
12:           counter++;
13:           cout << "Looping!   ";
14:       }
15:
16:       cout << "\nCounter: " << counter << ".\n";
17:        return 0;
18:    }
```

OUTPUT
```
Looping! Looping! Looping! Looping! Looping!
Counter: 5.
```

ANALYSIS   The condition is set on line 8: counter is initialized to 0. On line 10, counter is tested to see whether it is less than 5. counter is incremented on line 12. On line 16, a simple message is printed, but you can imagine that more important work could be done for each increment of the counter.

A `for` loop combines three steps into one statement. The three steps are initialization, test, and increment. A `for` statement consists of the keyword `for` followed by a pair of parentheses. Within the parentheses are three statements separated by semicolons.

The first statement is the initialization. Any legal C++ statement can be put here, but typically this is used to create and initialize a counting variable. Statement 2 is the test, and any legal C++ expression can be used here. This plays the same role as the condition in the `while` loop. Statement 3 is the action. Typically a value is incremented or decremented, though any legal C++ statement can be put here. Note that statements 1 and 3 can be any legal C++ statement, but statement 2 must be an expression—a C++ statement that returns a value. Listing 7.9 demonstrates a `for` loop.

INPUT **LISTING 7.9** Demonstrating the for Loop

```
1:      // Listing 7.9
2:      // Looping with for
3:
4:      #include <iostream.h>
5:
6:      int main()
7:      {
8:        int counter;
9:        for (counter = 0; counter < 5; counter++)
10:          cout << "Looping! ";
11:
12:        cout << "\nCounter: " << counter << ".\n";
13:        return 0;
14:      }
```

OUTPUT
```
Looping! Looping! Looping! Looping! Looping!
Counter: 5.
```

ANALYSIS   The `for` statement on line 9 combines the initialization of `counter`, the test that `counter` is less than 5, and the increment of `counter` all into one line. The body of the `for` statement is on line 10. Of course, a block could be used here as well.

The for Statement

The syntax for the `for` statement is as follows:

```
for (initialization; test; action )
    statement;
```

The `initialization` statement is used to initialize the state of a counter, or to otherwise prepare for the loop. `test` is any C++ expression and is evaluated each time through the

7

loop. If test is true, the body of the for loop is executed and then the action in the header is executed (typically the counter is incremented).

Example 1

```
// print Hello ten times
for (int i = 0; i<10; i++)
cout << "Hello! ";
```

Example 2

```
for (int i = 0; i < 10; i++)
{
    cout << "Hello!" << endl;
    cout << "the value of i is: " << i << endl;
}
```

Advanced for Loops

for statements are powerful and flexible. The three independent statements (initialization, test, and action) lend themselves to a number of variations.

A for loop works in the following sequence:

1. Performs the operations in the initialization

2. Evaluates the condition

3. If the condition is true, executes the body of the for loop;otherwise the loop is ended

4. Executes the action statement

After each time through the body of the loop, the steps 4 occurs and the loop repeats steps 2 and 3.

Multiple Initialization and Increments

It is not uncommon to initialize more than one variable, to test a compound logical expression, and to execute more than one statement. The initialization and the action may be replaced by multiple C++ statements, each separated by a comma. Listing 7.10 demonstrates the initialization and increment of two variables.

INPUT   LISTING 7.10   Demonstrating Multiple Statements in for Loop

```
1:  //listing 7.10
2:  // demonstrates multiple statements in
3:  // for loops
```

```
4:
5:  #include <iostream.h>
6:
7:  int main()
8:  {
9:      for (int i=0, j=0; i<3; i++, j++)
10:         cout << "i: " << i << " j: " << j << endl;
11:     return 0;
12: }
```

OUTPUT

```
i: 0  j: 0
i: 1  j: 1
i: 2  j: 2
```

ANALYSIS On line 9, two variables, i and j, are each initialized with the value 0. The test (i<3) is evaluated, and because it is true, the body of the for statement is executed, and the values are printed. Finally, the third clause in the for statement is executed, and i and j are incremented.

After line 10 completes, the condition is evaluated again, and if it remains true, the actions are repeated (i and j are again incremented), and the body of the loop is executed again. This continues until the test fails, in which case the action statement (body of the loop, cout in this case) is not executed, and control falls out of the loop.

Null Statements in for Loops

Any or all the statements in a for loop can be null. To accomplish this, use the semicolon (;) to mark where the statement would have been. To create a for loop that acts exactly like a while loop, leave out the first and third statements. Listing 7.11 illustrates this idea.

INPUT **LISTING 7.11** Null Statements in for Loops

```
1:   // Listing 7.11
2:   // For loops with null statements
3:
4:   #include <iostream.h>
5:
6:   int main()
7:   {
8:       int counter = 0;
9:
10:      for( ; counter < 5; )
11:      {
12:          counter++;
```

continues

LISTING 7.11   CONTINUED

```
13:            cout << "Looping!   ";
14:        }
15:
16:        cout << "\nCounter: " << counter << ".\n";
17:        return 0;
18:    }
```

OUTPUT

```
Looping!  Looping!  Looping!  Looping!  Looping!
Counter: 5.
```

ANALYSIS   You may recognize this as exactly like the while loop illustrated in Listing 7.8. On line 8, the counter variable is initialized. The for statement on line 10 does not initialize any values, but it does include a test for counter < 5. No increment statement exists, so this loop behaves exactly as if it had been written as follows:

```
while (counter < 5)
```

Once again, C++ gives you several ways to accomplish the same thing. No experienced C++ programmer would use a for loop in this way, but it does illustrate the flexibility of the for statement. In fact, it is possible, using break and continue, to create a for loop with none of the three statements. Listing 7.12 illustrates how.

LISTING 7.12   Illustrating an Empty for Loop Statement

```
1:     //Listing 7.12 illustrating
2:     //empty for loop statement
3:
4:     #include <iostream.h>
5:
6:     int main()
7:     {
8:         int counter=0;        // initialization
9:         int max;
10:        cout << "How many hellos?";
11:        cin >> max;
12:        for (;;)              // a for loop that doesn't end
13:        {
14:          if (counter < max)      // test
15:          {
16:            cout << "Hello!\n";
17:            counter++;          // increment
18:          }
19:          else
20:              break;
```

```
21:        }
22:        return 0;
23:    }
```

OUTPUT
```
How many hellos?3
Hello!
Hello!
Hello!
```

ANALYSIS The for loop has now been pushed to its absolute limit. initialization, test, and action have all been taken out of the for statement. The initialization is done on line 8, before the for loop begins. The test is done in a separate if statement on line 14, and if the test succeeds, the action, an increment to counter, is performed on line 17. If the test fails, breaking out of the loop occurs on line 20.

Although this particular program is somewhat absurd, sometimes a for(;;)loop or a while (true) loop is just what you want. An example of a more reasonable use of such loops is presented when switch statements are discussed later today.

Empty for Loops

Because so much can be done in the header of a for statement, at times you will not need the body to do anything at all. In that case, be sure to put a null statement (;) as the body of the loop. The semicolon can be on the same line as the header, but this is easy to overlook. Listing 7.13 illustrates how to use a null body in a for loop.

INPUT   **LISTING 7.13**   Illustrates the Null Statement in a for Loop

```
1:     //Listing 7.13
2:     //Demonstrates null statement
3:     // as body of for loop
4:
5:     #include <iostream.h>
6:     int main()
7:     {
8:        for (int i = 0; i<5; cout << "i: " << i++ << endl)
9:           ;
10:       return 0;
11:    }
```

OUTPUT
```
i: 0
i: 1
i: 2
i: 3
i: 4
```

7

ANALYSIS The `for` loop on line 8 includes three statements: the `initialization` statement establishes the counter `i` and initializes it to `0`. The `condition` statement tests for `i<5`, and the `action` statement prints the value in `i` and increments it.

Nothing is left to do in the body of the `for` loop, so the null statement (`;`) is used. Note that this is not a well-designed `for` loop: the `action` statement is doing far too much. This would be better rewritten as

```
8:          for (int i = 0; i<5; i++)
9:                  cout << "i: " << i << endl;
```

Although both do the same thing, this example is easier to understand.

Nested Loops

Loops may be nested with one loop sitting in the body of another. The inner loop will be executed in full for every execution of the outer loop. From experience, it seems that `for` loops are the type most commonly nested. All three of the loop types can be nested, but the `while` and `do...while` are just less common. Listing 7.14 illustrates writing marks into a matrix using nested `for` loops.

INPUT   **LISTING 7.14**   Illustrates Nested `for` Loops

```
1:    //Listing 7.14
2:    //Illustrates nested for loops
3:
4:    #include <iostream.h>
5:
6:    int main()
7:    {
8:        int rows, columns;
9:        char theChar;
10:        cout << "How many rows? ";
11:        cin >> rows;
12:        cout << "How many columns? ";
13:        cin >> columns;
14:        cout << "What character? ";
15:        cin >> theChar;
16:        for (int i = 0; i<rows; i++)
17:        {
18:           for (int j = 0; j<columns; j++)
19:               cout << theChar;
20:           cout << "\n";
21:        }
22:        return 0;
23:    }
```

OUTPUT
```
How many rows? 4
How many columns? 12
What character? x
xxxxxxxxxxxx
xxxxxxxxxxxx
xxxxxxxxxxxx
xxxxxxxxxxxx
```

ANALYSIS The user is prompted for the number of rows and columns and for a character to print. The first `for` loop, on line 16, initializes a counter (i) to 0, the condition is checked, and then the body of the outer `for` loop is run.

On line 18, the first line of the body of the outer `for` loop, another `for` loop, is established. A second counter (j) is also initialized to 0, the condition is checked, and the body of the inner `for` loop is executed. On line 19, the chosen character is printed, and control returns to the header of the inner `for` loop. Note that the inner `for` loop is only one statement (the printing of the character). The variable j is incremented and the condition is tested (j < columns), if it evaluates true, the next character is printed. This continues until j equals the number of columns.

After the inner `for` loop fails its test, in this case after 12 Xs are printed, execution falls through to line 20, and a new line is printed. The outer `for` loop now returns to its header, where i is incremented and its condition (i < rows) is tested. If this evaluates true, the body of the loop is executed.

In the second iteration of the outer `for` loop, the inner `for` loop is started over. Thus, j is reinitialized to 0, the condition is tested, and the entire inner loop is run again.

The important idea here is that by using a nested loop, the inner loop is executed for each iteration of the outer loop. Thus, the character is printed columns times for each row.

Note

As an aside, many C++ programmers use the letters i and j as counting variables. This tradition goes all the way back to FORTRAN, in which the letters i, j, k, l, m, and n were automatically integers (any variable beginning with the letters i through n inclusive) and integers were the only legal counting variables.

Other programmers prefer to use more descriptive counter variable names, such as Ctr1 and Ctr2. Using i and j in for loop headers should not cause much confusion, however.

7

Scoping in for Loops

In the past, variables declared in the for loop were scoped to the outer block. The new
ANSI standard changes this to scope these variables only to the block of the for loop
itself; however, not every compiler supports this change. If you are using something
other than a GNU compiler, you can test your compiler with the following code:

```
#include <iostream.h>
int main()
{
    // i scoped to the for loop?
    for (int i = 0; i<5; i++)
    {
        cout << "i: " << i << endl;
    }

    i = 7;  // should not be in scope!
    return 0;
}
```

The GNU compiler gives you a warning with this code; you can also force it to be strict
and give you an error. The warning looks like:

```
example.cxx: In function `int main()':
example.cxx:10: warning: name lookup of `i' changed for new ANSI `for' scoping
example.cxx:5: warning:   using obsolete binding at `i'
```

If this compiles without complaint, your (non-GNU) compiler does not yet support this
aspect of the ANSI standard.

If your compiler complains that i is not yet defined (in the line i=7), your compiler does
support the new standard. You can write code that will compile on either compiler by
changing this to

```
#include <iostream.h>
int main()
{
    int i; //declare outside the for loop
    for (int i = 0; i<5; i++)
    {
        cout << "i: " << i << endl;
    }

    i = 7;  // now this is in scope for all compilers
    return 0;
}
```

Summary of Loops

On Day 5 you learned how to solve the Fibonacci series problem using recursion. To review briefly, a Fibonacci series starts with 1, 1, 2, 3, and all subsequent numbers are the sum of the previous two:

1,1,2,3,5,8,13,21,34...

The nth Fibonacci number is the sum of the n–1 and the n–2 Fibonacci numbers. The problem solved on Day 5 was finding the value of the nth Fibonacci number. This was done with recursion. Listing 7.15 offers a solution using iteration.

INPUT **LISTING 7.15**   Solving the nth Fibonacci Number Using Iteration

```
1:   // Listing 7.15
2:   // Demonstrates solving the nth
3:   // Fibonacci number using iteration
4:
5:   #include <iostream.h>
6:
8:
9:   int fib(int position);
10:  int main()
11:  {
12:      int answer, position;
13:      cout << "Which position? ";
14:      cin >> position;
15:      cout << "\n";
16:
17:      answer = fib(position);
18:      cout << answer << " is the ";
19:      cout << position << "th Fibonacci number.\n";
20:      return 0;
21:  }
22:
23:  int fib(int n)
24:  {
25:      int minusTwo=1, minusOne=1, answer=2;
26:
27:      if (n < 3)
28:          return 1;
29:
30:      for (n -= 3; n; n--)
31:      {
32:          minusTwo = minusOne;
33:          minusOne = answer;
```

7

continues

LISTING 7.15 CONTINUED

```
34:          answer = minusOne + minusTwo;
35:      }
36:
37:      return answer;
38:  }
```

OUTPUT

```
Which position? 4
3 is the 4th Fibonacci number.
```

Running the program a second time:

```
Which position? 5
5 is the 5th Fibonacci number.
```

Running the program again:

```
Which position? 20
6765 is the 20th Fibonacci number.
```

Running the program yet again:

```
Which position? 70
885444751 is the 70th Fibonacci number.
```

ANALYSIS Listing 7.15 solves the Fibonacci series using iteration rather than recursion. This approach is faster and uses less memory than the recursive solution.

On line 13, the user is asked for the position to check. The function fib() is called, which evaluates the position. If the position is less than 3, the function returns the value 1. Starting with position 3, the function iterates using the following algorithm:

1. Establish the starting position: Fill variable answer with 2, minusTwo with 1, and minusOne with 1. Decrement the position by 3 because the first two numbers are handled by the starting position.

2. For every number, count up the Fibonacci series. This is done by

   a. Putting the value currently in minusOne into minusTwo.

   b. Putting the value currently in answer into minusOne.

   c. Adding minusOne and minusTwo and putting the sum in answer.

   d. Decrementing n.

3. When n reaches 0, return the answer.

This is exactly how you would solve this problem with pencil and paper. If you were asked for the fifth Fibonacci number, you would write

1, 1, 2,

and think, "two more to do." You would then add 2+1 and write 3, and think, "one more to find." Finally, you would write 3+2 and the answer would be 5. In effect, you are shifting your attention right one number each time through and decrementing the number remaining to be found.

Note the condition tested on line 30 (n). This is a C++ idiom, and is equivalent to n != 0. This `for` loop relies on the fact that when n reaches 0, it will evaluate `false`, because 0 is false in C++. The `for` loop header could have been written

```
for (n-=3; n!=0; n--)
```

which might have been clearer. However, this idiom is so common in C++ that there is little sense in fighting it.

Compile, link, and run this program, along with the recursive solution offered on Day 5. Try finding position 25 and compare the time it takes each program. Recursion is elegant, but because the function call brings a performance overhead, and because it is called so many times, its performance is noticeably slower than iteration. Microcomputers tend to be optimized for the arithmetic operations, so the iterative solution should be blazingly fast.

Be careful how large a number you enter. `fib` grows quickly, and long integers will overflow after a while.

switch Statements

On Day 4, you saw how to write `if` and `if/else` statements. These can become quite confusing when nested too deeply, and C++ offers an alternative. Unlike `if`, which evaluates one value, `switch` statements enable you to branch on any of several values. The general form of the `switch` statement is

```
switch (expression)
{
case valueOne:  statement;
                break;
case valueTwo:  statement;
                another_statement;
                break;
....
case valueN:    statement;
                break;
default:        statement;
}
```

`expression` is any legal C++ expression, and the statements are any legal C++ statements or block of statements that evaluate (or can be unambiguously converted to) an

7

integer value. Note, however, that the evaluation is for equality only; relational operators may not be used here, nor can Boolean operations.

If one of the case values matches the expression, execution jumps to those statements and continues to the end of the switch block unless a break statement is encountered. If nothing matches, execution branches to the optional default statement. If no default and no matching value exist, execution falls through the switch statement and the statement ends.

> **Note**
>
> It is almost always a good idea to have a default case in switch statements. If you have no other need for the default, use it to test for the supposedly impossible case, and print out an error message; this can be a tremendous aid in debugging.

It is important to note that if no break statement is at the end of a case statement, execution will fall through to the next case statement. This is sometimes necessary, but usually is an error. If you decide to let execution fall through, be sure to put a comment indicating that you did not just forget the break.

Listing 7.16 illustrates use of the switch statement.

INPUT   **LISTING 7.16**   Demonstrating the switch Statement

```
1:  //Listing 7.16
2:  // Demonstrates switch statement
3:
4:  #include <iostream.h>
5:
6:  int main()
7:  {
8:      unsigned short int number;
9:      cout << "Enter a number between 1 and 5: ";
10:     cin >> number;
11:     switch (number)
12:     {
13:         case 0:   cout << "Too small, sorry!";
14:                   break;
15:         case 5:   cout << "Good job!\n";  // fall through
16:         case 4:   cout << "Nice Pick!\n"; // fall through
17:         case 3:   cout << "Excellent!\n"; // fall through
18:         case 2:   cout << "Masterful!\n"; // fall through
19:         case 1:   cout << "Incredible!\n";
20:                   break;
```

```
21:        default: cout << "Too large!\n";
22:                 break;
23:    }
24:    cout << "\n\n";
25:      return 0;
26:  }
```

OUTPUT

```
Enter a number between 1 and 5: 3
Excellent!
Masterful!
Incredible!
```

Running the program a second time:

```
Enter a number between 1 and 5: 8
Too large!
```

ANALYSIS The user is prompted for a number. That number is given to the switch statement. If the number is 0, the case statement on line 13 matches, the message Too small, sorry! is printed, and the break statement ends the switch. If the value is 5, execution switches to line 15 where a message is printed, and then falls through to line 16, another message is printed, and so forth until hitting the break on line 20.

The net effect of these statements is that for a number between 1 and 5, that many messages are printed. If the value of the number is not 0 to 5, it is assumed to be too large, and the default statement is invoked on line 21.

The switch Statement

The syntax for the switch statement is as follows:

```
switch (expression)
{
case valueOne: statement;
case valueTwo: statement;
....
case valueN: statement;
default: statement;
}
```

The switch statement allows for branching on multiple values of expression. The expression is evaluated, and if it matches any of the case values, execution jumps to that line. Execution continues until either the end of the switch statement or a break statement is encountered.

If expression does not match any of the case statements, and if there is a default statement, execution switches to the default statement; otherwise, the switch statement ends.

7

```
switch (choice)
{
case 0:
        cout << "Zero!" << endl;
        break;
case 1:
        cout << "One!" << endl;
        break;
case 2:
        cout << "Two!" << endl;
default:
        cout << "Default!" << endl;
}
```

Example 2

```
switch (choice)
{
case 0:
case 1:
case 2:
        cout << "Less than 3!";
        break;
case 3:
        cout << "Equals 3!";
        break;
default:
        cout << "greater than 3!";
}
```

Using a switch Statement with a Menu

Listing 7.17 returns to the for(;;) loop discussed earlier. These loops are also called forever loops, as they will loop forever if a break is not encountered. The forever loop is used to put up a menu, solicit a choice from the user, act on the choice, and then return to the menu. This will continue until the user chooses to exit.

 Note

Some programmers like to write

```
#define EVER ;;
for (EVER)
{
    // statements...
}
```

A `forever` loop is a loop that does not have an exit condition. In order to exit the loop, a `break` statement must be used. Forever loops are also known as eternal loops.

INPUT **LISTING 7.17** Demonstrating a `forever` Loop

```
1:    //Listing 7.17
2:    //Using a forever loop to manage
3:    //user interaction
4:    #include <iostream.h>
5:
6:    // prototypes
7:    int menu();
8:    void DoTaskOne();
9:    void DoTaskMany(int);
10:
11:   int main()
12:   {
13:
14:       bool exit = false;
15:       for (;;)
16:       {
17:           int choice = menu();
18:           switch(choice)
19:           {
20:             case (1):
21:                 DoTaskOne();
22:                 break;
23:             case (2):
24:                 DoTaskMany(2);
25:                 break;
26:             case (3):
27:                 DoTaskMany(3);
28:                 break;
29:             case (4):
30:                 continue;   // redundant!
31:                 break;
32:             case (5):
33:                 exit=true;
34:                 break;
35:             default:
36:                 cout << "Please select again!\n";
37:                 break;
38:           }         // end switch
39:
40:           if (exit)
41:                 break;
42:       }             // end forever
43:       return 0;
```

continues

7

LISTING 7.17 CONTINUED

```
44:      }                        // end main()
45:
46:      int menu()
47:      {
48:          int choice;
49:
50:          cout << " **** Menu ****\n\n";
51:          cout << "(1) Choice one.\n";
52:          cout << "(2) Choice two.\n";
53:          cout << "(3) Choice three.\n";
54:          cout << "(4) Redisplay menu.\n";
55:          cout << "(5) Quit.\n\n";
56:          cout << ": ";
57:          cin >> choice;
58:          return choice;
59:      }
60:
61:      void DoTaskOne()
62:      {
63:          cout << "Task One!\n";
64:      }
65:
66:      void DoTaskMany(int which)
67:      {
68:          if (which == 2)
69:              cout << "Task Two!\n";
70:          else
71:              cout << "Task Three!\n";
72:      }
```

OUTPUT

```
 **** Menu ****

(1) Choice one.
(2) Choice two.
(3) Choice three.
(4) Redisplay menu.
(5) Quit.

: 1
Task One!
 **** Menu ****
(1) Choice one.
(2) Choice two.
(3) Choice three.
(4) Redisplay menu.
(5) Quit.

: 3
```

```
Task Three!
 **** Menu ****
(1) Choice one.
(2) Choice two.
(3) Choice three.
(4) Redisplay menu.
(5) Quit.

 : 5
```

ANALYSIS This program brings together a number of concepts from today and previous days. It also shows a common use of the switch statement.

The forever loop begins on line 15. The menu() function is called, which prints the menu to the screen and returns the user's selection. The switch statement, which begins on line 18 and ends on line 38, switches on the user's choice.

If the user enters 1, execution jumps to the case 1: statement on line 20. Line 21 switches execution to the DoTaskOne() function, which prints a message and returns. On its return, execution resumes on line 22, where the break ends the switch statement, and execution falls through to line 39. On line 40, the variable exit is evaluated. If it evaluates true, the break on line 41 will be executed and the for(;;) loop will end; but if it evaluates false, execution resumes at the top of the loop on line 15.

Note that the continue statement on line 30 is redundant. If it was left out and the break statement was encountered, the switch would end, exit would evaluate false, the loop would reiterate, and the menu would be reprinted. The continue does, however, bypass the test of exit.

Do	Don't
DO use switch statements to avoid deeply nested if statements. **DO** carefully document all intentional fall-through cases. **DO** put a default case in switch statements, if only to detect seemingly impossible situations.	**DON'T** forget break at the end of each case unless you want to fall through.

7

Summary

Different ways exist to cause a C++ program to loop. while loops check a condition, and if it is true, execute the statements in the body of the loop. do...while loops execute the body of the loop and then test the condition. for loops initialize a value and then test an expression. If an expression is true, the body of the loop is executed. Each subsequent time through the loop, the final statement in for the for header is executed, the expression is tested again, and the whole process repeats.

The goto statement is generally avoided because it causes an unconditional jump to a seemingly arbitrary location in the code and thus makes source code difficult to understand and maintain. continue causes while, do...while, and for loops to start over, and break causes while, do...while, for, and switch statements to end.

Q&A

Q How do you choose between if/else and switch?

A If more than just one or two else clauses are used, and all are testing the same value, consider using a switch statement.

Q How do you choose between while and do...while?

A If the body of the loop should always execute at least once, consider a do...while loop; otherwise, try to use the while loop.

Q How do you choose between while and for?

A If you are initializing a counting variable, testing that variable, and incrementing it each time through the loop, consider the for loop. If your variable is already initialized and is not incremented on each loop, a while loop may be the better choice.

Q How do you choose between recursion and iteration?

A Some problems cry out for recursion, but most problems will yield to iteration as well. Put recursion in your back pocket; it may come in handy someday.

Q Is it better to use while (true) or for (;;)?

A No significant difference exists.

Workshop

The Workshop provides quiz questions to help you solidify your understanding of the material covered as well as exercises to provide you with experience in using what you learned today. Try to answer the quiz and exercise questions before checking the answers in Appendix D, "Answers to Exercises and Quizzes," and make sure you understand the answers before continuing to the next day.

Quiz

1. How do I initialize more than one variable in a `for` loop?

2. Why is `goto` avoided?

3. Is it possible to write a `for` loop with a body that is never executed?

4. Is it possible to nest `while` loops within `for` loops?

5. Is it possible to create a loop that never ends? Give an example.

6. What happens if you create a loop that never ends?

Exercises

1. What is the value of x when the `for` loop completes?

```
for (int x = 0; x < 100; x++)
```

2. Write a nested `for` loop that prints a 10×10 pattern of 0s.

3. Write a `for` statement to count from 100 to 200 by twos.

4. Write a `while` loop to count from 100 to 200 by twos.

5. Write a `do...while` loop to count from 100 to 200 by twos.

6. **BUG BUSTER:** What is wrong with this code?

```
int counter = 0;
while (counter < 10)
{
    cout << "counter: " << counter;
}
```

7. **BUG BUSTER:** What is wrong with this code?

```
for (int counter = 0; counter < 10; counter++);
    cout << counter << " ";
```

8. **BUG BUSTER:** What is wrong with this code?

```
int counter = 100;
while (counter < 10)
{
    cout << "counter now: " << counter;
    counter--;
}
```

9. **BUG BUSTER:** What is wrong with this code?

```
cout << "Enter a number between 0 and 5: ";
```

7

```
cin >> theNumber;
switch (theNumber)
{
    case 0:
          doZero();
    case 1:                 // fall through
    case 2:                 // fall through
    case 3:                 // fall through
    case 4:                 // fall through
    case 5:
          doOneToFive();
          break;
    default:
          doDefault();
          break;
}
```

WEEK 1

In Review

You just finished your first of three weeks of learning C++ for Linux. You should be proud of yourself. But before you relax too much, there is more to do.

Take a look at Listing R1.1 and think about all you have learned during this first week. The C++ code in the listing uses most of the techniques covered during this time.

INPUT   **LISTING R1.1**   Week 1 in Review Listing

```
1:   #include <iostream.h>
2:   // Listing file lstr1-01.cxx
3:   enum CHOICE { DrawRect = 1, GetArea,
4:      GetPerim, ChangeDimensions, Quit};
5:   // Rectangle class declaration
6:   class Rectangle
7:   {
8:     public:
9:        // constructors
10:       Rectangle(int width, int height);
11:       ~Rectangle();
12:
13:       // accessors
14:       int GetHeight() const { return itsHeight; }
15:       int GetWidth() const { return itsWidth; }
16:       int GetArea() const { return itsHeight *
➥itsWidth; }
17:       int GetPerim() const { return 2*itsHeight +
➥2*itsWidth; }
18:       void SetSize(int newWidth, int newHeight);
19:
20:       // Misc. methods
21:
22:
23:     private:
24:       int itsWidth;
25:       int itsHeight;
26:   };
```

continues

LISTING R1.1 CONTINUED

```
27:
28: // Class method implementations
29: void Rectangle::SetSize(int newWidth, int newHeight)
30: {
31:    itsWidth = newWidth;
32:    itsHeight = newHeight;
33: }
34:
35:
36: Rectangle::Rectangle(int width, int height)
37: {
38:    itsWidth = width;
39:    itsHeight = height;
40: }
41:
42: Rectangle::~Rectangle() {}
43:
44: int DoMenu();
45: void DoDrawRect(Rectangle);
46: void DoGetArea(Rectangle);
47: void DoGetPerim(Rectangle);
48:
49: int main ()
50: {
51:    // initialize a rectangle to 30,5
52:    Rectangle theRect(30,5);
53:
54:    int choice = DrawRect;
55:    int fQuit = false;
56:
57:    while (!fQuit)
58:    {
59:      choice = DoMenu();
60:      if (choice < DrawRect || choice >  Quit)
61:      {
62:        cout << "\nInvalid Choice, please try again.\n\n";
63:        continue;
64:      }
65:      switch (choice)
66:      {
67:      case  DrawRect:
68:        DoDrawRect(theRect);
69:        break;
70:      case GetArea:
71:        DoGetArea(theRect);
72:        break;
73:      case GetPerim:
74:        DoGetPerim(theRect);
```

```
75:          break;
76:        case ChangeDimensions:
77:          int newLength, newWidth;
78:          cout << "\nNew width: ";
79:          cin >> newWidth;
80:          cout << "New height: ";
81:          cin >> newLength;
82:          theRect.SetSize(newWidth, newLength);
83:          DoDrawRect(theRect);
84:          break;
85:        case Quit:
86:          fQuit = true;
87:          cout << "\nExiting...\n\n";
88:          break;
89:        default:
90:          cout << "Error in choice!\n";
91:          fQuit = true;
92:          break;
93:      }    // end switch
94:    }      // end while
95:  return 0;
96: }        // end main
97:
98: int DoMenu()
99: {
100:   int choice;
101:     cout << "\n\n   *** Menu *** \n";
102:     cout << "(1) Draw Rectangle\n";
103:     cout << "(2) Area\n";
104:     cout << "(3) Perimeter\n";
105:     cout << "(4) Resize\n";
106:     cout << "(5) Quit\n";
107:
108:  cin >> choice;
109:  return choice;
110: }
111:
112: void DoDrawRect(Rectangle theRect)
113: {
114:    int height = theRect.GetHeight();
115:    int width = theRect.GetWidth();
116:
117:    for (int i = 0; i<height; i++)
118:    {
119:      for (int j = 0; j< width; j++)
120:         cout << "*";
121:      cout << "\n";
122:    }
123: }
124:
```

continues

LISTING R1.1   CONTINUED

```
125:
126: void DoGetArea(Rectangle theRect)
127: {
128:   cout << "Area: " <<  theRect.GetArea() << endl;
129: }
130:
131: void DoGetPerim(Rectangle theRect)
132: {
133:   cout << "Perimeter: " <<  theRect.GetPerim() << endl;
134: }
```

OUTPUT

```
*** Menu ***
(1) Draw Rectangle
(2) Area
(3) Perimeter
(4) Resize
(5) Quit
1
*****************************
*****************************
*****************************
*****************************
*****************************

    *** Menu ***
(1) Draw Rectangle
(2) Area
(3) Perimeter
(4) Resize
(5) Quit
2
Area: 150

    *** Menu ***
(1) Draw Rectangle
(2) Area
(3) Perimeter
(4) Resize
(5) Quit
3
Perimeter: 70

    *** Menu ***
(1) Draw Rectangle
(2) Area
(3) Perimeter
(4) Resize
(5) Quit
```

```
4

New Width: 10
New height: 8
**********
**********
**********
**********
**********
**********
**********
**********

      *** Menu ***
(1) Draw Rectangle
(2) Area
(3) Perimeter
(4) Resize
(5) Quit
2
Area: 80

      *** Menu ***
(1) Draw Rectangle
(2) Area
(3) Perimeter
(4) Resize
(5) Quit
3
Perimeter: 36

      *** Menu ***
(1) Draw Rectangle
(2) Area
(3) Perimeter
(4) Resize
(5) Quit
5

Exiting...
```

ANALYSIS The program shown in Listing R1.1 utilizes most of the skills you learned this week. You should not only be able to enter, compile, link, and run this program, but also understand what it does and how it works, based on the work you did this week.

The first six lines set up the new types and definitions that will be used throughout the program.

Lines 6–26 declare the `Rectangle` class. There are public accessor methods for obtaining and setting the width and height of the rectangle, as well as for computing the area and perimeter. Lines 29–40 contain the class function definitions that were not declared inline.

The function prototypes, for the non-class member functions, are on lines 44–47, and the program begins on line 49. The essence of this program is to generate a rectangle, and then to print out a menu offering five options: Draw the rectangle, determine its area, determine its perimeter, resize the rectangle, or quit.

A flag is set on line 55, and when that flag is not set to `true`, the menu loop continues. The flag is only set to `true` if the user picks Quit from the menu.

Each of the other choices, with the exception of `ChangeDimensions`, calls out to a function. This makes the `switch` statement cleaner. `ChangeDimensions` cannot call out to a function because it must change the dimensions of the rectangle. If the rectangle were passed (by value) to a function such as `DoChangeDimensions()`, the dimensions would be changed on the local copy of the rectangle in `DoChangeDimensions()`, and not on the rectangle in `main()`. On Day 8, "Pointers," and Day 10, "Advanced Functions," you will learn how to overcome this restriction, but for now the change is made in the `main()` function.

Note how the use of an enumeration makes the `switch` statement much cleaner and easier to understand. Had the `switch` depended on the numeric choices (1–5) of the user, you would have to constantly refer to the description of the menu to see which pick was which.

On line 60, the user's choice is checked to make sure it is in range. If not, an error message is printed and the menu is reprinted. Note that the `switch` statement includes an "impossible" default condition. This is an aid in debugging. If the program is working, that statement can never be reached.

Week in Review

Congratulations! You just completed the first week! Now you can create and understand sophisticated C++ programs. Of course, there is plenty more to do, and next week starts with one of the most difficult concepts in C++: pointers. Do not give up now—you are about to delve deeply into the meaning and use of object-oriented programming, virtual functions, and many of the advanced features of this powerful language.

You even learned how to use the compiler. That is one skill that you will use for every program! And after you learn one compiler, the others are easy (because it is the same process).

Take a break, bask in the glory of your accomplishment, and then turn the page to start Week 2.

WEEK 2

At a Glance

You have finished the first week of learning how to program in C++. By now you should feel comfortable entering programs, using your compiler, and thinking about objects, classes, and program flow.

Where You Are Going

Week 2 begins with pointers. Pointers are traditionally a difficult subject for new C++ programmers, but you will find them explained fully and clearly, and they should not be a stumbling block. Day 8, "Pointers," discusses pointers, and Day 9, "References," teaches references, which are a close cousin to pointers. On Day 10, "Advanced Functions," you will see how to overload functions, and Day 11, "Inheritance," introduces inheritance, a fundamental concept in object-oriented programming. On Day 12, "Arrays, C Strings, and Linked Lists," you will learn how to work with arrays, strings, and collections. Day 13, "Polymorphism," extends the lessons of Day 11 to discuss polymorphism, and Day 14, "Special Classes and Functions," ends the week with a discussion of static functions and friends.

DAY 8

Pointers

One of the most powerful tools available to a C++ programmer is the capability to manipulate computer memory directly by using pointers. Today you will learn:

- What pointers are
- How to declare and use pointers
- What the free store is and how to manipulate memory

Pointers present two special challenges when you are learning C++: They can be somewhat confusing, and it is not immediately obvious why they are needed. This lesson explains how pointers work, step by step. You will fully understand the need for pointers, as you continue to work through the rest of the book.

What Is a Pointer?

A *pointer* is a variable that holds a memory address.

To understand pointers, you must know a little about computer memory. Computer memory is divided into sequentially numbered memory locations.

Each variable is located at a unique location in memory, known as its address. Figure 8.1 shows a schematic representation of the storage of an unsigned long integer variable theAge.

FIGURE 8.1

A schematic represen-tation of theAge.

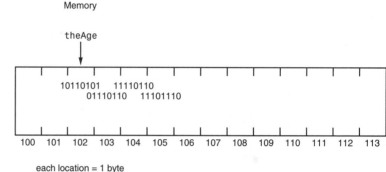

Memory

theAge

10110101   11110110
   01110110   11101110

100   101   102   103   104   105   106   107   108   109   110   111   112   113

each location = 1 byte
unsigned long int theAge = 4 bytes = 32 bits
variable name theAge points to 1st byte
the address of theAge is 102

Different computers number this memory using different, complex schemes. Usually, programmers do not need to know the particular address of any given variable because the compiler handles the details. If you want this information, though, you can use the address of operator (&), which is illustrated in Listing 8.1.

INPUT   **LISTING 8.1**   Demonstrating the Address of Operator

```
1:    // Listing 8.1 Demonstrates address of operator
2:    // and addresses of local variables
3:
4:    #include <iostream.h>
5:
6:    int main()
7:    {
8:        unsigned short shortVar=5;
9:        unsigned long  longVar=65535;
10:       long sVar = -65535;
11:
12:       cout << "shortVar:\t" << shortVar;
13:       cout << " Address of shortVar:\t";
14:       cout <<   &shortVar  << "\n";
15:
16:       cout << "longVar:\t"  << longVar;
17:       cout  <<  " Address of longVar:\t" ;
18:       cout <<   &longVar  << "\n";
19:
```

```
20:      cout << "sVar:\t"      << sVar;
21:      cout     << " Address of sVar:\t" ;
22:      cout     << &sVar     << "\n";
23:
24:      return 0;
25:   }
```

OUTPUT

```
shortVar: 5          Address of shortVar: b39fd2
longVar: 65535       Address of longVar:  b39fcc
sVar:    -65535      Address of sVar:     b39fc8
```

(Your printout may look different depending on the configuration of your system; some GNU compilers will show all the addresses as the value 1 (one). You may want to use the `printf()` with a format specifier of %p if that happens to you.)

ANALYSIS Three variables are declared and initialized: an unsigned `short` in line 8, an unsigned `long` in line 9, and a `long` in line 10. Their values and addresses are printed in lines 12–16 by using the address of the operator (&).

The value of `shortVar` is 5, as expected, and its address is b39fd2. This complicated address is specific to the computer, the compiler, and the operating system, and it may change slightly each time the program is run. Your results will be different. What does not change, however, is that the difference in the first two addresses is 2 bytes if your computer uses 2-byte short integers. The difference between the second and third is 4 bytes if your computer uses 4-byte long integers. Figure 8.2 illustrates how the variables in this program would be stored in memory.

FIGURE 8.2

Illustration of variable storage.

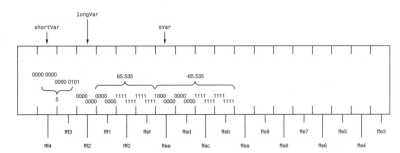

You do not need to know the actual numeric value of the address of each variable. What you care about is that each one has an address and that the right amount of memory is set aside. You tell the compiler how much memory to allow for your variables by declaring the variable type; the compiler automatically assigns an address for it. A long integer is typically 4 bytes, for example, meaning that the variable has an address to 4 bytes of memory.

There is no connection between the size of a data type and the size of the pointer used to point to that data type. A long int and a pointer to that long int each being 4 bytes is just a coincidence. You should make no assumptions about the size of a pointer and should not try to store an address in anything other than a pointer (do not try to store an address in an unsigned long integer).

Storing the Address in a Pointer

Every variable has an address. Even without knowing the specific address of a given variable, you can store that address in a pointer.

Suppose, for example, that howOld is an integer. To declare a pointer called pAge to hold its address, you would write

```
int *pAge = NULL;
```

This declares pAge to be a pointer to int. That is, pAge is declared to hold the address of an int.

Note that pAge is a variable the same as any of the variables. When you declare an integer variable (type int), it is set up to hold an integer. When you declare a pointer variable such as pAge, it is set up to hold an address. pAge is just a different type of variable.

In this example, pAge is initialized to the address constant NULL. A pointer whose value is NULL is called a *null pointer*. All pointers, when they are created, should be initialized to something. If you do not know what you want to assign to the pointer, assign NULL. A pointer that is not initialized is called a *wild pointer*. Wild pointers are very dangerous.

 Note

> Practice safe computing: Initialize your pointers! Some programmers like to use the value 0 (zero) to initialize their pointers. The better practice is to use the constant NULL.

If you do initialize the pointer to NULL, you must specifically assign the address of howOld to pAge. The following example shows how to do that:

```
unsigned short int howOld = 50;        // make a variable
unsigned short int * pAge = NULL;      // make a pointer
pAge = &howOld;                        // put howOld's address in pAge
```

The first line creates a variable—howOld, whose type is unsigned short int—and initializes it with the value 50. The second line declares pAge to be a pointer to type unsigned short int and initializes it to NULL. You know that pAge is a pointer because of the asterisk (*) after the variable type and before the variable name.

The third and final line assigns the address of howOld to the pointer pAge. You can tell that the address of howOld is being assigned because of the address of the operator (&). If the address of the operator had not been used, the value of howOld would have been assigned. That might, or might not, have been a valid address.

At this point, pAge has as its value the address of howOld. howOld, in turn, has the value 50. You could have accomplished this with one less step, as in

```
unsigned short int howOld = 50;        // make a variable
unsigned short int * pAge = &howOld;   // make pointer to howOld
```

pAge is a pointer that now contains the address of the howOld variable. Using pAge, you can actually determine the value of howOld, which in this case is 50. Accessing howOld by using the pointer pAge is called indirection because you are indirectly accessing howOld by means of pAge. Later today, you will see how to use indirection to access a variable's value.

Indirection means accessing the value at the address held by a pointer. The pointer provides an indirect way to get the value held at that address.

Selecting Pointer Names

Pointers can have any name that is legal for other variables. Many programmers follow the convention of naming all pointers with an initial p, as in pAge or pNumber.

Using the Indirection Operator

The indirection operator (*) is also called the *dereference operator*. When a pointer is dereferenced, the value at the address stored by the pointer is retrieved.

Normal variables provide direct access to their own values. If you create a new variable of type unsigned short int called yourAge, and you want to assign the value in howOld to that new variable, you would write

```
unsigned short int yourAge;
yourAge = howOld;
```

A pointer provides indirect access to the value of the variable whose address it stores. To assign the value in howOld to the new variable yourAge by way of the pointer pAge, you would write

```
unsigned short int yourAge;
yourAge = *pAge;
```

The indirection operator (*) in front of the variable pAge means "the value stored at." This assignment says, "Take the value stored at the address in pAge and assign it to yourAge."

> The indirection operator (*) is used in two distinct ways with pointers: declaration and dereference. When a pointer is declared, the star indicates that it is a pointer, not a normal variable. For example,
>
> ```
> unsigned short * pAge = NULL; // make a pointer to an unsigned short
> ```
>
> When the pointer is dereferenced, the indirection operator indicates that the value at the memory location stored in the pointer is to be accessed, rather than the address itself.
>
> ```
> *pAge = 5; // assign 5 to the value at pAge
> ```
>
> Also note that this same character (*) is used as the multiplication operator. The compiler knows which operator to call, based on context.

Understanding Pointers, Addresses, and Variables

It is important to distinguish between a pointer, the address that the pointer holds, and the value at the address held by the pointer. This is the source of much of the confusion about pointers.

Consider the following code fragment:

```
int theVariable = 5;
int * pPointer = &theVariable ;
```

theVariable is declared to be an integer variable initialized with the value 5. pPointer is declared to be a pointer to an integer; it is initialized with the address of theVariable. pPointer is the pointer. The address that pPointer holds is the address of theVariable. The value at the address that pPointer holds is 5. Figure 8.3 shows a schematic representation of theVariable and pPointer.

FIGURE 8.3

A schematic representation of memory.

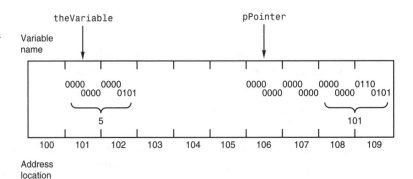

Manipulating Data by Using Pointers

After a pointer is assigned the address of a variable, you can use that pointer to access the data in that variable. Listing 8.2 demonstrates how the address of a local variable is assigned to a pointer and how the pointer manipulates the values in that variable.

INPUT **LISTING 8.2** Manipulating Data by Using Pointers

```
1:    // Listing 8.2 Using pointers
2:
3:    #include <iostream.h>
4:
5:    typedef unsigned short int USHORT;
6:    int main()
7:    {
8:       USHORT myAge;          // a variable
9:       USHORT * pAge = NULL; // a pointer
10:      myAge = 5;
11:      cout << "myAge: " << myAge << "\n";
12:      pAge = &myAge;        // assign address of myAge to pAge
13:      cout << "*pAge: " << *pAge << "\n\n";
14:      cout << "*pAge = 7\n";
15:      *pAge = 7;            // sets myAge to 7
16:      cout << "*pAge: " << *pAge << "\n";
17:      cout << "myAge: " << myAge << "\n\n";
18:      cout << "myAge = 9\n";
19:      myAge = 9;
20:      cout << "myAge: " << myAge << "\n";
21:      cout << "*pAge: " << *pAge << "\n";
22:
23:      return 0;
24:   }
```

OUTPUT
```
myAge: 5
*pAge: 5

*pAge = 7
*pAge: 7
myAge: 7

myAge = 9
myAge: 9
*pAge: 9
```

ANALYSIS This program declares two variables: an unsigned short, myAge, and a pointer to an unsigned short, pAge. myAge is assigned the value 5 on line 10; this is verified by the printout in line 11.

On line 12, pAge is assigned the address of myAge. On line 13, pAge is dereferenced and printed, showing that the value at the address that pAge stores is the 5 stored in myAge. In line 15, the value 7 is assigned to the variable at the address stored in pAge. This sets myAge to 7, and the printouts in lines 16–17 confirm this.

In line 19, the value 9 is assigned to the variable myAge. This value is obtained directly in line 20 and indirectly (by dereferencing pAge) in line 21.

Examining the Address

Pointers enable you to manipulate addresses without ever knowing their real value. After today, you can take it on faith that when you assign the address of a variable to a pointer, it really has the address of that variable as its value. But just this once, why not check to make sure? Listing 8.3 illustrates this idea.

INPUT   **LISTING 8.3** Finding Out What Is Stored in Pointer

```
1:      // Listing 8.3 What is stored in a pointer.
2:
3:      #include <iostream.h>
4:
5:
6:      int main()
7:      {
8:          unsigned short int myAge = 5, yourAge = 10;
9:          unsigned short int * pAge = &myAge;  // a pointer
10:         cout << "myAge:\t" << myAge <<  "\tyourAge:\t"
➥<< yourAge << "\n";
11:         cout << "&myAge:\t" << &myAge <<  "\t&yourAge:\t"
➥<< &yourAge <<"\n";
12:         cout << "pAge:\t" << pAge << "\n";
13:         cout << "*pAge:\t" << *pAge << "\n";
14:         pAge = &yourAge;         // reassign the pointer
15:         cout << "myAge:\t" << myAge <<  "\tyourAge:\t"
➥<< yourAge << "\n";
16:         cout << "&myAge:\t" << &myAge <<  "\t&yourAge:\t"
➥<< &yourAge <<"\n";
17:         cout << "pAge:\t" << pAge << "\n";
18:         cout << "*pAge:\t" << *pAge << "\n";
19:         cout << "&pAge:\t" << &pAge << "\n";
20:         return 0;
21:     }
```

OUTPUT

```
myAge:      5              yourAge:   10
&myAge:     0x355C         &yourAge:  0x355E
pAge:       0x355C
*pAge:      5
myAge:      5              yourAge:   10
&myAge:     0x355C         &yourAge:  0x355E
pAge:       0x355E
*pAge:      10
&pAge:      0x355A
```

(Your output may look different.)

ANALYSIS   In line 8, myAge and yourAge are declared to be variables of type unsigned short integer. In line 9, pAge is declared to be a pointer to an unsigned short integer, and it is initialized with the address of the variable myAge.

Lines 10 and 11 print the values and the addresses of myAge and yourAge. Line 12 prints the contents of pAge, which is the address of myAge. Line 13 prints the result of dereferencing pAge, which prints the value at pAge—the value in myAge, or 5.

This is the essence of pointers. Line 12 shows that pAge stores the address of myAge, and line 13 shows how to get the value stored in myAge by dereferencing the pointer pAge. Make sure that you understand this fully before you go on. Study the code and look at the output.

In line 14, pAge is reassigned to point to the address of yourAge. The values and addresses are printed again. The output shows that pAge now has the address of the variable yourAge and that dereferencing obtains the value in yourAge.

Line 19 prints the address of pAge itself. Like any variable, it has an address, and that address can be stored in a pointer. (Assigning the address of a pointer to another pointer will be discussed shortly.)

Do	Don't
DO use the indirection operator (*) to access the data stored at the address in a pointer.	
DO initialize all pointers either to a valid address or to NULL.	
DO remember the difference between the address in a pointer and the value at that address.	

Using Pointers

To declare a pointer, write the type of the variable or object whose address will be stored in the pointer, followed by the pointer operator (*) and the name of the pointer. For example,

```
unsigned short int * pPointer = NULL;
```

To assign or initialize a pointer, prepend the name of the variable whose address is being assigned with the address of operator (&). For example,

```
unsigned short int theVariable = 5;
unsigned short int * pPointer = & theVariable;
```

To dereference a pointer, prepend the pointer name with the dereference operator (*). For example,

```
unsigned short int theValue = *pPointer
```

Why Would You Use Pointers?

So far you have seen step-by-step details of assigning a variable's address to a pointer. In practice, though, you would never do this. After all, why bother with a pointer when you already have a variable with access to that value? The only reason for this kind of pointer manipulation of an automatic variable is to demonstrate how pointers work.

Now that you are comfortable with the syntax of pointers, you can put them to good use. Pointers are used, most often, for three tasks:

- Managing data on the free store
- Accessing class member data and functions
- Passing variables by reference to functions

The rest of this lesson focuses on managing data on the free store and accessing class member data and functions. Tomorrow you will learn about passing variables by reference.

The Stack and the Free Store

On Day 5, "Functions," in the section "How Functions Work—A Look Under the Hood," five areas of memory are mentioned:

- Global name space
- The free store

- Registers
- Code space
- The stack

Local variables are on the stack, along with function parameters. Code is in code space, of course, and global variables are in global name space. The registers are used for internal housekeeping functions, such as keeping track of the top of the stack and the instruction pointer. Just about all remaining memory is given over to the free store, which is sometimes referred to as the *heap*.

The problem with local variables is that they do not persist; when the function returns, the local variables are thrown away. Global variables solve that problem at the cost of unrestricted access throughout the program, which leads to the creation of code that is difficult to understand and maintain. Putting data in the free store solves both of these problems.

You can think of the free store as a massive section of memory in which thousands of sequentially numbered cubbyholes lie waiting for your data. You cannot label these cubbyholes, though, as you can the stack. You must ask for the address of the cubbyhole that you reserve and then stash that address away in a pointer.

One way to think about this is with an analogy: A friend gives you the 800 number for Acme Mail Order. You go home and program your telephone with that number, and then you throw away the piece of paper with the number on it. If you push the button, a telephone rings somewhere, and Acme Mail Order answers. You do not remember the number, nor do you know where the other telephone is located, but the button gives you access to Acme Mail Order. Acme Mail Order is your data on the free store. You do not know where it is, but you know how to get to it. You access it by using its address—in this case, the telephone number. You do not have to know that number; you just have to put it into a pointer (the button). The pointer gives you access to your data without bothering you with the details.

The stack is cleaned automatically when a function returns. All the local variables go out of scope, and they are removed from the stack. The free store is not cleaned until your program ends, and it is your responsibility to free any memory that you reserved when you are done with it.

The advantage to the free store is that the memory you reserve remains available until you explicitly free it. If you reserve memory on the free store while in a function, the memory is still available when the function returns.

The advantage of accessing memory in this way, rather than using global variables, is that only functions with access to the pointer have access to the data. This provides a tightly controlled interface to that data, and it eliminates the problem of one function changing that data in unexpected and unanticipated ways.

For this to work, you must be able to create a pointer to an area on the free store and to pass that pointer among functions. The following sections describe how to do this.

new

You allocate memory on the free store in C++ by using the new keyword. new is followed by the type of the object that you want to allocate, so that the compiler knows how much memory is required. Therefore, new unsigned short int allocates 2 bytes in the free store, and new long allocates 4.

The return value from new is a memory address. It must be assigned to a pointer. To create an unsigned short on the free store, you might write

```
unsigned short int * pPointer;
pPointer = new unsigned short int;
```

You can, of course, initialize the pointer at its creation with

```
unsigned short int * pPointer = new unsigned short int;
```

In either case, pPointer now points to an unsigned short int on the free store. You can use this like any other pointer to a variable and assign a value into that area of memory by writing

```
*pPointer = 72;
```

This means, "Put 72 at the value in pPointer," or "Assign the value 72 to the area on the free store to which pPointer points."

If new cannot create memory on the free store (memory is, after all, a limited resource), it throws an exception (see Day 20, "Exceptions and Error Handling").

delete

When you are finished with your area of memory, you must call delete on the pointer. delete returns the memory to the free store. Remember that the pointer itself—as opposed to the memory to which it points—is a local variable. When the function in which it is declared returns, that pointer goes out of scope and is lost. The memory allocated with new is not freed automatically, however. That memory becomes unavailable because you have no way of referencing it (you have no idea where it is)—a situation called a *memory leak*. It is known as a memory leak because that memory cannot be recovered until the program ends. It is as though the memory has leaked out of your computer.

To restore the memory to the free store, you use the keyword `delete`. For example,

`delete pPointer;`

When you delete the pointer, what you are really doing is freeing up the memory whose address is stored in the pointer. You are saying, "Return to the free store the memory that this pointer points to." The pointer is still a pointer, and it can be reassigned. Listing 8.4 demonstrates allocating a variable on the heap, using that variable, and deleting it.

Caution

When you call `delete` on a pointer, the memory it points to is freed. Calling `delete` on that pointer again will crash your program! When you delete a pointer, set it to NULL. Calling `delete` on a null pointer is guaranteed to be safe. For example,

```
Animal *pDog = new Animal;
delete pDog;    //frees the memory
  pDog = NULL; //sets pointer to null
  //...
delete pDog; //harmless
```

INPUT   **LISTING 8.4**   Allocating, Using, and Deleting Pointers

```
 1:     // Listing 8.4
 2:     // Allocating and deleting a pointer
 3:
 4:     #include <iostream.h>
 5:     int main()
 6:     {
 7:        int localVariable = 5;
 8:        int * pLocal= &localVariable;
 9:        int * pHeap = new int;
10:        *pHeap = 7;
11:        cout << "localVariable: " << localVariable << "\n";
12:        cout << "*pLocal: " << *pLocal << "\n";
13:        cout << "*pHeap: " << *pHeap << "\n";
14:        delete pHeap;
15:        pHeap = new int;
16:        *pHeap = 9;
17:        cout << "*pHeap: " << *pHeap << "\n";
18:        delete pHeap;
19:        return 0;
20:     }
```

OUTPUT
```
localVariable: 5
*pLocal: 5
*pHeap: 7
*pHeap: 9
```

ANALYSIS Line 7 declares and initializes a local variable. Line 8 declares and initializes a pointer with the address of the local variable. Line 9 declares another pointer but initializes it with the result obtained from calling for a new int. This allocates space on the free store for an int. Line 10 verifies that memory was allocated and the pointer is valid (not null) by using it. If no memory can be allocated, the pointer is null and an error message is printed.

To keep things simple, real error checking is often not included in the sample programs in this book, but you must include some sort of error checking in your own programs. A better way of error checking would be to test for a null pointer before initializing the value. You could replace line 10 in Listing 8.4 with the following:

```
if (pHeap == NULL)

{
    // handle the error here:
    // report the problem.  In most cases the next steps
    // are to perform cleanup (close files, set statuses, etc.)
    // and exit the program.
}
*pHeap = 7;
```

Line 10 assigns the value 7 to the newly allocated memory. Line 11 prints the value of the local variable, and line 12 prints the value pointed to by pLocal. As expected, these are the same. Line 13 prints the value pointed to by pHeap. It shows that the value assigned in line 10 is, in fact, accessible.

In line 14, the memory allocated in line 9 is returned to the free store by a call to delete. This frees the memory and disassociates the pointer from that memory. pHeap is now free to point to other memory. It is reassigned in lines 15 and 16, and line 17 prints the result. Line 18 restores that memory to the free store.

Although line 18 is redundant (the end of the program would have returned that memory), it is a good idea to free this memory explicitly. If the program changes or is extended, having already taken care of this step will be beneficial.

8

Memory Leaks

Another way you might inadvertently create a memory leak is by reassigning your pointer before deleting the memory to which it points. Consider this code fragment:

```
1:    unsigned short int * pPointer = new unsigned short int;
2:    *pPointer = 72;
3:    pPointer = new unsigned short int;
4:    *pPointer = 84;
```

Line 1 creates pPointer and assigns it the address of an area on the free store. Line 2 stores the value 72 in that area of memory. Line 3 reassigns pPointer to another area of memory. Line 4 places the value 84 in that area. The original area—in which the value 72 is now held—is unavailable because the pointer to that area of memory has been reassigned. No way exists to access that original area of memory, nor is there any way to free it before the program ends.

The code should have been written like this:

```
1: unsigned short int * pPointer = new unsigned short int;
2: *pPointer = 72;
3: delete pPointer;
4: pPointer = new unsigned short int;
5: *pPointer = 84;
```

Now the memory originally pointed to by pPointer is deleted, and thus freed, in line 3.

 Note

For every time that you use new in your program, there should a corresponding delete. It is important to keep track of which pointer owns an area of memory and to ensure that the memory is returned to the free store when you are done with it.

Objects on the Free Store

There are still many things to learn about using and creating objects. The following sections will cover:

- Creating Objects on the free store
- Deleting Objects
- Accessing Data Members
- Member Data on the Free Store

Creating Objects on the Free Store

Just as you can create a pointer to an integer, you can create a pointer to any object.
If you have declared an object of type Cat, you can declare a pointer to that class and
instantiate a Cat object on the free store, just as you can make one on the stack. The
syntax is the same as for integers:

```
Cat *pCat = new Cat;
```

This calls the default constructor—the constructor that takes no parameters. The
constructor is called whenever an object is created (on the stack or on the free store).

Deleting Objects

When you call delete on a pointer to an object on the free store, that object's destructor
is called before the memory is released. This gives your class a chance to clean up, just
as it does for objects destroyed on the stack. Listing 8.5 illustrates creating and deleting
objects on the free store.

INPUT   **LISTING 8.5**   Creating and Deleting Objects on the Free Store

```
1:      // Listing 8.5
2:      // Creating objects on the free store
3:
4:      #include <iostream.h>
5:
6:      class SimpleCat
7:      {
8:      public:
9:              SimpleCat();
10:             ~SimpleCat();
11:     private:
12:             int itsAge;
13:         };
14:
15:     SimpleCat::SimpleCat()
16:         {
17:             cout << "Constructor called.\n";
18:             itsAge = 1;
19:         }
20:
21:     SimpleCat::~SimpleCat()
22:         {
23:             cout << "Destructor called.\n";
24:         }
25:
26:     int main()
27:         {
```

```
28:                    cout << "SimpleCat Frisky...\n";
29:                    SimpleCat Frisky;
30:                    cout << "SimpleCat *pRags = new SimpleCat...\n";
31:                    SimpleCat * pRags = new SimpleCat;
32:                    cout << "delete pRags...\n";
33:                    delete pRags;
34:                    cout << "Exiting, watch Frisky go...\n";
35:                    return 0;
36:            }
```

OUTPUT

```
SimpleCat Frisky...
Constructor called.
SimpleCat *pRags = new SimpleCat...
Constructor called.
delete pRags...
Destructor called.
Exiting, watch Frisky go...
Destructor called.
```

ANALYSIS Lines 6–13 declare the stripped-down class SimpleCat. Line 9 declares
SimpleCat's constructor, and lines 15–19 contain its definition. Line 10 declares
SimpleCat's destructor, and lines 21–24 contain its definition.

In line 29, Frisky is created on the stack, which causes the constructor to be called. In
line 31, the SimpleCat pointed to by pRags is created on the heap; the constructor is
called again. In line 33, delete is called on pRags, and the destructor is called. When the
function ends, Frisky goes out of scope, and the destructor is called.

Accessing Data Members

You accessed data members and functions by using the dot (.) operator for Cat objects
created locally. To access the Cat object on the free store, you must dereference the
pointer and call the dot operator on the object pointed to by the pointer. Therefore, to
access the GetAge member function, you would write

```
(*pRags).GetAge();
```

Parentheses are used to ensure that pRags is dereferenced before GetAge() is accessed.

Because this is cumbersome, C++ provides a shorthand operator for indirect access: the
points-to operator (->), which is created by typing the dash (-) immediately followed by
the greater-than symbol (>). C++ treats this as a single symbol. Listing 8.6 demonstrates
accessing member variables and functions of objects created on the free store.

LISTING 8.6   Accessing Member Data of Objects on the Free Store

```
1:      // Listing 8.6
2:      // Accessing data members of objects on the heap
3:
4:      #include <iostream.h>
5:
6:      class SimpleCat
7:      {
8:      public:
9:            SimpleCat() {itsAge = 2; }
10:           ~SimpleCat() {}
11:           int GetAge() const { return itsAge; }
12:           void SetAge(int age) { itsAge = age; }
13:     private:
14:           int itsAge;
15:       };
16:
17:      int main()
18:      {
19:            SimpleCat * Frisky = new SimpleCat;
20:            cout << "Frisky is " << Frisky->GetAge() <<
➥" years old\n";
21:            Frisky->SetAge(5);
22:            cout << "Frisky is " << Frisky->GetAge()
➥<< " years old\n";
23:            delete Frisky;
24:            return 0;
25:        }
```

Frisky is 2 years old
Frisky is 5 years old

In line 19, a `SimpleCat` object is instantiated on the free store. The default constructor sets its age to 2, and the `GetAge()` method is called in line 20. Because this is a pointer, the indirection operator (`->`) is used to access the member data and functions. In line 21, the `SetAge()` method is called, and `GetAge()` is accessed again in line 22.

Member Data on the Free Store

One or more of the data members of a class can be a pointer to an object on the free store. The memory can be allocated in the class constructor or in one of its methods, and it can be deleted in its destructor, as Listing 8.7 illustrates.

INPUT   **LISTING 8.7**   Pointers as Member Data

```
1:   // Listing 8.7
2:   // Pointers as data members
3:
4:      #include <iostream.h>
5:
6:      class SimpleCat
7:      {
8:      public:
9:              SimpleCat();
10:             ~SimpleCat();
11:             int GetAge() const { return *itsAge; }
12:             void SetAge(int age) { *itsAge = age; }
13:
14:             int GetWeight() const { return *itsWeight; }
15:             void setWeight (int weight) { *itsWeight = weight; }
16:
17:      private:
18:             int * itsAge;
19:             int * itsWeight;
20:         };
21:
22:      SimpleCat::SimpleCat()
23:      {
24:             itsAge = new int(2);
25:             itsWeight = new int(5);
26:      }
27:
28:      SimpleCat::~SimpleCat()
29:      {
30:          delete itsAge;
31:          delete itsWeight;
32:      }
33:
34:      int main()
35:      {
36:             SimpleCat *Frisky = new SimpleCat;
37:             cout << "Frisky is " << Frisky->GetAge()
➥<< " years old\n";
38:             Frisky->SetAge(5);
39:             cout << "Frisky is " << Frisky->GetAge()
➥<< " years old\n";
40:             delete Frisky;
41:             return 0;
42:      }
```

OUTPUT

```
Frisky is 2 years old
Frisky is 5 years old
```

ANALYSIS   The class SimpleCat is declared to have two member variables—both of which are pointers to integers—on lines 18 and 19. The constructor (lines 22–26) initializes the pointers to memory on the free store and to the default values.

The destructor (lines 28–32) cleans up the allocated memory. Because this is the destructor, there is no point in assigning these pointers to NULL because they will no longer be accessible. This is one of the safe places to break the rule that deleted pointers should be assigned to NULL, although following the rule does not hurt.

The calling function (in this case, main()) is unaware that itsAge and itsWeight are pointers to memory on the free store. main() continues to call GetAge() and SetAge(), and the details of the memory management are hidden in the implementation of the class—as they should be.

When Frisky is deleted in line 40, its destructor is called. The destructor deletes each of its member pointers. If these, in turn, point to objects of other user-defined classes, their destructors are called as well.

Frequently Asked Questions

FAQ: If I declare an object on the stack that has member variables on the heap, what is on the stack and what is on the heap? For example,

```cpp
#include <iostream.h>

class SimpleCat
{
public:
    SimpleCat();
    ~SimpleCat();
    int GetAge() const { return *itsAge; }
    // other methods

private:
    int * itsAge;
    int * itsWeight;
};

SimpleCat::SimpleCat()
{
    itsAge = new int(2);
    itsWeight = new int(5);
}

SimpleCat::~SimpleCat()
{
    delete itsAge;
    delete itsWeight;
```

```
        }

        int main()
        {
            SimpleCat Frisky;
            cout << "Frisky is " <<
                        Frisky.GetAge() <<
                            " years old\n";
            Frisky.SetAge(5);
            cout << "Frisky is " <<
                    Frisky.GetAge() << " years old\n";
            return 0;
        }
```

Answer: What is on the stack is the local variable `Frisky`. That variable has two pointers, each of which is taking up some stack space and holding the address of an integer allocated on the heap. Thus, in the example, 8 bytes are on the stack (assuming 4-byte pointers) and 8 bytes are on the heap.

Now this would be pretty silly in a real program unless a good reason existed for the `Cat` object to hold its members by reference. In this case, there is no good reason, but in other cases, this would make a lot of sense.

This begs the question: What are you trying to accomplish? Understand, too, that you must start with design. If what you designed is an object that refers to another object, but the second object may come into existence before the first object and continue after the first object is gone, the first object must contain the second by reference.

For example, the first object might be a window and the second object might be a document. The window needs access to the document, but it does not control the lifetime of the document. Thus, the window needs to hold the document by reference.

You implement this in C++ by using pointers or references. References are covered on Day 9, "References."

Special Pointers and More issues

There are still many things to learn about using and pointers. The following sections will cover:

- The `this` Pointer
- Stray, Wild, or Dangling Pointers
- `const` Pointers

The this Pointer

Every class member function has a hidden parameter: the this pointer. this points to the individual object. Therefore, in each call to GetAge() or SetAge(), the this pointer for the object is included as a hidden parameter.

It is possible to use the this pointer explicitly, as Listing 8.8 illustrates.

INPUT   **LISTING 8.8**   Using the this Pointer

```
1:     // Listing 8.8
2:     // Using the this pointer
3:
4:     #include <iostream.h>
5:
6:     class Rectangle
7:     {
8:     public:
9:         Rectangle();
10:         ~Rectangle();
11:         void SetLength(int length) { this->itsLength = length; }
12:         int GetLength() const { return this->itsLength; }
13:
14:         void SetWidth(int width) { itsWidth = width; }
15:         int GetWidth() const { return itsWidth; }
16:
17:     private:
18:         int itsLength;
19:         int itsWidth;
20:     };
21:
22:     Rectangle::Rectangle()
23:     {
24:         itsWidth = 5;
25:         itsLength = 10;
26:     }
27:     Rectangle::~Rectangle()
28:     {}
29:
30:     int main()
31:     {
32:         Rectangle theRect;
33:         cout << "theRect is " << theRect.GetLength()
        ➥<< " feet long.\n";
34:         cout << "theRect is " << theRect.GetWidth()
        ➥<< " feet wide.\n";
35:         theRect.SetLength(20);
36:         theRect.SetWidth(10);
37:         cout << "theRect is " << theRect.GetLength()
```

```
➥<< " feet long.\n";
38:             cout << "theRect is " << theRect.GetWidth()
➥<< " feet wide.\n";
39:             return 0;
40:         }
```

OUTPUT
```
theRect is 10 feet long.
theRect is 5 feet wide.
theRect is 20 feet long.
theRect is 10 feet wide.
```

ANALYSIS The >SetLength() and GetLength() accessor functions explicitly use the this pointer to access the member variables of the Rectangle object. The SetWidth and GetWidth accessors do not. No difference exists in their behavior, although the syntax is easier to understand.

If that were all there was to the this pointer, there would be little point in bothering you with it. The this pointer, however, is a pointer; it stores the memory address of an object. As such, it can be a powerful tool.

You will see a practical use for the this pointer on Day 10, "Advanced Functions," when operator overloading is discussed. For now, your goal is to know about the this pointer and to understand what it is: a pointer to the object itself.

You do not have to worry about creating or deleting the this pointer. The compiler takes care of that.

Stray, Wild, or Dangling Pointers

One source of bugs that are nasty and difficult to find is stray pointers. A *stray pointer* (also called a wild or dangling pointer) is created when you call delete on a pointer—thereby freeing the memory that it points to—and then you do not set it to NULL. If you then try to use that pointer again without reassigning it, the result is unpredictable and, if you are lucky, your program will crash.

It is as though the Acme Mail Order company moved away, but you still pressed the programmed button on your phone. It is possible that nothing terrible happens—a telephone rings in a deserted warehouse. Perhaps the telephone number has been reassigned to a munitions factory, and your call detonates an explosive and blows up your whole city!

In short, be careful not to use a pointer after you have called delete on it. The pointer still points to the old area of memory, but the compiler is free to put other data there; using the pointer can cause your program to crash. Worse, your program might proceed merrily on its way and crash several minutes later. This is called a time bomb, and it is no fun. To be safe, after you delete a pointer, set it to NULL. This disarms the pointer.

Note   Stray pointers are often called wild pointers or dangling pointers. This is just a terminology difference.

Listing 8.9 illustrates creating a stray pointer.

Caution   This program intentionally creates a stray pointer. Do NOT run this program—it will crash, if you are lucky.

INPUT   **LISTING 8.9**   Creating a Stray Pointer

```
1:    // Listing 8.9
2:    // Demonstrates a stray pointer
3:    typedef unsigned short int USHORT;
4:    #include <iostream.h>
5:
6:    int main()
7:    {
8:        USHORT * pInt = new USHORT;
9:        *pInt = 10;
10:       cout << "*pInt: " << *pInt << endl;
11:       delete pInt;
12:
13:       long * pLong = new long;
14:       *pLong = 90000;
15:       cout << "*pLong: " << *pLong << endl;
16:
17:       *pInt = 20;      // uh oh, this was deleted!
18:
19:       cout << "*pInt: " << *pInt   << endl;
20:       cout << "*pLong: " << *pLong  << endl;
21:       delete pLong;
22:       return 0;
23:   }
```

OUTPUT
```
*pInt:    10
*pLong:   90000
*pInt:    20
*pLong:   65556
```

(Your output may look different.)

ANALYSIS Line 8 declares pInt to be a pointer to USHORT, and pInt is pointed to newly allocated memory. Line 9 puts the value 10 in that memory, and line 10 prints its value. After the value is printed, delete is called on the pointer. pInt is now a stray, or dangling, pointer.

Line 13 declares a new pointer, pLong, which is pointed at the memory allocated by new. Line 14 assigns the value 90000 to pLong, and line 15 prints its value.

Line 17 assigns the value 20 to the memory that pInt points to, but pInt no longer points anywhere that is valid. The memory that pInt points to was freed by the call to delete, so assigning a value to that memory is certain disaster.

Line 19 prints the value at pInt. Sure enough, it is 20. Line 20 prints 20, the value at pLong; it has suddenly been changed to 65556. Two questions arise:

1. How could pLong's value change, given that pLong was not touched?
2. Where did the 20 go when pInt was used in line 17?

As you might guess, these are related questions. When a value was placed at pInt in line 17, the compiler happily placed the value 20 at the memory location that pInt previously pointed to. However, because that memory was freed in line 11, the compiler was free to reassign it. When pLong was created in line 13, it was given pInt's old memory location. (On some computers this may not happen, depending on where in memory these values are stored.) When the value 20 was assigned to the location that pInt previously pointed to, it wrote over the value pointed to by pLong. This is called "stomping on a pointer." It is often the unfortunate outcome of using a stray pointer.

This is a particularly nasty bug because the value that changed was not associated with the stray pointer. The change to the value at pLong was a side effect of the misuse of pInt. In a large program, this would be very difficult to track down.

Just for fun, here are the details of how 65,556 got into that memory address:

1. pInt was pointed at a particular memory location, and the value 10 was assigned.
2. delete was called on pInt, which told the compiler that it could put something else at that location. Then pLong was assigned the same memory location.
3. The value 90000 was assigned to *pLong. The particular computer used in this example stored the 4-byte value of 90,000 (00 01 5F 90) in byte-swapped order. Therefore, it was stored as 5F 90 00 01.
4. pInt was assigned the value 20—or 00 14 in hexadecimal notation. Because pInt still pointed to the same address, the first two bytes of pLong were overwritten, leaving 00 14 00 01.

5. The value at pLong was printed, reversing the bytes back to their correct order of 00 01 00 14, which was translated into the value of 65556.

Do	Don't
DO use new to create objects on the free store.	**DON'T** forget to balance all new statements with a delete statement.
DO use delete to destroy objects on the free store and to return their memory.	**DON'T** forget to assign NULL to all pointers on which you call delete.
DO check the value returned by new.	

Frequently Asked Questions

FAQ: What is the difference between a null pointer and a stray pointer?

Answer: When you delete a pointer, you tell the compiler to free the memory, but the pointer itself continues to exist. It is now a stray pointer.

When you then write myPtr = NULL;, you change it from being a stray pointer to being a null pointer.

Normally, if you delete a pointer and then delete it again, your program is undefined. That is, anything might happen—if you are lucky, the program will crash. If you delete a null pointer, nothing happens; it is safe.

Using a stray *or* a null pointer (for example, writing myPtr = 5;) is illegal, and it might crash. If the pointer is null, it *will* crash, another benefit of null over stray. The authors prefer predictable crashes because they are easier to debug.

const Pointers

You can use the keyword const for pointers before the type, after the type, or in both places. For example, all the following are legal declarations:

```
const int * pOne;
int * const pTwo;
const int * const pThree;
```

pOne is a pointer to a constant integer. The value that is pointed to cannot be changed.

pTwo is a constant pointer to an integer. The integer can be changed, but pTwo cannot point to anything else.

8

pThree is a constant pointer to a constant integer. The value that is pointed to cannot be changed, and pThree cannot be changed to point to anything else.

The trick to keeping this straight is to look to the right of the keyword const to find out what is being declared constant. If the type is to the right of the keyword, it is the value that is constant. If the variable is to the right of the keyword const, it is the pointer variable itself that is constant.

```
const int * p1;   // the int pointed to is constant
int * const p2;   // p2 is constant, it can't point to anything else
```

const Pointers and const Member Functions

On Day 6, "Basic Classes," you learned that you can apply the keyword const to a member function. When a function is declared const, the compiler flags as an error any attempt to change data in the object from within that function.

If you declare a pointer to a const object, the only methods that you can call with that pointer are const methods. Listing 8.10 illustrates this.

INPUT   **LISTING 8.10**   Using Pointers to const Objects

```
1:    // Listing 8.10
2:    // Using pointers with const methods
3:
4:    #include <iostream.h>
5:
6:    class Rectangle
7:    {
8:    public:
9:        Rectangle();
10:        ~Rectangle();
11:        void SetLength(int length) { itsLength = length; }
12:        int GetLength() const { return itsLength; }
13:        void SetWidth(int width) { itsWidth = width; }
14:        int GetWidth() const { return itsWidth; }
15:
16:    private:
17:        int itsLength;
18:        int itsWidth;
19:    };
20:
21:    Rectangle::Rectangle()
22:    {
23:    itsWidth = 5;
24:    itsLength = 10;
25:    }
26:
```

continues

LISTING **8.10**   CONTINUED

```
27:        Rectangle::~Rectangle()
28:        {}
29:
30:        int main()
31:        {
32:            Rectangle* pRect =  new Rectangle;
33:            const Rectangle * pConstRect = new Rectangle;
34:            Rectangle * const pConstPtr = new Rectangle;
35:
36:            cout << "pRect width: " << pRect->GetWidth()
➡      << " feet\n";
37:            cout << "pConstRect width: " << pConstRect->
➡      GetWidth() << " feet\n";
38:            cout << "pConstPtr width: " << pConstPtr->
➡      GetWidth() << " feet\n";
39:
40:            pRect->SetWidth(10);
41:            // pConstRect->SetWidth(10);
42:            pConstPtr->SetWidth(10);
43:
44:            cout << "pRect width: " << pRect->GetWidth()
➡      << " feet\n";
45:            cout << "pConstRect width: "
➡      << pConstRect->GetWidth() << " feet\n";
46:            cout << "pConstPtr width: "
➡      << pConstPtr->GetWidth() << " feet\n";
47:      return 0;
48:        }
```

OUTPUT
```
pRect width: 5 feet
pConstRect width: 5 feet
pConstPtr width: 5 feet
pRect width: 10 feet
pConstRect width: 5 feet
pConstPtr width: 10 feet
```

ANALYSIS Lines 6–19 declare Rectangle. Line 14 declares the GetWidth() member method const. Line 32 declares a pointer to Rectangle. Line 33 declares pConstRect, which is a pointer to a constant Rectangle. Line 34 declares pConstPtr, which is a constant pointer to Rectangle.

Lines 36–38 print their values.

In line 40, pRect is used to set the width of the rectangle to 10. In line 41, pConstRect would be used, but it was declared to point to a constant Rectangle. Therefore, it cannot legally call a non-const member function; it is commented out. In line 42, pConstPtr calls SetWidth(). pConstPtr is declared to be a constant pointer to a rectangle. In other words, the pointer is constant and cannot point to anything else, but the rectangle is not constant.

const this Pointers

When you declare an object to be const, you are in effect declaring that the this pointer is a pointer to a const object. A const this pointer can be used only with const member functions.

Constant objects and constant pointers will be discussed again tomorrow, when references to constant objects are discussed.

Do	Don't
DO protect objects passed by reference with const if they should not be changed.	
DO pass by reference when the object can be changed.	
DO pass by value when small objects should not be changed.	

Pointer Arithmetic

Pointers can be subtracted one from another. One powerful technique is to point two pointers at different elements in an array and to take their difference to see how many elements separate the two members. This can be useful when parsing arrays of characters, as shown in Listing 8.11.

INPUT   **LISTING 8.11**   Illustrating How to Parse Out Words from a Character String

```
1:     #include <iostream.h>
2:     #include <ctype.h>
3:     #include <string.h>
4:     bool GetWord(char* string, char* word, int& wordOffset);
5:     // driver program
6:     int main()
7:     {
8:         const int bufferSize = 255;
9:         char buffer[bufferSize+1];  // hold the entire string
10:        char word[bufferSize+1];     // hold the word
```

continues

LISTING 8.11   CONTINUED

```
11:         int wordOffset = 0;                  // start at the beginning
12:
13:         cout << "Enter a string: ";
14:         cin.getline(buffer,bufferSize);
15:
16:         while (GetWord(buffer,word,wordOffset))
17:         {
18:             cout << "Got this word: " << word << endl;
19:         }
20:
21:         return 0;
22:
23:     }
24:
25:
26:     // function to parse words from a string.
27:     bool GetWord(char* string, char* word, int& wordOffset)
28:     {
29:
30:         if (!string[wordOffset])  // end of string?
31:             return false;
32:
33:         char *p1, *p2;
34:         p1 = p2 = string+wordOffset;  // point to the next word
35:
36:         // eat leading spaces
37:         for (int i = 0; i<(int)strlen(p1) && !isalnum(p1[0]); i++)
38:             p1++;
39:
40:         // see if you have a word
41:         if (!isalnum(p1[0]))
42:             return false;
43:
44:         // p1 now points to start of next word
45:         // point p2 there as well
46:         p2 = p1;
47:
48:         // march p2 to end of word
49:         while (isalnum(p2[0]))
50:             p2++;
51:
52:         // p2 is now at end of word
53:         // p1 is at beginning of word
54:         // length of word is the difference
55:         int len = int (p2 - p1);
56:
57:         // copy the word into the buffer
58:         strncpy (word,p1,len);
```

```
59:
60:          // null terminate it
61:          word[len]='\0';
62:
63:          // now find the beginning of the next word
64:          for (int i = int(p2-string); i<(int)strlen
➡    (string) && !isalnum(p2[0]); i++)
65:              p2++;
66:
67:          wordOffset = int(p2-string);
68:
69:          return true;
70:     }
```

OUTPUT

```
Enter a string: this code first appeared in C++ Report
Got this word: this
Got this word: code
Got this word: first
Got this word: appeared
Got this word: in
Got this word: C
Got this word: Report
```

ANALYSIS On line 13, the user is prompted to enter a string. This is fed to GetWord on line 16, along with a buffer to hold the first word and an integer variable WordOffset, which is initialized on line 11 to zero. As words are returned from GetWord, they are printed until GetWord() returns false.

Each call to GetWord causes a jump to line 27. On line 30, we check to see if the value of string[wordOffset]) is zero. This will be true if the code is past the end of the string, at which time GetWord() will return false.

On line 33, two character pointers, p1 and p2, are declared, and on line 34, they are set to point into string offset by wordOffset. Initially, wordOffset is zero, so they point to the beginning of the string.

Lines 37 and 38 tick through the string, pushing p1 to the first alphanumeric character. Lines 41 and 42 ensure that it finds an alphanumeric character; if not, it returns false.

p1 now points to the start of the next word, and line 46 sets p2 to point to the same position.

Lines 49 and 50 then cause p2 to march through the word, stopping at the first nonalphanumeric character. p2 is now pointing to the end of the word that p1 points to the beginning of. By subtracting p1 from p2 on line 55 and casting the result to an integer, the code is able to establish the length of the word. It then copies that word into the buffer *word*, passing in as the starting point p1 and as the length the difference just established.

On line 61, the code appends a null to mark the end of the word. p2 is then incremented to point to the beginning of the next word, and the offset of that word is pushed into the integer reference wordOffset. Finally, it returns true to indicate that a word has been found.

This is a classic example of code that is best understood by putting it into a debugger and stepping through its execution.

Summary

Pointers provide a powerful way to access data by indirection. Every variable has an address, which can be obtained using the address of operator (&). The address can be stored in a pointer.

Pointers are declared by writing the type of object that they point to, followed by the indirection operator (*) and the name of the pointer. Pointers should be initialized to point to an object or to NULL.

You access the value at the address stored in a pointer by using the indirection operator (*). You can declare const pointers, which cannot be reassigned to point to other objects, and pointers to const objects, which cannot be used to change the objects to which they point.

To create new objects on the free store, you use the new keyword and assign the address that is returned to a pointer. You free that memory by calling the delete keyword on the pointer. delete frees the memory, but it does not destroy the pointer. Therefore, you must reassign the pointer after its memory has been freed.

Q&A

Q Why are pointers so important?

A Today you saw how pointers are used to hold the address of objects on the free store and how they are used to pass arguments by reference. In addition, on Day 13, "Polymorphism," you will see how pointers are used in class polymorphism.

Q Why should I bother to declare anything on the free store?

A Objects on the free store persist after the return of a function. Additionally, the capability to store objects on the free store enables you to decide at runtime how many objects you need, instead of having to declare this in advance. This is explored in greater depth tomorrow.

Q Why should I declare an object `const` if it limits what I can do with it?

A As a programmer, you want to enlist the compiler in helping you find bugs. One serious bug that is difficult to find is a function that changes an object in ways that are not obvious to the calling function. Declaring an object `const` prevents such changes.

Workshop

The Workshop provides quiz questions to help you solidify your understanding of the material covered and exercises to provide you with experience in using what you learned. Try to answer the quiz and exercise questions before checking the answers in Appendix D, "Answers to Exercises and Quizzes," and make sure you understand the answers before continuing to the next day.

Quiz

1. What operator is used to determine the address of a variable?

2. What operator is used to find the value stored at an address held in a pointer?

3. What is a pointer?

4. What is the difference between the address stored in a pointer and the value at that address?

5. What is the difference between the indirection operator and the address of operator?

6. What is the difference between `const int * ptrOne` and `int * const ptrTwo`?

Exercises

1. What do these declarations do?

   a. `int * pOne;`

   b. `int vTwo;`

   c. `int * pThree = &vTwo;`

2. If you have an unsigned short variable named `yourAge`, how would you declare a pointer to manipulate `yourAge`?

3. Assign the value `50` to the variable `yourAge` by using the pointer that you declared in Exercise 2.

4. Write a small program that declares an integer and a pointer to the integer. Assign the address of the integer to the pointer. Use the pointer to set a value in the integer variable.

5. **BUG BUSTER**: What is wrong with this code?

```
#include <iostream.h>
int main()
{
    int *pInt;
    *pInt = 9;
    cout << "The value at pInt: " << *pInt;
    return 0;
}
```

6. **BUG BUSTER**: What is wrong with this code?

```
int main()
{
    int SomeVariable = 5;
    cout << "SomeVariable: " << SomeVariable << "\n";
    int *pVar = & SomeVariable;
    pVar = 9;
    cout << "SomeVariable: " << *pVar << "\n";
    return 0;
}
```

DAY 9

References

Yesterday you learned how to use pointers to manipulate objects on the free store and how to refer to those objects indirectly. References, the topic of today's lesson, give you almost all the power of pointers but with a much easier syntax. Today you will learn:

- What references are
- How references differ from pointers
- How to create references and use them
- What the limitations of references are
- How to pass values and objects into and out of functions by reference

What Is a Reference?

A *reference* is an alias or synonym; when you create a reference, you initialize it with the name of another object, the target. From that moment on, the reference acts as an alternative name for the target, and anything you do to the reference is really done to the target.

You create a reference by writing the type of the target object, followed by the reference operator (&), followed by the name of the reference. References can use any legal variable name, but many programmers prefer to prefix all reference names with "r." Thus, if you have an integer variable named someInt, you can make a reference to that variable by writing the following:

```
int &rSomeRef = someInt;
```

This is read as rSomeRef and is a reference to an integer that is initialized to refer to someInt. Listing 9.1 shows how references are created and used.

Note

Note that the reference operator (&) is the same symbol as the one used for the address of the operator. These are not the same operators, however, although clearly they are related.

INPUT   **LISTING 9.1**   Creating and Using References

```
1:      //Listing 9.1
2:      // Demonstrating the use of References
3:
4:      #include <iostream.h>
5:
6:      int main()
7:      {
8:          int  intOne;
9:          int &rSomeRef = intOne;
10:
11:         intOne = 5;
12:         cout << "intOne: " << intOne << endl;
13:         cout << "rSomeRef: " << rSomeRef << endl;
14:
15:         rSomeRef = 7;
16:         cout << "intOne: " << intOne << endl;
17:         cout << "rSomeRef: " << rSomeRef << endl;
18:         return 0;
19:     }
```

OUTPUT
```
intOne: 5
rSomeRef: 5
intOne: 7
rSomeRef: 7
```

ANALYSIS   On line 8, a local int variable, intOne, is declared. On line 9, a reference to an int, rSomeRef, is declared and initialized to refer to intOne. If you declare a reference but do not initialize it, you will get a compile-time error. References must be initialized.

On line 11, intOne is assigned the value 5. On lines 12 and 13, the values in intOne and rSomeRef are printed, and are, of course, the same.

On line 15, 7 is assigned to rSomeRef. Because this is a reference, it is an alias for intOne, and thus the 7 is really assigned to intOne, as is shown by the printouts on lines 16 and 17.

Using the Address of Operator & on References

If you ask a reference for its address, it returns the address of its target. That is the nature of references: They are aliases for the target. Listing 9.2 demonstrates this.

INPUT   **LISTING 9.2**   Taking the Address of a Reference

```
1:    //Listing 9.2
2:    // Demonstrating the use of References
3:
4:    #include <iostream.h>
5:
6:    int main()
7:    {
8:        int  intOne;
9:        int &rSomeRef = intOne;
10:
11:       intOne = 5;
12:       cout << "intOne: " << intOne << endl;
13:       cout << "rSomeRef: " << rSomeRef << endl;
14:
15:       cout << "&intOne: "  << &intOne << endl;
16:       cout << "&rSomeRef: " << &rSomeRef << endl;
17:
18:    return 0;
19:    }
```

```
intOne: 5
rSomeRef: 5
&intOne:  0x3500
&rSomeRef: 0x3500
```

> **Note**
>
> Your output may differ on the last two lines.

ANALYSIS Once again, rSomeRef is initialized as a reference to intOne. This time the addresses of the two variables are printed, and they are identical. C++ gives you no way to access the address of the reference itself because it is not meaningful as it would be if you were using a pointer or other variable. References are initialized when created, and they always act as a synonym for their target, even when the address of the operator is applied.

For example, if you have a class called President, you might declare an instance of that class as follows:

```
President William_Jefferson_Clinton;
```

You might then declare a reference to President and initialize it with this object:

```
President &Bill_Clinton = William_Jefferson_Clinton;
```

Only one President exists; both identifiers refer to the same object of the same class. Any action you take on Bill_Clinton will be taken on William_Jefferson_Clinton as well.

Be careful to distinguish between the & symbol on line 9 of Listing 9.2, which declares a reference to int named rSomeRef, and the & symbols on lines 15 and 16, which return the addresses of the integer variable intOne and the reference rSomeRef.

Normally, when you use a reference, you do not use the address of the operator. You simply use the reference as you would use the target variable. This is shown on line 13.

References Cannot Be Reassigned

Even experienced C++ programmers who know the rule—that references cannot be reassigned and are always aliases for their target—can be confused by what happens when you try to reassign a reference. What appears to be a reassignment turns out to be the assignment of a new value to the target. Listing 9.3 illustrates this fact.

INPUT   **LISTING 9.3**   Assigning to a Reference

```
1:    //Listing 9.3
2:    //Reassigning a reference
3:
4:    #include <iostream.h>
5:
6:    int main()
7:    {
8:        int  intOne;
9:        int &rSomeRef = intOne;
10:
11:       intOne = 5;
12:       cout << "intOne:\t" << intOne << endl;
13:       cout << "rSomeRef:\t" << rSomeRef << endl;
14:       cout << "&intOne:\t"  << &intOne << endl;
15:       cout << "&rSomeRef:\t" << &rSomeRef << endl;
16:
17:       int intTwo = 8;
18:       rSomeRef = intTwo;  // not what you think!
19:       cout << "\nintOne:\t" << intOne << endl;
20:       cout << "intTwo:\t" << intTwo << endl;
21:       cout << "rSomeRef:\t" << rSomeRef << endl;
22:       cout << "&intOne:\t"  << &intOne << endl;
23:       cout << "&intTwo:\t"  << &intTwo << endl;
24:       cout << "&rSomeRef:\t" << &rSomeRef << endl;
25:       return 0;
26:    }
```

OUTPUT

```
intOne:       5
rSomeRef:     5
&intOne:      0x213e
&rSomeRef:    0x213e

intOne:       8
intTwo:       8
rSomeRef:     8
&intOne:      0x213e
&intTwo:      0x2130
&rSomeRef:    0x213e
```

ANALYSIS   Once again, on lines 8 and 9, an integer variable and a reference to an integer are declared. The integer is assigned the value 5 on line 11, and the values and their addresses are printed on lines 12–15.

On line 17, a new variable, intTwo, is created and initialized with the value 8. On line 18, the programmer tries to reassign rSomeRef to now be an alias to the variable intTwo, but that is not what happens. What actually happens is that rSomeRef continues to act as an alias for intOne, so this assignment is equivalent to the following:

```
intOne = intTwo;
```

Sure enough, when the values of intOne and rSomeRef are printed (lines 19–21), they are the same as intTwo. In fact, when the addresses are printed on lines 22–24, you see that rSomeRef continues to refer to intOne and not intTwo.

Do	Don't
DO use references to create an alias to an object. **DO** initialize all references.	**DON'T** try to reassign a reference. **DON'T** confuse the address of operator with the reference operator.

What Can Be Referenced?

Any object can be referenced, including user-defined objects. Note that you create a reference to an object, but not to a class. You do not write this:

```
int & rIntRef = int;    // wrong
```

You must initialize rIntRef to a particular integer, such as this:

```
int howBig = 200;
int & rIntRef = howBig;
```

In the same way, you do not initialize a reference to a CAT:

```
CAT & rCatRef = CAT;    // wrong
```

You must initialize rCatRef to a particular CAT object:

```
CAT frisky;
CAT & rCatRef = frisky;
```

References to objects are used just like the object itself. Member data and methods are accessed using the normal class member access operator (.), and just as with the built-in types, the reference acts as an alias to the object. Listing 9.4 illustrates this.

INPUT   **LISTING 9.4**   References to Objects

```
1:    // Listing 9.4
2:    // References to class objects
3:
4:    #include <iostream.h>
```

```
5:
6:     class SimpleCat
7:     {
8:        public:
9:            SimpleCat (int age, int weight);
10:           ~SimpleCat() {}
11:           int GetAge() { return itsAge; }
12:           int GetWeight() { return itsWeight; }
13:       private:
14:           int itsAge;
15:           int itsWeight;
16:    };
17:
18:    SimpleCat::SimpleCat(int age, int weight)
19:    {
20:         itsAge = age;
21:         itsWeight = weight;
22:    }
23:
24:    int main()
25:    {
26:         SimpleCat Frisky(5,8);
27:         SimpleCat & rCat = Frisky;
28:
29:         cout << "Frisky is: ";
30:         cout << Frisky.GetAge() << " years old. \n";
31:         cout << "And Frisky weighs: ";
32:         cout << rCat.GetWeight() << " pounds. \n";
33:        return 0;
34:    }
```

9

OUTPUT   Frisky is: 5 years old.
             And Frisky weighs: 8 pounds.

ANALYSIS   On line 26, Frisky is declared to be a SimpleCat object. On line 27, a
               SimpleCat reference, rCat, is declared and initialized to refer to Frisky. On
lines 30 and 32, the SimpleCat accessor methods are accessed by using first the
SimpleCat object and then the SimpleCat reference. Note that the access is identical.
Again, the reference is an alias for the actual object.

References

Declare a reference by writing the type, followed by the reference operator (&), followed
by the reference name. References must be initialized at the time of creation.

```
Example 1:
        int hisAge;
        int &rAge = hisAge;

Example 2:
        CAT boots;
        CAT &rCatRef = boots;
```

Using Null Pointers and Null References

When pointers are not initialized or when they are deleted, they ought to be assigned to NULL. This is not true for references. In fact, a reference cannot be null, and a program with a reference to a null object is considered an invalid program. When a program is invalid, just about anything can happen. It can appear to work, or it can write weird (and incorrect) data to files on your disk. Both are possible outcomes of an invalid program.

Most compilers will support a null object without much complaint, with your program crashing only if you try to use the object in some way. Taking advantage of this, however, is still not a good idea. When you move your program to another machine or compiler, mysterious bugs may develop if you have null objects.

Passing Function Arguments by Reference

On Day 5, "Functions," you learned that functions have two limitations: Arguments are passed by value, and the return statement can return only one value.

Passing values to a function by reference can overcome both of these limitations. In C++, passing by reference is accomplished in two ways: using pointers and using references. Note the difference: You pass *by* reference using a pointer, or you pass *by* reference using a reference.

The syntax of using a pointer is different from that of using a reference, but the net effect is the same. Rather than a copy being created within the scope of the function, the actual original object is passed into the function.

On Day 5 you learned that functions are passed their parameters on the stack. When a function is passed a value by reference (using either pointers or references), the address of the object is put on the stack, not the entire object.

In fact, on some computers the address is actually held in a register and nothing is put on the stack. In either case, the compiler now knows how to get to the original object, and changes are made there and not in a copy.

Passing an object by reference enables the function to change the object being referred to.

Recall that Listing 5.5 in Day 5 demonstrated that a call to the swap() function did not affect the values in the calling function. Listing 5.5 is reproduced here as Listing 9.5, for your convenience.

INPUT   **LISTING 9.5**   Demonstrating Passing by Value

```
1:      //Listing 9.5 Demonstrates passing by value
2:
3:      #include <iostream.h>
4:
5:      void swap(int x, int y);
6:
7:      int main()
8:      {
9:         int x = 5, y = 10;
10:
11:        cout << "Main. Before swap, x: " << x << " y: "
➡    << y << "\n";
12:        swap(x,y);
13:        cout << "Main. After swap, x: " << x << " y: "
➡    << y << "\n";
14:     return 0;
15:     }
16:
17:     void swap (int x, int y)
18:     {
19:        int temp;
20:
21:        cout << "Swap. Before swap, x: " << x << " y: "
➡    << y << "\n";
22:
23:        temp = x;
24:        x = y;
25:        y = temp;
26:
27:        cout << "Swap. After swap, x: " << x << " y: "
➡    << y << "\n";
28:
29:     }
```

9

OUTPUT
```
Main. Before swap, x: 5 y: 10
Swap. Before swap, x: 5 y: 10
Swap. After swap, x: 10 y: 5
Main. After swap, x: 5 y: 10
```

ANALYSIS This program initializes two variables in `main()` and then passes them to the swap() function, which appears to swap them. When they are examined again in `main()`, they are unchanged!

The problem here is that x and y are being passed to swap() by value. That is, local copies were made in the function. What you want is to pass x and y by reference.

Two ways to solve this problem are possible in C++: You can make the parameters of swap() pointers to the original values, or you can pass in references to the original values.

Making swap() Work with Pointers

When you pass in a pointer, you pass in the address of the object, and thus the function can manipulate the value at that address. To make swap() change the actual values using pointers, the function, swap(), should be declared to accept two int pointers. Then, by dereferencing the pointers, the values of x and y will, in fact, be swapped. Listing 9.6 demonstrates this idea.

INPUT   **LISTING 9.6**   Simulating Pass by Reference Using Pointers

```
1:       // Demonstrates simulated pass by
2:       // reference Using pointers
3:       #include <iostream.h>
4:
5:       void swap(int *x, int *y);
6:
7:       int main()
8:       {
9:         int x = 5, y = 10;
10:
11:         cout << "Main. Before swap, x: " << x
 ➥   << " y: " << y << "\n";
12:         swap(&x,&y);
13:         cout << "Main. After swap, x: " << x
 ➥   << " y: " << y << "\n";
14:      return 0;
15:       }
16:
17:       void swap (int *px, int *py)
18:       {
19:         int temp;
```

```
20:
21:            cout << "Swap. Before swap, *px: "
➥    << *px << " *py: " << *py << "\n";
22:
23:               temp = *px;
24:               *px = *py;
25:               *py = temp;
26:
27:               cout << "Swap. After swap, *px: " << *px
➥    << " *py: " << *py << "\n";
28:
29:       }
```

OUTPUT
```
Main. Before swap, x: 5 y: 10
Swap. Before swap, *px: 5 *py: 10
Swap. After swap, *px: 10 *py: 5
Main. After swap, x: 10 y: 5
```

ANALYSIS Success!

On line 5, the prototype of swap() is changed to indicate that its two parameters will be pointers to int rather than int variables. When swap() is called on line 12, the addresses of x and y are passed as the arguments.

On line 19, a local variable, temp, is declared in the swap() function. temp need not be a pointer; it will just hold the value of *px (that is, the value of x in the calling function) for the life of the function. After the function returns, temp will no longer be needed.

On line 23, temp is assigned the value at px. On line 24, the value at px is assigned to the value at py. On line 25, the value stashed in temp (that is, the original value at px) is put into py.

The net effect of this is that the values in the calling function, whose address was passed to swap(), are, in fact, swapped.

Implementing swap() with References

The preceding program works, but the syntax of the swap() function is cumbersome in two ways. First, the repeated need to dereference the pointers within the swap() function makes it error-prone and hard to read. Second, the need to pass the address of the variables in the calling function makes the inner workings of swap() overly apparent to its users.

It is a goal of C++ to prevent the user of a function from worrying about how it works. Passing by pointers puts the burden on the calling function rather than where it belongs—on the called function. Listing 9.7 rewrites the swap() function, using references.

LISTING 9.7 swap() Rewritten with References

```
1:      //Listing 9.7 Demonstrates passing by reference
2:      // using references!
3:
4:        #include <iostream.h>
5:
6:        void swap(int &x, int &y);
7:
8:        int main()
9:        {
10:            int x = 5, y = 10;
11:
12:            cout << "Main. Before swap, x: " << x <<
➥ " y: " << y << "\n";
13:            swap(x,y);
14:            cout << "Main. After swap, x: " << x <<
➥ " y: " << y << "\n";
15:            return 0;
16:        }
17:
18:        void swap (int &rx, int &ry)
19:        {
20:            int temp;
21:
22:            cout << "Swap. Before swap, rx: " << rx <<
➥ " ry: " << ry << "\n";
23:
24:            temp = rx;
25:            rx = ry;
26:            ry = temp;
27:
28:            cout << "Swap. After swap, rx: " << rx << "
➥ ry: " << ry << "\n";
29:
30:                }
```

```
Main. Before swap, x: 5 y: 10
Swap. Before swap, rx: 5 ry: 10
Swap. After swap, rx: 10 ry: 5
Main. After swap, x: 10, y: 5
```

Just as in the example with pointers, two variables are declared on line 10, and their values are printed on line 12. On line 13, the function swap() is called, but note that x and y, not their addresses, are passed. The calling function simply passes the variables.

When swap() is called, program execution jumps to line 18, where the variables are identified as references. Their values are printed on line 22, but note that no special operators are required. These are aliases for the original values and can be used as such.

On lines 24–26, the values are swapped, and then printed on line 28. Program execution jumps back to the calling function, and on line 14, the values are printed in `main()`. Because the parameters to `swap()` are declared to be references, the values from `main()` are passed by reference, and thus are changed in `main()` as well. Another successful method.

References provide the convenience and ease of use of normal variables, with the power and pass-by-reference capability of pointers!

9

Understanding Function Headers and Prototypes

Listing 9.6 shows `swap()` using pointers, and Listing 9.7 shows it using references. Using the function that takes references is easier, and the code is easier to read, but how does the calling function know if the values are passed by reference or by value? As a client (or user) of `swap()`, the programmer must ensure that `swap()` will, in fact, change the parameters.

This is another use for the function prototype. By examining the parameters declared in the prototype, which is typically in a header file along with all the other prototypes, the programmer knows that the values passed into `swap()` are passed by reference, and thus will be swapped properly.

If `swap()` had been a member function of a class, the class declaration, also available in a header file, would have supplied this information.

In C++, clients of classes and functions rely on the header file to tell all that is needed; it acts as the interface to the class or function. The actual implementation is hidden from the client. This enables the programmer to focus on the problem at hand and to use the class or function without concern for how it works.

When Colonel John Roebling designed the Brooklyn Bridge, he worried in detail about how the concrete was poured and how the wire for the bridge was manufactured. He was intimately involved in the mechanical and chemical processes required to create his materials. Today, however, engineers make more efficient use of their time by using well-understood building materials, without regard to how their manufacturer produced them.

It is the goal of C++ to enable programmers to rely on well-understood classes and functions without regard to their internal workings. These "component parts" can be assembled to produce a program, much the same way wires, pipes, clamps, and other parts are assembled to produce buildings and bridges.

In much the same way that an engineer examines the spec sheet for a pipe to determine its load-bearing capacity, volume, fitting size, and so forth, a C++ programmer reads the interface of a function or class to determine what services it provides, what parameters it takes, and what values it returns.

This is also known as taking the *black box* approach. You know the inputs to the black box, you have a general idea what it does, and you get the expected outputs. But you have no idea how this happened because you cannot see the inner workings (nor should you care—there are plenty of other things to worry about).

A simple example of this is the sqrt() function in the standard library. You know it takes a floating-point argument and it returns the square root of that argument. You know the interface (input and output), you know the general details (calculate the square root), but you don't know the intimate details of how that calculation occurs.

Returning Multiple Values Using Pointers

As discussed, functions can only return one value. What if you need to get two values back from a function? One way to solve this problem is to pass two objects into the function, by reference. The function can then fill the objects with the correct values. Because passing by reference allows a function to change the original objects, this effectively enables the function to return two pieces of information. This approach bypasses the return value of the function, which can then be reserved for reporting errors.

Again, this can be done with references or pointers. Listing 9.8 demonstrates a function that returns three values: two as pointer parameters and one as the return value of the function.

INPUT   **LISTING 9.8**   Returning Values with Pointers

```
1:      //Listing 9.8
2:      // Returning multiple values from a function
3:      // using pointers
4:      #include <iostream.h>
5:
6:      short Factor(int n, int* pSquared, int* pCubed);
7:
8:      int main()
9:      {
10:         int number, squared, cubed;
11:         short error;
12:
13:         cout << "Enter a number (0 - 20): ";
14:         cin >> number;
```

```
15:
16:        error = Factor(number, &squared, &cubed);
17:
18:        if (!error)
19:        {
20:            cout << "number: " << number << "\n";
21:            cout << "square: " << squared << "\n";
22:            cout << "cubed: "  << cubed   << "\n";
23:        }
24:        else
25:            cout << "Error encountered!!\n";
26:        return 0;
27:    }
28:
29:    short Factor(int n, int *pSquared, int *pCubed)
30:    {
31:    short Value = 0;
32:        if (n > 20)
33:            Value = 1;
34:        else
35:        {
36:            *pSquared = n*n;
37:            *pCubed = n*n*n;
38:            Value = 0;
39:        }
40:        return Value;
41:    }
```

OUTPUT

```
Enter a number (0 - 20): 3
number: 3
square: 9
cubed: 27
```

ANALYSIS On line 10, number, squared, and cubed are defined as int's. number is assigned a value based on user input. This value and the addresses of squared and cubed are passed to the function Factor().

Factor() examines the first parameter, which is passed by Value. If it is greater than 20 (the maximum value this function can handle), it sets return Value to a simple error value. Note that the return value from Function() is reserved for either this error value or the value 0, indicating all went well, and note that the function returns this value on line 40.

The actual values needed, the square and cube of number, are returned not by using the return mechanism, but rather by changing the original variables (whose addresses are contained in the pointers that were passed into the function).

On lines 36 and 37, the original variables (referenced via pointers) are assigned their return values. On line 38, return Value is assigned a success value. On line 40, return Value is returned.

One improvement to this program might be to declare the following:

```
enum ERROR_VALUE { SUCCESS, FAILURE};
```

Then, rather than returning 0 or 1, the program could return SUCCESS or FAILURE.

Returning Values by Reference

Although Listing 9.8 works, it can be made easier to read and maintain by using references rather than pointers. Listing 9.9 shows the same program rewritten to use references and to incorporate the ERROR enumeration.

INPUT   **LISTING 9.9**   Listing 9.8 Rewritten Using References

```
1:      //Listing 9.9
2:      // Returning multiple values from a function
3:      // using references
4:
5:      #include <iostream.h>
6:
7:      typedef unsigned short USHORT;
8:      enum ERR_CODE { SUCCESS, ERROR };
9:
10:     ERR_CODE Factor(USHORT, USHORT&, USHORT&);
11:
12:     int main()
13:     {
14:         USHORT number, squared, cubed;
15:         ERR_CODE result;
16:
17:         cout << "Enter a number (0 - 20): ";
18:         cin >> number;
19:
20:         result = Factor(number, squared, cubed);
21:
22:         if (result == SUCCESS)
23:         {
24:             cout << "number: " << number << "\n";
25:             cout << "square: " << squared << "\n";
26:             cout << "cubed: " << cubed   << "\n";
27:         }
28:         else
29:         cout << "Error encountered!!\n";
30:     return 0;
31:       }
```

```
32:
33:     ERR_CODE Factor(USHORT n, USHORT &rSquared, USHORT &rCubed)
34:     {
35:         if (n > 20)
36:             return ERROR;    // simple error code
37:         else
38:         {
39:             rSquared = n*n;
40:             rCubed = n*n*n;
41:             return SUCCESS;
42:         }
43:     }
```

OUTPUT

```
Enter a number (0 - 20): 3
number: 3
square: 9
cubed: 27
```

ANALYSIS Listing 9.9 is identical to Listing 9.8, with two exceptions. The ERR_CODE enumeration makes the error reporting a bit more explicit on lines 36 and 41, as well as the error handling on line 22.

The larger change, however, is that Factor() is now declared to take references to squared and cubed rather than to pointers. This makes the manipulation of these parameters far simpler and easier to understand.

Passing by Reference for Efficiency

Each time you pass an object into a function by value, a copy of the object is made. Each time you return an object from a function by value, another copy is made.

On Day 5, you learned that these objects are copied onto the stack. Doing so takes time and memory. For small objects, such as the built-in integer values, this is a trivial cost.

However, with larger, user-created objects, the cost is greater. The size of a user-created object on the stack is the sum of each of its member variables. These, in turn, can each be user-created objects, and passing such a massive structure by copying it onto the stack can be very expensive in performance and memory consumption.

Another cost occurs as well. With the classes you create, each of these temporary copies is created when the compiler calls a special constructor: the copy constructor. Tomorrow you will learn how copy constructors work and how you can make your own, but for now it is enough to know that the copy constructor is called each time a temporary copy of the object is put on the stack.

When the temporary object is destroyed, which happens when the function returns, the object's destructor is called. If an object is returned by the function by value, a copy of that object must be made and destroyed as well.

With large objects, these constructor and destructor calls can be expensive in speed and use of memory. To illustrate this idea, Listing 9.10 creates a stripped-down, user-created object: SimpleCat. A real object would be larger and more expensive, but this is sufficient to show how often the copy constructor and destructor are called.

Listing 9.10 creates the SimpleCat object and then calls two functions. The first function receives the Cat by value and then returns it by value. The second one receives a pointer to the object, rather than the object itself, and returns a pointer to the object.

INPUT   **LISTING 9.10**   Passing Objects by Reference Using Pointers

```
1:    //Listing 9.10
2:    // Passing pointers to objects
3:
4:    #include <iostream.h>
5:
6:    class SimpleCat
7:    {
8:    public:
9:            SimpleCat ();                    // constructor
10:           SimpleCat(SimpleCat&);      // copy constructor
11:           ~SimpleCat();                    // destructor
12:    };
13:
14:    SimpleCat::SimpleCat()
15:    {
16:            cout << "Simple Cat Constructor...\n";
17:    }
18:
19:    SimpleCat::SimpleCat(SimpleCat&)
20:    {
21:            cout << "Simple Cat Copy Constructor...\n";
22:    }
23:
24:    SimpleCat::~SimpleCat()
25:    {
26:            cout << "Simple Cat Destructor...\n";
27:    }
28:
29:    SimpleCat FunctionOne (SimpleCat theCat);
30:    SimpleCat* FunctionTwo (SimpleCat *theCat);
31:
32:    int main()
33:    {
```

```
34:            cout << "Making a cat...\n";
35:            SimpleCat Frisky;
36:            cout << "Calling FunctionOne...\n";
37:            FunctionOne(Frisky);
38:            cout << "Calling FunctionTwo...\n";
39:            FunctionTwo(&Frisky);
40:        return 0;
41:    }
42:
43:    // FunctionOne, passes by value
44:    SimpleCat FunctionOne(SimpleCat theCat)
45:    {
46:                    cout << "Function One. Returning...\n";
47:                    return theCat;
48:    }
49:
50:    // functionTwo, passes by reference
51:    SimpleCat* FunctionTwo (SimpleCat  *theCat)
52:    {
53:                    cout << "Function Two. Returning...\n";
54:                    return theCat;
55:    }
```

OUTPUT

```
1:  Making a cat...
2:  Simple Cat Constructor...
3:  Calling FunctionOne...
4:  Simple Cat Copy Constructor...
5:  Function One. Returning...
6:  Simple Cat Copy Constructor...
7:  Simple Cat Destructor...
8:  Simple Cat Destructor...
9:  Calling FunctionTwo...
10: Function Two. Returning...
11: Simple Cat Destructor...
```

Note

Line numbers in the above output will not print. They were added to aid in the analysis.

ANALYSIS   A very simplified SimpleCat class is declared on lines 6 to 12. The constructor, copy constructor, and destructor all print an informative message so that you can tell when they are called.

On line 34, main() prints out a message that is seen on output line 1. On line 35, a SimpleCat object is instantiated. This causes the constructor to be called, and the output from the constructor is seen on output line 2.

On line 36, main() reports that it is calling FunctionOne, which creates output line 3. Because FunctionOne() is called passing the SimpleCat object by value, a copy of the SimpleCat object is made on the stack as an object local to the called function. This causes the copy constructor to be called, which creates output line 4.

Program execution jumps to line 46 in the called function, which prints an informative message, output line 5. The function then returns the SimpleCat object by value. This creates yet another copy of the object, calling the copy constructor and producing line 6.

The return value from FunctionOne() is not assigned to any object, so the temporary value created for the return is thrown away, calling the destructor, which produces output line 7. Because FunctionOne() has ended, its local copy goes out of scope and is destroyed, calling the destructor and producing output line 8.

Program execution returns to main(), and FunctionTwo() is called, but the parameter is passed by reference. No copy is produced, so there is no output. FunctionTwo() prints the message that appears as output line 10 and then returns the SimpleCat object, again by reference, and so again produces no calls to the constructor or destructor.

Finally, the program ends and Frisky goes out of scope, causing one final call to the destructor and printing output line 11.

The net effect of this is that the call to FunctionOne(), because it passed the cat by value, produced two calls to the copy constructor and two to the destructor, whereas the call to FunctionTwo() produced none.

Passing a const Pointer

Although passing a pointer to FunctionTwo() is more efficient, it is dangerous. FunctionTwo() is not meant to be allowed to change the SimpleCat object that it is passed, yet it is given the address of the SimpleCat. This seriously exposes the object to change and defeats the protection offered in passing by value.

Passing by value is like giving a museum a photograph of your masterpiece instead of the real thing. If vandals mark it up, there is no harm done to the original. Passing by reference is like sending your home address to the museum and inviting guests to come over and look at the real thing.

The solution is to pass a pointer to a constant SimpleCat. Doing so prevents calling any non-const method on SimpleCat, and thus protects the object from change. Listing 9.11 demonstrates this idea.

INPUT   **LISTING 9.11**   Passing const Pointers

```
1:  //Listing 9.11
2:      // Passing const pointers to objects
3:
4:      #include <iostream.h>
5:
6:      class SimpleCat
7:      {
8:      public:
9:              SimpleCat();
10:             SimpleCat(SimpleCat&);
11:             ~SimpleCat();
12:
13:             int GetAge() const { return itsAge; }
14:             void SetAge(int age) { itsAge = age; }
15:
16:      private:
17:             int itsAge;
18:         };
19:
20:      SimpleCat::SimpleCat()
21:      {
22:             cout << "Simple Cat Constructor...\n";
23:             itsAge = 1;
24:      }
25:
26:      SimpleCat::SimpleCat(SimpleCat&)
27:      {
28:             cout << "Simple Cat Copy Constructor...\n";
29:      }
30:
31:      SimpleCat::~SimpleCat()
32:      {
33:             cout << "Simple Cat Destructor...\n";
34:      }
35:
36:const SimpleCat * const FunctionTwo (const SimpleCat * const theCat);
37:
38:          int main()
39:          {
40:             cout << "Making a cat...\n";
41:             SimpleCat Frisky;
42:             cout << "Frisky is " ;
43:             cout << Frisky.GetAge();
44:             cout << " years old\n";
45:             int age = 5;
46:             Frisky.SetAge(age);
47:             cout << "Frisky is " ;
48:             cout << Frisky.GetAge();
```

9

continues

LISTING 9.11 CONTINUED

```
49:                        cout << " years old\n";
50:                        cout << "Calling FunctionTwo...\n";
51:                        FunctionTwo(&Frisky);
52:                        cout << "Frisky is " ;
53:                        cout << Frisky.GetAge();
54:                        cout << " years old\n";
55:     return 0;
56:             }
57:
58:     // functionTwo, passes a const pointer
59:     const SimpleCat * const FunctionTwo
➥(const SimpleCat * const theCat)
60:     {
61:             cout << "Function Two. Returning...\n";
62:             cout << "Frisky is now " << theCat->GetAge();
63:             cout << " years old \n";
64:             // theCat->SetAge(8);    const!
65:             return theCat;
66:             }
```

OUTPUT

```
Making a cat...
Simple Cat constructor...
Frisky is 1 years old
Frisky is 5 years old
Calling FunctionTwo...
FunctionTwo. Returning...
Frisky is now 5 years old
Frisky is 5 years old
Simple Cat Destructor...
```

ANALYSIS SimpleCat has added two accessor functions, GetAge() on line 13, which is a const function, and SetAge() on line 14, which is not a const function. It has also added the member variable itsAge on line 17.

The constructor, copy constructor, and destructor are still defined to print their messages. The copy constructor is never called, however, because the object is passed by reference and no copies are made. On line 41, an object is created, and its default age is printed, starting on line 42.

On line 46, itsAge is set using the accessor SetAge, and the result is printed on line 47. FunctionOne is not used in this program, but FunctionTwo() is called. FunctionTwo() has changed slightly; the parameter and return value are now declared, on line 36, to take a constant pointer to a constant object and to return a constant pointer to a constant object.

Because the parameter and return value are still passed by reference, no copies are made and the copy constructor is not called. The pointer in FunctionTwo(), however, is now constant, and thus cannot call the non-const method, SetAge(). If the call to SetAge() on line 64 was not commented out, the program would not compile.

Note that the object created in main() is not constant, and Frisky can call SetAge(). The address of this non-constant object is passed to FunctionTwo(), but because FunctionTwo()'s declaration declares the pointer to be a constant pointer to a constant object, the object is treated as if it were constant!

References as an Alternative to Pointers

Listing 9.11 solves the problem of making extra copies, and thus saves the calls to the copy constructor and destructor. It uses constant pointers to constant objects, and thereby solves the problem of the function changing the object. It is still somewhat cumbersome, however, because the objects passed to the function are pointers.

Because you know the object will never be null, it would be easier to work within the function if a reference was passed in, rather than a pointer. Listing 9.12 illustrates this.

INPUT   **LISTING 9.12**   Passing References to Objects

```
1: //Listing 9.12
2: // Passing references to objects
3:
4:    #include <iostream.h>
5:
6:    class SimpleCat
7:    {
8:    public:
9:            SimpleCat();
10:            SimpleCat(SimpleCat&);
11:            ~SimpleCat();
12:
13:            int GetAge() const { return itsAge; }
14:            void SetAge(int age) { itsAge = age; }
15:
16:    private:
17:            int itsAge;
18:        };
19:
20:        SimpleCat::SimpleCat()
21:        {
22:                cout << "Simple Cat Constructor...\n";
23:                itsAge = 1;
24:        }
25:
```

continues

LISTING **9.12**   CONTINUED

```
26:      SimpleCat::SimpleCat(SimpleCat&)
27:      {
28:              cout << "Simple Cat Copy Constructor...\n";
29:      }
30:
31:      SimpleCat::~SimpleCat()
32:      {
33:              cout << "Simple Cat Destructor...\n";
34:      }
35:
36:      const    SimpleCat & FunctionTwo (const SimpleCat & theCat);
37:
38:      int main()
39:      {
40:              cout << "Making a cat...\n";
41:              SimpleCat Frisky;
42:              cout << "Frisky is " << Frisky.GetAge() << " years old\n";
43:              int age = 5;
44:              Frisky.SetAge(age);
45:              cout << "Frisky is " << Frisky.GetAge() << " years old\n";
46:              cout << "Calling FunctionTwo...\n";
47:              FunctionTwo(Frisky);
48:              cout << "Frisky is " << Frisky.GetAge() << " years old\n";
49:      return 0;
50:      }
51:
52:      // functionTwo, passes a ref to a const object
53:      const SimpleCat & FunctionTwo (const SimpleCat & theCat)
54:      {
55:                  cout << "Function Two. Returning...\n";
56:                  cout << "Frisky is now " << theCat.GetAge();
57:                  cout << " years old \n";
58:                  // theCat.SetAge(8);    const!
59:                  return theCat;
60:      }
```

OUTPUT
```
Making a cat...
Simple Cat constructor...
Frisky is 1 years old
Frisky is 5 years old
Calling FunctionTwo...
FunctionTwo. Returning...
Frisky is now 5 years old
Frisky is 5 years old
Simple Cat Destructor...
```

ANALYSIS The output is identical to that produced by Listing 9.11. The only significant change is that FunctionTwo() now takes and returns a reference to a constant object. Again, working with references is somewhat simpler than working with pointers, and the same savings and efficiency are achieved, as well as the safety provided by using const.

9

---

const References

C++ programmers do not usually differentiate between "constant reference to a SimpleCat object" and "reference to a constant SimpleCat object." References themselves can never be reassigned to refer to another object, and so they are always constant. If the keyword const is applied to a reference, it is to make the object referred to be constant.

Understanding When to Use References and When to Use Pointers

C++ programmers strongly prefer references to pointers. References are cleaner and easier to use, and they do a better job of hiding information, as you saw in the previous example.

References cannot be reassigned, however. If you need to point first to one object and then to another, you must use a pointer. References cannot be null, so if any chance exists that the object in question may be null, you must not use a reference. You must use a pointer.

An example of the latter concern is the operator new. If new cannot allocate memory on the free store, it returns a null pointer. Because a reference cannot be null, you must not initialize a reference to this memory until you check that it is not null. The following example shows how to handle this:

```
int *pInt = new int;
if (pInt != NULL)
int &rInt = *pInt;
```

In this example a pointer to int, pInt, is declared and initialized with the memory returned by the operator new. The address in pInt is tested, and if it is not null, pInt is dereferenced. The result of dereferencing an int variable is an int object, and rInt is initialized to refer to that object. Thus, rInt becomes an alias to the int returned by the operator new.

Do	Don't
DO pass parameters by reference whenever possible.	**DON'T** use pointers if references will work.
DO return by reference whenever possible.	**DON'T** return a reference to a local object.
DO use const to protect references and pointers whenever possible.	

Mixing References and Pointers

It is perfectly legal to declare both pointers and references in the same function parameter list, along with objects passed by value. Here is an example:

```
CAT * SomeFunction (Person &theOwner, House *theHouse, int age);
```

This declaration says that SomeFunction takes three parameters. The first is a reference to a Person object, the second is a pointer to a House object, and the third is an integer. It returns a pointer to a CAT object.

The question of where to put the reference (&) or indirection (*) operator when declaring these variables is a great controversy. You may legally write any of the following:

```
1:   CAT&  rFrisky;

2:   CAT & rFrisky;

3:   CAT  &rFrisky;
```

Note

Whitespace is completely ignored, so anywhere you see a space here you may put as many spaces, tabs, and new lines as you like.

Setting aside freedom of expression issues, which is best? Here are arguments for all three:

The argument for case 1 is that rFrisky is a variable whose name is rFrisky and whose type can be thought of as "reference to CAT object." Thus, this argument goes, the & should be with the type.

The counter-argument is that the type is CAT. The & is part of the "declarator," which includes the variable name and the ampersand. More important, having the & near the CAT can lead to the following bug:

```
CAT&  rFrisky, rBoots;
```

Casual examination of this line would lead you to think that both rFrisky and rBoots are references to CAT objects, but you would be wrong. This really says that rFrisky is a reference to a CAT, and rBoots (despite its name) is not a reference but a plain old CAT variable. This should be rewritten as follows:

```
CAT     &rFrisky, rBoots;
```

The answer to this objection is that declarations of references and variables should never be combined like this. The right answer is

```
CAT& rFrisky;
CAT  boots;
```

Finally, many programmers opt out of the argument and go with the middle position, that of putting the & in the middle of the two, as illustrated in case 2.

Of course, everything said so far about the reference operator (&) applies equally well to the indirection operator (*). The important thing is to recognize that reasonable people differ in their perceptions of the one true way. Choose a style that works for you, and be consistent within any one program; clarity is, and remains, the goal.

Many programmers like the following conventions for declaring references and pointers:

1. Put the ampersand and asterisk in the middle, with a space on either side.

2. Never declare references, pointers, and variables all on the same line.

Do Not Return a Reference to an Object That Is Not in Scope!

When C++ programmers learn to pass by reference, they have a tendency to go hog-wild. It is possible, however, to overdo it. Remember that a reference is always an alias to some other object. If you pass a reference into or out of a function, be sure to ask yourself, "What is the object I'm aliasing, and will it still exist every time it's used?"

Listing 9.13 illustrates the danger of returning a reference to an object that no longer exists.

INPUT   **LISTING 9.13**   Returning a Reference to a Non-existent Object

```
1:     // Listing 9.13
2:     // Returning a reference to an object
```

continues

LISTING 9.13   CONTINUED

```
 3:        // which no longer exists
 4:
 5:        #include <iostream.h>
 6:
 7:        class SimpleCat
 8:        {
 9:        public:
10:               SimpleCat (int age, int weight);
11:               ~SimpleCat() {}
12:               int GetAge() { return itsAge; }
13:               int GetWeight() { return itsWeight; }
14:          private:
15:               int itsAge;
16:               int itsWeight;
17:          };
18:
19:        SimpleCat::SimpleCat(int age, int weight)
20:        {
21:          itsAge = age;
22:          itsWeight = weight;
23:        }
24:
25:        SimpleCat &TheFunction();
26:
27:        int main()
28:        {
29:               SimpleCat &rCat = TheFunction();
30:               int age = rCat.GetAge();
31:               cout << "rCat is " << age << " years old!\n";
32:          return 0;
33:          }
34:
35:        SimpleCat &TheFunction()
36:        {
37:               SimpleCat Frisky(5,9);
38:               return Frisky;
39:          }
```

OUTPUT

```
./lst09-13.cxx: In function `class SimpleCat & TheFunction()':
./lst09-13.cxx:38: warning: reference to local variable `Frisky'
returned
```

Caution

The GNU compilers will not compile this program. It also will not compile on the Borland compiler, but it will on Microsoft compilers.

Returning a reference to a local variable is a bad coding practice.

ANALYSIS On lines 7–17, SimpleCat is declared. On line 29, a reference to a SimpleCat is initialized with the results of calling TheFunction(), which is declared on line 25 to return a reference to a SimpleCat.

The body of TheFunction() declares a local object of type SimpleCat and initializes its age and weight. It then returns that local object by reference. The GNU compilers are smart enough to catch this error and will not let you run the program. Some other compilers will let you run the program, with unpredictable results.

When TheFunction() returns, the local object, Frisky, will be destroyed (painlessly, I assure you). The reference returned by this function will be an alias to a non-existent object, and this is a bad thing.

Returning a Reference to an Object on the Heap

You might be tempted to solve the problem in Listing 9.13 by having TheFunction() create Frisky on the heap. That way, when you return from TheFunction(), Frisky will still exist.

The problem with this approach is: What do you do with the memory allocated for Frisky when you are done with it? Listing 9.14 illustrates this problem.

INPUT **LISTING 9.14** Memory Leaks

```
1:      // Listing 9.14
2:      // Resolving memory leaks
3:      #include <iostream.h>
4:
5:      class SimpleCat
6:      {
7:      public:
8:              SimpleCat (int age, int weight);
9:              ~SimpleCat() {}
10:             int GetAge() { return itsAge; }
11:             int GetWeight() { return itsWeight; }
12:
13:     private:
14:             int itsAge;
15:             int itsWeight;
16:     };
17:
18:     SimpleCat::SimpleCat(int age, int weight)
19:     {
```

continues

LISTING 9.14   CONTINUED

```
20:          itsAge = age;
21:          itsWeight = weight;
22:      }
23:
24:      SimpleCat & TheFunction();
25:
26:      int main()
27:      {
28:          SimpleCat & rCat = TheFunction();
29:          int age = rCat.GetAge();
30:          cout << "rCat is " << age << " years old!\n";
31:          cout << "&rCat: " << &rCat << endl;
32:          // How do you get rid of that memory?
33:          SimpleCat * pCat = &rCat;
34:          delete pCat;
35:          // Uh oh, rCat now refers to ??
36:      return 0;
37:      }
38:
39:      SimpleCat &TheFunction()
40:      {
41:          SimpleCat * pFrisky = new SimpleCat(5,9);
42:          cout << "pFrisky: " << pFrisky << endl;
43:          return *pFrisky;
44:      }
```

```
pFrisky: 0x620b0
rCat is 5 years old!
&rCat: 0x620b0
```

> **Caution**   The code shown in Listing 9.14 compiles, links, and appears to work. But it is a time bomb waiting to go off because there is a hidden memory leak.

ANALYSIS   TheFunction() has been changed so that it no longer returns a reference to a local variable. Memory is allocated on the free store and assigned to a pointer on line 41. The address that pointer holds is printed, and then the pointer is dereferenced and the SimpleCat object is returned by reference.

On line 28, the return of TheFunction() is assigned to a reference to SimpleCat, and that object is used to obtain the cat's age, which is printed on line 30.

To prove that the reference declared in main() is referring to the object put on the free store in TheFunction(), the address of operator is applied to rCat. Sure enough, it displays the address of the object it refers to, and this matches the address of the object on the free store.

So far, so good. But how will that memory be freed? You cannot use delete on the reference. One clever solution is to create another pointer and initialize it with the address obtained from rCat. This does delete the memory, and it plugs the memory leak. One small problem, though: What is rCat referring to after line 34? As stated earlier, a reference must always alias an actual object; if it references a null object (as this does now), the program is invalid.

Note

> It cannot be overemphasized that a program with a reference to a null object may compile, but it is invalid and its performance is unpredictable.

Three solutions exist to this problem. The first is to declare a SimpleCat object on line 28 and to return that cat from TheFunction by value. The second is to go ahead and declare the SimpleCat on the free store in TheFunction(), but have TheFunction() return a pointer to that memory. Then the calling function can delete the pointer when it is done.

The third workable solution, and the right one, is to declare the object in the calling function and then to pass it to TheFunction() by reference.

Pointer, Pointer, Who Has the Pointer?

When your program allocates memory on the free store, a pointer is returned. It is imperative that you keep a pointer to that memory because after the pointer is lost, the memory cannot be deleted and becomes a memory leak.

As you pass this block of memory between functions, someone will "own" the pointer. Typically, the value in the block will be passed using references, and the function that created the memory is the one that deletes it. But this is a general rule, not an ironclad one.

It is dangerous for one function to create memory and another to free it, however. Ambiguity about who owns the pointer can lead to one of two problems: forgetting to delete a pointer or deleting it twice. Either one can cause serious problems in your program. It is safer to build your functions so that they delete the memory they create.

If you are writing a function that needs to create memory and then pass it back to the calling function, consider changing your interface. Have the calling function allocate the memory and then pass it into your function by reference. This moves all memory management out of your program and back to the function that is prepared to delete it.

Do	Don't
DO pass parameters by value when you must.	DON'T pass by reference if the item referred to may go out of scope.
DO return by value when you must.	DON'T use references to null objects.

Summary

Today you learned what references are and how they compare to pointers. You saw that references must be initialized to refer to an existing object and cannot be reassigned to refer to anything else. Any action taken on a reference is in fact taken on the reference's target object. Proof of this is that taking the address of a reference returns the address of the target.

You saw that passing objects by reference can be more efficient than passing by value. Passing by reference also allows the called function to change the value in the arguments back in the calling function.

You saw that arguments to functions and values returned from functions can be passed by reference, and that this can be implemented with pointers or with references.

You saw how to use pointers to constant objects and constant references to pass values between functions safely while achieving the efficiency of passing by reference.

Q&A

Q Why have references if pointers can do everything references can?

A References are easier to use and to understand. The indirection is hidden, and no need exists to repeatedly dereference the variable.

Q Why have pointers if references are easier?

A References cannot be null, and they cannot be reassigned. Pointers offer greater flexibility but are slightly more difficult to use.

Q **Why would you ever return by value from a function?**

A If the object being returned is local, you must return by value or you will be returning a reference to a non-existent object.

Q **Given the danger in returning by reference, why not always return by value?**

A Far greater efficiency is achieved in returning by reference. Memory is saved and the program runs faster.

Workshop

The Workshop contains quiz questions to help solidify your understanding of the material covered and exercises to provide you with experience in using what you learned. Try to answer the quiz and exercise questions before checking the answers in Appendix D, "Answers to Exercises and Quizzes," and make sure you understand the answers before continuing tomorrow.

Quiz

1. What is the difference between a reference and a pointer?
2. When must you use a pointer rather than a reference?
3. What does new return if there is insufficient memory to make your new object?
4. What is a constant reference?
5. What is the difference between passing by reference and passing a reference?

Exercises

1. Write a program that declares an int, a reference to an int, and a pointer to an int. Use the pointer and the reference to manipulate the value in the int.
2. Write a program that declares a constant pointer to a constant integer. Initialize the pointer to an integer variable, varOne. Assign 6 to varOne. Use the pointer to assign 7 to varOne. Create a second integer variable, varTwo. Reassign the pointer to varTwo. Do not compile this exercise yet.
3. Now compile the program in Exercise 2. What produces errors? What produces warnings?
4. Write a program that produces a stray pointer.
5. Fix the program from Exercise 4.
6. Write a program that produces a memory leak.
7. Fix the program from Exercise 6.

8. **BUG BUSTER**: What is wrong with this program?

```
1:      #include <iostream.h>
2:
3:      class CAT
4:      {
5:        public:
6:            CAT(int age) { itsAge = age; }
7:            ~CAT(){}
8:            int GetAge() const { return itsAge;}
9:        private:
10:           int itsAge;
11:     };
12:
13:     CAT & MakeCat(int age);
14:     int main()
15:     {
16:        int age = 7;
17:        CAT Boots = MakeCat(age);
18:        cout << "Boots is " << Boots.GetAge() << " years old\n";
           return 0;
19:     }
20:
21:     CAT & MakeCat(int age)
22:     {
23:        CAT * pCat = new CAT(age);
24:        return *pCat;
25:     }
```

9. Fix the program from Exercise 8.

DAY 10

Advanced Functions

On Day 5, "Functions," you learned the fundamentals of working with functions. Now that you know how pointers and references work, you can do more with functions. Today you will learn:

- How to overload member functions
- How to overload operators
- How to write functions to support classes with dynamically allocated variables

Overloading Member Functions

On Day 5, you learned how to implement function polymorphism, or function overloading, by writing two or more functions with the same name but with different parameters. Class member functions can be overloaded as well, in much the same way.

The `Rectangle` class, demonstrated in Listing 10.1, has two `DrawShape()` functions. One, which takes no parameters, draws the rectangle based on the class's current values. The other takes two values, `width` and `height`, and draws the rectangle based on those values, ignoring the current class values.

```
1:      //Listing 10.1 Overloading class member functions
2:      #include <iostream.h>
3:
4: 5:      // Rectangle class declaration
6:      class Rectangle
7:      {
8:      public:
9:          // constructors
10:         Rectangle(int width, int height);
11:         ~Rectangle(){}
12:
13:         // overloaded class function DrawShape
14:         void DrawShape() const;
15:         void DrawShape(int aWidth, int aHeight) const;
16:
17:     private:
18:         int itsWidth;
19:         int itsHeight;
20:     };
21:
22:     //Constructor implementation
23:     Rectangle::Rectangle(int width, int height)
24:     {
25:         itsWidth = width;
26:         itsHeight = height;
27:     }
28:
29:
30:     // Overloaded DrawShape - takes no values
31:     // Draws based on current class member values
32:     void Rectangle::DrawShape() const
33:     {
34:         DrawShape( itsWidth, itsHeight);
35:     }
36:
37:
38:     // overloaded DrawShape - takes two values
39:     // draws shape based on the parameters
40:     void Rectangle::DrawShape(int width, int height) const
41:     {
42:         for (int i = 0; i<height; i++)
43:         {
44:           for (int j = 0; j< width; j++)
45:           {
46:              cout << "*";
47:           }
48:           cout << "\n";
49:         }
```

```
50:     }
51:
52:     // Driver program to demonstrate overloaded functions
53:     int main()
54:     {
55:         // initialize a rectangle to 30,5
56:         Rectangle theRect(30,5);
57:         cout << "DrawShape(): \n";
58:         theRect.DrawShape();
59:         cout << "\nDrawShape(40,2): \n";
60:         theRect.DrawShape(40,2);
61:     return 0;
62:     }
```

OUTPUT

```
DrawShape():
******************************
******************************
******************************
******************************
******************************

DrawShape(40,2):
****************************************
****************************************
```

ANALYSIS Listing 10.1 represents a stripped-down version of the Week in Review project from Week 1. The test for illegal values has been taken out to save room, as have some of the accessor functions. The main program has been stripped down to a simple driver program, rather than a menu.

The important code, however, is on lines 14 and 15, where DrawShape() is overloaded. The implementation for these overloaded class methods is on lines 30–50. Note that the version of DrawShape() that takes no parameters simply calls the version that takes two parameters, passing in the current member variables. Try very hard to avoid duplicating code in two functions. Otherwise, keeping them in sync when changes are made to one or the other will be difficult and error-prone.

The driver program on lines 52–62 creates a rectangle object and then calls DrawShape(), first passing in no parameters and then passing in two integers.

The compiler decides which method to call based on the number and type of parameters entered. One can imagine a third overloaded function named DrawShape() that takes one dimension and an enumeration for whether it is the width or height, at the user's choice.

Using Default Values

Just as nonclass functions can have one or more default values, so can each member
function of a class. The same rules apply for declaring the default values, as illustrated in
Listing 10.2.

LISTING 10.2   Using Default Values

```
1:      //Listing 10.2 Default values in member functions
2:      #include <iostream.h>
3:
4:
5:
6:      // Rectangle class declaration
7:      class Rectangle
8:      {
9:      public:
10:         // constructors
11:         Rectangle(int width, int height);
12:         ~Rectangle(){}
13:         void DrawShape(int aWidth, int aHeight, bool UseCurrentVals =
        ↦false) const;
14:
15:     private:
16:         int itsWidth;
17:         int itsHeight;
18:     };
19:
20:     //Constructor implementation
21:     Rectangle::Rectangle(int width, int height):
22:     itsWidth(width),          // initializations
23:     itsHeight(height)
24:     {}                        // empty body
25:
26:
27:     // default values used for third parameter
28:     void Rectangle::DrawShape(
29:         int width,
30:         int height,
31:         bool UseCurrentValue
32:         ) const
33:     {
34:         int printWidth;
35:         int printHeight;
36:
37:         if (UseCurrentValue == true)
38:         {
39:             printWidth = itsWidth;          // use current class values
40:             printHeight = itsHeight;
```

```
41:         }
42:         else
43:         {
44:             printWidth = width;          // use parameter values
45:             printHeight = height;
46:         }
47:
48:
49:         for (int i = 0; i<printHeight; i++)
50:         {
51:             for (int j = 0; j< printWidth; j++)
52:             {
53:                 cout << "*";
54:             }
55:             cout << "\n";
56:         }
57:     }
58:
59:     // Driver program to demonstrate overloaded functions
60:     int main()
61:     {
62:         // initialize a rectangle to 30,5
63:         Rectangle theRect(30,5);
64:         cout << "DrawShape(0,0,true)...\n";
65:         theRect.DrawShape(0,0,true);
66:         cout <<"DrawShape(40,2)...\n";
67:         theRect.DrawShape(40,2);
68:         return 0;
69:     }
```

10

OUTPUT
```
DrawShape(0,0,true)...
******************************
******************************
******************************
******************************
******************************
DrawShape(40,2)...
****************************************
****************************************
```

ANALYSIS Listing 10.2 replaces the overloaded DrawShape() function with a single function with default parameters. The function is declared on line 13 to take three parameters. The first two, aWidth and aHeight, are integer variables, and the third, UseCurrentVals, is a bool that defaults to false.

The implementation for this somewhat awkward function begins on line 28. The third parameter, UseCurrentValue, is evaluated. If it is true, the member variables itsWidth and itsHeight are used to set the local variables printWidth and printHeight, respectively.

If `UseCurrentValue` is false, either because it has defaulted false or was set by the user, the first two parameters are used for setting `printWidth` and `printHeight`.

Note that if `UseCurrentValue` is true, the values of the other two parameters are completely ignored.

Lines 22 and 23, which initialize private member data variables, are explained in the "Initializing Objects" section later today.

Choosing Between Default Values and Overloaded Functions

Listings 10.1 and 10.2 accomplish the same thing, but the overloaded functions in Listing 10.1 are easier to understand and more natural to use. Also, if a third variation is needed—perhaps the user wants to supply either the width or the height, but not both—it is easy to extend the overloaded functions. The default value, however, will quickly become unusually complex as new variations are added.

How do you decide whether to use function overloading or default values? A good rule of thumb is to use function overloading under the following conditions:

- No reasonable default value exists.
- You need different algorithms.
- You need to support variant types in your parameter list (different data types or class for different calls).

Understanding Default Constructors

As discussed on Day 6, "Basic Classes," if you do not explicitly declare a constructor for your class, a default constructor is created that takes no parameters and does nothing. You are free to make your own default constructor, however, that takes no arguments but that "sets up" your object as required.

The constructor provided for you by the compiler is called the "default" constructor, but by convention so is any constructor that takes no parameters. This can be a bit confusing, but it is usually clear from the context which one is meant.

Take note that if you code any constructors at all, the default constructor is not made by the compiler. So if you want a constructor that takes no parameters and you have already created any other constructors, you must code your own default constructor yourself!

Overloading Constructors

The point of a constructor is to establish the object; for example, the point of a Rectangle constructor is to make a rectangle. Before the constructor runs, no rectangle exists, only an area of memory. After the constructor finishes, there is a complete, ready-to-use rectangle object.

Constructors, like all member functions, can be overloaded. The capability to overload constructors is very powerful and very flexible.

For example, you might have a rectangle object that has two constructors: The first takes a length and a width and makes a rectangle of that size. The second takes no values and makes a default-sized rectangle. Listing 10.3 implements this idea.

INPUT **LISTING 10.3** Overloading the Constructor

```
1:     // Listing 10.3
2:     // Overloading constructors
3:
4:     #include <iostream.h>
5:
6:     class Rectangle
7:     {
8:     public:
9:          Rectangle();
10:          Rectangle(int width, int length);
11:          ~Rectangle() {}
12:          int GetWidth() const { return itsWidth; }
13:          int GetLength() const { return itsLength; }
14:     private:
15:          int itsWidth;
16:          int itsLength;
17:     };
18:
19:     Rectangle::Rectangle()
20:     {
21:          itsWidth = 5;
22:          itsLength = 10;
23:     }
24:
25:     Rectangle::Rectangle (int width, int length)
26:     {
27:          itsWidth = width;
28:          itsLength = length;
29:     }
30:
31:     int main()
32:     {
```

continues

LISTING **10.3**   CONTINUED

```
33:             Rectangle Rect1;
34:             cout << "Rect1 width: " << Rect1.GetWidth() << endl;
35:             cout << "Rect1 length: " << Rect1.GetLength() << endl;
36:
37:             int aWidth, aLength;
38:             cout << "Enter a width: ";
39:             cin >> aWidth;
40:             cout << "\nEnter a length: ";
41:             cin >> aLength;
42:
43:             Rectangle Rect2(aWidth, aLength);
44:             cout << "\nRect2 width: " << Rect2.GetWidth() << endl;
45:             cout << "Rect2 length: " << Rect2.GetLength() << endl;
46:             return 0;
47:     }
```

OUTPUT
```
Rect1 width: 5
Rect1 length: 10
Enter a width: 20

Enter a length: 50

Rect2 width: 20
Rect2 length: 50
```

ANALYSIS The Rectangle class is declared on lines 6–17. Two constructors are declared: the "default constructor" on line 9 and a constructor taking two integer variables.

On line 33, a rectangle is created using the default constructor, and its values are printed on lines 34 and 35. On lines 37–41, the user is prompted for a width and length, and the constructor taking two parameters is called on line 43. Finally, the width and length for this rectangle are printed on lines 44–45.

Just as it does with any overloaded function, the compiler chooses the right constructor, based on the number and type of the parameters.

Initializing Objects

With the exception of lines 22 and 23 of listing 10.2, up to now, you were setting the member variables of objects in the body of the constructor. Constructors, however, are invoked in two stages: the initialization stage and the body.

Most variables can be set in either stage, either by initializing in the initialization stage
or by assigning in the body of the constructor. It is cleaner, and often more efficient, to
initialize member variables at the initialization stage. The following example shows how
to initialize member variables:

```
CAT():          // constructor name and parameters
itsAge(5),      // initialization list
itsWeight(8)
{ }                    // body of constructor
```

After the closing parentheses on the constructor's parameter list, write a colon. Then
write the name of the member variable and a pair of parentheses. Inside the parentheses,
write the expression to be used to initialize that member variable. If more than one initialization exists, separate each one with a comma. Listing 10.4 shows the definition of
the constructors from Listing 10.3 with initialization of the member variables rather than
assignment.

10

> **Caution**
>
> The file for Listing 10.4 on the CD-ROM will not compile—it is just a piece of
> code (code *segment*), not a program.

INPUT   **LISTING 10.4**   A Code Snippet Showing Initialization of Member Variables

```
1:   Rectangle::Rectangle():
2:        itsWidth(5),
3:        itsLength(10)
4:   {
5:   }
6:
7:   Rectangle::Rectangle (int width, int length):
8:        itsWidth(width),
9:        itsLength(length)
10:  {
11:  }
```

OUTPUT   No output.

Some variables must be initialized and cannot be assigned to, such as references and
constants. It is common to have other assignments or action statements in the body of
the constructor; however, it is best to use initialization as much as possible.

Using the Copy Constructor

In addition to providing a default constructor and destructor, the compiler provides a default copy constructor. The copy constructor is called every time a copy of an object is made.

When you pass an object by value, either into a function or as a function's return value, a temporary copy of that object is made. If the object is a user-defined object, the class's copy constructor is called. Yesterday, in Listings 9.5 and 9.6, you saw how temporary copies of regular variables is created. Today you get to see how it works with objects.

All copy constructors take one parameter, a reference to an object of the same class. It is a good idea to make it a constant reference because the constructor will not have to alter the object passed in. For example:

```
CAT(const CAT & theCat);
```

Here the CAT constructor takes a constant reference to an existing CAT object. The goal of the copy constructor is to make a copy of theCat.

The default copy constructor simply copies each member variable from the object passed as a parameter to the member variables of the new object. This is called a *memberwise* (or shallow) copy, and although this is fine for most member variables, it breaks pretty quickly for member variables that are pointers to objects on the free store.

A shallow or memberwise copy copies the exact values of one object's member variables into another object. Pointers in both objects end up pointing to the same memory. A deep copy copies the values allocated on the heap to newly allocated memory.

If the CAT class includes a member variable, itsAge, that points to an integer on the free store, the default copy constructor will copy the passed-in CAT's itsAge member variable to the new CAT's itsAge member variable. The two objects will now point to the same memory, as illustrated in Figure 10.1.

This will lead to a disaster when either CAT goes out of scope. As mentioned on Day 8, "Pointers," the job of the destructor is to clean up this memory. If the original CAT's destructor frees this memory and the new CAT is still pointing to the memory, a stray pointer has been created, and the program is in mortal danger. Figure 10.2 illustrates this problem.

FIGURE 10.1

Using the default copy constructor.

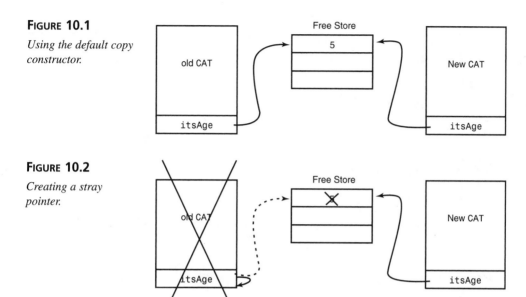

FIGURE 10.2

Creating a stray pointer.

The solution to this is to create your own copy constructor and to allocate the memory as required. After the memory is allocated, the old values can be copied into the new memory. This is called a deep copy. Listing 10.5 illustrates how to do this.

INPUT   **LISTING 10.5**   Copy Constructors

```
1:   // Listing 10.5
2:   // Copy constructors
3:
4:   #include <iostream.h>
5:
6:   class CAT
7:   {
8:       public:
9:           CAT();                              // default constructor
10:          CAT (const CAT &);     // copy constructor
11:          ~CAT();                             // destructor
12:          int GetAge() const { return *itsAge; }
13:          int GetWeight() const { return *itsWeight; }
14:          void SetAge(int age) { *itsAge = age; }
15:
16:      private:
17:          int *itsAge;
18:          int *itsWeight;
19:  };
```

continues

LISTING 10.5   CONTINUED

```
20:
21:   CAT::CAT()
22:   {
23:       itsAge = new int;
24:       itsWeight = new int;
25:       *itsAge = 5;
26:       *itsWeight = 9;
27:   }
28:
29:   CAT::CAT(const CAT & rhs)
30:   {
31:       itsAge = new int;
32:       itsWeight = new int;
33:       *itsAge = rhs.GetAge();   // public access
34:       *itsWeight = *(rhs.itsWeight); // private access
35:   }
36:
37:   CAT::~CAT()
38:   {
39:       delete itsAge;
40:       itsAge = NULL;
41:       delete itsWeight;
42:       itsWeight = NULL;
43:   }
44:
45:   int main()
46:   {
47:       CAT frisky;
48:       cout << "frisky's age: " << frisky.GetAge() << endl;
49:       cout << "Setting frisky to 6...\n";
50:       frisky.SetAge(6);
51:       cout << "Creating boots from frisky\n";
52:       CAT boots(frisky);
53:       cout << "frisky's age: " <<     frisky.GetAge() << endl;
54:       cout << "boots' age: " << boots.GetAge() << endl;
55:       cout << "setting frisky to 7...\n";
56:       frisky.SetAge(7);
57:       cout << "frisky's age: " <<     frisky.GetAge() << endl;
58:       cout << "boot's age: " << boots.GetAge() << endl;
59:       return 0;
60:   }
```

OUTPUT

```
frisky's age: 5
Setting frisky to 6...
Creating boots from frisky
frisky's age: 6
boots' age:  6
setting frisky to 7...
frisky's age: 7
boots' age: 6
```

ANALYSIS On lines 6–19, the CAT class is declared. Note that on line 9 a default constructor is declared, and on line 10 a copy constructor is declared.

On lines 17 and 18, two member variables are declared, each as a pointer to an integer. Typically there would be little reason for a class to store int member variables as pointers, but this was done to illustrate how to manage member variables on the free store.

The default constructor on lines 21–27 allocates room on the free store for two int variables and then assigns values to them.

The copy constructor begins on line 29. Note that the parameter is rhs. It is common to refer to the parameter to a copy constructor as rhs, which stands for "right-hand side." When you look at the assignments in lines 33 and 34, you should see that the object passed in as a parameter is on the right side of the equal sign. It works this way:

On lines 31 and 32, memory is allocated on the free store. Then, on lines 33 and 34, the value at the new memory location is assigned the values from the existing CAT.

The parameter rhs is a CAT that is passed into the copy constructor as a constant reference. As a CAT object, rhs has all the member variables of any other CAT.

Any CAT object can access private member variables of any other CAT object; however, it is good programming practice to use public accessor methods when possible. The member function rhs.GetAge() returns the value stored in the memory pointed to by rhs's member variable itsAge.

Figure 10.3 diagrams what is happening here. The values pointed to by the existing CAT's member variables are copied to the memory allocated for the new CAT.

FIGURE 10.3

Deep copy illustrated.

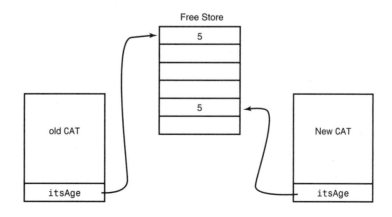

On line 47, a CAT called frisky is created. frisky's age is printed, and then his age is set to 6 on line 50. On line 52, a new CAT, boots, is created, using the copy constructor and passing in frisky. Had frisky been passed as a parameter to a function, this same call to the copy constructor would have been made by the compiler.

On lines 53 and 54, the ages of both CATs are printed. Sure enough, boots has frisky's age, 6, not the default age of 5. On line 56, frisky's age is set to 7, and then the ages are printed again. This time frisky's age is 7, but boots's age is still 6, demonstrating that they are stored in separate areas of memory.

When the CATs fall out of scope, their destructors are automatically invoked. The implementation of the CAT destructor is shown on lines 37–43. delete is called on both pointers, itsAge and itsWeight, returning the allocated memory to the free store. Also, for safety, the pointers are reassigned to NULL.

Overloading Operators

C++ has a number of built-in types, including int, real, char, and so forth. Each of these has a number of built-in operators, such as addition (+) and multiplication (*). C++ enables you to add these operators to your own classes as well.

To explore operator overloading fully, Listing 10.6 creates a new class, Counter. A Counter object will be used in counting (surprise!) in loops and other applications where a number must be incremented, decremented, or otherwise tracked.

INPUT   **LISTING 10.6**   The Counter Class

```
1:     // Listing 10.6
2:     // The Counter class
3:
4:
5:     #include <iostream.h>
6:
7:     class Counter
8:     {
9:        public:
10:           Counter();
11:           ~Counter(){}
12:           int GetItsVal()const { return itsVal; }
13:           void SetItsVal(int x) {itsVal = x; }
14:
15:        private:
16:           int itsVal;
17:
18:     };
```

```
19:
20:    Counter::Counter():
21:    itsVal(0)
22:    {}
23:
24:    int main()
25:    {
26:       Counter i;
27:       cout << "The value of i is " << i.GetItsVal() << endl;
28:      return 0;
29:    }
```

OUTPUT The value of i is 0

ANALYSIS As it stands, this is a pretty useless class. It is defined on lines 7–18. Its only member variable is an `int`. The default constructor, which is defined on line 10 and whose implementation is on line 20, initializes the one member variable, `itsVal`, to zero.

Unlike a regular, compiler-defined `int`, the `Counter` object cannot be incremented, decremented, added, assigned, or otherwise manipulated. This is a feature, not a problem. In exchange for this, it makes printing its value far more difficult! Printing is more difficult because there is no compiler-defined format, so you have to create it.

Writing an Increment Function

Operator overloading restores much of the functionality that has been stripped out of this class. Two ways exist, for example, to add the capability to increment a `Counter` object. The first is to write an increment method, as shown in Listing 10.7.

INPUT **LISTING 10.7** Adding an Increment Operator

```
1:    // Listing 10.7
2:    // The Counter class
3:
4:
5:    #include <iostream.h>
6:
7:    class Counter
8:    {
9:       public:
10:          Counter();
11:          ~Counter(){}
12:          int GetItsVal()const { return itsVal; }
13:          void SetItsVal(int x) {itsVal = x; }
14:          void Increment() { ++itsVal; }
```

continues

LISTING **10.7**   CONTINUED

```
15:
16:        private:
17:            int itsVal;
18:
19:    };
20:
21:    Counter::Counter():
22:    itsVal(0)
23:    {}
24:
25:    int main()
26:    {
27:        Counter i;
28:        cout << "The value of i is " << i.GetItsVal() << endl;
29:        i.Increment();
30:        cout << "The value of i is " << i.GetItsVal() << endl;
31:    return 0;
32:    }
```

OUTPUT
```
The value of i is 0
The value of i is 1
```

ANALYSIS Listing 10.7 adds an Increment function, defined on line 14. Although this works, it is cumbersome to use. The program cries out for the capability to add a ++ operator, and of course, this can be done.

Overloading the Prefix Operator

Prefix operators can be overloaded by declaring functions with the following form:

```
returnType Operator op (parameters)
```

Here, op is the operator to overload. Thus, the ++ operator can be overloaded with the following syntax:

```
void operator++ ()
```

Listing 10.8 demonstrates this alternative.

INPUT   LISTING **10.8**   Overloading operator++

```
1:    // Listing 10.8
2:    // The Counter class
3:
4:
5:    #include <iostream.h>
```

```
6:
7:      class Counter
8:      {
9:        public:
10:           Counter();
11:           ~Counter(){}
12:           int GetItsVal()const { return itsVal; }
13:           void SetItsVal(int x) {itsVal = x; }
14:           void Increment() { ++itsVal; }
15:           void operator++ () { ++itsVal; }
16:
17:        private:
18:           int itsVal;
19:
20:      };
21:
22:      Counter::Counter():
23:      itsVal(0)
24:      {}
25:
26:      int main()
27:      {
28:        Counter i;
29:        cout << "The value of i is " << i.GetItsVal() << endl;
30:        i.Increment();
31:        cout << "The value of i is " << i.GetItsVal() << endl;
32:        ++i;
33:        cout << "The value of i is " << i.GetItsVal() << endl;
34:      return 0;
35:      }
```

10

OUTPUT
```
The value of i is 0
The value of i is 1
The value of i is 2
```

ANALYSIS On line 15, operator++ is overloaded, and is used on line 32. This is much closer to the syntax you would expect with the Counter object. At this point, you might consider putting in the extra capabilities for which Counter was created in the first place, such as detecting when the Counter overruns its maximum size.

A significant defect exists in the way the increment operator was written, however. If you want to put the Counter on the right side of an assignment, it will fail. For example:

```
Counter a = ++i;
```

This code intends to create a new `Counter`, a, and then assign to it the value in i after i is incremented. The built-in copy constructor will handle the assignment, but the current increment operator does not return a `Counter` object. It returns void. You cannot assign a void object to a `Counter` object. (You cannot make something from nothing!)

Returning Types in Overloaded Operator Functions

Clearly, what you want is to return a `Counter` object so that it can be assigned to another `Counter` object. Which object should be returned? One approach would be to create a temporary object and return that. Listing 10.9 illustrates this approach.

INPUT   **LISTING 10.9**   Returning a Temporary Object

```
1:      // Listing 10.9
2:      // operator++ returns a temporary object
3:
4:
5:      #include <iostream.h>
6:
7:      class Counter
8:      {
9:        public:
10:           Counter();
11:           ~Counter(){}
12:           int GetItsVal()const { return itsVal; }
13:           void SetItsVal(int x) {itsVal = x; }
14:           void Increment() { ++itsVal; }
15:           Counter operator++ ();
16:
17:        private:
18:           int itsVal;
19:
20:      };
21:
22:      Counter::Counter():
23:      itsVal(0)
24:      {}
25:
26:      Counter Counter::operator++()
27:      {
28:          ++itsVal;
29:          Counter temp;
30:          temp.SetItsVal(itsVal);
31:          return temp;
32:      }
33:
34:      int main()
35:      {
```

```
36:        Counter i;
37:        cout << "The value of i is " << i.GetItsVal() << endl;
38:        i.Increment();
39:        cout << "The value of i is " << i.GetItsVal() << endl;
40:        ++i;
41:        cout << "The value of i is " << i.GetItsVal() << endl;
42:        Counter a = ++i;
43:        cout << "The value of a: " << a.GetItsVal();
44:        cout << " and i: " << i.GetItsVal() << endl;
45:        return 0;
46:    }
```

OUTPUT
```
The value of i is 0
The value of i is 1
The value of i is 2
The value of a: 3 and i: 3
```

ANALYSIS In this version, operator++ has been declared on line 15 to return a Counter object. On line 29, a temporary variable, temp, is created, and its value is set to match that in the current object. That temporary variable is returned and immediately assigned to a on line 42.

Returning Nameless Temporaries

There is really no need to name the temporary object created on line 29. If Counter had a constructor that took a value, you could simply return the result of that constructor as the return value of the increment operator. Listing 10.10 illustrates this idea.

INPUT   **LISTING 10.10**   Returning a Nameless Temporary Object

```
1:     // Listing 10.10
2:     // operator++ returns a nameless temporary object
3:
4:
5:     #include <iostream.h>
6:
7:     class Counter
8:     {
9:        public:
10:          Counter();
11:          Counter(int val);
12:          ~Counter(){}
13:          int GetItsVal()const { return itsVal; }
14:          void SetItsVal(int x) {itsVal = x; }
15:          void Increment() { ++itsVal; }
16:          Counter operator++ ();
17:
```

continues

LISTING 10.10 CONTINUED

```
18:        private:
19:            int itsVal;
20:
21:    };
22:
23:    Counter::Counter():
24:    itsVal(0)
25:    {}
26:
27:    Counter::Counter(int val):
28:    itsVal(val)
29:    {}
30:
31:    Counter Counter::operator++()
32:    {
33:        ++itsVal;
34:        return Counter (itsVal);
35:    }
36:
37:    int main()
38:    {
39:        Counter i;
40:        cout << "The value of i is " << i.GetItsVal() << endl;
41:        i.Increment();
42:        cout << "The value of i is " << i.GetItsVal() << endl;
43:        ++i;
44:        cout << "The value of i is " << i.GetItsVal() << endl;
45:        Counter a = ++i;
46:        cout << "The value of a: " << a.GetItsVal();
47:        cout << " and i: " << i.GetItsVal() << endl;
48:        return 0;
49:    }
```

OUTPUT

```
The value of i is 0
The value of i is 1
The value of i is 2
The value of a: 3 and i: 3
```

ANALYSIS On line 11, a new constructor is declared that takes an `int`. The implementation is on lines 27–29. It initializes `itsVal` with the passed-in value.

The implementation of `operator++` is now simplified. On line 33, `itsVal` is incremented. Then on line 34, a temporary `Counter` object is created, initialized to the value in `itsVal`, and then returned as the result of the `operator++`.

This is more elegant, but begs the question, "Why create a temporary object at all?" Remember that each temporary object must be constructed and later destroyed—each one potentially an expensive operation. Also, the object i already exists and already has the right value, so why not return it? We can solve this problem by using the this pointer.

Using the this Pointer

The this pointer, as discussed on Day 9, "References," was passed to the operator++ member function as to all member functions. The this pointer points to i, and if dereferenced, it will return the object i, which already has the right value in its member variable itsVal. Listing 10.11 illustrates returning the dereferenced this pointer and avoiding the creation of an unneeded temporary object.

10

INPUT   **LISTING 10.11**   Returning the this Pointer

```
1:     // Listing 10.11
2:     // Returning the dereferenced this pointer
3:
4:
5:     #include <iostream.h>
6:
7:     class Counter
8:     {
9:        public:
10:           Counter();
11:           ~Counter(){}
12:           int GetItsVal()const { return itsVal; }
13:           void SetItsVal(int x) {itsVal = x; }
14:           void Increment() { ++itsVal; }
15:           const Counter& operator++ ();
16:
17:        private:
18:           int itsVal;
19:
20:     };
21:
22:     Counter::Counter():
23:     itsVal(0)
24:     {};
25:
26:     const Counter& Counter::operator++()
27:     {
28:         ++itsVal;
29:         return *this;
30:     }
31:
```

continues

LISTING 10.11 CONTINUED

```
32:    int main()
33:    {
34:        Counter i;
35:        cout << "The value of i is " << i.GetItsVal() << endl;
36:        i.Increment();
37:        cout << "The value of i is " << i.GetItsVal() << endl;
38:        ++i;
39:        cout << "The value of i is " << i.GetItsVal() << endl;
40:        Counter a = ++i;
41:        cout << "The value of a: " << a.GetItsVal();
42:        cout << " and i: " << i.GetItsVal() << endl;
43:        return 0;
44:    }
```

OUTPUT

```
The value of i is 0
The value of i is 1
The value of i is 2
The value of a: 3 and i: 3
```

ANALYSIS The implementation of operator++, on lines 26–30, has been changed to dereference the this pointer and to return the current object. This provides a Counter
object to be assigned to a. As discussed earlier, if the Counter object allocated memory,
it would be important to override the copy constructor. In this case, the default copy constructor works fine.

Note that the value returned is a Counter reference, thereby avoiding the creation of an
extra temporary object. It is a const reference because the value should not be changed
by the function using this Counter.

Overloading the Postfix Operator

So far, you have overloaded the prefix operator. What if you want to overload the postfix
increment operator? Here the compiler has a problem: How is it to differentiate between
prefix and postfix? By convention, an integer variable is supplied as a parameter to the
operator declaration. The parameter's value is ignored; it is just a signal that this is the
postfix operator. This is demonstrated in Listing 10.12.

Learning the Differences Between Prefix and Postfix

Before you can write the postfix operator, you must understand how it is different from
the prefix operator. We reviewed this in detail on Day 4, "Expressions and Statements"
(see Listing 4.3).

To review, prefix says "increment, and then fetch," but postfix says "fetch, and then increment."

Thus, although the prefix operator can simply increment the value and then return the object itself, the postfix must return the value that existed before it was incremented. To do this, we must create a temporary object that will hold the original value, increment the value of the original object, and then return the temporary.

We should go over that again. Consider the following line of code:

```
a = x++;
```

If x was 5, after this statement a is 5, but x is 6. Thus, we returned the value in x and assigned it to a, and then we increased the value of x. If x is an object, its postfix increment operator must stash away the original value (5) in a temporary object, increment x's value to 6, and then return that temporary to assign its value to a.

Note that because we are returning the temporary, we must return it by value and not by reference because the temporary will go out of scope as soon as the function returns.

Listing 10.12 demonstrates the use of both the prefix and the postfix operators.

INPUT **LISTING 10.12** Prefix and Postfix Operators

```
1:     // Listing 10.12
2:     // Prefix and Postfix Operators
3:
4:
5:     #include <iostream.h>
6:
7:     class Counter
8:     {
9:     public:
10:        Counter();
11:        ~Counter(){}
12:        int GetItsVal()const { return itsVal; }
13:        void SetItsVal(int x) {itsVal = x; }
14:        const Counter& operator++ ();      // prefix
15:        const Counter operator++ (int); // postfix
16:
17:    private:
18:        int itsVal;
19:    };
20:
21:    Counter::Counter():
22:    itsVal(0)
23:    {}
24:
```

continues

LISTING 10.12 CONTINUED

```
25:    const Counter& Counter::operator++()
26:    {
27:        ++itsVal;
28:        return *this;
29:    }
30:
31:    const Counter Counter::operator++(int x)
32:    {
33:        Counter temp(*this);
34:        ++itsVal;
35:        return temp;
36:    }
37:
38:    int main()
39:    {
40:        Counter i;
41:        cout << "The value of i is " << i.GetItsVal() << endl;
42:        i++;
43:        cout << "The value of i is " << i.GetItsVal() << endl;
44:        ++i;
45:        cout << "The value of i is " << i.GetItsVal() << endl;
46:        Counter a = ++i;
47:        cout << "The value of a: " << a.GetItsVal();
48:        cout << " and i: " << i.GetItsVal() << endl;
49:        a = i++;
50:        cout << "The value of a: " << a.GetItsVal();
51:        cout << " and i: " << i.GetItsVal() << endl;
52:        return 0;
53:    }
```

OUTPUT
```
The value of i is 0
The value of i is 1
The value of i is 2
The value of a: 3 and i: 3
The value of a: 3 and i: 4
```

ANALYSIS The postfix operator is declared on line 15 and implemented on lines 31–36. Note that the prototype of the prefix operator on line 14 does not include the flag integer (x), but is used with its normal syntax. The postfix operator uses a flag value (x) to signal that it is the postfix and not the prefix. The flag value (x) is never used, however.

Operator Overloading: Unary Operators

Declare an overloaded operator the same as you would a function. Use the keyword operator, followed by the operator to overload. Unary operator functions do not take parameters, with the exception of the postfix increment and decrement, which take an integer as a flag.

Example 1

```
const Counter& Counter::operator++ ();
```

Example 2

```
Counter Counter::operator--(int);
```

Using the Addition Operator

10

The increment operator is a unary operator. It operates on only one object. The addition operator (+) is a binary operator, in which two objects are involved. How do you implement overloading the + operator for Count?

The goal is to be able to declare two Counter variables and then add them, as in the following example:

```
Counter varOne, varTwo, varThree;
VarThree = VarOne + VarTwo;
```

Once again, you could start by writing a function, Add(), which would take a Counter as its argument, add the values, and then return a Counter with the result. Listing 10.13 illustrates this approach.

INPUT   **LISTING 10.13**   The Add() Function

```
1:    // Listing 10.13
2:    // Add function
3:
4:
5:    #include <iostream.h>
6:
7:    class Counter
8:    {
9:    public:
10:       Counter();
11:       Counter(int initialValue);
12:       ~Counter(){}
13:       int GetItsVal()const { return itsVal; }
14:       void SetItsVal(int x) {itsVal = x; }
15:       Counter Add(const Counter &);
```

continues

LISTING 10.13 CONTINUED

```
16:
17:      private:
18:          int itsVal;
19:
20:      };
21:
22:      Counter::Counter(int initialValue):
23:      itsVal(initialValue)
24:      {}
25:
26:      Counter::Counter():
27:      itsVal(0)
28:      {}
29:
30:      Counter Counter::Add(const Counter & rhs)
31:      {
32:          return Counter(itsVal+ rhs.GetItsVal());
33:      }
34:
35:      int main()
36:      {
37:          Counter varOne(2), varTwo(4), varThree;
38:          varThree = varOne.Add(varTwo);
39:          cout << "varOne: " << varOne.GetItsVal()<< endl;
40:          cout << "varTwo: " << varTwo.GetItsVal() << endl;
41:          cout << "varThree: " << varThree.GetItsVal() << endl;
42:
43:       return 0;
44:      }
```

OUTPUT

```
varOne: 2
varTwo: 4
varThree: 6
```

ANALYSIS The Add() function is declared on line 15. It takes a constant Counter reference, which is the number to add to the current object. It returns a Counter object, which is the result to be assigned to the left side of the assignment statement, as shown on line 38. That is, varOne is the object, varTwo is the parameter to the Add() function, and the result is assigned to varThree.

In order to create varThree without having to initialize a value for it, a default constructor is required. The default constructor initializes itsVal to 0, as shown on lines 26–28. Because varOne and varTwo need to be initialized to a nonzero value, another constructor was created, as shown on lines 22–24. Another solution to this problem is to provide the default value 0 to the constructor declared on line 11.

Overloading operator+

The Add() function itself is shown on lines 30–33. It works, but its use is unnatural. Overloading the + operator would make for a more natural use of the Counter class. Listing 10.14 illustrates this.

INPUT **LISTING 10.14**   operator+

```
1:     // Listing 10.14
2:     //Overload operator plus (+)
3:
4:
5:     #include <iostream.h>
6:
7:     class Counter
8:     {
9:     public:
10:        Counter();
11:        Counter(int initialValue);
12:        ~Counter(){}
13:        int GetItsVal()const { return itsVal; }
14:        void SetItsVal(int x) {itsVal = x; }
15:        Counter operator+ (const Counter &);
16:     private:
17:        int itsVal;
18:     };
19:
20:     Counter::Counter(int initialValue):
21:     itsVal(initialValue)
22:     {}
23:
24:     Counter::Counter():
25:     itsVal(0)
26:     {}
27:
28:     Counter Counter::operator+ (const Counter & rhs)
29:     {
30:        return Counter(itsVal + rhs.GetItsVal());
31:     }
32:
33:     int main()
34:     {
35:        Counter varOne(2), varTwo(4), varThree;
36:        varThree = varOne + varTwo;
37:        cout << "varOne: " << varOne.GetItsVal()<< endl;
38:        cout << "varTwo: " << varTwo.GetItsVal() << endl;
39:        cout << "varThree: " << varThree.GetItsVal() << endl;
40:
41:      return 0;
42:     }
```

10

OUTPUT
```
varOne: 2
varTwo: 4
varThree: 6
```

ANALYSIS operator+ is declared on line 15 and defined on lines 28–31. Compare these with the declaration and definition of the Add() function in the previous listing; they are nearly identical. The syntax of their use, however, is quite different. It is more natural to say this:

```
varThree = varOne + varTwo;
```

than to say:

```
varThree = varOne.Add(varTwo);
```

Not a big change, but enough to make the program easier to use and understand.

> **Note** The techniques used for overloading operator++ can be applied to the other unary operators, such as operator--.

Operator Overloading: Binary Operators

Binary operators are created like unary operators, except that they do take a parameter. The parameter is a constant reference to an object of the same type.

Example 1

```
Counter Counter::operator+ (const Counter & rhs);
```

Example 2

```
Counter Counter::operator-(const Counter & rhs);
```

Additional Issues in Operator Overloading

Overloaded operators can be member functions, as described in this lesson, or nonmember functions. The latter will be described on Day 14, "Special Classes and Functions," when we discuss friend functions.

The only operators that must be class members are the assignment (=), subscript([ ]), function call (()), and indirection (->) operators.

Operator [ ] will be discussed on Day 11, "Inheritance," when arrays are covered.

Examining the Limitations on Operator Overloading

Operators on built-in types (such as int) cannot be overloaded. The precedence order cannot be changed, and the arity of the operator, that is, whether it is unary or binary, cannot be changed. You cannot make up new operators, so you cannot declare ** to be the "power of" operator.

Arity refers to how many terms are used in the operator. Some C++ operators are unary and use only one term (myValue++). Some operators are binary and use two terms (a + b). Only one operator is ternary and uses three terms. The ?: operator is often called the ternary operator because it is the only ternary operator in C++ (a > b ? x : y).

What to Overload

Operator overloading is one of the aspects of C++ most overused and abused by new programmers. It is tempting to create new and interesting uses for some of the more obscure operators, but these invariably lead to code that is confusing and difficult to read.

Of course, making the + operator subtract and the * operator add can be fun, but no professional programmer would do that. The greater danger lies in the well-intentioned but idiosyncratic use of an operator—using + to mean concatenate a series of letters or / to mean split a string. There is good reason to consider these uses, but there is even better reason to proceed with caution. Remember, the goal of overloading operators is to increase usability and understanding.

Do	Don't
DO use operator overloading when it will clarify the program. **DO** return an object of the class from overloaded operators.	**DON'T** create counterintuitive operators.

Using The Assignment Operator

The fourth and final function that is supplied by the compiler, if you do not specify one, is the assignment operator (operator=()). This operator is called whenever you assign to an object. For example:

```
CAT catOne(5,7);
CAT catTwo(3,4);
// ... other code here
catTwo = catOne;
```

10

Here, catOne is created and initialized with itsAge equal to 5 and itsWeight equal to 7. catTwo is then created and assigned the values 3 and 4.

After a while, catTwo is assigned the values in catOne. Two issues are raised here: What happens if itsAge is a pointer, and what happens to the original values in catTwo?

Handling member variables that store their values on the free store was discussed earlier during the examination of the copy constructor. The same issues arise here, as you saw illustrated in Figures 10.1 and 10.2.

C++ programmers differentiate between a shallow, or memberwise, copy on the one hand and a deep copy on the other. A shallow copy just copies the members, and both objects end up pointing to the same area on the free store. A deep copy allocates the necessary memory. This is illustrated in Figure 10.3.

An added wrinkle occurs with the assignment operator, however. The object catTwo already exists and has memory already allocated. That memory must be deleted if there is to be no memory leak. But what happens if you assign catTwo to itself?

```
catTwo = catTwo;
```

No one is likely to do this on purpose, but the program must be able to handle it. More important, it is possible for this to happen by accident when references and dereferenced pointers hide the fact that the assignment is to itself.

If you did not handle this problem carefully, catTwo would delete its memory allocation. Then, when it was ready to copy in the memory from the right side of the assignment, it would have a very big problem: The memory would be gone.

To protect against this, your assignment operator must check to see whether the right side of the assignment operator is the object itself. It does this by examining the this pointer. Listing 10.15 shows a class with an assignment operator.

INPUT   **LISTING 10.15**   An Assignment Operator

```
1:      // Listing 10.15
2:      // Copy constructors
3:
4:      #include <iostream.h>
5:
6:      class CAT
7:      {
8:          public:
9:              CAT();                              // default constructor
10:     // copy constructor and destructor elided!
11:             int GetAge() const { return *itsAge; }
```

```
12:                    int GetWeight() const { return *itsWeight; }
13:                    void SetAge(int age) { *itsAge = age; }
14:                    CAT & operator=(const CAT &);
15:
16:              private:
17:                    int *itsAge;
18:                    int *itsWeight;
19:         };
20:
21:      CAT::CAT()
22:      {
23:            itsAge = new int;
24:         itsWeight = new int;
25:         *itsAge = 5;
26:         *itsWeight = 9;
27:  }
28:
29:
30: CAT & CAT::operator=(const CAT & rhs)
31: {
32:    if (this == &rhs)
33:        return *this;
34:    *itsAge = rhs.GetAge();
35:    *itsWeight = rhs.GetWeight();
36:    return *this;
37: }
38:
39:
40:    int main()
41:    {
42:        CAT frisky;
43:        cout << "frisky's age: " << frisky.GetAge() << endl;
44:        cout << "Setting frisky to 6...\n";
45:        frisky.SetAge(6);
46:        CAT whiskers;
47:        cout << "whiskers' age: " << whiskers.GetAge() << endl;
48:        cout << "copying frisky to whiskers...\n";
49:        whiskers = frisky;
50:        cout << "whiskers' age: " << whiskers.GetAge() << endl;
51:        return 0;
52:    }
```

OUTPUT

```
frisky's age: 5
Setting frisky to 6...
whiskers' age: 5
copying frisky to whiskers...
whiskers' age: 6
```

ANALYSIS Listing 10.15 brings back the CAT class and leaves out the copy constructor and destructor to save room. On line 14, the assignment operator is declared, and on lines 30–37, it is defined.

On line 32, the current object (the CAT being assigned to) is tested to see whether it is the same as the CAT being assigned. This is done by checking whether the address of rhs is the same as the address stored in the this pointer.

Of course, the equality operator (==) can be overloaded as well, enabling you to determine for yourself what it means for your objects to be equal.

Understanding Conversion Operators

What happens when you try to assign a variable of a built-in type, such as int or unsigned short, to an object of a user-defined class? Listing 10.16 brings back the Counter class and attempts to assign a variable of type int to a Counter object.

Caution

Listing 10.16 will not compile!

INPUT **LISTING 10.16**   Attempting to Assign an int to a Counter

```
1:      // Listing 10.16
2:      // This code won't compile!
3:
4:
5:      #include <iostream.h>
6:
7:      class Counter
8:      {
9:        public:
10:          Counter();
11:          ~Counter(){}
12:          int GetItsVal()const { return itsVal; }
13:          void SetItsVal(int x) {itsVal = x; }
14:        private:
15:          int itsVal;
16:
17:      };
18:
19:      Counter::Counter():
20:      itsVal(0)
21:      {}
22:
```

```
23:     int main()
24:     {
25:        int theShort = 5;
26:        Counter theCtr = theShort;
27:        cout << "theCtr: " << theCtr.GetItsVal() << endl;
28:      return 0;
29:     }
```

OUTPUT

```
lst10-16.cxx: In function `int main()':
lst10-16.cxx:26: no matching function for call to `Counter::Counter
(int)'
lst10-16.cxx:17: candidates are: Counter::Counter(const Counter &)
lst10-16.cxx:19:                      Counter::Counter()
lst10-16.cxx:26: in base initialization for class `Counter'
```

10

ANALYSIS   The Counter class declared on lines 7–17 has only a default constructor. It
declares no particular method for turning an int into a Counter object, and so
line 26 causes a compile error. The compiler cannot figure out, unless you tell it, that
given an int, it should assign that value to the member variable itsVal.

Most compilers give you a much shorter message, something like "Unable to convert int
to Counter."

Listing 10.17 corrects this by creating a conversion operator: a constructor that takes an
int and produces a Counter object.

INPUT   **LISTING 10.17** Converting int to Counter

```
1:       // Listing 10.17
2:       // Constructor as conversion operator
3:
4:
5:       #include <iostream.h>
6:
7:       class Counter
8:       {
9:          public:
10:            Counter();
11:            Counter(int val);
12:            ~Counter(){}
13:            int GetItsVal()const { return itsVal; }
14:            void SetItsVal(int x) {itsVal = x; }
15:          private:
16:            int itsVal;
17:
18:       };
19:
20:       Counter::Counter():
```

continues

LISTING **10.17**   CONTINUED

```
21:          itsVal(0)
22:          {}
23:
24:      Counter::Counter(int val):
25:      itsVal(val)
26:      {}
27:
28:
29:      int main()
30:      {
31:          int theShort = 5;
32:          Counter theCtr = theShort;
33:          cout << "theCtr: " << theCtr.GetItsVal() << endl;
34:          return 0;
35:      }
```

OUTPUT   theCtr: 5

ANALYSIS   The important change is on line 11, where the constructor is overloaded to take an int, and on lines 24–26, where the constructor is implemented. The effect of this constructor is to create a Counter out of an int.

Given this, the compiler is able to call the constructor that takes an int as its argument. Here is the way to do it:

Step 1: Create a counter called theCtr.

This is like saying: int x = 5; which creates an integer variable x and then initializes it with the value 5. In this case, we create a Counter object theCtr and initialize it with the short integer variable theShort.

Step 2: Assign to theCtr *the value of* theShort.

But theShort is a short, not a *counter*! First we have to convert it into a Counter. The compile will try to make certain conversions for you automatically, but you have to teach it how. You teach the compiler how to make the conversion by creating a constructor for Counter that takes as its only parameter, for example, a short:

```
class Counter
{
Counter (short int x);
// ..
};
```

This constructor creates `Counter` objects from `shorts`. It does this by creating a temporary and unnamed *counter*. For illustration purposes, suppose that the temporary `Counter` object we create from the `short` is called `wasShort`.

Step 3: Assign `wasShort` *to* `theCtr`, *which is equivalent to*

```
"theCtr = wasShort";
```

In this step, `wasShort` (the temporary created when you ran the constructor) is substituted for what was on the right side of the assignment operator. That is, now that the compiler has made a temporary for you, it initializes `theCtr` with that temporary.

To understand this, you must understand that ALL operator overloading works the same way—you declare an overloaded operator using the keyword `operator`. With binary operators (such as = or +) the right side variable becomes the parameter. This is done by the constructor. Thus,

```
a = b;
```

becomes

```
a.operator=(b);
```

What happens, however, if you try to reverse the assignment with the following?

```
1:  Counter theCtr(5);
2:  int theShort = theCtr;
3:  cout << "theShort : " << theShort  << endl;
```

Again, this will generate a compile error. Although the compiler now knows how to create a `Counter` out of an `int`, it does not know how to reverse the process (unless you tell it how to).

Creating Your Conversion Operators

To solve this and similar problems, C++ provides conversion operators that can be added to your class. This enables your class to specify how to do implicit conversions to built-in types. Listing 10.18 illustrates this. One note, however: Conversion operators do not specify a return value, even though they do, in effect, return a converted value.

INPUT   **LISTING 10.18**   Converting from `Counter` to `unsigned short()`

```
1:  #include <iostream.h>
2:
3:  class Counter
4:  {
5:    public:
```

continues

LISTING 10.18   CONTINUED

```
6:        Counter();
7:        Counter(int val);
8:        ~Counter(){}
9:        int GetItsVal()const { return itsVal; }
10:       void SetItsVal(int x) {itsVal = x; }
11:       operator unsigned short();
12:    private:
13:       int itsVal;
14:
15:    };
16:
17:   Counter::Counter():
18:   itsVal(0)
19:   {}
20:
21:  Counter::Counter(int val):
22:  itsVal(val)
23:  {}
24:
25:  Counter::operator unsigned short ()
26:  {
27:      return ( int (itsVal) );
28:  }
29:
30:  int main()
31:  {
32:      Counter ctr(5);
33:      int theShort = ctr;
34:      cout << "theShort: " << theShort << endl;
35:      return 0;
36:  }
```

OUTPUT   theShort: 5

ANALYSIS   On line 11, the conversion operator is declared. Note that it has no return value. The implementation of this function is on lines 25–28. Line 27 returns the value of itsVal, converted to an int.

Now the compiler knows how to turn int variables into Counter objects and vice versa, and they can be assigned to one another freely.

Summary

Today you learned how to overload member functions of your classes. You also learned how to supply default values to functions and how to decide when to use default values and when to overload.

Overloading class constructors enables you to create flexible classes that can be created from other objects. Initialization of objects happens at the initialization stage of construction and is more efficient than assigning values in the body of the constructor.

The copy constructor and the assignment operator are supplied by the compiler if you do not create your own, but they do a memberwise copy of the class. In classes in which member data includes pointers to the free store, these methods must be overridden so that you allocate memory for the target object.

Almost all C++ operators can be overloaded, although you want to be careful not to create operators whose use is counterintuitive. You cannot change the arity of operators, nor can you invent new operators.

The `this` pointer refers to the current object and is an invisible parameter to all member functions. The dereferenced `this` pointer is often returned by overloaded operators.

Conversion operators enable you to create classes that can be used in expressions that expect a different type of object. They are exceptions to the rule that all functions return an explicit value; like constructors and destructors, they have no return type.

Q&A

Q Why would you ever use default values when you can overload a function?

A It is easier to maintain one function than two, and it is often easier to understand a function with default parameters than to study the bodies of two functions. Furthermore, updating one of the functions and neglecting to update the second is a common source of bugs.

Q Given the problems with overloaded functions, why not always use default values instead?

A Overloaded functions supply capabilities not available with default variables, such as varying the list of parameters by type rather than just by number.

Q When writing a class constructor, how do you decide what to put in the initialization and what to put in the body of the constructor?

A A simple rule of thumb is to do as much as possible in the initialization phase—that is, initialize all member variables there. Some things, like computations and print statements, must be in the body of the constructor.

Q   Can an overloaded function have a default parameter?

A Yes. No reason exists not to combine these powerful features. One or more of the overloaded functions can have its own default values, following the normal rules for default variables in any function.

Q   Why are some member functions defined within the class declaration and others are not?

A Defining the implementation of a member function within the declaration makes it inline. Generally, this is done only if the function is extremely simple. Note that you can also make a member function inline by using the keyword `inline`, even if the function is declared outside the class declaration.

Workshop

The Workshop provides quiz questions to help solidify your understanding of the material covered and exercises to provide you with experience in using what you have learned. Try to answer the quiz and exercise questions before checking the answers in Appendix D, "Answers to Exercises and Quizzes," and make sure you understand the answers before continuing to tomorrow's lesson.

Quiz

1. When you overload member functions, in what ways must they differ?
2. What is the difference between a declaration and a definition?
3. When is the copy constructor called?
4. When is the destructor called?
5. How does the copy constructor differ from the assignment operator (=)?
6. What is the `this` pointer?
7. How do you differentiate between overloading the prefix and postfix increment operators?
8. Can you overload the `operator+` for short integers?
9. Is it legal in C++ to overload the `operator++` so that it decrements a value in your class?
10. What return value must conversion operators have in their declarations?

Exercises

1. Write a `SimpleCircle` class declaration (only) with one member variable: `itsRadius`. Include a default constructor, a destructor, and accessor methods for radius.

2. Using the class you created in Exercise 1, write the implementation of the default constructor, initializing `itsRadius` with the value 5.

3. Using the same class, add a second constructor that takes a value as its parameter and assigns that value to `itsRadius`.

4. Create a prefix and postfix increment operator for your `SimpleCircle` class that increments `itsRadius`.

5. Change `SimpleCircle` to store `itsRadius` on the free store, and fix the existing methods.

6. Provide a copy constructor for `SimpleCircle`.

7. Provide an assignment operator for `SimpleCircle`.

8. Write a program that creates two `SimpleCircle` objects. Use the default constructor on one and instantiate the other with the value 9. Call the increment operator on each and then print their values. Finally, assign the second to the first and print its values.

9. **BUG BUSTER:** What is wrong with this implementation of the assignment operator?

```
SQUARE SQUARE ::operator=(const SQUARE & rhs)
{
        itsSide = new int;
        *itsSide = rhs.GetSide();
        return *this;
}
```

10. **BUG BUSTER:** What is wrong with this implementation of the addition operator?

```
VeryShort  VeryShort::operator+ (const VeryShort& rhs)
{
    itsVal += rhs.GetItsVal();
    return *this;
}
```

Inheritance

It is a fundamental aspect of human intelligence to seek out, recognize, and create relationships among concepts. We build hierarchies, matrices, networks, and other interrelationships to explain and understand the ways in which things interact. C++ attempts to capture this in inheritance hierarchies. Today you will learn:

- What inheritance is
- How to derive one class from another
- What protected access is and how to use it
- What virtual functions are

What Is Inheritance?

What is a dog? When you look at your pet, what do you see? I see four legs in service to a mouth. A biologist sees a network of interacting organs, a physicist sees atoms and forces at work, and a taxonomist sees a representative of the species *Canis domesticus*.

It is that last assessment that interests us at the moment. A dog is a kind of canine, a canine is a kind of mammal, and so forth. Taxonomists divide the world of living things into Kingdom, Phylum, Class, Order, Family, Genus, and Species.

This hierarchy establishes an *is-a* relationship. A member of the species *Homo sapiens is a* kind of primate. You see this relationship everywhere: A station wagon *is a* kind of car, which *is a* kind of vehicle. A sundae *is a* kind of dessert, which *is a* kind of food.

When we say something is a kind of something else, we imply that it is a specialization of that thing. That is, a car is a special kind of vehicle.

Any object that is *is-a* has some characteristics of the higher order description. A car is a vehicle. So is a truck. A car is not a truck. But they both have certain similar characteristics that they share with the common description *vehicle*. Some of these inherited similarities are wheels, a body, some form of engine, and others.

Inheritance and Derivation

The concept dog inherits—that is, it automatically gets—all the features of a mammal. Because it is a mammal, we know that it moves and that it breathes air. All mammals, by definition, move and breathe air. The concept of a dog adds the idea of barking, wagging its tail, eating my revisions to this lesson just when I was finally done, barking when I'm trying to sleep, and so on.

We can divide dogs into working dogs, sporting dogs, and terriers; and we can divide sporting dogs into retrievers, spaniels, and so forth. Finally, each of these can be specialized further; for example, retrievers can be subdivided into Labradors and Goldens.

A Golden is a kind of retriever, which is a sporting dog, which is a dog, and thus a kind of mammal, which is a kind of animal, and therefore, a kind of living thing. This hierarchy is represented in Figure 11.1 using the Unified Modeling Language (UML). Arrows point from more specialized types to more general types.

C++ attempts to represent these relationships by enabling you to define classes that derive from one another. Derivation is a way of expressing the *is-a* relationship. You derive a new class, Dog, from the class Mammal. You do not have to state explicitly that dogs move because they inherit that from Mammal.

A class that adds new functionality to an existing class is said to derive from that original class. The original class is said to be the new class's base class.

If the Dog class derives from the Mammal class, Mammal is a base class of Dog. Derived classes are supersets of their base classes. Just as dog adds certain features to the idea of mammal, the Dog class will add certain methods or data to the Mammal class.

FIGURE 11.1

Hierarchy of animals.

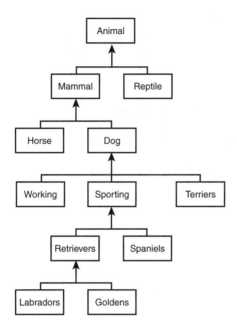

Typically, a base class has more than one derived class. Because dogs, cats, and horses are all types of mammals, their classes all derive from the `Mammal` class.

Building Classes that Represent Animals

To facilitate the discussion of derivation and inheritance, this lesson will focus on the relationships among a number of classes representing animals. You can imagine that you have been asked to design a children's game—a simulation of a farm.

In time you will develop a whole set of farm animals, including horses, cows, dogs, cats, sheep, and so forth. You will create methods for these classes so that they can act in the ways the child might expect, but for now you can stub-out each method with a simple print statement.

Stubbing-out a function means that you write only enough to show that the function was called, leaving the details for later when you have more time. Please feel free to extend the minimal code provided in this lesson to enable the animals to act more realistically.

The Syntax of Derivation

When you declare a class, you can indicate what class it derives from by writing a colon after the class name, the type of derivation (public or otherwise), and the class from which it derives. The following is an example:

```
class Dog : public Mammal
```

The type of derivation will be discussed later in this lesson. For now, always use public. The class from which you derive must have been declared earlier, or you will get a compiler error. Listing 11.1 illustrates how to declare a Dog class that is derived from a Mammal class.

LISTING 11.1 Simple Inheritance

```
1:      //Listing 11.1 Simple inheritance
2:
3:      #include <iostream.h>
4:      enum BREED { GOLDEN, CAIRN, DANDIE, SHETLAND, DOBERMAN, LAB };
5:
6:      class Mammal
7:      {
8:      public:
9:          // constructors
10:         Mammal();
11:         ~Mammal();
12:
13:         //accessors
14:         int GetAge()const;
15:         void SetAge(int);
16:         int GetWeight() const;
17:         void SetWeight();
18:
19:         //Other methods
20:         void Speak() const;
21:         void Sleep() const;
22:
23:
24:     protected:
25:         int itsAge;
26:         int itsWeight;
27:     };
28:
29:     class Dog : public Mammal
30:     {
31:     public:
32:
33:         // Constructors
34:         Dog();
35:         ~Dog();
36:
37:         // Accessors
38:         BREED GetBreed() const;
39:         void SetBreed(BREED);
40:
41:         // Other methods
42:          WagTail();
```

```
43:        BegForFood();
44:
45:    protected:
46:       BREED itsBreed;
47:    };
```

OUTPUT The above program has no output because it is only a set of class declarations without their implementations. It is not a full program. Nonetheless, there is much to see here.

ANALYSIS On lines 6–27, the Mammal class is declared. Note that in this example, Mammal does not derive from any other class. In the real world, mammals do derive—that is, mammals are kinds of animals. In a C++ program, you can represent only a fraction of the information you have about any given object. Reality is far too complex to capture all of it, so every C++ hierarchy is an arbitrary representation of the data available. The trick of good design is to represent the areas that you care about in a way that maps back to reality in a reasonably faithful manner.

The hierarchy has to begin somewhere; this program begins with Mammal. Because of this decision, some member variables that might properly belong in a higher base class are now represented here. Certainly all animals have an age and weight, for example, if Mammal is derived from Animal, we might expect to inherit those attributes. As it is, the attributes appear in the Mammal class.

To keep the program reasonably simple and manageable, only six methods have been put in the Mammal class—four accessor methods, Speak(), and Sleep().

The Dog class inherits from Mammal, as indicated on line 29. Every Dog object will have three member variables: itsAge, itsWeight, and itsBreed. Note that the class declaration for Dog does not include the member variables itsAge and itsWeight. Dog objects inherit these variables from the Mammal class, along with all Mammal's methods except the copy operator and the constructors and destructor.

Private Versus Protected

You may have noticed that a new access keyword, protected, was introduced on lines 24 and 45 of Listing 11.1. Previously, class data had been declared private. However, private members are not available to derived classes. You could make itsAge and itsWeight public, but that is not desirable. You do not want other classes accessing these data members directly.

11

What you want is a designation that says, "Make these visible to this class and to classes that derive from this class." That designation is protected. Protected data members and functions are fully visible to derived classes, but are otherwise private.

In total, three access specifiers exist: public, protected, and private. If a function has an object of your class, it can access all the public member data and functions. The member functions, in turn, can access all private data members and functions of their own class, and all protected data members and functions of any class from which they derive.

Thus, the function Dog::WagTail() can access the private data itsBreed and can access the protected data in the Mammal class.

Even if other classes are layered between Mammal and Dog (for example, DomesticAnimals), the Dog class will still be able to access the protected members of Mammal, assuming that these other classes all use public inheritance. Private inheritance is discussed on Day 15, "Advanced Inheritance."

Listing 11.2 demonstrates how to create objects of type Dog and access the data and functions of that type.

INPUT   **LISTING 11.2**   Using a Derived Object

```
1:      //Listing 11.2 Using a derived object
2:
3:      #include <iostream.h>
4:      enum BREED { GOLDEN, CAIRN, DANDIE, SHETLAND, DOBERMAN, LAB };
5:
6:      class Mammal
7:      {
8:      public:
9:          // constructors
10:         Mammal():itsAge(2), itsWeight(5){}
11:         ~Mammal(){}
12:
13:         //accessors
14:         int GetAge()const { return itsAge; }
15:         void SetAge(int age) { itsAge = age; }
16:         int GetWeight() const { return itsWeight; }
17:         void SetWeight(int weight) { itsWeight = weight; }
18:
19:         //Other methods
20:         void Speak()const { cout << "Mammal sound!\n"; }
21:         void Sleep()const { cout << "shhh. I'm sleeping.\n"; }
22:
23:
```

```
24:    protected:
25:        int itsAge;
26:        int itsWeight;
27:    };
28:
29:    class Dog : public Mammal
30:    {
31:    public:
32:
33:        // Constructors
34:        Dog():itsBreed(GOLDEN){}
35:        ~Dog(){}
36:
37:        // Accessors
38:        BREED GetBreed() const { return itsBreed; }
39:        void SetBreed(BREED breed) { itsBreed = breed; }
40:
41:        // Other methods
42:        void WagTail() const { cout << "Tail wagging...\n"; }
43:        void BegForFood() const { cout << "Begging for food...\n"; }
44:
45:    private:
46:        BREED itsBreed;
47:    };
48:
49:    int main()
50:    {
51:        Dog fido;
52:        fido.Speak();
53:        fido.WagTail();
54:        cout << "Fido is " << fido.GetAge() << " years old\n";
55:     return 0;
56:    }
```

OUTPUT

```
Mammal sound!
Tail wagging...
Fido is 2 years oldt
```

ANALYSIS On lines 6–27, the Mammal class is declared (all its functions are inline to save space here). On lines 29–47, the Dog class is declared as a derived class of Mammal. Thus, by these declarations, all Dogs have an age, a weight, and a breed.

On line 51, a Dog is defined: Fido. Fido inherits all the attributes of a Mammal, as well as all the attributes of a Dog. Thus, Fido knows how to WagTail(), but he also knows how to Speak() and Sleep().

Constructors and Destructors

Dog objects are Mammal objects. This is the essence of the *is-a* relationship. When Fido is created, his base constructor is called first, creating a Mammal. Then the Dog constructor is called, completing the construction of the Dog object. Because we gave Fido no parameters, the default constructor was called in each case. Fido does not exist until he is completely constructed, which means that both his Mammal part and his Dog part must be constructed. Thus, both constructors must be called.

When Fido is destroyed, first the Dog destructor will be called and then the destructor for the Mammal part of Fido. Each destructor is given an opportunity to clean up after its own part of Fido. Remember to clean up after your Dog! Listing 11.3 demonstrates this.

INPUT   **LISTING 11.3**   Constructors and Destructors Called

```
1:     //Listing 11.3 Constructors and destructors called.
2:
3:     #include <iostream.h>
4:     enum BREED { GOLDEN, CAIRN, DANDIE, SHETLAND, DOBERMAN, LAB };
5:
6:     class Mammal
7:     {
8:     public:
9:         // constructors
10:        Mammal();
11:        ~Mammal();
12:
13:        //accessors
14:        int GetAge() const { return itsAge; }
15:        void SetAge(int age) { itsAge = age; }
16:        int GetWeight() const { return itsWeight; }
17:        void SetWeight(int weight) { itsWeight = weight; }
18:
19:        //Other methods
20:        void Speak() const { cout << "Mammal sound!\n"; }
21:        void Sleep() const { cout << "shhh. I'm sleeping.\n"; }
22:
23:
24:     protected:
25:        int itsAge;
26:        int itsWeight;
27:     };
28:
29:     class Dog : public Mammal
30:     {
31:     public:
32:
```

```
33:        // Constructors
34:        Dog();
35:        ~Dog();
36:
37:        // Accessors
38:        BREED GetBreed() const { return itsBreed; }
39:        void SetBreed(BREED breed) { itsBreed = breed; }
40:
41:        // Other methods
42:        void WagTail() const { cout << "Tail wagging...\n"; }
43:        void BegForFood() const { cout << "Begging for food...\n"; }
44:
45:    private:
46:        BREED itsBreed;
47:    };
48:
49:    Mammal::Mammal():
50:    itsAge(1),
51:    itsWeight(5)
52:    {
53:        cout << "Mammal constructor...\n";
54:    }
55:
56:    Mammal::~Mammal()
57:    {
58:        cout << "Mammal destructor...\n";
59:    }
60:
61:    Dog::Dog():
62:    itsBreed(GOLDEN)
63:    {
64:        cout << "Dog constructor...\n";
65:    }
66:
67:    Dog::~Dog()
68:    {
69:        cout << "Dog destructor...\n";
70:    }
71:    int main()
72:    {
73:        Dog fido;
74:        fido.Speak();
75:        fido.WagTail();
76:        cout << "Fido is " << fido.GetAge() << " years old\n";
77:      return 0;
78:    }
```

11

```
Mammal constructor...
Dog constructor...
Mammal sound!
Tail wagging...
Fido is 1 years old
Dog destructor...
Mammal destructor...
```

ANALYSIS Listing 11.3 is like Listing 11.2, except that the constructors and destructors now print to the screen when called. Mammal's constructor is called, then Dog's. At that point the Dog fully exists, and its methods can be called. When Fido goes out of scope, Dog's destructor is called, followed by a call to Mammal's destructor.

Passing Arguments to Base Constructors

It is possible that you will want to overload the constructor of Mammal to take a specific age and overload the Dog constructor to take a breed. How do you get the age and weight parameters passed up to the right constructor in Mammal? What if Dogs want to initialize weight but Mammals do not?

Base class initialization can be performed during class initialization by writing the base class name, followed by the parameters expected by the base class. Listing 11.4 demonstrates this.

INPUT   **LISTING 11.4**   Overloading Constructors in Derived Classes

```
1:     //Listing 11.4 Overloading constructors in derived classes
2:
3:     #include <iostream.h>
4:     enum BREED { GOLDEN, CAIRN, DANDIE, SHETLAND, DOBERMAN, LAB };
5:
6:     class Mammal
7:     {
8:     public:
9:         // constructors
10:        Mammal();
11:        Mammal(int age);
12:        ~Mammal();
13:
14:        //accessors
15:        int GetAge() const { return itsAge; }
16:        void SetAge(int age) { itsAge = age; }
17:        int GetWeight() const { return itsWeight; }
18:        void SetWeight(int weight) { itsWeight = weight; }
19:
20:        //Other methods
21:        void Speak() const { cout << "Mammal sound!\n"; }
```

```
22:        void Sleep() const { cout << "shhh. I'm sleeping.\n"; }
23:
24:
25:    protected:
26:        int itsAge;
27:        int itsWeight;
28:    };
29:
30:    class Dog : public Mammal
31:    {
32:    public:
33:
34:        // Constructors
35:        Dog();
36:        Dog(int age);
37:        Dog(int age, int weight);
38:        Dog(int age, BREED breed);
39:        Dog(int age, int weight, BREED breed);
40:        ~Dog();
41:
42:        // Accessors
43:        BREED GetBreed() const { return itsBreed; }
44:        void SetBreed(BREED breed) { itsBreed = breed; }
45:
46:        // Other methods
47:        void WagTail() const { cout << "Tail wagging...\n"; }
48:        void BegForFood() const { cout << "Begging for food...\n"; }
49:
50:    private:
51:        BREED itsBreed;
52:    };
53:
54:    Mammal::Mammal():
55:    itsAge(1),
56:    itsWeight(5)
57:    {
58:        cout << "Mammal constructor...\n";
59:    }
60:
61:    Mammal::Mammal(int age):
62:    itsAge(age),
63:    itsWeight(5)
64:    {
65:        cout << "Mammal(int) constructor...\n";
66:    }
67:
68:    Mammal::~Mammal()
69:    {
70:        cout << "Mammal destructor...\n";
71:    }
72:
```

continues

LISTING **11.4**   CONTINUED

```
73:    Dog::Dog():
74:    Mammal(),
75:    itsBreed(GOLDEN)
76:    {
77:        cout << "Dog constructor...\n";
78:    }
79:
80:    Dog::Dog(int age):
81:    Mammal(age),
82:    itsBreed(GOLDEN)
83:    {
84:        cout << "Dog(int) constructor...\n";
85:    }
86:
87:    Dog::Dog(int age, int weight):
88:    Mammal(age),
89:    itsBreed(GOLDEN)
90:    {
91:        itsWeight = weight;
92:        cout << "Dog(int, int) constructor...\n";
93:    }
94:
95:    Dog::Dog(int age, int weight, BREED breed):
96:    Mammal(age),
97:    itsBreed(breed)
98:    {
99:        itsWeight = weight;
100:       cout << "Dog(int, int, BREED) constructor...\n";
101:    }
102:
103:   Dog::Dog(int age, BREED breed):
104:   Mammal(age),
105:   itsBreed(breed)
106:   {
107:       cout << "Dog(int, BREED) constructor...\n";
108:   }
109:
110:   Dog::~Dog()
111:   {
112:       cout << "Dog destructor...\n";
113:   }
114:   int main()
115:   {
116:       Dog fido;
117:       Dog rover(5);
118:       Dog buster(6,8);
119:       Dog yorkie (3,GOLDEN);
120:       Dog dobbie (4,20,DOBERMAN);
```

```
121:      fido.Speak();
122:      rover.WagTail();
123:      cout << "Yorkie is " << yorkie.GetAge() << " years old\n";
124:      cout << "Dobbie weighs ";
125:      cout << dobbie.GetWeight() << " pounds\n";
126:    return 0;
127:  }
```

Note
> The output has been numbered here so that each line can be referred to in the analysis.

OUTPUT
```
1:  Mammal constructor...
2:  Dog constructor...
3:  Mammal(int) constructor...
4:  Dog(int) constructor...
5:  Mammal(int) constructor...
6:  Dog(int, int) constructor...
7:  Mammal(int) constructor...
8:  Dog(int, BREED) constructor...
9:  Mammal(int) constructor...
10: Dog(int, int, BREED) constructor...
11: Mammal sound!
12: Tail wagging...
13: Yorkie is 3 years old
14: Dobbie weighs 20 pounds.
15: Dog destructor...
16: Mammal destructor...
17: Dog destructor...
18: Mammal destructor...
19: Dog destructor...
20: Mammal destructor...
21: Dog destructor...
22: Mammal destructor...
23: Dog destructor...
24: Mammal destructor...
```

11

ANALYSIS In Listing 11.4, the Mammal's constructor has been overloaded on line 11 to take an integer, the Mammal's age. The implementation on lines 61–66 initializes itsAge with the value passed into the constructor and initializes itsWeight with the value 5.

Dog has overloaded five constructors on lines 35–39. The first is the default constructor. The second takes the age, which is the same parameter that the Mammal constructor takes. The third constructor takes both the age and the weight, the fourth takes the age and the breed, and the fifth takes the age, the weight, and the breed.

Note that on line 74, Dog's default constructor calls Mammal's default constructor. Although it is not strictly necessary to do this, it serves as documentation that you intended to call the base constructor, which takes no parameters. The base constructor would be called in any case, but actually doing so makes your intentions explicit.

The implementation for the Dog constructor, which takes an integer, is on lines 80–85. In its initialization phase (lines 81–82), Dog initializes its base class, passing in the parameter, and then it initializes its breed.

Another Dog constructor is on lines 87–93. This one takes two parameters. Once again it initializes its base class by calling the appropriate constructor, but this time it also assigns weight to its base class's variable itsWeight. Note that you cannot assign to the base class variable in the initialization phase. Because Mammal does not have a constructor that takes this parameter, you must do this within the body of the Dog's constructor.

Walk through the remaining constructors to make sure you are comfortable with how they work. Note what is initialized and what must wait for the body of the constructor.

The output has been numbered so that each line can be referred to in this analysis. The first two lines of output represent the instantiation of Fido, using the default constructor.

In the output, lines 3 and 4 represent the creation of rover. Lines 5 and 6 represent buster. Note that the Mammal constructor that was called is the constructor that takes one integer, but the Dog constructor is the constructor that takes two integers.

After all the objects are created, they are used and then go out of scope. As each object is destroyed, first the Dog destructor and then the Mammal destructor is called, five of each in total.

Overriding Functions

A Dog object has access to all the member functions in class Mammal, as well as to any member functions, such as WagTail(), that the declaration of the Dog class might add. It can also override a base class function. Overriding a function means changing the implementation of a base class function in a derived class. When you make an object of the derived class, the correct function is called.

When a derived class creates a function with the same return type and signature as a member function in the base class, but with a new implementation, it is said to be overriding that method.

When you override a function, it must agree in return type and in signature with the function in the base class. The signature is the function prototype other than the return type: that is, the name, the parameter list, and the keyword const, if used.

Listing 11.5 illustrates what happens if the Dog class overrides the Speak() method in Mammal. To save room, the accessor functions have been left out of these classes.

LISTING 11.5 Overriding a Base Class Method in a Derived Class

```
1:     //Listing 11.5 Overriding a base class method in a derived class
2:
3:     #include <iostream.h>
4:     enum BREED { GOLDEN, CAIRN, DANDIE, SHETLAND, DOBERMAN, LAB };
5:
6:     class Mammal
7:     {
8:     public:
9:        // constructors
10:        Mammal() { cout << "Mammal constructor...\n"; }
11:        ~Mammal() { cout << "Mammal destructor...\n"; }
12:
13:        //Other methods
14:        void Speak()const { cout << "Mammal sound!\n"; }
15:        void Sleep()const { cout << "shhh. I'm sleeping.\n"; }
16:
17:
18:     protected:
19:        int itsAge;
20:        int itsWeight;
21:     };
22:
23:     class Dog : public Mammal
24:     {
25:     public:
26:
27:        // Constructors
28:        Dog(){ cout << "Dog constructor...\n"; }
29:        ~Dog(){ cout << "Dog destructor...\n"; }
30:
31:        // Other methods
32:        void WagTail() const { cout << "Tail wagging...\n"; }
33:        void BegForFood() const { cout << "Begging for food...\n"; }
34:        void Speak() const { cout << "Woof!\n"; }
35:
36:     private:
37:        BREED itsBreed;
38:     };
39:
40:     int main()
41:     {
42:        Mammal bigAnimal;
43:        Dog fido;
44:        bigAnimal.Speak();
45:        fido.Speak();
46:      return 0;
47:     }
```

11

```
Mammal constructor...
Mammal constructor...
Dog constructor...
Mammal sound!
Woof!
Dog destructor...
Mammal destructor...
Mammal destructor...
```

ANALYSIS On line 34, the Dog class overrides the Speak() method, causing Dog objects to say Woof! when the Speak() method is called. On line 42, a Mammal object, bigAnimal, is created, causing the first line of output when the Mammal constructor is called. On line 43, a Dog object, fido, is created, causing the next two lines of output, where the Mammal constructor and then the Dog constructor are called.

On line 44, the Mammal object calls its Speak() method; then on line 45, the Dog object calls its Speak() method. The output reflects that the correct methods were called. Finally, the two objects go out of scope and the destructors are called.

Overloading Versus Overriding

These terms are similar, and they do similar things. When you overload a method, you create more than one method with the same name, but with a different signature. When you override a method, you create a method in a derived class with the same name as a method in the base class and the same signature.

Hiding the Base Class Method

In the previous listing, the Dog class's Speak() method hides the base class's method. This is just what is wanted, but it can have unexpected results. If Mammal has a method, Move(), which is overloaded, and Dog overrides that method, the Dog method will hide all the Mammal methods with that name.

If Mammal overloads Move() as three methods—one that takes no parameters, one that takes an integer, and one that takes an integer and a direction—and Dog overrides just the Move() method that takes no parameters, it will not be easy to access the other two methods using a Dog object. Listing 11.6 illustrates this problem.

INPUT **LISTING 11.6** Hiding Methods

```
1:    //Listing 11.6 Hiding methods
2:
3:    #include <iostream.h>
4:
```

```
5:      class Mammal
6:      {
7:      public:
8:          void Move() const { cout << "Mammal move one step\n"; }
9:          void Move(int distance) const
10:         {
11:             cout << "Mammal move ";
12:             cout << distance <<" steps.\n";
13:         }
14:     protected:
15:         int itsAge;
16:         int itsWeight;
17:     };
18:
19:     class Dog : public Mammal
20:     {
21:     public:
22: // Other compilers may give a warning that you are hiding a function!
23:         void Move() const { cout << "Dog move 5 steps.\n"; }
24:     };
25:
26:     int main()
27:     {
28:         Mammal bigAnimal;
29:         Dog fido;
30:         bigAnimal.Move();
31:         bigAnimal.Move(2);
32:         fido.Move();
33:         // fido.Move(10);
34:         return 0;
35:     }
```

11

OUTPUT
```
Mammal move one step
Mammal move 2 steps.
Dog move 5 steps.
```

ANALYSIS All the extra methods and data have been removed from these classes. On lines 8 and 9, the Mammal class declares the overloaded Move() methods. On line 23, Dog overrides the version of Move() with no parameters. These are invoked on lines 30–32, and the output reflects this as executed.

Line 33, however, is commented out because it causes a compile-time error. Although the Dog class could have called the Move(int) method if it had not overridden the version of Move() without parameters, now that it has done so, it must override both if it wants to use both. Otherwise, it will *hide* the method that it does not override. This is reminiscent of the rule that if you supply any constructor, the compiler will no longer supply a default constructor. The GNU compilers give the following message if you uncomment line 33:

```
lst11-06.cxx: In function `int main()':
lst11-06.cxx:33: too many arguments for method `void Dog::Move() const'
```

The rule is this: When you override any overloaded method, all the other overloads of that method are hidden. If you do not want them hidden, you must override them all.

It is a common mistake to hide a base class method when you intend to override it, by forgetting to include the keyword const. const is part of the signature, and leaving it off changes the signature and thus hides the method rather than overriding it.

Overriding Versus Hiding

In the next section, virtual methods are described. Overriding a virtual method supports polymorphism—hiding it undermines polymorphism. You will see more on this very soon.

Calling the Base Method

If you have overridden the base method, it is still possible to call it by fully qualifying the name of the method. You do this by writing the base name, followed by two colons and then the method name, for example: Mammal::Move().

It would have been possible to rewrite line 32 in Listing 11.6 so that it would compile, by writing

```
32:    fido.Mammal::Move(10);
```

This calls the Mammal method explicitly. Listing 11.7 fully illustrates this idea.

INPUT   **LISTING 11.7**   Calling Base Method from Overridden Method

```
1:    //Listing 11.7 Calling base method from overridden method.
2:
3:    #include <iostream.h>
4:
5:    class Mammal
6:    {
7:    public:
8:       void Move() const { cout << "Mammal move one step\n"; }
9:       void Move(int distance) const
10:      {
11:           cout << "Mammal move " << distance;
12:           cout << " steps.\n";
13:      }
14:
15:    protected:
```

```
16:        int itsAge;
17:        int itsWeight;
18:    };
19:
20:    class Dog : public Mammal
21:    {
22:    public:
23:        void Move()const;
24:
25:    };
26:
27:    void Dog::Move() const
28:    {
29:        cout << "In dog move...\n";
30:        Mammal::Move(3);
31:    }
32:
33:    int main()
34:    {
35:        Mammal bigAnimal;
36:        Dog fido;
37:        bigAnimal.Move(2);
38:        fido.Mammal::Move(6);
39:      return 0;
40:    }
```

OUTPUT

```
Mammal move 2 steps.
Mammal move 6 steps.
```

ANALYSIS On line 35, a `Mammal`, `bigAnimal`, is created, and on line 36, a `Dog`, `fido`, is created. The method call on line 37 invokes the `Move()` method of `Mammal`, which takes an `int`.

The programmer wanted to invoke `Move(int)` on the `Dog` object, but had a problem. `Dog` overrides the `Move()` method, but does not overload it and does not provide a version that takes an `int`. This is solved by the explicit call to the base class `Move(int)` method on line 38.

Do	Don't
DO extend the functionality of tested classes by deriving. **DO** change the behavior of certain functions in the derived class by overriding the base class methods.	**DON'T** hide a base class function by changing the function signature.

Virtual Methods

This lesson has emphasized the fact that a Dog object is a Mammal object. So far that has meant only that the Dog object has inherited the attributes (data) and capabilities (methods) of its base class. In C++ the *is-a* relationship runs deeper than that, however.

C++ extends its polymorphism to allow pointers to base classes to be assigned to derived class objects. Thus, you can write

```
Mammal* pMammal = new Dog;
```

This creates a new Dog object on the heap and returns a pointer to that object, which it assigns to a pointer to Mammal. This is fine because a dog is a mammal.

 Note

This is the essence of polymorphism. For example, you could create many types of windows, including dialog boxes, scrollable windows, and list boxes, and give them each a virtual draw() method. By creating a pointer to a window and assigning dialog boxes and other derived types to that pointer, you can call draw() without regard to the actual runtime type of the object pointed to. The correct draw() function will be called.

You can then use this pointer to invoke any method on Mammal. What you would like is for those methods that are overridden in Dog() to call the correct function. Virtual functions enable you to do that. Listing 11.8 illustrates how this works, and what happens with nonvirtual methods.

INPUT   **LISTING 11.8**   Using Virtual Methods

```
1:     //Listing 11.8 Using virtual methods
2:
3:     #include <iostream.h>
4:
5:     class Mammal
6:     {
7:     public:
8:         Mammal():itsAge(1) { cout << "Mammal constructor...\n"; }
9:         virtual ~Mammal() { cout << "Mammal destructor...\n"; }
10:        void Move() const { cout << "Mammal move one step\n"; }
11:        virtual void Speak() const { cout << "Mammal speak!\n"; }
12:    protected:
13:        int itsAge;
14:
15:    };
```

```
16:
17:    class Dog : public Mammal
18:    {
19:    public:
20:       Dog() { cout << "Dog Constructor...\n"; }
21:       virtual ~Dog() { cout << "Dog destructor...\n"; }
22:       void WagTail() { cout << "Wagging Tail...\n"; }
23:       void Speak()const { cout << "Woof!\n"; }
24:       void Move()const { cout << "Dog moves 5 steps...\n"; }
25:    };
26:
27:    int main()
28:    {
29:
30:       Mammal *pDog = new Dog;
31:       pDog->Move();
32:       pDog->Speak();
33:
34:     return 0;
35:    }
```

OUTPUT

```
Mammal constructor...
Dog Constructor...
Mammal move one step
Woof!
```

ANALYSIS On line 11, Mammal is provided a virtual method—speak(). The designer of this class thereby signals that she expects this class eventually to be another class's base type. The derived class will probably want to override this function.

On line 30, a pointer to Mammal is created (pDog), but it is assigned the address of a new Dog object. Because a dog is a mammal, this is a legal assignment. The pointer is then used to call the Move() function. Because the compiler knows pDog only to be a Mammal, it looks to the Mammal object to find the Move() method.

On line 32, the pointer then calls the Speak() method. Because Speak() is virtual, the Speak() method overridden in Dog is invoked.

This is almost magical. As far as the calling function knew, it had a Mammal pointer, but here a method on Dog was called. In fact, if you had an array of pointers to Mammal, each of which pointed to a subclass of Mammal, you could call each in turn, and the correct function would be called. Listing 11.9 illustrates this idea.

11

LISTING 11.9   Multiple Virtual Functions Called in Turn

```
1:      //Listing 11.9 Multiple virtual functions called in turn
2:
3:      #include <iostream.h>
4:
5:      class Mammal
6:      {
7:      public:
8:         Mammal():itsAge(1) {  }
9:         virtual ~Mammal() { }
10:        virtual void Speak() const { cout << "Mammal speak!\n"; }
11:     protected:
12:        int itsAge;
13:     };
14:
15:     class Dog : public Mammal
16:     {
17:     public:
18:        void Speak()const { cout << "Woof!\n"; }
19:     };
20:
21:
22:     class Cat : public Mammal
23:     {
24:     public:
25:        void Speak()const { cout << "Meow!\n"; }
26:     };
27:
28:
29:     class Horse : public Mammal
30:     {
31:     public:
32:        void Speak()const { cout << "Whinny!\n"; }
33:     };
34:
35:     class Pig : public Mammal
36:     {
37:     public:
38:        void Speak()const { cout << "Oink!\n"; }
39:     };
40:
41:     int main()
42:     {
43:        Mammal* theArray[5];
44:        Mammal* ptr;
45:        int choice, i;
46:        for ( i = 0; i<5; i++)
47:        {
48:           cout << "(1)dog (2)cat (3)horse (4)pig: ";
```

```
49:            cin >> choice;
50:            switch (choice)
51:            {
52:               case 1: ptr = new Dog;
53:               break;
54:               case 2: ptr = new Cat;
55:               break;
56:               case 3: ptr = new Horse;
57:               break;
58:               case 4: ptr = new Pig;
59:               break;
60:               default: ptr = new Mammal;
61:               break;
62:            }
63:            theArray[i] = ptr;
64:        }
65:        for (i=0;i<5;i++)
66:            theArray[i]->Speak();
67:        return 0;
68:    }
```

OUTPUT

```
(1)dog (2)cat (3)horse (4)pig: 1
(1)dog (2)cat (3)horse (4)pig: 2
(1)dog (2)cat (3)horse (4)pig: 3
(1)dog (2)cat (3)horse (4)pig: 4
(1)dog (2)cat (3)horse (4)pig: 5
Woof!
Meow!
Whinny!
Oink!
Mammal speak!
```

11

ANALYSIS This stripped-down program, which provides only the barest functionality to each class, illustrates virtual functions in their purest form. Four classes are declared: Dog, Cat, Horse, and Pig are all derived from Mammal.

On line 10, Mammal's Speak() function is declared to be virtual. On lines 18, 25, 32, and 38, the four derived classes override the implementation of Speak().

The user is prompted to pick which objects to create, and the pointers are added to the array on lines 46–64.

Note

At compile time, it is impossible to know which objects will be created, and thus which Speak() methods will be invoked. The pointer ptr is bound to its object at runtime. This is called dynamic binding, or runtime binding, as opposed to static binding, or compile-time binding.

How Virtual Functions Work

When a derived object, such as a Dog object, is created, first the constructor for the base class is called, and then the constructor for the derived class is called. Figure 11.2 shows what the Dog object looks like after it is created. Note that the Mammal part of the object is contiguous in memory with the Dog part.

FIGURE 11.2

The Dog *object after it is created.*

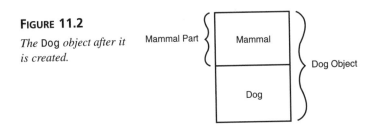

When a virtual function is created in an object, the object must keep track of that function. Many compilers build a *virtual function table*, called a v-table. One of these is kept for each type, and each object of that type keeps a virtual table pointer (called a vptr or v-pointer), which points to that table.

Although implementations vary, all compilers must accomplish the same thing, so you will not be too wrong with this description.

Each object's vptr points to the v-table which, in turn, has a pointer to each of the virtual functions. (Note: Pointers to functions will be discussed in depth on Day 14, "Special Classes and Functions.") When the Mammal part of the Dog is created, the vptr is initialized to point to the correct part of the v-table, as shown in Figure 11.3.

When the Dog constructor is called, and the Dog part of this object is added, the vptr is adjusted to point to the virtual function overrides (if any) in the Dog object (see Figure 11.4).

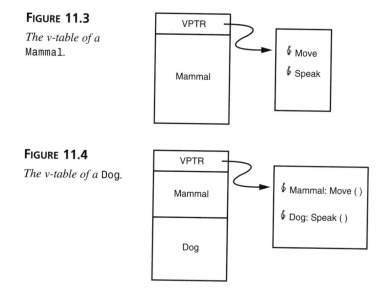

FIGURE 11.3

The v-table of a `Mammal`.

FIGURE 11.4

The v-table of a `Dog`.

When a pointer to a `Mammal` is used, the `vptr` continues to point to the correct function, depending on the "real" type of the object. Thus, when `Speak()` is invoked, the correct function is invoked.

You Cannot Get There from Here

If the `Dog` object had a method, `WagTail()`, which is not in the `Mammal`, you could not use the pointer to `Mammal` to access that method (unless you cast it to be a pointer to `Dog`). Because `WagTail()` is not a virtual function, and because it is not in a `Mammal` object, you cannot get there without either a `Dog` object or a `Dog` pointer.

Although you can transform the `Mammal` pointer into a `Dog` pointer, usually much better and safer ways exist to call the `WagTail()` method. C++ frowns on explicit casts because they are error-prone. This subject will be addressed in depth when multiple inheritance is covered on Day 13, " Polymorphism," and again when templates are covered on Day 20, "Exceptions and Error Handling."

Data Slicing

Data Slicing is what happens when the compiler selects the virtual function that is part of a base class instead of one in a derived class. Normally, you would want to execute a function with the same name in the derived class. The term *virtual function magic* is often applied to this process.

Note that the virtual function magic operates only on pointers and references. Passing an object by value will not enable the virtual functions to be invoked. Listing 11.10 illustrates this problem.

　　LISTING 11.10　Data Slicing When Passing by Value

```
1:    //Listing 11.10 Data slicing when passing by value
2:
3:    #include <iostream.h>
4:
5:    class Mammal
6:    {
7:    public:
8:       Mammal():itsAge(1) {  }
9:       virtual ~Mammal() { }
10:      virtual void Speak() const { cout << "Mammal speak!\n"; }
11:   protected:
12:      int itsAge;
13:   };
14:
15:   class Dog : public Mammal
16:   {
17:   public:
18:      void Speak()const { cout << "Woof!\n"; }
19:   };
20:
21:   class Cat : public Mammal
22:   {
23:   public:
24:      void Speak()const { cout << "Meow!\n"; }
25:   };
26:
27:   void ValueFunction (Mammal);
28:   void PtrFunction    (Mammal*);
29:   void RefFunction (Mammal&);
30:   int main()
31:   {
32:      Mammal* ptr=NULL;
33:      int choice;
34:      while (1)
35:      {
36:         bool fQuit = false;
37:         cout << "(1)dog (2)cat (0)Quit: ";
38:         cin >> choice;
39:         switch (choice)
40:         {
41:            case 0: fQuit = true;
42:            break;
43:            case 1: ptr = new Dog;
```

```
44:                break;
45:                case 2: ptr = new Cat;
46:                break;
47:                default: ptr = new Mammal;
48:                break;
49:            }
50:            if (fQuit)
51:                break;
52:            PtrFunction(ptr);
53:            RefFunction(*ptr);
54:            ValueFunction(*ptr);
55:        }
56:        return 0;
57:    }
58:
59:    void ValueFunction (Mammal MammalValue)
60:    {
61:        MammalValue.Speak();
62:    }
63:
64:    void PtrFunction (Mammal * pMammal)
65:    {
66:        pMammal->Speak();
67:    }
68:
69:    void RefFunction (Mammal & rMammal)
70:    {
71:        rMammal.Speak();
72:    }
```

OUTPUT

```
(1)dog (2)cat (0)Quit: 1
Woof
Woof
Mammal Speak!
(1)dog (2)cat (0)Quit: 2
Meow!
Meow!
Mammal Speak!
(1)dog (2)cat (0)Quit: 0
```

ANALYSIS On lines 5–25, stripped-down versions of the Mammal, Dog, and Cat classes are declared. Three functions are declared—PtrFunction(), RefFunction(), and ValueFunction(). They take a pointer to a Mammal, a Mammal reference, and a Mammal object, respectively. All three functions then do the same thing—they call the Speak() method.

The user is prompted to choose a Dog or a Cat, and based on the choice he makes, a pointer to the correct type is created on lines 43–46.

11

In the first line of the output, the user chooses `Dog`. The `Dog` object is created on the free store on line 43. The `Dog` is then passed as a pointer, as a reference, and by value to the three functions.

The pointer and references all invoke the virtual functions, and the `Dog->Speak()` member function is invoked. This is shown on the first two lines of output after the user's choice.

The dereferenced pointer, however, is passed by value. The function expects a `Mammal` object, and so the compiler slices down the `Dog` object to just the `Mammal` part. At that point, the `Mammal Speak()` method is called, as reflected in the third line of output after the user's choice.

This experiment is then repeated for the `Cat` object, with similar results.

Virtual Destructors

It is legal and common to pass a pointer to a derived object when a pointer to a base object is expected. What happens when that pointer to a derived subject is deleted? If the destructor is virtual, as it should be, the right thing happens—the derived class's destructor is called. Because the derived class's destructor will automatically invoke the base class's destructor, the entire object will be properly destroyed.

The rule of thumb is this: If any of the functions in your class are virtual, the destructor should be as well.

Virtual Copy Constructors

Constructors cannot be virtual, and so, technically, no such thing exists as a virtual copy constructor. Nonetheless, at times your program desperately needs to be able to pass in a pointer to a base object and have a copy of the correct derived object that is created. A common solution to this problem is to create a `Clone()` method in the base class and to make that virtual. The `Clone()` method creates a new object copy of the current class and returns that object.

Because each derived class overrides the `Clone()` method, a copy of the derived class is created. Listing 11.11 illustrates how this is used.

INPUT   **LISTING 11.11**   Virtual Copy Constructor

```
1:      //Listing 11.11 Virtual copy constructor
2:
3:      #include <iostream.h>
4:
```

```
5:     class Mammal
6:     {
7:     public:
8:         Mammal():itsAge(1) { cout << "Mammal constructor...\n"; }
9:         virtual ~Mammal() { cout << "Mammal destructor...\n"; }
10:        Mammal (const Mammal & rhs);
11:        virtual void Speak() const { cout << "Mammal speak!\n"; }
12:        virtual Mammal* Clone() { return new Mammal(*this); }
13:        int GetAge()const { return itsAge; }
14:    protected:
15:        int itsAge;
16:    };
17:
18:    Mammal::Mammal (const Mammal & rhs):itsAge(rhs.GetAge())
19:    {
20:        cout << "Mammal Copy Constructor...\n";
21:    }
22:
23:    class Dog : public Mammal
24:    {
25:    public:
26:        Dog() { cout << "Dog constructor...\n"; }
27:        virtual ~Dog() { cout << "Dog destructor...\n"; }
28:        Dog (const Dog & rhs);
29:        void Speak()const { cout << "Woof!\n"; }
30:        virtual Mammal* Clone() { return new Dog(*this); }
31:    };
32:
33:    Dog::Dog(const Dog & rhs):
34:    Mammal(rhs)
35:    {
36:        cout << "Dog copy constructor...\n";
37:    }
38:
39:    class Cat : public Mammal
40:    {
41:    public:
42:        Cat() { cout << "Cat constructor...\n"; }
43:        ~Cat() { cout << "Cat destructor...\n"; }
44:        Cat (const Cat &);
45:        void Speak()const { cout << "Meow!\n"; }
46:        virtual Mammal* Clone() { return new Cat(*this); }
47:    };
48:
49:    Cat::Cat(const Cat & rhs):
50:    Mammal(rhs)
51:    {
52:        cout << "Cat copy constructor...\n";
53:    }
54:
55:    enum ANIMALS { MAMMAL, DOG, CAT};
```

continues

LISTING 11.11 CONTINUED

```
56:    const int NumAnimalTypes = 3;
57:    int main()
58:    {
59:       Mammal *theArray[NumAnimalTypes];
60:       Mammal* ptr;
61:       int choice, i;
62:       for ( i = 0; i<NumAnimalTypes; i++)
63:       {
64:          cout << "(1)dog (2)cat (3)Mammal: ";
65:          cin >> choice;
66:          switch (choice)
67:          {
68:             case DOG: ptr = new Dog;
69:             break;
70:             case CAT: ptr = new Cat;
71:             break;
72:             default: ptr = new Mammal;
73:             break;
74:          }
75:          theArray[i] = ptr;
76:       }
77:       Mammal *OtherArray[NumAnimalTypes];
78:       for (i=0;i<NumAnimalTypes;i++)
79:       {
80:          theArray[i]->Speak();
81:          OtherArray[i] = theArray[i]->Clone();
82:       }
83:       for (i=0;i<NumAnimalTypes;i++)
84:          OtherArray[i]->Speak();
85:       return 0;
86:    }
```

OUTPUT

```
1:  (1)dog (2)cat (3)Mammal: 1
2:  Mammal constructor...
3:  Dog constructor...
4:  (1)dog (2)cat (3)Mammal: 2
5:  Mammal constructor...
6:  Cat constructor...
7:  (1)dog (2)cat (3)Mammal: 3
8:  Mammal constructor...
9:  Woof!
10: Mammal Copy Constructor...
11: Dog copy constructor...
12: Meow!
13: Mammal Copy Constructor...
14: Cat copy constructor...
15: Mammal speak!
16: Mammal Copy Constructor...
```

```
17: Woof!
18: Meow!
19: Mammal speak!
```

ANALYSIS Listing 11.11 is very similar to the previous two listings, except that a new virtual method has been added to the `Mammal` class: `Clone()`. This method returns a pointer to a new `Mammal` object by calling the copy constructor, passing in itself (`*this`) as a `const` reference.

`Dog` and `Cat` both override the `Clone()` method, initializing their data and passing in copies of themselves to their own copy constructors. Because `Clone()` is virtual, this will effectively create a virtual copy constructor, as shown on line 81.

The user is prompted to choose dogs, cats, or mammals, and these are created on lines 62–74. A pointer to each choice is stored in an array on line 75.

As the program iterates over the array, each object has its `Speak()` and its `Clone()` methods called, in turn, on lines 80 and 81. The result of the `Clone()` call is a pointer to a copy of the object, which is then stored in a second array on line 81.

On line 1 of the output, the user is prompted and responds with 1, choosing to create a dog. The `Mammal` and `Dog` constructors are invoked. This is repeated for `Cat` and for `Mammal` on lines 4 and 7 of the output.

Line 9 of the output represents the call to `Speak()` on the first object, the `Dog`. The virtual `Speak()` method is called, and the correct version of `Speak()` is invoked. The `Clone()` function is then called, and because this is also virtual, `Dog`'s `Clone()` method is invoked, causing the `Mammal` constructor and the `Dog` copy constructor to be called.

The same is repeated for `Cat` on lines 12–14, and then for `Mammal` on lines 15 and 16. Finally, the new array is iterated, and each of the new objects has `Speak()` invoked.

The Cost of Virtual Methods

Because objects with virtual methods must maintain a v-table, some overhead occurs in having virtual methods. If you have a very small class from which you do not expect to derive other classes, there may be no reason to have any virtual methods at all.

When you declare any methods virtual, you have already paid most of the price of the v-table (although each entry does add a small memory overhead). At that point, you want the destructor to be virtual, and the assumption will be that all other methods probably will be virtual as well. Take a long, hard look at any nonvirtual methods, and be certain you understand why they are not virtual.

11

Do	Don't
DO use virtual methods when you expect to derive from a class.	**DON'T** mark the constructor as virtual.
DO use a virtual destructor if any methods are virtual.	

Summary

Today you learned how derived classes inherit from base classes. This lesson discussed public inheritance and virtual functions. Classes inherit all the public and protected data and functions from their base classes.

Protected access is public to derived classes and private to all other objects. Even derived classes cannot access private data or functions in their base classes.

Constructors can be initialized before the body of the constructor. At that time, the base constructors are invoked and parameters can be passed to the base class.

Functions in the base class can be overridden in the derived class. If the base class functions are virtual, and if the object is accessed by pointer or reference, the derived class's functions will be invoked, based on the runtime type of the object pointed to.

Methods in the base class can be invoked by explicitly naming the function with the prefix of the base class name and two colons. For example, if Dog inherits from Mammal, Mammal's walk() method can be called with Mammal::walk().

In classes with virtual methods, the destructor should almost always be made virtual. A virtual destructor ensures that the derived part of the object will be freed when delete is called on the pointer. Constructors cannot be virtual. Virtual copy constructors can be effectively created by making a virtual member function that calls the copy constructor.

Q&A

Q Are inherited members and functions passed along to subsequent generations? If Dog derives from Mammal, and Mammal derives from Animal, does Dog inherit Animal's functions and data?

A Yes. As derivation continues, derived classes inherit the sum of all the functions and data in all their base classes.

Q If, in the preceding example, `Mammal` overrides a function in `Animal`, which does `Dog` get, the original or the overridden function?

A If `Dog` inherits from `Mammal`, it gets the function in the state `Mammal` has it: the overridden function.

Q Can a derived class make a public base function private?

A Yes, the derived class can override the method and make it private. It then remains private for all subsequent derivation.

Q Why not make all class functions virtual?

A Overhead occurs with the first virtual function in the creation of a v-table. After that, the overhead is trivial. Many C++ programmers feel that if one function is virtual, all others should be. Other programmers disagree, feeling that there should always be a reason for what you do.

Q If a function (`SomeFunc()`) is virtual in a base class and is also overloaded, so as to take either an integer or two integers, and the derived class overrides the form taking one integer, what is called when a pointer to a derived object calls the two-integer form?

A The overriding of the one-`int` form hides the entire base class function, and thus you will get a compile error complaining that that function requires only one `int`.

Workshop

The Workshop provides quiz questions to help you solidify your understanding of the material that was covered and exercises to provide you with experience in using what you learned today. Try to answer the quiz and exercise questions before checking the answers in Appendix D, "Answers to Exercises and Quizzes," and make sure you understand the answers before continuing to tomorrow's lesson.

Quiz

1. What is a v-table?
2. What is a virtual destructor?
3. How do you show the declaration of a virtual constructor?
4. How can you create a virtual copy constructor?
5. How do you invoke a base member function from a derived class in which you've overridden that function?
6. How do you invoke a base member function from a derived class in which you have not overridden that function?

7. If a base class declares a function to be virtual, and a derived class does not use the term virtual when overriding that class, is it still virtual when inherited by a third-generation class?

8. What is the protected keyword used for?

Exercises

1. Show the declaration of a virtual function that takes an integer parameter and returns void.

2. Show the declaration of a class Square, which derives from Rectangle, which in turn derives from Shape.

3. If, in Exercise 2, Shape takes no parameters, Rectangle takes two (length and width), but Square takes only one (length), show the constructor initialization for Square.

4. Write a virtual copy constructor for the class Square (in Exercise 3).

5. **BUG BUSTER**: What is wrong with this code snippet?

```
void SomeFunction (Shape);
Shape * pRect = new Rectangle;
SomeFunction(*pRect);
```

6. **BUG BUSTER:** What is wrong with this code snippet?

```
class Shape()
{
public:
     Shape();
     virtual ~Shape();
     virtual Shape(const Shape&);
};
```

DAY 12

Arrays, C Strings, and Linked Lists

In previous lessons, you declared a single `int`, `char`, or other object. You often want to declare a collection of objects, such as 20 `ints` or a litter of `CATs`. Today, you will learn:

- What arrays are and how to declare them
- What strings are and how to use character arrays to make them
- The relationship between arrays and pointers
- How to use pointer arithmetic with arrays

What Is an Array?

An *array* is a collection of data storage locations, each of which holds the same type of data. Each storage location is called an *element* of the array.

You declare an array by writing the type, followed by the array name and the subscript. The *subscript* is the number of elements in the array, surrounded by square brackets. Another word for subscript is *offset* since it represents the distance from the beginning of the array. For example:

```
long LongArray[25];
```

This example declares an array of 25 long integers, named `LongArray`. When the compiler sees this declaration, it sets aside enough memory to hold all 25 elements. Because each long integer requires 4 bytes, this declaration sets aside 100 contiguous bytes of memory, as illustrated in Figure 12.1.

FIGURE 12.1

Declaring an array.

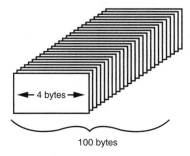

Accessing Array Elements

You access each of the array elements by referring to an offset from the array name. Array elements are counted from zero. Therefore, the first array element is `arrayName[0]`. In the `LongArray` example, `LongArray[0]` is the first array element, `LongArray[1]` the second, and so forth.

This can be somewhat confusing. The array `SomeArray[3]` has three elements. They are `SomeArray[0]`, `SomeArray[1]`, and `SomeArray[2]`. More generally, `SomeArray[n]` has n elements that are numbered `SomeArray[0]` through `SomeArray[n-1]`.

Therefore, `LongArray[25]` is numbered from `LongArray[0]` through `LongArray[24]`. Listing 12.1 shows how to declare an array of five integers and fill each with a value.

INPUT   **LISTING 12.1**   Using an Integer Array

```
1:      //Listing 12.1 - Arrays
2:      #include <iostream.h>
3:
4:      int main()
5:      {
6:          int myArray[5];
7:          int i;
8:          for ( i=0; i<5; i++)   // 0-4
9:          {
```

```
10:             cout << "Value for myArray[" << i << "]: ";
11:          cin >> myArray[i];
12:      }
13:      for (i = 0; i<5; i++)
14:          cout << i << ": " << myArray[i] << "\n";
15:      return 0;
16:    }
```

OUTPUT
```
Value for myArray[0]:  3
Value for myArray[1]:  6
Value for myArray[2]:  9
Value for myArray[3]:  12
Value for myArray[4]:  15
0: 3
1: 6
2: 9
3: 12
4: 15
```

ANALYSIS Line 6 declares an array called myArray, which holds five integer variables. Line 8 establishes a loop that counts from 0 through 4, which is the proper set of offsets for a five-element array. The user is prompted for a value, and that value is saved at the correct offset into the array.

The first value is saved at myArray[0], the second at myArray[1], and so forth. The second for loop prints each value to the screen.

Note Arrays count from 0, not from 1. This is the cause of many bugs in programs written by C++ novices. Whenever you use an array, remember that an array with 10 elements counts from ArrayName[0] to ArrayName[9]. ArrayName[10] is not used.

12

Writing Past the End of an Array

When you write a value to an element in an array, the compiler computes where to store the value based on the size of each element and the subscript. Suppose that you ask to write over the value at LongArray[5], which is the sixth element. The compiler multiplies the offset (5) by the size of each element—in this case, 4. It then moves that many bytes (20) from the beginning of the array and writes the new value at that location.

Remember that *subscript* and *offset* are synonyms.

If you ask to write at LongArray[50], the compiler ignores the fact that no such element exists. It computes how far past the first element it should look (200 bytes) and then writes over whatever is at that location. This can be virtually any data, and writing your new value there might have unpredictable results. If you are lucky, your program will crash immediately. If not, you will eventually get strange results much later in your program, and you will have a difficult time figuring out what went wrong.

In a robust operating system like Linux, a program crash will not affect the operating system itself. In a non-robust environment (like MS-DOS), a program can overwrite portions of the operating system, causing your machine to freeze. These problems are particularly difficult to debug. In rare cases, a rogue program can affect Linux—primarily when it runs with root privileges.

The compiler is like a blind man pacing off the distance from a house. He starts out at the first house, MainStreet[0]. When you ask him to go to the sixth house on Main Street, he says to himself, "I must go five more houses. Each house is four big paces from the other. I must go an additional 20 steps." If you ask him to go to MainStreet[100] and Main Street is only 25 houses long, he will pace off 400 steps. Long before he gets there, he will, no doubt, step in front of a moving bus. So be careful where you send him.

Listing 12.2 shows what happens when you write past the end of an array.

Caution Do not run this program; it may crash a non-Linux system!

INPUT   **LISTING 12.2** Writing Past the End of an Array

```
1:      //Listing 12.2
2:      // Demonstrates what happens when you write past the end
3:      // of an array
4:
5:      #include <iostream.h>
6:      int main()
7:      {
8:         // sentinels
9:         long sentinelOne[3];
10:        long TargetArray[25]; // array to fill
11:        long sentinelTwo[3];
12:        int i;
13:        for (i=0; i<3; i++)
14:            sentinelOne[i] = sentinelTwo[i] = 0;
15:
```

```
16:        for (i=0; i<25; i++)
17:           TargetArray[i] = 0;
18:
19:        cout << "Test 1: \n";   // test current values (should be 0)
20:        cout << "TargetArray[0]: " << TargetArray[0] << "\n";
21:        cout << "TargetArray[24]: " << TargetArray[24] << "\n\n";
22:
23:        for (i = 0; i<3; i++)
24:        {
25:           cout << "sentinelOne[" << i << "]: ";
26:           cout << sentinelOne[i] << "\n";
27:           cout << "sentinelTwo[" << i << "]: ";
28:            cout << sentinelTwo[i]<< "\n";
29:        }
30:
31:        cout << "\nAssigning...";
32:        for (i = 0; i<=25; i++)
33:           TargetArray[i] = 20;
34:
35:        cout << "\nTest 2: \n";
36:        cout << "TargetArray[0]: " << TargetArray[0] << "\n";
37:        cout << "TargetArray[24]: " << TargetArray[24] << "\n";
38:        cout << "TargetArray[25]: " << TargetArray[25] << "\n\n";
39:        for (i = 0; i<3; i++)
40:        {
41:           cout << "sentinelOne[" << i << "]: ";
42:           cout << sentinelOne[i]<< "\n";
43:           cout << "sentinelTwo[" << i << "]: ";
44:           cout << sentinelTwo[i]<< "\n";
45:        }
46:
47:     return 0;
48:     }
```

12

OUTPUT
```
Test 1:
TargetArray[0]: 0
TargetArray[24]: 0

SentinelOne[0]: 0
SentinelTwo[0]: 0
SentinelOne[1]: 0
SentinelTwo[1]: 0
SentinelOne[2]: 0
SentinelTwo[2]: 0

Assigning...
Test 2:
TargetArray[0]: 20
TargetArray[24]: 20
TargetArray[25]: 20
```

```
SentinelOne[0]: 20
SentinelTwo[0]: 0
SentinelOne[1]: 0
SentinelTwo[1]: 0
SentinelOne[2]: 0
SentinelTwo[2]: 0
```

ANALYSIS Lines 9 and 11 declare two arrays of three integers that act as sentinels around TargetArray. These sentinel arrays are initialized with the value 0. If memory is written to beyond the end of TargetArray, the sentinels are likely to be changed. Some compilers count down in memory; others count up. For this reason, the sentinels are placed on both sides of TargetArray.

Lines 19–29 confirm the sentinel values in Test 1. In line 33, TargetArray's members are all initialized to the value 20, but the counter counts to TargetArray offset 25, which does not exist in TargetArray.

Lines 36–38 print TargetArray's values in Test 2. Note that TargetArray[25] is perfectly happy to print the value 20. However, when SentinelOne and SentinelTwo are printed, SentinelOne[0] reveals that its value has changed. This is because the memory that is 25 elements after TargetArray[0] is the same memory that is at SentinelOne[0]. When the nonexistent TargetArray[25] was accessed, what was actually accessed was SentinelOne[0].

This nasty bug can be very hard to find, because SentinelOne[0]'s value was changed in a part of the code that was not writing to SentinelOne at all.

This code uses "magic numbers" such as 3 for the size of the sentinel arrays and 25 for the size of TargetArray. It is safer to use constants so that you can change all these values in one place.

Note that because all compilers use memory differently, your results may vary.

Fence Post Errors

Because it is so common to write to one past the end of an array, this bug has its own name. It is called a *fence post error*. This refers to the problem in counting how many fence posts you need for a 10-foot fence if you need one post for every foot. Most people answer 10, but of course you need 11. Figure 12.2 makes this clear.

This type of "off by one" counting can be the bane of any programmer's life. Over time, however, you'll get used to the idea that a 25-element array counts only to element 24, and that everything counts from 0.

FIGURE 12.2

Fence post errors.

> **Note**
>
> Some programmers refer to ArrayName[0] as the zeroth element. Getting into this habit is a big mistake. If ArrayName[0] is the zeroth element, what is ArrayName[1]? The oneth? If so, when you see ArrayName[24], will you realize that it is not the 24th element, but rather the 25th? It is far better to say that ArrayName[0] is at offset zero and is the first element.
>
> Pay attention to that: offset zero and first element—different numbers describing the same location. Be sure you do not switch the two in your mind.

Initializing Arrays

You can initialize a simple array of built-in types, such as integers and characters, when you first declare the array. After the array name, you put an equal sign (=) and a list of comma-separated values enclosed in braces. For example,

```
int IntegerArray[5] = { 10, 20, 30, 40, 50 };
```

declares IntegerArray to be an array of five integers. It assigns IntegerArray[0] the value 10, IntegerArray[1] the value 20, and so forth.

If you omit the size of the array, an array just big enough to hold the initialization is created. Therefore, if you write

```
int IntegerArray[] = { 10, 20, 30, 40, 50 };
```

you will create the same array as you did in the previous example.

If you need to know the size of the array, you can ask the compiler to compute it for you. For example,

```
const USHORT IntegerArrayLength;
IntegerArrayLength = sizeof(IntegerArray)/sizeof(IntegerArray[0]);
```

sets the constant USHORT variable IntegerArrayLength to the result obtained from dividing the size of the entire array by the size of each individual entry in the array. That quotient is the number of members in the array.

You cannot initialize more elements than you declared for the array. Therefore,

12

```
int IntegerArray[5] = { 10, 20, 30, 40, 50, 60};
```

generates a compiler error because you declared a five-member array and initialized six values. It is legal, however, to write

```
int IntegerArray[5] = { 10, 20};
```

Although uninitialized array members have no guaranteed values, aggregates will be initialized to 0. Thus, if you do not initialize an array member, its value will be set to 0.

Do	Don't
DO let the compiler set the size of initialized arrays.	**DON'T** write past the end of the array.
DO give arrays meaningful names, as you would with any variable.	
DO remember that the first member of the array is at offset 0.	

Declaring Arrays

Arrays can have any legal variable name, but they cannot have the same name as another variable or array within their scope. Therefore, you cannot have an array named myCats[5] and a variable named myCats at the same time.

You can dimension the array size with a const or with an enumeration. Listing 12.3 illustrates this.

INPUT   **LISTING 12.3**   Using consts and enums in Arrays

```
1:     // Listing 12.3
2:     // Dimensioning arrays with consts and enumerations
3:
4:     #include <iostream.h>
5:     int main()
6:     {
7:        enum WeekDays { Sun, Mon, Tue,
8:            Wed, Thu, Fri, Sat, DaysInWeek };
9:        int ArrayWeek[DaysInWeek] = { 10, 20, 30, 40, 50, 60, 70 };
10:
11:        cout << "The value at Tuesday is: " << ArrayWeek[Tue];
12:     return 0;
13:     }
```

OUTPUT `The value at Tuesday is: 30`

ANALYSIS Line 7 creates an enumeration called WeekDays. It has eight members. Sunday is equal to 0, and DaysInWeek is equal to 7.

Line 11 uses the enumerated constant Tue as an offset into the array. Because Tue evaluates to 2, the third element of the array, ArrayWeek[2], is returned and printed in line 11.

Arrays

To declare an array, write the type of object stored, followed by the name of the array and a subscript with the number of objects to be held in the array.

Example 1

```
int MyIntegerArray[90];
```

Example 2

```
long * ArrayOfPointersToLongs[100];
```

To access members of the array, use the subscript operator.

Example 1

```
int theNinethInteger = MyIntegerArray[8];
```

Example 2

```
long * pLong = ArrayOfPointersToLongs[8];
```

Arrays count from zero. An array of *n* items is numbered from 0–*n*–1.

12

Arrays of Objects

Any object, whether built-in or user-defined, can be stored in an array. When you declare the array, you tell the compiler the type of object to store and the number of objects for which to allocate room. The compiler knows how much room is needed for each object based on the class declaration. The class must have a default constructor that takes no arguments so that the objects can be created when the array is defined.

Accessing member data in an array of objects is a two-step process. You identify the member of the array by using the index operator ([ ]), and then you add the member operator (.) to access the particular member variable. Listing 12.4 demonstrates how you would create an array of five CATs.

INPUT
LISTING 12.4 Creating an Array of Objects

```
1:     // Listing 12.4 - An array of objects
2:
3:     #include <iostream.h>
4:
5:     class CAT
6:     {
7:        public:
8:           CAT() { itsAge = 1; itsWeight=5; }
9:           ~CAT() {}
10:          int GetAge() const { return itsAge; }
11:          int GetWeight() const { return itsWeight; }
12:          void SetAge(int age) { itsAge = age; }
13:
14:       private:
15:          int itsAge;
16:          int itsWeight;
17:    };
18:
19:    int main()
20:    {
21:       CAT Litter[5];
22:       int i;
23:       for (i = 0; i < 5; i++)
24:          Litter[i].SetAge(2*i +1);
25:
26:       for (i = 0; i < 5; i++)
27:       {
28:          cout << "Cat #" << i+1<< ": ";
29:          cout << Litter[i].GetAge() << endl;
30:       }
31:       return 0;
32:    }
```

OUTPUT
```
cat #1: 1
cat #2: 3
cat #3: 5
cat #4: 7
cat #5: 9
```

ANALYSIS
Lines 5–17 declare the CAT class. The CAT class must have a default constructor so that CAT objects can be created in an array. Remember that if you create any other constructor, the compiler-supplied default constructor is not created; you must create your own.

The first for loop (lines 23 and 24) sets the age of each of the five CATs in the array. The second for loop (lines 26–30) accesses each member of the array and calls GetAge().

Each individual CAT's GetAge() method is called by accessing the member in the array, Litter[i], followed by the dot operator (.), and the member function.

Working with Multidimensional Arrays

It is possible to have arrays of more than one dimension. Each dimension is represented as a subscript in the array. Therefore, a two-dimensional array has two subscripts; a three-dimensional array has three subscripts; and so on. Arrays can have any number of dimensions, although it is likely that most of the arrays you create will be of one or two dimensions.

A good example of a two-dimensional array is a chessboard. One dimension represents the eight rows; the other dimension represents the eight columns. Figure 12.3 illustrates this idea.

FIGURE 12.3

A chessboard and a two-dimensional array.

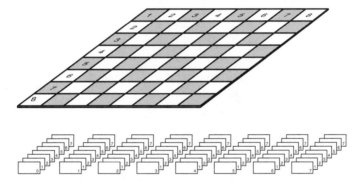

Suppose that you have a class named SQUARE. The declaration of an array named Board that represents it would be

```
SQUARE Board[8][8];
```

You could also represent the same data with a one-dimensional, 64-square array. For example:

```
SQUARE Board[64];
```

This does not correspond as closely to the real-world object as the two-dimensional array. When the game begins, the king is located in the fourth position in the first row. Counting from zero array, that position corresponds to

```
Board[0][3];
```

assuming that the first subscript corresponds to row and the second to column. The layout of positions for the entire board is illustrated in Figure 12.3.

Initializing Multidimensional Arrays

You can initialize multidimensional arrays. Assign the list of values to array elements in order, with the last array subscript changing while each of the former holds steady. Therefore, if you have an array

```
int theArray[5][3];
```

the first three elements go into `theArray[0]`; the next three into `theArray[1]`; and so forth.

You initialize this array by writing

```
int theArray[5][3] = { 1,2,3,4,5,6,7,8,9,10,11,12,13,14,15 };
```

For the sake of clarity, you could group the initializations with braces. For example:

```
int theArray[5][3] = {  {1,2,3},
{4,5,6},
{7,8,9},
{10,11,12},
{13,14,15} };
```

The compiler ignores the inner braces, which make it easier to understand how the numbers are distributed.

Each value must be separated by a comma, without regard to the braces. The entire initialization set must be within braces, and it must end with a semicolon.

Listing 12.5 creates a two-dimensional array. The first dimension is the set of numbers from 0–4. The second dimension consists of the double of each value in the first dimension.

INPUT   **LISTING 12.5**   Creating a Multidimensional Array

```
1:     #include <iostream.h>
2:     int main()
3:     {
4:         int SomeArray[5][2] = { {0,0}, {1,2}, {2,4}, {3,6}, {4,8}};
5:         for (int i = 0; i<5; i++)
6:             for (int j=0; j<2; j++)
7:             {
8:                 cout << "SomeArray[" << i << "][" << j << "]: ";
9:                 cout << SomeArray[i][j]<< endl;
10:            }
11:
12:     return 0;
13:     }
```

OUTPUT
```
SomeArray[0][0]: 0
SomeArray[0][1]: 0
SomeArray[1][0]: 1
SomeArray[1][1]: 2
SomeArray[2][0]: 2
SomeArray[2][1]: 4
SomeArray[3][0]: 3
SomeArray[3][1]: 6
SomeArray[4][0]: 4
SomeArray[4][1]: 8
```

ANALYSIS Line 4 declares `SomeArray` to be a two-dimensional array. The first dimension consists of five integers; the second dimension consists of two integers. This creates a 5×2 grid, as Figure 12.4 shows.

FIGURE 12.4

A 5×2 array.

Some Array [5] [2]

The values are initialized in pairs, although they could be computed as well. Lines 5 and 6 create a nested `for` loop. The outer `for` loop ticks through each member of the first dimension. For every member in that dimension, the inner `for` loop ticks through each member of the second dimension. This is consistent with the printout. `SomeArray[0][0]` is followed by `SomeArray[0][1]`. The first dimension is incremented only after the second dimension is incremented by 1. Then the second dimension starts over.

A Word About Arrays and Memory

When you declare an array, you tell the compiler exactly how many objects you expect to store in it. The compiler sets aside memory for all the objects, even if you never use it. This is not a problem with arrays for which you have a good idea of how many objects you will need. For example, a chessboard has 64 squares, and cats have between 1 and 10 kittens. When you have no idea of how many objects you will need, however, you must use more advanced data structures.

This book looks at arrays of pointers, arrays built on the free store, and various other collections. We will look at a few advanced data structures, and you can learn more in advanced books like *C++ Unleashed* by Sams Publishing. Two of the great things about programming are that there are always more things to learn and that there are always more books from which to learn.

12

Using the Free Store to Solve Memory Issues

The arrays discussed so far store all their members on the stack. Usually stack memory is severely limited, whereas free store memory is much larger. The size of arrays is of a static nature. Once you declare an array and compile your program, the size cannot change during execution. But there are ways around this limitation. Taking advantage of the free store allows you to have data structures that behave as if they were dynamic arrays.

Arrays of Pointers

It is possible to declare each object on the free store and then to store only a pointer to the object in the array. This dramatically reduces the amount of stack memory used. Listing 12.6 rewrites the array from Listing 12.4, but it stores all the objects on the free store. As an indication of the greater memory that this enables, the array is expanded from 5–500, and the name is changed from `Litter` to `Family`.

INPUT   **LISTING 12.6**   Storing an Array on the Free Store

```
1:    // Listing 12.6 - An array of pointers to objects
2:
3:    #include <iostream.h>
4:
5:    class CAT
6:    {
7:       public:
8:          CAT() { itsAge = 1; itsWeight=5; }
9:          ~CAT() {}                              // destructor
10:         int GetAge() const { return itsAge; }
11:         int GetWeight() const { return itsWeight; }
12:         void SetAge(int age) { itsAge = age; }
13:
14:      private:
15:         int itsAge;
16:         int itsWeight;
17:    };
18:
19:    int main()
20:    {
21:       CAT * Family[500];
22:       int i;
23:       CAT * pCat;
24:       for (i = 0; i < 500; i++)
25:       {
26:          pCat = new CAT;
27:          pCat->SetAge(2*i +1);
```

```
28:          Family[i] = pCat;
29:      }
30:
31:     for (i = 0; i < 500; i++)
32:     {
33:         cout << "Cat #" << i+1 << ": ";
34:         cout << Family[i]->GetAge() << endl;
35:     }
36:   return 0;
37:   }
```

OUTPUT

```
Cat #1: 1
Cat #2: 3
Cat #3: 5
...
Cat #499: 997
Cat #500: 999
```

ANALYSIS   The CAT object declared in lines 5–17 is identical with the CAT object declared in Listing 12.4. This time, however, the array declared in line 21 is named Family, and it is declared to hold 500 pointers to CAT objects.

In the initial loop (lines 24–29), 500 new CAT objects are created on the free store, and each one has its age set to twice the index plus one. Therefore, the first CAT is set to 1, the second CAT to 3, the third CAT to 5, and so on. Finally, the pointer is added to the array.

Because the array has been declared to hold pointers, the pointer—rather than the dereferenced value in the pointer—is added to the array.

The second loop (lines 31–35) prints each of the values. The pointer is accessed by using the index, Family[i]. That address is then used to access the GetAge() method.

In this example, the array Family and all its pointers are stored on the stack, but the 500 CATs that are created are stored on the free store.

Declaring Arrays on the Free Store

It is possible to put the entire array on the free store, also known as the *heap*. You do this by calling new and using the subscript operator. The result is a pointer to an area on the free store that holds the array. For example,

```
CAT *Family = new CAT[500];
```

declares Family to be a pointer to the first in an array of 500 CATs. In other words, Family points to—or has the address of—Family[0].

The advantage of using `Family` in this way is that you can use pointer arithmetic to access each member of `Family`. For example, you can write

```
CAT *Family = new CAT[500];
CAT *pCat = Family;              //pCat points to Family[0]
pCat->SetAge(10);               // set Family[0] to 10
pCat++;                         // advance to Family[1]
pCat->SetAge(20);               // set Family[1] to 20
```

This declares a new array of 500 CATs and a pointer to point to the start of the array. Using that pointer, the first CAT's `SetAge()` function is called with a value of 10. The pointer is then incremented to point to the next CAT, and the second CAT's `SetAge()` method is then called.

Using a Pointer to an Array Versus an Array of Pointers

Examine the following three declarations:

```
1:  Cat    FamilyOne[500];
2:  CAT * FamilyTwo[500];
3:  CAT * FamilyThree = new CAT[500];
```

`FamilyOne` is an array of 500 CATs. `FamilyTwo` is an array of 500 pointers to CATs. `FamilyThree` is a pointer to an array of 500 CATs.

The differences among these three code lines dramatically affect how these arrays operate. What is perhaps even more surprising is that `FamilyThree` is a variant of `FamilyOne`, but it is very different from `FamilyTwo`.

This raises the thorny issue of how pointers relate to arrays. In the third case, `FamilyThree` is a pointer to an array. That is, the address in `FamilyThree` is the address of the first item in that array. This is exactly the case for `FamilyOne`.

Using Pointers with Array Names

In C++ an array name is a constant pointer to the first element of the array. Therefore, in the declaration

```
CAT Family[50];
```

`Family` is a pointer to `&Family[0]`, which is the address of the first element of the array `Family`.

It is legal to use array names as constant pointers, and vice versa. Therefore, `Family + 4` is a legitimate way of accessing the data at `Family[4]`.

The compiler does all the arithmetic when you add to, increment, and decrement pointers. The address accessed when you write Family + 4 is not 4 bytes past the address of Family—it is 4 objects. If each object is 4 bytes long, Family + 4 is 16 bytes past the start of the array. If each object is a CAT that has 4 long member variables of 4 bytes each and two short member variables of 2 bytes each, each CAT is 20 bytes, and Family + 4 is 80 bytes past the start of the array.

Listing 12.7 illustrates declaring and using an array on the free store.

INPUT **LISTING 12.7** Creating an Array by Using new

```
1:      // Listing 12.7 - An array on the free store
2:
3:      #include <iostream.h>
4:
5:      class CAT
6:      {
7:         public:
8:            CAT() { itsAge = 1; itsWeight=5; }
9:            ~CAT();
10:           int GetAge() const { return itsAge; }
11:           int GetWeight() const { return itsWeight; }
12:           void SetAge(int age) { itsAge = age; }
13:
14:        private:
15:           int itsAge;
16:           int itsWeight;
17:      };
18:
19:      CAT :: ~CAT()
20:      {
21:        // cout << "Destructor called!\n";
22:      }
23:
24:      int main()
25:      {
26:        CAT * Family = new CAT[500];
27:        int i;
28:
29:        for (i = 0; i < 500; i++)
30:        {
31:            Family[i].SetAge(2*i +1);
32:        }
33:
34:        for (i = 0; i < 500; i++)
35:        {
36:           cout << "Cat #" << i+1 << ": ";
37:           cout << Family[i].GetAge() << endl;
```

continues

12

LISTING 12.7 CONTINUED

```
38:        }
39:
40:        delete [] Family;
41:
42:    return 0;
43:    }
```

```
Cat #1: 1
Cat #2: 3
Cat #3: 5
...
Cat #499: 997
Cat #500: 999
```

ANALYSIS Line 26 declares the array Family, which holds 500 CAT objects. The entire array is created on the free store with the call to new CAT[500].

Deleting Arrays on the Free Store

What happens to the memory allocated for these CAT objects when the array is destroyed? Is there a chance of a memory leak? Deleting Family automatically returns all the memory set aside for the array if you use the delete [ ] operator, remembering to include the square brackets. The compiler is smart enough to destroy each object in the array and to return its memory to the free store.

To see this, change the size of the array from 500 to 10 in lines 26, 29, and 34. Then uncomment the cout statement in line 21. When line 43 is reached and the array is destroyed, each CAT object destructor is called.

When you create an item on the heap by using new, you always delete that item and free its memory with delete. Similarly, when you create an array by using new <class>[size], you delete that array and free all its memory with delete[ ]. The brackets signal the compiler that this array is being deleted.

If you leave the brackets off, only the first object in the array will be deleted. You can prove this to yourself by removing the bracket on line 38. If you edited line 21 so that the destructor prints, you should now see only one CAT object destroyed. Congratulations! You just created a memory leak.

Do	Don't
DO remember that an array of *n* items is numbered from zero through *n*–1.	**DON'T** write or read past the end of an array.
DO use array indexing with pointers that point to arrays.	**DON'T** confuse an array of pointers with a pointer to an array.

What are char Arrays?

A string is a series of characters. The only strings you have seen until now have been unnamed string constants used in cout statements, such as

```
cout << "hello world.\n";
```

In C++ a string is an array of chars ending with a null character. You can declare and initialize a string the same as you would any other array. For example:

```
char Greeting[] =
{ 'H', 'e', 'l', 'l', 'o', ' ', 'W','o','r','l','d', '\0' };
```

The last character, '\0', is the null character, which many C++ functions recognize as the terminator for a string. Although this character-by-character approach works, it is difficult to type and it admits too many opportunities for error. C++ enables you to use a shorthand form of the previous line of code. It is

```
char Greeting[] = "Hello World";
```

You should note two things about this syntax:

- Instead of single-quoted characters separated by commas and surrounded by braces, you have a double-quoted string, no commas, and no braces.
- You do not need to add the null character because the compiler adds it for you.

The string Hello World is 12 bytes. Hello is 5 bytes, the space 1, World 5, and the null character 1.

You can also create uninitialized character arrays. As with all arrays, it is important to ensure that you do not put more into the buffer than there is room for.

Listing 12.8 demonstrates the use of an uninitialized buffer.

12

INPUT **LISTING 12.8** Filling an Array

```
1:     //Listing 12.8 char array buffers
2:
3:     #include <iostream.h>
4:
5:     int main()
6:     {
7:        char buffer[80];
8:        cout << "Enter the string: ";
9:        cin >> buffer;
10:       cout << "Here's the buffer:  " << buffer << endl;
11:    return 0;
12:    }
```

OUTPUT
```
Enter the string: Hello World
Here's the buffer:  Hello
```

ANALYSIS On line 7, a buffer is declared to hold 80 characters. This is large enough to hold a 79-character string and a terminating null character.

On line 8, the user is prompted to enter a string, which is entered into buffer on line 9. It is the syntax of cin to write a terminating null to buffer after it writes the string.

Two problems occur with the program in Listing 12.8. First, if the user enters more than 79 characters, cin writes past the end of the buffer. Second, if the user enters a space, cin thinks that it is the end of the string, and it stops writing to the buffer.

To solve these problems, you must call a special method on cin: get(). cin.get() takes three parameters:

- The buffer to fill
- The maximum number of characters to get
- The delimiter to terminate input

The default delimiter is newline. Listing 12.9 illustrates its use.

INPUT **LISTING 12.9** Filling an Array

```
1:     //Listing 12.9 using cin.get()
2:
3:     #include <iostream.h>
4:
5:     int main()
6:     {
7:        char buffer[80];
8:        cout << "Enter the string: ";
```

```
9:          cin.get(buffer, 79);        // get up to 79 or newline
10:         cout << "Here's the buffer:  " << buffer << endl;
11:         return 0;
12:     }
```

OUTPUT
Enter the string: Hello World
Here's the buffer: Hello World

ANALYSIS Line 9 calls the method get() of cin. The buffer declared in line 7 is passed in as the first argument. The second argument is the maximum number of characters to get. In this case, it must be 79 to allow for the terminating null. No need exists to provide a terminating character because the default value of newline is sufficient.

Using String Functions

C++ inherits from C a library of functions for dealing with strings. Among those many functions, the most commonly used are: strcpy(), strncpy(), strcat(), and strlen(). strcpy() copies the entire contents of one string into a designated buffer; strncpy() copies the specified number of characters from one string into the other; strlen() tells you how long the string is (which can be different from the array size); and strcat() appends strings together. Listing 12.10 demonstrates the use of these functions.

INPUT **LISTING 12.10** Using Common String Functions

```
1: // listing 12.10 - strcpy, strncpy, strlen, and strcat
2:     #include <iostream.h>
3:     #include <string.h>
4:     int main()
5:     {
6:         char String1[] = "No man is an island";
7:         char String2[80] = "";
8:         char String3[80] = "";
9:         cout << "String1: " << String1 << endl;
10:        strcpy(String2,String1);
11:        cout << "String2: " << String2 << endl;
12:        strncpy (String3, String1, 5); // not entire string
13:        String3[5] = '\0';              // you need a null terminator
14:        cout << "String3 after strncpy: " << String3 << endl;
15:        cout << "String1 is " << strlen (String1) <<
16:            " bytes long, \n  String2 is " <<
17:            strlen (String2) <<
18:            " bytes long, \n  and String3 is " <<
19:            strlen (String3) << " bytes long" << endl;
20:        strcat(String3, String1);
21:        cout << "String3 after strcat: " << String3 << endl;
22:        cout << "String1 is still " << strlen (String1) <<
```

12

continues

LISTING 12.10   CONTINUED

```
23:                    " bytes long, \n  String2 is still " <<
24:                    strlen (String2) <<
25:                    " bytes long, \n  and String3 is now " <<
26:                    strlen (String3) << " bytes long" << endl;
27:           return 0;
28:      }
```

OUTPUT

```
String1: No man is an island
String2: No man is an island
String3 after strncpy: No ma
String1 is 19 bytes long,
   String2 is 19 bytes long,
   and String3 is 5 bytes long
String3 after strcat: No maNo man is an island
String1 is still 19 bytes long,
   String2 is still 19 bytes long,
   and String3 is now 24 bytes long
```

ANALYSIS The header file `string.h` is included in line 3. This file contains the prototypes of the string functions. Lines 6, 7, and 8 allocate three character arrays; the first is initialized to "No man is an island," and the other two are empty.

On line 10, the `strcpy()` function takes two character arrays—a destination followed by a source. If the source were larger than the destination, `strcpy()` would overwrite past the end of the buffer.

To protect against this, the standard library also includes `strncpy()` as shown on line 12. This variation takes a maximum number of characters to copy. `strncpy()` copies up to the first null character or the maximum number of characters specified into the destination buffer. If this maximum is less than the length of the string, a null terminator is not included in the destination string. So you have to put one there yourself, as shown on line 13.

`strlen()` takes one character array argument and returns the length of that string up to, but not including, the null terminator. This should be at least one less than the size of the array containing the string.

On line 20, the `strcat()` function takes two character arrays—a destination followed by a source. The source array will be appended to the end of the string stored in the destination array. If the size of source plus the size of the original destination were larger than the destination array can contain, `strcat()` would overwrite past the end of the buffer (`strncat()` can be used to prevent this).

Of course, there are many other string functions available.

Using Strings and Pointers

As you learned earlier today, when you use the array name alone (without a subscript contained in square brackets), you are referencing the address of the array. This variable is behaving like a pointer. It is a special pointer—a constant pointer. It is a constant pointer because you are not allowed to change where it points to. The reason behind that is: arrays do not move; if you changed the pointer itself, you would not be able to reference the memory allocated for that array.

Notice that in Listing 12.10, it is the array name that is used as arguments to the string functions. You can also use pointers to strings in place of arrays. The only difference is that you are not allowed to change a string in place (you are not allowed to concatenate another string to it as was done to the String3 array). The language standard does not prohibit this but the compiler or operating system may not allow you (treating strings as being read-only). Even if you are not prevented from doing so, you should not change a string in place. Trust me on this one—it can cause all kinds of side effects and is not portable.

Listing 12.11 illustrates the use of strings and pointers.

INPUT **LISTING 12.11** Using Strings and Pointers

```
1: // listing 12.11 - Strings and Pointers
2:      #include <iostream.h>
3:      #include <string.h>
4:      int main()
5:      {
6:          char *String1 = "No man is an island";
7:          char String2[80] = "";
8:          char String3[80] = "";
9:          cout << "String1: " << String1 << endl;
10:         strcpy(String2,String1);
11:         cout << "String2: " << String2 << endl;
12:         strncpy (String3, String1, 5); // not entire string
13:         String3[5] = '\0';              // you need a null terminator
14:         cout << "String3 after strncpy: " << String3 << endl;
15:         cout << "String1 is " << strlen (String1) <<
16:             " bytes long, \n  String2 is " <<
17:             strlen (String2) <<
18:             " bytes long, \n  and String3 is " <<
19:             strlen (String3) << " bytes long" << endl;
20:         strcat(String3, String1);
21:         cout << "String3 after strcat: " << String3 << endl;
22:         cout << "String1 is still " << strlen (String1) <<
23:             " bytes long, \n  String2 is still " <<
24:             strlen (String2) <<
```

12

continues

LISTING **12.11**   CONTINUED

```
25:                 " bytes long, \n  and String3 is now " <<
26:                 strlen (String3) << " bytes long" << endl;
27:          String1 = "Now is the time for all good people...";
28:          cout << "String1: " << String1 << endl;
29:          strcat(String3, String1);
30:          cout << "String3 after strcat2: " << String3 << endl;
31:          cout << "String1 is now " << strlen (String1) <<
32:                 " bytes long, \n  String2 is still " <<
33:                 strlen (String2) <<
34:                 " bytes long, \n  and String3 is now " <<
35:                 strlen (String3) << " bytes long" << endl;
36:          return 0;
37:     }
```

OUTPUT

```
String1: No man is an island
String2: No man is an island
String3 after strncpy: No ma
String1 is 19 bytes long,
   String2 is 19 bytes long,
   and String3 is 5 bytes long
String3 after strcat: No maNo man is an island
String1 is still 19 bytes long,
   String2 is still 19 bytes long,
   and String3 is now 24 bytes long
String1: Now is the time for all good people...
String3 after strcat2: [ccc:ic]
No maNo man is an islandNow is the time for all good people...
String1 is now 38 bytes long,
   String2 is still 19 bytes long,
   and String3 is now 62 bytes long
```

ANALYSIS   The header file string.h is included in line 3. This file contains the prototypes of the string functions. Line 6 allocates a pointer to a character string ("No man is an island"), and lines 7 and 8 allocate two character arrays.

Through line 26, Listing 12.11 is exactly the same as Listing 12.10 (see that listing if you need an explanation of those lines).

Line 27 changes String1. It does not modify the original contents ("No man is an island"); it causes String1 to point to a different string in memory ("Now is the time for all good people..."). This is a subtle distinction but very important because you should not use a string pointer (like String1) as the destination of strcpy(), strncpy(), strcat(), or similar functions.

You also cannot code something like the following:

```
String2 = "this will not compile";
```

This does not work because the variable String2 was allocated as an array and you are not allowed to change the address constant that is the beginning of the array.

Line 29 is the same as line 20. The output of line 30 will be different from that of line 21 because String1 is different and String3 retains its contents from line 20.

The final version of String3 is not very readable because there are no separators between the strings concatenated into it. A good technique is to strcat() another character into the destination string (like a blank) as follows:

```
strcpy(result_string, original_string);
strcat(result_string, " ");
strcat(result_string, next_string);
```

A space will appear between the contents of original_string and next_string in the result_string variable. The strcat() function requires a string, which is why the single space in the first call is enclosed in double quotes—to make it a string (of length one).

You can use string pointers with any of the string functions.

String Classes

Most C++ compilers come with a class library that includes a large set of classes for data manipulation. A standard component of a class library is a String class.

C++ inherited the null-terminated string and the library of functions that includes strcpy() from C, but these functions are not integrated into an object-oriented framework. A String class provides an encapsulated set of data and functions for manipulating that data, as well as accessor functions so that the data itself is hidden from the clients of the String class.

If your compiler does not already provide a String class—and perhaps even if it does— you might want to write your own. GNU provides a String class. The remainder of this lesson discusses the design and partial implementation of String classes.

At a minimum, a String class should overcome the basic limitations of character arrays. Like all arrays, character arrays are static. You define how large they are. They always take up that much room in memory, even if you do not need it all. Writing past the end of the array is disastrous.

A good String class allocates only as much memory as it needs and always enough to hold whatever it is given. If it cannot allocate enough memory, it should fail gracefully.

Listing 12.12 provides a first approximation of a String class.

LISTING 12.12   Using a String Class

```
1:     //Listing 12.12
2:
3:     #include <iostream.h>
4:     #include <string.h>
5:
6:     // Rudimentary string class
7:     class String
8:     {
9:        public:
10:          // constructors
11:          String();
12:          String(const char *const);
13:          String(const String &);
14:          ~String();
15:
16:          // overloaded operators
17:          char & operator[](unsigned short offset);
18:          char operator[](unsigned short offset) const;
19:          String operator+(const String&);
20:          void operator+=(const String&);
21:          String & operator= (const String &);
22:
23:          // General accessors
24:          unsigned short GetLen()const { return itsLen; }
25:          const char * GetString() const { return itsString; }
26:
27:        private:
28:          String (unsigned short);          // private constructor
29:          char * itsString;
30:          unsigned short itsLen;
31:     };
32:
33:     // default constructor creates string of 0 bytes
34:     String::String()
35:     {
36:        itsString = new char[1];
37:        itsString[0] = '\0';
38:        itsLen=0;
39:     }
40:
41:     // private (helper) constructor, used only by
42:     // class methods for creating a new string of
43:     // required size. Null filled.
44:     String::String(unsigned short len)
45:     {
46:        itsString = new char[len+1];
47:        for (unsigned short i = 0; i<=len; i++)
48:           itsString[i] = '\0';
```

```
49:        itsLen=len;
50:     }
51:
52:     // Converts a character array to a String
53:     String::String(const char * const cString)
54:     {
55:        itsLen = strlen(cString);
56:        itsString = new char[itsLen+1];
57:        for (unsigned short i = 0; i<itsLen; i++)
58:           itsString[i] = cString[i];
59:        itsString[itsLen]='\0';
60:     }
61:
62:     // copy constructor
63:     String::String (const String & rhs)
64:     {
65:        itsLen=rhs.GetLen();
66:        itsString = new char[itsLen+1];
67:        for (unsigned short i = 0; i<itsLen;i++)
68:           itsString[i] = rhs[i];
69:        itsString[itsLen] = '\0';
70:     }
71:
72:     // destructor, frees allocated memory
73:     String::~String ()
74:     {
75:        delete [] itsString;
76:        itsLen = 0;
77:     }
78:
79:     // operator equals, frees existing memory
80:     // then copies string and size
81:     String& String::operator=(const String & rhs)
82:     {
83:        if (this == &rhs)
84:           return *this;
85:        delete [] itsString;
86:        itsLen=rhs.GetLen();
87:        itsString = new char[itsLen+1];
88:        for (unsigned short i = 0; i<itsLen;i++)
89:           itsString[i] = rhs[i];
90:        itsString[itsLen] = '\0';
91:        return *this;
92:     }
93:
94:     //nonconstant offset operator, returns
95:     // reference to character so it can be
96:     // changed!
97:     char & String::operator[](unsigned short offset)
98:     {
99:        if (offset > itsLen)
```

continues

12

LISTING 12.12   CONTINUED

```
100:          return itsString[itsLen-1];
101:      else
102:          return itsString[offset];
103:   }
104:
105:   // constant offset operator for use
106:   // on const objects (see copy constructor!)
107:   char String::operator[](unsigned short offset) const
108:   {
109:      if (offset > itsLen)
110:          return itsString[itsLen-1];
111:      else
112:          return itsString[offset];
113:   }
114:
115:   // creates a new string by adding current
116:   // string to rhs
117:   String String::operator+(const String& rhs)
118:   {
119:      unsigned short  totalLen = itsLen + rhs.GetLen();
120:      String temp(totalLen);
121:          unsigned short i;
122:      for ( i= 0; i<itsLen; i++)
123:          temp[i] = itsString[i];
124:      for (unsigned short j = 0; j<rhs.GetLen(); j++, i++)
125:          temp[i] = rhs[j];
126:      temp[totalLen]='\0';
127:      return temp;
128:   }
129:
130:   // changes current string, returns nothing
131:   void String::operator+=(const String& rhs)
132:   {
133:      unsigned short rhsLen = rhs.GetLen();
134:      unsigned short totalLen = itsLen + rhsLen;
135:      String  temp(totalLen);
136:          unsigned short i;
137:      for (i = 0; i<itsLen; i++)
138:          temp[i] = itsString[i];
139:      for (unsigned short j = 0; j<rhs.GetLen(); j++, i++)
140:          temp[i] = rhs[i-itsLen];
141:      temp[totalLen]='\0';
142:      *this = temp;
143:   }
144:
145:   int main()
146:   {
147:      String s1("initial test");
```

```
148:        cout << "S1:\t" << s1.GetString() << endl;
149:
150:        char * temp = "Hello World";
151:        s1 = temp;
152:        cout << "S1:\t" << s1.GetString() << endl;
153:
154:        char tempTwo[20];
155:        strcpy(tempTwo,"; nice to be here!");
156:        s1 += tempTwo;
157:        cout << "tempTwo:\t" << tempTwo << endl;
158:        cout << "S1:\t" << s1.GetString() << endl;
159:
160:        cout << "S1[4]:\t" << s1[4] << endl;
161:        s1[4]='x';
162:        cout << "S1:\t" << s1.GetString() << endl;
163:
164:        cout << "S1[999]:\t" << s1[999] << endl;
165:
166:        String s2(" Another string");
167:        String s3;
168:        s3 = s1+s2;
169:        cout << "S3:\t" << s3.GetString() << endl;
170:
171:        String s4;
172:        s4 = "Why does this work?";
173:        cout << "S4:\t" << s4.GetString() << endl;
174:      return 0;
175:    }
```

OUTPUT

```
S1:        initial test
S1:        Hello world
tempTwo:        ; nice to be here!
S1:        Hello world; nice to be here!
S1[4]:     o
S1:        Hellx World; nice to be here!
S1[999]:        !
S3:        Hellx World; nice to be here! Another string
S4:        Why does this work?
```

12

ANALYSIS Lines 7–31 are the declaration of a simple String class. Lines 11–13 contain three constructors: the default constructor, the copy constructor, and a constructor that takes an existing null-terminated (C-style) string.

This String class overloads the offset operator ([ ]), operator plus (+), and operator plus-equals (+=). The offset operator is overloaded twice: once as a constant function returning a char and again as a nonconstant function returning a reference to a char.

The nonconstant version is used in statements such as

```
SomeString[4]='x';
```

as seen in line 161. This enables direct access to each of the characters in the string. A reference to the character is returned so that the calling function can manipulate it.

The constant version is used when a constant String object is being accessed, such as in the implementation of the copy constructor (line 63). Note that rhs[i] is accessed, yet rhs is declared as a const String &. It is not legal to access this object by using a nonconstant member function. Therefore, the offset operator must be overloaded with a constant accessor.

If the object being returned was large, you might want to declare the return value to be a constant reference. However, because a char is only 1 byte, there would be no point in doing that.

The default constructor is implemented in lines 33–39. It creates a string whose length is 0. It is the convention of this String class to report its length not counting the terminating null. This default string contains only a terminating null.

The copy constructor is implemented in lines 63–70. It sets the new string's length to that of the existing string—plus 1 for the terminating null. It copies each character from the existing string to the new string, and it null-terminates the new string.

Lines 53–60 implement the constructor that takes an existing C-style string. This constructor is similar to the copy constructor. The length of the existing string is established by a call to the standard String library function strlen().

On line 28, another constructor, String(unsigned short), is declared to be a private member function. It is the intent of the designer of this class that no client class ever create a String of arbitrary length. This constructor exists only to help in the internal creation of Strings as required, for example, by operator+=, on line 131. This will be discussed in depth when operator+= is described later.

The String(unsigned short) constructor fills every member of its array with NULL. Therefore, the for loop checks for i<=len rather than i<len.

The destructor, implemented in lines 73–77, deletes the character string maintained by the class. Be sure to include the brackets in the call to the delete operator so that every member of the array is deleted, instead of only the first.

The assignment operator first checks whether the right side of the assignment is the same as the left side. If it is not, the current string is deleted, and the new string is created and copied into place. A reference is returned to facilitate assignments such as

```
String1 = String2 = String3;
```

The offset operator is overloaded twice. Rudimentary bounds checking is performed both times. If the user attempts to access a character at a location beyond the end of the array, the last character—that is, `len-1`—is returned.

Lines 117–128 implement operator plus (+) as a concatenation operator. It is convenient to be able to write

```
String3 = String1 + String2;
```

and have `String3` be the concatenation of the other two strings. To accomplish this, the operator plus (+) function computes the combined length of the two strings and creates a temporary string `temp`. This invokes the private constructor, which takes an integer, and creates a string filled with nulls. The nulls are then replaced by the contents of the two strings. The left side string (`*this`) is copied first, followed by the right side string (`rhs`).

The first `for` loop counts through the string on the left side and adds each character to the new string. The second `for` loop counts through the right side. Note that i continues to count the place for the new string, even as j counts into the `rhs` string.

Operator plus returns the `temp` string by value, which is assigned to the string on the left side of the assignment (`string1`). Operator += operates on the existing string—that is, the left side of the statement `string1 += string2`. It works the same as operator plus, except that the `temp` value is assigned to the current string (`*this = temp`) in line 142.

The `main()` function (lines 145–175) acts as a test driver program for this class. Line 147 creates a `String` object by using the constructor that takes a null-terminated C-style string. Line 148 prints its contents by using the accessor function `GetString()`. Line 150 creates another C-style string. Line 151 tests the assignment operator, and line 152 prints the results.

Line 154 creates a third C-style string, `tempTwo`. Line 155 invokes `strcpy` to fill the buffer with the characters `; nice to be here!` Line 156 invokes operator += and concatenates `tempTwo` onto the existing string s1. Line 158 prints the results.

In line 160, the fifth character in s1 is accessed and printed. It is assigned a new value in line 161. This invokes the nonconstant offset operator (`[ ]`). Line 162 prints the result, which shows that the actual value has, in fact, been changed.

Line 164 attempts to access a character beyond the end of the array. The last character of the array is returned, as designed.

Lines 166 and 167 create two more `String` objects, and line 168 calls the addition operator. Line 169 prints the results.

Line 171 creates a new `String` object, s4. Line 172 invokes the assignment operator.

12

Line 173 prints the results. You might be thinking, "The assignment operator is defined to take a constant `String` reference in line 21, but here the program passes in a C-style string. Why is this legal?"

The answer is that the compiler expects a `String`, but it is given a character array. Therefore, it checks whether it can create a `String` from what it is given. In line 12, you declared a constructor that creates `Strings` from character arrays. The compiler creates a temporary `String` from the character array and passes it to the assignment operator. This is known as implicit casting, or promotion. If you had not declared—and provided the implementation for—the constructor that takes a character array, this assignment would have generated a compiler error.

Linked Lists and Other Structures

Arrays are much like Tupperware. They are great containers, but they are of a fixed size. If you pick a container that is too large, you waste space in your storage area. If you pick one that is too small, its contents spill all over and you have a big mess.

One way to solve this problem is with a linked list. A linked list is a data structure that consists of small containers that are designed to fit and that are linked together as needed. The idea is to write a class that holds one object of your data—such as one `CAT` or one `Rectangle`—and that can point at the next container. You create one container for each object that you need to store, and you chain them together as needed.

The containers are called *nodes*. The first node in the list is called the *head*, and the last node in the list is called the *tail*.

Lists come in three fundamental forms. From simplest to most complex, they are

- Singly linked
- Doubly linked
- Trees

In a singly linked list, each node points forward to the next one, but not backward. To find a particular node, start at the top and go from node to node, as in a treasure hunt ("The next node is under the sofa"). A doubly linked list enables you to move backward and forward in the chain. A tree is a complex structure built from nodes, each of which can point in two or three directions. Figure 12.5 shows these three fundamental structures.

FIGURE 12.5

Linked lists.

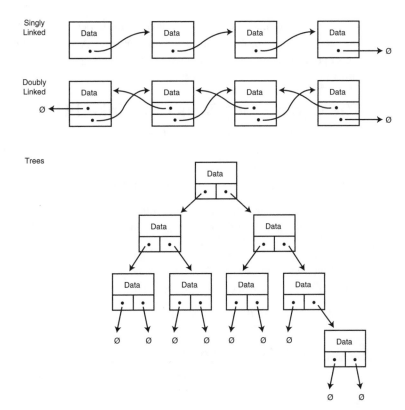

Examining A Linked List Case Study

12

In this section, we will examine a linked list in detail as a case study both of how you create complex structures and, more importantly, how you use inheritance, polymorphism, and encapsulation to manage large projects.

Delegation of Responsibility

A fundamental premise of object-oriented programming is that each object does *one* thing very well and delegates to other objects anything that is not its core mission.

An automobile is a perfect example of this idea in hardware: the engine's job is to produce the power. Distribution of that power is not the engine's job; that is up to the transmission. Turning is not the job of the engine nor the transmission; that is delegated to the wheels.

A well-designed machine has lots of small, well-understood parts, each doing its own job and working together to accomplish a greater good. A well-designed program is much the same: each class sticks to its own knitting, but together they create one heck of an afghan.

The Component Parts of a Linked List

The linked list will consist of nodes. The node class itself will be abstract; we will use three subtypes to accomplish the work. There will be a head node whose job is to manage the head of the list, a tail node (guess what its job is!), and zero or more internal nodes. The internal nodes will keep track of the actual data to be held in the list.

Note that the data and the list are quite distinct. You can, in theory, save any type of data you like in a list. It is not the data that is linked together; it is the node that *holds* the data.

The driver program does not know about the nodes; it works with the list. The list, however, does little work; it simply delegates to the nodes.

Listing 12.13 shows the code; we will examine it in excruciating detail.

INPUT   **LISTING 12.13**   Linked List

```
0:     // ************************************************
1:     //    FILE:         Listing 12.13
2:     //
3:     //    PURPOSE:      Demonstrate linked list
4:     //    NOTES:
5:     //
6:     //
7:     //
8:     //
9:     // Demonstrates an object-oriented approach to
10:    // linked lists. The list delegates to the node.
11:    // The node is an abstract data type. Three types of
12:    // nodes are used, head nodes, tail nodes and internal
13:    // nodes. Only the internal nodes hold data.
14:    //
15:    // The Data class is created to serve as an object to
16:    // hold in the linked list.
17:    //
18:    // ************************************************
19:
20:
21:    #include <iostream.h>
22:
23:    enum { kIsSmaller, kIsLarger, kIsSame};
```

```
24:
25:     // Data class to put into the linked list
26:     // Any class in this linked list must support two methods:
27:     // Show (displays the value) and Compare (returns relative
➡position)
28:     class Data
29:     {
30:     public:
31:         Data(int val):myValue(val){}
32:         ~Data(){}
33:         int Compare(const Data &);
34:         void Show() { cout << myValue << endl; }
35:     private:
36:         int myValue;
37:     };
38:
39:     // Compare is used to decide where in the list
40:     // a particular object belongs.
41:     int Data::Compare(const Data & theOtherData)
42:     {
43:         if (myValue < theOtherData.myValue)
44:             return kIsSmaller;
45:         if (myValue > theOtherData.myValue)
46:             return kIsLarger;
47:         else
48:             return kIsSame;
49:     }
50:
51:     // forward declarations
52:     class Node;
53:     class HeadNode;
54:     class TailNode;
55:     class InternalNode;
56:
57:     // ADT representing the node object in the list
58:     // Every derived class must override Insert and Show
59:     class Node
60:     {
61:     public:
62:         Node(){}
63:         virtual ~Node(){}
64:         virtual Node * Insert(Data * theData)=0;
65:         virtual void Show() = 0;
66:     private:
67:     };
68:
69:     // This is the node which holds the actual object
70:     // In this case the object is of type Data
71:     // We'll see how to make this more general when
72:     // we cover templates
73:     class InternalNode: public Node
```

12

continues

LISTING **12.13** CONTINUED

```
74:     {
75:     public:
76:         InternalNode(Data * theData, Node * next);
77:         ~InternalNode(){ delete myNext; delete myData; }
78:         virtual Node * Insert(Data * theData);
79:         virtual void Show() { myData->Show(); myNext->Show(); }
➥// delegate!
80:
81:     private:
82:             Data * myData;  // the data itself
83:             Node * myNext;   // points to next node in the linked list
84:     };
85:
86:     // All the constructor does is to initialize
87:     InternalNode::InternalNode(Data * theData, Node * next):
88:     myData(theData),myNext(next)
89:     {
90:     }
91:
92:     // the meat of the list
93:     // When you put a new object into the list
94:     // it is passed to the node which figures out
95:     // where it goes and inserts it into the list
96:     Node * InternalNode::Insert(Data * theData)
97:     {
98:
99:         // is the new guy bigger or smaller than me?
100:         int result = myData->Compare(*theData);
101:
102:
103:         switch(result)
104:         {
105:             // by convention if it is the same as me it comes first
106:         case kIsSame:        // fall through
107:         case kIsLarger:      // new data comes before me
108:             {
109:                 InternalNode * dataNode = new
➥InternalNode(theData, this);
110:                 return dataNode;
111:             }
112:
113:             // it is bigger than I am so pass it on to the next
114:             // node and let HIM handle it.
115:         case kIsSmaller:
116:             myNext = myNext->Insert(theData);
117:             return this;
118:         }
119:         return this;  // appease compiler
```

```
120:    }
121:
122:
123:    // Tail node is just a sentinel
124:
125:    class TailNode : public Node
126:    {
127:    public:
128:        TailNode(){}
129:        ~TailNode(){}
130:        virtual Node * Insert(Data * theData);
131:        virtual void Show() { }
132:
133:    private:
134:
135:    };
136:
137:    // If data comes to me, it must be inserted before me
138:    // as I am the tail and NOTHING comes after me
139:    Node * TailNode::Insert(Data * theData)
140:    {
141:        InternalNode * dataNode = new InternalNode(theData, this);
142:        return dataNode;
143:    }
144:
145:    // Head node has no data, it just points
146:    // to the very beginning of the list
147:    class HeadNode : public Node
148:    {
149:    public:
150:        HeadNode();
151:        ~HeadNode() { delete myNext; }
152:        virtual Node * Insert(Data * theData);
153:        virtual void Show() { myNext->Show(); }
154:    private:
155:        Node * myNext;
156:    };
157:
158:    // As soon as the head is created
159:    // it creates the tail
160:    HeadNode::HeadNode()
161:    {
162:        myNext = new TailNode;
163:    }
164:
165:    // Nothing comes before the head so just
166:    // pass the data on to the next node
167:    Node * HeadNode::Insert(Data * theData)
168:    {
169:        myNext = myNext->Insert(theData);
170:        return this;
```

continues

LISTING 12.13   CONTINUED

```
171:    }
172:
173:    // I get all the credit and do none of the work
174:    class LinkedList
175:    {
176:    public:
177:        LinkedList();
178:        ~LinkedList() { delete myHead; }
179:        void Insert(Data * theData);
180:        void ShowAll() { myHead->Show(); }
181:    private:
182:        HeadNode * myHead;
183:    };
184:
185:    // At birth, i create the head node
186:    // It creates the tail node
187:    // So an empty list points to the head that
188:    // points to the tail and has nothing between
189:    LinkedList::LinkedList()
190:    {
191:        myHead = new HeadNode;
192:    }
193:
194:    // Delegate, delegate, delegate
195:    void LinkedList::Insert(Data * pData)
196:    {
197:        myHead->Insert(pData);
198:    }
199:
200:    // test driver program
201:    int main()
202:    {
203:        Data * pData;
204:        int val;
205:        LinkedList ll;
206:
207:        // ask the user to produce some values
208:        // put them in the list
209:        for (;;)
210:        {
211:            cout << "What value? (0 to stop): ";
212:            cin >> val;
213:            if (!val)
214:                break;
215:            pData = new Data(val);
216:            ll.Insert(pData);
217:        }
218:
```

```
219:        // now walk the list and show the data
220:        ll.ShowAll();
221:        return 0;  // ll falls out of scope and is destroyed!
222:    }
```

OUTPUT

```
What value? (0 to stop): 5
What value? (0 to stop): 8
What value? (0 to stop): 3
What value? (0 to stop): 9
What value? (0 to stop): 2
What value? (0 to stop): 10
What value? (0 to stop): 0
2
3
5
8
9
10
```

ANALYSIS The first thing to note is the enumerated constant, which provides three constant values: kIsSmaller, kIsLarger, and kIsSame. Every object that may be held in this linked list must support a Compare() method. These constants will be the result value returned by the Compare() method.

For illustration purposes, the class Data is created on lines 28–37, and the Compare() method is implemented on lines 39–49. A Data object holds a value and can compare itself with other Data objects. It also supports a Show() method to display the value of the Data object.

The easiest way to understand the workings of the linked list is to step through an example of using one. On line 201 a driver program is declared; on line 203 a pointer to a Data object is declared; and on line 205 a local linked list is defined.

When the linked list is created, the constructor on line 189 is called. The only work done in the constructor is to allocate a HeadNode object and to assign that object's address to the pointer held in the linked list on line 182.

This allocation of a HeadNode invokes the HeadNode constructor shown on lines 160–163. This in turn allocates a TailNode and assigns its address to the head node's myNext pointer. The creation of the TailNode calls the TailNode constructor shown on line 128, which is inline and which does nothing.

Thus, by the simple act of allocating a linked list on the stack, the list is created, a head and a tail node are created, and their relationship is established, as illustrated in Figure 12.6.

12

FIGURE 12.6

Line 209 begins an infinite loop. The user will be prompted for values to add to the linked list. He can add as many values as he likes, entering 0 when he is finished. The code on line 213 evaluates the value entered; if it is 0, it breaks out of the loop.

If the value is not 0, a new Data object is created on line 215, and that is inserted into the list on line 216. For illustration purposes, assume the user enters the value 15. This invokes the Insert method on line 195.

The linked list immediately delegates responsibility for inserting the object to its head node. This invokes the method Insert on line 167. The head node immediately passes the responsibility to whatever node its myNext is pointing to. In this (first) case, it is pointing to the tail node (remember, when the head node was born, it created a link to a tail node). This, therefore, invokes the method Insert on line 139.

TailNode::Insert knows that the object it has been handed must be inserted immediately before itself—that is, the new object will be in the list right before the tail node. Therefore, on line 141 it creates a new InternalNode object, passing in the data and a pointer to itself. This invokes the constructor for the InternalNode object, shown on line 87.

The InternalNode constructor does nothing more than initialize its Data pointer with the address of the Data object it was passed and its myNext pointer with the node's address it was passed. In this case, the node it will point to is the tail node (remember, the tail node passed in its own this pointer).

Now that the InternalNode has been created, the address of that internal node is assigned to the pointer dataNode on line 141, and that address is in turn returned from the TailNode::Insert() method. This returns us to HeadNode::Insert(), where the address of the InternalNode is assigned to the HeadNode's myNext pointer (on line 169). Finally, the HeadNode's address is returned to the linked list where, on line 197, it is thrown away (nothing is done with it because the linked list already knows the address of the head node).

Why bother returning the address if it is not used? Insert is declared in the base class, Node. The return value is needed by the other implementations. If you change the return value of HeadNode::Insert(), you will get a compiler error; it is simpler just to return the HeadNode and let the linked list throw its address on the floor.

So what happened? The data was inserted into the list. The list passed it to the head. The head, blindly, passed the data to whatever the head happened to be pointing to. In this (first) case, the head was pointing to the tail. The tail immediately created a new internal node, initializing the new node to point to the tail. The tail then returned the address of the new node to the head, which reassigned its myNext pointer to point to the new node. Presto! The data is in the list in the right place, as illustrated in Figure 12.7.

FIGURE 12.7

The linked list after the first node is inserted.

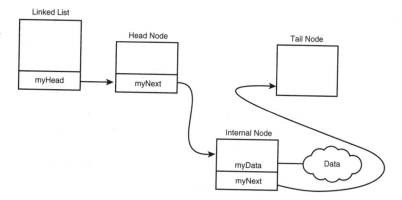

After inserting the first node, program control resumes at line 211. Once again, the value is evaluated. For illustration purposes, assume that the value 3 is entered. This causes a new Data object to be created on line 215 and to be inserted into the list on line 216.

Once again, on line 197, the list passes the data to its HeadNode. The HeadNode::Insert() method, in turn, passes the new value to whatever its myNext happens to be pointing to. As you know, it is now pointing to the node that contains the Data object whose value is 15. This invokes the InternalNode::Insert() method on line 96.

On line 100, the InternalNode uses its myData pointer to tell its Data object (the one whose value is 15) to call its Compare() method, passing in the new Data object (whose value is 3). This invokes the Compare() method shown on line 41.

The two values are compared, and, because myValue will be 15 and theOtherData.myValue will be 3, the returned value will be kIsLarger. This will cause program flow to jump to line 109.

A new InternalNode is created for the new Data object. The new node will point to the current InternalNode object, and the new InternalNode's address is returned from the

`InternalNode::Insert()` method to the `HeadNode`. Thus, the new node, whose object's value is smaller than the current node's object's value, is inserted into the list, and the list now looks like Figure 12.8.

FIGURE 12.8

The linked list after the second node is inserted.

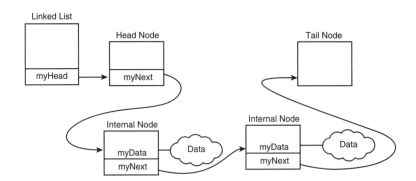

In the third invocation of the loop, the customer adds the value 8. This is larger than 3 but smaller than 15, and so it should be inserted between the two existing nodes. Progress will be like the previous example, except that when the node whose object's value is 3 does the comparing, rather than returning `kIsLarger`, it will return `kIsSmaller` (meaning that the object whose value is 3 is smaller than the new object, whose value is 8).

This will cause the `InternalNode::Insert()` method to branch to line 116. Rather than creating a new node and inserting it, the `InternalNode` will just pass the new data on to the `Insert` method of whatever its `myNext` pointer happens to be pointing to. In this case, it will invoke `InsertNode` on the `InternalNode` whose `Data` object's value is 15.

The comparison will be done again, and a new `InternalNode` will be created. This new `InternalNode` will point to the `InternalNode` whose `Data` object's value is 15, and its address will be passed back to the `InternalNode` whose `Data` object's value is 3, as shown on line 116.

The net effect is that the new node will be inserted into the list at the right location.

If at all possible, you will want to step through the insertion of a number of nodes in your debugger. You should be able to watch these methods invoke one another and the pointers be properly adjusted.

What Have You Learned?

Dorothy said, "If I ever go looking for my heart's desire again, I won't look any further than my own backyard." Although it is true there is no place like home, it is also true that this is nothing like procedural programming. In procedural programming, a controlling method would examine data and invoke functions.

In this object-oriented approach, each individual object is given a narrow and well-defined set of responsibilities. The linked list is responsible for maintaining the head node. The head node immediately passes the new data on to whatever it points to, without regard to what that might be.

The tail node creates a new node and inserts it whenever it is handed data. It knows only one thing: if this came to me, it gets inserted right before me.

Internal nodes are marginally more complicated; they ask their existing object to compare itself with the new object. Depending on the result, they then insert or they just pass it along.

Note that the InternalNode has *no idea* how to do the comparison; that is properly left to the object itself. All the InternalNode knows is to ask the objects to compare themselves and to expect one of three possible answers. Given one answer, it inserts; otherwise, it just passes it along, not knowing or caring where it will end up.

So which object is in charge? In a well-designed object-oriented program, *no one* is in charge. Each object does its own little job, and the net effect is a well-running machine.

Using Array Classes Instead of Built-in Arrays

Writing your own array class has many advantages over using the built-in arrays. For starters, you can prevent array overruns. You might also consider making your array class dynamically sized: At creation it might have only one member, growing as needed during the course of the program.

You might want to sort or otherwise order the members of the array. You might consider a number of powerful array variants. Among the most popular are

- Ordered collection: Each member is in sorted order.
- Set: No member appears more than once.
- Dictionary: This uses matched pairs in which one value acts as a key to retrieve the other value.

12

- Sparse array: Indices are permitted for a large set, but only those values actually added to the array consume memory. Thus, you can ask for `SparseArray[5]` or `SparseArray[200]`, but it is possible that memory is allocated only for a small number of entries.
- Bag: An unordered collection that is added to and retrieved in random order.

By overloading the index operator (`[ ]`), you can turn a linked list into an ordered collection. By excluding duplicates, you can turn a collection into a set. If each object in the list has a pair of matched values, you can use a linked list to build a dictionary or a sparse array.

Summary

Today you learned how to create arrays in C++. An array is a fixed-size collection of objects that are all the same type.

Arrays do not do bounds checking. Therefore it is legal—even if disastrous—to read or write past the end of an array. Arrays count from 0. A common mistake is to write to off-set *n* of an array of *n* members.

Arrays can be one-dimensional or multidimensional. In either case, the members of the array can be initialized, as long as the array contains either built-in types, such as `int`, or objects of a class that has a default constructor.

Arrays and their contents can be on the free store or on the stack. If you delete an array on the free store, remember to use the brackets in the call to `delete`.

Array names are constant pointers to the first elements of the array. Pointers and arrays use pointer arithmetic to find the next element of an array.

You can create linked lists to manage collections with sizes you will not know at compile time. From linked lists, you can create any number of more complex data structures.

Strings are arrays of characters, or `chars`. C++ provides special features for managing `char` arrays, including the capability to initialize them with quoted strings.

Q&A

Q What happens if I write to element 25 in a 24-member array?

A You will write to other memory, with potentially disastrous effects on your program.

Q What is in an uninitialized array element?

A Whatever happens to be in memory at a given time. The results of using this member without assigning a value are unpredictable.

Q Can I combine arrays?

A Yes. With simple arrays you can use pointers to combine them into a new, larger array. With strings, you can use some of the built-in functions, such as `strcat`, to combine strings.

Q Why should I create a linked list if an array will work?

A An array must have a fixed size, whereas a linked list can be sized dynamically at runtime.

Q Why would I ever use built-in arrays if I can make a better array class?

A Built-in arrays are quick and easy to use.

Q Must a string class use a `char *` to hold the contents of the string?

A No. It can use any memory storage the designer thinks is best.

Workshop

The Workshop provides quiz questions to help you solidify your understanding of the material covered and exercises to provide you with experience in using what you have learned. Try to answer the quiz and exercise questions before checking the answers in Appendix D, "Answers to Exercises and Quizzes," and make sure you understand the answers before continuing to Day 13.

Quiz

1. What are the first and last elements in `SomeArray[25]`?
2. How do you declare a multidimensional array?
3. Initialize the members of the array in Question 2.
4. How many elements are in the array `SomeArray[10][5][20]`?
5. What is the maximum number of elements that you can add to a linked list?
6. Can you use subscript notation on a linked list?
7. What is the last character in the string "Brad is a nice guy"?

Exercises

1. Declare a two-dimensional array that represents a tic-tac-toe game board.

2. Write the code that initializes all the elements in the array you created in Exercise 1 to the value 0.

3. Write the declaration for a Node class that holds integers.

4. **BUG BUSTER:** What is wrong with this code fragment?

```
unsigned short SomeArray[5][4];
for (int i = 0; i<4; i++)
    for (int j = 0; j<5; j++)
        SomeArray[i][j] = i+j;
```

5. **BUG BUSTER:** What is wrong with this code fragment?

```
unsigned short SomeArray[5][4];
for (int i = 0; i<=5; i++)
    for (int j = 0; j<=4; j++)
        SomeArray[i][j] = 0;
```

DAY **13**

Polymorphism

Yesterday, you learned how to write virtual functions in derived classes. This is the fundamental building block of polymorphism: the capability to bind specific, derived class objects to base class pointers at runtime. Today, you will learn:

- What multiple inheritance is and how to use it
- What virtual inheritance is
- What abstract data types are
- What pure virtual functions are

Problems with Single Inheritance

Suppose you were working with your animal classes for a while, and you divided the class hierarchy into Birds and Mammals. The Bird class includes the member function Fly(). The Mammal class has been divided into a number of types of Mammals, including Horse. The Horse class includes the member functions Whinny() and Gallop().

Suddenly, you realize you need a Pegasus object: a cross between a Horse and a Bird. A Pegasus can Fly(), it can Whinny(), and it can Gallop(). With single inheritance, you are in quite a jam.

You can make Pegasus a Bird, but then it will not be able to Whinny() or Gallop(). You can make it a Horse, but then it will not be able to Fly().

Your first solution is to copy the Fly() method into the Pegasus class and derive Pegasus from Horse. This works fine, at the cost of having the Fly() method in two places (Bird and Pegasus). If you change one, you must remember to change the other. Of course, a developer who comes along months or years later to maintain your code must also know to fix both places.

Soon, however, you have a new problem. You want to create a list of Horse objects and a list of Bird objects. You would like to be able to add your Pegasus objects to either list, but if a Pegasus is a Horse, you cannot add it to a list of Birds.

You have a couple of potential solutions. You can rename the Horse method Gallop() to Move(), and then override Move() in your Pegasus object to do the work of Fly(). You would then override Move() in your other horses to do the work of Gallop(). Perhaps Pegasus could be clever enough to gallop short distances and fly longer distances.

```
Pegasus::Move(long distance)
{
if (distance > veryFar)
fly(distance);
else
gallop(distance);
}
```

This is a bit limiting. Perhaps one day Pegasus will want to fly a short distance or gallop a long distance. Your next solution might be to move Fly() up into Horse, as illustrated in Listing 13.1. The problem is that most horses cannot fly, so you have to make this method do nothing unless it is a Pegasus.

INPUT   **LISTING 13.1**   If Horses Could Fly...

```
1:      // Listing 13.1. If horses could fly...
2:      // Percolating Fly() up into Horse
3:
4:      #include <iostream.h>
5:
6:      class Horse
7:      {
8:      public:
9:          void Gallop(){ cout << "Galloping...\n"; }
10:         virtual void Fly() { cout << "Horses can't fly.\n" ; }
11:     private:
12:         int itsAge;
13:     };
14:
```

```
15:     class Pegasus : public Horse
16:     {
17:     public:
18:        virtual void Fly() { cout <<
➥"I can fly! I can fly! I can fly!\n"; }
19:     };
20:
21:     const int NumberHorses = 5;
22:     int main()
23:     {
24:        Horse* Ranch[NumberHorses];
25:        Horse* pHorse;
26:        int choice,i;
27:        for (i=0; i<NumberHorses; i++)
28:        {
29:           cout << "(1)Horse (2)Pegasus: ";
30:           cin >> choice;
31:           if (choice == 2)
32:              pHorse = new Pegasus;
33:           else
34:              pHorse = new Horse;
35:           Ranch[i] = pHorse;
36:        }
37:        cout << "\n";
38:        for (i=0; i<NumberHorses; i++)
39:        {
40:           Ranch[i]->Fly();
41:           delete Ranch[i];
42:        }
43:     return 0;
44:     }
```

OUTPUT

```
(1)Horse (2)Pegasus: 1
(1)Horse (2)Pegasus: 2
(1)Horse (2)Pegasus: 1
(1)Horse (2)Pegasus: 2
(1)Horse (2)Pegasus: 1

Horses can't fly.
I can fly! I can fly! I can fly!
Horses can't fly.
I can fly! I can fly! I can fly!
Horses can't fly.
```

13

ANALYSIS This program certainly works, although at the expense of the Horse class having a Fly() method. On line 10, the method Fly() is provided to Horse. In a real-world class, you might have it issue an error, or fail quietly. On line 18, the Pegasus class overrides the Fly() method to "do the right thing," represented here by printing a happy message.

The array of Horse pointers on line 24 is used to demonstrate that the correct Fly()
method is called, based on the runtime binding of the Horse or Pegasus object.

 Note These examples have been stripped down to their bare essentials to illustrate the points under consideration. Constructors, virtual destructors, and
so on have been removed to keep the code simple.

Percolating Upward

Putting the required function higher in the class hierarchy is a common solution to this
problem and results in many functions "percolating up" into the base class. The base
class is then in grave danger of becoming a global namespace for all the functions that
might be used by any of the derived classes. This can seriously undermine the class
typing of C++, and can create a large and cumbersome base class.

In general, you want to percolate shared functionality up the hierarchy, without migrat-
ing the interface of each class. This means that if two classes that share a common base
class (for example, Horse and Bird both share Animal) and have a function in common
(both birds and horses eat, for example), you would want to move that functionality up
into the base class and create a virtual function.

What you want to avoid, however, is percolating an interface (such as Fly) up where it
does not belong just so that you can call that function only on some derived classes.

Casting Down

An alternative to this approach, still within single inheritance, is to keep the Fly()
method within Pegasus and only call it if the pointer is actually pointing to a Pegasus
object. To make this work, you will need to be able to ask your pointer what type it is
really pointing to. This is known as Runtime Type Identification (RTTI). Using RTTI has
only recently become an official part of C++.

If your compiler does not support RTTI, you can mimic it by putting a method that
returns an enumerated type in each of the classes. You can then test that type at runtime
and call Fly() if it returns Pegasus.

Earlier versions of the GNU compilers (2.7.2 and earlier) do not support RTTI on all
platforms. The version included on the CD-ROM (2.9.5) does support it—by default.

> **Note**
>
> Beware of using RTTI in your programs. Its use may be an indication of poor design. Consider using virtual functions, templates, or multiple inheritance instead.

To call `Fly()`, however, you must cast the pointer, telling it that the object it is pointing to is a `Pegasus` object, not a `Horse`. This is called casting down because you are casting the `Horse` object down to a more derived type.

C++ now officially, though perhaps reluctantly, supports casting down using the new `dynamic_cast` operator. It works this way:

If you have a pointer to a base class such as `Horse`, and you assign to it a pointer to a derived class, such as `Pegasus`, you can use the `Horse` pointer polymorphically. If you then need to get at the `Pegasus` object, you create a `Pegasus` pointer and use the `dynamic_cast` operator to make the conversion.

At runtime, the base pointer will be examined. If the conversion is proper, your new `Pegasus` pointer will be fine. If the conversion is improper, if you did not really have a `Pegasus` object after all, your new pointer will be null. Listing 13.2 illustrates this point.

INPUT **LISTING 13.2** Casting Down

```
1:    // Listing 13.2 Using dynamic_cast.
2:    // Using rtti
3:
4:    #include <iostream.h>
5:    enum TYPE { HORSE, PEGASUS };
6:
7:    class Horse
8:    {
9:    public:
10:       virtual void Gallop(){ cout << "Galloping...\n"; }
11:
12:    private:
13:        int itsAge;
14:    };
15:
16:    class Pegasus : public Horse
17:    {
18:    public:
19:
20:        virtual void Fly() { cout <<
➥"I can fly! I can fly! I can fly!\n"; }
21:    };
```

continues

LISTING 13.2 CONTINUED

```
22:
23:    const int NumberHorses = 5;
24:    int main()
25:    {
26:        Horse* Ranch[NumberHorses];
27:        Horse* pHorse;
28:        int choice,i;
29:        for (i=0; i<NumberHorses; i++)
30:        {
31:            cout << "(1)Horse (2)Pegasus: ";
32:            cin >> choice;
33:            if (choice == 2)
34:                pHorse = new Pegasus;
35:            else
36:                pHorse = new Horse;
37:            Ranch[i] = pHorse;
38:        }
39:        cout << "\n";
40:        for (i=0; i<NumberHorses; i++)
41:        {
42:            Pegasus *pPeg = dynamic_cast< Pegasus *> (Ranch[i]);
42:            if (pPeg)
43:                pPeg->Fly();
44:            else
45:                cout << "Just a horse\n";
46:
47:            delete Ranch[i];
48:        }
49:    return 0;
50: }
```

OUTPUT
```
(1)Horse (2)Pegasus: 1
(1)Horse (2)Pegasus: 2
(1)Horse (2)Pegasus: 1
(1)Horse (2)Pegasus: 2
(1)Horse (2)Pegasus: 1

Just a horse
I can fly! I can fly! I can fly!
Just a horse
I can fly! I can fly! I can fly!
Just a horse
```

Frequently Asked Questions

FAQ: When compiling, I got an error from my GNU g++ compiler (version 2.7.2 or earlier):

```
lst13-02.cxx: In function `int main()':
lst13-02.cxx:42: cannot take typeid of object when -frtti is not specified
lst13-02.cxx:42: invalid type argument
lst13-02.cxx:42: failed to build type descriptor node of 'Pegasus',
➥maybe typeinfo.h not included
```

FAQ: What should I do?

Answer: This is one of the GNU compiler's more confusing error messages. Unfortunately, the version you are using may not support RTTI even though it suggests ways around it.

You can try recompiling with the -frtti option, but if you get the warning that the option is not recognized, your platform and specific version does not support this capability.

Version 2.9.5 supports RTTI by default.

ANALYSIS This solution also works. Fly() is kept out of Horse, and it is not called on Horse objects. When it is called on Pegasus objects, however, they must be explicitly cast; Horse objects do not have the method Fly(), so the pointer must be told it is pointing to a Pegasus object before being used.

The need for you to cast the Pegasus object is a warning that something may be wrong with your design. This program effectively undermines the virtual function polymorphism because it depends on casting the object to its real runtime type.

Adding to Two Lists

The other problem with these solutions is that because you declared Pegasus to be a type of Horse, you cannot add a Pegasus object to a list of Birds. You have paid the price of either moving Fly() up into Horse or casting down the pointer, and yet you still do not have the full functionality you need.

One final, single inheritance solution presents itself. You can push Fly(), Whinny(), and Gallop() all up into a common base class of both Bird and Horse: Animal. Now, instead of having a list of Birds and a list of Horses, you can have one unified list of Animals. This works, but percolates more functionality up into the base classes.

13

Alternatively, you can leave the methods where they are but cast down Horses and Birds and Pegasus objects, but that is even worse!

Do	**Don't**
DO move functionality up the inheritance hierarchy.	**DON'T** cast pointers to base objects down to derived objects.
DO avoid switching on the runtime type of the object—use virtual methods, templates, and multiple inheritance.	**DON'T** move interface up the inheritance hierarchy.

Multiple Inheritance

It is possible to derive a new class from more than one base class. This is called multiple inheritance. To derive from more than the base class, you separate each base class by commas in the class designation. Listing 13.3 illustrates how to declare Pegasus so that it derives from both Horses and Birds. The program then adds Pegasus objects to both types of lists.

INPUT **LISTING 13.3** Multiple Inheritance

```
1:     // Listing 13.3. Multiple inheritance.
2:     // Multiple Inheritance
3:
4:     #include <iostream.h>
5:
6:     class Horse
7:     {
8:     public:
9:         Horse() { cout << "Horse constructor... "; }
10:        virtual ~Horse() { cout << "Horse destructor... "; }
11:        virtual void Whinny() const { cout << "Whinny!... "; }
12:    private:
13:        int itsAge;
14:    };
15:
16:    class Bird
17:    {
18:    public:
19:        Bird() { cout << "Bird constructor... "; }
20:        virtual ~Bird() { cout << "Bird destructor... "; }
21:        virtual void Chirp() const { cout << "Chirp... ";  }
22:        virtual void Fly() const
23:        {
```

```
24:            cout << "I can fly! I can fly! I can fly! ";
25:         }
26:     private:
27:         int itsWeight;
28:     };
29:
30:     class Pegasus : public Horse, public Bird
31:     {
32:     public:
33:         void Chirp() const { Whinny(); }
34:         Pegasus() { cout << "Pegasus constructor... "; }
35:         ~Pegasus() { cout << "Pegasus destructor...   "; }
36:     };
37:
38:     const int MagicNumber = 2;
39:     int main()
40:     {
41:         Horse* Ranch[MagicNumber];
42:         Bird* Aviary[MagicNumber];
43:         Horse * pHorse;
44:         Bird * pBird;
45:         int choice,i;
46:         for (i=0; i<MagicNumber; i++)
47:         {
48:             cout << "\n(1)Horse (2)Pegasus: ";
49:             cin >> choice;
50:             if (choice == 2)
51:                 pHorse = new Pegasus;
52:             else
53:                 pHorse = new Horse;
54:             Ranch[i] = pHorse;
55:         }
56:         for (i=0; i<MagicNumber; i++)
57:         {
58:             cout << "\n(1)Bird (2)Pegasus: ";
59:             cin >> choice;
60:             if (choice == 2)
61:                 pBird = new Pegasus;
62:             else
63:                 pBird = new Bird;
64:             Aviary[i] = pBird;
65:         }
66:
67:         cout << "\n";
68:         for (i=0; i<MagicNumber; i++)
69:         {
70:             cout << "\nRanch[" << i << "]: " ;
71:             Ranch[i]->Whinny();
72:             delete Ranch[i];
73:         }
74:
```

13

continues

LISTING **13.3**   CONTINUED

```
75:          for (i=0; i<MagicNumber; i++)
76:          {
77:             cout << "\nAviary[" << i << "]: " ;
78:             Aviary[i]->Chirp();
79:             Aviary[i]->Fly();
80:             delete Aviary[i];
81:          }
82:       return 0;
83:    }
```

OUTPUT

```
(1)Horse (2)Pegasus: 1
Horse constructor...
(1)Horse (2)Pegasus: 2
Horse constructor... Bird constructor... Pegasus constructor...
(1)Bird (2)Pegasus: 1
Bird constructor...
(1)Bird (2)Pegasus: 2
Horse constructor... Bird constructor... Pegasus constructor...

Ranch[0]: Whinny!... Horse destructor...
Ranch[1]: Whinny!... Pegasus destructor...  Bird destructor...
Horse destructor...
Aviary[0]: Chirp... I can fly! I can fly! I can fly! Bird destructor...
Aviary[1]: Whinny!... I can fly! I can fly! I can fly!
Pegasus destructor... Bird destructor... Horse destructor...
```

ANALYSIS On lines 6–14, a Horse class is declared. The constructor and destructor print out a message, and the Whinny() method prints the word Whinny!

On lines 16–28, a Bird class is declared. In addition to its constructor and destructor, this class has two methods: Chirp() and Fly(), both of which print identifying messages. In a real program these might, for example, activate the speaker or generate animated images.

Finally, on lines 30–36, the class Pegasus is declared. It derives both from Horse and from Bird. The Pegasus class overrides the Chirp() method to call the Whinny() method, which it inherits from Horse.

Two lists are created: a Ranch with pointers to Horse on line 41, and an Aviary with pointers to Bird on line 42. On lines 46–55, Horse and Pegasus objects are added to the Ranch. On lines 56–65, Bird and Pegasus objects are added to the Aviary.

Invocations of the virtual methods on both the Bird pointers and the Horse pointers do the right things for Pegasus objects. For example, on line 78 the members of the Aviary array are used to call Chirp() on the objects to which they point. The Bird class declares this to be a virtual method, so the right function is called for each object.

Note that each time a `Pegasus` object is created, the output reflects that both the `Bird` part and the `Horse` part of the `Pegasus` object are also created. When a `Pegasus` object is destroyed, the `Bird` and `Horse` parts are destroyed as well, thanks to the destructors being made virtual.

Declaring Multiple Inheritance

Declare an object to inherit from more than one class by listing the base classes following the colon after the class name. Separate the base classes by commas.

Example 1

```
class Pegasus : public Horse, public Bird
```

Example 2

```
class Schnoodle : public Schnauzer, public Poodle
```

The Parts of a Multiply Inherited Object

When the `Pegasus` object is created in memory, both the base classes form part of the `Pegasus` object, as illustrated in Figure 13.1.

FIGURE 13.1

Multiply inherited objects.

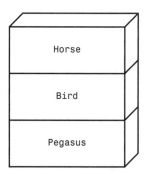

Several issues arise with objects with multiple base classes. For example, what happens if two base classes that happen to have the same name have virtual functions or data? How are multiple base class constructors initialized? What happens if both multiple base classes derive from the same class? The following sections will answer these questions and explore how multiple inheritance can be put to work.

13

Constructors in Multiply Inherited Objects

If `Pegasus` derives from both `Horse` and `Bird`, and each of the base classes has constructors that take parameters, the `Pegasus` class initializes these constructors in turn. Listing
13.4 illustrates how this is done.

INPUT   **LISTING 13.4**   Calling Multiple Constructors

```
1:      // Listing 13.4
2:      // Calling multiple constructors
3:      #include <iostream.h>
4:      typedef int HANDS;
5:      enum COLOR { Red, Green, Blue, Yellow, White, Black, Brown } ;
6:
7:      class Horse
8:      {
9:      public:
10:         Horse(COLOR color, HANDS height);
11:         virtual ~Horse() { cout << "Horse destructor...\n"; }
12:         virtual void Whinny()const { cout << "Whinny!... "; }
13:         virtual HANDS GetHeight() const { return itsHeight; }
14:         virtual COLOR GetColor() const { return itsColor; }
15:      private:
16:         HANDS itsHeight;
17:         COLOR itsColor;
18:      };
19:
20:      Horse::Horse(COLOR color, HANDS height):
21:          itsColor(color),itsHeight(height)
22:      {
23:          cout << "Horse constructor...\n";
24:      }
25:
26:      class Bird
27:      {
28:      public:
29:          Bird(COLOR color, bool migrates);
30:          virtual ~Bird() {cout << "Bird destructor...\n";  }
31:          virtual void Chirp()const { cout << "Chirp... ";  }
32:          virtual void Fly()const
33:          {
34:             cout << "I can fly! I can fly! I can fly! ";
35:          }
36:          virtual COLOR GetColor()const { return itsColor; }
37:          virtual bool GetMigration() const { return itsMigration; }
38:
39:      private:
40:          COLOR itsColor;
41:          bool itsMigration;
```

```
42:    };
43:
44:    Bird::Bird(COLOR color, bool migrates):
45:        itsColor(color), itsMigration(migrates)
46:    {
47:        cout << "Bird constructor...\n";
48:    }
49:
50:    class Pegasus : public Horse, public Bird
51:    {
52:    public:
53:        void Chirp()const { Whinny(); }
54:        Pegasus(COLOR, HANDS, bool,long);
55:        ~Pegasus() {cout << "Pegasus destructor...\n";}
56:        virtual long GetNumberBelievers() const
57:         {
58:            return  itsNumberBelievers;
59:         }
60:
61:    private:
62:        long itsNumberBelievers;
63:    };
64:
65:    Pegasus::Pegasus(
66:        COLOR aColor,
67:        HANDS height,
68:        bool migrates,
69:        long NumBelieve):
70:    Horse(aColor, height),
71:    Bird(aColor, migrates),
72:    itsNumberBelievers(NumBelieve)
73:    {
74:        cout << "Pegasus constructor...\n";
75:    }
76:
77:    int main()
78:    {
79:        Pegasus *pPeg = new Pegasus(Red, 5, true, 10);
80:        pPeg->Fly();
81:        pPeg->Whinny();
82:        cout << "\nYour Pegasus is " << pPeg->GetHeight();
83:        cout << " hands tall and ";
84:        if (pPeg->GetMigration())
85:           cout << "it does migrate.";
86:        else
87:           cout << "it does not migrate.";
88:        cout << "\nA total of " << pPeg->GetNumberBelievers();
89:        cout << " people believe it exists.\n";
90:        delete pPeg;
91:     return 0;
92:    }
```

13

OUTPUT

```
Horse constructor...
Bird constructor...
Pegasus constructor...
I can fly! I can fly! I can fly! Whinny!...
Your Pegasus is 5 hands tall and it does migrate.
A total of 10 people believe it exists.

Pegasus destructor...
Bird destructor...
Horse destructor...
```

ANALYSIS On lines 7–18, the Horse class is declared. The constructor takes two parameters: one is an enumeration declared on line 5, and the other is a typedef declared on line 4. The implementation of the constructor on lines 20–24 simply initializes the member variables and prints a message.

On lines 26–42, the Bird class is declared, and the implementation of its constructor is on lines 45–49. Again, the Bird class takes two parameters. Interestingly, the Horse constructor takes color (so that you can detect horses of different colors), and the Bird constructor takes the color of the feathers (so those of one feather can stick together). This leads to a problem when you want to ask the Pegasus for its color, which you will see in the next example.

The Pegasus class itself is declared on lines 50–63, and its constructor is on lines 65–75. The initialization of the Pegasus object includes three statements. First, the Horse constructor is initialized with color and height. Then the Bird constructor is initialized with color and the Boolean. Finally, the Pegasus member variable itsNumberBelievers is initialized. After all that is accomplished, the body of the Pegasus constructor is called.

In the main() function, a Pegasus pointer is created and used to access the member functions of the base objects.

Ambiguity Resolution

In Listing 13.4, both the Horse class and the Bird class have a method GetColor(). You may need to ask the Pegasus object to return its color, but you have a problem: The Pegasus class inherits from both Bird and Horse. They both have a color, and their methods for getting that color have the same names and signature. This creates an ambiguity for the compiler, which you must resolve.

If you simply write

```
COLOR currentColor = pPeg->GetColor();
```

g++ will give you the compiler error:

```
request for method `GetColor' is ambiguous
```

You can resolve the ambiguity with an explicit call to the function you want to invoke:

```
COLOR currentColor = pPeg->Horse::GetColor();
```

Any time you need to resolve which class a member function or member data inherits from, you can fully qualify the call by prepending the class name to the base class data or function.

Note that if `Pegasus` were to override this function, the problem would be moved, as it should be, into the `Pegasus` member function:

```
virtual COLOR GetColor()const { return Horse::GetColor(); }
```

This hides the problem from clients of the `Pegasus` class and encapsulates within `Pegasus` the knowledge of which base class it wants to inherit its color from. A client is still free to force the issue by writing

```
COLOR currentColor = pPeg->Bird::GetColor();
```

Inheriting from Shared Base Class

What happens if both `Bird` and `Horse` inherit from a common base class, such as `Animal`? Figure 13.2 shows what this looks like.

FIGURE 13.2

Common base classes.

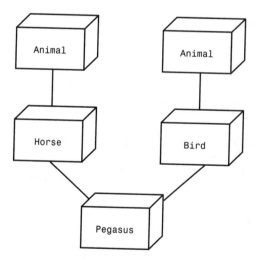

13

As you can see in Figure 13.2, two base class objects exist. When a function or data member is called in the shared base class, another ambiguity exists. For example, if `Animal` declares `itsAge` as a member variable and `GetAge()` as a member function, and you call `pPeg->GetAge()`, did you mean to call the `GetAge()` function you inherited from `Animal` by way of `Horse`, or by way of `Bird`? You must resolve this ambiguity as well, as illustrated in Listing 13.5.

INPUT **LISTING 13.5** Common Base Classes

```
1:      // Listing 13.5
2:      // Common base classes
3:      #include <iostream.h>
4:
5:      typedef int HANDS;
6:      enum COLOR { Red, Green, Blue, Yellow, White, Black, Brown } ;
7:
8:      class Animal         // common base to both horse and bird
9:      {
10:     public:
11:         Animal(int);
12:         virtual ~Animal() { cout << "Animal destructor...\n"; }
13:         virtual int GetAge() const { return itsAge; }
14:         virtual void SetAge(int age) { itsAge = age; }
15:     private:
16:         int itsAge;
17:     };
18:
19:     Animal::Animal(int age):
20:     itsAge(age)
21:     {
22:         cout << "Animal constructor...\n";
23:     }
24:
25:     class Horse : public Animal
26:     {
27:     public:
28:         Horse(COLOR color, HANDS height, int age);
29:         virtual ~Horse() { cout << "Horse destructor...\n"; }
30:         virtual void Whinny()const { cout << "Whinny!... "; }
31:         virtual HANDS GetHeight() const { return itsHeight; }
32:         virtual COLOR GetColor() const { return itsColor; }
33:     protected:
34:         HANDS itsHeight;
35:         COLOR itsColor;
36:     };
37:
38:     Horse::Horse(COLOR color, HANDS height, int age):
39:         Animal(age),
```

```
40:         itsColor(color),itsHeight(height)
41:     {
42:         cout << "Horse constructor...\n";
43:     }
44:
45:     class Bird : public Animal
46:     {
47:     public:
48:         Bird(COLOR color, bool migrates, int age);
49:         virtual ~Bird() {cout << "Bird destructor...\n"; }
50:         virtual void Chirp()const { cout << "Chirp... "; }
51:         virtual void Fly()const
52:             { cout << "I can fly! I can fly! I can fly! "; }
53:         virtual COLOR GetColor()const { return itsColor; }
54:         virtual bool GetMigration() const { return itsMigration; }
55:     protected:
56:         COLOR itsColor;
57:         bool itsMigration;
58:     };
59:
60:     Bird::Bird(COLOR color, bool migrates, int age):
61:         Animal(age),
62:         itsColor(color), itsMigration(migrates)
63:     {
64:         cout << "Bird constructor...\n";
65:     }
66:
67:     class Pegasus : public Horse, public Bird
68:     {
69:     public:
70:         void Chirp()const { Whinny(); }
71:         Pegasus(COLOR, HANDS, bool, long, int);
72:         virtual ~Pegasus() {cout << "Pegasus destructor...\n";}
73:         virtual long GetNumberBelievers() const
74:             { return  itsNumberBelievers; }
75:         virtual COLOR GetColor()const { return Horse::itsColor; }
76:         virtual int GetAge() const { return Horse::GetAge(); }
77:     private:
78:         long itsNumberBelievers;
79:     };
80:
81:     Pegasus::Pegasus(
82:         COLOR aColor,
83:         HANDS height,
84:         bool migrates,
85:         long NumBelieve,
86:         int age):
87:     Horse(aColor, height,age),
88:     Bird(aColor, migrates,age),
89:     itsNumberBelievers(NumBelieve)
90:     {
```

continues

13

LISTING **13.5** CONTINUED

```
91:        cout << "Pegasus constructor...\n";
92:    }
93:
94:    int main()
95:    {
96:        Pegasus *pPeg = new Pegasus(Red, 5, true, 10, 2);
97:        int age = pPeg->GetAge();
98:        cout << "This pegasus is " << age << " years old.\n";
99:        delete pPeg;
100:       return 0;
101:   }<
```

OUTPUT

```
Animal constructor...
Horse constructor...
Animal constructor...
Bird constructor...
Pegasus constructor...
This pegasus is 2 years old.
Pegasus destructor...
Bird destructor...
Animal destructor...
Horse destructor...
Animal destructor...
```

ANALYSIS Several interesting features are in this listing. The Animal class is declared on lines 8–17. Animal adds one member variable, itsAge and two accessors: GetAge() and SetAge().

On line 25, the Horse class is declared to derive from Animal. The Horse constructor now has a third parameter, age, which it passes to its base class, Animal. Note that the Horse class does not override GetAge(); it simply inherits it.

On line 46, the Bird class is declared to derive from Animal. Its constructor also takes an age and uses it to initialize its base class, Animal. It also inherits GetAge() without overriding it.

Pegasus inherits from both Bird and from Animal, and so has two Animal classes in its inheritance chain. If you were to call GetAge() on a Pegasus object, you would have to disambiguate, or fully qualify, the method you want if Pegasus did not override the method.

This is solved on line 77 when the Pegasus object overrides GetAge() to do nothing more than to *chain up*—that is, to call the same method in a base class.

Chaining up is done for two reasons: either to disambiguate which base class to call, as in this case, or to do some work and then let the function in the base class do some more work. At times, you may want to do work and then chain up, or chain up and then do the work when the base class function returns.

The Pegasus constructor takes five parameters: the creature's color, its height (in hands), whether it migrates, how many believe in it, and its age. The constructor initializes the Horse part of the Pegasus with the color, height, and age on line 87. It initializes the Bird part with color, whether it migrates, and age on line 88. Finally, it initializes itsNumberBelievers on line 89.

The call to the Horse constructor on line 87 invokes the implementation shown on line 38. The Horse constructor uses the age parameter to initialize the Animal part of the Horse part of the Pegasus. It then goes on to initialize the two member variables of Horse—itsColor and itsHeight.

The call to the Bird constructor on line 88 invokes the implementation shown on line 60. Here too, the age parameter is used to initialize the Animal part of the Bird.

Note that the color parameter to the Pegasus is used to initialize member variables in both Bird and Horse. Note also that the age is used to initialize itsAge in the Horse's base Animal and in the Bird's base Animal.

Virtual Inheritance

In Listing 13.5, the Pegasus class went to some lengths to disambiguate which of its Animal base classes it meant to invoke. Most of the time, the decision as to which one to use is arbitrary—after all, the Horse and the Bird have the same base class.

It is possible to tell C++ that you do not want two copies of the shared base class, as shown in Figure 13.2, but would rather have a single shared base class, as shown in Figure 13.3.

You accomplish this by making Animal a virtual base class of both Horse and Bird. The Animal class does not change at all. The Horse and Bird classes change only in their use of the term virtual in their declarations. Pegasus, however, changes substantially.

Normally, a class's constructor initializes only its own variables and its base class. Virtually inherited base classes are an exception, however. They are initialized by their most derived class. Thus, Animal is initialized not by Horse and Bird, but by Pegasus. Horse and Bird have to initialize Animal in their constructors, but these initializations will be ignored when a Pegasus object is created.

13

FIGURE 13.3

A diamond inheritance.

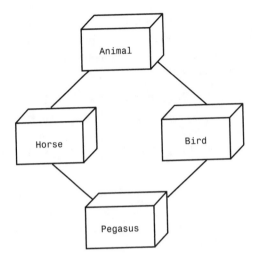

Listing 13.6 rewrites Listing 13.5 to take advantage of virtual derivation.

INPUT **LISTING 13.6** Illustration of the Use of Virtual Inheritance

```
1:    // Listing 13.6
2:    // Virtual inheritance
3:    #include <iostream.h>
4:
5:    typedef int HANDS;
6:    enum COLOR { Red, Green, Blue, Yellow, White, Black, Brown } ;
7:
8:    class Animal          // common base to both horse and bird
9:    {
10:   public:
11:       Animal(int);
12:       virtual ~Animal() { cout << "Animal destructor...\n"; }
13:       virtual int GetAge() const { return itsAge; }
14:       virtual void SetAge(int age) { itsAge = age; }
15:   private:
16:       int itsAge;
17:   };
18:
19:   Animal::Animal(int age):
20:   itsAge(age)
21:   {
22:       cout << "Animal constructor...\n";
23:   }
24:
25:   class Horse : virtual public Animal
26:   {
```

```
27:    public:
28:       Horse(COLOR color, HANDS height, int age);
29:       virtual ~Horse() { cout << "Horse destructor...\n"; }
30:       virtual void Whinny()const { cout << "Whinny!... "; }
31:       virtual HANDS GetHeight() const { return itsHeight; }
32:       virtual COLOR GetColor() const { return itsColor; }
33:    protected:
34:       HANDS itsHeight;
35:       COLOR itsColor;
36:    };
37:
38:    Horse::Horse(COLOR color, HANDS height, int age):
39:       Animal(age),
40:       itsColor(color),itsHeight(height)
41:    {
42:       cout << "Horse constructor...\n";
43:    }
44:
45:    class Bird : virtual public Animal
46:    {
47:    public:
48:       Bird(COLOR color, bool migrates, int age);
49:       virtual ~Bird() {cout << "Bird destructor...\n";  }
50:       virtual void Chirp()const { cout << "Chirp... ";  }
51:       virtual void Fly()const
52:          { cout << "I can fly! I can fly! I can fly! "; }
53:       virtual COLOR GetColor()const { return itsColor; }
54:       virtual bool GetMigration() const { return itsMigration; }
55:    protected:
56:       COLOR itsColor;
57:       bool itsMigration;
58:    };
59:
60:    Bird::Bird(COLOR color, bool migrates, int age):
61:       Animal(age),
62:       itsColor(color), itsMigration(migrates)
63:    {
64:       cout << "Bird constructor...\n";
65:    }
66:
67:    class Pegasus : public Horse, public Bird
68:    {
69:    public:
70:       void Chirp()const { Whinny(); }
71:       Pegasus(COLOR, HANDS, bool, long, int);
72:       virtual ~Pegasus() {cout << "Pegasus destructor...\n";}
73:       virtual long GetNumberBelievers() const
74:          { return  itsNumberBelievers; }
75:       virtual COLOR GetColor()const { return Horse::itsColor; }
76:    private:
77:       long itsNumberBelievers;
```

continues

13

LISTING 13.6   CONTINUED

```
78:    };
79: >
80:    Pegasus::Pegasus(
81:       COLOR aColor,
82:       HANDS height,
83:       bool migrates,
84:       long NumBelieve,
85:       int age):
86:    Horse(aColor, height,age),
87:    Bird(aColor, migrates,age),
88:    Animal(age*2),
89:    itsNumberBelievers(NumBelieve)
90:    {
91:       cout << "Pegasus constructor...\n";
92:    }
93:
94:    int main()
95:    {
96:       Pegasus *pPeg = new Pegasus(Red, 5, true, 10, 2);
97:       int age = pPeg->GetAge();
98:       cout << "This pegasus is " << age << " years old.\n";
99:      delete pPeg;
100:     return 0;
101:    }
```

OUTPUT
```
Animal constructor...
Horse constructor...
Bird constructor...
Pegasus constructor...
This pegasus is 4 years old.
Pegasus destructor...
Bird destructor...
Horse destructor...
Animal destructor...
```

ANALYSIS   On line 25, Horse declares that it inherits virtually from Animal, and on line 45, Bird makes the same declaration. Note that the constructors for both Bird and Animal still initialize the Animal object.

Pegasus inherits from both Bird and Animal, and as the most derived object of Animal, it also initializes Animal. It is Pegasus's initialization that is called, however, and the calls to Animal's constructor in Bird and Horse are ignored. You can see this because the value 2 is passed in, and Horse and Bird pass it along to Animal, but Pegasus doubles it. The result, 4, is reflected in the printout on line 98 and as shown in the output.

`Pegasus` no longer has to disambiguate the call to `GetAge()`, and so it is free to simply inherit this function from `Animal`. Note that `Pegasus` must still disambiguate the call to `GetColor()` because this function is in both of its base classes and not in `Animal`.

Declaring Classes for Virtual Inheritance

To ensure that derived classes have only one instance of common base classes, declare the intermediate classes to inherit virtually from the base class.

Example 1

```
class Horse : virtual public Animal
class Bird : virtual public Animal
class Pegasus : public Horse, public Bird
```

Example 2

```
class Schnauzer : virtual public Dog
class Poodle : virtual public Dog
class Schnoodle : public Schnauzer, public Poodle
```

Problems with Multiple Inheritance

Although multiple inheritance offers several advantages over single inheritance, many C++ programmers are reluctant to use it. The problems they cite are that many compilers do not yet support it, that it makes debugging harder, and that nearly everything that can be done with multiple inheritance can be done without it.

These are valid concerns, and you will want to be on your guard against installing needless complexity into your programs. Some debuggers have a hard time with multiple inheritance, and some designs are needlessly made complex by using multiple inheritance when it is not needed.

Do	Don't
DO use multiple inheritance when a new class needs functions and features from more than one base class.	**DON'T** use multiple inheritance when single inheritance will do.
DO use virtual inheritance when the most derived classes must have only one instance of the shared base class.	
DO initialize the shared base class from the most derived class when using virtual base classes.	

13

Mixins and Capabilities Classes

One way to strike a middle ground between multiple inheritance and single inheritance is to use what are called mixins. Thus, you might have your `Horse` class derive from `Animal` and from `Displayable`. `Displayable` would just add a few methods for displaying any object onscreen.

A *mixin*, or *capability* class, is a class that adds functionality without adding much or any data.

Capability classes are mixed into a derived class the same as any other class might be, by declaring the derived class to inherit publicly from them. The only difference between a capability class and any other class is that the capability class has little or no data. This is an arbitrary distinction, of course, and is just a shorthand way of noting that at times all you want to do is mix in some additional capabilities without complicating the derived class.

This will, for some debuggers, make it easier to work with mixins than with more complex multiply inherited objects. In addition, less likelihood exists of ambiguity in accessing the data in the other principal base class.

For example, if `Horse` derives from `Animal` and from `Displayable`, `Displayable` would have no data. `Animal` would be just as it always was, so all the data in `Horse` would derive from `Animal`, but the functions in `Horse` would derive from both.

The term mixin comes from an ice cream store in Somerville, Massachusetts, where candies and cakes were mixed into the basic ice cream flavors. This seemed like a good metaphor to some of the object-oriented programmers who used to take a summer break there, especially while working with the object-oriented programming language SCOOPS.

Abstract Data Types

Often, you will create a hierarchy of classes together. For example, you might create a `Shape` class, and derive from that `Rectangle` and `Circle`. From `Rectangle`, you might derive `Square` as a special case of `Rectangle`.

Each of the derived classes will override the `Draw()` method, the `GetArea()` method, and so forth. Listing 13.7 illustrates a bare-bones implementation of the `Shape` class and its derived `Circle` and `Rectangle` classes.

LISTING 13.7 Shape Classes

```
1:    //Listing 13.7. Shape classes.
2:
3:    #include <iostream.h>
4:
5:
6:    class Shape
7:    {
8:    public:
9:      Shape(){}
10:     virtual ~Shape(){}
11:     virtual long GetArea() { return -1; }
12:     virtual long GetPerim() { return -1; }
13:     virtual void Draw() {}
14:   private:
15:   };
16:
17:   class Circle : public Shape
18:   {
19:   public:
20:        Circle(int radius):itsRadius(radius){}
21:        ~Circle(){}
22:        long GetArea() { return 3 * itsRadius * itsRadius; }
23:        long GetPerim() { return 6 * itsRadius; }
24:        void Draw();
25:   private:
26:        int itsRadius;
27:        int itsCircumference;
28:   };
29:
30:   void Circle::Draw()
31:   {
32:        cout << "Circle drawing routine here!\n";
33:   }
34:
35:
36:   class Rectangle : public Shape
37:   {
38:   public:
39:        Rectangle(int len, int width):
40:            itsLength(len), itsWidth(width){}
41:        virtual ~Rectangle(){}
42:        virtual long GetArea() { return itsLength * itsWidth; }
43:        virtual long GetPerim() {return 2*itsLength + 2*itsWidth; }
44:        virtual int GetLength() { return itsLength; }
45:        virtual int GetWidth() { return itsWidth; }
46:        virtual void Draw();
47:   private:
48:        int itsWidth;
```

continues

13

LISTING **13.7**   CONTINUED

```
49:       int itsLength;
50:    };
51:
52:    void Rectangle::Draw()
53:    {
54:      for (int i = 0; i<itsLength; i++)
55:      {
56:        for (int j = 0; j<itsWidth; j++)
57:          cout << "x ";
58:
59:        cout << "\n";
60:      }
61:    }
62:
63:    class Square : public Rectangle
64:    {
65:    public:
66:        Square(int len);
67:        Square(int len, int width);
68:        ~Square(){}
69:        long GetPerim() {return 4 * GetLength();}
70:    };
71:
72:    Square::Square(int len):
73:      Rectangle(len,len)
74:    {}
75:
76:    Square::Square(int len, int width):
77:      Rectangle(len,width)
78:
79:    {
80:      if (GetLength() != GetWidth())
81:        cout << "Error, not a square... a Rectangle??\n";
82:    }
83:
84:    int main()
85:    {
86:      int choice;
87:      bool fQuit = false;
88:      Shape * sp;
89:
90:      while ( ! fQuit )
91:      {
92:        cout << "(1)Circle (2)Rectangle (3)Square (0)Quit: ";
93:        cin >> choice;
94:
95:        switch (choice)
96:        {
```

```
97:              case 0: fQuit = true;
98:              break;
99:             case 1: sp = new Circle(5);
100:              break;
101:             case 2: sp = new Rectangle(4,6);
102:              break;
103:             case 3: sp = new Square(5);
104:              break;
105:             default: cout << "Please enter a number between 0 and 3"
               ➥<< endl;
106:             continue;
107:             break;
108:          }
109:        if(fQuit) break;
110:        sp->Draw();
111:         delete sp;
112:        cout << "\n";
113:      }
114:    return 0;
115:  }
```

OUTPUT

```
(1)Circle (2)Rectangle (3)Square (0)Quit: 2
x x x x x x
x x x x x x
x x x x x x
x x x x x x

(1)Circle (2)Rectangle (3)Square (0)Quit:3
x x x x x
x x x x x
x x x x x
x x x x x
x x x x x

(1)Circle (2)Rectangle (3)Square (0)Quit:0
```

ANALYSIS   On lines 6–15, the Shape class is declared. The GetArea() and GetPerim()
methods return an error value, and Draw() takes no action. After all, what does it
mean to draw a Shape? Only types of shapes (circles, rectangle, and so on) can be drawn;
Shapes as an abstraction cannot be drawn.

Circle derives from Shape and overrides the three virtual methods. Note that no reason
exists to add the word "virtual," because that is part of their inheritance. But there is no
harm in doing so either, as shown in the Rectangle class on lines 42, 43, and 46. It is a
good idea to include the term virtual as a reminder, a form of documentation.

Square derives from Rectangle, and it, too, overrides the GetPerim() method, inheriting
the rest of the methods defined in Rectangle.

13

It is troubling, though, that a client might try to instantiate a Shape object, and it might be desirable to make that impossible. The Shape class exists only to provide an interface for the classes derived from it; as such, it is an abstract data type, or ADT.

An abstract data type represents a concept (such as shape) rather than an object (such as circle). In C++, an ADT is always the base class to other classes, and it is not valid to make an instance of an ADT.

Pure Virtual Functions

C++ supports the creation of abstract data types with pure virtual functions. A virtual function is made pure by initializing it with zero, as in

```
virtual void Draw() = 0;
```

Any class with one or more pure virtual functions is an ADT, and it is illegal to instantiate an object of a class that is an ADT. Trying to do so will cause a compile-time error. Putting a pure virtual function in your class signals two things to clients of your class:

- Do not make an object of this class; derive from it.
- Make sure you override the pure virtual function.

Any class that derives from an ADT inherits the pure virtual function as pure, and so must override every pure virtual function if it wants to instantiate objects. Thus, if Rectangle inherits from Shape, and Shape has three pure virtual functions, Rectangle must override all three or it, too, will be an ADT. Listing 13.8 rewrites the Shape class to be an abstract data type. To save space, the rest of Listing 13.7 is not reproduced here. Replace the declaration of Shape in Listing 13.7, lines 7–16, with the declaration of Shape in Listing 13.8 and run the program again.

INPUT **LISTING 13.8** Abstract Data Types

```
1:  class Shape
2:  {
3:  public:
4:        Shape(){}
5:        ~Shape(){}
6:        virtual long GetArea() = 0; // error
7:        virtual long GetPerim()= 0;
8:        virtual void Draw() = 0;
9:  private:
10: };
```

OUTPUT

```
(1)Circle (2)Rectangle (3)Square (0)Quit: 2
x x x x x x
x x x x x x
x x x x x x
x x x x x x

(1)Circle (2)Rectangle (3)Square (0)Quit: 3
x x x x x
x x x x x
x x x x x
x x x x x
x x x x x

(1)Circle (2)Rectangle (3)Square (0)Quit: 0
```

ANALYSIS As you can see, the workings of the program are totally unaffected. The only difference is that it would now be impossible to make an object of class Shape.

Abstract Data Types

Declare a class to be an abstract data type by including one or more pure virtual functions in the class declaration. Declare a pure virtual function by writing = 0 after the function declaration.

One example looks like:

```
class Shape
{
virtual void Draw() = 0;    // pure virtual
};
```

Implementing Pure Virtual Functions

Typically, the pure virtual functions in an abstract base class are never implemented. Because no objects of that type are ever created, no reason exists to provide implementations, and the ADT works purely as the definition of an interface to objects that derive from it.

It is possible, however, to provide an implementation to a pure virtual function. The function can then be called by objects derived from the ADT, perhaps to provide common functionality to all the overridden functions. Listing 13.9 reproduces Listing 13.7, this time with Shape as an ADT and with an implementation for the pure virtual function Draw(). The Circle class overrides Draw(), as it must, but it then chains up to the base class function for additional functionality.

13

In this example, the additional functionality is simply an additional message printed, but one can imagine that the base class provides a shared drawing mechanism, perhaps setting up a window that all derived classes will use.

INPUT   **LISTING 13.9**   Implementing Pure Virtual Functions

```
1:     //Implementing pure virtual functions
2:
3:     #include <iostream.h>
4:
5:     class Shape
6:     {
7:     public:
8:         Shape(){}
9: virtual ~Shape(){}
10:        virtual long GetArea() = 0;
11:        virtual long GetPerim()= 0;
12:        virtual void Draw() = 0;
13:     private:
14:     };
15:
16:      void Shape::Draw()
17:      {
18:         cout << "Abstract drawing mechanism!\n";
19:      }
20:
21:     class Circle : public Shape
22:     {
23:     public:
24:            Circle(int radius):itsRadius(radius){}
25: virtual ~Circle(){}
26:            long GetArea() { return 3 * itsRadius * itsRadius; }
27:            long GetPerim() { return 9 * itsRadius; }
28:            void Draw();
29:     private:
30:        int itsRadius;
31:        int itsCircumference;
32:     };
33:
34:     void Circle::Draw()
35:     {
36:         cout << "Circle drawing routine here!\n";
37:         Shape::Draw();
38:     }
39:
40:
41:     class Rectangle : public Shape
42:     {
43:     public:
```

```
44:           Rectangle(int len, int width):
45:              itsLength(len), itsWidth(width){}
46: virtual ~Rectangle(){}
47:           long GetArea() { return itsLength * itsWidth; }
48:           long GetPerim() {return 2*itsLength + 2*itsWidth; }
49:           virtual int GetLength() { return itsLength; }
50:           virtual int GetWidth() { return itsWidth; }
51:           void Draw();
52:    private:
53:       int itsWidth;
54:       int itsLength;
55:    };
56:
57:    void Rectangle::Draw()
58:    {
59:       for (int i = 0; i<itsLength; i++)
60:       {
61:          for (int j = 0; j<itsWidth; j++)
62:             cout << "x ";
63:
64:          cout << "\n";
65:       }
66:       Shape::Draw();
67:    }
68:
69:
70:    class Square : public Rectangle
71:    {
72:    public:
73:          Square(int len);
74:          Square(int len, int width);
75: virtual ~Square(){}
76:          long GetPerim() {return 4 * GetLength();}
77:    };
78:
79:    Square::Square(int len):
80:       Rectangle(len,len)
81:    {}
82:
83:    Square::Square(int len, int width):
84:       Rectangle(len,width)
85:
86:    {
87:       if (GetLength() != GetWidth())
88:          cout << "Error, not a square... a Rectangle??\n";
89:    }
90:
91:    int main()
92:    {
93:       int choice;
94:       bool fQuit = false;
```

continues

13

LISTING **13.9**   CONTINUED

```
95:      Shape * sp;
96:
97:      while (1)
98:      {
99:        cout << "(1)Circle (2)Rectangle (3)Square (0)Quit: ";
100:       cin >> choice;
101:
102:       switch (choice)
103:       {
104:          case 1: sp = new Circle(5);
105:          break;
106:          case 2: sp = new Rectangle(4,6);
107:          break;
108:          case 3: sp = new Square (5);
109:          break;
110:          default: fQuit = true;
111:          break;
112:       }
113:       if (fQuit)
114:          break;
115:
116:       sp->Draw();
117:        delete sp;
118:       cout << "\n";
119:     }
120:    return 0;
121:  }
```

OUTPUT

```
(1)Circle (2)Rectangle (3)Square (0)Quit: 2
x x x x x x
x x x x x x
x x x x x x
x x x x x x
Abstract drawing mechanism!

(1)Circle (2)Rectangle (3)Square (0)Quit: 3
x x x x x
x x x x x
x x x x x
x x x x x
x x x x x
Abstract drawing mechanism!

(1)Circle (2)Rectangle (3)Square (0)Quit: 0
```

ANALYSIS On lines 5–14, the abstract data type Shape is declared, with all three of its accessor methods declared to be pure virtual. Note that this is not necessary. If any one were declared pure virtual, the class would have been an ADT.

The GetArea() and GetPerim() methods are not implemented, but Draw() is. Circle and Rectangle both override Draw(), and both chain up to the base method, taking advantage of shared functionality in the base class.

Complex Hierarchies of Abstraction

At times, you will derive ADTs from other ADTs. It may be that you will want to make some of the derived pure virtual functions non-pure, and leave others pure.

If you create the Animal class, you may make Eat(), Sleep(), Move(), and Reproduce() all pure virtual functions. Perhaps from Animal you derive Mammal and Fish.

On examination, you decide that every Mammal will reproduce in the same way, and so you make Mammal::Reproduce() be non-pure, but you leave Eat(), Sleep(), and Move() as pure virtual functions.

From Mammal you derive Dog, and Dog must override and implement the three remaining pure virtual functions so that you can make objects of type Dog.

What you are saying, as the class designer, is that no Animals or Mammals can be instantiated, but that all Mammals may inherit the provided Reproduce() method without overriding it.

Listing 13.10 illustrates this technique with a bare-bones implementation of these classes.

INPUT   **LISTING 13.10**   Deriving ADTs from Other ADTs

```
1:      // Listing 13.10
2:      // Deriving ADTs from other ADTs
3:      #include <iostream.h>
4:
5:      enum COLOR { Red, Green, Blue, Yellow, White, Black, Brown } ;
6:
7:      class Animal        // common base to both Mammal and Fish
8:      {
9:      public:
10:         Animal(int);
11:         virtual ~Animal() { cout << "Animal destructor...\n"; }
12:         virtual int GetAge() const { return itsAge; }
13:         virtual void SetAge(int age) { itsAge = age; }
14:         virtual void Sleep() const = 0;
```

13

continues

Listing 13.10   CONTINUED

```
15:        virtual void Eat() const = 0;
16:        virtual void Reproduce() const = 0;
17:        virtual void Move() const = 0;
18:        virtual void Speak() const = 0;
19:    private:
20:        int itsAge;
21:    };
22:
23:    Animal::Animal(int age):
24:    itsAge(age)
25:    {
26:        cout << "Animal constructor...\n";
27:    }
28:
29:    class Mammal : public Animal
30:    {
31:    public:
32:        Mammal(int age):Animal(age)
33:            { cout << "Mammal constructor...\n";}
34:        virtual ~Mammal() { cout << "Mammal destructor...\n";}
35:        virtual void Reproduce() const
36:            { cout << "Mammal reproduction depicted...\n"; }
37:    };
38:
39:    class Fish : public Animal
40:    {
41:    public:
42:        Fish(int age):Animal(age)
43:            { cout << "Fish constructor...\n";}
44:        virtual ~Fish() {cout << "Fish destructor...\n";   }
45:        virtual void Sleep() const { cout << "fish snoring...\n"; }
46:        virtual void Eat() const { cout << "fish feeding...\n"; }
47:        virtual void Reproduce() const
48:            { cout << "fish laying eggs...\n"; }
49:        virtual void Move() const
50:            { cout << "fish swimming...\n";    }
51:        virtual void Speak() const { }
52:    };
53:
54:    class Horse : public Mammal
55:    {
56:    public:
57:        Horse(int age, COLOR color ):
58:        Mammal(age), itsColor(color)
59:            { cout << "Horse constructor...\n"; }
60:        virtual ~Horse() { cout << "Horse destructor...\n"; }
61:        virtual void Speak()const { cout << "Whinny!... \n"; }
62:        virtual COLOR GetItsColor() const { return itsColor; }
```

```
63:        virtual void Sleep() const
64:            { cout << "Horse snoring...\n"; }
65:        virtual void Eat() const { cout << "Horse feeding...\n"; }
66:        virtual void Move() const { cout << "Horse running...\n";}
67:
68:    protected:
69:        COLOR itsColor;
70:    };
71:
72:    class Dog : public Mammal
73:    {
74:    public:
75:        Dog(int age, COLOR color ):
76:            Mammal(age), itsColor(color)
77:                { cout << "Dog constructor...\n"; }
78:        virtual ~Dog() { cout << "Dog destructor...\n"; }
79:        virtual void Speak()const { cout << "Woof!... \n"; }
80:        virtual void Sleep() const { cout << "Dog snoring...\n"; }
81:        virtual void Eat() const { cout << "Dog eating...\n"; }
82:        virtual void Move() const  { cout << "Dog running...\n"; }
83:        virtual void Reproduce() const
84:            { cout << "Dogs reproducing...\n"; }
85:
86:    protected:
87:        COLOR itsColor;
88:    };
89:
90:    int main()
91:    {
92:        Animal *pAnimal=NULL;
93:        int choice;
94:        bool fQuit = false;
95:
96:        while (1)
97:        {
98:            cout << "(1)Dog (2)Horse (3)Fish (0)Quit: ";
99:            cin >> choice;
100:
101:            switch (choice)
102:            {
103:                case 1: pAnimal = new Dog(5,Brown);
104:                break;
105:                case 2: pAnimal = new Horse(4,Black);
106:                break;
107:                case 3: pAnimal = new Fish (5);
108:                break;
109:                default: fQuit = true;
110:                break;
111:            }
112:            if (fQuit)
113:                break;
```

continues

13

LISTING 13.10   CONTINUED

```
114:
115:        pAnimal->Speak();
116:        pAnimal->Eat();
117:        pAnimal->Reproduce();
118:        pAnimal->Move();
119:        pAnimal->Sleep();
120:        delete pAnimal;
121:        cout << "\n";
122:     }
123:     return 0;
124:  }
```

OUTPUT

```
(1)Dog (2)Horse (3)Bird (0)Quit: 1
Animal constructor...
Mammal constructor...
Dog constructor...
Woof!...
Dog eating...
Dog reproducing....
Dog running...
Dog snoring...
Dog destructor...
Mammal destructor...
Animal destructor...

(1)Dog (2)Horse (3)Bird (0)Quit: 0
```

ANALYSIS   On lines 7–21, the abstract data type Animal is declared. Animal has non-pure virtual accessors for itsAge, which are shared by all Animal objects. It has five pure virtual functions, Sleep(), Eat(), Reproduce(), Move(), and Speak().

Mammal is derived from Animal, is declared on lines 29–37, and adds no data. It overrides Reproduce(), however, providing a common form of reproduction for all mammals. Fish must override Reproduce() because Fish derives directly from Animal and cannot take advantage of mammalian reproduction (and a good thing, too!).

Mammal classes no longer have to override the Reproduce() function, but they are free to do so if they choose, as Dog does on line 83. Fish, Horse, and Dog all override the remaining pure virtual functions, so that objects of their type can be instantiated.

In the body of the program, an Animal pointer is used to point to the various derived objects in turn. The virtual methods are invoked, and based on the runtime binding of the pointer, the correct method is called in the derived class.

It would be a compile-time error to try to instantiate an Animal or a Mammal, as both are abstract data types.

Which Types Are Abstract?

In one program, the class `Animal` is abstract; in another, it is not. What determines whether to make a class abstract?

The answer to this question is decided not by any real-world intrinsic factor, but by what makes sense in your program. If you are writing a program that depicts a farm or a zoo, you may want `Animal` to be an abstract data type, but `Dog` to be a class from which you can instantiate objects.

On the other hand, if you are making an animated kennel, you may want to keep `Dog` as an abstract data type and only instantiate types of dogs: retrievers, terriers, and so forth. The level of abstraction is a function of how finely you need to distinguish your types.

Do	Don't
DO use abstract data types to provide common functionality for a number of related classes. **DO** override all pure virtual functions. **DO** make pure virtual any function that must be overridden.	**DON'T** try to instantiate an object of an abstract data type.

The Observer Pattern

A very hot trend in C++ is the creation and dissemination of design patterns. These are well-documented solutions to common problems encountered by C++ programmers. As an example, the observer pattern solves a common problem in inheritance.

Imagine that you develop a timer class that knows how to count elapsed seconds. Such a class might have a class member `itsSeconds`, which is an integer, and it would have methods to set, get, and increment `itsSeconds`.

Now suppose we further assume that your program wants to be informed every time the timer's `itsSeconds` member is incremented. One obvious solution would be to put a notification method into the timer. However, notification is not an intrinsic part of timing, and the complex code for registering those classes that need to be informed whenever the clock increments does not really belong in your timer class.

More importantly, after you work out the logic of registering those who are interested in these changes and then notifying them, you would like to abstract this out into a class of its own and be able to reuse it with other classes that might be "observed" in this way.

13

Therefore, a better solution is to create an observer class. Make this observer an abstract data type with a pure virtual function Update().

Now create a second abstract data type, called Subject. Subject keeps an array of Observer objects and also provides two methods: register() (which adds observers to its list) and Notify(), which is called when there is something to report.

Those classes that want to be notified of your timer's changes inherit from Observer. The timer itself inherits from Subject. The Observer class registers itself with the Subject class. The Subject class calls Notify when it changes (in this case when the timer updates).

Finally, we note that not every client of timer wants to be observable, and thus we create a new class called ObservedTimer, which inherits both from timer and from Subject. This gives the ObservedTimer the timer characteristics and the capability to be observed.

A Word About Multiple Inheritance, Abstract Data Types, and Java

Many C++ programmers are aware that Java was based in large part on C++, and yet the creators of Java chose to leave out multiple inheritance. It was their opinion that multiple inheritance introduced complexity that worked against the ease of use of Java. They felt they could meet 90% of the multiple inheritance functionality using what are called interfaces.

An *interface* is much like an abstract data type in that it defines a set of functions that can only be implemented in a derived class. However, with interfaces, you do not directly derive from the interface; you derive from another class and implement the interface, much like multiple inheritance. Thus, this marriage of an abstract data type and multiple inheritance gives you something akin to a capability class without the complexity or overhead of multiple inheritance. In addition, because interfaces can have neither implementations nor data members, the need for virtual inheritance is eliminated.

Whether this is a bug or a feature is in the eyes of the beholder. In either case, if you understand multiple inheritance and abstract data types in C++, you will be in a good position to move on to using some of the more advanced features of Java should you decide to learn that language as well.

The observer pattern and how it is implemented both in Java and C++ is covered in detail in Robert Martin's article "C++ and Java: A Critical Comparison," in the January 1997 issue of *C++ Report*.

Summary

Today you learned how to overcome some of the limitations in single inheritance. You learned about the danger of percolating interfaces up the inheritance hierarchy and the risks in casting down the inheritance hierarchy. You also learned how to use multiple inheritance, what problems multiple inheritance can create, and how to solve them using virtual inheritance.

You also learned what abstract data types are and how to create abstract classes using pure virtual functions. You learned how to implement pure virtual functions and when and why you might do so. Finally, you saw how to implement the observer pattern using multiple inheritance and abstract data types.

Q&A

Q What does percolating functionality upward mean?

A This refers to the idea of moving shared functionality upward into a common base class. If more than one class shares a function, it is desirable to find a common base class in which that function can be stored.

Q Is percolating upward always a good thing?

A Yes, if you are percolating shared functionality upward. No, if all you are moving is interface. That is, if all the derived classes can't use the method, it is a mistake to move it up into a common base class. If you do, you'll have to switch on the runtime type of the object before deciding if you can invoke the function.

Q Why is switching on the runtime type of an object bad?

A With large programs, the switch statements become big and hard to maintain. The point of virtual functions is to let the virtual table, rather than the programmer, determine the runtime type of the object.

Q Why is casting bad?

A Casting isn't bad if it is done in a way that is type-safe. If a function is called that knows that the object must be of a particular type, casting to that type is fine. Casting can be used to undermine the strong type checking in C++, and that is what you want to avoid. If you are switching on the runtime type of the object and then casting a pointer, that may be a warning sign that something is wrong with your design.

13

Q Why not make all functions virtual?

A Virtual functions are supported by a virtual function table, which incurs runtime overhead, both in the size of the program and in the performance of the program. The v-ptr, or virtual-function pointer, is an implementation detail of virtual functions. Each object in a class with virtual functions has a v-ptr, which points to the virtual function table for that class. If you have very small classes that you don't expect to subclass, you may not want to make any of the functions virtual.

Q When should the destructor be made virtual?

A Any time you think the class will be subclassed, and a pointer to the base class will be used to access an object of the subclass. As a general rule of thumb, if you've made any functions in your class virtual, be sure to make the destructor virtual as well.

Q Why bother making an Abstract Data Type—why not just make it non-abstract and avoid creating any objects of that type?

A The purpose of many of the conventions in C++ is to enlist the compiler in finding bugs, so as to avoid runtime bugs in code that you give your customers. Making a class abstract—that is, giving it pure virtual functions—causes the compiler to flag any objects created of that abstract type as errors.

Workshop

The Workshop provides quiz questions to help you solidify your understanding of the material covered and exercises to provide you with experience in using what you have learned. Try to answer the quiz and exercise questions before checking the answers in Appendix D, "Answers to Exercises and Quizzes," and make sure you understand the answers before continuing to tomorrow's lesson.

Quiz

1. What is a down cast?

2. What is the v-ptr?

3. If a round-rectangle has straight edges and rounded corners, and your RoundRect class inherits both from Rectangle and from Circle, and they in turn both inherit from Shape, how many Shapes are created when you create a RoundRect?

4. If Horse and Bird inherit from Animal using public virtual inheritance, do their constructors initialize the Animal constructor? If Pegasus inherits from both Horse and Bird, how does it initialize Animal's constructor?

5. Declare a class vehicle and make it an abstract data type.

6. If a base class is an ADT, and it has three pure virtual functions, how many of these must be overridden in its derived classes?

Exercises

1. Show the declaration for a class `JetPlane`, which inherits from `Rocket` and `Airplane`.

2. Show the declaration for `777`, which inherits from the `JetPlane` class described in Exercise 1.

3. Write a program that derives `Car` and `Bus` from the class `Vehicle`. Make `Vehicle` be an ADT with two pure virtual functions. Make `Car` and `Bus` not be ADTs.

4. Modify the program in Exercise 3 so that `Car` is an ADT, and derive `SportsCar`, `Wagon`, and `Coupe` from `Car`. In the `Car` class, provide an implementation for one of the pure virtual functions in `Vehicle` and make it non-pure.

13

DAY 14

Special Classes and Functions

C++ offers several ways to limit the scope and impact of variables and pointers. So far, you have seen how to create global variables, local function variables, pointers to variables, and class member variables. Today you will learn:

- What static member data (variables) and static member functions are
- How to use static member variables and static member functions
- How to create and manipulate pointers to functions and pointers to member functions
- How to work with arrays of pointers to functions

Static Member Data

Until now, you have probably thought of the data in each object as unique to that object and not shared among objects in a class. If you have five Cat objects, for example, each has its own age, weight, and other data. The age of one does not affect the age of another.

At times, however, you will want to keep track of a pool of data. For example, you might want to know how many objects for a specific class have been created in your program, and how many are still in existence. Static member variables are shared among all instances of a class. They are a compromise between global data, which is available to all parts of your program, and member data, which is usually available only to each object.

You can think of a static member as belonging to the class rather than to the object. Normal member data is one per object, but static members are one per class. Listing 14.1 declares a Cat object with a static data member, HowManyCats. This variable keeps track of how many Cat objects have been created. This is done by incrementing the static variable, HowManyCats, with each construction and decrementing it with each destruction.

INPUT   **LISTING 14.1**   Static Member Data

```
1:     //Listing 14.1 static data members
2:
3:     #include <iostream.h>
4:
5:     class Cat
6:     {
7:     public:
8:         Cat(int age):itsAge(age){HowManyCats++; }
9:         virtual ~Cat() { HowManyCats—; }
10:        virtual int GetAge() { return itsAge; }
11:        virtual void SetAge(int age) { itsAge = age; }
12:        static int HowManyCats;
13:
14:    private:
15:        int itsAge;
16:
17:    };
18:
19:    int Cat::HowManyCats = 0;
20:
21:    int main()
22:    {
23:        const int MaxCats = 5; int i;
24:        Cat *CatHouse[MaxCats];
25:        for (i = 0; i<MaxCats; i++)
26:            CatHouse[i] = new Cat(i);
27:
28:        for (i = 0; i<MaxCats; i++)
29:        {
30:            cout << "There are ";
31:            cout << Cat::HowManyCats;
32:            cout << " cats left!\n";
33:            cout << "Deleting the one which is ";
```

```
34:              cout << CatHouse[i]->GetAge();
35:              cout << " years old\n";
36:              delete CatHouse[i];
37:              CatHouse[i] = 0;
38:          }
39:      return 0;
40:      }
```

OUTPUT
```
There are 5 cats left!
Deleting the one which is 0 years old
There are 4 cats left!
Deleting the one which is 1 years old
There are 3 cats left!
Deleting the one which is 2 years old
There are 2 cats left!
Deleting the one which is 3 years old
There are 1 cats left!
Deleting the one which is 4 years old
```

ANALYSIS On lines 5–17, the simplified class Cat is declared. On line 12, HowManyCats is declared to be a static member variable of type int.

The declaration of HowManyCats does not define an integer; no storage space is set aside. Unlike the non-static member variables, no storage space is set aside by instantiating a Cat object because the HowManyCats member variable is not in the object. Thus, on line 19, the variable is defined and initialized.

It is a common mistake to forget to define the static member variables of classes. Do not let this happen to you! Of course, if it does, the GNU compiler will catch it with a number of pithy error messages such as the following:

```
lst14-01.cxx: In method `Cat::Cat(int)':
lst14-01.cxx:8: `HowManyCats' undeclared (first use this function)
lst14-01.cxx:8: (Each undeclared identifier is reported only once
lst14-01.cxx:8: for each function it appears in.)
lst14-01.cxx: In method `Cat::~Cat()':
lst14-01.cxx:9: `HowManyCats' undeclared (first use this function)
lst14-01.cxx: At top level:
lst14-01.cxx:19: `int Cat::HowManyCats' is not a static member of `class Cat'
lst14-01.cxx: In function `int main()':
lst14-01.cxx:31: `HowManyCats' is not a member of type `Cat'
```

Some compilers do not detect the problem, and the linker gives you a message like:

```
undefined symbol Cat::HowManyCats
```

You do not need to do this for itsAge because it is a non-static member variable and is defined each time you make a Cat object, which you do here on line 26.

14

The constructor for Cat increments the static member variable on line 8. The destructor decrements it on line 9. Thus, at any moment, HowManyCats has an accurate measure of how many Cat objects were created but not yet destroyed.

The driver program on lines 21–40 instantiates five Cats and puts them in an array. This calls five Cat constructors, and thus HowManyCats is incremented five times from its initial value of 0.

The program then loops through each of the five positions in the array and prints out the value of HowManyCats before deleting the current Cat pointer. The printout reflects that the starting value is 5 (after all, 5 are constructed), and that each time the loop is run, one fewer Cat remains.

Note that HowManyCats is public and is accessed directly by main(). No reason exists to expose this member variable in this way. It is preferable to make it private along with the other member variables and provide a public accessor method, as long as you will always access the data through an instance of Cat. On the other hand, if you want to access this data directly, without necessarily having a Cat object available, you have two options: keep it public, as shown in Listing 14.2, or provide a static member function, as discussed later today.

INPUT   **LISTING 14.2**   Accessing Static Members Without an Object

```
1:      //Listing 14.2 static data members
2:
3:      #include <iostream.h>
4:
5:      class Cat
6:      {
7:      public:
8:          Cat(int age):itsAge(age){HowManyCats++; }
9:          virtual ~Cat() { HowManyCats—; }
10:         virtual int GetAge() { return itsAge; }
11:         virtual void SetAge(int age) { itsAge = age; }
12:         static int HowManyCats;
13:
14:     private:
15:         int itsAge;
16:
17:     };
18:
19:     int Cat::HowManyCats = 0;
20:
21:     void TelepathicFunction();
22:
23:     int main()
```

```
24:    {
25:        const int MaxCats = 5; int i;
26:        Cat *CatHouse[MaxCats];
27:        for (i = 0; i<MaxCats; i++)
28:        {
29:            CatHouse[i] = new Cat(i);
30:            TelepathicFunction();
31:        }
32:
33:        for ( i = 0; i<MaxCats; i++)
34:        {
35:            delete CatHouse[i];
36:            TelepathicFunction();
37:        }
38:        return 0;
39:    }
40:
41:    void TelepathicFunction()
42:    {
43:        cout << "There are ";
44:        cout << Cat::HowManyCats << " cats alive!\n";
45:    }
```

OUTPUT

```
There are 1 cats alive!
There are 2 cats alive!
There are 3 cats alive!
There are 4 cats alive!
There are 5 cats alive!
There are 4 cats alive!
There are 3 cats alive!
There are 2 cats alive!
There are 1 cats alive!
There are 0 cats alive!
```

ANALYSIS Listing 14.2 is much like Listing 14.1 except for the addition of a new function, TelepathicFunction(). This function does not create a Cat object, nor does it take a Cat object as a parameter, yet it can access the HowManyCats member variable. Again, it is worth re-emphasizing that this member variable is not in any particular object; it is in the class as a whole, and, if public, can be accessed by any function in the program.

The alternative to making this member variable public is to make it private. If you do, you can access it through a member function, but then you must have an object of that class available. Listing 14.3 shows this approach. The alternative, static member functions, is discussed immediately after the analysis of Listing 14.3.

14

INPUT **LISTING 14.3** Accessing Static Members Using Non-static Member Functions

```
1:      //Listing 14.3 private static data members
2:
3:      #include <iostream.h>
4:
5:      class Cat
6:      {
7:      public:
8:          Cat(int age):itsAge(age){HowManyCats++; }
9:          virtual ~Cat() { HowManyCats—; }
10:         virtual int GetAge() { return itsAge; }
11:         virtual void SetAge(int age) { itsAge = age; }
12:         virtual int GetHowMany() { return HowManyCats; }
13:
14:
15:     private:
16:         int itsAge;
17:         static int HowManyCats;
18:     };
19:
20:     int Cat::HowManyCats = 0;
21:
22:     int main()
23:     {
24:         const int MaxCats = 5; int i;
25:         Cat *CatHouse[MaxCats];
26:         for (i = 0; i<MaxCats; i++)
27:             CatHouse[i] = new Cat(i);
28:
29:         for (i = 0; i<MaxCats; i++)
30:         {
31:             cout << "There are ";
32:             cout << CatHouse[i]->GetHowMany();
33:             cout << " cats left!\n";
34:             cout << "Deleting the one which is ";
35:             cout << CatHouse[i]->GetAge()+2;
36:             cout << " years old\n";
37:             delete CatHouse[i];
38:             CatHouse[i] = 0;
39:         }
40:         return 0;
41:     }
```

OUTPUT
```
There are 5 cats left!
Deleting the one which is 2 years old
There are 4 cats left!
Deleting the one which is 3 years old
There are 3 cats left!
Deleting the one which is 4 years old
```

```
There are 2 cats left!
Deleting the one which is 5 years old
There are 1 cats left!
Deleting the one which is 6 years old
```

ANALYSIS On line 17, the static member variable HowManyCats is declared to have private access. Now you cannot access this variable from nonmember functions, such as TelepathicFunction from the previous listing.

Even though HowManyCats is static, it is still within the scope of the class. Any class function, such as GetHowMany(), can access it, just as member functions can access any member data. However, for a function to call GetHowMany(), it must have an object on which to call the function.

Do	**Don't**
DO use static member variables to share data among all instances of a class. **DO** make static member variables protected or private if you want to restrict access to them.	**DON'T** use static member variables to store data for one object. Static member data is shared among all objects of its class.

Static Member Functions

Static member functions are like static member variables: They exist not in an object but in the scope of the class. Thus, they can be called without having an object of that class, as illustrated in Listing 14.4.

INPUT **LISTING 14.4** Static Member Functions

```
1:    //Listing 14.4 Static member functions
2:
3:    #include <iostream.h>
4:
5:    class Cat
6:    {
7:    public:
8:       Cat(int age):itsAge(age){HowManyCats++; }
9:       virtual ~Cat() { HowManyCats—; }
10:      virtual int GetAge() { return itsAge; }
11:      virtual void SetAge(int age) { itsAge = age; }
12:      static int GetHowMany() { return HowManyCats; }
13:   private:
14:      int itsAge;
```

14

continues

LISTING **14.4**   CONTINUED

```
15:        static int HowManyCats;
16:    };
17:
18:    int Cat::HowManyCats = 0;
19:
20:    void TelepathicFunction();
21:
22:    int main()
23:    {
24:        const int MaxCats = 5;
25:        Cat *CatHouse[MaxCats]; int i;
26:        for (i = 0; i<MaxCats; i++)
27:        {
28:            CatHouse[i] = new Cat(i);
29:            TelepathicFunction();
30:        }
31:
32:        for ( i = 0; i<MaxCats; i++)
33:        {
34:            delete CatHouse[i];
35:            TelepathicFunction();
36:        }
37:        return 0;
38:    }
39:
40:    void TelepathicFunction()
41:    {
42:        cout << "There are " << Cat::GetHowMany() << " cats alive!\n";
43:    }
```

OUTPUT
```
There are 1 cats alive!
There are 2 cats alive!
There are 3 cats alive!
There are 4 cats alive!
There are 5 cats alive!
There are 4 cats alive!
There are 3 cats alive!
There are 2 cats alive!
There are 1 cats alive!
There are 0 cats alive!
```

ANALYSIS   The static member variable HowManyCats is declared to have private access on line 15 of the Cat declaration. The public accessor function, GetHowMany(), is declared to be both public and static on line 12.

Because GetHowMany() is public, it can be accessed by any function, and because it is static, no need exists to have an object of type Cat on which to call it. Thus, on line 42, the function TelepathicFunction() is able to access the public static accessor, even though it has no access to a Cat object. Of course, you could have called GetHowMany() on the Cat objects available in main(), the same as with any other accessor functions.

> **Note**
>
> Static member functions do not have a this pointer. Therefore, they cannot be declared const. Also, because member data variables are accessed in member functions using the this pointer, static member functions cannot access any non-static member variables!

Static Member Functions

You can access static member functions by calling them on an object of the class the same as you do any other member function, or you can call them without an object by fully qualifying the class and object name.

Here's an example:

```
class Cat
{
public:
static int GetHowMany() { return HowManyCats; }
private:
static int HowManyCats;
};
int Cat::HowManyCats = 0;
int main()
{
int howMany;
Cat theCat;                               // define a cat
howMany = theCat.GetHowMany();   // access through an object
howMany = Cat::GetHowMany();      // access without an object
}
```

Pointers to Functions

Just as an array name is a constant pointer to the first element of the array, a function name is a constant pointer to the function. It is possible to declare a pointer variable that points to a function and to invoke the function by using that pointer. This can be very useful; it enables you to create programs that decide which functions to invoke based on user input.

14

The only tricky part about function pointers is understanding the type of the object being pointed to. A pointer to int points to an integer variable, and a pointer to a function must point to a function of the appropriate return type and signature.

In the following declaration

```
long (* funcPtr) (int);
```

funcPtr is declared to be a pointer (note the * in front of the name) that points to a function that takes an integer parameter and returns a long. The parentheses around * funcPtr are necessary because the parentheses around int bind more tightly, that is they have higher precedence than the indirection operator (*). Without the first parentheses, this would declare a function that takes an integer and returns a pointer to a long. (Remember that spaces are meaningless here.)

Examine these two declarations:

```
long * Function (int);
```

```
long (* funcPtr) (int);
```

The first, Function (), is a function taking an integer and returning a pointer to a variable of type long. The second, funcPtr, is a pointer to a function taking an integer and returning a variable of type long.

The declaration of a function pointer will always include the return type and the parentheses indicating the type of the parameters, if any. Listing 14.5 illustrates the declaration and use of function pointers.

INPUT **LISTING 14.5** Pointers to Functions

```
1:     // Listing 14.5 Using function pointers
2:
3:     #include <iostream.h>
4:
5:     void Square (int&,int&);
6:     void Cube (int&, int&);
7:     void Swap (int&, int &);
8:     void GetVals(int&, int&);
9:     void PrintVals(int, int);
10:
11:    int main()
12:    {
13:        void (* pFunc) (int &, int &);
14:        bool fQuit = false;
15:
16:        int valOne=1, valTwo=2;
```

```
17:        int choice;
18:        while (fQuit == false)
19:        {
20:            cout << "(0)Quit (1)Change Values (2)Square
➡(3)Cube (4)Swap: ";
21:            cin >> choice;
22:            switch (choice)
23:            {
24:                case 1: pFunc = GetVals; break;
25:                case 2: pFunc = Square; break;
26:                case 3: pFunc = Cube; break;
27:                case 4: pFunc = Swap; break;
28:                default : fQuit = true; break;
29:            }
30:
31:            if (fQuit)
32:                break;
33:
34:            PrintVals(valOne, valTwo);
35:            pFunc(valOne, valTwo);
36:            PrintVals(valOne, valTwo);
37:        }
38:     return 0;
39:    }
40:
41:    void PrintVals(int x, int y)
42:    {
43:        cout << "x: " << x << " y: " << y << endl;
44:    }
45:
46:    void Square (int & rX, int & rY)
47:    {
48:        rX *= rX;
49:        rY *= rY;
50:    }
51:
52:    void Cube (int & rX, int & rY)
53:    {
54:        int tmp;
55:
56:        tmp = rX;
57:        rX *= rX;
58:        rX = rX * tmp;
59:
60:        tmp = rY;
61:        rY *= rY;
62:        rY = rY * tmp;
63:    }
64:
65:    void Swap(int & rX, int & rY)
66:    {
```

continues

14

LISTING 14.5 CONTINUED

```
67:          int temp;
68:          temp = rX;
69:          rX = rY;
70:          rY = temp;
71:      }
72:
73:      void GetVals (int & rValOne, int & rValTwo)
74:      {
75:          cout << "New value for ValOne: ";
76:          cin >> rValOne;
77:          cout << "New value for ValTwo: ";
78:          cin >> rValTwo;
79:      }
```

OUTPUT

```
(0)Quit (1)Change Values (2)Square (3)Cube (4)Swap: 1
x: 1 y: 2
New value for ValOne: 2
New value for ValTwo: 3
x: 2 y: 3
(0)Quit (1)Change Values (2)Square (3)Cube (4)Swap: 3
x: 2 y: 3
x: 8 y: 27
(0)Quit (1)Change Values (2)Square (3)Cube (4)Swap: 2
x: 8 y: 27
x: 64 y: 729
(0)Quit (1)Change Values (2)Square (3)Cube (4)Swap: 4
x: 64 y: 729
x: 729 y: 64
(0)Quit (1)Change Values (2)Square (3)Cube (4)Swap: 0
```

ANALYSIS On lines 5–8, four functions are declared, each with the same return type and signature, returning void and taking two references to integers.

On line 13, pFunc is declared to be a pointer to a function that returns void and takes two integer reference parameters. Any of the previous functions can be pointed to by pFunc. The user is repeatedly offered the choice of which functions to invoke, and pFunc is assigned accordingly. On lines 34–36, the current value of the two integers is printed, the currently assigned function is invoked, and then the values are printed again.

Pointer to Function

A pointer to function is invoked the same as the functions it points to, except that the function pointer name is used instead of the function name.

Assign a pointer to function to a specific function by assigning to the function name without the parentheses. The function name is a constant pointer to the function itself. Use the pointer to function the same as you would the function name. The pointer to function must agree in return value and signature with the function to which you assign it.

Here is one example:

```
long (*pFuncOne) (int, int);
long SomeFunction (int, int);
pFuncOne = SomeFunction;
pFuncOne(5,7);
```

Why Use Function Pointers?

You certainly could write the program in Listing 14.5 without function pointers, but the use of these pointers makes the intent and use of the program explicit: Pick a function from a list, and then invoke it.

Listing 14.6 uses the function prototypes and definitions from Listing 14.5, but the body of the program does not use a function pointer. Examine the differences between these two listings.

INPUT   **LISTING 14.6**   Rewriting Listing 14.5 Without the Pointer to Function

```
1:     // Listing 14.6 Without function pointers
2:
3:     #include <iostream.h>
4:
5:     void Square (int&,int&);
6:     void Cube (int&, int&);
7:     void Swap (int&, int &);
8:     void GetVals(int&, int&);
9:     void PrintVals(int, int);
10:
11:    int main()
12:    {
13:        bool fQuit = false;
14:        int valOne=1, valTwo=2;
15:        int choice;
16:        while (fQuit == false)
17:        {
18:            cout << "(0)Quit (1)Change Values (2)Square
➥(3)Cube (4)Swap: ";
19:            cin >> choice;
20:            switch (choice)
```

continues

14

LISTING **14.6**   CONTINUED

```
21:              {
22:                 case 1:
23:                     PrintVals(valOne, valTwo);
24:                     GetVals(valOne, valTwo);
25:                     PrintVals(valOne, valTwo);
26:                     break;
27:
28:                 case 2:
29:                     PrintVals(valOne, valTwo);
30:                     Square(valOne,valTwo);
31:                     PrintVals(valOne, valTwo);
32:                     break;
33:
34:                 case 3:
35:                     PrintVals(valOne, valTwo);
36:                     Cube(valOne, valTwo);
37:                     PrintVals(valOne, valTwo);
38:                     break;
39:
40:                 case 4:
41:                     PrintVals(valOne, valTwo);
42:                     Swap(valOne, valTwo);
43:                     PrintVals(valOne, valTwo);
44:                     break;
45:
46:                 default :
47:                     fQuit = true;
48:                     break;
49:             }
50:
51:          if (fQuit)
52:              break;
53:      }
54:    return 0;
55:    }
56:
57:    void PrintVals(int x, int y)
58:    {
59:       cout << "x: " << x << " y: " << y << endl;
60:    }
61:
62:    void Square (int & rX, int & rY)
63:    {
64:       rX *= rX;
65:       rY *= rY;
66:    }
67:
68:    void Cube (int & rX, int & rY)
```

```
69:      {
70:          int tmp;
71:
72:          tmp = rX;
73:          rX *= rX;
74:          rX = rX * tmp;
75:
76:          tmp = rY;
77:          rY *= rY;
78:          rY = rY * tmp;
79:      }
80:
81:      void Swap(int & rX, int & rY)
82:      {
83:          int temp;
84:          temp = rX;
85:          rX = rY;
86:          rY = temp;
87:      }
88:
89:      void GetVals (int & rValOne, int & rValTwo)
90:      {
91:          cout << "New value for ValOne: ";
92:          cin >> rValOne;
93:          cout << "New value for ValTwo: ";
94:          cin >> rValTwo;
95:      }
```

OUTPUT

```
(0)Quit (1)Change Values (2)Square (3)Cube (4)Swap: 1
x: 1 y: 2
New value for ValOne: 2
New value for ValTwo: 3
(0)Quit (1)Change Values (2)Square (3)Cube (4)Swap: 3
x: 2 y: 3
x: 8 y: 27
(0)Quit (1)Change Values (2)Square (3)Cube (4)Swap: 2
x: 8 y: 27
x: 64 y: 729
(0)Quit (1)Change Values (2)Square (3)Cube (4)Swap: 4
x: 64 y: 729
x: 729 y: 64
(0)Quit (1)Change Values (2)Square (3)Cube (4)Swap: 0
```

ANALYSIS   The implementation of the functions has been left out because it is identical to that provided in Listing 14.5. As you can see, the output is unchanged, but the body of the program has expanded from 22 lines to 46. The calls to PrintVals() must be repeated for each case.

14

It was tempting to put PrintVals() at the top of the while loop and again at the bottom, rather than in each case statement. However, this would have called PrintVals() even for the exit case, and that was not part of the specification.

Setting aside the increased size of the code and the repeated calls to do the same thing, the overall clarity is somewhat diminished. This is an artificial case, however, created to show how pointers to functions work. In real-world conditions, the advantages are even clearer: Pointers to functions can eliminate duplicate code, clarify your program, and enable you to make tables of functions to call based on runtime conditions.

Shorthand Invocation

The pointer to function does not need to be dereferenced, although you are free to do so. Therefore, if pFunc is a pointer to a function taking an integer and returning a variable of type long, and you assign pFunc to a matching function, you can invoke that function with either

pFunc(x);

or

(*pFunc)(x);

The two forms are identical. The former is just a shorthand version of the latter.

Using Arrays of Pointers to Functions

Just as you can declare an array of pointers to integers, you can declare an array of pointers to functions returning a specific value type and with a specific signature. Listing 14.7 again rewrites Listing 14.5, this time using an array to invoke all the choices at once.

INPUT   **LISTING 14.7**   Demonstrates Use of an Array of Pointers to Functions

```
1:     // Listing 14.7 demonstrates use of an array of
➥pointers to functions
2:
3:     #include <iostream.h>
4:
5:     void Square (int&,int&);
6:     void Cube (int&, int&);
7:     void Swap (int&, int &);
8:     void GetVals(int&, int&);
9:     void PrintVals(int, int);
10:
11:    int main()
```

```
12:     {
13:         int valOne=1, valTwo=2;
14:         int choice, i;
15:         const int MaxArray = 5;
16:         void (*pFuncArray[MaxArray])(int&, int&);
17:
18:         for (i=0;i<MaxArray;i++)
19:         {
20:             cout << "(1)Change Values (2)Square (3)Cube (4)Swap: ";
21:             cin >> choice;
22:             switch (choice)
23:             {
24:                 case 1:pFuncArray[i] = GetVals; break;
25:                 case 2:pFuncArray[i] = Square; break;
26:                 case 3:pFuncArray[i] = Cube; break;
27:                 case 4:pFuncArray[i] = Swap; break;
28:                 default:pFuncArray[i] = 0;
29:             }
30:         }
31:
32:         for (i=0;i<MaxArray; i++)
33:         {
34:             if ( pFuncArray[i] == 0 )
35:                 continue;
36:             pFuncArray[i](valOne,valTwo);
37:             PrintVals(valOne,valTwo);
38:         }
39:      return 0;
40:     }
41:
42:     void PrintVals(int x, int y)
43:     {
44:         cout << "x: " << x << " y: " << y << endl;
45:     }
46:
47:     void Square (int & rX, int & rY)
48:     {
49:         rX *= rX;
50:         rY *= rY;
51:     }
52:
53:     void Cube (int & rX, int & rY)
54:     {
55:         int tmp;
56:
57:         tmp = rX;
58:         rX *= rX;
59:         rX = rX * tmp;
60:
61:         tmp = rY;
62:         rY *= rY;
```

14

continues

LISTING 14.7   CONTINUED

```
63:          rY = rY * tmp;
64:      }
65:
66:      void Swap(int & rX, int & rY)
67:      {
68:          int temp;
69:          temp = rX;
70:          rX = rY;
71:          rY = temp;
72:      }
73:
74:      void GetVals (int & rValOne, int & rValTwo)
75:      {
76:          cout << "New value for ValOne: ";
77:          cin >> rValOne;
78:          cout << "New value for ValTwo: ";
79:          cin >> rValTwo;
80:      }
```

OUTPUT

```
(1)Change Values (2)Square (3)Cube (4)Swap: 1
(1)Change Values (2)Square (3)Cube (4)Swap: 2
(1)Change Values (2)Square (3)Cube (4)Swap: 3
(1)Change Values (2)Square (3)Cube (4)Swap: 4
(1)Change Values (2)Square (3)Cube (4)Swap: 2
New Value for ValOne: 2
New Value for ValTwo: 3
x: 2 y: 3
x: 4 y: 9
x: 64 y: 729
x: 729 y: 64
x: 531441 y:4096
```

ANALYSIS   Once again, the implementation of the functions has been left out to save space, but it is the same as in Listing 14.5. On line 16, the array pFuncArray is declared to be an array of five pointers to functions that return void and that take two integer references.

On lines 18–30, the user is asked to pick the functions to invoke, and each member of the array is assigned the address of the appropriate function. On lines 32–38, each function is invoked in turn. The result is printed after each invocation.

Passing Pointers to Functions to Other Functions

The pointers to functions (and arrays of pointers to functions, for that matter) can be passed to other functions, which may take action and then call the right function using the pointer.

You might improve Listing 14.5, for example, by passing the chosen function pointer to another function (outside of main()), which prints the values, invokes the function, and then prints the values again. Listing 14.8 illustrates this variation.

INPUT **LISTING 14.8** Passing Pointers to Functions as Function Arguments

```
1:      // Listing 14.8 Without function pointers
2:
3:      #include <iostream.h>
4:
5:      void Square (int&,int&);
6:      void Cube (int&, int&);
7:      void Swap (int&, int &);
8:      void GetVals(int&, int&);
9:      void PrintVals(void (*)(int&, int&),int&, int&);
10:
11:     int main()
12:     {
13:         int valOne=1, valTwo=2;
14:         int choice;
15:         bool fQuit = false;
16:
17:         void (*pFunc)(int&, int&);
18:
19:         while (fQuit == false)
20:         {
21:             cout << "(0)Quit (1)Change Values (2)Square
➥(3)Cube (4)Swap: ";
22:             cin >> choice;
23:             switch (choice)
24:             {
25:                 case 1:pFunc = GetVals; break;
26:                 case 2:pFunc = Square; break;
27:                 case 3:pFunc = Cube; break;
28:                 case 4:pFunc = Swap; break;
29:                 default:fQuit = true; break;
30:             }
31:             if (fQuit == true)
32:                 break;
33:             PrintVals ( pFunc, valOne, valTwo);
34:         }
35:
36:      return 0;
37:     }
38:
39:     void PrintVals( void (*pFunc)(int&, int&),int& x, int& y)
40:     {
41:         cout << "x: " << x << " y: " << y << endl;
42:         pFunc(x,y);
```

continues

14

LISTING **14.8**   CONTINUED

```
43:            cout << "x: " << x << " y: " << y << endl;
44:      }
45:
46:      void Square (int & rX, int & rY)
47:      {
48:         rX *= rX;
49:         rY *= rY;
50:      }
51:
52:      void Cube (int & rX, int & rY)
53:      {
54:         int tmp;
55:
56:         tmp = rX;
57:         rX *= rX;
58:         rX = rX * tmp;
59:
60:         tmp = rY;
61:         rY *= rY;
62:         rY = rY * tmp;
63:      }
64:
65:      void Swap(int & rX, int & rY)
66:      {
67:         int temp;
68:         temp = rX;
69:         rX = rY;
70:         rY = temp;
71:      }
72:
73:      void GetVals (int & rValOne, int & rValTwo)
74:      {
75:         cout << "New value for ValOne: ";
76:         cin >> rValOne;
77:         cout << "New value for ValTwo: ";
78:         cin >> rValTwo;
79:      }
```

OUTPUT
```
(0)Quit (1)Change Values (2)Square (3)Cube (4)Swap: 1
x: 1 y: 2
New value for ValOne: 2
New value for ValTwo: 3
x: 2 y: 3
(0)Quit (1)Change Values (2)Square (3)Cube (4)Swap: 3
x: 2 y: 3
x: 8 y: 27
(0)Quit (1)Change Values (2)Square (3)Cube (4)Swap: 2
x: 8 y: 27
```

```
x: 64  y: 729
(0)Quit (1)Change Values (2)Square (3)Cube (4)Swap: 4
x: 64  y: 729
x: 729 y:64
(0)Quit (1)Change Values (2)Square (3)Cube (4)Swap: 0
```

ANALYSIS On line 17, pFunc is declared to be a pointer to a function returning void and taking two parameters, both integer references. On line 9, PrintVals is declared to be a function taking three parameters. The first is a pointer to a function that returns void but takes two integer reference parameters, and the second and third arguments to PrintVals are integer references. The user is again prompted for which functions to call, and then on line 33 PrintVals is called.

A good way to test a C++ programmer's level of knowledge is to ask them what this declaration means:

```
void PrintVals(void (*)(int&, int&),int&, int&);
```

This is the kind of declaration that you use infrequently and probably look up in the book each time you need it, but it will save your program on those rare occasions when it is exactly the required construct.

Using typedef with Pointers to Functions

The construct void (*)(int&, int&) is cumbersome, at best. You can use typedef to simplify this, by declaring a type (in this case it is called VPF) as a pointer to a function returning void and taking two integer references. Listing 14.9 rewrites Listing 14.8 using this typedef statement.

INPUT **LISTING 14.9**   Using typedef to Make Pointers to Functions More Readable

```
1:   // Listing 14.9. Using typedef to make pointers to
➥functions more readable
2:
3:   #include <iostream.h>
4:
5:   void Square (int&,int&);
6:   void Cube (int&, int&);
7:   void Swap (int&, int &);
8:   void GetVals(int&, int&);
9:   typedef  void (*VPF) (int&, int&) ;
10:   void PrintVals(VPF,int&, int&);
11:
12:   int main()
13:   {
14:   int valOne=1, valTwo=2;
15:   int choice;
```

14

continues

LISTING 14.9 CONTINUED

```
16:    bool fQuit = false;
17:
18:    VPF pFunc;
19:
20:    while (fQuit == false)
21:    {
22:    cout << "(0)Quit (1)Change Values (2)Square (3)Cube (4)Swap: ";
23:    cin >> choice;
24:    switch (choice)
25:    {
26:    case 1:pFunc = GetVals; break;
27:    case 2:pFunc = Square; break;
28:    case 3:pFunc = Cube; break;
29:    case 4:pFunc = Swap; break;
30:    default:fQuit = true; break;
31:    }
32:    if (fQuit == true)
33:    break;
34:    PrintVals ( pFunc, valOne, valTwo);
35:    }
36:    return 0;
37:    }
38:
39:    void PrintVals( VPF pFunc,int& x, int& y)
40:    {
41:    cout << "x: " << x << " y: " << y << endl;
42:    pFunc(x,y);
43:    cout << "x: " << x << " y: " << y << endl;
44:    }
45:
46:     void Square (int & rX, int & rY)
47:     {
48:        rX *= rX;
49:        rY *= rY;
50:     }
51:
52:     void Cube (int & rX, int & rY)
53:     {
54:        int tmp;
55:
56:        tmp = rX;
57:        rX *= rX;
58:        rX = rX * tmp;
59:
60:        tmp = rY;
61:        rY *= rY;
62:        rY = rY * tmp;
63:     }
```

```
64:
65:     void Swap(int & rX, int & rY)
66:     {
67:        int temp;
68:        temp = rX;
69:        rX = rY;
70:        rY = temp;
71:     }
72:
73:     void GetVals (int & rValOne, int & rValTwo)
74:     {
75:        cout << "New value for ValOne: ";
76:        cin >> rValOne;
77:        cout << "New value for ValTwo: ";
78:        cin >> rValTwo;
79:     }
```

OUTPUT

```
(0)Quit (1)Change Values (2)Square (3)Cube (4)Swap: 1
x: 1 y: 2
New value for ValOne: 2
New value for ValTwo: 3
x: 2 y: 3
(0)Quit (1)Change Values (2)Square (3)Cube (4)Swap: 3
x: 2 y: 3
x: 8 y: 27
(0)Quit (1)Change Values (2)Square (3)Cube (4)Swap: 2
x: 8 y: 27
x: 64 y: 729
(0)Quit (1)Change Values (2)Square (3)Cube (4)Swap: 4
x: 64 y: 729
x: 729 y: 64
(0)Quit (1)Change Values (2)Square (3)Cube (4)Swap: 0
```

ANALYSIS On line 9, `typedef` is used to declare `VPF` to be of the type "pointer to function that returns void and takes two parameters, both integer references."

On line 10, the function `PrintVals()` is declared to take three parameters: a `VPF` and two integer references. On line 18, `pFunc` is now declared to be of type `VPF`.

After the type `VPF` is defined, all subsequent uses to declare `pFunc` and `PrintVals()` are much cleaner. As you can see, the output is identical.

Pointers to Member Functions

Until this point, all the function pointers you created have been for general, nonclass functions. It is also possible to create pointers to functions that are members of classes.

14

To create a pointer-to-member function, use the same syntax as with a pointer to function, but include the class name and the scoping operator (::). Thus, if pFunc points to a member function of the class Shape, which takes two integers and returns void, the declaration for pFunc is the following:

```
void (Shape::*pFunc) (int, int);
```

Pointers to member functions are used in the same way as pointers to functions, except that they require an object of the correct class on which to invoke them. Listing 14.10 illustrates the use of pointers to member functions.

INPUT   LISTING **14.10**   Pointers to Member Functions

```
1:     //Listing 14.10 Pointers to member functions using virtual methods
2:
3:     #include <iostream.h>
4:
5:     class Mammal
6:     {
7:     public:
8:         Mammal():itsAge(1) {  }
9:        virtual ~Mammal() { }
10:        virtual void Speak() const = 0;
11:        virtual void Move() const = 0;
12:    protected:
13:        int itsAge;
14:    };
15:
16:    class Dog : public Mammal
17:    {
18:    public:
19:        void Speak()const { cout << "Woof!\n"; }
20:        void Move() const { cout << "Walking to heel...\n"; }
21:    };
22:
23:
24:    class Cat : public Mammal
25:    {
26:    public:
27:        void Speak()const { cout << "Meow!\n"; }
28:        void Move() const { cout << "slinking...\n"; }
29:    };
30:
31:
32:    class Horse : public Mammal
33:    {
34:    public:
35:        void Speak()const { cout << "Whinny!\n"; }
```

```
36:      void Move() const { cout << "Galloping...\n"; }
37:    };
38:
39:
40:    int main()
41:    {
42:      void (Mammal::*pFunc)() const =0;
43:      Mammal* ptr =NULL;
44:      int Animal;
45:      int Method;
46:      bool fQuit = false;
47:
48:      while (fQuit == false)
49:      {
50:        cout << "(0)Quit (1)dog (2)cat (3)horse: ";
51:        cin >> Animal;
52:        switch (Animal)
53:        {
54:          case 1: ptr = new Dog; break;
55:          case 2: ptr = new Cat; break;
56:          case 3: ptr = new Horse; break;
57:          default: fQuit = true; break;
58:        }
59:        if (fQuit)
60:          break;
61:
62:        cout << "(1)Speak  (2)Move: ";
63:        cin >> Method;
64:        switch (Method)
65:        {
66:          case 1: pFunc = Mammal::Speak; break;
67:          default: pFunc = Mammal::Move; break;
68:        }
69:
70:        (ptr->*pFunc)();
71:        delete ptr;
72:      }
73:    return 0;
74:    }
```

OUTPUT

```
(0)Quit (1)dog (2)cat (3)horse: 1
(1)Speak (2)Move: 1
Woof!
(0)Quit (1)dog (2)cat (3)horse: 2
(1)Speak (2)Move: 1
Meow!
(0)Quit (1)dog (2)cat (3)horse: 3
(1)Speak (2)Move: 2
Galloping
(0)Quit (1)dog (2)cat (3)horse: 0
```

14

On lines 4–14, the abstract data type Mammal is declared with two pure virtual methods, Speak() and Move(). Mammal is subclassed into Dog, Cat, and Horse, each of which overrides Speak() and Move().

The driver program in main() asks the user to choose which type of animal to create, and then a new subclass of Animal is created on the free store and assigned to ptr on lines 54–56.

The user is then prompted for which method to invoke, and that method is assigned to the pointer pFunc on line 66 or 67. g++ version 2.7.2 compiles this without complaint; 2.9.5 gives you the following warnings (because you are passing addresses around):

```
./lst14-10.cxx: In function `int main()':
./lst14-10.cxx:66: warning: assuming & on `Mammal::Speak() const'
./lst14-10.cxx:67: warning: assuming & on `Mammal::Move() const'
```

On line 70, the method chosen is invoked by the object created, by using the pointer ptr to access the object and pFunc to access the function.

Finally, on line 71, delete is called on the pointer ptr to return the memory set aside for the object to the free store. Note that no reason exists to call delete on pFunc because this is a pointer to code, not to an object on the free store. In fact, attempting to do so will generate a compile-time error.

Arrays of Pointers to Member Functions

As with pointers to functions, pointers to member functions can be stored in an array. The array can be initialized with the addresses of various member functions, and these can be invoked by offsets into the array. Listing 14.11 illustrates this technique.

INPUT   **LISTING 14.11**   Array of Pointers to Member Functions

```
1:     //Listing 14.11 Array of pointers to member functions
2:
3:     #include <iostream.h>
4:
5:     class Dog
6:     {
7:     public:
8:         void Speak()const { cout << "Woof!\n"; }
9:         void Move() const { cout << "Walking to heel...\n"; }
10:        void Eat() const { cout << "Gobbling food...\n"; }
11:        void Growl() const { cout << "Grrrrr\n"; }
12:        void Whimper() const { cout << "Whining noises...\n"; }
13:        void RollOver() const { cout << "Rolling over...\n"; }
14:        void PlayDead() const { cout << "Is this the end of
                             ➥Little Caesar?\n"; }
```

```
15:    };
16:
17:    typedef void (Dog::*PDF)()const ;
18:    int main()
19:    {
20:       const int MaxFuncs = 7;
21:       PDF DogFunctions[MaxFuncs] =
22:          {  Dog::Speak,
23:             Dog::Move,
24:             Dog::Eat,
25:             Dog::Growl,
26:             Dog::Whimper,
27:             Dog::RollOver,
28:             Dog::PlayDead };
29:
30:       Dog* pDog =NULL;
31:       int Method;
32:       bool fQuit = false;
33:
34:       while (!fQuit)
35:       {
36:          cout <<    "(0)Quit (1)Speak (2)Move (3)Eat (4)Growl";
37:          cout << " (5)Whimper (6)Roll Over (7)Play Dead: ";
38:          cin >> Method;
39:          if (Method == 0)
40:          {
41:             fQuit = true;
42:          }
43:          else
44:          {
45:             pDog = new Dog;
46:             (pDog->*DogFunctions[Method-1])();
47:             delete pDog;
48:          }
49:       }
50:    return 0;
51:    }
```

OUTPUT

```
 (0)Quit (1)Speak (2)Move (3)Eat (4)Growl (5)Whimper (6)Roll Over
(7)Play Dead: 1
Woof!
 (0)Quit (1)Speak (2)Move (3)Eat (4)Growl (5)Whimper (6)Roll Over
(7)Play Dead: 4
Grrr
 (0)Quit (1)Speak (2)Move (3)Eat (4)Growl (5)Whimper (6)Roll Over
(7)Play Dead: 7
Is this the end of Little Caesar?
 (0)Quit (1)Speak (2)Move (3)Eat (4)Growl (5)Whimper (6)Roll Over
(7)Play Dead: 0>
```

14

ANALYSIS On lines 5–15, the class `Dog` is created, with seven member functions all sharing the same return type and signature. On line 17, a `typedef` declares `PDF` to be a pointer to a member function of `Dog` that takes no parameters and returns no values, and that is `const`: the signature of the seven member functions of `Dog`.

On lines 21–28, the array `DogFunctions` is declared to hold seven such member functions, and it is initialized with the addresses of these functions. As with Listing 14.10, g++ version 2.7.2 did not complain about this code; 2.9.5 produced the following:

```
./lst14-11.cxx: In function `int main()':
./lst14-11.cxx:28: warning: assuming & on `Dog::Speak() const'
./lst14-11.cxx:28: warning: assuming & on `Dog::Move() const'
./lst14-11.cxx:28: warning: assuming & on `Dog::Eat() const'
./lst14-11.cxx:28: warning: assuming & on `Dog::Growl() const'
./lst14-11.cxx:28: warning: assuming & on `Dog::Whimper() const'
./lst14-11.cxx:28: warning: assuming & on `Dog::RollOver() const'
./lst14-11.cxx:28: warning: assuming & on `Dog::PlayDead() const'
```

On lines 36 and 37, the user is prompted to pick a method. Unless `Quit` is picked, a new `Dog` is created on the heap, and then the correct method is invoked on the array on line 46. This is another good line to show to the hotshot C++ programmers in your company; ask them what it does:

```
(pDog->*DogFunctions[Method-1])();
```

What do you think would happen if an out-of-range value was entered (like –1 or 8)? Because C++ has no array bound checking, you would not get a compile or runtime error. You may get completely unexpected results as your program attempts to use the address stored in that memory as a function. Because you did not set the value in that memory (as was done in lines 21–28), you have no idea what is there. That location may be some numeric value that will be treated as if it was the address of a function with unpredictable results.

Once again, this is a bit esoteric, but when you need a table built from member functions, it can make your program much easier to read and understand.

Do	Don't
DO invoke pointers to member functions on a specific object of a class.	**DON'T** use pointer-to-member functions when simpler solutions are possible.
DO use `typedef` to make pointer-to-member function declarations easier to read.	

Summary

Today you learned how to create static member variables in your class. Each class, rather than each object, has one instance of the static member variable. It is possible to access this member variable without an object of the class type by fully qualifying the name (assuming that you declared the static member to have public access).

Static member variables can be used as counters across instances of the class. Because they are not part of the object, the declaration of static member variables does not allocate memory, and static member variables must be defined and initialized outside the declaration of the class.

Static member functions are part of the class in the same way that static member variables are. They can be accessed without a particular object of the class and can be used to access static member data. Static member functions cannot be used to access non-static member data because they do not have a `this` pointer.

Because static member functions do not have a `this` pointer, they also cannot be made `const`. `const` in a member function indicates that the `this` pointer is `const`.

You also learned how to declare and use pointers to functions and pointers to member functions. You saw how to create arrays of these pointers and how to pass them to functions.

Pointers to functions and pointers to member functions can be used to create tables of functions that can be selected from at runtime. This can give your program flexibility that is not easily achieved without these pointers.

Q&A

Q Why use static data when you can use global data?

A Static data is scoped to the class. In this manner, static data is available only through an object of the class, through an explicit call using the class name if it is public, or by using a static member function. However, static data is typed to the class type, and the restricted access and strong typing makes static data safer than global data.

Q Why use static member functions when you can use global functions?

A Static member functions are scoped to the class and can be called only by using an object of the class or an explicit full specification (such as `ClassName::FunctionName()`).

14

Q **Is it common to use many pointers to functions and pointers to member functions?**

A No, these have their special uses, but are not common constructs. Many complex and powerful programs have neither.

Workshop

The Workshop contains quiz questions to help solidify your understanding of the material covered and exercises to provide you with experience in using what you learned today. Try to answer the quiz and exercise questions before checking the answers in Appendix D, "Answers to Exercises and Quizzes," and make sure you understand the answers before continuing tomorrow.

Quiz

1. Can static member variables be private?
2. Show the declaration for a static member variable.
3. Show the declaration for a static function.
4. Show the declaration for a pointer to function returning `long` and taking an integer parameter.
5. Modify the pointer in Question 4 so that it's a pointer to member function of class `Car`.
6. Show the declaration for an array of 10 pointers as defined in Question 5.

Exercises

1. Write a short program declaring a class with one member variable and one static member variable. Have the constructor initialize the member variable and increment the static member variable. Have the destructor decrement the member variable.
2. Using the program from Exercise 1, write a short driver program that makes three objects and then displays their member variables and the static member variable. Then destroy each object and show the effect on the static member variable.
3. Modify the program from Exercise 2 to use a static member function to access the static member variable. Make the static member variable private.

4. Write a pointer to member function to access the non-static member data in the program in Exercise 3, and use that pointer to print the value of that data.

5. Add two more member variables to the class from the previous questions. Add accessor functions that get the value of these values and give all the member functions the same return values and signatures. Use the pointer to member function to access these functions.

14

WEEK 2

In Review

The Week in Review program for Week 2 brings together many of the skills you acquired over the past fortnight and produces a powerful program.

This demonstration of linked lists utilizes virtual functions, pure virtual functions, function overriding, polymorphism, public inheritance, function overloading, forever loops, pointers, references, and more. Note that this is a different linked list from the one shown on Day 12, "Arrays, C Strings, and Linked Lists"; in C++ there are many ways to accomplish the same thing.

The goal of this program is to create a linked list. The nodes on the list are designed to hold parts, as might be used in a factory. Although this is not the final form of this program, it does make a good demonstration of a fairly advanced data structure. The code list is 303 lines. Try to analyze the code on your own before reading the analysis that follows the output.

INPUT　**LISTING R2.1**　Week 2 in Review Listing

```
1:     //
********************************************************
2:     //
3:     // Title:       Week 2 in Review
4:     //
5:     // File:        Week2
6:     //
7:     // Description:   Provide a linked list
➥demonstration program
8:     //
9:     // Classes:      PART - holds part numbers and
➥potentially other
10:    //                    information about parts
```

continues

8

9

10

11

12

13

14

LISTING R2.1   CONTINUED

```
11:    //
12:    //                    PartNode - acts as a node in a PartsList
13:    //
14:    //                    PartsList - provides the mechanisms for a linked list
                                                        ➥of parts
15:    //
16:    //
17:    // ***************************************************
18:
19:    #include <iostream.h>
20:
21:
22:
23:    // *************** Part ************
24:
25:    // Abstract base class of parts
26:    class Part
27:    {
28:    public:
29:        Part():itsPartNumber(1) {}
30:        Part(int PartNumber):itsPartNumber(PartNumber){}
31:        virtual ~Part(){};
32:        int GetPartNumber() const { return itsPartNumber; }
33:        virtual void Display() const =0;   // must be overridden
34:    private:
35:        int itsPartNumber;
36:    };
37:
38:    // implementation of pure virtual function so that
39:    // derived classes can chain up
40:    void Part::Display() const
41:    {
42:        cout << "\nPart Number: " << itsPartNumber << endl;
43:    }
44:
45:    // *************** Car Part ************
46:
47:    class CarPart : public Part
48:    {
49:    public:
50:        CarPart():itsModelYear(94){}
51:        CarPart(int year, int partNumber);
52:        virtual void Display() const
53:      {
54:          Part::Display(); cout << "Model Year: ";
55:          cout << itsModelYear << endl;
56:      }
57:    private:
```

```
58:        int itsModelYear;
59:     };
60:
61:     CarPart::CarPart(int year, int partNumber):
62:        itsModelYear(year),
63:        Part(partNumber)
64:     {}
65:
66:
67:     // **************** AirPlane Part ************
68:
69:     class AirPlanePart : public Part
70:     {
71:     public:
72:        AirPlanePart():itsEngineNumber(1){};
73:        AirPlanePart(int EngineNumber, int PartNumber);
74:        virtual void Display() const
75:      {
76:         Part::Display(); cout << "Engine No.: ";
77:         cout << itsEngineNumber << endl;
78:      }
79:     private:
80:        int itsEngineNumber;
81:     };
82:
83:     AirPlanePart::AirPlanePart(int EngineNumber, int PartNumber):
84:        itsEngineNumber(EngineNumber),
85:        Part(PartNumber)
86:     {}
87:
88:     // **************** Part Node ************
89:     class PartNode
90:     {
91:     public:
92:        PartNode (Part*);
93:        ~PartNode();
94:        void SetNext(PartNode * node) { itsNext = node; }
95:        PartNode * GetNext() const;
96:        Part * GetPart() const;
97:     private:
98:        Part *itsPart;
99:        PartNode * itsNext;
100:     };
101:
102:     // PartNode Implementations...
103:
104:     PartNode::PartNode(Part* pPart):
105:     itsPart(pPart),
106:     itsNext(0)
107:     {}
```

continues

```
108:
109:    PartNode::~PartNode()
110:    {
111:       delete itsPart;
112:       itsPart = 0;
113:       delete itsNext;
114:       itsNext = 0;
115:    }
116:
117:    // Returns NULL if no next PartNode
118:    PartNode * PartNode::GetNext() const
119:    {
120:          return itsNext;
121:    }
122:
123:    Part * PartNode::GetPart() const
124:    {
125:       if (itsPart)
126:          return itsPart;
127:       else
128:          return NULL; //error
129:    }
130:
131:    // *************** Part List ***********
132:    class PartsList
133:    {
134:    public:
135:       PartsList();
136:       ~PartsList();
137:       // needs copy constructor and operator equals!
138:       Part*      Find(int & position, int PartNumber)  const;
139:       int      GetCount() const { return itsCount; }
140:       Part*      GetFirst() const;
141:       static      PartsList& GetGlobalPartsList()
142:      {
143:         return  GlobalPartsList;
144:      }
145:       void      Insert(Part *);
146:       void      Iterate(void (Part::*f)()const) const;
147:       Part*      operator[](int) const;
148:    private:
149:       PartNode * pHead;
150:       int itsCount;
151:       static PartsList GlobalPartsList;
152:    };
153:
154:    PartsList PartsList::GlobalPartsList;
155:
```

```
156:    // Implementations for Lists...
157:
158:    PartsList::PartsList():
159:        pHead(0),
160:        itsCount(0)
161:        {}
162:
163:    PartsList::~PartsList()
164:    {
165:        delete pHead;
166:    }
167:
168:    Part*   PartsList::GetFirst() const
169:    {
170:       if (pHead)
171:          return pHead->GetPart();
172:       else
173:          return NULL;  // error catch here
174:    }
175:
176:    Part *  PartsList::operator[](int offSet) const
177:    {
178:        PartNode* pNode = pHead;
179:
180:        if (!pHead)
181:           return NULL; // error catch here
182:
183:        if (offSet > itsCount)
184:            return NULL; // error
185:
186:        for (int i=0;i<offSet; i++)
187:           pNode = pNode->GetNext();
188:
189:      return    pNode->GetPart();
190:    }
191:
192:    Part*   PartsList::Find(int & position, int PartNumber)  const
193:    {
194:        PartNode * pNode =NULL;
195:        for (pNode = pHead, position = 0;
196:             pNode!=NULL;
197:             pNode = pNode->GetNext(), position++)
198:        {
199:           if (pNode->GetPart()->GetPartNumber() == PartNumber)
200:              break;
201:        }
202:        if (pNode == NULL)
203:           return NULL;
204:        else
205:           return pNode->GetPart();
```

continues

LISTING R2.1 CONTINUED

```
206:    }
207:
208:    void PartsList::Iterate(void (Part::*func)()const) const
209:    {
210:        if (!pHead)
211:            return;
212:        PartNode* pNode = pHead;
213:        do
214:            (pNode->GetPart()->*func)();
215:        while (pNode = pNode->GetNext());
216:    }
217:
218:    void PartsList::Insert(Part* pPart)
219:    {
220:        PartNode * pNode = new PartNode(pPart);
221:        PartNode * pCurrent = pHead;
222:        PartNode * pNext = NULL;
223:
224:        int New =  pPart->GetPartNumber();
225:        int Next = 0;
226:        itsCount++;
227:
228:        if (!pHead)
229:        {
230:            pHead = pNode;
231:            return;
232:        }
233:
234:        // if this one is smaller than head
235:        // this one is the new head
236:        if (pHead->GetPart()->GetPartNumber() > New)
237:        {
238:            pNode->SetNext(pHead);
239:            pHead = pNode;
240:            return;
241:        }
242:
243:        for (;;)
244:        {
245:            // if there is no next, append this new one
246:            if (!pCurrent->GetNext())
247:            {
248:                pCurrent->SetNext(pNode);
249:                return;
250:            }
251:
252:            // if this goes after this one and before the next
253:            // then insert it here, otherwise get the next
```

```
254:              pNext = pCurrent->GetNext();
255:              Next = pNext->GetPart()->GetPartNumber();
256:              if (Next > New)
257:              {
258:                 pCurrent->SetNext(pNode);
259:                 pNode->SetNext(pNext);
260:                 return;
261:              }
262:              pCurrent = pNext;
263:          }
264:      }
265:
266:     int main()
267:     {
268:        PartsList&pl = PartsList::GetGlobalPartsList();
269:        Part * pPart = NULL;
270:        int PartNumber;
271:        int value;
272:        int choice;
273:
274:        while (1)
275:        {
276:           cout << "(0)Quit (1)Car (2)Plane: ";
277:           cin >> choice;
278:
279:           if (!choice)
280:               break;
281:
282:           cout << "New PartNumber?: ";
283:           cin >>  PartNumber;
284:
285:           if (choice == 1)
286:           {
287:              cout << "Model Year?: ";
288:              cin >> value;
289:              pPart = new CarPart(value,PartNumber);
290:           }
291:           else
292:           {
293:              cout << "Engine Number?: ";
294:              cin >> value;
295:              pPart = new AirPlanePart(value,PartNumber);
296:           }
297:
298:           pl.Insert(pPart);
299:        }
300:      void (Part::*pFunc)()const = Part::Display;
301:      pl.Iterate(pFunc);
302:     return 0;
303:    }
```

OUTPUT
```
   (0)Quit (1)Car (2)Plane: 1
New PartNumber?: 2837
Model Year? 90
   (0)Quit (1)Car (2)Plane: 2
New PartNumber?: 378
Engine Number?: 4938
   (0)Quit (1)Car (2)Plane: 1
New PartNumber?: 4499
Model Year? 94
   (0)Quit (1)Car (2)Plane: 1
New PartNumber?: 3000
Model Year? 93
   (0)Quit (1)Car (2)Plane: 0

Part Number: 378
Engine No.: 4938

Part Number: 2837
Model Year: 90

Part Number: 3000
Model Year: 93

Part Number: 4499
Model Year: 94
```

ANALYSIS Listing R2.1 provides a linked list implementation for Part objects. A linked list is a dynamic data structure; that is, it is like an array but it is sized to fit as objects are added and deleted.

This particular linked list is designed to hold objects of class Part, where Part is an abstract data type serving as a base class to any objects with a part number. In this example, Part has been subclassed into CarPart and AirPlanePart.

Class Part, which is declared on lines 26–36, consists of a part number and some accessors. Presumably this class could be fleshed out to hold other important information about the parts, such as what components they are used in, how many are in stock, and so forth. Part is an abstract data type, enforced by the pure virtual function Display().

Note that Display() does have an implementation, on lines 40–43. It is the designer's intention that derived classes will be forced to create their own Display() method, but may chain up to this method as well.

Two simple derived classes, CarPart and AirPlanePart, are provided on lines 47–59 and 69–87, respectively. Each provides an overridden Display() method, which does in fact chain up to the base class Display() method.

The class `PartNode` serves as the interface between the `Part` class and the `PartList` class. It contains a pointer to a part and a pointer to the next node in the list. Its only methods are to get and set the next node in the list and to return the `Part` to which it points.

The intelligence of the list is, appropriately, in the class `PartsList`, whose declaration is on lines 132–152. `PartsList` keeps a pointer to the first element in the list (`pHead`) and uses that to access all other methods by walking the list. Walking the list means asking each node in the list for the next node, until you reach a node whose next pointer is `NULL`.

This is only a partial implementation; a fully developed list would provide either greater access to its first and last nodes, or would provide an iterator object, which allows clients to easily walk the list.

`PartsList` nonetheless provides a number of interesting methods, which are listed in alphabetical order. This is often a good idea, because it makes finding the functions easier.

`Find()` takes a `PartNumber` and an `int`. If the part corresponding to `PartNumber` is found, it returns a pointer to the `Part` and fills the `int` with the position of that part in the list. If `PartNumber` is not found, it returns `NULL`, and the position is meaningless.

`GetCount()` returns the number of elements in the list. `PartsList` keeps this number as a member variable, `itsCount`, though it could, of course, compute this number by walking the list.

`GetFirst()` returns a pointer to the first `Part` in the list, or returns `NULL` if the list is empty.

`GetGlobalPartsList()` returns a reference to the static member variable `GlobalPartsList`. This is a static instance of this class; every program with a `PartsList` also has one `GlobalPartsList`, though, of course, it is free to make other `PartsLists` as well. A full implementation of this idea would modify the constructor of `Part` to ensure that every part is created on the `GlobalPartsList`.

`Insert` takes a pointer to a `Part`, creates a `PartNode` for it, and adds the `Part` to the list, ordered by `PartNumber`.

`Iterate` takes a pointer to a member function of `Part`, which takes no parameters, returns void, and is const. It calls that function for every `Part` object in the list. In the sample program this is called on `Display()`, which is a virtual function, so the appropriate `Display()` method will be called based on the runtime type of the `Part` object called.

Operator[] allows direct access to the Part at the offset provided. Rudimentary bounds checking is provided; if the list is NULL, or if the offset requested is greater than the size of the list, NULL is returned as an error condition.

Note that in a real program, these comments on the functions would be written into the class declaration.

The driver program is on lines 266–303. A reference to PartsList is declared on line 268 and initialized with GlobalPartsList. Note that GlobalPartsList is initialized on line 154. This is necessary because the declaration of a static member variable does not define it; definition must be done outside the declaration of the class.

On lines 274–299, the user is repeatedly prompted to choose whether to enter a car part or an airplane part. Depending on the choice, the right value is requested, and the appropriate part is created. After the part is created, it is inserted into the list on line 298.

The implementation for the Insert() method of PartsList is on lines 218–264. When the first part number is entered, 2837, a CarPart with that part number and the model year 90 is created and passed in to LinkedList::Insert().

On line 220, a new PartNode is created with that part, and the variable New is initialized with the part number. The PartsList's itsCount member variable is incremented on line 226.

On line 228, the test that pHead is NULL will evaluate true. Because this is the first node, it is true that the PartsList's pHead pointer has zero. Thus, on line 230, pHead is set to point to the new node, and this function returns.

The user is prompted to enter a second part, and this time an AirPlane part with part number 37 and engine number 4938 is entered. Once again PartsList::Insert() is called, and once again pNode is initialized with the new node. The static member variable itsCount is incremented to 2, and pHead is tested. Because pHead was assigned last time, it is no longer null and the test fails.

On line 236, the part number held by pHead, 2837, is compared against the current part number, 378. Because the new one is smaller than the one held by pHead, the new one must become the new head pointer, and the test on line 236 is true.

On line 238, the new node is set to point to the node currently pointed to by pHead. Note that this does not point the new node to pHead, but rather to the node that pHead was pointing to! On line 239, pHead is set to point to the new node.

The third time through the loop, the user enters the part number 4499 for a Car with model year 94. The counter is incremented and the number this time is not less than the number pointed to by pHead, so the for loop that begins on line 243 is entered.

The value pointed to by pHead is 378. The value pointed to by the second node is 2837. The current value is 4499. The pointer pCurrent points to the same node as pHead, and so has a next value; pCurrent points to the second node, and so the test on line 246 fails.

The pointer pCurrent is set to point to the next node, and the loop repeats. This time the test on line 246 succeeds. There is no next item, so the current node is told to point to the new node on line 248, and the insert is finished.

The fourth time through, the part number 3000 is entered. This proceeds just like the previous iteration, but this time when the current node is pointing to 2837, and the next node has 4499, the test on line 256 returns true, and the new node is inserted into position.

When the user finally presses 0, the test on line 279 evaluates true and the while(1) loop breaks. On line 300, the member function Display() is assigned to the pointer to member function pFunc. In a real program this would be assigned dynamically, based on the user's choice of method.

The pointer to member function is passed to the PartsList Iterate() method. On line 208, the Iterate() method ensures that the list is not empty. Then, on lines 213–215, each Part on the list is called using the pointer to member function. This calls the appropriate Display() method for the Part, as shown in the output.

WEEK 3

At a Glance

You have finished the second week of learning C++. By now you should feel comfortable with some of the more advanced aspects of object-oriented programming, including encapsulation and polymorphism.

Where You Are Going

The last regular week begins with a discussion of advanced inheritance. On Day 16, "Streams," you will learn about streams in depth, and on Day 17, "Namespaces," you will learn how to work with this exciting addition to the C++ Standard. Day 18, "Object-Oriented Analysis and Design," is a departure: Rather than focusing on the syntax of the language, you take a day out to learn about object-oriented analysis and design. On Day 19, "Templates," templates are introduced, and on Day 20, "Exceptions and Error Handling," exceptions are explained. Day 21, "What's Next," the last regular day of this book, covers some miscellaneous subjects not covered elsewhere, and then there is a discussion of the next steps to take in becoming a C++ guru.

## 17

DAY 15

Advanced Inheritance

So far, you have worked with single and multiple inheritance to create *is-a* relationships. Today you will learn:

- What containment is and how to model it
- What delegation is and how to model it
- How to implement one class in terms of another
- How to use private inheritance

Containment

As you have seen in previous examples, it is possible for the member data of a class to include objects of another class. C++ programmers say that the outer class contains the inner class. Thus, an `Employee` class might contain string objects (for the name of the employee), as well as integers (for the employee's salary and so forth).

Listing 15.1 describes an incomplete, but still useful, `String` class. This listing does not produce any output. Instead, Listing 15.1 will be used with later listings.

```
1:// Listing 15.1: The String Class - string.hpp - used by listing 15.2
2:    #include <iostream.h>
3:    #include <string.h>
4:    class String
5:    {
6:      public:
7:          // constructors
8:          String();
9:           String(const char *const);
10:          String(const String &);
11:          ~String();
12:
13:          // overloaded operators
14:          char & operator[](int offset);
15:          char operator[](int offset) const;
16:          String operator+(const String&);
17:          void operator+=(const String&);
18:          String & operator= (const String &);
19:
20:          // General accessors
21:          int GetLen()const { return itsLen; }
22:          const char * GetString() const { return itsString; }
23:          // static int ConstructorCount;
24:
25:      private:
26:          String (int);           // private constructor
27:          char * itsString;
28:          unsigned short itsLen;
29:
30:    };
31:
32:    // default constructor creates string of 0 bytes
33:    String::String()
34:    {
35:        itsString = new char[1];
36:        itsString[0] = '\0';
37:        itsLen=0;
38:        // cout << "\tDefault string constructor\n";
39:        // ConstructorCount++;
40:    }
41:
42:    // private (helper) constructor, used only by
43:    // class methods for creating a new string of
44:    // required size.  Null filled.
45:    String::String(int len)
46:    {
47:        itsString = new char[len+1];
48:        for (int i = 0; i<=len; i++)
```

```
49:            itsString[i] = '\0';
50:         itsLen=len;
51:         // cout << "\tString(int) constructor\n";
52:         // ConstructorCount++;
53:      }
54:
55:      // Converts a character array to a String
56:      String::String(const char * const cString)
57:      {
58:         itsLen = strlen(cString);
59:         itsString = new char[itsLen+1];
60:         for (int i = 0; i<itsLen; i++)
61:            itsString[i] = cString[i];
62:         itsString[itsLen]='\0';
63:         // cout << "\tString(char*) constructor\n";
64:         // ConstructorCount++;
65:      }
66:
67:      // copy constructor
68:      String::String (const String & rhs)
69:      {
70:         itsLen=rhs.GetLen();
71:         itsString = new char[itsLen+1];
72:         for (int i = 0; i<itsLen;i++)
73:            itsString[i] = rhs[i];
74:         itsString[itsLen] = '\0';
75:         // cout << "\tString(String&) constructor\n";
76:         // ConstructorCount++;
77:      }
78:
79:      // destructor, frees allocated memory
80:      String::~String ()
81:      {
82:         delete [] itsString;
83:         itsLen = 0;
84:         // cout << "\tString destructor\n";
85:      }
86:
87:      // operator equals, frees existing memory
88:      // then copies string and size
89:      String& String::operator=(const String & rhs)
90:      {
91:         if (this == &rhs)
92:            return *this;
93:         delete [] itsString;
94:         itsLen=rhs.GetLen();
95:         itsString = new char[itsLen+1];
96:         for (int i = 0; i<itsLen;i++)
97:            itsString[i] = rhs[i];
```

continues

LISTING 15.1 CONTINUED

```
98:          itsString[itsLen] = '\0';
99:          // cout << "\tString operator=\n";
100:         return *this;
101:     }
102:
103:     //non constant offset operator, returns
104:     // reference to character so it can be
105:     // changed!
106:     char & String::operator[](int offset)
107:     {
108:        if (offset > itsLen)
109:            return itsString[itsLen-1];
110:        else
111:            return itsString[offset];
112:     }
113:
114:     // constant offset operator for use
115:     // on const objects (see copy constructor!)
116:     char String::operator[](int offset) const
117:     {
118:        if (offset > itsLen)
119:            return itsString[itsLen-1];
120:        else
121:            return itsString[offset];
122:     }
123:
124:     // creates a new string by adding current
125:     // string to rhs
126:     String String::operator+(const String& rhs)
127:     {
128:        int  totalLen = itsLen + rhs.GetLen();
129:        String temp(totalLen);
130:        int i, j;
131:        for (i = 0; i<itsLen; i++)
132:            temp[i] = itsString[i];
133:        for (j = 0; j<rhs.GetLen(); j++, i++)
134:            temp[i] = rhs[j];
135:        temp[totalLen]='\0';
136:        return temp;
137:     }
138:
139:     // changes current string, returns nothing
140:     void String::operator+=(const String& rhs)
141:     {
142:        unsigned short rhsLen = rhs.GetLen();
143:        unsigned short totalLen = itsLen + rhsLen;
144:        String  temp(totalLen);
145:        int i, j;
146:        for (i = 0; i<itsLen; i++)
```

```
147:            temp[i] = itsString[i];
148:        for (j = 0; j<rhs.GetLen(); j++, i++)
149:            temp[i] = rhs[i-itsLen];
150:        temp[totalLen]='\0';
151:        *this = temp;
152:    }
153:
154:    // int String::ConstructorCount = 0;
```

OUTPUT None.

ANALYSIS Listing 15.1 provides a String class much like the one used in Listing 12.12 of Day 12, "Arrays, C Strings, and Linked Lists." The significant difference here is that the constructors and a few other functions in Listing 12.12 have print statements to show their use, which are currently commented out in Listing 15.1. These functions will be used in later examples.

On line 23, the static member variable ConstructorCount is declared, and on line 154 it is initialized. This variable is incremented in each string constructor. All this is currently commented out; it will be used in a later listing.

Listing 15.2 describes an Employee class that contains three string objects.

INPUT **LISTING 15.2** The Employee Class and Driver Program

```
1:    #include "String.hpp"
2:
3:    class Employee
4:    {
5:
6:    public:
7:        Employee();
8:        Employee(char *, char *, char *, long);
9:        ~Employee();
10:       Employee(const Employee&);
11:       Employee & operator= (const Employee &);
12:
13:       const String & GetFirstName() const
14:           { return itsFirstName; }
15:       const String & GetLastName() const { return itsLastName; }
16:       const String & GetAddress() const { return itsAddress; }
17:       long GetSalary() const { return itsSalary; }
18:
19:       void SetFirstName(const String & fName)
20:           { itsFirstName = fName; }
```

continues

LISTING 15.2 CONTINUED

```
21:        void SetLastName(const String & lName)
22:           { itsLastName = lName; }
23:        void SetAddress(const String & address)
24:             { itsAddress = address; }
25:        void SetSalary(long salary) { itsSalary = salary; }
26:     private:
27:        String    itsFirstName;
28:        String    itsLastName;
29:        String    itsAddress;
30:        long      itsSalary;
31:     };
32:
33:     Employee::Employee():
34:        itsFirstName(""),
35:        itsLastName(""),
36:        itsAddress(""),
37:        itsSalary(0)
38:     {}
39:
40:     Employee::Employee(char * firstName, char * lastName,
41:        char * address, long salary):
42:        itsFirstName(firstName),
43:        itsLastName(lastName),
44:        itsAddress(address),
45:        itsSalary(salary)
46:     {}
47:
48:     Employee::Employee(const Employee & rhs):
49:        itsFirstName(rhs.GetFirstName()),
50:        itsLastName(rhs.GetLastName()),
51:        itsAddress(rhs.GetAddress()),
52:        itsSalary(rhs.GetSalary())
53:     {}
54:
55:     Employee::~Employee() {}
56:
57:     Employee & Employee::operator= (const Employee & rhs)
58:     {
59:        if (this == &rhs)
60:           return *this;
61:
62:        itsFirstName = rhs.GetFirstName();
63:        itsLastName = rhs.GetLastName();
64:        itsAddress = rhs.GetAddress();
65:        itsSalary = rhs.GetSalary();
66:
67:        return *this;
68:     }
69:
```

```
70:    int main()
71:    {
72:        Employee Edie("Jane","Doe","1461 Shore Parkway", 20000);
73:        Edie.SetSalary(50000);
74:        String LastName("Levine");
75:        Edie.SetLastName(LastName);
76:        Edie.SetFirstName("Edythe");
77:
78:        cout << "Name: ";
79:        cout << Edie.GetFirstName().GetString();
80:        cout << " " << Edie.GetLastName().GetString();
81:        cout << ".\nAddress: ";
82:        cout << Edie.GetAddress().GetString();
83:        cout << ".\nSalary: " ;
84:        cout << Edie.GetSalary();
85:        return 0;
86:    }
```

15

Note

Put the code from Listing 15.1 into a file called String.hpp. Then, any time you need the String class you can include Listing 15.1 by using #include "String.hpp", as in Listing 15.2.

For convenience in this book, I included the implementation with the declaration of the class. In a real program, you would save the class declaration in String.hpp and the implementation in String.cpp. You would then add String.cpp into your program (using a makefile) and have String.cpp #include String.hpp.

OUTPUT

```
Name: Edythe Levine.
Address: 1461 Shore Parkway.
Salary: 50000
```

ANALYSIS Listing 15.2 shows the Employee class, which contains three string objects: itsFirstName, itsLastName, and itsAddress.

On line 72, an Employee object is created, and four values are passed in to initialize the Employee object. On line 73, the Employee access function SetSalary() is called, with the constant value 50000. Note that in a real program, this would be either a dynamic value (set at runtime) or a constant.

On line 74, a string is created and initialized using a C++ string constant. This string object is then used as an argument to SetLastName() on line 75.

On line 76, the Employee function SetFirstName() is called with yet another string constant. However, if you are paying close attention, you will notice that Employee does not have a function `SetFirstName()` that takes a character string as its argument; `SetFirstName()` requires a constant string reference.

The compiler resolves this because it knows how to make a string from a constant character string. It knows this because you told it how to do so on line 9 of Listing 15.1.

Accessing Members of the Contained Class

Employee objects do not have special access to the member variables of `String`. If the `Employee` object `Edie` tried to access the member variable `itsLen` of its own `itsFirstName` member variable, it would get a compile-time error. This is not much of a burden, however. The accessor functions provide an interface for the `String` class, and the `Employee` class need not worry about the implementation details, just as it does not worry about how the integer variable, `itsSalary`, stores its information.

Filtering Access to Contained Members

Note that the `String` class provides the `operator+`. The designer of the `Employee` class has blocked access to the `operator+` being called on `Employee` objects by declaring that all the string accessors, such as `GetFirstName()`, return a constant reference. Because `operator+` is not (and cannot be) a `const` function (it changes the object it is called on), attempting to write the following will cause a compile-time error:

```
String buffer = Edie.GetFirstName() + Edie.GetLastName();
```

`GetFirstName()` returns a constant `String`, and you cannot call `operator+` on a constant object.

To fix this, overload `GetFirstName()` to be non-const:

```
const String & GetFirstName() const { return itsFirstName; }
String & GetFirstName()  { return itsFirstName; }
```

Note that the return value is no longer `const` and that the member function itself is no longer `const`. Changing the return value is not sufficient to overload the function name; you must change the constancy of the function itself.

Cost of Containment

It is important to note that the user of an `Employee` class pays the price of each of those string objects each time one is constructed or a copy of the `Employee` is made.

Uncommenting the `cout` statements in Listing 15.1, lines 38, 51, 63, 75, 84, and 99, reveals how often these are called. Listing 15.3 rewrites the driver program to add `print` statements indicating where in the program objects are being created.

> **Note**
>
> To compile this listing, uncomment lines 38, 51, 63, 75, 84, and 99 in Listing 15.1.

INPUT   **LISTING 15.3**   Contained Class Constructors

```cpp
1:  #include "String.hpp"
2:
3:  class Employee
4:  {
5:
6:  public:
7:      Employee();
8:      Employee(char *, char *, char *, long);
9:      ~Employee();
10:      Employee(const Employee&);
11:      Employee & operator= (const Employee &);
12:
13:      const String & GetFirstName() const
14:          { return itsFirstName; }
15:      const String & GetLastName() const { return itsLastName; }
16:      const String & GetAddress() const { return itsAddress; }
17:      long GetSalary() const { return itsSalary; }
18:
19:      void SetFirstName(const String & fName)
20:          { itsFirstName = fName; }
21:      void SetLastName(const String & lName)
22:          { itsLastName = lName; }
23:      void SetAddress(const String & address)
24:          { itsAddress = address; }
25:      void SetSalary(long salary) { itsSalary = salary; }
26:  private:
27:      String    itsFirstName;
28:      String    itsLastName;
29:      String    itsAddress;
30:      long      itsSalary;
31:  };
32:
33:  Employee::Employee():
34:      itsFirstName(""),
35:      itsLastName(""),
36:      itsAddress(""),
37:      itsSalary(0)
38:  {}
39:
40:  Employee::Employee(char * firstName, char * lastName,
41:      char * address, long salary):
```

continues

LISTING 15.3 CONTINUED

```
42:          itsFirstName(firstName),
43:          itsLastName(lastName),
44:          itsAddress(address),
45:          itsSalary(salary)
46:     {}
47:
48:     Employee::Employee(const Employee & rhs):
49:          itsFirstName(rhs.GetFirstName()),
50:          itsLastName(rhs.GetLastName()),
51:          itsAddress(rhs.GetAddress()),
52:          itsSalary(rhs.GetSalary())
53:     {}
54:
55:     Employee::~Employee() {}
56:
57:     Employee & Employee::operator= (const Employee & rhs)
58:     {
59:         if (this == &rhs)
60:             return *this;
61:
62:         itsFirstName = rhs.GetFirstName();
63:         itsLastName = rhs.GetLastName();
64:         itsAddress = rhs.GetAddress();
65:         itsSalary = rhs.GetSalary();
66:
67:         return *this;
68:     }
69:
70:      int main()
71:      {
72:         cout << "Creating Edie...\n";
73:         Employee Edie("Jane","Doe","1461 Shore Parkway", 20000);
74:         Edie.SetSalary(20000);
75:         cout << "Calling SetFirstName with char *...\n";
76:         Edie.SetFirstName("Edythe");
77:         cout << "Creating temporary string LastName...\n";
78:         String LastName("Levine");
79:         Edie.SetLastName(LastName);
80:
81:         cout << "Name: ";
82:         cout << Edie.GetFirstName().GetString();
83:         cout << " " << Edie.GetLastName().GetString();
84:         cout << "\nAddress: ";
85:         cout << Edie.GetAddress().GetString();
86:         cout << "\nSalary: " ;
87:         cout << Edie.GetSalary();
88:         cout << endl;
89:      return 0;
90:      }
```

15

```
OUTPUT   1:   Creating Edie...
         2:           String(char*) constructor
         3:           String(char*) constructor
         4:           String(char*) constructor
         5:   Calling SetFirstName with char *...
         6:           String(char*) constructor
         7:           String destructor
         8:   Creating temporary string LastName...
         9:           String(char*) constructor
        10:   Name: Edythe Levine
        11:   Address: 1461 Shore Parkway
        12:   Salary: 20000
        13:           String destructor
        14:           String destructor
        15:           String destructor
        16:           String destructor
```

ANALYSIS Listing 15.3 uses the same class declarations as Listings 15.1 and 15.2. However, the cout statements have been uncommented. The output from Listing 15.3 has been numbered to make analysis easier.

On line 3 of Listing 15.3, the statement Creating Edie... is printed, as reflected on line 1 of the output. On line 73, an Employee object, Edie, is created with four parameters. The output reflects the constructor for String being called three times, as expected.

Line 75 prints an information statement, and then on line 76 is the statement Edie.SetFirstName("Edythe"). This statement causes a temporary string to be created from the character string "Edythe", as reflected on lines 6 and 7 of the output. Note that the temporary string is destroyed immediately after it is used in the assignment statement.

On line 78, a String object is created in the body of the program. Here the programmer is doing explicitly what the compiler did implicitly on the previous statement. This time you see the constructor on line 9 of the output, but no destructor. This object will not be destroyed until it goes out of scope at the end of the function.

On lines 82–88, the strings in the employee object are destroyed as the Employee object falls out of scope, and the string LastName, created on line 78, is destroyed as well when it falls out of scope.

Copying by Value

Listing 15.3 illustrates how the creation of one Employee object caused five string constructor calls. Listing 15.4 again rewrites the driver program. This time the print statements are not used, but the string static member variable ConstructorCount is uncommented and used.

Examination of Listing 15.1 shows that ConstructorCount is incremented each time a
string constructor is called. The driver program in Listing 15.4 calls the print functions,
passing in the Employee object, first by reference and then by value. ConstructorCount
keeps track of how many string objects are created when the employee is passed as a
parameter.

> **Note**
>
> To compile this listing, leave in the lines that you uncommented in Listing
> 15.1 to run Listing 15.3, and in addition, uncomment lines 23, 39, 52, 64, 76,
> and 153 from Listing 15.1.

INPUT   **LISTING 15.4**   Passing by Value

```
1:    #include "String.hpp"
2:
3:    class Employee
4:    {
5:
6:    public:
7:        Employee();
8:        Employee(char *, char *, char *, long);
9:        ~Employee();
10:        Employee(const Employee&);
11:        Employee & operator= (const Employee &);
12:
13:        const String & GetFirstName() const
14:            { return itsFirstName; }
15:        const String & GetLastName() const { return itsLastName; }
16:        const String & GetAddress() const { return itsAddress; }
17:        long GetSalary() const { return itsSalary; }
18:
19:        void SetFirstName(const String & fName)
20:            { itsFirstName = fName; }
21:        void SetLastName(const String & lName)
22:            { itsLastName = lName; }
23:        void SetAddress(const String & address)
24:            { itsAddress = address; }
25:        void SetSalary(long salary) { itsSalary = salary; }
26:    private:
27:        String    itsFirstName;
28:        String    itsLastName;
29:        String    itsAddress;
30:        long      itsSalary;
31:    };
32:
```

15

```
33:     Employee::Employee():
34:         itsFirstName(""),
35:         itsLastName(""),
36:         itsAddress(""),
37:         itsSalary(0)
38:     {}
39:
40:     Employee::Employee(char * firstName, char * lastName,
41:         char * address, long salary):
42:         itsFirstName(firstName),
43:         itsLastName(lastName),
44:         itsAddress(address),
45:         itsSalary(salary)
46:     {}
47:
48:     Employee::Employee(const Employee & rhs):
49:         itsFirstName(rhs.GetFirstName()),
50:         itsLastName(rhs.GetLastName()),
51:         itsAddress(rhs.GetAddress()),
52:         itsSalary(rhs.GetSalary())
53:     {}
54:
55:     Employee::~Employee() {}
56:
57:     Employee & Employee::operator= (const Employee & rhs)
58:     {
59:         if (this == &rhs)
60:             return *this;
61:
62:         itsFirstName = rhs.GetFirstName();
63:         itsLastName = rhs.GetLastName();
64:         itsAddress = rhs.GetAddress();
65:         itsSalary = rhs.GetSalary();
66:
67:         return *this;
68:     }
69:
70:      void PrintFunc(Employee);
71:      void rPrintFunc(const Employee&);
72:
73:      int main()
74:      {
75:         Employee Edie("Jane","Doe","1461 Shore Parkway", 20000);
76:         Edie.SetSalary(20000);
77:         Edie.SetFirstName("Edythe");
78:         String LastName("Levine");
79:         Edie.SetLastName(LastName);
80:
81:         cout << "Constructor count: " ;
```

continues

LISTING 15.4   CONTINUED

```
82:         cout << String::ConstructorCount << endl;
83:         rPrintFunc(Edie);
84:         cout << "Constructor count: ";
85:          cout << String::ConstructorCount << endl;
86:         PrintFunc(Edie);
87:         cout << "Constructor count: ";
88:          cout << String::ConstructorCount << endl;
89:      return 0;
90:      }
91:     void PrintFunc (Employee Edie)
92:     {
93:
94:         cout << "Name: ";
95:         cout << Edie.GetFirstName().GetString();
96:         cout << " " << Edie.GetLastName().GetString();
97:         cout << ".\nAddress: ";
98:         cout << Edie.GetAddress().GetString();
99:         cout << ".\nSalary: " ;
100:         cout << Edie.GetSalary();
101:         cout << endl;
102:
103:     }
104:
105:     void rPrintFunc (const Employee& Edie)
106:     {
107:         cout << "Name: ";
108:         cout << Edie.GetFirstName().GetString();
109:         cout << " " << Edie.GetLastName().GetString();
110:         cout << "\nAddress: ";
111:         cout << Edie.GetAddress().GetString();
112:         cout << "\nSalary: " ;
113:         cout << Edie.GetSalary();
114:         cout << endl;
115:     }
```

OUTPUT

```
String(char*) constructor
        String(char*) constructor
        String(char*) constructor
        String(char*) constructor
        String destructor
        String(char*) constructor
Constructor count: 5
Name: Edythe Levine
Address: 1461 Shore Parkway
Salary: 20000
Constructor count: 5
        String(String&) constructor
        String(String&) constructor
```

```
        String(String&) constructor
Name: Edythe Levine.
Address: 1461 Shore Parkway.
Salary: 20000
        String destructor
        String destructor
        String destructor
Constructor count: 8
String destructor
        String destructor
        String destructor
        String destructor
```

ANALYSIS The output shows that five string objects were created as part of creating one
Employee object. When the Employee object is passed to rPrintFunc() by reference, no additional Employee objects are created, and so no additional String objects are
created. (They, too, are passed by reference.)

When, on line 83, the Employee object is passed to PrintFunc() by value, a copy of the
Employee is created, and three more string objects are created (by calls to the copy constructor).

Implementation in Terms of Inheritance/Containment Versus Delegation

At times, one class wants to draw on some of the attributes of another class. For example, suppose you need to create a PartsCatalog class. The specification you were given
defines a PartsCatalog as a collection of parts; each part has a unique part number. The
PartsCatalog does not allow duplicate entries and does allow access by part number.

The listing for the Week in Review for Week 2 provides a PartsList class. This
PartsList is well-tested and understood, and you can build on that technology when
making your PartsCatalog, rather than inventing it from scratch. Reuse is one of the
most productive ways of programming—build on what you already have.

You could create a new PartsCatalog class and have it contain a PartsList. The
PartsCatalog could delegate management of the linked list to its contained PartsList
object.

An alternative would be to make the PartsCatalog derive from PartsList and thereby
inherit the properties of a PartsList. Remembering, however, that public inheritance
provides an *is-a* relationship, you should question whether a PartsCatalog really is a
type of PartsList.

One way to answer the question of whether PartsCatalog is a PartsList is to assume that PartsList is the base and PartsCatalog is the derived class, and then to ask these other questions:

1. Is anything in the base class that should not be in the derived class? For example, does the PartsList base class have functions that are inappropriate for the PartsCatalog class? If so, you probably do not want public inheritance.

2. Might the class you are creating have more than one of the base? For example, might a PartsCatalog need two PartsLists in each object? If it might, you almost certainly want to use containment.

3. Do you need to inherit from the base class so that you can take advantage of virtual functions or access protected members? If so, you must use inheritance, public or private.

Based on the answers to these questions, you must choose between public inheritance (the *is-a* relationship) and either private inheritance (explained later today) or containment.

- Contained—An object declared as a member of another class contained by that class.
- Delegation—Using the attributes of a contained class to accomplish functions not otherwise available to the containing class.
- Implemented in terms of—Building one class on the capabilities of another without using public inheritance.

Delegation

Why not derive PartsCatalog from PartsList? The PartsCatalog is not a PartsList because PartsLists are ordered collections, and each member of the collection can repeat. The PartsCatalog has unique entries that are not ordered. The fifth member of the PartsCatalog is not part number 5.

Certainly, it would have been possible to inherit publicly from PartsList and then override Insert() and the offset operators ([]) to do the right thing, but then you would have changed the essence of the PartsList class. Instead, you can build a PartsCatalog that has no offset operator, does not allow duplicates, and defines the operator+ to combine two sets.

The first way to accomplish this is with containment. The PartsCatalog will delegate list management to a contained PartsList. Listing 15.5 illustrates this approach.

LISTING 15.5 Delegating to a Contained `PartsList`

```
1:      #include <iostream.h>
2:
3:      // **************** Part ************
4:
5:      // Abstract base class of parts
6:      class Part
7:      {
8:      public:
9:         Part():itsPartNumber(1) {}
10:        Part(int PartNumber):
11:            itsPartNumber(PartNumber){}
12:        virtual ~Part(){}
13:        int GetPartNumber() const
14:            { return itsPartNumber; }
15:        virtual void Display() const =0;
16:      private:
17:         int itsPartNumber;
18:      };
19:
20:      // implementation of pure virtual function so that
21:      // derived classes can chain up
22:      void Part::Display() const
23:      {
24:          cout << "\nPart Number: " << itsPartNumber << endl;
25:      }
26:
27:      // **************** Car Part ************
28:
29:      class CarPart : public Part
30:      {
31:      public:
32:         CarPart():itsModelYear(94){}
33:         CarPart(int year, int partNumber);
34:         virtual void Display() const
35:         {
36:             Part::Display();
37:             cout << "Model Year: ";
38:             cout << itsModelYear << endl;
39:         }
40:      private:
41:         int itsModelYear;
42:      };
43:
44:      CarPart::CarPart(int year, int partNumber):
45:         itsModelYear(year),
46:         Part(partNumber)
```

continues

15

LISTING 15.5 CONTINUED

```
47:        {}
48:
49:
50:        // *************** AirPlane Part ************
51:
52:        class AirPlanePart : public Part
53:        {
54:        public:
55:           AirPlanePart():itsEngineNumber(1){};
56:           AirPlanePart
57:              (int EngineNumber, int PartNumber);
58:           virtual void Display() const
59:           {
60:              Part::Display();
61:              cout << "Engine No.: ";
62:              cout << itsEngineNumber << endl;
63:           }
64:        private:
65:           int itsEngineNumber;
66:        };
67:
68:        AirPlanePart::AirPlanePart
69:           (int EngineNumber, int PartNumber):
70:           itsEngineNumber(EngineNumber),
71:           Part(PartNumber)
72:        {}
73:
74:        // *************** Part Node ************
75:        class PartNode
76:        {
77:        public:
78:           PartNode (Part*);
79:           ~PartNode();
80:           void SetNext(PartNode * node)
81:              { itsNext = node; }
82:           PartNode * GetNext() const;
83:           Part * GetPart() const;
84:        private:
85:           Part *itsPart;
86:           PartNode * itsNext;
87:        };
88:         // PartNode Implementations...
89:
90:         PartNode::PartNode(Part* pPart):
91:         itsPart(pPart),
92:         itsNext(0)
93:            {}
94:
```

15

```
95:        PartNode::~PartNode()
96:        {
97:          delete itsPart;
98:          itsPart = NULL;
99:          delete itsNext;
100:          itsNext = NULL;
101:        }
102:
103:        // Returns NULL if no next PartNode
104:        PartNode * PartNode::GetNext() const
105:        {
106:            return itsNext;
107:        }
108:
109:        Part * PartNode::GetPart() const
110:        {
111:          if (itsPart)
112:            return itsPart;
113:          else
114:            return NULL; //error
115:        }
116:
117:
118:
119:        // *************** Part List ***********
120:        class PartsList
121:        {
122:        public:
123:          PartsList();
124:          ~PartsList();
125:          // needs copy constructor and operator equals!
126:          void      Iterate(void (Part::*f)()const) const;
127:          Part*     Find(int & position, int PartNumber)  const;
128:          Part*     GetFirst() const;
129:          void      Insert(Part *);
130:          Part*     operator[](int) const;
131:          int     GetCount() const { return itsCount; }
132:          static    PartsList& GetGlobalPartsList()
133:          {
134:              return  GlobalPartsList;
135:          }
136:        private:
137:          PartNode * pHead;
138:          int itsCount;
139:          static PartsList GlobalPartsList;
140:        };
141:
142:        PartsList PartsList::GlobalPartsList;
143:
```

continues

LISTING 15.5   CONTINUED

```
144:
145:        PartsList::PartsList():
146:            pHead(0),
147:            itsCount(0)
148:            {}
149:
150:        PartsList::~PartsList()
151:        {
152:            delete pHead;
153:        }
154:
155:        Part*    PartsList::GetFirst() const
156:        {
157:            if (pHead)
158:                return pHead->GetPart();
159:            else
160:                return NULL;  // error catch here
161:        }
162:
163:        Part * PartsList::operator[](int offSet) const
164:        {
165:            PartNode* pNode = pHead;
166:
167:            if (!pHead)
168:                return NULL; // error catch here
169:
170:            if (offSet > itsCount)
171:                return NULL; // error
172:
173:            for (int i=0;i<offSet; i++)
174:                pNode = pNode->GetNext();
175:
176:            return    pNode->GetPart();
177:        }
178:
179:        Part*    PartsList::Find(
180:            int & position,
181:            int PartNumber)   const
182:        {
183:            PartNode * pNode = NULL;
184:            for (pNode = pHead, position = 0;
185:                    pNode!=NULL;
186:                    pNode = pNode->GetNext(), position++)
187:            {
188:                if (pNode->GetPart()->GetPartNumber() == PartNumber)
189:                    break;
190:            }
191:            if (pNode == NULL)
```

```
192:                return NULL;
193:           else
194:                return pNode->GetPart();
195:      }
196:
197:      void PartsList::Iterate(void (Part::*func)()const) const
198:      {
199:           if (!pHead)
200:                return;
201:           PartNode* pNode = pHead;
202:           do
203:                (pNode->GetPart()->*func)();
204:           while (pNode = pNode->GetNext());
205:      }
206:
207:      void PartsList::Insert(Part* pPart)
208:      {
209:           PartNode * pNode = new PartNode(pPart);
210:           PartNode * pCurrent = pHead;
211:           PartNode * pNext = NULL;
212:
213:           int New =  pPart->GetPartNumber();
214:           int Next = 0;
215:           itsCount++;
216:
217:           if (!pHead)
218:           {
219:                pHead = pNode;
220:                return;
221:           }
222:
223:           // if this one is smaller than head
224:           // this one is the new head
225:           if (pHead->GetPart()->GetPartNumber() > New)
226:           {
227:                pNode->SetNext(pHead);
228:                pHead = pNode;
229:                return;
230:           }
231:
232:           for (;;)
233:           {
234:                // if there is no next, append this new one
235:                if (!pCurrent->GetNext())
236:                {
237:                     pCurrent->SetNext(pNode);
238:                     return;
239:                }
```

continues

LISTING 15.5   CONTINUED

```
240:
241:                // if this goes after this one and before the next
242:                // then insert it here, otherwise get the next
243:                pNext = pCurrent->GetNext();
244:                Next = pNext->GetPart()->GetPartNumber();
245:                if (Next > New)
246:                {
247:                   pCurrent->SetNext(pNode);
248:                   pNode->SetNext(pNext);
249:                   return;
250:                }
251:                pCurrent = pNext;
252:           }
253:        }
254:
255:
256:
257:     class PartsCatalog
258:     {
259:     public:
260:        void Insert(Part *);
261:        int Exists(int PartNumber);
262:        Part * Get(int PartNumber);
263:        operator+(const PartsCatalog &);
264:        void ShowAll() { thePartsList.Iterate(Part::Display); }
265:     private:
266:        PartsList thePartsList;
267:     };
268:
269:     void PartsCatalog::Insert(Part * newPart)
270:     {
271:        int partNumber =  newPart->GetPartNumber();
272:        int offset;
273:
274:        if (!thePartsList.Find(offset, partNumber))
275:
276:           thePartsList.Insert(newPart);
277:        else
278:        {
279:           cout << partNumber << " was the ";
280:           switch (offset)
281:           {
282:              case 0:  cout << "first "; break;
283:              case 1:  cout << "second "; break;
284:              case 2:  cout << "third "; break;
285:              default: cout << offset+1 << "th ";
286:           }
287:           cout << "entry. Rejected!\n";
```

```
288:              }
289:          }
290:
291:      int PartsCatalog::Exists(int PartNumber)
292:      {
293:          int offset;
294:          thePartsList.Find(offset,PartNumber);
295:              return offset;
296:      }
297:
298:      Part * PartsCatalog::Get(int PartNumber)
299:      {
300:          int offset;
301:          Part * thePart = thePartsList.Find(offset, PartNumber);
302:          return thePart;
303:      }
304:
305:
306:      int main()
307:      {
308:          PartsCatalog pc;
309:          Part * pPart = NULL;
310:          int PartNumber;
311:          int value;
312:          int choice;
313:
314:          while (1)
315:          {
316:              cout << "(0)Quit (1)Car (2)Plane: ";
317:              cin >> choice;
318:
319:              if (!choice)
320:                  break;
321:
322:              cout << "New PartNumber?: ";
323:              cin >>  PartNumber;
324:
325:              if (choice == 1)
326:              {
327:                  cout << "Model Year?: ";
328:                  cin >> value;
329:                  pPart = new CarPart(value,PartNumber);
330:              }
331:              else
332:              {
333:                  cout << "Engine Number?: ";
334:                  cin >> value;
335:                  pPart = new AirPlanePart(value,PartNumber);
```

continues

LISTING 15.5 CONTINUED

```
336:              }
337:              pc.Insert(pPart);
338:          }
339:          pc.ShowAll();
340:       return 0;
341:    }
```

OUTPUT

```
(0)Quit (1)Car (2)Plane:  1
New PartNumber?: 1234
Model Year?: 94
(0)Quit (1)Car (2)Plane:  1
New PartNumber?: 4434
Model Year?: 93
(0)Quit (1)Car (2)Plane:  1
New PartNumber?: 1234
Model Year?: 94
1234 was the first entry. Rejected!
(0)Quit (1)Car (2)Plane:  1
New PartNumber?: 2345
Model Year?: 93
(0)Quit (1)Car (2)Plane:  0

Part Number: 1234
Model Year: 94

Part Number: 2345
Model Year: 93

Part Number: 4434
Model Year: 93
```

Note

Some compilers (other than g++) cannot compile line 267, even though it is legal C++. If your compiler complains about this line, change it to

```
267:            void ShowAll() { thePartsList.Iterate(&Part::
➥Display); }
```

(Note the addition of the ampersand in front of Part::Display). If that works, immediately call your compiler vendor and complain.

ANALYSIS Listing 15.5 reproduces the Part, PartNode, and PartsList classes from Week 2 in Review.

A new class, PartsCatalog, is declared on lines 257 to 267. PartsCatalog has a PartsList as its data member, to which it delegates list management. Another way to say this is that the PartsCatalog is implemented in terms of this PartsList.

Note that clients of the PartsCatalog do not have access to the PartsList directly. The interface is through the PartsCatalog, and as such, the behavior of the PartsList is dramatically changed. For example, the PartsCatalog::Insert() method does not allow duplicate entries into the PartsList.

The implementation of PartsCatalog::Insert() starts on line 269. The Part that is passed in as a parameter is asked for the value of its itsPartNumber member variable. This value is fed to the PartsList's Find() method, and if no match is found, the number is inserted; otherwise, an informative error message is printed.

Note that PartsCatalog does the actual insert by calling Insert() on its member variable, pl, which is a PartsList. The mechanics of the actual insertion and the maintenance of the linked list, as well as searching and retrieving from the linked list, are maintained in the contained PartsList member of PartsCatalog. No reason exists for PartsCatalog to reproduce this code; it can take full advantage of the well-defined interface.

This is the essence of reusability within C++: PartsCatalog can reuse the PartsList code, and the designer of PartsCatalog is free to ignore the implementation details of PartsList. The interface to PartsList (that is, the class declaration) provides all the information needed by the designer of the PartsCatalog class.

Private Inheritance

If PartsCatalog needed access to the protected members of PartsList (in this case, none exist), or needed to override any of the PartsList methods, PartsCatalog would be forced to inherit from PartsList.

Because a PartsCatalog is not a PartsList object, and because you do not want to expose the entire set of functionality of PartsList to clients of PartsCatalog, you need to use private inheritance.

The first thing to know about private inheritance is that all the base member variables and functions are treated as if they were declared to be private, regardless of their actual access level in the base. Thus, to any function that is not a member function of PartsCatalog, every function inherited from PartsList is inaccessible. This is critical: private inheritance does not involve inheriting interface, only implementation.

To clients of the PartsCatalog class, the PartsList class is invisible. None of its interface is available to them: they cannot call any of its methods. They can call PartsCatalog methods, however; PartsCatalog methods can then access all of PartsList because PartsCatalog is derived from PartsList. The important thing here is that the PartsCatalog is not a PartsList, as would have been implied by public inheritance. It is implemented in terms of a PartsList, just as would have been the case with containment. The private inheritance is just a convenience.

Listing 15.6 demonstrates the use of private inheritance by rewriting the PartsCatalog class as privately derived from PartsList.

INPUT   **LISTING 15.6**   Private Inheritance

```
1:      //listing 15.6 demonstrates private inheritance
2:      #include <iostream.h>
3:
4:      // *************** Part ************
5:
6:      // Abstract base class of parts
7:      class Part
8:          {
9:      public:
10:         Part():itsPartNumber(1) {}
11:         Part(int PartNumber):
12:             itsPartNumber(PartNumber){}
13:         virtual ~Part(){}
14:         int GetPartNumber() const
15:             { return itsPartNumber; }
16:         virtual void Display() const =0;
17:     private:
18:         int itsPartNumber;
19:         };
20:
21:     // implementation of pure virtual function so that
22:     // derived classes can chain up
23:     void Part::Display() const
24:         {
25:         cout << "\nPart Number: " << itsPartNumber << endl;
26:         }
27:
28:     // *************** Car Part ************
29:
30:     class CarPart : public Part
31:         {
32:     public:
33:         CarPart():itsModelYear(94){}
34:         CarPart(int year, int partNumber);
35:         virtual void Display() const
```

```
36:            {
37:                Part::Display();
38:                cout << "Model Year: ";
39:                cout << itsModelYear << endl;
40:            }
41:        private:
42:            int itsModelYear;
43:        };
44:
45:        CarPart::CarPart(int year, int partNumber):
46:            itsModelYear(year),
47:            Part(partNumber)
48:        {}
49:
50:
51:        // *************** AirPlane Part ***********
52:
53:        class AirPlanePart : public Part
54:        {
55:        public:
56:            AirPlanePart():itsEngineNumber(1){};
57:            AirPlanePart
58:                (int EngineNumber, int PartNumber);
59:            virtual void Display() const
60:            {
61:                Part::Display();
62:                cout << "Engine No.: ";
63:                cout << itsEngineNumber << endl;
64:            }
65:        private:
66:            int itsEngineNumber;
67:        };
68:
69:        AirPlanePart::AirPlanePart
70:            (int EngineNumber, int PartNumber):
71:            itsEngineNumber(EngineNumber),
72:            Part(PartNumber)
73:        {}
74:
75:        // *************** Part Node ***********
76:        class PartNode
77:        {
78:        public:
79:            PartNode (Part*);
80:            ~PartNode();
81:            void SetNext(PartNode * node)
82:                { itsNext = node; }
83:            PartNode * GetNext() const;
```

continues

LISTING 15.6   CONTINUED

```
84:          Part * GetPart() const;
85:      private:
86:          Part *itsPart;
87:          PartNode * itsNext;
88:      };
89:       // PartNode Implementations...
90:
91:       PartNode::PartNode(Part* pPart):
92:       itsPart(pPart),
93:       itsNext(0)
94:       {}
95:
96:       PartNode::~PartNode()
97:       {
98:          delete itsPart;
99:         itsPart = NULL;
100:          delete itsNext;
101:          itsNext = NULL;
102:       }
103:
104:       // Returns NULL if no next PartNode
105:       PartNode * PartNode::GetNext() const
106:       {
107:            return itsNext;
108:       }
109:
110:       Part * PartNode::GetPart() const
111:       {
112:          if (itsPart)
113:            return itsPart;
114:          else
115:            return NULL; //error
116:       }
117:
118:
119:
120:       // *************** Part List ***********
121:      class PartsList
122:      {
123:      public:
124:          PartsList();
125:          ~PartsList();
126:          // needs copy constructor and operator equals!
127:          void      Iterate(void (Part::*f)()const) const;
128:          Part*     Find(int & position, int PartNumber)  const;
129:          Part*     GetFirst() const;
130:          void      Insert(Part *);
131:          Part*     operator[](int) const;
```

```
132:        int    GetCount() const { return itsCount; }
133:        static    PartsList& GetGlobalPartsList()
134:        {
135:            return  GlobalPartsList;
136:        }
137:    private:
138:        PartNode * pHead;
139:        int itsCount;
140:        static PartsList GlobalPartsList;
141:    };
142:
143:    PartsList PartsList::GlobalPartsList;
144:
145:
146:     PartsList::PartsList():
147:        pHead(0),
148:        itsCount(0)
149:        {}
150:
151:     PartsList::~PartsList()
152:     {
153:        delete pHead;
154:     }
155:
156:     Part*   PartsList::GetFirst() const
157:     {
158:        if (pHead)
159:            return pHead->GetPart();
160:        else
161:            return NULL;   // error catch here
162:     }
163:
164:     Part *  PartsList::operator[](int offSet) const
165:     {
166:        PartNode* pNode = pHead;
167:
168:        if (!pHead)
169:            return NULL; // error catch here
170:
171:        if (offSet > itsCount)
172:            return NULL; // error
173:
174:        for (int i=0;i<offSet; i++)
175:            pNode = pNode->GetNext();
176:
177:        return   pNode->GetPart();
178:     }
179:
```

continues

LISTING 15.6 CONTINUED

```
180:     Part*   PartsList::Find(
181:         int & position,
182:         int PartNumber)  const
183:     {
184:         PartNode * pNode = NULL;
185:         for (pNode = pHead, position = 0;
186:              pNode!=NULL;
187:              pNode = pNode->GetNext(), position++)
188:         {
189:             if (pNode->GetPart()->GetPartNumber() == PartNumber)
190:                 break;
191:         }
192:         if (pNode == NULL)
193:             return NULL;
194:         else
195:             return pNode->GetPart();
196:     }
197:
198:     void PartsList::Iterate(void (Part::*func)()const) const
199:     {
200:         if (!pHead)
201:             return;
202:         PartNode* pNode = pHead;
203:         do
204:             (pNode->GetPart()->*func)();
205:         while (pNode = pNode->GetNext());
206:     }
207:
208:     void PartsList::Insert(Part* pPart)
209:     {
210:         PartNode * pNode = new PartNode(pPart);
211:         PartNode * pCurrent = pHead;
212:         PartNode * pNext = NULL;
213:
214:         int New =  pPart->GetPartNumber();
215:         int Next = 0;
216:         itsCount++;
217:
218:         if (!pHead)
219:         {
220:             pHead = pNode;
221:             return;
222:         }
223:
224:         // if this one is smaller than head
225:         // this one is the new head
226:         if (pHead->GetPart()->GetPartNumber() > New)
227:         {
```

```
228:              pNode->SetNext(pHead);
229:              pHead = pNode;
230:              return;
231:          }
232:
233:          for (;;)
234:          {
235:              // if there is no next, append this new one
236:              if (!pCurrent->GetNext())
237:              {
238:                  pCurrent->SetNext(pNode);
239:                  return;
240:              }
241:
242:              // if this goes after this one and before the next
243:              // then insert it here, otherwise get the next
244:              pNext = pCurrent->GetNext();
245:              Next = pNext->GetPart()->GetPartNumber();
246:              if (Next > New)
247:              {
248:                  pCurrent->SetNext(pNode);
249:                  pNode->SetNext(pNext);
250:                  return;
251:              }
252:              pCurrent = pNext;
253:          }
254:      }
255:
256:
257:
258:  class PartsCatalog : private PartsList
259:  {
260:  public:
261:    void Insert(Part *);
262:    int Exists(int PartNumber);
263:    Part * Get(int PartNumber);
264:    operator+(const PartsCatalog &);
265:    void ShowAll() { Iterate(Part::Display); }
266:  private:
267:  };
268:
269:  void PartsCatalog::Insert(Part * newPart)
270:  {
271:      int partNumber =  newPart->GetPartNumber();
272:      int offset;
273:
274:      if (!Find(offset, partNumber))
275:          PartsList::Insert(newPart);
276:      else
```

continues

LISTING 15.6   CONTINUED

```
277:        {
278:            cout << partNumber << " was the ";
279:            switch (offset)
280:            {
281:                case 0:  cout << "first "; break;
282:                case 1:  cout << "second "; break;
283:                case 2:  cout << "third "; break;
284:                default: cout << offset+1 << "th ";
285:            }
286:            cout << "entry. Rejected!\n";
287:        }
288:    }
289:
290:    int PartsCatalog::Exists(int PartNumber)
291:    {
292:        int offset;
293:        Find(offset,PartNumber);
294:        return offset;
295:    }
296:
297:    Part * PartsCatalog::Get(int PartNumber)
298:    {
299:        int offset;
300:        return (Find(offset, PartNumber));
301:
302:    }
303:
304:    int main()
305:    {
306:        PartsCatalog pc;
307:        Part * pPart = NULL;
308:        int PartNumber;
309:        int value;
310:        int choice;
311:
312:        while (1)
313:        {
314:            cout << "(0)Quit (1)Car (2)Plane: ";
315:            cin >> choice;
316:
317:            if (!choice)
318:                break;
319:
320:            cout << "New PartNumber?: ";
321:            cin >>  PartNumber;
322:
323:            if (choice == 1)
324:            {
```

```
325:                    cout << "Model Year?: ";
326:                    cin >> value;
327:                    pPart = new CarPart(value,PartNumber);
328:                }
329:                else
330:                {
331:                    cout << "Engine Number?: ";
332:                    cin >> value;
333:                    pPart = new AirPlanePart(value,PartNumber);
334:                }
335:                pc.Insert(pPart);
336:            }
337:        pc.ShowAll();
338:    return 0;
339:    }
```

OUTPUT

```
(0)Quit (1)Car (2)Plane:  1
New PartNumber?: 1234
Model Year?: 94
(0)Quit (1)Car (2)Plane:  1
New PartNumber?: 4434
Model Year?: 93
(0)Quit (1)Car (2)Plane:  1
New PartNumber?: 1234
Model Year?: 94
1234 was the first entry. Rejected!
(0)Quit (1)Car (2)Plane:  1
New PartNumber?: 2345
Model Year?: 93
(0)Quit (1)Car (2)Plane:  0

Part Number: 1234
Model Year: 94

Part Number: 2345
Model Year: 93

Part Number: 4434
Model Year: 93
```

ANALYSIS   Listing 15.6 shows a changed interface to PartsCatalog and the rewritten driver program. The interfaces to the other classes are unchanged from Listing 15.5.

On line 258 of Listing 15.6, PartsCatalog is declared to derive privately from PartsList. The interface to PartsCatalog does not change from Listing 15.5, although, of course, it no longer needs an object of type PartsList as member data.

The PartsCatalog ShowAll() function calls PartsList Iterate() with the appropriate pointer to member function of class Part. ShowAll() acts as a public interface to

`Iterate()`, providing the correct information but preventing client classes from calling `Iterate()` directly. Although `PartsList` might allow other functions to be passed to `Iterate()`, `PartsCatalog` does not.

The `Insert()` function has changed as well. Note, on line 274, that `Find()` is now called directly because it is inherited from the base class. The call on line 275 to `Insert()` must be fully qualified, of course, or it would endlessly recurse into itself.

In short, when methods of `PartsCatalog` want to call `PartsList` methods, they may do so directly. The only exception is when `PartsCatalog` has overridden the method and the `PartsList` version is needed, in which case the function name must be qualified fully.

Private inheritance enables the `PartsCatalog` to inherit what it can use, but still provides mediated access to `Insert` and other methods to which client classes should not have direct access.

Do	Don't
DO inherit publicly when the derived object is a kind of the base class.	DON'T use private inheritance when you need to use more than one of the base class. You must use containment. For example, if `PartsCatalog` needed two `PartsLists`, you could not have used private inheritance.
DO use containment when you want to delegate functionality to another class, but you do not need access to its protected members.	
DO use private inheritance when you need to implement one class in terms of another, and you need access to the base class's protected members.	DON'T use public inheritance when members of the base class should not be available to clients of the derived class.

Friend Classes

Sometimes you will create classes together, as a set. For example, `PartNode` and `PartsList` were tightly coupled, and it would have been convenient if `PartsList` could have read `PartNode`'s `Part` pointer, `itsPart`, directly.

You would not want to make `itsPart` public, or even protected, because this is an implementation detail of `PartNode` and you want to keep it private. You do want to expose it to `PartsList`, however.

If you want to expose your private member data or functions to another class, you must declare that class to be a friend. This extends the interface of your class to include the friend class.

After `PartsNode` declares `PartsList` to be a friend, all `PartsNode`'s member data and functions are public as far as `PartsList` is concerned.

It is important to note that friendship cannot be transferred. Although you are my friend and Joe is your friend, that does not mean Joe is my friend. Friendship is not inherited, either. Again, although you are my friend and share my secrets with you, that does not mean I am willing to share my secrets with your children.

Finally, friendship is not commutative. Assigning Class One to be a friend of Class Two does not make Class Two a friend of Class One. You may be willing to tell me your secrets, but that does not mean I am willing to tell you mine.

Listing 15.7 illustrates friendship by rewriting the example from Listing 15.6, making `PartsList` a friend of `PartNode`. Note that this does not make `PartNode` a friend of `PartsList`.

INPUT   **LISTING 15.7**   Friend Class Illustrated

```
 1:      #include <iostream.h>
 2: // Listing 15.7: friend class illustrated
 3:
 4:
 5:
 6:      // *************** Part ***********
 7:
 8:      // Abstract base class of parts
 9:      class Part
10:        {
11:        public:
12:           Part():itsPartNumber(1) {}
13:           Part(int PartNumber):
14:               itsPartNumber(PartNumber){}
15:           virtual ~Part(){}
16:           int GetPartNumber() const
17:               { return itsPartNumber; }
18:           virtual void Display() const =0;
19:        private:
20:           int itsPartNumber;
21:        };
22:
23:      // implementation of pure virtual function so that
24:      // derived classes can chain up
25:      void Part::Display() const
26:      {
27:          cout << "\nPart Number: ";
28:          cout << itsPartNumber << endl;
```

continues

LISTING 15.7 CONTINUED

```
29:      }
30:
31:      // *************** Car Part ************
32:
33:      class CarPart : public Part
34:      {
35:      public:
36:         CarPart():itsModelYear(94){}
37:         CarPart(int year, int partNumber);
38:         virtual void Display() const
39:         {
40:             Part::Display();
41:             cout << "Model Year: ";
42:             cout << itsModelYear << endl;
43:         }
44:      private:
45:         int itsModelYear;
46:      };
47:
48:      CarPart::CarPart(int year, int partNumber):
49:         itsModelYear(year),
50:         Part(partNumber)
51:      {}
52:
53:
54:      // *************** AirPlane Part ************
55:
56:      class AirPlanePart : public Part
57:      {
58:      public:
59:         AirPlanePart():itsEngineNumber(1){};
60:         AirPlanePart
61:             (int EngineNumber, int PartNumber);
62:         virtual void Display() const
63:         {
64:             Part::Display();
65:             cout << "Engine No.: ";
66:             cout << itsEngineNumber << endl;
67:         }
68:      private:
69:         int itsEngineNumber;
70:      };
71:
72:      AirPlanePart::AirPlanePart
73:          (int EngineNumber, int PartNumber):
74:         itsEngineNumber(EngineNumber),
75:         Part(PartNumber)
76:      {}
```

15

```
77:
78:    // *************** Part Node ************
79:    class PartNode
80:    {
81:    public:
82:        friend class PartsList;
83:        PartNode (Part*);
84:        ~PartNode();
85:        void SetNext(PartNode * node)
86:            { itsNext = node; }
87:        PartNode * GetNext() const;
88:        Part * GetPart() const;
89:    private:
90:        Part *itsPart;
91:        PartNode * itsNext;
92:    };
93:
94:
95:        PartNode::PartNode(Part* pPart):
96:        itsPart(pPart),
97:        itsNext(0)
98:        {}
99:
100:        PartNode::~PartNode()
101:        {
102:            delete itsPart;
103:            itsPart = NULL;
104:            delete itsNext;
105:            itsNext = NULL;
106:        }
107:
108:        // Returns NULL if no next PartNode
109:        PartNode * PartNode::GetNext() const
110:        {
111:                return itsNext;
112:        }
113:
114:        Part * PartNode::GetPart() const
115:        {
116:            if (itsPart)
117:                return itsPart;
118:            else
119:                return NULL; //error
120:        }
121:
122:
123:    // *************** Part List ************
124:    class PartsList
```

continues

LISTING 15.7 CONTINUED

```
125:    {
126:    public:
127:        PartsList();
128:        ~PartsList();
129:        // needs copy constructor and operator equals!
130:        void     Iterate(void (Part::*f)()const) const;
131:        Part*    Find(int & position, int PartNumber) const;
132:        Part*    GetFirst() const;
133:        void      Insert(Part *);
134:        Part*    operator[](int) const;
135:        int    GetCount() const { return itsCount; }
136:        static    PartsList& GetGlobalPartsList()
137:                {
138:                    return  GlobalPartsList;
139:                }
140:    private:
141:        PartNode * pHead;
142:        int itsCount;
143:        static PartsList GlobalPartsList;
144:    };
145:
146:    PartsList PartsList::GlobalPartsList;
147:
148:    // Implementations for Lists...
149:
150:    PartsList::PartsList():
151:        pHead(0),
152:        itsCount(0)
153:        {}
154:
155:    PartsList::~PartsList()
156:    {
157:        delete pHead;
158:    }
159:
160:    Part*   PartsList::GetFirst() const
161:    {
162:        if (pHead)
163:            return pHead->itsPart;
164:        else
165:            return NULL;   // error catch here
166:    }
167:
168:    Part * PartsList::operator[](int offSet) const
169:    {
170:        PartNode* pNode = pHead;
171:
172:        if (!pHead)
```

```
173:            return NULL; // error catch here
174:
175:        if (offSet > itsCount)
176:            return NULL; // error
177:
178:        for (int i=0;i<offSet; i++)
179:            pNode = pNode->itsNext;
180:
181:      return    pNode->itsPart;
182:    }
183:
184:    Part* PartsList::Find(int & position, int PartNumber) const
185:    {
186:        PartNode * pNode = NULL;
187:        for (pNode = pHead, position = 0;
188:             pNode!=NULL;
189:             pNode = pNode->itsNext, position++)
190:        {
191:            if (pNode->itsPart->GetPartNumber() == PartNumber)
192:            break;
193:        }
194:        if (pNode == NULL)
195:            return NULL;
196:        else
197:            return pNode->itsPart;
198:    }
199:
200:    void PartsList::Iterate(void (Part::*func)()const) const
201:    {
202:        if (!pHead)
203:            return;
204:        PartNode* pNode = pHead;
205:        do
206:            (pNode->itsPart->*func)();
207:        while (pNode = pNode->itsNext);
208:    }
209:
210:    void PartsList::Insert(Part* pPart)
211:    {
212:        PartNode * pNode = new PartNode(pPart);
213:        PartNode * pCurrent = pHead;
214:        PartNode * pNext = NULL;
215:
216:        int New =  pPart->GetPartNumber();
217:        int Next = 0;
218:        itsCount++;
219:
220:        if (!pHead)
221:        {
```

continues

LISTING 15.7   CONTINUED

```
222:            pHead = pNode;
223:            return;
224:        }
225:
226:        // if this one is smaller than head
227:        // this one is the new head
228:        if (pHead->itsPart->GetPartNumber() > New)
229:        {
230:            pNode->itsNext = pHead;
231:            pHead = pNode;
232:            return;
233:        }
234:
235:        for (;;)
236:        {
237:            // if there is no next, append this new one
238:            if (!pCurrent->itsNext)
239:            {
240:                pCurrent->itsNext = pNode;
241:                return;
242:            }
243:
244:            // if this goes after this one and before the next
245:            // then insert it here, otherwise get the next
246:            pNext = pCurrent->itsNext;
247:            Next = pNext->itsPart->GetPartNumber();
248:            if (Next > New)
249:            {
250:                pCurrent->itsNext = pNode;
251:                pNode->itsNext = pNext;
252:                return;
253:            }
254:            pCurrent = pNext;
255:        }
256:    }
257:
258:    class PartsCatalog : private PartsList
259:    {
260:    public:
261:        void Insert(Part *);
262:        int Exists(int PartNumber);
263:        Part * Get(int PartNumber);
264:        operator+(const PartsCatalog &);
265:        void ShowAll() { Iterate(Part::Display); }
266:    private:
267:    };
268:
269:    void PartsCatalog::Insert(Part * newPart)
```

```
270:     {
271:         int partNumber = newPart->GetPartNumber();
272:         int offset;
273:
274:         if (!Find(offset, partNumber))
275:             PartsList::Insert(newPart);
276:         else
277:         {
278:             cout << partNumber << " was the ";
279:             switch (offset)
280:             {
281:                 case 0:  cout << "first "; break;
282:                 case 1:  cout << "second "; break;
283:                 case 2:  cout << "third "; break;
284:                 default: cout << offset+1 << "th ";
285:             }
286:             cout << "entry. Rejected!\n";
287:         }
288:     }
289:
290:     int PartsCatalog::Exists(int PartNumber)
291:     {
292:         int offset;
293:         Find(offset,PartNumber);
294:         return offset;
295:     }
296:
297:     Part * PartsCatalog::Get(int PartNumber)
298:     {
299:         int offset;
300:         return (Find(offset, PartNumber));
301:
302:     }
303:
304:     int main()
305:     {
306:         PartsCatalog pc;
307:         Part * pPart = NULL;
308:         int PartNumber;
309:         int value;
310:         int choice;
311:
312:         while (1)
313:         {
314:             cout << "(0)Quit (1)Car (2)Plane: ";
315:             cin >> choice;
316:
317:             if (!choice)
318:                 break;
```

continues

15

LISTING 15.7   CONTINUED

```
319:
320:            cout << "New PartNumber?: ";
321:            cin >>  PartNumber;
322:
323:            if (choice == 1)
324:            {
325:               cout << "Model Year?: ";
326:               cin >> value;
327:               pPart = new CarPart(value,PartNumber);
328:            }
329:            else
330:            {
331:               cout << "Engine Number?: ";
332:               cin >> value;
333:               pPart = new AirPlanePart(value,PartNumber);
334:            }
335:            pc.Insert(pPart);
336:         }
337:       pc.ShowAll();
338:       return 0;
339:     }
```

OUTPUT

```
 (0)Quit (1)Car (2)Plane:  1
New PartNumber?: 1234
Model Year?: 94
(0)Quit (1)Car (2)Plane:  1
New PartNumber?: 4434
Model Year?: 93
(0)Quit (1)Car (2)Plane:  1
New PartNumber?: 1234
Model Year?: 94
1234 was the first entry. Rejected!
(0)Quit (1)Car (2)Plane:  1
New PartNumber?: 2345
Model Year?: 93
(0)Quit (1)Car (2)Plane:  0

Part Number: 1234
Model Year: 94

Part Number: 2345
Model Year: 93

Part Number: 4434
Model Year: 93
```

15

ANALYSIS On line 82, the class `PartsList` is declared to be a friend to the `PartNode` class.

This listing places the friend declaration in the public section, but this is not required; it can be put anywhere in the class declaration without changing the meaning of the statement. Because of this statement, all the private member data and functions are available to any member function of class `PartsList`.

On line 160, the implementation of the member function `GetFirst()` reflects this change. Rather than returning `pHead->GetPart`, this function can now return the otherwise private member data by writing `pHead->itsPart`. Similarly, the `Insert()` function can now write `pNode->itsNext = pHead`, rather than writing `pNode->SetNext(pHead)`.

Admittedly, these are trivial changes, and a good enough reason does not exist to make `PartsList` a friend of `PartNode`, but they do serve to illustrate how the keyword `friend` works.

Declarations of `friend` classes should be used with extreme caution. If two classes are inextricably entwined, and one must frequently access data in the other, good reason may exist to use this declaration. But use it sparingly; it is often just as easy to use the public accessor methods, and doing so enables you to change one class without having to recompile the other.

Note

You will often hear novice C++ programmers complain that friend declarations "undermine" the encapsulation so important to object-oriented programming. This is, frankly, errant nonsense. The friend declaration makes the declared friend part of the class interface and is no more an undermining of encapsulation than is public derivation.

Friend Class

Declare one class to be a friend of another by putting the word `friend` into the class granting the access rights. That is, I can declare you to be my friend, but you cannot declare yourself to be my friend.

Here's an example:

```
class PartNode{
public:
friend class PartsList;
➥// declares PartsList to be a friend of PartNode
};
```

Friend Functions

At times, you will want to grant this level of access not to an entire class, but only to one or two functions of that class. You can do this by declaring the member functions of the other class to be friends, rather than declaring the entire class to be a friend. In fact, you can declare any function, whether or not it is a member function of another class, to be a friend function.

Friend Functions and Operator Overloading

Listing 15.1 provided a String class that overrode the operator+. It also provided a constructor that took a constant character pointer, so that string objects could be created from C-style strings. This enabled you to create a string and add to it with a C-style string.

> **Tip** C-style strings are null-terminated character arrays, such as char myString[] = "Hello World"."

What you could not do, however, was create a C-style string (a character string) and add to it using a string object, as shown in this example:

```
char cString[] = {"Hello"};
String sString(" World");
String sStringTwo = cString + sString;   //error!
```

C-style strings do not have an overloaded operator+. As discussed on Day 10, "Advanced Functions," when you say cString + sString; what you are really calling is cString.operator+(sString). Because you cannot call operator+() on a C-style string, this causes a compile-time error.

You can solve this problem by declaring a friend function in String, which overloads operator+ but takes two string objects. The C-style string will be converted to a string object by the appropriate constructor, and then operator+ will be called using the two string objects. Listing 15.8 shows the use of a friend operator.

INPUT   **LISTING 15.8**   Friendly operator+

```
1:     //Listing 15.8 - friendly operators
2:
3:     #include <iostream.h>
4:     #include <string.h>
```

15

```
5:
6:      // Rudimentary string class
7:      class String
8:      {
9:         public:
10:           // constructors
11:           String();
12:           String(const char *const);
13:           String(const String &);
14:           ~String();
15:
16:           // overloaded operators
17:           char & operator[](int offset);
18:           char operator[](int offset) const;
19:           String operator+(const String&);
20:           friend String operator+(const String&, const String&);
21:           void operator+=(const String&);
22:           String & operator= (const String &);
23:
24:           // General accessors
25:           int GetLen()const { return itsLen; }
26:           const char * GetString() const { return itsString; }
27:
28:         private:
29:           String (int);          // private constructor
30:           char * itsString;
31:           unsigned short itsLen;
32:      };
33:
34:      // default constructor creates string of 0 bytes
35:      String::String()
36:      {
37:         itsString = new char[1];
38:         itsString[0] = '\0';
39:         itsLen=0;
40:         // cout << "\tDefault string constructor\n";
41:         // ConstructorCount++;
42:      }
43:
44:      // private (helper) constructor, used only by
45:      // class methods for creating a new string of
46:      // required size.  Null filled.
47:      String::String(int len)
48:      {
49:         itsString = new char[len+1];
50:         for (int i = 0; i<=len; i++)
51:            itsString[i] = '\0';
52:         itsLen=len;
53:         // cout << "\tString(int) constructor\n";
```

continues

LISTING 15.8 CONTINUED

```
54:        // ConstructorCount++;
55:     }
56:
57:     // Converts a character array to a String
58:     String::String(const char * const cString)
59:     {
60:        itsLen = strlen(cString);
61:        itsString = new char[itsLen+1];
62:        for (int i = 0; i<itsLen; i++)
63:           itsString[i] = cString[i];
64:        itsString[itsLen]='\0';
65:        // cout << "\tString(char*) constructor\n";
66:        // ConstructorCount++;
67:     }
68:
69:     // copy constructor
70:     String::String (const String & rhs)
71:     {
72:        itsLen=rhs.GetLen();
73:        itsString = new char[itsLen+1];
74:        for (int i = 0; i<itsLen;i++)
75:           itsString[i] = rhs[i];
76:        itsString[itsLen] = '\0';
77:        // cout << "\tString(String&) constructor\n";
78:        // ConstructorCount++;
79:     }
80:
81:     // destructor, frees allocated memory
82:     String::~String ()
83:     {
84:        delete [] itsString;
85:        itsLen = 0;
86:        // cout << "\tString destructor\n";
87:     }
88:
89:     // operator equals, frees existing memory
90:     // then copies string and size
91:     String& String::operator=(const String & rhs)
92:     {
93:        if (this == &rhs)
94:           return *this;
95:        delete [] itsString;
96:        itsLen=rhs.GetLen();
97:        itsString = new char[itsLen+1];
98:        for (int i = 0; i<itsLen;i++)
99:           itsString[i] = rhs[i];
100:       itsString[itsLen] = '\0';
101:       return *this;
```

```
102:          // cout << "\tString operator=\n";
103:      }
104:
105:      //non constant offset operator, returns
106:      // reference to character so it can be
107:      // changed!
108:      char & String::operator[](int offset)
109:      {
110:          if (offset > itsLen)
111:              return itsString[itsLen-1];
112:          else
113:              return itsString[offset];
114:      }
115:
116:      // constant offset operator for use
117:      // on const objects (see copy constructor!)
118:      char String::operator[](int offset) const
119:      {
120:          if (offset > itsLen)
121:              return itsString[itsLen-1];
122:          else
123:              return itsString[offset];
124:      }
125:      // creates a new string by adding current
126:      // string to rhs
127:      String String::operator+(const String& rhs)
128:      {
129:          int  totalLen = itsLen + rhs.GetLen();
130:          String temp(totalLen);
131:          int i, j;
132:          for (i = 0; i<itsLen; i++)
133:              temp[i] = itsString[i];
134:          for (j = 0, i = itsLen; j<rhs.GetLen(); j++, i++)
135:              temp[i] = rhs[j];
136:          temp[totalLen]='\0';
137:          return temp;
138:      }
139:
140:      // creates a new string by adding
141:      // one string to another
142:      String operator+(const String& lhs, const String& rhs)
143:      {
144:          int  totalLen = lhs.GetLen() + rhs.GetLen();
145:          String temp(totalLen);
146:          int i, j;
147:          for (i = 0; i<lhs.GetLen(); i++)
148:              temp[i] = lhs[i];
149:          for (j = 0, i = lhs.GetLen(); j<rhs.GetLen(); j++, i++)
150:              temp[i] = rhs[j];
```

continues

LISTING 15.8   CONTINUED

```
151:            temp[totalLen]='\0';
152:            return temp;
153:    }
154:
155:    int main()
156:    {
157:        String s1("String One ");
158:        String s2("String Two ");
159:        char *c1 = { "C-String One " } ;
160:        String s3;
161:        String s4;
162:        String s5;
163:
164:        cout << "s1: " << s1.GetString() << endl;
165:        cout << "s2: " << s2.GetString() << endl;
166:        cout << "c1: " << c1 << endl;
167:        s3 = s1 + s2;
168:        cout << "s3: " << s3.GetString() << endl;
169:        s4 = s1 + c1;
170:        cout << "s4: " << s4.GetString() << endl;
171:        s5 = c1 + s2;
172:        cout << "s5: " << s5.GetString() << endl;
173:     return 0;
174:    }
```

OUTPUT
```
s1: String One
s2: String Two
c1: C-String One
s3: String One String Two
s4: String One C-String One
s5: C-String One String Two
```

ANALYSIS   The implementation of all the string methods except operator+ is unchanged from Listing 15.1. On line 20, a new operator+ is overloaded to take two constant string references and to return a string, and this function is declared to be a friend.

Note that this operator+ is not a member function of this or any other class. It is declared within the declaration of the String class only so that it can be made a friend, but because it is declared, no other function prototype is needed.

The implementation of this operator+ is on lines 142–153. Note that it is similar to the earlier operator+, except that it takes two strings and accesses them both through their public accessor methods.

The driver program demonstrates the use of this function on line 171, where operator+ is now called on a C-style string!

Friend Functions

Declare a function to be a friend by using the keyword `friend` and then the full specification of the function. Declaring a function to be a friend does not give the `friend` function access to your `this` pointer, but it does provide full access to all private and protected member data and functions.

Here's an example:

```
class PartNode
{   // ...
    // make another class's member function a _friend
    friend void PartsList::Insert(Part *);
    // make a global function a friend
    friend int SomeFunction();
    // ...
};
```

Overloading the Insertion Operator

You are finally ready to give your `String` class the capability to use `cout` the same as any other type. Until now, when you wanted to print a string, you were forced to write the following:

```
cout << theString.GetString();
```

What you can do instead is write this:

```
cout << theString;
```

To accomplish this, you must override `operator<<()`. Day 16, "Streams," presents the ins and outs (`cins` and `couts`?) of working with `iostreams`; for now, Listing 15.9 illustrates how `operator<<` can be overloaded using a `friend` function.

INPUT   **LISTING 15.9**   Overloading operator<<()

```
1:    #include <iostream.h>
2:    #include <string.h>
3: // Listing 15.9: Overloading the << operator
4:    class String
5:    {
6:       public:
7:          // constructors
8:          String();
9:           String(const char *const);
```

continues

LISTING **15.9**   CONTINUED

```
10:              String(const String &);
11:              ~String();
12:
13:              // overloaded operators
14:              char & operator[](int offset);
15:              char operator[](int offset) const;
16:              String operator+(const String&);
17:              void operator+=(const String&);
18:              String & operator= (const String &);
19:              friend ostream& operator<<
20:                  ( ostream& theStream,String& theString);
21:              // General accessors
22:              int GetLen()const { return itsLen; }
23:              const char * GetString() const { return itsString; }
24:
25:          private:
26:              String (int);          // private constructor
27:              char * itsString;
28:              unsigned short itsLen;
29:          };
30:
31:
32:      // default constructor creates string of 0 bytes
33:      String::String()
34:      {
35:          itsString = new char[1];
36:          itsString[0] = '\0';
37:          itsLen=0;
38:          // cout << "\tDefault string constructor\n";
39:          // ConstructorCount++;
40:      }
41:
42:      // private (helper) constructor, used only by
43:      // class methods for creating a new string of
44:      // required size.  Null filled.
45:      String::String(int len)
46:      {
47:          itsString = new char[len+1];
48:          for (int i = 0; i<=len; i++)
49:              itsString[i] = '\0';
50:          itsLen=len;
51:          // cout << "\tString(int) constructor\n";
52:          // ConstructorCount++;
53:      }
54:
55:      // Converts a character array to a String
56:      String::String(const char * const cString)
57:      {
```

15

```
58:        itsLen = strlen(cString);
59:        itsString = new char[itsLen+1];
60:        for (int i = 0; i<itsLen; i++)
61:            itsString[i] = cString[i];
62:        itsString[itsLen]='\0';
63:        // cout << "\tString(char*) constructor\n";
64:        // ConstructorCount++;
65:    }
66:
67:    // copy constructor
68:    String::String (const String & rhs)
69:    {
70:        itsLen=rhs.GetLen();
71:        itsString = new char[itsLen+1];
72:        for (int i = 0; i<itsLen;i++)
73:            itsString[i] = rhs[i];
74:        itsString[itsLen] = '\0';
75:        // cout << "\tString(String&) constructor\n";
76:        // ConstructorCount++;
77:    }
78:
79:    // destructor, frees allocated memory
80:    String::~String ()
81:    {
82:        delete [] itsString;
83:        itsLen = 0;
84:        // cout << "\tString destructor\n";
85:    }
86:
87:    // operator equals, frees existing memory
88:    // then copies string and size
89:    String& String::operator=(const String & rhs)
90:    {
91:        if (this == &rhs)
92:            return *this;
93:        delete [] itsString;
94:        itsLen=rhs.GetLen();
95:        itsString = new char[itsLen+1];
96:        for (int i = 0; i<itsLen;i++)
97:            itsString[i] = rhs[i];
98:        itsString[itsLen] = '\0';
99:        return *this;
100:        // cout << "\tString operator=\n";
101:    }
102:
103:    //non constant offset operator, returns
104:    // reference to character so it can be
105:    // changed!
106:    char & String::operator[](int offset)
```

continues

LISTING **15.9**   CONTINUED

```
107:    {
108:        if (offset > itsLen)
109:            return itsString[itsLen-1];
110:        else
111:            return itsString[offset];
112:    }
113:
114:    // constant offset operator for use
115:    // on const objects (see copy constructor!)
116:    char String::operator[](int offset) const
117:    {
118:        if (offset > itsLen)
119:            return itsString[itsLen-1];
120:        else
121:            return itsString[offset];
122:    }
123:
124:    // creates a new string by adding current
125:    // string to rhs
126:    String String::operator+(const String& rhs)
127:    {
128:        int  totalLen = itsLen + rhs.GetLen();
129:        String temp(totalLen);
130:        int i, j;
131:        for (i = 0; i<itsLen; i++)
132:            temp[i] = itsString[i];
133:        for (j = 0; j<rhs.GetLen(); j++, i++)
134:            temp[i] = rhs[j];
135:        temp[totalLen]='\0';
136:        return temp;
137:    }
138:
139:    // changes current string, returns nothing
140:    void String::operator+=(const String& rhs)
141:    {
142:        unsigned short rhsLen = rhs.GetLen();
143:        unsigned short totalLen = itsLen + rhsLen;
144:        String  temp(totalLen);
145:        int i, j;
146:        for (i = 0; i<itsLen; i++)
147:            temp[i] = itsString[i];
148:        for (j = 0, i = 0; j<rhs.GetLen(); j++, i++)
149:            temp[i] = rhs[i-itsLen];
150:        temp[totalLen]='\0';
151:        *this = temp;
152:    }
153:
154:    // int String::ConstructorCount =
```

```
155:     ostream& operator<< ( ostream& theStream,String& theString)
156:     {
157:         theStream << theString.itsString;
158:         return theStream;
159:     }
160:
161:     int main()
162:     {
163:         String theString("Hello world.");
164:         cout << theString;
165:       return 0;
166:     }
```

OUTPUT   Hello world.

ANALYSIS   On line 19, `operator<<` is declared to be a `friend` function that takes an `ostream` reference and a `String` reference and then returns an `ostream` reference. Note that this is not a member function of `String`. It returns a reference to an `ostream` so that you can concatenate calls to `operator<<`, such as this:

```
cout << "myAge: " << itsAge << " years.";
```

The implementation of this `friend` function is on lines 155–159. All this really does is hide the implementation details of feeding the string to the `ostream`, and that is just as it should be. You will see more about overloading this operator and `operator>>` on Day 16.

Summary

Today you saw how to delegate functionality to a contained object. You also saw how to implement one class in terms of another by using either containment or private inheritance. Containment is restricted in that the new class does not have access to the protected members of the contained class, and it cannot override the member functions of the contained object. Containment is simpler to use than private inheritance, and should be used when possible.

You also saw how to declare both friend functions and friend classes. Using a friend function, you saw how to overload the extraction operator, to allow your new classes to use `cout` the same as the built-in classes do.

Remember that public inheritance expresses *is-a*, containment expresses *has-a*, and private inheritance expresses *implemented in terms of*. The relationship *delegates to* can be expressed using either containment or private inheritance, although containment is more common.

Q&A

Q Why is it so important to distinguish between *is-a*, *has-a*, and *implemented in terms of*?

A The point of C++ is to implement well-designed, object-oriented programs. Keeping these relationships straight helps to ensure that your design corresponds to the reality of what you are modeling. Furthermore, a well-understood design will more likely be reflected in well-designed code.

Q Why is containment preferred over private inheritance?

A The challenge in modern programming is to cope with complexity. The more you can use objects as black boxes, the fewer details you have to worry about and the more complexity you can manage. Contained classes hide their details; private inheritance exposes the implementation details.

Q Why not make all classes friends of all the classes they use?

A Making one class a friend of another exposes the implementation details and reduces encapsulation. The ideal is to keep as many of the details of each class hidden from all other classes as possible.

Q If a function is overloaded, do you need to declare each form of the function to be a friend?

A Yes, if you overload a function and declare it to be a friend of another class, you must declare `friend` for each form that you want to grant this access to.

Workshop

The Workshop contains quiz questions to help solidify your understanding of the material covered and exercises to provide you with experience in using what you learned today. Try to answer the quiz and exercise questions before checking the answers in Appendix D, "Answers to Exercises and Quizzes," and make sure you understand the answers before going to the next day.

Quiz

1. How do you establish an *is-a* relationship?
2. How do you establish a *has-a* relationship?
3. What is the difference between containment and delegation?
4. What is the difference between delegation and *implemented in terms of*?
5. What is a `friend` function?

6. What is a `friend` class?

7. If `Dog` is a friend of `Boy`, is `Boy` a friend of `Dog`?

8. If `Dog` is a friend of `Boy`, and `Terrier` derives from `Dog`, is `Terrier` a friend of `Boy`?

9. If `Dog` is a friend of `Boy` and `Boy` is a friend of `House`, is `Dog` a friend of `House`?

10. Where must the declaration of a `friend` function appear?

Exercises

1. Show the declaration of a class, `Animal`, that contains a data member that is a string object.

2. Show the declaration of a class, `BoundedArray`, that is an array.

3. Show the declaration of a class, `Set`, that is declared in terms of an array.

4. Modify Listing 15.1 to provide the `String` class with an extraction operator (`>>`).

5. **BUG BUSTER:** What is wrong with this program?

```
1:     #include <iostream.h>
2:
3:     class Animal;
4:
5:     void setValue(Animal& , int);
6:
7:
8:     class Animal
9:     {
10:    public:
11:       int GetWeight()const { return itsWeight; }
12:       int GetAge() const { return itsAge; }
13:    private:
14:       int itsWeight;
15:       int itsAge;
16:    };
17:
18:    void setValue(Animal& theAnimal, int theWeight)
19:    {
20:       friend class Animal;
21:       theAnimal.itsWeight = theWeight;
22:    }
23:
24:    int main()
25:    {
26:       Animal peppy;
27:       setValue(peppy,5);
28:    }
```

6. Fix the listing in Exercise 5 so that it compiles.

7. **BUG BUSTER:** What is wrong with this code?

```
1:      #include <iostream.h>
2:
3:      class Animal;
4:
5:      void setValue(Animal& , int);
6:      void setValue(Animal& ,int,int);
7:
8:      class Animal
9:      {
10:     friend void setValue(Animal& ,int);
11:     private:
12:         int itsWeight;
13:         int itsAge;
14:     };
15:
16:     void setValue(Animal& theAnimal, int theWeight)
17:     {
18:         theAnimal.itsWeight = theWeight;
19:     }
20:
21:
22:     void setValue(Animal& theAnimal, int theWeight, int theAge)
23:     {
24:         theAnimal.itsWeight = theWeight;
25:         theAnimal.itsAge = theAge;
26:     }
27:
28:     int main()
29:     {
30:         Animal peppy;
31:         setValue(peppy,5);
32:         setValue(peppy,7,9);
33:     }
```

8. Fix Exercise 7 so that it compiles.

DAY **16**

Streams

Until now, you were using cout to write to the screen and cin to read from the keyboard, without a full understanding of how they work. Today you will learn:

- What streams are and how they are used
- How to manage input and output using streams
- How to write to and read from files using streams

Overview of Streams

C++ does not, as part of the language, define how data is written to the screen or to a file, nor how data is read into a program. However, these are clearly essential parts of working with C++, and the standard C++ library includes the iostream library, which facilitates input and output (I/O).

The advantage of having the input and output kept apart from the language and handled in libraries is that it is easier to make the language "platform-independent." That is, you can write C++ programs on a PC and then recompile them and run them on a Sun workstation. Or you can compile using the GNU compiler on the PC (during the day at work for instance) and take that code home to use under Linux. The compiler creator supplies the right library, and everything works. At least that is the general theory.

A library is a collection of object files (.o under Linux, .obj on a PC) that can be linked to your program to provide additional functionality. This is the most basic form of code reuse and has been around since ancient programmers punched 1s and 0s into the punched cards.

Encapsulation

The iostream classes view the flow of data from your program to the screen as being a stream of data, one byte following another. If the destination of the stream is a file or the screen, the source is usually some part of your program. If the stream is reversed, the data can come from the keyboard or a disk file and be "poured" into your data variables.

One principal goal of streams is to encapsulate the problems of getting the data to and from the disk or the screen. After a stream is created, your program works with the stream and the stream sweats the details. Figure 16.1 illustrates this fundamental idea.

FIGURE 16.1

Encapsulation through streams.

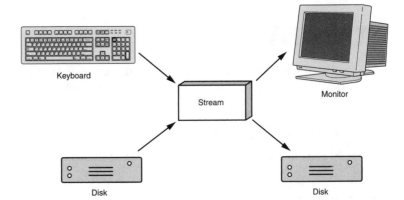

Buffering

Writing to the disk (and to a lesser extent the screen) is very "expensive." It takes a long time (relatively speaking) to write data to the disk or to read data from the disk, and execution of the program is generally blocked by disk writes and reads. To solve this problem, streams provide "buffering." Data is written into the stream, but it is not written back out to the disk immediately. Instead, the stream's buffer fills and fills, and when it is full, it writes to the disk all at once.

Picture water trickling into the top of a tank and the tank filling and filling, but no water running out of the bottom. Figure 16.2 illustrates this idea.

FIGURE 16.2

Filling the buffer.

When the water (data) reaches the top, the valve opens and all the water flows out in a rush. Figure 16.3 illustrates this idea.

FIGURE 16.3

Emptying the buffer.

After the buffer is empty, the bottom valve closes, the top valve opens, and more water flows into the buffer tank, as illustrated in Figure 16.4.

FIGURE **16.4**

Refilling the buffer.

Every once in a while you need to get the water out of the tank even before it is full. This is called "flushing the buffer." Figure 16.5 illustrates this idea.

FIGURE **16.5**

Flushing the buffer.

Streams and Buffers

As you might expect, C++ takes an object-oriented view toward implementing streams and buffers.

- The streambuf class manages the buffer, and its member functions provide the capability to fill, empty, flush, and otherwise manipulate the buffer.

- The `ios` class is the base class to the input and output stream classes. The `ios` class has a `streambuf` object as a member variable.

- The `istream` and `ostream` classes derive from the `ios` class and specialize input and output stream behavior, respectively.

- The `iostream` class is derived from both the `istream` and the `ostream` classes and provides input and output methods for writing to the screen.

- The `fstream` classes provide input and output from files.

Standard I/O Objects

When a C++ program that includes the `iostream` classes starts, four objects are created and initialized:

- `cin` (pronounced "see-in") handles input from the standard input, the keyboard.

- `cout` (pronounced "see-out") handles output to the standard output, the screen.

- `cerr` (pronounced "see-err") handles unbuffered output to the standard error device, the screen. Because this is unbuffered, everything sent to `cerr` is written to the standard error device immediately, without waiting for the buffer to fill or for a flush command to be received.

- `clog` (pronounced "see-log") handles buffered error messages that are output to the standard error device, the screen. It is common for this to be "redirected" to a log file, as described in the following section.

Note The `iostream` class library is added automatically to your program by the compiler. All you need to do to use these functions is put the appropriate `include` statement at the top of your program listing.

Redirection

Each of the standard devices, input, output, and error, can be redirected to other devices. Standard error is often redirected to a file, and standard input and output can be piped to files using operating system commands.

Redirecting refers to sending output (or input) to a place different than the default. The redirection operators for Linux (as well as other UNIX versions and DOS) are (<) redirect input and (>) redirect output.

Piping refers to using the output of one program as the input of another.

Linux (and other UNIX versions) provides advanced redirection capabilities: redirect output (>), redirect input (<), and redirect output to the input of a second program (|).

DOS provides rudimentary redirection commands, such as redirect output (>) and (redirect output operator)> The general idea is the same in DOS, Linux, and UNIX: Take the output intended for the screen and write it to a file, or pipe it into another program. Alternatively, the input for a program can be extracted from a file rather than from the keyboard.

Redirection is more a function of the operating system than of the `iostream` libraries. C++ just provides access to the four standard devices; it is up to the user to redirect the devices to whatever alternatives are needed.

Input Using `cin`

The global object `cin` is responsible for input and is made available to your program when you include `iostream.h`. In previous examples, you used the overloaded extraction operator (>>) to put data into your program's variables. How does this work? The syntax, as you may remember, is the following:

```
int someVariable;
cout << "Enter a number: ";
cin >> someVariable;
```

The global object `cout` is discussed later today; for now, focus on the third line, `cin >> someVariable;`. What can you guess about `cin`?

Clearly, it must be a global object because you did not define it in your own code. You know from previous operator experience that `cin` has overloaded the extraction operator (>>) and that the effect is to write whatever data `cin` has in its buffer into your local variable, `someVariable`.

What may not be immediately obvious is that `cin` has overloaded the extraction operator for a great variety of parameters, among them `int&`, `short&`, `long&`, `double&`, `float&`, `char&`, `char*`, and so forth. When you write `cin >> someVariable;`, the type of `someVariable` is assessed. In the preceding example, `someVariable` is an integer, so the following function is called:

```
istream & operator>> (int &)
```

Note that because the parameter is passed by reference, the extraction operator is able to act on the original variable. Listing 16.1 illustrates the use of `cin`.

INPUT **LISTING 16.1** cin Handles Different Data Types

```
1:   //Listing 16.1 — character strings and cin
2:
3:   #include <iostream.h>
4:
5:   int main(ef)
6:   {
7:       int myInt;
8:       long myLong;
9:       double myDouble;
10:      float myFloat;
11:      unsigned int myUnsigned;
12:
13:      cout << "int: ";
14:      cin >> myInt;
15:      cout << "Long: ";
16:      cin >> myLong;
17:      cout << "Double: ";
18:      cin >> myDouble;
19:      cout << "Float: ";
20:      cin >> myFloat;
21:      cout << "Unsigned: ";
22:      cin >> myUnsigned;
23:
24:      cout << "\n\nInt:\t" << myInt << endl;
25:      cout << "Long:\t" << myLong << endl;
26:      cout << "Double:\t" << myDouble << endl;
27:      cout << "Float:\t" << myFloat << endl;
28:      cout << "Unsigned:\t" << myUnsigned << endl;
29:      return 0;
30:  }
```

OUTPUT
```
int: 2
Long: 70000
Double: 987654321
Float: 3.33
Unsigned: 25

Int:    2
Long:    70000
Double: 9.87654e+08
Float:   3.33
Unsigned:        25
```

ANALYSIS On lines 7–11, variables of various types are declared. On lines 13–22, the user is prompted to enter values for these variables, and the results are printed (using cout) on lines 24–28.

The output reflects that the variables were put into the right "kinds" of variables, and the program works as you might expect.

Strings

cin can also handle character pointer (char*) arguments; thus, you can create a character buffer and use cin to fill it. For example, you can write the following:

```
char YourName[50]
cout << "Enter your name: ";
cin >> YourName;
```

If you enter "Jesse", the variable YourName will be filled with the characters J, e, s, s, e, \0. The last character is a *null character*; cin automatically ends the string with a null character, and you must have enough room in the buffer to allow for the entire string plus the null. The null signals "end of string" to the standard library functions discussed on Day 21, "What's Next."

Note

> The null character ('\0') is different from the NULL pointer. They may contain the same value in memory (binary zeroes), but they serve different purposes. Because of that, you should treat them differently. Do not set a pointer to the value '\0'. Do not end a string with the constant NULL.

String Problems

After all this success with cin, you might be surprised when you try to enter a full name into a string. cin believes that whitespace is a separator. When it sees a space or a newline character, it assumes the input for the parameter is complete, and in the case of strings, it adds a null character right then and there. Listing 16.2 illustrates this problem.

INPUT   **LISTING 16.2**   Trying to Write More Than One Word to cin

```
1:    //Listing 16.2 — character strings and cin
2:
3:    #include <iostream.h>
4:
5:    int main()
6:    {
7:        char YourName[50];
8:        cout << "Your first name: ";
9:        cin >> YourName;
10:       cout << "Here it is: " << YourName << endl;
11:       cout << "Your entire name: ";
12:       cin >> YourName;
13:       cout << "Here it is: " << YourName << endl;
14:     return 0;
15:    }
```

OUTPUT

```
Your first name: Jesse
Here it is: Jesse
Your entire name: Jesse Liberty
Here it is: Jesse
```

ANALYSIS On line 7, a character array is created to hold the user's input. On line 8, the user is prompted to enter one name, and that name is stored properly, as shown in the output.

On line 11, the user is again prompted, this time for a full name. cin reads the input, and when it sees the space between the names, it puts a null character after the first word and terminates input. This is not exactly what was intended.

To understand why this works this way, examine Listing 16.3, which shows input for several fields.

INPUT **LISTING 16.3** Multiple Input

```
1:    //Listing 16.3 - character strings and cin
2:
3:    #include <iostream.h>
4:
5:    int main()
6:    {
7:        int myInt;
8:        long myLong;
9:        double myDouble;
10:       float myFloat;
11:       unsigned int myUnsigned;
12:       char myWord[50];
13:
14:       cout << "int: ";
15:       cin >> myInt;
16:       cout << "Long: ";
17:       cin >> myLong;
18:       cout << "Double: ";
19:       cin >> myDouble;
20:       cout << "Float: ";
21:       cin >> myFloat;
22:       cout << "Word: ";
23:       cin >> myWord;
24:       cout << "Unsigned: ";
25:       cin >> myUnsigned;
26:
27:       cout << "\n\nInt:\t" << myInt << endl;
28:       cout << "Long:\t" << myLong << endl;
29:       cout << "Double:\t" << myDouble << endl;
30:       cout << "Float:\t" << myFloat << endl;
31:       cout << "Word: \t" << myWord << endl;
```

continues

LISTING 16.3 CONTINUED

```
32:        cout << "Unsigned:\t" << myUnsigned << endl;
33:
34:        cout << "\n\nInt, Long, Double, Float, Word, Unsigned: ";
35:        cin >> myInt >> myLong >> myDouble;
36:        cin >> myFloat >> myWord >> myUnsigned;
37:        cout << "\n\nInt:\t" << myInt << endl;
38:        cout << "Long:\t" << myLong << endl;
39:        cout << "Double:\t" << myDouble << endl;
40:        cout << "Float:\t" << myFloat << endl;
41:        cout << "Word: \t" << myWord << endl;
42:        cout << "Unsigned:\t" << myUnsigned << endl;
43:
44:
45:     return 0;
46:    }
```

OUTPUT

```
Int: 2
Long: 30303
Double: 393939397834
Float: 3.33
Word: Hello
Unsigned: 85

Int:     2
Long:    30303
Double: 3.93939e+11
Float:   3.33
Word:    Hello
Unsigned:        85

Int, Long, Double, Float, Word, Unsigned: 3 304938 393847473 6.66 bye -2

Int:     3
Long:    304938
Double: 3.93847e+08
Float:   6.66
Word:    bye
Unsigned: 4294967294
```

ANALYSIS Again, several variables are created, this time including a char array. The user is prompted for input and the output is faithfully printed.

On line 34, the user is prompted for all the input at once, and then each "word" of input is assigned to the appropriate variable. It is to facilitate this kind of multiple assignment that cin must consider each word in the input to be the full input for each variable. If cin was to consider the entire input to be part of one variable's input, this kind of concatenated input would be impossible.

Note that on line 42, the last object requested was an unsigned integer, but the user entered -2. Because cin believes it is writing to an unsigned integer, the bit pattern of -2 was evaluated as an unsigned integer, and when written out by cout, the value 4294967294 was displayed. The unsigned value 4294967294 has the exact bit pattern of the signed value -2.

Later in this lesson, you will see how to enter an entire string into a buffer, including multiple words. For now, the question arises, "How does the extraction operator manage this trick of concatenation?"

operator>> Returns a Reference to an istream Object

The return value of cin is a reference to an istream object. Because cin itself is an istream object, the return value of one extraction operation can be the input to the next extraction.

```
int VarOne, varTwo, varThree;
cout << "Enter three numbers: "
cin >> VarOne >> varTwo >> varThree;
```

When you write cin >> VarOne >> varTwo >> varThree;, the first extraction is evaluated (cin >> VarOne). The return value from this is another istream object, and that object's extraction operator gets the variable varTwo. It is as if you had written this:

```
((cin >> varOne) >> varTwo) >> varThree;
```

You will see this technique repeated later when cout is discussed.

Other Member Functions of cin

In addition to overloading operator>>, cin has a number of other member functions. These are used when finer control over the input is required.

Single Character Input

operator>> taking a character reference can be used to get a single character from the standard input. The member function get() can also be used to obtain a single character, and can do so in two ways: get() can be used with no parameters, in which case the return value is used, or it can be used with a reference to a character.

Using get() with No Parameters

The first form of get() is without parameters. This returns the value of the character found and will return EOF (end of file) if the end of the file is reached. get() with no parameters is not often used. It is not possible to concatenate this use of get() for multiple input because the return value is not an iostream object. Thus, the following will not work:

```
cin.get() >>myVarOne >> myVarTwo; //   illegal
```

The return value of `cin.get() >> myVarOne` is an integer, not an iostream object.

A common use of `get()` with no parameters is illustrated in Listing 16.4.

INPUT **LISTING 16.4** Using `get()` with No Parameters

```
1:   // Listing 16.4 - Using get() with no parameters
2:   #include <iostream.h>
3:
4:   int main()
5:   {
6:      char ch;
7:      while ( (ch = cin.get()) != EOF)
8:      {
9:         cout << "ch: " << ch << endl;
10:     }
11:     cout << "\nDone!\n";
12:   return 0;
13:   }
```

Note

On many platforms (such as DOS), you have to press the Enter key before any of the characters are echoed. Some platforms echo each character as entered.

To exit this program, you must send end of file from the keyboard. Under Linux, you use Ctrl+D; on DOS computers, use Ctrl+Z.

OUTPUT

```
Hello
ch: H
ch: e
ch: l
ch: l
ch: o
ch:

World
ch: W
ch: o
ch: r
ch: l
ch: d
ch:

 (ctrl-d)
Done!
```

ANALYSIS On line 6, a local character variable is declared. The `while` loop assigns the input received from `cin.get()` to `ch`, and if it is not EOF, the string is printed out. This output is buffered until an end of line is read, however. When EOF is encountered (when you press Ctrl+D under Linux , or Ctrl+Z on a DOS machine), the loop exits.

Note that not every implementation of `istream` supports this version of `get()`, although it is now part of the ANSI/ISO standard. Of course, the GNU compilers do.

Using `get()` with a Character Reference Parameter

16

When a character is passed as input to `get()`, that character is filled with the next character in the input stream. The return value is an `iostream` object, and so this form of `get()` can be concatenated, as illustrated in Listing 16.5.

INPUT **LISTING 16.5**   Using `get()` with Parameters

```
1:     // Listing 16.5 - Using get() with parameters
2:     #include <iostream.h>
3:
4:     int main()
5:     {
6:        char a, b, c;
7:
8:        cout << "Enter three letters: ";
9:
10:       cin.get(a).get(b).get(c);
11:
12:       cout << "a: " << a << "\nb: " << b << "\nc: " << c << endl;
13:    return 0;
14:    }
```

OUTPUT
```
Enter three letters: one
a: o
b: n
c: e
```

ANALYSIS On line 6, three character variables are created. On line 10, `cin.get()` is called three times, concatenated. First `cin.get(a)` is called. This puts the first letter into a and returns `cin` so that when it is done, `cin.get(b)` is called, putting the next letter into b. The end result of this is that `cin.get(c)` is called and the third letter is put in c.

Because `cin.get(a)` evaluates to `cin`, you could have written this:

`cin.get(a) >> b;`

In this form, `cin.get(a)` evaluates to `cin`, so the second phrase is `cin >> b;`.

Do	**Don't**
DO use the extraction operator (>>) when you need to skip over whitespace. **DO** use `get()` with a character parameter when you need to examine every character, including whitespace.	

Strings Input from the Standard Input Device

The extraction operator (>>) can be used to fill a character array, as can the member functions `get()` and `getline()`.

The final form of `get()` takes three parameters. The first parameter is a pointer to a character array, the second parameter is the maximum number of characters to read plus one, and the third parameter is the termination character. This is a good example of function overloading; depending on the arguments passed in the function call, the proper form of the function is selected.

If you enter 20 as the second parameter, `get()` will read 19 characters and then will null-terminate the string, which it will store in the first parameter. The third parameter, the termination character, defaults to a newline character (`'\n'`). If a termination character is reached before the maximum number of characters is read, a null is written and the termination character is left in the buffer.

Listing 16.6 illustrates the use of this form of `get()`.

INPUT   **LISTING 16.6**   Using `get()` with a Character Array

```
1:     // Listing 16.6 - Using get() with a character array
2:     #include <iostream.h>
3:
4:     int main()
5:     {
6:         char stringOne[256];
7:         char stringTwo[256];
8:
9:         cout << "Enter string one: ";
10:        cin.get(stringOne,256);
11:        cout << "stringOne: " << stringOne << endl;
12:
13:        cout << "Enter string two: ";
14:        cin >> stringTwo;
15:        cout << "StringTwo: " << stringTwo << endl;
16:     return 0;
17:     }
```

OUTPUT

```
Enter string one: Now is the time
stringOne: Now is the time
Enter string two: For all good
StringTwo: For
```

ANALYSIS On lines 6 and 7, two character arrays are created. On line 9, the user is prompted to enter a string, and `cin.get()` is called on line 10. The first parameter is the buffer to fill, and the second is one more than the maximum number for `get()` to accept (the extra position being given to the null character, (`'\0'`)). The defaulted third parameter is a newline character.

The user enters "Now is the time." Because the user ends the phrase with a newline character, that phrase is put into `stringOne`, followed by a terminating null.

The user is prompted for another string on line 13, and this time the extraction operator is used. Because the extraction operator takes everything up to the first whitespace, the string `For`, with a terminating null character, is stored in the second string, which, of course, is not what was intended.

Another way to solve this problem is to use `getline()`, as illustrated in Listing 16.7.

INPUT   **LISTING 16.7**   Using getline()

```
1:      // Listing 16.7 - Using getline()
2:      #include <iostream.h>
3:
4:      int main()
5:      {
6:          char stringOne[256];
7:          char stringTwo[256];
8:          char stringThree[256];
9:
10:         cout << "Enter string one: ";
11:         cin.getline(stringOne,256);
12:         cout << "stringOne: " << stringOne << endl;
13:
14:         cout << "Enter string two: ";
15:         cin >> stringTwo;
16:         cout << "stringTwo: " << stringTwo << endl;
17:
18:         cout << "Enter string three: ";
19:         cin.getline(stringThree,256);
20:         cout << "stringThree: " << stringThree << endl;
21:      return 0;
22:      }
```

16

OUTPUT

```
Enter string one: one two three
stringOne: one two three
Enter string two: four five six
stringTwo: four
Enter string three: stringThree: five six
```

ANALYSIS   This example warrants careful examination; it contains some potential surprises. On lines 6–8, three character arrays are declared.

On line 10, the user is prompted to enter a string, and that string is read by `getline()`. Like `get()`, `getline()` takes a buffer and a maximum number of characters. Unlike `get()`, however, `getline()` reads the terminating newline character and throws it away. With `get()`, the terminating newline character is not thrown away. It is left in the input buffer.

On line 14, the user is prompted again, and this time the extraction operator is used. The user enters "four five six" and the first word, four, is put in `stringTwo`. The string "Enter string three" is then displayed, and `getline()` is called again. Because "five six" is still in the input buffer, it is immediately read up to the newline character; `getline()` terminates and the string in `stringThree` is printed on line 20.

The user has no chance to enter string "three" because the second `getline()` call is fulfilled by the string remaining in the input buffer after the call to the extraction operator on line 15. There is no way for the user to ever enter string "three" because `stringTwo` ends when the Enter key is pressed, but the Enter key remains in the input buffer and immediately satisfies the second `getline()` call.

The extraction operator (>>) reads up to the first whitespace and puts the word into the character array.

The member function `get()` is overloaded. In one version, it takes no parameters and returns the value of the character it receives. In the second version, it takes a single character reference and returns the `istream` object by reference.

In the third and final version, `get()` takes a character array, a number of characters to get, and a termination character (which defaults to a newline character). This version of `get()` reads characters into the array until it gets to one fewer than its maximum number of characters or it encounters the termination character, whichever comes first. If `get()` encounters the termination character, it leaves that character in the input buffer and stops reading characters.

The member function `getline()` also takes three parameters: the buffer to fill, one more than the maximum number of characters to get, and the termination character. `getline()` functions the same as `get()` does with these parameters, except `getline()` throws away the terminating character.

cin.ignore() for Input Cleanup

At times, you want to ignore the remaining characters on a line until you hit either end of line (EOL) or end of file (EOF). The member function ignore() serves this purpose. ignore() takes two parameters: the maximum number of characters to ignore and the termination character. If you write ignore(80,'\n'), up to 80 characters will be thrown away until a newline character is found. The newline character is then thrown away and the ignore() statement ends. Listing 16.8 illustrates the use of ignore().

16

INPUT   **LISTING 16.8**   Using ignore()

```
1:     // Listing 16.8 - Using ignore()
2:     #include <iostream.h>
3:
4:     int main()
5:     {
6:        char stringOne[255];
7:        char stringTwo[255];
8:
9:        cout << "Enter string one:";
10:       cin.get(stringOne,255);
11:       cout << "String one: " << stringOne << endl;
12:
13:       cout << "Enter string two: ";
14:       cin.getline(stringTwo,255);
15:       cout << "String two: " << stringTwo << endl;
16:
17:       cout << "\n\nNow try again...\n";
18:
19:       cout << "Enter string one: ";
20:       cin.get(stringOne,255);
21:       cout << "String one: " << stringOne<< endl;
22:
23:       cin.ignore(255,'\n');
24:
25:       cout << "Enter string two: ";
26:       cin.getline(stringTwo,255);
27:       cout << "String Two: " << stringTwo<< endl;
28:    return 0;
29:    }
```

OUTPUT

```
Enter string one:once upon a time
String one: once upon a time
Enter string two: String two:

Now try again...
Enter string one: once upon a time
String one: once upon a time
Enter string two: there was a
String Two: there was a
```

On lines 6 and 7, two character arrays are created. On line 9, the user is prompted for input and types "once upon a time" and presses Enter. On line 10, get() is used to read this string. get() fills stringOne and terminates on the newline character, but leaves the newline character in the input buffer.

On line 13, the user is prompted again, but the getline() on line 14 reads the newline character that is already in the buffer and terminates immediately, before the user can enter any input.

On line 19, the user is prompted again and puts in the same first line of input. This time, however, on line 23, ignore() is used to "eat" the newline character. Thus, when the getline() call on line 26 is reached, the input buffer is empty, and the user can input the next line of the story.

peek() and putback()

The input object cin has two additional methods that can come in rather handy: peek(), which looks at but does not extract the next character, and putback(), which inserts a character into the input stream. Listing 16.9 illustrates how these might be used.

INPUT   **LISTING 16.9**   Using peek() and putback()

```
1:    // Listing 16.9 - Using peek() and putback()
2:    #include <iostream.h>
3:
4:    int main()
5:    {
6:       char ch;
7:       cout << "enter a phrase: ";
8:       while ( cin.get(ch) )
9:       {
10:         if (ch == '!')
11:            cin.putback('$');
12:         else
13:            cout << ch;
14:         while (cin.peek() == '#')
15:            cin.ignore(1,'#');
16:      }
17:    return 0;
18:    }
```

OUTPUT
```
enter a phrase: Now!is#the!time#for!fun#!
Now$isthe$timefor$fun$
```

ANALYSIS   On line 6, a character variable, ch, is declared, and on line 7, the user is prompted to enter a phrase. The purpose of this program is to turn any exclamation marks (!) into dollar signs ($) and to remove any pound symbols (#).

The program loops as long as it is getting characters other than the end of file (Ctrl+D under Linux, Ctrl+C or Ctrl+D on other operating systems). (Remember that `cin.get()` returns 0 for the end of the file). If the current character is an exclamation point, it is thrown away and the $ symbol is put back into the input buffer; it will be read the next time. If the current item is not an exclamation point, it is printed. The next character is "peeked" at, and when pound symbols are found, they are removed.

This example is not the most efficient way to do either of these things (and it will not find a pound symbol if it is the first character), but it does illustrate how these methods work. They are relatively obscure, so do not spend a lot of time worrying about when you might really use them. Put them into your bag of tricks; they will come in handy eventually.

 Tip

> `peek()` and `putback()` are typically used for parsing strings and other data, such as when writing a compiler.

Output with cout

You have used `cout` along with the overloaded insertion operator (<<) to write strings, integers, and other numeric data to the screen. It is also possible to format the data, aligning columns and writing the numeric data in decimal and hexadecimal form. This section shows you how.

Flushing the Output

You already saw that using `endl` will flush the output buffer. `endl` calls `cout`'s member function `flush()`, which writes all the data it is buffering. You can call the `flush()` method directly, either by calling the `flush()` member method or by writing the following:

```
cout << flush
```

This can be convenient when you need to ensure that the output buffer is emptied and that the contents are written to the screen.

Related Functions

Just as the extraction operator can be supplemented with `get()` and `getline()`, the insertion operator can be supplemented with `put()` and `write()`.

The function `put()` is used to write a single character to the output device. Because `put()` returns an `ostream` reference and because `cout` is an `ostream` object, you can concatenate `put()` the same as you do the insertion operator. Listing 16.10 illustrates this idea.

INPUT   **LISTING 16.10**   Using put()

```
1:      // Listing 16.10 - Using put()
2:      #include <iostream.h>
3:
4:      int main()
5:      {
6:         cout.put('H').put('e').put('l').put('l').put('o').put('\n');
7:      return 0;
8:      }
```

OUTPUT   Hello

Note   Some compilers (other than GNU) have trouble printing using this code. If
              your compiler will not print the word Hello, you may want to skip this listing.

ANALYSIS Line 6 is evaluated like this: cout.put('H') writes the letter H to the screen and
              returns the cout object. This leaves the following:

```
cout.put('e').put('l').put('l').put('o').put('\n');
```

The letter e is written, leaving cout.put('l'). This process repeats, each letter being
written and the cout object returned until the final character ('\n') is written and the
function returns.

The function write() works the same as the insertion operator (<<), except that it takes a
parameter that tells the function the maximum number of characters to write. Listing
16.11 illustrates its use.

INPUT   **LISTING 16.11**   Using write()

```
1:      // Listing 16.11 - Using write()
2:      #include <iostream.h>
3:      #include <string.h>
4:
5:      int main()
6:      {
7:         char One[] = "One if by land";
8:
9:
10:
11:        int fullLength = strlen(One);
12:        int tooShort = fullLength -4;
13:        int tooLong = fullLength + 6;
14:
```

```
15:     cout.write(One,fullLength) << "\n";
16:     cout.write(One,tooShort) << "\n";
17:     cout.write(One,tooLong) << "\n";
18:   return 0;
19:   }
```

OUTPUT

```
One if by land
One if by
One if by land i?!
```

16

 Note The last line of output may look different on your computer—really it is just garbage.

ANALYSIS On line 7, one phrase is created. On line 11, the integer `fullLength` is set to the length of the phrase, `tooShort` is set to that length minus four, and `tooLong` is set to `fullLength` plus six.

On line 15, the complete phrase is printed using `write()`. The length is set to the actual length of the phrase, and the correct phrase is printed.

On line 16, the phrase is printed again, but it is four characters shorter than the full phrase, and that is reflected in the output.

On line 17, the phrase is printed again, but this time `write()` is instructed to write an extra six characters. After the phrase is written, the next six bytes of contiguous memory are written.

Manipulators, Flags, and Formatting Instructions

The output stream maintains a number of state flags, determining which base (decimal or hexadecimal) to use, how wide to make the fields, and what character to use to fill in fields. A state flag is a byte whose individual bits are each assigned a special meaning. Manipulating bits in this way is discussed on Day 21, "What's Next." Each of `ostream`'s flags can be set using member functions and manipulators.

Using `cout.width()`

The default width of your output will be just enough space to print the number, character, or string in the output buffer. You can change this by using `width()`. Because `width()` is a member function, it must be invoked with a `cout` object. It only changes the width of the very next output field and then immediately reverts to the default. Listing 16.12 illustrates its use.

LISTING 16.12   Adjusting the Width of Output

```
 1:    // Listing 16.12 - Adjusting the width of output
 2:    #include <iostream.h>
 3:
 4:    int main()
 5:    {
 6:       cout << "Start >";
 7:       cout.width(25);
 8:       cout << 123 << "< End\n";
 9:
10:       cout << "Start >";
11:       cout.width(25);
12:       cout << 123<< "< Next >";
13:       cout << 456 << "< End\n";
14:
15:       cout << "Start >";
16:       cout.width(4);
17:       cout << 123456 << "< End\n";
18:
19:     return 0;
20:    }
```

```
Start >                    123< End
Start >                    123< Next >456< End
Start >123456< End
```

The first output, on lines 6–8, prints the number 123 within a field whose width is set to 25 on line 7. This is reflected in the first line of output.

The second line of output first prints the value 123 in the same field whose width is set to 25, and then prints the value 456. Note that 456 is printed in a field whose width is reset to just large enough; as stated, the effect of width() lasts only as long as the very next output.

The final output reflects that setting a width that is smaller than the output is the same as setting a width that is just large enough.

Setting the Fill Characters

Normally cout fills the empty field created by a call to width() with spaces, as shown in Listing 16.12. At times, you may want to fill the area with other characters, such as asterisks. To do this, you call fill() and pass in as a parameter the character you want used as a fill character. Listing 16.13 illustrates this.

LISTING 16.13 Using `fill()`

```
1:    // Listing 16.13 - fill()
2:
3:    #include <iostream.h>
4:
5:    int main()
6:    {
7:        cout << "Start >";
8:        cout.width(25);
9:        cout << 123 << "< End\n";
10:
11:
12:        cout << "Start >";
13:        cout.width(25);
14:        cout.fill('*');
15:        cout << 123 << "< End\n";
16:    return 0;
17:    }
```

16

```
Start >                  123< End
Start >******************123< End
```

Lines 7–9 repeat the functionality from the previous example. Lines 12–15 repeat this again, but this time, on line 14, the fill character is set to asterisks, as reflected in the output.

Setting `iostream` Flags

The `iostream` objects keep track of their state by using flags. You can set these flags by calling `setf()` and passing in one or another of the predefined enumerated constants.

Objects are said to have state when some or all of their data represents a condition that can change during the course of the program.

For example, you can set whether to show trailing zeros (so that 20.00 does not become truncated to 20). To turn trailing zeros on, call `setf(ios::showpoint)`.

The enumerated constants are scoped to the `iostream` class (`ios`) and thus are called with the full qualification `ios::flagname`, such as `ios::showpoint`.

You can turn on the plus sign (+) before positive numbers by using `ios::showpos`. You can change the alignment of the output by using `ios::left`, `ios::right`, or `ios::internal`.

Finally, you can set the base of the numbers for display by using `ios::dec` (decimal), `ios::oct` (octal—base eight), or `ios::hex` (hexadecimal—base sixteen). These flags can also be concatenated into the insertion operator. Listing 16.14 illustrates these settings.

As a bonus, Listing 16.14 also introduces the setw manipulator, which sets the width, but can also be concatenated with the insertion operator.

LISTING 16.14 Using setf

```
1:     // Listing 16.14 - Using setf
2:     #include <iostream.h>
3:     #include <iomanip.h>
4:
5:     int main()
6:     {
7:        const int number = 185;
8:        cout << "The number is " << number << endl;
9:
10:       cout << "The number is " << hex <<  number << endl;
11:
12:       cout.setf(ios::showbase);
13:       cout << "The number is " << hex <<  number << endl;
14:
15:       cout << "The number is " ;
16:       cout.width(10);
17:       cout << hex << number << endl;
18:
19:       cout << "The number is " ;
20:       cout.width(10);
21:       cout.setf(ios::left);
22:       cout << hex << number << endl;
23:
24:       cout << "The number is " ;
25:       cout.width(10);
26:       cout.setf(ios::internal);
27:       cout << hex << number << endl;
28:
29:       cout << "The number is:" << setw(10) << hex << number << endl;
30:       return 0;
31:    }
```

```
The number is 185
The number is b9
The number is 0xb9
The number is         0xb9
The number is 0xb9
The number is         0xb9
The number is:        0xb9
```

On line 7, the constant int number is initialized to the value 185. This is displayed on line 8.

The value is displayed again on line 10, but this time the manipulator hex is concatenated, causing the value to be displayed in hexadecimal form as b9. (The value b in hexadecimal form represents 11. Eleven times 16 equals 176; add the 9 for a total of 185.)

On line 12, the flag showbase is set. This causes the prefix 0x to be added to all hexadecimal numbers, as reflected in the output.

On line 16, the width is set to 10, and the value is pushed to the extreme right. On line 20, the width is again set to 10, but this time the alignment is set to the left, and the number is again printed flush left.

On line 25, again the width is set to 10, but this time the alignment is internal. Thus the 0x is printed flush left, but the value b9 is printed flush right.

Finally, on line 29, the concatenation operator setw() is used to set the width to 10, and the value is printed again.

Streams Versus the `printf()` Function

Most C++ implementations also provide the standard C I/O libraries, including the printf() statement. Although printf() is in some ways easier to use than cout, it is much less desirable.

printf() does not provide type safety, so it is easy to inadvertently tell it to display an integer as if it was a character, and vice versa. printf() also does not support classes, and so it is not possible to teach it how to print your class data; you must feed each class member to printf() one by one.

On the other hand, printf() does make formatting much easier because you can put the formatting characters directly into the printf() statement. Because printf() has its uses and many programmers still make extensive use of it, this section briefly reviews its use.

To use printf(), be sure to include the stdio.h header file. In its simplest form, printf() takes a formatting string as its first parameter and then a series of values as its remaining parameters.

The formatting string is a quoted string of text and conversion specifiers. All conversion specifiers must begin with the percent symbol (%). The common conversion specifiers are presented in Table 16.1.

TABLE 16.1   The Common Conversion Specifiers

Specifier	Used For
Â	Strings
Â	Integers
Â	Long integer
Â	Double
Â	Float

Each of the conversion specifiers can also provide a width statement and a precision statement, expressed as a float, where the digits to the left of the decimal are used for the total width, and the digits to the right of the decimal provide the precision for floats. Thus, `%5d` is the specifier for a 5-digit-wide integer, and `%15.5f` is the specifier for a 15-digit-wide `float`, of which the final five digits are dedicated to the decimal portion. Listing 16.15 illustrates various uses of `printf()`.

INPUT   **LISTING 16.15**   Printing with `printf()`

```
1:  #include <stdio.h>
2:  int main()
3:  {
4:      printf("%s","hello world\n");
5:
6:      char *phrase = "Hello again!\n";
7:      printf("%s",phrase);
8:
9:      int x = 5;
10:     printf("%d\n",x);
11:
12:     char *phraseTwo = "Here's some values: ";
13:     char *phraseThree = " and also these: ";
14:     int y = 7, z = 35;
15:     long longVar = 98456;
16:     float floatVar =  8.8f;
17:
18:     printf("%s %d %d %s %ld %f\n",phraseTwo,y,z,
    phraseThree,longVar,floatVar);
19:
20:     char *phraseFour = "Formatted: ";
21:     printf("%s %5d %10d  %10.5f\n",phraseFour,y,z,floatVar);
22:     return 0;
23: }
```

OUTPUT
```
hello world
Hello again!
5
```

```
Here's some values: 7 35  and also these: 98456 8.800000
Formatted:      7        35     8.800000
```

ANALYSIS The first `printf()` statement, on line 4, uses the standard form: the term `printf`, followed by a quoted string with a conversion specifier (in this case `%s`), followed by a value to insert into the conversion specifier.

The `%s` indicates that this is a string, and the value for the string is, in this case, the quoted string "hello world."

The second `printf()` statement is the same as the first, but this time a `char` pointer is used, rather than quoting the string right in place in the `printf()` statement.

The third `printf()`, on line 10, uses the integer conversion specifier, and for its value the integer variable x. The fourth `printf()` statement, on line 18, is more complex. Here six values are concatenated. Each conversion specifier is supplied, and then the values are provided, separated by commas.

Finally, on line 21, format specifications are used to specify width and precision. As you can see, all this is somewhat easier than using manipulators.

As stated previously, however, the limitation here is that no type checking occurs and `printf()` cannot be declared a friend or member function of a class. So if you want to print the various member data of a class, you must feed each accessor method to the `printf()` statement explicitly.

16

Frequently Asked Questions

FAQ: Can you summarize how I manipulate output?

Answer (with special thanks to Robert Francis): To format output in C++, you use a combination of special characters, output manipulators, and flags.

The following special characters are included in an output string being sent to Â using the insertion operator:

  \n—Newline character

  \r—Carriage return

  \t—Tab

  \\—Backslash

  \ddd (octal number)—ASCII character

  \a—Alarm (ring bell)

Example:

```
cout << "\aAn error occured\t"
```

Rings the bell, prints an error message, and moves to the next tab stop. Manipulators are used with the `cout` operator. Those manipulators that take arguments require that you include `iomanip.h` in your file.

The following is a list of manipulators that do *not* require `imanip.h`:

> `flush`—Flushes the output buffer

> `endl`—Inserts newline character and flushes the output buffer

> `oct`—Sets output base to octal

> `dec`—Sets output base to decimal

> `hex`—Sets output base to hexadecimal

The following is a list of manipulators that *do* require `imanip.h` `setbase(base)`—Sets output base (0 = decimal, 8 = octal, 10 = decimal, 16 = hex)

> `setw (width)`—Sets minimum output field width

> `setfill (ch)`—Fills character to be used when width is defined

> `setprecision (p)`—Sets precision for floating-point numbers

> `setiosflags (f)`—Sets one or more ios flags

> `resetiosflags (f)`—Resets one or more ios flags

Example:

> `cout << setw(12) << setfill('#') << hex << x << endl;`

sets the field width to 12, sets the fill character to `'#'`, specifies hex output, prints the value of `'x'`, puts a newline character in the buffer, and flushes the buffer. All the manipulators except `flush`, `enal`, and `setw` remain in effect until changed or until the end of the program. `setw` returns to the default after the current `cout`.

The following ios flags can be used with the `setiosflags` and `resetiosflags` manipulators:

> `ios::left`—Left-justifies output in specified width

> `ios::right`—Right-justifies output in specified width

> `ios::internal`—Sign is left-justified, value is right-justified

> `ios::dec`—Decimal output

> `ios::oct`—Octal output

> `ios::hex`—Hexadecimal output

> `ios::showbase`—Adds 0x to hexadecimal numbers, 0 to octal numbers

> `ios::showpoint`—Adds trailing zeros as required by precision

> `ios::uppercase`—Hex and scientific notation numbers shown in uppercase

> `ios::showpos`—The + sign shown for positive numbers

> `ios::scientific`—Shows floating point in scientific notation

> `ios::fixed`—Shows floating point in decimal notation

Additional information can be obtained from file `ios.h` and from the GNU library documentation.

File Input and Output

Streams provide a uniform way of dealing with data coming from the keyboard or the hard disk and going out to the screen or hard disk. In either case, you can use the insertion and extraction operators or the other related functions and manipulators. To open and close files, you create `ifstream` and `ofstream` objects (for input and output respectively) as described in the next few sections. Because `ifstream` objects are similar to `ofsteam` objects, the material covered is limited. Just apply `ofstream` techniques.

Using `ofstream`

The particular objects used to read from or write to files are called `ofstream` objects. These are derived from the `iostream` objects you already used.

To get started with writing to a file, you must first create an `ofstream` object, and then associate that object with a particular file on your disk. To use `ofstream` objects, you must be sure to include `fstream.h` in your program.

 Note

> Because `fstream.h` includes `iostream.h`, you do not need to include `iostream` explicitly.

Condition States

The `iostream` objects maintain flags that report on the state of your input and output. You can check each of these flags using the Boolean functions `eof()`, `bad()`, `fail()`, and `good()`. The function `eof()` returns `true` if the `iostream` object has encountered EOF, end of file. The function `bad()` returns `true` if you attempt an invalid operation. The function `fail()` returns `true` anytime `bad()` is `true` or an operation fails. Finally, the function `good()` returns `true` anytime all three of the other functions are `false`.

Opening Files for Input and Output

To open the file `myfile.cpp` with an `ofstream` object, declare an instance of an `ofstream` object and pass in the filename as a parameter:

```
ofstream fout("myfile.cpp");
```

Opening this file for input works the same way, except that it uses an `ifstream` object:

```
ifstream fin("myfile.cpp");
```

Note that `fout` and `fin` are names you assign; here `fout` has been used to reflect its similarity to `cout`, and `fin` has been used to reflect its similarity to `cin`.

One important file stream function that you will need right away is `close()`. Every file stream object you create opens a file for either reading or writing (or both). It is important to `close()` the file after you finish reading or writing; this ensures that the file will not be corrupted and that the data you wrote is flushed to the disk.

After the stream objects are associated with files, they can be used the same as any other stream objects. Listing 16.16 illustrates this.

INPUT   **LISTING 16.16**   Opening Files for Read and Write

```
1:    #include <fstream.h>
2:    int main()
3:    {
4:        char fileName[80];
5:        char buffer[255];     // for user input
6:        cout << "File name: ";
7:        cin >> fileName;
8:
9:        ofstream fout(fileName);  // open for writing
10:       fout << "This line written directly to the file...\n";
11:       cout << "Enter text for the file: ";
12:       cin.ignore(1,'\n');  // eat the newline after the file name
13:       cin.getline(buffer,255);  // get the user's input
14:       fout << buffer << "\n";   // and write it to the file
15:       fout.close();             // close the file, ready for reopen
16:
17:       ifstream fin(fileName);    // reopen for reading
18:       cout << "Here's the contents of the file:\n";
19:       char ch;
20:       while (fin.get(ch))
21:           cout << ch;
22:
23:       cout << "\n***End of file contents.***\n";
24:
25:       fin.close();              // always pays to be tidy
26:       return 0;
27:    }
```

OUTPUT

```
File name: test1
Enter text for the file: This text is written to the file!
Here's the contents of the file:
This line written directly to the file...
This text is written to the file!

***End of file contents.***
```

ANALYSIS   On line 4, a buffer is set aside for the filename, and on line 5, another buffer is set aside for user input. The user is prompted to enter a filename on line 6, and this response is written to the `fileName` buffer. On line 9, an `ofstream` object is created, fout, which is associated with the new filename. This opens the file; if the file already exists, its contents are thrown away.

On line 10, a string of text is written directly to the file. On line 11, the user is prompted for input. The newline character left over from the user's input of the filename is eaten on line 12, and the user's input is stored into buffer on line 13. That input is written to the file along with a newline character on line 14, and then the file is closed on line 15.

On line 17, the file is reopened, this time in input mode, and the contents are read, one character at a time, on lines 20 and 21.

Changing the Default Behavior of ofstream on Open

The default behavior upon opening a file is to create the file if it does not yet exist and to truncate the file (that is, delete all its contents) if it does exist. If you do not want this default behavior, you can explicitly provide a second argument to the constructor of your ofstream object.

Valid arguments include

- ios::app—Appends to the end of existing files rather than truncating them.
- ios::ate—Places you at the end of the file, but you can write data anywhere in the file.
- ios::trunc—The default. Causes existing files to be truncated.
- ios::nocreate—If the file does not exist, the open fails.
- ios::noreplace—If the file does already exist, the open fails.

Note that app is short for append; ate is short for at end, and trunc is short for truncate. Listing 16.17 illustrates using append by reopening the file from Listing 16.16 and appending to it.

INPUT **LISTING 16.17** Appending to the End of a File

```
1:     #include <fstream.h>
2:     int main()   // returns 1 on error
3:     {
4:         char fileName[80];
5:         char buffer[255];
6:         cout << "Please re-enter the file name: ";
7:         cin >> fileName;
8:
9:         ifstream fin(fileName);
10:        if (fin)                 // already exists?
11:        {
12:            cout << "Current file contents:\n";
```

continues

LISTING 16.17   CONTINUED

```
13:        char ch;
14:        while (fin.get(ch))
15:           cout << ch;
16:        cout << "\n***End of file contents.***\n";
17:     }
18:     fin.close();
19:
20:     cout << "\nOpening " << fileName << " in append mode...\n";
21:
22:     ofstream fout(fileName,ios::app);
23:     if (!fout)
24:     {
25:        cout << "Unable to open " << fileName << " for appending.\n";
26:        return(1);
27:     }
28:
29:     cout << "\nEnter text for the file: ";
30:     cin.ignore(1,'\n');
31:     cin.getline(buffer,255);
32:     fout << buffer << "\n";
33:     fout.close();
34:
35:     fin.open(fileName);  // reassign existing fin object!
36:     if (!fin)
37:     {
38:        cout << "Unable to open " << fileName << " for reading.\n";
39:        return(1);
40:     }
41:     cout << "\nHere's the contents of the file:\n";
42:     char ch;
43:     while (fin.get(ch))
44:        cout << ch;
45:     cout << "\n***End of file contents.***\n";
46:     fin.close();
47:     return 0;
48:  }
```

OUTPUT

```
Please re-enter the file name: test1
Current file contents:
This line written directly to the file...
This text is written to the file!

***End of file contents.***

Opening test1 in append mode...

Enter text for the file: More text for the file!
```

```
Here's the contents of the file:
This line written directly to the file...
This text is written to the file!
More text for the file!

***End of file contents.***
```

ANALYSIS The user is again prompted to enter the filename. This time an input file stream object is created on line 9. That open is tested on line 10, and if the file already exists, its contents are printed on lines 12–16. Note that if(fin) is synonymous with if (fin.good()).

The input file is then closed, and the same file is reopened, this time in append mode, on line 22. After this open (and every open), the file is tested to ensure that the file was opened properly. Note that if(!fout) is the same as testing if (fout.fail()). The user is then prompted to enter text, and the file is closed again on line 33.

Finally, as in Listing 16.16, the file is reopened in read mode; however, this time fin does not need to be redeclared. It is just reassigned to the same filename. Again the open is tested, on line 36, and if all is well, the contents of the file are printed to the screen, and the file is closed for the final time.

Do	**DON'T**
DO test each open of a file to ensure that it opened successfully.	**DON'T** try to close or reassign cin or cout.
DO reuse existing ifstream and ofstream objects.	
DO close all fstream objects when you are done using them.	

Binary Versus Text Files

Some operating systems, such as DOS, distinguish between text files and binary files. Text files store everything as text (as you might have guessed), so large numbers such as 54,325 are stored as a string of numerals ('5', '4', ',', '3', '2', '5'). This can be inefficient, but has the advantage that the text can be read and manipulated using the standard Linux commands like cat, more, vi, head, tail, grep, and so on, as well as simple programs such as the DOS type command.

To help the runtime library distinguish between text and binary files, C++ provides the ios::binary flag. On many systems, this flag is ignored because all data is stored in binary format. On some rather prudish systems, the ios::binary flag is illegal and will not compile—or even worse, is silently ignored.

Caution | Under Linux, the operating system views files as a stream of bytes—it is up to the programmers to impose structure on that stream in their programs. The GNU compiler under Linux handles the ios:binary flag properly. Under other operating systems, it may not.

Binary files can store not only integers and strings, but also entire data structures. You can write all the data at one time by using the write() method of fstream.

If you use write(), you can recover the data using read(). Each of these functions expects a pointer to character, however, so you must cast the address of your class to be a pointer to character.

The second argument to these functions is the number of characters to write, which you can determine using sizeof(). Note that what is being written is the data, not the methods. What is recovered is only data. Listing 16.18 illustrates writing the contents of a class to a file.

INPUT   **LISTING 16.18**   Writing a Class to a File

```
1:     #include <fstream.h>
2:
3:     class Animal
4:     {
5:     public:
6:         Animal(int weight, long days):itsWeight(weight),
itsNumberDaysAlive(days){}
7:         ~Animal(){}
8:
9:         int GetWeight()const { return itsWeight; }
10:        void SetWeight(int weight) { itsWeight = weight; }
11:
12:        long GetDaysAlive()const { return  itsNumberDaysAlive; }
13:        void SetDaysAlive(long days) { itsNumberDaysAlive = days; }
14:
15:    private:
16:        int itsWeight;
17:        long itsNumberDaysAlive;
18:    };
19:
20:    int main()    // returns 1 on error
21:    {
22:        char fileName[80];
23:
24:
25:        cout << "Please enter the file name: ";
```

```
26:        cin >> fileName;
27:        ofstream fout(fileName,ios::binary);
28:        if (!fout)
29:        {
30:           cout << "Unable to open " << fileName << " for writing.\n";
31:           return(1);
32:        }
33:
34:        Animal Bear(50,100);
35:        fout.write((char*) &Bear,sizeof Bear);
36:
37:        fout.close();
38:
39:        ifstream fin(fileName,ios::binary);
40:        if (!fin)
41:        {
42:           cout << "Unable to open " << fileName << " for reading.\n";
43:           return(1);
44:        }
45:
46:        Animal BearTwo(1,1);
47:
48:        cout << "BearTwo weight: " << BearTwo.GetWeight() << endl;
49:        cout << "BearTwo days: " << BearTwo.GetDaysAlive() << endl;
50:
51:        fin.read((char*) &BearTwo, sizeof BearTwo);
52:
53:        cout << "BearTwo weight: " << BearTwo.GetWeight() << endl;
54:        cout << "BearTwo days: " << BearTwo.GetDaysAlive() << endl;
55:        fin.close();
56:        return 0;
57:    }
```

OUTPUT

```
Please enter the file name: Animals
BearTwo weight: 1
BearTwo days: 1
BearTwo weight: 50
BearTwo days: 1005
```

ANALYSIS On lines 3–18, a stripped-down Animal class is declared. On lines 22–32, a file is created and opened for output in binary mode. An animal whose weight is 50 and who is 100 days old is created on line 34, and its data is written to the file on line 35.

The file is closed on line 37 and reopened for reading in binary mode on line 39. A second animal is created, on line 46, whose weight is 1 and who is only one day old. The data from the file is read into the new animal object on line 51, wiping out the existing data and replacing it with the data from the file.

Command-Line Processing

Many operating systems, such as DOS and UNIX, enable the user to pass parameters to your program when the program starts. These are called command-line options and are typically separated by spaces on the command line. For example:

```
SomeProgram Param1 Param2 Param3
```

These parameters are not passed to `main()` directly. Instead, every program's `main()` function is passed two parameters. The first is an integer count of the number of arguments on the command line. The program name itself is counted, so every program has at least one parameter. The example of a command line shown previously has four. (The name `SomeProgram` plus the three parameters make a total of four command-line arguments.)

The second parameter passed to `main()` is an array of pointers to character strings. Because an array name is a constant pointer to the first element of the array, you can declare this argument to be a pointer to a pointer to `char`, a pointer to an array of `char`, or an array of arrays of `char`.

Typically, the first argument is called `argc` (argument count), but you may call it anything you like. The second argument is often called `argv` (argument vector), but again this is just a convention.

It is common to test `argc` to ensure that you received the expected number of arguments and to use `argv` to access the strings themselves. Note that `argv[0]` is the name of the program, and `argv[1]` is the first parameter to the program, represented as a string. If your program takes two numbers as arguments, you will need to translate these numbers to strings. On Day 21 you will see how to use the standard library conversions. Listing 16.19 illustrates how to use the command-line arguments.

INPUT   **LISTING 16.19**   Using Command-line Arguments

```
1:    #include <iostream.h>
2:    int main(int argc, char **argv)
3:    {
4:       cout << "Received " << argc << " arguments...\n";
5:       for (int i=0; i<argc; i++)
6:          cout << "argument " << i << ": " << argv[i] << endl;
7:    return 0;
8:    }
```

```
TestProgram  Teach Yourself C++ In 21 Days
Received 7 arguments...
argument 0: TestProgram.exe
```

```
argument 1: Teach
argument 2: Yourself
argument 3: C++
argument 4: In
argument 5: 21
argument 6: Days
```

Note

> This works best when run from a command line. If you are using a GUI inter-
> face like K Desktop Environment (KDE), you need to open a terminal session.
> If you are using an operating system other than Linux, you may need to
> either run this code from the command line (that is, from a DOS box) or you
> must set the command-line parameters in your compiler (see your compiler
> documentation).

ANALYSIS The function `main()` declares two arguments: `argc` is an integer that contains the count of command-line arguments, and `argv` is a pointer to the array of strings. Each string in the array pointed to by `argv` is a command-line argument. Note that `argv` could have easily been declared as `char *argv[]` or `char argv[][]`. It is a matter of programming style how you declare `argv`; even though this program declared it as a pointer to a pointer, array offsets were still used to access the individual strings.

On line 4, `argc` is used to print the number of command-line arguments: seven in all, counting the program name itself.

On lines 5 and 6, each of the command-line arguments is printed, passing the null-terminated strings to `cout` by indexing into the array of strings.

A more common use of command-line arguments is illustrated in Listing 16.20 by modifying the code from Listing 16.18 to take the filename as a command-line argument.

INPUT **LISTING 16.20** Using Command-line Arguments

```
1:    #include <fstream.h>
2:
3:    class Animal
4:    {
5:    public:
6:        Animal(int weight, long days):itsWeight(weight),
       ➥itsNumberDaysAlive(days){}
7:        ~Animal(){}
8:
9:        int GetWeight()const { return itsWeight; }
10:       void SetWeight(int weight) { itsWeight = weight; }
```

continues

LISTING **16.20**   CONTINUED

```
11:
12:        long GetDaysAlive()const { return  itsNumberDaysAlive; }
13:        void SetDaysAlive(long days) { itsNumberDaysAlive = days; }
14:
15:    private:
16:       int itsWeight;
17:       long itsNumberDaysAlive;
18:    };
19:
20:     int main(int argc, char *argv[])    // returns 1 on error
21:     {
22:       if (argc != 2)
23:       {
24:          cout << "Usage: " << argv[0] << " <filename>" << endl;
25:          return(1);
26:       }
27:
28:       ofstream fout(argv[1],ios::binary);
29:       if (!fout)
30:       {
31:          cout << "Unable to open " << argv[1] << " for writing.\n";
32:          return(1);
33:       }
34:
35:       Animal Bear(50,100);
36:       fout.write((char*) &Bear,sizeof Bear);
37:
38:       fout.close();
39:
40:       ifstream fin(argv[1],ios::binary);
41:       if (!fin)
42:       {
43:          cout << "Unable to open " << argv[1] << " for reading.\n";
44:          return(1);
45:       }
46:
47:       Animal BearTwo(1,1);
48:
49:       cout << "BearTwo weight: " << BearTwo.GetWeight() << endl;
50:       cout << "BearTwo days: " << BearTwo.GetDaysAlive() << endl;
51:
52:       fin.read((char*) &BearTwo, sizeof BearTwo);
53:
54:       cout << "BearTwo weight: " << BearTwo.GetWeight() << endl;
55:       cout << "BearTwo days: " << BearTwo.GetDaysAlive() << endl;
56:       fin.close();
57:       return 0;
58:     }
```

OUTPUT
```
BearTwo weight: 1
BearTwo days: 1
BearTwo weight: 50
BearTwo days: 100s
```

ANALYSIS The declaration of the Animal class is the same as in Listing 16.18. This time, however, rather than prompting the user for the filename, command-line arguments are used. On line 2, main() is declared to take two parameters: the count of the command-line arguments and a pointer to the array of command-line argument strings.

On lines 22–26, the program ensures that the expected number of arguments (exactly two) is received. If the user fails to supply a single filename, an error message is printed:

```
Usage TestProgram <filename>
```

Then the program exits. Note that by using argv[0] rather than hard-coding a program name, you can compile this program to have any name, and this usage statement will work automatically.

On line 28, the program attempts to open the supplied filename for binary output. No reason exists to copy the filename into a local temporary buffer. It can be used directly by accessing argv[1].

This technique is repeated on line 40 when the same file is reopened for input, and it is used in the error condition statements when the files cannot be opened, on lines 25 and 31.

Summary

Today streams were introduced, and the global objects cout and cin were described. The goal of the istream and ostream objects is to encapsulate the work of writing to device drivers and buffering input and output.

Four standard stream objects are created in every program: cout, cin, cerr, and clog. Each of these can be "redirected" by many operating systems.

The istream object cin is used for input, and its most common use is with the overloaded extraction operator (>>). The ostream object cout is used for output, and its most common use is with the overloaded insertion operator (<<).

Each of these objects has a number of other member functions, such as get() and put(). Because the common forms of each of these methods returns a reference to a stream object, it is easy to concatenate each of these operators and functions.

The state of the stream objects can be changed by using manipulators. These can set the formatting and display characteristics and various other attributes of the stream objects.

16

File I/O can be accomplished by using the `fstream` classes, which derive from the stream classes. In addition to supporting the normal insertion and extraction operators, these objects also support `read()` and `write()` for storing and retrieving large binary objects.

Q&A

Q How do you know when to use the insertion and extraction operators and when to use the other member functions of the stream classes?

A In general, it is easier to use the insertion and extraction operators, and they are preferred when their behavior is what is needed. In those unusual circumstances when these operators don't do the job (such as reading in a string of words), the other functions can be used.

Q What is the difference between `cerr` and `clog`?

A `cerr` is not buffered. Everything written to `cerr` is immediately written out. This is fine for errors that are written to the screen, but it may have a performance cost that is too high for writing logs to disk. `clog` buffers its output, and thus can be more efficient.

Q Why were streams created if `printf()` works well?

A `printf()` does not support the strong type system of C++, and it does not support user-defined classes.

Q When would you ever use `putback()`?

A When one read operation is used to determine whether a character is valid, but a different read operation (perhaps by a different object) needs the character to be in the buffer. This is most often used when parsing a file; for example, the C++ compiler might use `putback()`.

Q When would you use `ignore()`?

A A common use of this is after using `get()`. Because `get()` leaves the terminating character in the buffer, it is not uncommon to immediately follow a call to `get()` with a call to `ignore(1,'\n');`. This is often used in parsing.

Q My friends use `printf()` in their C++ programs. Can I?

A Sure. You'll gain some convenience, but you'll sacrifice type safety.

Workshop

The Workshop contains quiz questions to help solidify your understanding of the material covered and exercises to provide you with experience in using what you learned. Try to answer the quiz and exercise questions before checking the answers in Appendix D, "Answers to Exercises and Quizzes," and make sure you understand the answers before going to the next day.

Quiz

1. What is the insertion operator, and what does it do?
2. What is the extraction operator, and what does it do?
3. What are the three forms of `cin.get()`, and what are their differences?
4. What is the difference between `cin.read()` and `cin.getline()`?
5. What is the default width for outputting a long integer using the insertion operator?
6. What is the return value of the insertion operator?
7. What parameter does the constructor to an `ofstream` object take?
8. What does the `ios::ate` argument do?

Exercises

1. Write a program that writes to the four standard iostream objects: `cin`, `cout`, `cerr`, and `clog`.
2. Write a program that prompts the user to enter her full name and then displays it on the screen.
3. Rewrite Listing 16.9 to do the same thing, but without using `putback()` or `ignore()`.
4. Write a program that takes a filename as a parameter and opens the file for reading. Read every character of the file and display only the letters and punctuation to the screen. (Ignore all nonprinting characters.) Then close the file and exit.
5. Write a program that displays its command-line arguments in reverse order and does not display the program name.

DAY **17**

Namespaces

A new addition to ANSI C++ is the use of namespaces to help programmers avoid name clashes when using more than one library. Today you will learn:

- How functions and classes are resolved by name
- How to create a namespace
- How to use a namespace
- How to use the standard namespace `std`

Getting Started with Namespaces

Name conflicts have been a source of aggravation to both C and C++ developers. The ANSI standardization offered a chance to resolve this problem through the use of *namespaces,* but be warned: Not all compilers support this feature yet. g++ 2.9.5 and newer do support this feature. g++ version 2.7.2 is one of those that does not really support it and will give you the following message:

```
warning: namespaces are mostly broken in this version of g++
```

A name clash happens when a duplicate name with matching scope is found in two parts of your program. The most common occurrence can be found in different library packages. For example, a container class library will most certainly declare and implement a List class. (You will learn more about container classes on Day 19, "Templates.")

It is not a surprise to find a List class also being used in a windowing library. Suppose that you want to maintain a list of windows for your application, or assume that you are using the List class found in the container class library. You declare an instance of the window library's List to hold your windows, and you discover that the member functions you want to call are not available. The compiler has matched your List declaration to the List container in the standard library, but what you really want is the List found in the vendor-specific window library.

Namespaces are used to partition the global namespace and to eliminate, or at least reduce, name conflicts. Namespaces are similar in some ways to classes, and the syntax is very similar.

Items declared within the namespace are owned by the namespace. All items within a namespace have public visibility. Namespaces can be nested within other namespaces. Functions can be defined within the body of the namespace or defined outside the body of the namespace. If a function is defined outside the body of the namespace, it must be qualified by the namespace's name.

Resolving Functions and Classes by Name

As it parses source code and builds a list of function and variable names, the compiler checks for name conflicts. Those conflicts that cannot be resolved by the compiler might be resolved by the linker.

The compiler cannot check for name clashes across translation units (for example, object files); that is the purpose of the linker. Thus, the compiler will not even offer a warning.

It is not uncommon for the linker (ld under Linux) to fail with the message *Identifier* multiply defined (*identifier* is some named type). You see this linker message if you have defined the same name with the same scope in different translation units. You get a compiler error if you redefine a name within a single file having the same scope. The following example, when compiled and linked, will produce an error message by the linker:

```
// file first.cpp
int integerValue = 0 ;
int main( ) {
    int integerValue = 0 ;
    // . . .
```

```
    return 0 ;
} ;

// file second.cpp
int integerValue = 0 ;
// end of second.cpp
```

The GNU linker announces the following diagnostic messages:

```
second.cc: multiple definition of `integerValue'
first.cc: first defined here
```

If these names were in a different scope, the compiler and linker would not complain.

It is also possible to receive a warning from the compiler concerning *identifier hiding*. The compiler should warn, in first.cpp, that integerValue in main() is hiding the global variable with the same name.

To use the integerValue declared outside main(), you must explicitly scope the variable to global scope. Consider this example, which assigns the value 10 to the integerValue outside main() and not to the integerValue declared within main():

```
// file first.cpp
int integerValue = 0 ;
int main( )
{
    int integerValue = 0 ;
    ::integerValue = 10 ; //assign to global "integerValue"
    // . . .
    return 0 ;
} ;

// file second.cpp
int integerValue = 0 ;
// end of second.cpp
```

> **Note**
>
> Note the use of the scope resolution operator : :, indicating that the integerValue being referred to is global, not local.

The problem with the two global integers defined outside of any functions is that they have the same name and visibility, and thus will cause a linker error.

Note

The term *visibility* is used to designate the scope of a defined object, whether it is a variable, a class, or a function. For example, a variable declared and defined outside any function has *file*, or *global*, scope. The visibility of this variable is from the point of its definition through the end of the file. A variable having a *block*, or *local*, scope is found within a block structure. The most common examples are variables defined within functions. The following example shows the scope of variables.

```
int globalScopeInt  = 5 ;
void f( )
{
    int localScopeInt = 10 ;
}
int main( )
{
    int localScopeInt = 15 ;
    {
        int anotherLocal = 20 ;
        int localScopeInt = 30 ;
    }
    return 0 ;
}
```

The first int definition, globalScopeInt, is visible within the functions f() and main(). The next definition is found within the function f() and is named localScopeInt. This variable has local scope, meaning that it is visible only within the block defining it.

The main() function cannot access f()'s localScopeInt. When the function returns, localScopeInt goes out of scope. The third definition, also named localScopeInt, is found in the main() function. This variable has block scope.

Note that main()'s localScopeInt does not conflict with f()'s localScopeInt. The next two definitions, anotherLocal and localScopeInt, both have block scope. As soon as the execution of the program reaches the closing brace, these two variables lose their visibility.

Notice that this localScopeInt is hiding the localScopeInt defined just before the opening brace (the second localScopeInt defined in the program). When the program moves past the closing brace, the second localScopeInt defined resumes visibility. Any change made to the localScopeInt defined within the braces does not affect the contents of the outer localScopeInt.

> **Note**
>
> Names can have *internal* and *external linkage*. These two terms refer to the use or availability of a name across multiple translation units or within a single translation unit. Any name having internal linkage can only be referred to within the translation unit in which it is defined. For example, a variable defined to have internal linkage can be shared by functions within the same translation unit. Names having external linkage are available to other translation units. The following example demonstrates internal and external linkage.

```
// file: first.cpp
int externalInt = 5 ;
const int j = 10 ;
int main()
{
    return 0 ;
}

// file: second.cpp
extern int externalInt ;
int anExternalInt = 10 ;
const int j = 10 ;
```

The `externalInt` variable defined in `first.cpp` has external linkage. Although it is defined in `first.cpp`, `second.cpp` can also access it. The two `j`s found in both files are `const` and thus by default have internal linkage. You can override the `const` default by providing an explicit declaration, as shown here:

```
// file: first.cpp
extern const int j = 10 ;

// file: second.cpp
extern const int j ;
#include <iostream>
int main()
{
    std::cout << "j is " << j << std::endl ;
    return 0 ;
}
```

Note that this example calls `cout` with the namespace designation of `std`; this allows you to refer to all the "standard" objects in the ANSI standard library. When built, this example displays the following:

```
j is 10
```

The standards committee deprecates the following type of usage:

```
static int staticInt = 10 ;
int main()
{
    //...
}
```

The use of static to limit the scope of external variables is no longer recommended and may eventually become illegal. You should now use namespaces instead of static.

Do	Don't
DO use namespaces instead of the static keyword.	DON'T apply the static keyword to a variable defined at file scope.

Creating a Namespace

The syntax for a namespace declaration is similar to the syntax for a struct or class declaration: First, apply the keyword namespace followed by an optional namespace name, and then an opening curly brace. The namespace is concluded with a closing brace but no terminating semicolon.

Here is an example:

```
namespace Window
{
    void move( int x, int y) ;
}
```

The name Window uniquely identifies the namespace. You can have many occurrences of a named namespace. These multiple occurrences can occur within a single file or across multiple translation units. The C++ standard library namespace, std, is a prime example of this feature. This makes sense because the standard library is a logical grouping of functionality.

The main concept behind namespaces is to group related items into a specified (named) area. The following is a brief example of a namespace that spans multiple header files:

```
// header1.h
namespace Window
{
    void move( int x, int y) ;
}

// header2.h
```

```
namespace Window
{
    void resize( int x, int y ) ;
}
```

Declaring and Defining Types

You can declare and define types and functions within namespaces. Of course, this is a design and maintenance issue. Good design dictates that you should separate interface from implementation. You should follow this principle not only with classes but also with namespaces. The following example demonstrates a cluttered and poorly defined namespace:

```
namespace Window {
    // . . . other declarations and variable definitions.
    void move( int x, int y) ; // declarations
    void resize( int x, int y ) ;
    // . . . other declarations and variable definitions.

    void move( int x, int y )
    {
        if( x < MAX_SCREEN_X  && x > 0 )
            if( y < MAX_SCREEN_Y  && y > 0 )
                platform.move( x, y ) ; // specific routine
    }

    void resize( int x, int y )
    {
        if( x < MAX_SIZE_X  && x > 0 )
            if( y < MAX_SIZE_Y  && y > 0 )
                platform.resize( x, y ) ; // specific routine
    }
    // . . . definitions continue
}
```

You can see how quickly the namespace becomes cluttered! The previous example is approximately 20 lines in length; imagine if this namespace were four times longer.

Defining Functions Outside a Namespace

You should define namespace functions outside the namespace body. Doing so illustrates a clear separation of the declaration of the function and its definition—and also keeps the namespace body uncluttered. Separating the function definition from the namespace also enables you to put the namespace and its embodied declarations within a header file; the definitions can be placed into an implementation file.

17

Here is an example:

```
// file header.h
namespace Window {
    void move( int x, int y) ;
    // other declarations …
}

// file impl.cpp
void Window::move( int x, int y )
{
    // code to move the window
}
```

Adding New Members

New members can be added to a namespace only within its body. You cannot define new members using qualifier syntax. The most you can expect from this style of definition is a complaint from your compiler. The following example demonstrates this error:

```
namespace Window {
    // lots of declarations
}
//…some code
int Window::newIntegerInNamespace ; // sorry, can't do this
```

The preceding line of code is illegal. Your (conforming) compiler will issue a diagnostic reflecting the error. To correct the error—or avoid it altogether—move the declaration within the namespace body.

All members within a namespace are public. The following code does not compile:

```
namespace Window {
    private:
        void move( int x, int y ) ;
}
```

Nesting Namespaces

A namespace can be nested within another namespace. The reason they can be nested is because the definition of a namespace is also a declaration. As with any other namespace, you must qualify a name using the enclosing namespace. If you have nested namespaces, you must qualify each namespace in turn. For example, the following shows a named namespace nested within another named namespace:

```
namespace Window {
    namespace Pane {
        void size( int x, int y ) ;
    }
}
```

To access the function `size()` outside of `Window`, you must qualify the function with both enclosing namespace names. The following code demonstrates the qualification:

```
int main( )
{
    Window::Pane::size( 10, 20 ) ;
    return 0 ;
}
```

Using a Namespace

Now take a look at an example of using a namespace and the associated use of the scope resolution operator. The code first declares all types and functions for use within the namespace `Window`. After defining everything required, the example then defines any member functions declared. These member functions are defined outside of the namespace; the names are explicitly identified using the scope resolution operator. Listing 17.1 illustrates using a namespace.

INPUT   **LISTING 17.1**   Using a Namespace

```
1: #include <iostream>
2: // Listing 17.1 Using a Namespace
3: namespace Window
4: {
5:     const int MAX_X = 30 ;
6:     const int MAX_Y = 40 ;
7:     class Pane
8:     {
9:         public:
10:             Pane() ;
11:             ~Pane() ;
12:             void size( int x, int y ) ;
13:             void move( int x, int y ) ;
14:             void show( ) ;
15:         private:
16:             static int cnt ;
17:             int x ;
18:             int y ;
19:     };
20: }
21:
22: int Window::Pane::cnt = 0 ;
23: Window::Pane::Pane() : x(0), y(0) { }
24: Window::Pane::~Pane() { }
```

continues

LISTING 17.1 CONTINUED

```
25:
26: void Window::Pane::size( int x, int y )
27: {
28:     if( x < Window::MAX_X  &&  x > 0 )
29:         Pane::x = x ;
30:     if( y < Window::MAX_Y  &&  y > 0 )
31:         Pane::y = y ;
32: }
33: void Window::Pane::move( int x, int y )
34: {
35:     if( x < Window::MAX_X  &&  x > 0 )
36:         Pane::x = x ;
37:     if( y < Window::MAX_Y  &&  y > 0 )
38:         Pane::y = y ;
39: }
40: void Window::Pane::show( )
41: {
42:     std::cout << "x " << Pane::x ;
43:     std::cout << " y " << Pane::y << std::endl ;
44: }
45:
46: int main( )
47: {
48:     Window::Pane pane ;
49:
50:     pane.move( 20, 20 ) ;
51:     pane.show( ) ;
52:
53:     return 0 ;
54: }
```

OUTPUT x 20 y 20

ANALYSIS Note that class `Pane` is nested inside the namespace `Window`. This is the reason you have to qualify the name `Pane` with the `Window::` qualifier.

The static variable `cnt`, which is declared in `Pane` on line 16, is defined as usual. Within the function `Pane::size()` on lines 26–32, notice that `MAX_X` and `MAX_Y` are fully qualified. This is because `Pane` is in scope; otherwise, the compiler would issue an error diagnostic. This also holds true for the function `Pane::move()`.

If you compile this code with g++ version 2.7.2, you will get the following message:

```
warning: namespaces are mostly broken in this version of g++
```

The only solution is to use a newer version that supports the namespaces.

Also interesting is the qualification of `Pane::x` and `Pane::y` inside both function definitions. Why is this? Well, if the function `Pane::move()` were written like this, you would have a problem:

```
void Window::Pane::move( int x, int y )
{
    if( x < Window::MAX_X  &&  x > 0 )
        x = x ;
    if( y < Window::MAX_Y  &&  y > 0 )
        y = y ;
    Platform::move( x, y ) ;
}
```

Can you spot the issue? You probably will not get much of an answer from your compiler; some do not issue any kind of diagnostic message at all.

The source of the problem is the function's arguments. Arguments x and y hide the private x and y instance variables declared within class `Pane`. Effectively, the statements assign both x and y to itself:

```
x = x ;
y = y ;
```

Introducing the `using` Keyword

The `using` keyword is used for both the `using` directive and the `using` declaration. The syntax of the `using` keyword determines whether the context is a directive or a declaration.

The `using` Directive

The `using` directive effectively exposes all names declared in a namespace to be in the current scope. You can refer to the names without qualifying them with their respective namespace name. The following example shows the `using` directive:

```
namespace Window {
    int value1 = 20 ;
    int value2 = 40 ;
}
. . .
Window::value1 = 10 ;

using namespace Window ;
value2 = 30 ;
```

The scope of the `using` directive begins at its declaration and continues on to the end of the current scope. Notice that `value1` must be qualified in order to reference it. The variable `value2` does not require the qualification because the directive introduces all names in a namespace into the current scope.

The `using` directive can be used at any level of scope. This enables you to use the directive within block scope; when that block goes out of scope, so do all the names within the namespace. The following sample shows this behavior:

```
namespace Window {
    int value1 = 20 ;
    int value2 = 40 ;
}
//. . .
void f()
{
    {
        using namespace Window ;
        value2 = 30 ;
    }
    value2 = 20 ; //error!
}
```

The last line of code in `f()`, `value2 = 20 ;` is an error because `value2` is not defined. The name is accessible in the previous block because the directive pulls the name into that block. When that block goes out of scope, so do the names in namespace `Window`.

Variable names declared within a local scope hide any namespace names introduced in that scope. This behavior is similar to how a local variable hides a global variable. Even if you introduce a namespace after a local variable, that local variable will hide the namespace name. The following example shows this:

```
namespace Window {
    int value1 = 20 ;
    int value2 = 40 ;
}
//. . .
void f()
{
    int value2 = 10 ;
    using namespace Window ;
    std::cout << value2 << std::endl ;
}
```

The output of this function is `10`, not `40`. This output confirms the fact that the `value2` in namespace `Window` is hidden by the `value2` in `f()`. If you need to use a name within a namespace, you must qualify the name with the namespace name.

An ambiguity can arise using a name that is both globally defined and defined within a namespace. The ambiguity surfaces only if the name is used, and not just when a namespace is introduced. This is demonstrated in the following code fragment:

```
namespace Window {
    int value1 = 20 ;
}
//. . .
using namespace Window ;
int value1 = 10 ;
void f( )
{
    value1 = 10 ;
}
```

The ambiguity occurs within function f(). The directive effectively brings Window::value1 into the global namespace; because a value1 is already globally defined, the use of value1 in f() is an error. Note that if the line of code in f() were removed, no error would exist.

The using Declaration

The using declaration is similar to the using directive except that the declaration provides a finer level of control. More specifically, the using declaration is used to declare a specific name (from a namespace) to be in the current scope. You can then refer to the specified object by its name only. The following example demonstrates the use of the using declaration:

```
namespace Window {
    int value1 = 20 ;
    int value2 = 40 ;
    int value3 = 60 ;
}
//. . .
using Window::value2 ; //bring value2 into current scope
Window::value1 = 10 ;   //value1 must be qualified
value2 = 30 ;
Window::value3 = 10 ;   //value3 must be qualified
```

The using declaration adds the specified name to the current scope. The declaration does not affect the other names within the namespace. In the previous example, value2 is referenced without qualification, but value1 and value3 require qualification. The using declaration provides more control over namespace names that you bring into a scope. This is in contrast with the directive that brings all names in a namespace into scope.

17

After a name is brought into a scope, it is visible until the end of that scope. This behavior is the same as any other declaration. A using declaration may be used in the global namespace or within any local scope.

It is an error to introduce a name into a local scope where a namespace name has been declared. The reverse is also true. The following example shows this:

```
namespace Window {
    int value1 = 20 ;
    int value2 = 40 ;
}
//. . .
void f()
{
   int value2 = 10 ;
   using Window::value2 ; // multiple declaration
   std::cout << value2 << std::endl  ;
}
```

The second line in function f() will produce a compiler error because the name value2 is already defined. The same error occurs if the using declaration is introduced before the definition of the local value2.

Any name introduced at local scope with a using declaration hides any name outside that scope. The following code snippet demonstrates this behavior:

```
namespace Window {
    int value1 = 20 ;
    int value2 = 40 ;
}
int value2 = 10 ;
//. . .
void f()
{
    using Window::value2 ;
    std::cout << value2 << std::endl  ;
}
```

The using declaration in f() hides the value2 defined in the global namespace.

As mentioned earlier, a using declaration gives you finer control over the names introduced from a namespace. A using directive brings all names from a namespace into the current scope. It is preferable to use a declaration over a directive because a directive effectively defeats the purpose of the namespace mechanism. A declaration is more definitive because you are explicitly identifying the names you want to introduce into a scope. A using declaration will not pollute the global namespace, as is the case with a using directive (unless, of course, you declare all names found in the namespace). Name hiding, global namespace pollution, and ambiguity all are reduced to a more manageable level by using the using declaration.

Using Namespace Alias

A namespace *alias* is designed to provide another name for a named namespace. An alias provides a shorthand term for you to use to refer to a namespace. This is especially true if a namespace name is very long; creating an alias can help cut down on lengthy, repetitive typing. Look at this example:

```
namespace the_software_company {
    int value ;
    // . . .
}
the_software_company::value = 10 ;
. . .
namespace TSC = the_software_company ;
TSC::value = 20 ;
```

A drawback, of course, is that your alias may collide with an existing name. If this is the case, the compiler will catch the conflict and you can resolve it by renaming the alias.

Using the Unnamed Namespace

An unnamed namespace is simply that—a namespace that does not have a name. A common use of unnamed spaces is to shield global data from potential name clashes between translation units. Every translation unit has its own unique, unnamed namespace. All names defined within the unnamed namespace (within each translation unit) can be referred to without explicit qualification. The following is an example of two unnamed namespaces found in two separate files:

```
// file: one.cpp
namespace {
    int value ;
    char p( char *p ) ;
    //. . .
}

// file: two.cpp
namespace {
    int value ;
    char p( char *p ) ;
    //. . .
}
int main( )
{
    char c = p( ptr ) ;
}
```

17

Each of the names, `value` and function `p()`, is distinct to its respective file. To refer to a (unnamed namespace) name within a translation unit, use the name without qualification. This usage is demonstrated in the previous example with the call to function `p()`. This use implies a `using` directive for objects referred to from an unnamed namespace. Because of this, you cannot access members of an unnamed namespace in another translation unit. The behavior of an unnamed namespace is the same as a `static` object having external linkage. Consider this example:

```
static int value = 10 ;
```

Remember that this use of the `static` keyword is deprecated by the standards committee. Namespaces now exist to replace code as previously shown. Another way to think of unnamed namespaces is that they are global variables with internal linkage.

Using the Standard Namespace `std`

The best example of namespaces is found in the C++ standard library. The standard library is completely encased within the namespace named `std`. All functions, classes, objects, and templates are declared within the namespace `std`.

You will, no doubt, see code such as the following:

```
#include <iostream>
using namespace std ;
```

Remember that the `using` directive pulls everything in from the named namespace. It is bad form to employ the `using` directive when using the standard library. Why? Because doing so defeats the purpose of using a namespace; the global namespace will be polluted with all the names found in the header. Keep in mind that all header files use the namespace feature, so if you include multiple standard header files and specify the `using` directive, everything declared in the headers will be in the global namespace. Please note that most of the examples in this book violate this rule; this action is not an intent to advocate violating the rule, but it is used to ensure brevity of the examples. You should use the `using` declaration instead, as in the following example:

```
#include <iostream>
using std::cin ;
using std::cout ;
using std::endl ;
int main( )
{
    int value = 0 ;
    cout << "So, how many eggs did you say you wanted?" << endl ;
    cin >> value ;
    cout << value << " eggs, sunny-side up!" << endl ;
```

```
    return( 0 ) ;
}
```

The following shows a sample run of the program:

```
So, how many eggs did you say you wanted?
4
4 eggs, sunny-side up!
```

As an alternative, you could fully qualify the names that you use, as in the following code sample:

```
#include <iostream>
int main( )
{
    int value = 0 ;
    std::cout << "How many eggs did you want?" << std::endl ;
    std::cin >> value ;
    std::cout << value << " eggs, sunny-side up!" << std::endl ;
    return( 0 ) ;
}
```

Sample output from this program is shown here:

```
How many eggs did you want?
4
4 eggs, sunny-side up!
```

This might be appropriate for shorter programs but can become quite cumbersome for any significant amount of code. Imagine having to prefix std:: for every name you use that is found in the standard library!

Summary

Creating a namespace is very similar to a class declaration. A couple of differences are worth noting. First, a semicolon does not follow a namespace's closing brace. Second, a namespace is open, whereas a class is closed. This means that you can continue to define the namespace in other files or in separate sections of a single file.

Anything that can be declared can be inserted into a namespace. If you are designing classes for a reusable library, you should be using the namespace feature. Functions declared within a namespace should be defined outside that namespace's body. This promotes a separation of interface from implementation and also keeps the namespace from becoming cluttered.

Namespaces can be nested. A namespace is a declaration; this fact enables you to nest namespaces. Do not forget that you must fully qualify names that are nested.

The using directive is used to expose all names in a namespace to the current scope. This effectively pollutes the global namespace with all names found in the named namespace. It is generally bad practice to use the using directive, especially with respect to the standard library. Use using declarations instead.

The using declaration is used to expose a specific namespace name into the current scope. This allows you to refer to the object by its name only.

A namespace alias is similar in nature to a typedef. A namespace alias enables you to create another name for a named namespace. This can be quite useful when you are using a namespace with a long name.

Every file can contain an unnamed namespace. An unnamed namespace, as its name implies, is a namespace without a name. An unnamed namespace allows you to use the names within the namespace without qualification. It keeps the namespace names local to the translation unit. Unnamed namespaces are the same as declaring a global variable with the static keyword.

The C++ standard library is enclosed in a namespace named std. Avoid using the using directive when using the standard library; instead, use the using declaration.

Q&A

Q Do I have to use namespaces?

A No, you can write simple programs and ignore namespaces altogether. Be sure to use the old standard libraries (for example, #include <string.h>) rather than the new libraries (for example, #include <cstring>).

Q What are the two forms of statements with the using keyword? What are the differences between those two forms?

A The using keyword can be used for the using directives and the using declarations. A using directive allows all names in a namespace to be used as if they are normal names. A using declaration, on the other hand, enables the program to use an individual name from a namespace without qualifying it with the namespace qualifier.

Q What are the unnamed namespaces? Why do we need unnamed namespaces?

A Unnamed namespaces are namespaces without names. They are used to wrap a collection of declarations against possible name clashes. Names in an unnamed namespace cannot be used outside of the translation unit where the namespace is declared.

Workshop

The Workshop contains quiz questions to help solidify your understanding of the materi-al covered and exercises to provide you with experience in using what you learned. Try to answer the quiz and exercise questions before checking the answers in Appendix D, "Answers to Exercises and Quizzes," and make sure you understand the answers before going on to the next day.

Quiz

1. Can I use names defined in a namespace without using the using keyword?

2. What are the major differences between normal and unnamed namespaces?

3. What is the standard namespace?

Exercises

1. **BUG BUSTER:** What is wrong in this program?

```
#include <iostream>

int main()
{
    cout << "Hello world!" << end;
    return 0;
}
```

2. List three ways of fixing the problem found in Exercise 1.

17

DAY **18**

Object-Oriented Analysis and Design

It is easy to become focused on the syntax of C++ and to lose sight of how and why you use these techniques to build programs. Today you will learn:

- How to use object-oriented analysis to understand the problem you are trying to solve
- How to use object-oriented design to create a robust, extensible, and reliable solution
- How to use the Unified Modeling Language (UML) to document your analysis and design

Is C++ Object-Oriented?

C++ was created as a bridge between object-oriented programming and C, the world's most popular programming language for commercial software development. The goal was to provide object-oriented design to a fast, commercial software development platform.

C was developed as a middle ground between high-level business application languages such as COBOL and the pedal-to-the-metal, high-performance, but difficult-to-use Assembler language. C was to enforce "structured" programming, in which problems were "decomposed" into smaller units of repeatable activities called *procedures*.

The programs we are writing at the beginning of the new century are much more complex than those written at the beginning of the last decade. Programs created in procedural languages tend to be difficult to manage, hard to maintain, and impossible to extend. Graphical user interfaces, the Internet, digital telephony, and a host of new technologies have dramatically increased the complexity of programming projects at the same time that consumer expectations for the quality of the user interface are rising.

In the face of this increasing complexity, developers took a long, hard look at the state of the industry. What they found was disheartening, at best. Software was late, broken, defective, bug-ridden, unreliable, and expensive. Projects routinely ran over budget and were delivered late to market. The cost of maintaining and building on these projects was prohibitive, and a tremendous amount of money was being wasted.

Object-oriented software development offers a path out of the abyss. Object-oriented programming languages build a strong link between the data structures and the methods that manipulate that data. More important, in object-oriented programming, you no longer think about data structures and manipulating functions; you think instead about objects—things.

The world is populated by things: cars, dogs, trees, clouds, flowers. Each *thing* has characteristics (fast, friendly, brown, puffy, pretty). Most things have behavior (move, bark, grow, rain, wilt). We do not think about a dog's data and how we might manipulate it—we think about a dog as a thing in the world, what it is like, and what it does.

What Models Are

If we are to manage complexity, we must create a model of the universe. The goal of the model is to create a meaningful abstraction of the real world. Such an abstraction should be simpler than the real world but should also accurately reflect the real world so that we can use the model to predict the behavior of things in the real world.

A child's globe is a classic model. The model is not the thing itself; we would never confuse a child's globe with the Earth, but one maps the other well enough that we can learn about the Earth by studying the globe.

There are, of course, significant simplifications. A child's globe never has rain, floods, globe-quakes and so forth, but I can use that globe to predict how long it will take me to fly from my home to Indianapolis should I ever need to come in and explain myself to the Sams senior management when they ask me why my manuscript was late ("you see, I was doing great, but then I got lost in a metaphor and it took me hours to get out").

A model that is not simpler than the thing being modeled is not much use. Steven Wright jokes about just such a thing: "I have a map on which one inch equals one inch. I live at E5."

Object-oriented software design is about building good models. It consists of two significant pieces: a modeling language and a process.

Software Design: The Modeling Language

The *modeling language* is the least important aspect of object-oriented analysis and design; unfortunately, it tends to get the most attention. A modeling language is nothing more than a convention for how to draw a model on paper. We can easily decide to draw our classes as triangles and the inheritance relationship as a dotted line. If so, we might model a geranium as shown in Figure 18.1.

FIGURE 18.1

Generalization/ specialization.

In the figure, you see that a Geranium is a special kind of flower. If you and I agree to draw our inheritance (generalization/specialization) diagrams like this, we will understand each other perfectly. Over time, we would probably want to model lots of complex relationships to develop our own complicated set of diagramming conventions and rules.

Of course, we need to explain our conventions to everyone else with whom we work, and each new employee or collaborator will have to learn our conventions. We may interact with other companies that have their own conventions, and we need to allow time to negotiate a common convention and to compensate for the inevitable misunderstandings.

It would be more convenient if everyone in the industry agreed on a common modeling language. (For that matter, it would be convenient if everyone in the world agreed on a spoken language, but one thing at a time.) The *lingua franca* of software development is UML—the Unified Modeling Language. The job of the UML is to answer questions such as, "How do we draw an inheritance relationship?" The geranium drawing shown in Figure 18.1 would be drawn in UML as shown in Figure 18.2.

FIGURE 18.2

UML drawing of specialization.

In UML, classes are drawn as rectangles, and inheritance is drawn as a line with an arrowhead. Interestingly, the arrowhead points from the more specialized class to the more general class. The direction of the arrow is counter-intuitive for most folks, but it does not matter much; when we all agree, the system works just fine.

The details of the UML are rather straightforward. The diagrams are not hard to use or to understand, and they are explained as we go along in this lesson, rather than trying to teach the UML out of context. Although it is possible to write a whole book on the UML, the truth is that 90 percent of the time, you use only a small subset of the UML notation, and that subset is easily learned.

Software Design: The Process

The *process* of object-oriented analysis and design is much more complex and important than the modeling language. So of course, it is what you hear much less about. That is because the debate about modeling languages is pretty much settled; as an industry, we decided to use the UML. The debate about process rages on.

A *methodologist* is someone who develops or studies one or more methods. Typically, methodologists develop and publish their own methods. A *method* is a modeling language and a process. Three of the leading methodologists and their methods are Grady Booch, who developed the Booch method; Ivar Jacobson, who developed object-oriented software engineering; and James Rumbaugh, who developed Object Modeling Technology (OMT). Together, these three men have created *Objectory*, a method and a commercial product from Rational Software, Inc. All three men are employed at Rational Software, where they are affectionately known as the *Three Amigos*.

This lesson loosely follows *Objectory*. I will not follow it rigidly because I do not believe in slavish adherence to academic theory—I am much more interested in shipping product than in adhering to a method. Other methods have something to offer, and I tend to be eclectic; picking up bits and pieces as I go along and stitching them together into a workable framework.

The process of software design is *iterative*. That means that as we develop software, we go through the entire process repeatedly as we strive for enhanced understanding of the requirements. The design directs the implementation, but the details uncovered during implementation feed back into the design. Most important, we do not try to develop any sizable project in a single, orderly, straight line; rather, we iterate over pieces of the project, constantly improving our design and refining our implementation.

Iterative development can be distinguished from waterfall development. In waterfall development, the output from one stage becomes the input to the next, and there is no going back (see Figure 18.3). In a waterfall development process, the requirements are detailed, and the clients sign off ("Yes, this is what I want"); the requirements are then passed on to the designer, set in stone. The designer creates the design (and a wonder to behold it is) and passes it off to the programmer who implements the design. The programmer in turn hands the code to a QA person who tests the code and then releases it to the customer. Great in theory, disaster in practice.

18

FIGURE 18.3

The waterfall method.

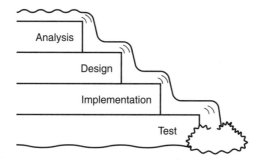

Analysis

Design

Implementation

Test

In iterative design, the visionary comes up with a concept, and then we begin to work on fleshing out the requirements. As we examine the details, the vision may grow and evolve. When we have a good start on the requirements, we begin the design, knowing full well that the questions that arise during design may cause modifications back in the requirements. As we work on design, we begin prototyping and then implementing the product. The issues that arise in development feed back into design and may even influence our understanding of the requirements. Most important, we design and implement only pieces of the full product, iterating over the design and implementation phases repeatedly.

Although the steps of the process are repeated iteratively, it is nearly impossible to describe them in such a cyclical manner. Therefore, I will describe them in sequence: conceptualization, analysis, design, implementation, testing, and rollout. Do not misunderstand me—in reality, we run through each of these steps many times during the course of the development of a single product. The iterative design process is just hard to present and understand if we cycle through each step, so I describe them one after the other.

The following are the steps of the iterative design process:

1. Conceptualization—when the vision and overall purpose of the project is developed.
2. Analysis—determining the needs of the organization (figuring out what the software should do), this is where you model your classes.
3. Design—creating the blueprint for a solution to the problem set.
4. Implementation—building the system from the design blueprint, this is where the code is developed (in C++ for example).
5. Testing—making sure the system does what it is supposed to do.
6. Rollout—getting the system out for the users.

These steps are a piece of cake. All the rest is details.

 Note   This lesson only covers the first three steps: conceptualization, analysis, and design. The other steps are well beyond the scope of this introductory lesson. You can find plenty of books that will cover all of these topics in excruciating detail.

Controversies

Endless controversies exist about what happens in each stage of the iterative design process, and even about what you name those stages. Here is the secret: *it does not matter*. The essential steps are the same in just about every process: Find out what you need to build, design a solution, and implement that design.

Although the newsgroups and object-technology mailing lists thrive on splitting hairs, the essentials of object-oriented analysis and design are fairly straightforward. In this lesson, I lay out a practical approach to the process as the bedrock on which you can build the architecture of your application.

The goal of all this work is to produce code that meets the stated requirements and that is reliable, extensible, and maintainable. Most important, the goal is to produce high-quality code on time and on budget.

Conceptualization: The Vision

All great software starts with a vision. One individual has an insight into a product he thinks would be good to build. Rarely do committees create compelling visions. The very first phase of object-oriented analysis and design is to capture this vision in a single sentence (or at most, a short paragraph). The vision becomes the guiding principle of development, and the team that comes together to implement the vision ought to refer back to it—and update it if necessary—as it goes forward.

Even if the vision statement comes out of a committee in the marketing department, one person should be designated as the "visionary." It is that person's job to be the keeper of the sacred light. As you progress, the requirements will evolve. Scheduling and time-to-market demands may modify what you try to accomplish in the first iteration of the program, but the visionary must keep an eye on the essential idea, to ensure that whatever is produced reflects the core vision with high fidelity. It is this ruthless dedication—this passionate commitment—that sees the project through to completion. If you lose sight of the vision, your product is doomed.

Requirements Analysis

The conceptualization phase, in which the vision is articulated, is very brief. It may be no longer than a flash of insight followed by the time it takes to write down what the visionary has in mind. Often, as the object-oriented expert, you join the project after the vision is already articulated.

18

Some companies confuse the vision statement with the requirements. A strong vision is necessary, but it is not sufficient. To move on to analysis, you must understand how the product will be used and how it must perform. The goal of the analysis phase is to articulate and capture these requirements. The outcome of the analysis phase is the production of a requirements document. The first section in the requirements document is the use-case analysis.

Use Cases

The driving force in analysis, design, and implementation is the use cases. A *use case* is nothing more than a high-level description of how the product will be used. Use cases don't just drive the analysis—they drive the design, they help you find the classes, and they are especially important in testing the product.

Creating a robust and comprehensive set of use cases may be the single most important task in analysis. It is here that you depend most heavily on your domain experts; the domain experts have the most information about the business requirements you are trying to capture.

Use cases pay little attention to user interface, and they pay no attention to the internals of the system you are building. Any system or person who interacts with the system is called an *actor*.

To summarize, the following are some definitions:

- Use case—A description of how the software will be used.
- Domain experts—People with expertise in the *domain* (area) of business for which you are creating the product.
- Actor—Any person or system that interacts with the system you are developing.

A use case is a description of the interaction between an actor and the system itself. For purposes of use-case analysis, the system is treated as a "black box." An actor "sends a message" to the system, and something happens: information is returned, the state of the system is changed, the space ship changes direction, or whatever.

Identify the Actors

It is important to note that not all actors are people. Systems that interact with the system you are building are also actors. Thus, if we were building an automated teller machine, the customer and the bank clerk can both be actors—as can other systems with which our new system interacts, such as a mortgage-tracking or student-loan system. The essential characteristics of actors are as follows:

- They are external to the system
- They interact with the system

Getting started is often the hardest part of use-case analysis. Often, the best way to get going is with a "brainstorming" session. Simply write down the list of people and systems that will interact with your new system. Remember that when we discuss *people*, we really mean *roles*—the bank clerk, the manager, the customer, and so forth. One person can have more than one role.

For the ATM example just mentioned, we can expect such a list to include the following roles:

- The customer
- The bank personnel
- A back-office system
- The person who fills the ATM with money and supplies

You do not need to go beyond the obvious list at first. Generating even three or four actors may be enough to get you started on generating use cases. Each of these actors interacts with the system in different ways. You want to capture these interactions in your use cases.

Determine the First Use Cases

18

We should start with the customer role. We might brainstorm the following use cases for a *customer*:

- Customer checks account balances.
- Customer deposits money to her account.
- Customer withdraws money from her account.
- Customer transfers money between accounts.
- Customer opens an account.
- Customer closes an account.

Should we distinguish between "Customer deposits money in her checking account" and "Customer deposits money in her savings account," or should we combine these actions (as we did in the preceding list) into "Customer deposits money to her account?" The answer to this question lies in whether this distinction is meaningful in the domain.

To determine whether these actions are one use case or two, you must ask whether the *mechanisms* are different (does the customer do something significantly different with these deposits) and whether the *outcomes* are different (does the system reply in a different way). The answer to both questions for the deposit issue is "no": The customer deposits money to either account in essentially the same way, and the outcome is pretty much the same; the ATM responds by incrementing the balance in the appropriate account.

Given that the actor and the system behave and respond more or less identically, regard-less of whether the deposit is made to the checking or the savings account, these two use cases are actually a single use case. Later, when we flesh out use-case scenarios, we can try the two variations to see whether they make any difference at all.

As you think about each actor, you may discover additional use cases by asking these questions:

- Why is the actor using this system?

  The customer is using the system to get cash, to make a deposit, or to check an account balance.

- What outcome does the actor want from each request?

  Add cash to an account or get cash to make a purchase.

- What happened to cause the actor to use this system now?

  The actor may recently have been paid or may be on the way to make a purchase.

- What must the actor do to use the system?

  Put an ATM card into the slot in the machine.

  Aha! We need a use case for the customer logging in to the system.

- What information must the actor provide to the system?

  Enter a Personal ID number.

  Aha! We need use cases for obtaining and editing the Personal ID number.

- What information does the actor hope to get from the system?

  Balances, and so on.

You can often find additional use cases by focusing on the attributes of the objects in the domain. The customer has a name, a PIN (personal identification number), and an account number; do we have use cases to manage these objects? An account has an account number, a balance, and a transaction history; have we captured these elements in the use cases?

After we explore the customer use cases in detail, the next step in fleshing out the list of use cases is to develop the use cases for each of the other actors. The following list shows a reasonable first set of use cases for the ATM example:

- Customer checks account balances.
- Customer deposits money to her account.
- Customer withdraws money from her account.
- Customer transfers money between accounts.

- Customer opens an account.
- Customer closes an account.
- Customer logs in to her account.
- Customer checks recent transactions.
- Bank clerk logs in to special management account.
- Bank clerk makes an adjustment to a customer's account.
- A back office system updates a user's account based on external activity.
- Changes in a user's account are reflected in a back office system.
- The ATM signals it is out of cash to dispense.
- The bank technician fills the ATM with cash and supplies.

Create the Domain Model

After you have a first cut at your use cases, you can begin to flesh out your requirements document with a detailed domain model. The *domain model* is a document that captures all you know about the domain (the field of business you are working in). As part of your domain model, you create domain objects that describe all the objects mentioned in your use cases. So far, the ATM example includes these objects: customer, bank personnel, back office systems, checking account, savings account, and so forth.

For each of these domain objects, we want to capture such essential data as the name of the object (for example, customer, account, and so on), whether the object is an actor, the object's principal attributes and behavior, and so forth. Many modeling tools support capturing this information in "class" descriptions. Figure 18.4 shows how this information is captured with the Rational Rose program from Rational Software.

18

FIGURE 18.4

Capturing information with the Rational Rose program.

It is important to realize that the items we are describing here are *not* design objects, but rather objects in the domain. This is documentation of how the world works, not documentation of how our system will work.

We can diagram the relationship among the objects in the domain of the ATM example using the UML—with the same diagramming conventions we will use later to describe the relationships among classes in the domain. This is one of the great strengths of the UML: We can use the same tools at every stage of the project.

For example, we can capture that checking accounts and savings accounts are both specializations of the more general concept of bank account by using the UML conventions for classes and generalization relationships, as shown in Figure 18.5.

FIGURE 18.5

Specialization.

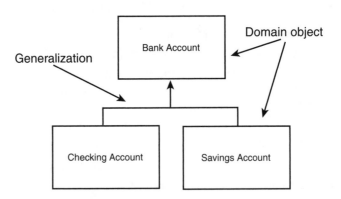

In the diagram in Figure 18.5, the boxes represent the various domain objects, and the line with an arrowhead indicates generalization. The UML specifies that this line is drawn from the *specialized* class to the more general "base" class. Thus, both Checking Account and Savings Account point up to Bank Account, indicating that each is a specialized form of Bank Account.

Note

Again, it is important to note that the relationships we are showing at this time are relationships among objects in the domain. Later, you may decide to have a CheckingAccount object in your design as well as a BankAccount object, and you may implement this relationship using inheritance; but these are design-time decisions. At analysis time, all we are doing is documenting our understanding of these objects in the domain.

The UML is a rich modeling language, and you can capture any number of relationships. The principal relationships captured in analysis, however, are generalization (or specialization), containment, and association.

Generalization

Generalization is often equated with "inheritance," but a sharp and meaningful distinction exists between the two. Generalization describes the relationship; inheritance is the programming implementation of generalization—it is how we manifest generalization in code.

Generalization implies that the derived object *is a* subtype of the base object. Thus, a checking account *is a* bank account. The relationship is symmetrical: Bank account *generalizes* the common behavior and attributes of checking and savings accounts.

During domain analysis, you seek to capture these relationships *as they exist in the real world.*

Containment

Often, one object is composed of many subobjects. For example, a car is composed of a steering wheel, tires, doors, radio, and so forth. A checking account is composed of a balance, a transaction history, a customer ID, and so on. We say that the checking account *has* these items; containment models have the *has-a* relationship. The UML illustrates the containment relationship by drawing a line with a diamond from the containing object to the contained object, as shown in Figure 18.6.

FIGURE 18.6

Containment.

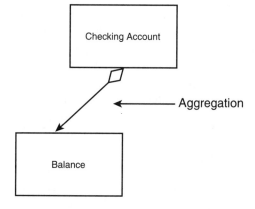

The diagram in Figure 18.6 suggests that the Checking Account *has a* Balance. You can combine these diagrams to show a fairly complex set of relationships (see Figure 18.7).

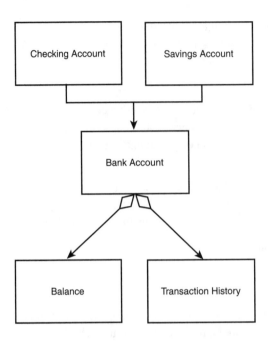

FIGURE 18.7

Object relationships.

The diagram in Figure 18.7 states that a Checking Account and a Savings Account are both Bank Accounts, and that all Bank Accounts have both a Balance and a Transaction History.

Association

The third relationship commonly captured in the domain analysis is a simple association. An *association* suggests that two objects know of one another and that the objects interact in some way. This definition will become much more precise in the design stage, but for analysis, we are suggesting only that Object A and Object B interact, but that neither contains the other and neither is a specialization of the other. We show this association in the UML with a simple straight line between the objects, as shown in Figure 18.8.

FIGURE 18.8

Association.

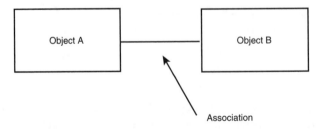

The diagram in Figure 18.8 indicates that Object A associates in some way with Object B.

Establish Scenarios

Now that we have a preliminary set of use cases and the tools with which to diagram the relationship among the objects in the domain, we are ready to formalize the use cases and give them more depth.

Each use case can be broken into a series of scenarios. A *scenario* is a description of a specific set of circumstances that distinguish among the various contingent elements of the use case. For example, the use case "Customer withdraws money from her account" might have the following scenarios:

- Customer requests a $300 withdrawal from checking, puts the cash in the cash slot, and the system prints a receipt.
- Customer requests a $300 withdrawal from checking, but her balance is $200. Customer is informed that not enough cash is in the checking account to accomplish the withdrawal.
- Customer requests a $300 withdrawal from checking, but she has already withdrawn $100 today and the limit is $300 per day. Customer is informed of the problem, and she chooses to withdraw only $200.
- Customer requests a $300 withdrawal from checking, but the receipt roll is out of paper. Customer is informed of the problem, and she chooses to proceed without a receipt.

And so forth. Each scenario explores a variation on the original use case. Often, these variations are exception conditions (not enough money in account, not enough money in machine, and so on). Sometimes, the variations explore nuances of decisions in the use case itself (for example, did the customer want to transfer money before making the withdrawal?).

Not every possible scenario must be explored. You are looking for those scenarios that tease out requirements of the system or details of the interaction with the actor.

Establish Guidelines

As part of your methodology, you will want to create guidelines for documenting each scenario. You capture these guidelines in your requirements document. Typically, you want to ensure that each scenario includes the following:

- Preconditions—What must be true for the scenario to begin
- Triggers—What causes the scenario to begin

18

- What actions the actors take
- What results or changes are caused by the system
- What feedback do the actors receive
- Whether repeating activities occur, and what causes them to conclude
- A description of the logical flow of the scenario
- What causes the scenario to end
- Postconditions—What must be true when the scenario is complete

In addition, you will want to name each use case and each scenario. Thus, you might have the following situation:

Use Case:	Customer withdraws cash.
Scenario:	Successful cash withdrawal from checking.
Preconditions:	Customer is already logged on to system.
Trigger:	Customer requests "withdrawal."
Description:	Customer chooses to withdraw cash from a checking account. Sufficient cash is in the account, sufficient cash and receipt paper are in the ATM, and the network is up and running. The ATM asks the customer to indicate the amount of the withdrawal, and the customer asks for $300, a legal amount to withdraw at this time. The machine dispenses $300 and prints a receipt, and the customer takes the money and the receipt.
Postconditions:	Customer account is debited $300, and customer has $300 cash.

This use case can be shown with the incredibly simple diagram given in Figure 18.9.

Little information is captured here except a high-level abstraction of an interaction between an actor (the customer) and the system. This diagram becomes slightly more useful when you show the interaction among use cases. I say only *slightly* more useful because only two interactions are possible: «uses» and «extends». The «uses» stereotype indicates that one use case is a superset of another. For example, it is not possible to *withdraw cash* without first *logging on*. We can show this relationship with the diagram shown in Figure 18.10.

FIGURE 18.9

Use-case diagram.

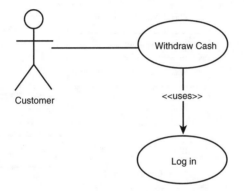

FIGURE 18.10

The «uses» *stereotype.*

18

Figure 18.10 indicates that the Withdraw Cash use case "uses" the Log In use case, and thus fully implements Log In as part of Withdraw Cash.

Tip

The «extends» use case was intended to indicate conditional relationships and something akin to inheritance, but so much confusion exists in the object-modeling community about the distinction between «uses» and «extends» that many developers have simply set aside «extends», feeling that its meaning is not sufficiently well-understood. Personally, I use «uses» when I would otherwise copy and paste the entire use case in place, and I use «extends» when I only *use* the use case under certain definable conditions.

Interaction Diagrams

Although the diagram of the use case itself may be of limited value, you can associate diagrams with the use case that can dramatically improve the documentation and understanding of the interactions. For example, we know that the Withdraw Cash scenario represents the interactions among the following domain objects: customer, checking account, and the user interface. We can document this interaction with an interaction diagram, as shown in Figure 18.11.

FIGURE 18.11

UML interaction diagram.

The interaction diagram in Figure 18.11 captures details of the scenario that may not be evident by reading the text. The objects that are interacting are *domain* objects, and the entire ATM/UI is treated as a single object, with only the specific bank account called out in any detail.

This rather simple ATM example shows only a fanciful set of interactions, but nailing down the specifics of these interactions can be a powerful tool in understanding both the problem domain and the requirements of your new system.

Create Packages

Because you generate many use cases for any problem of significant complexity, the UML enables you to group your use cases in packages.

A *package* is like a directory or a folder—it is a collection of modeling objects (classes, actors, and so forth). To manage the complexity of use cases, you can create packages aggregated by whatever characteristics make sense for your problem. Thus, you can aggregate your use cases by account type (everything affecting checking or savings), by credit or debit, by customer type, or by whatever characteristics make sense to you. More importantly, a single use case can appear in different packages, allowing you great flexibility of design.

Application Analysis

In addition to creating use cases, the requirements document will capture your customer's assumptions, constraints, and requirements about hardware and operating systems. Application requirements are your *particular* customer's prerequisites—those things that you would normally determine during design and implementation but that your client has decided for you.

The application requirements are often driven by the need to interface with existing (legacy) systems. In this case, understanding what the existing systems do and how they work is an essential component of your analysis.

Ideally, you analyze the problem, design the solution, and then decide which platform and operating system best fit your design. That scenario is as ideal as it is rare. More often, the client has a standing investment in a particular operating system or hardware platform. The client's business plan depends on your software running on the existing system, and you must capture these requirements early and design accordingly.

Systems Analysis

Some software is written to stand alone, interacting only with the end user. Often, however, you will be called on to interface to an existing system. *Systems analysis* is the process of collecting all the details of the systems with which you will interact. Will your new system be a server, providing services to the existing system, or will it be a client? Will you be able to negotiate an interface between the systems, or must you adapt to an existing standard? Will the other system be stable, or must you continually hit a moving target?

18

These and related questions must be answered in the analysis phase, before you begin to design your new system. In addition, you will want to try to capture the constraints and limitations implicit in interacting with the other systems. Will they slow down the responsiveness of your system? Will they put high demands on your new system, consuming resources and computing time?

Planning Documents

After you understand what your system must do and how it must behave, it is time to take a first stab at creating a time and budget document. Often, the timeline is dictated, top-down, by the client: "You have 18 months to get this done." Ideally, you examine the requirements and estimate the time it will take to design and implement the solution. That is the ideal. The practical reality is that most systems come with an imposed time limit and cost limit, and the real trick is to figure out how much of the required functionality you can build in the allotted time—and at the allotted cost.

Here are two guidelines to keep in mind when you are creating a project budget and timeline:

- If you are given a range, the outer number is probably optimistic.
- Hofstadter's Law: It always takes longer than you expect, even when you take into account Hofstadter's Law.

Given these realities, it is imperative that you prioritize your work. *You will not finish*—it is that simple. It is important that when you run out of time, what you have works and is adequate for a first release. If you are building a bridge and run out of time, if you did not get a chance to put in the bicycle path, that is too bad; but you can still open the bridge and start collecting tolls. If you run out of time and you are only halfway across the river, that is not as good.

An essential thing to know about planning documents is that they are wrong. This early in the process, it is virtually impossible to offer a reliable estimate of the duration of the project. After you have the requirements, you can get a good handle on how long the design will take, a fair estimate of how long the implementation will take, and a reasonable guesstimate of the testing time. Then you must allow yourself at least 20 to 25 percent "wiggle room," which you can tighten as you move forward and learn more.

Note

> The inclusion of "wiggle room" in your planning document is not an excuse to avoid planning documents. It is merely a warning not to rely on them too much early on. As the project goes forward, you strengthen your understanding of how the system works, and your estimates will become increasingly precise.

Visualizations

The final piece of the requirements document is the visualization. The visualization is a fancy name for the diagrams, pictures, screen shots, prototypes, and any other visual representations created to help you think through and design the graphical user interface of your product.

For many large projects, you may develop a full prototype to help you (and your customers) understand how the system will behave. On some teams, the prototype becomes the living requirements document; the "real" system is designed to implement the functionality demonstrated in the prototype.

Artifacts

At the end of each phase of analysis and design, you will create a series of documents or "artifacts." Table 18.1 shows some of the artifacts of the analysis phase. These documents are used by the customer to make sure that you understand what the customer needs, by end users to give feedback and guidance to the project, and by the project team to design and implement the code. Many of these documents also provide material crucial both to your documentation team and to Quality Assurance to tell them how the system *ought* to behave.

18

TABLE 18.1 Artifacts Created During the Analysis Stage of Project Development

Artifact	Description
Use case report	A document detailing the use cases, scenarios, stereotypes, preconditions, postconditions, and visualizations
Domain analysis	Document and diagrams describing the relationships among the domain objects
Analysis collaboration diagrams	Collaboration diagrams describing interactions among objects in the problem domain
Analysis activity diagrams	Activity diagrams describing interactions among objects in the problem domain
Systems analysis	Report and diagrams describing low-level and hardware systems on which the project will be built
Application analysis document	Report and diagrams describing the customer's requirements specific to this particular project
Operational constraints report	Report describing performance characteristics and constraints imposed by this client
Cost and planning document	Report with Gantt and Pert charts indicating projected scheduling, milestones, and costs

Design

Analysis focuses on understanding the problem domain, whereas design focuses on creating the solution. *Design* is the process of transforming your understanding of the requirements into a model that can be implemented in software. The result of this process is the production of a design document.

The design document is divided into two sections: Class Design and Architectural Mechanisms. The Class Design section, in turn, is divided into static design (which details the various classes and their relationships and characteristics) and dynamic design (which details how the classes interact).

The Architectural Mechanisms section of the design document provides details about how you will implement object persistence, concurrency, a distributed object system, and so forth. The rest of this lesson focuses on the class design aspect of the design document; other lessons in the rest of this book explain how to implement various architecture mechanisms.

What Are the Classes?

As a C++ programmer, you are used to creating classes. Formal design methodology requires you to separate the C++ class from the design class, although they will be intimately related. The C++ class you write in code is the implementation of the class you designed. These are isomorphic: Each class in your design will correspond to a class in your code, but do not confuse one for the other. It is certainly possible to implement your design classes in another language, and the *syntax* of the class definitions might be changed.

That said, most of the time we talk about these classes without distinguishing them because the differences are highly abstract. When you say that in your model your Cat class will have a Meow() method, understand that this means that you will put a Meow() method into your C++ class as well.

You capture the model's classes in UML diagrams, and you capture the C++ classes in code that can be compiled. The distinction is meaningful, yet subtle.

In any case, the biggest stumbling block for many novices is finding the initial set of classes and understanding what makes a well-designed class. One simplistic technique suggests writing out the use-case scenarios and then creating a class for every noun. Consider the following use-case scenario:

Customer chooses to withdraw **cash** from **checking**. Sufficient cash is in the **account**, sufficient cash and **receipts** are in the **ATM**, and the **network** is up and running. The ATM asks the customer to indicate an **amount** for the **withdrawal**, and the customer asks for $300, a legal amount to withdraw at this time. The **machine** dispenses $300 and prints a receipt, and the customer takes the **money** and the receipt.

You might pull out of this scenario the following classes:

- Customer
- Cash
- Checking
- Account
- Receipts
- ATM
- Network
- Amount
- Withdrawal
- Machine
- Money

You might then aggregate the synonyms to create this list, and then create classes for each of these nouns:

- Customer
- Cash (money, amount, withdrawal)
- Checking
- Account
- Receipts
- ATM (machine)
- Network

This is not a bad way to start, as far as it goes. You might then go on to diagram the obvious relationships among some of these classes as shown in Figure 18.12.

18

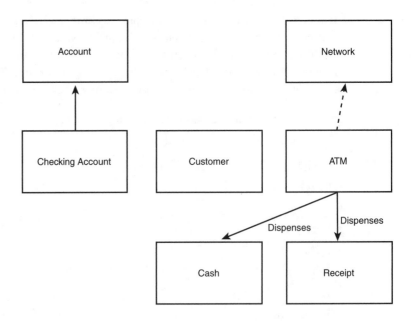

FIGURE 18.12

Preliminary classes.

Transformations

What you began to do in the preceding section was not so much extracting the nouns from the scenario as to begin transforming objects from the domain analysis into objects in the design. That is a fine first step. Often, many of the objects in the domain will have *surrogates* in the design. An object is called a surrogate to distinguish between the actual physical receipt dispensed by an ATM and the object in your design that is merely an intellectual abstraction implemented in code.

You will likely find that *most* of the domain objects have an isomorphic representation in the design—that is, a one-to-one correspondence exists between the domain object and the design object. Other times, however, a single domain object is represented in the design by an entire series of design objects. And at times, a series of domain objects may be represented by a single design object.

In Figure 18.12, note that we have already captured the fact that CheckingAccount is a specialization of Account. We did not set out to find the generalization relationship, but this one was self-evident, so we captured it. Similarly, we knew, from the domain analysis, that the ATM dispenses both Cash and Receipts, so we captured that information immediately in the design.

The relationship between Customer and CheckingAccount is less obvious. We know that such a relationship exists, but the details are not obvious, so we hold off.

Other Transformations

After you have transformed the domain objects, you can begin to look for other useful design-time objects. A good starting place is with interfaces. Each interface between your new system and any existing (legacy) systems should be encapsulated in an interface class. If you will interact with a database of any type, this is also a good candidate for an interface class.

These interface classes offer encapsulation of the interface protocol and thus shield your code from changes in the other system. Interface classes allow you to change your own design, or to accommodate changes in the design of other systems, without breaking the rest of the code. As long as the two systems continue to support the agreed-on interface, they can move independently of one another.

Data Manipulation

Similarly, you will create classes for data manipulation. If you have to transform data from one format into another format (for example, from Fahrenheit to Celsius or from inch/pound to metric), you may want to encapsulate these manipulations behind a data manipulation class. You can use this technique when messaging data into required formats for other systems or for transmission over the Internet—in short, any time you must manipulate data into a specified format, you will encapsulate the protocol behind a data manipulation class.

Views

Every "view" or "report" your system generates (or, if you generate many reports, every set of reports) is a candidate for a class. The rules behind the report—both how the information is gathered and how it is to be displayed—can be productively encapsulated inside a view class.

Devices

If your system interacts with or manipulates devices (such as printers, modems, scanners, and so forth), the specifics of the device protocol ought to be encapsulated in a class. Again, by creating classes for the interface to the device, you can plug in new devices with new protocols and not break any of the rest of your code; just create a new interface class that supports the same interface (or a derived interface), and off you go.

Static Model

When you have established your preliminary set of classes, it is time to begin modeling their relationships and interactions. For purposes of clarity, this lesson first explains the static model and then explains the dynamic model. In the actual design process, you will

18

move freely between the static and dynamic models, filling in details of both and, in fact, adding new classes and sketching them in as you go.

The static model focuses on three areas of concern: responsibilities, attributes, and relationships. The most important of these—and the one you focus on first—is the set of responsibilities for each class. The most important guiding principle is this: *Each class should be responsible for one thing.*

That is not to say that each class has only one method. Far from it; many classes will have dozens of methods. But all these methods must be coherent and cohesive; that is, they must all relate to one another and contribute to the class's capability to accomplish a single area of responsibility.

In a well-designed system, each object is an instance of a well-defined and well-understood class that is responsible for one area of concern. Classes typically delegate extraneous responsibilities to other, related classes. By creating classes that have only a single area of concern, you promote the creation of highly maintainable code.

To get a handle on the responsibilities of your classes, you may find it beneficial to begin your design work with the use of CRC cards.

CRC Cards

CRC stands for Class, Responsibility, and Collaboration. A CRC card is nothing more than a 4×6 index card. This simple, low-tech device enables you to work with other people in understanding the primary responsibilities of your initial set of classes. You assemble a stack of blank 4×6 index cards and meet around a conference table for a series of CRC card sessions.

How to Conduct a CRC Session

Each CRC session should be attended, ideally, by a group of three to six people; any more becomes unwieldy. You should have a *facilitator*, whose job it is to keep the session on track and to help the participants capture what they learn. At least one senior software architect should be present, ideally someone with significant experience in object-oriented analysis and design. In addition, you will want to include at least one or two "domain experts" who understand the system requirements and who can provide expert advice in how things ought to work.

The most essential ingredient in a CRC session is the conspicuous absence of managers. This is a creative, free-wheeling session that must be unencumbered by the need to impress one's boss. The goal here is to explore, to take risks, to tease out the responsibilities of the classes, and to understand how they might interact with one another.

You begin the CRC session by assembling your group around a conference table, with a small stack of 4×6 index cards. At the top of each CRC card you will write the name of a single class. Draw a line down the center of the card and write *Responsibilities* on the left and *Collaborations* on the right.

Begin by filling out cards for the most important classes you have identified. For each card, write a one-sentence or two-sentence definition on the back. You may also capture what other class this class specializes if that is obvious at the time you are working with the CRC card. Just write *Superclass:* below the class name and fill in the name of the class this class derives from.

Focus on Responsibilities

The point of the CRC session is to identify the *responsibilities* of each class. Pay little attention to the attributes, capturing only the most essential and obvious attributes as you go. The important work is to identify the responsibilities. If, in fulfilling a responsibility, the class must delegate work to another class, you capture that information under *collaborations*.

As you progress, keep an eye on your list of responsibilities. If you run out of room on your 4×6 card, it may make sense to wonder whether you are asking this class to do too much. Remember, each class should be responsible for one general area of work, and the various responsibilities listed should be cohesive and coherent—that is, they should work together to accomplish the overall responsibility of the class.

At this point, you do *not* want to focus on relationships, nor do you want to worry about the class interface or which methods will be public and which will be private. The focus is only on understanding what each class *does*.

Anthropomorphic and Use-Case Driven

The key feature of CRC cards is to make them *anthropomorphic*—that is, you attribute humanlike qualities to each class. It works this way: After you have a preliminary set of classes, return to your CRC scenarios. Divide the cards around the table arbitrarily, and walk through the scenario together. For example, return to the following banking scenario:

> Customer chooses to withdraw cash from checking. Sufficient cash is in the account, sufficient cash and receipts are in the ATM, and the network is up and running. The ATM asks the customer to indicate an amount for the withdrawal, and the customer asks for $300, a legal amount to withdraw at this time. The machine dispenses $300 and prints a receipt, and the customer takes the money and the receipt.

18

Assume we have five participants in our CRC session: Amy, the facilitator and object-oriented designer; Barry, the lead programmer; Charlie, the client; Dorris, the domain expert; and Ed, a programmer.

Amy holds up a CRC card representing `CheckingAccount` and says "I tell the customer how much money is available. He asks me to give him $300. I send a message to the dispenser telling him to give out $300 cash." Barry holds up his card and says "I'm the dispenser; I spit out $300 and send Amy a message telling her to decrement her balance by $300. Who do I tell that the machine now has $300 less? Do I keep track of that?" Charlie says, "I think we need an object to keep track of cash in the machine." Ed says, "No, the dispenser should know how much cash it has; that's part of being a dispenser." Amy disagrees: "No, someone has to coordinate the dispensing of cash. The dispenser needs to know whether cash is available and whether the customer has enough in the account, and it has to count out the money and know when to close the drawer. It should delegate responsibility for keeping track of cash on hand—some kind of internal account. Whoever knows about cash on hand can also notify the back office when it is time to be refilled. Otherwise, that's asking the dispenser to do too much."

The discussion continues. By holding up cards and interacting with one another, the requirements and opportunities to delegate are teased out; each class comes alive, and its responsibilities are clarified. When the group becomes bogged down in design questions, the facilitator can make a decision and help the group move on.

Limitations of CRC Cards

Although CRC cards can be a powerful tool for getting started with design, they have inherent limitations. The first problem is that they do not scale well. In a very complex project, you can be overwhelmed with CRC cards; just keeping track of them all can be difficult.

CRC cards also do not capture the interrelationship among classes. Although it is true that collaborations are noted, the nature of the collaboration is not modeled well. Looking at the CRC cards, you cannot tell whether classes aggregate one another, who creates whom, and so forth. CRC cards also do not capture attributes, so it is difficult to go from CRC cards to code. Most importantly, CRC cards are static; although you can act out the interactions among the classes, the CRC cards themselves do not capture this information.

In short, CRC cards are a good start, but you need to move the classes into the UML if you are to build a robust and complete model of your design. Although the transition *into* the UML is not terribly difficult, it is a one-way street. After you move your classes into UML diagrams, there is no turning back; you set aside the CRC cards and do not come back to them. It is simply too difficult to keep the two models synchronized with one another.

Transforming CRC Cards to UML

Each CRC card can be translated directly into a class modeled with the UML. Responsibilities are translated into class methods, and whatever attributes you have captured are added as well. The class definition from the back of the card is put into the class documentation. Figure 18.13 shows the relationship between the `CheckingAccount` CRC card and the UML class created from that card.

Class: CheckingAccount

SuperClass: Account

Responsibilities:

> Track current balance
>
> Accept deposits and transfers in
>
> Write checks
>
> Transfer cash out
>
> Keep current day's ATM withdrawal balance

Collaborations:

> Other accounts
>
> Back-office systems
>
> Cash dispenser

FIGURE 18.13

CRC card.

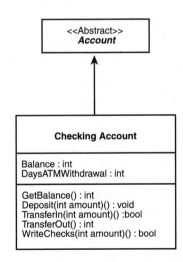

18

Class Relationships

After the classes are in the UML, you can begin to turn your attention to the relationships among the various classes. The principal relationships you will model are the following:

- Generalization
- Association
- Aggregation
- Composition

These are relationships in the domain model that are carried (translated) into the C++ classes.

The generalization relationship is implemented in C++ through public inheritance. From a design perspective, however, we focus less on the mechanism and more on the semantics: what it is that this relationship implies.

We examined the generalization relationship in the analysis phase, but now we turn our attention not just to the objects in the domain, but also to the objects in our design. Our efforts now are to "factor out" common functionality in related classes into base classes that can encapsulate the shared responsibilities.

When you "factor out" common functionality, you move that functionality out of the specialized classes and up into the more general class. Thus, if you notice that both your checking and your savings account need methods for transferring money in and out, you can move the `TransferFunds()` method up into the account base class. The more you factor out of the derived classes, the more polymorphic your design will be.

One of the capabilities available in C++, which is not available in Java, is *multiple inheritance* (although Java has a similar, if limited, capability with its *multiple interfaces*). Multiple inheritance allows a class to inherit from more than one base class, bringing in the members and methods of two or more classes.

Experience has shown that you should use multiple inheritance judiciously because it can complicate both your design and the implementation. Many problems initially solved with multiple inheritance are today solved using aggregation. That said, multiple inheritance is a powerful tool, and your design may require that a single class specializes the behavior of two or more other classes.

Multiple Inheritance Versus Containment

Is an object the sum of its parts? Does it make sense to model a `Car` object as a specialization of `SteeringWheel`, `Door`, and `Tire`, as shown in Figure 18.14?

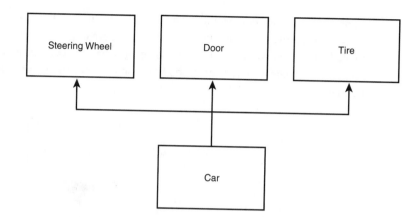

FIGURE 18.14

False inheritance.

It is important to come back to the fundamentals: Public inheritance should always model generalization. The common expression for this is that inheritance should model *is-a* relationships. If you want to model the *has-a* relationship (for example, a car *has-a* steering wheel), you do so with aggregation, as shown in Figure 18.15.

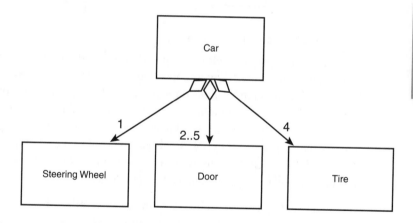

FIGURE 18.15

Aggregation.

18

The diagram in Figure 18.15 indicates that a car has a steering wheel, four wheels, and from two to five doors. This is a more accurate model of the relationship between a car and its parts. Notice that the diamond in the diagram is not filled in; this is so because we are modeling this relationship as an aggregation, not as a composition. Composition implies control for the lifetime of the object. Although the car *has* tires and a door, the tires and door can exist before they are part of the car and can continue to exist after they are no longer part of the car.

Figure 18.16 models composition. This model says that the body is not only an aggregation of a head, two arms, and two legs, but that these objects (head, arms, legs) are
created when the body is created and disappear when the body disappears. That is, they
have no independent existence; the body is composed of these things and their lifetimes
are intertwined.

FIGURE 18.16

Composition.

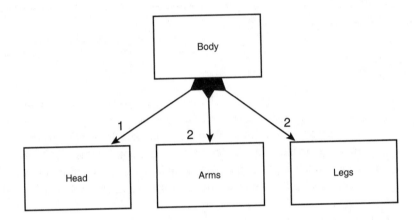

Discriminators and Powertypes

How might you design the classes required to reflect the various model lines of a
typical car manufacturer? Suppose that you are hired to design a system for Acme
Motors, which currently manufactures five cars: the Pluto (a slow, compact car with a
small engine); the Venus (a four-door sedan with a middle-sized engine); the Mars
(a sport coupe with the company's biggest engine, engineered for maximum performance); the Jupiter (a minivan with the same engine as the sports coupe but designed
to shift at a lower RPM and to use its power to move its greater weight); and the Earth
(a station wagon with a small engine but high RPM).

You might start by creating subtypes of the car that reflect the various models, and then
create instances of each model as it rolls off the assembly line, as shown in Figure 18.17.

How are these models differentiated? As you saw, they are differentiated by the engine
size, body type, and performance characteristics. These various discriminating characteristics can be mixed and matched to create various models. We can model this in the
UML with the *discriminator* stereotype, as shown in Figure 18.18.

FIGURE 18.17

Modeling subtypes.

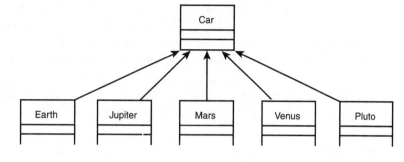

FIGURE 18.18

Modeling the di scriminator.

The diagram in Figure 18.18 indicates that classes can be derived from Car based on mixing and matching three discriminating attributes. The size of the engine dictates how powerful the car is, and the performance characteristics indicate how sporty the car is. Thus, you can have a powerful and sporty station wagon, a low-power family sedan, and so forth.

Each attribute can be implemented with a simple enumerator. Thus, the body type might be implemented with the following statement in code:

```
enum BodyType = { sedan, coupe, minivan, stationwagon };
```

It may turn out, however, that a simple value is insufficient to model a particular discriminator. For example, the performance characteristic may be rather complex. In this case, the discriminator can be modeled as a class, and the discrimination can be encapsulated in an instance of that type.

Thus, the car might model the performance characteristics in a *performance* type, which contains information about where the engine shifts and how fast it can turn. The UML stereotype for a class that encapsulates a discriminator, and that can be used to create *instances* of a class (Car) that are logically of different types (for example, SportsCar versus LuxuryCar) is «powertype». In this case, the Performance class is a powertype for car. When you instantiate Car, you also instantiate a Performance object, and you associate a given Performance object with a given Car, as shown in Figure 18.19.

FIGURE 18.19

A discriminator as a powertype.

Powertypes enable you to create a variety of *logical* types without using inheritance. You can thus manage a large and complex set of types without the combinatorial explosion you might encounter with inheritance.

Typically, you *implement* the powertype in C++ with pointers. In this case, the Car class holds a pointer to an instance of the PerformanceCharacteristics class (see Figure 18.20). I leave it as an exercise to the ambitious reader to convert the body and engine discriminators into powertypes.

FIGURE 18.20

The relationship between a Car object and its powertype.

```
Class Car : public Vehicle
{
public:
    Car();
    ~Car();
    // other public methods elided
private:
    PerformanceCharacteristics * pPerformance;
};
```

As a final note, powertypes enable you to create new *types* (not just instances) at run-time. Because each logical type is differentiated only by the attributes of the associated powertype, these attributes can be parameters to the powertype's constructor. This means that you can, at runtime, create new *types* of cars on-the-fly. That is, by passing different engine sizes and shift points to the powertype, you can effectively create new performance characteristics. By assigning those characteristics to various cars, you can effectively enlarge the set of types of cars *at runtime*.

Dynamic Model

In addition to modeling the relationships among the classes, it is critical to model how they interact. For example, going back to the banking scenario, the CheckingAccount, ATM, and Receipt classes may interact with the Customer in fulfilling the "Withdraw Cash" use case. We return to the kinds of sequence diagrams first used in analysis, but now we flesh out the details based on the methods we developed in the classes, as shown in Figure 18.21.

This simple interaction diagram shows the interaction among a number of design classes over time. It suggests that the ATM class will delegate to the CheckingAccount class all responsibility for managing the balance, while the CheckingAccount will call on the ATM to manage display to the user.

Interaction diagrams come in two flavors. The one in Figure 18.21 is called a *sequence diagram*. Another view on the same information is provided by the *collaboration diagram*. The sequence diagram emphasizes the sequence of events over time; the collaboration diagram emphasizes the interactions among the classes. You can generate a collaboration diagram directly from a sequence diagram; tools such as the Rational Rose program automate this task at the click of a button (see Figure 18.22).

FIGURE 18.21

Sequence diagram.

FIGURE 18.22

Collaboration diagram.

State Transition Diagrams

As we come to understand the interactions among the objects, we have to understand the various possible *states* of each individual object. We can model the transitions among the various states in a state diagram (or state transition diagram). Figure 18.23 shows the various states of the CustomerAccount class as the customer logs in to the system.

FIGURE 18.23

Customer account state.

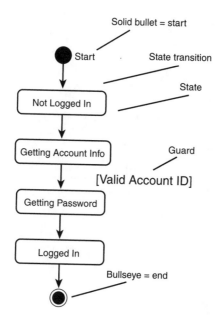

Every state diagram begins with a single start state and ends with zero or more end states. The individual states are named, and the transitions may be labeled. The guard indicates a condition that must be satisfied for an object to move from one state to another.

Super States

The customer can change his mind at any time and decide not to log in. He can do this after he swipes his card to identify his account or after he enters his password. In either case, the system must accept his request to cancel and return to the "not logged in state" (see Figure 18.24).

As you can see, in a more complicated diagram, the Canceled state will quickly become a distraction. This is particularly annoying because canceling is an exceptional condition that should not be given prominence in the diagram. You can simplify this diagram by using a *super state*, as shown in Figure 18.25.

18

FIGURE 18.24

User may cancel.

FIGURE 18.25

Super state.

The diagram in Figure 18.25 provides the same information in Figure 18.24 but is much cleaner and easier to read. From the time you start logging in until the system finalizes your login, you can cancel the process. If you do cancel, you return to the state "not logged in."

Do Not Rush to Code

One of the biggest problems in software development organizations is their rush to begin coding. There are always time pressures, and the coding/testing portions of the project tend to be the largest part. And usually a number of people are assigned to the task.

As a result, companies often rush through or skimp on the analysis phase to create the appearance of progress and keep the programmers busy. Unfortunately, this results in a solution that does not solve the underlying problem. This fact is discovered as the coding approaches completion. So the programmers have to go back and fix the discrepancies, resulting in harried programmers, software bugs, missed deadlines, and incomplete solutions.

Try to resist the organizational pressures. Work to get a complete analysis before the coding begins. If you need to, you can present information about failed projects that rushed to coding.

Of course, this is not an excuse to indulge in "analysis paralysis" where the analysis goes on and on forever with no results and no progress. There is a thin line between analysis being complete and going into paralysis. Unfortunately, experience is the only way to determine the difference.

There is a concept of "good enough." It is extremely difficult to make anything truly "complete." There is an axiom in this industry that 80% of the results take 20% of the time and the remaining 20% takes 80% of the time. At some point you make the decision to move on to the next step or you will begin to suffer from what is known as Analysis Paralysis—never getting to the final product because you are trying to get the perfect model.

Unfortunately, the best time to determine if the analysis and design is truly "good enough" is once the project is done. If the code delivered matches the organizational requirements, then it was good enough. Missing pieces or features missing, tend to indicate that not enough effort or time was expended. If there are features that no one wants or can figure out a purpose for, then that is a good indication that too much time was spent on the design.

Only retrospect and learning from the results will help you learn when the effort for a design is good enough.

How good or complete does your analysis have to be? How good is good enough? Only you and your organization can decide this. But think about it! Too many organizations do not think about the process and continually fail to deliver software on-time, on-budget, or with the needed features.

18

Summary

This lesson provided an introduction to the issues involved in object-oriented analysis and design. The essence of this approach is to analyze how your system will be used (use cases) and how it must perform, and then to design the classes and model their relationships and interactions.

In the old days, we sketched out a quick idea of what we wanted to accomplish and began writing code. The problem is that complex projects are never finished; and if they are, they are unreliable and brittle. By investing up front in understanding the requirements and modeling the design, we ensure a finished product that is correct (that is, it meets the design) and that is robust, reliable, and extensible.

Issues relating to testing and rollout are beyond the scope of this book, except to mention that you want to plan your unit testing as you implement, and that you will use your requirements document as the foundation of your test plan prior to rollout.

Q&A

Q In what way is object-oriented analysis and design fundamentally different from other approaches?

A Prior to the development of these object-oriented techniques, analysts and programmers tended to think of programs as groups of functions that acted on data. Object-oriented programming focuses on the integrated data and functionality as discrete units that have both knowledge (data) and capabilities (functions). Procedural programs, on the other hand, focus on functions and how they act on data. It has been said that Pascal and C programs are collections of procedures, and C++ programs are collections of classes.

Q Is object-oriented programming finally the silver bullet that will solve all programming problems?

A No, it was never intended to be. For large, complex problems, however, object-oriented analysis, design, and programming can provide the programmer with tools to manage enormous complexity in ways that were previously impossible.

Q Is C++ the perfect object-oriented language?

A C++ has a number of advantages and disadvantages when compared with alternative object-oriented programming languages, but it has one killer advantage above and beyond all others: It is the single most popular object-oriented programming language on the face of the Earth. Frankly, most programmers do not decide to program in C++ after an exhaustive analysis of the alternative object-oriented programming languages; they go where the action is, and currently the action is with C++. There are good reasons for that; C++ has a lot to offer, but this book exists because C++ is the development language of choice at so many corporations and Linux is such a growth area.

Workshop

The Workshop provides quiz questions to help you solidify your understanding of the material covered and exercises to provide you with experience in using what you have learned. Try to answer the quiz and exercise questions before checking the answers in Appendix D, "Answers to Exercises and Quizzes," and make sure you understand the answers before continuing tomorrow.

Quiz

1. What is the difference between object-oriented programming and procedural programming?

2. What are the phases of object-oriented analysis and design?

3. How are sequence diagrams and collaboration diagrams related?

Exercises

1. Suppose you had to simulate the intersection of Massachusetts Avenue and Vassar Street—two typical two-lane roads, with traffic lights and crosswalks. The purpose of the simulation is to determine whether the timing of the traffic signal allows for a smooth flow of traffic.

   What kinds of objects should be modeled in the simulation? What would the classes be for the simulation?

2. Suppose the intersection from Exercise 1 was in a suburb of Boston, which has arguably the most unfriendly streets in the United States. At any time three kinds of Boston drivers exist:

   Locals, who continue to drive through intersections after the light turns red; tourists, who drive slowly and cautiously (in a rental car, typically); and taxis, who have a wide variation of driving patterns, depending on the kinds of passengers in the cabs.

   Also, Boston has two kinds of pedestrians: locals, who cross the street whenever they feel like it and seldom use the crosswalk buttons; and tourists, who always use the crosswalk buttons and cross only when the Walk/Don't Walk light permits.

18

Finally, Boston has bicyclists who never pay attention to stoplights.

How do these considerations change the model?

3. You are asked to design a group scheduler. The software enables you to arrange meetings among individuals or groups and to reserve a limited number of conference rooms. Identify the principal subsystems.

4. Design and show the interfaces to the classes in the room reservation portion of the program discussed in Exercise 3.

Templates

A powerful new tool for C++ programmers is "parameterized types" or *templates*. Templates are so useful that the Standard Template Library (STL) has been adopted into the definition of the C++ language.

Today you will learn:

- What templates are and how to use them
- How to create class templates
- How to create function templates
- What the Standard Template Library is and how to learn to use it

What Are Templates?

At the end of Week 2, you saw how to build a PartsList object and how to use it to create a PartsCatalog. If you want to build on the PartsList object to make a list of cats, you have a problem: PartsList only knows about parts.

To solve this problem, you can create a List base class and derive from it the PartsList and CatsList classes. You could then cut and paste much of the

PartsList class into the new CatsList declaration. Next week, when you want to make a list of Car objects, you would then have to make a new class, and again you would cut and paste.

Needless to say, this is not a satisfactory solution. Over time, the List class and its derived classes will have to be extended. Making sure that all the changes are propagated to all the related classes would be a nightmare.

Templates solve this problem, and with the adoption of the ANSI standard, they are an integral part of the language. Like all of C++, they are type-safe and very flexible.

Parameterized Types

Templates enable you to teach the compiler how to make a list of any type of thing, rather than creating a set of type-specific lists—a PartsList is a list of parts, a CatsList is a list of cats. The only way in which they differ is the type of the thing on the list. With templates, the type of the thing on the list becomes a parameter to the definition of the class.

A common component of virtually all C++ libraries is an array class. As you saw with Lists, it is tedious and inefficient to create one array class for integers, another for doubles, and yet another for an array of Animals. Templates let you declare a parameterized array class and then specify what type of object each instance of the array will hold. Note that the Standard Template Library provides a standardized set of *container* classes, including arrays, lists, and so forth. This lesson explores what it takes to write your own so that you fully understand how templates work; however, in a commercial program, you would almost certainly use the STL classes rather than creating your own.

Instantiating an Instance of a Template

Instantiation is the act of creating a specific type from a template. The individual classes are called *instances* of the template.

Parameterized templates provide you with the capability to create a general class and pass types as parameters to that class to build specific instances.

Template Definition

You declare a parameterized Array object (a template for an array) by writing

```
1: template <class T>    // declare the template and the parameter
2: class Array           // the class being parameterized
3: {
```

```
4:    public:
5:        Array();
6:    // full class declaration here
7: };
```

The keyword `template` is used at the beginning of every declaration and definition of a template class. The parameters of the template follow the keyword `template`. The parameters are the things that will change with each instance. In the array template shown previously, for example, the type of the objects stored in the array will change. One instance might store an array of integers, and another might store an array of `Animals`.

In this example, the keyword `class` is used, followed by the identifier `T`. The keyword `class` indicates that this parameter is a type. The identifier `T` is used throughout the rest of the template definition to refer to the parameterized type. One instance of this class will substitute `int` everywhere `T` appears, and another will substitute `Cat`.

To declare an `int` and a `Cat` instance of the parameterized `Array` class, you would write

```
Array<int> anIntArray;
Array<Cat> aCatArray;
```

The object `anIntArray` is of the type *array of integers*; the object `aCatArray` is of the type *array of cats*. You can now use the type `Array<int>` anywhere you would normally use a type—as the return value from a function, as a parameter to a function, and so forth. Listing 19.1 provides the full declaration of this stripped-down `Array` template.

> **Note**
>
> Listing 19.1 is not a complete program and will not compile!

19

INPUT **LISTING 19.1** A Template of an Array Class

```
1: //Listing 19.1 A template of an array class
2:     #include <iostream.h>
3:     const int DefaultSize = 10;
4:
5:     template <class T>   // declare the template and the parameter
6:     class Array           // the class being parameterized
7:     {
8:     public:
9:         // constructors
10:        Array(int itsSize = DefaultSize);
11:        Array(const Array &rhs);
12:        ~Array() { delete [] pType; }
13:
```

continues

LISTING 19.1   CONTINUED

```
14:        // operators
15:        Array& operator=(const Array&);
16:        T& operator[](int offSet) { return pType[offSet]; }
17:
18:        // accessors
19:        int getSize() { return itsSize; }
20:
21:    private:
22:        T *pType;
23:        int  itsSize;
24:    };
```

OUTPUT   There is no output. This is an incomplete program.

ANALYSIS The definition of the template begins on line 5 with the keyword `template` followed by the parameter. In this case, the parameter is identified to be a type by the keyword `class`, and the identifier `T` is used to represent the parameterized type.

From line 6 until the end of the template on line 24, the rest of the declaration is like any other class declaration. The only difference is that wherever the type of the object would normally appear, the identifier `T` is used instead. For example, `operator[]` would be expected to return a reference to an object in the array, and in fact, it is declared to return a reference to a `T`.

When an instance of an integer array is declared, the `operator=` that is provided to that array will return a reference to an integer. When an instance of an `Animal` array is declared, the `operator=` provided to the `Animal` array will return a reference to an `Animal`.

Using the Name

Within the class declaration, the word `Array` may be used without further qualification. Elsewhere in the program, this class will be referred to as `Array<T>`. For example, if you do not write the constructor within the class declaration, you must write

```
template <class T>
Array<T>::Array(int size):
itsSize = size
{
    pType = new T[size];
    for (int i = 0; i<size; i++)
    pType[i] = 0;
}
```

The declaration on the first line of this code fragment is required to identify the type (class T). The template name is Array<T>, and the function name is Array(int size).

The remainder of the function is the same as it would be for a non-template function. It is a common and preferred method to get the class and its functions working as a simple declaration before turning it into a template.

Implementing the Template

The full implementation of the Array template class requires implementation of the copy constructor, operator=, and so forth. Listing 19.2 provides a simple driver program to exercise this template class.

Note

The GNU compilers 2.7.2 and newer support templates. Some older compilers, however, do not support templates. Templates are now part of the ANSI C++ standard. All major compiler vendors support templates in their current versions. If you have a very old compiler, you will not be able to compile and run the exercises in this lesson. It is still a good idea to read through the entire lesson, however, and return to this material when you upgrade your compiler. Remember that the CD-ROM has version 2.9.5, which does support templates.

INPUT   **LISTING 19.2**   The Implementation of the Template Array

```
1:     #include <iostream.h>
2:  // Listing 19.2: Implementing the template array
3:     const int DefaultSize = 10;
4:
5:     // declare a simple Animal class so that we can
6:     // create an array of animals
7:
8:     class Animal
9:     {
10:    public:
11:       Animal(int);
12:       Animal();
13:       ~Animal() {}
14:       int GetWeight() const { return itsWeight; }
15:       void Display() const { cout << itsWeight; }
16:    private:
17:       int itsWeight;
18:    };
19:
20:     Animal::Animal(int weight):
```

19

continues

LISTING 19.2   CONTINUED

```
21:     itsWeight(weight)
22:     {}
23:
24:     Animal::Animal():
25:     itsWeight(0)
26:     {}
27:
28:
29:     template <class T>  // declare the template and the parameter
30:     class Array               // the class being parameterized
31:     {
32:     public:
33:         // constructors
34:         Array(int itsSize = DefaultSize);
35:         Array(const Array &rhs);
36:         ~Array() { delete [] pType; }
37:
38:         // operators
39:         Array& operator=(const Array&);
40:         T& operator[](int offSet) { return pType[offSet]; }
41:         const T& operator[](int offSet) const
42:             { return pType[offSet]; }
43:         // accessors
44:         int GetSize() const { return itsSize; }
45:
46:     private:
47:         T *pType;
48:         int  itsSize;
49:     };
50:
51:     // implementations follow...
52:
53:     // implement the Constructor
54:     template <class T>
55:     Array<T>::Array(int size):
56:     itsSize(size)
57:     {
58:         pType = new T[size];
59:         for (int i = 0; i<size; i++)
60:             pType[i] = 0;
61:     }
62:
63:     // copy constructor
64:     template <class T>
65:     Array<T>::Array(const Array &rhs)
66:     {
67:         itsSize = rhs.GetSize();
68:         pType = new T[itsSize];
```

```
69:        for (int i = 0; i<itsSize; i++)
70:            pType[i] = rhs[i];
71:    }
72:
73:    // operator=
74:    template <class T>
75:    Array<T>& Array<T>::operator=(const Array &rhs)
76:    {
77:        if (this == &rhs)
78:            return *this;
79:        delete [] pType;
80:        itsSize = rhs.GetSize();
81:        pType = new T[itsSize];
82:        for (int i = 0; i<itsSize; i++)
83:            pType[i] = rhs[i];
84:        return *this;
85:    }
86:
87:    // driver program
88:    int main()
89:    {
90:        Array<int> theArray;        // an array of integers
91:        Array<Animal> theZoo;       // an array of Animals
92:        Animal *pAnimal;
93:
94:        // fill the arrays
95:        for (int i = 0; i < theArray.GetSize(); i++)
96:        {
97:            theArray[i] = i*2;
98:            pAnimal = new Animal(i*3);
99:            theZoo[i] = *pAnimal;
100:            delete pAnimal;
101:        }
102:        // print the contents of the arrays
103:        for (int j = 0; j < theArray.GetSize(); j++)
104:        {
105:            cout << "theArray[" << j << "]:\t";
106:            cout << theArray[j] << "\t\t";
107:            cout << "theZoo[" << j << "]:\t";
108:            theZoo[j].Display();
109:            cout << endl;
110:        }
111:
112:        return 0;
113:    }
```

19

OUTPUT		
theArray[0]:	0	theZoo[0]:	0

theArray[0]:   0   theZoo[0]:   0
theArray[1]:   2   theZoo[1]:   3
theArray[2]:   4   theZoo[2]:   6
theArray[3]:   6   theZoo[3]:   9
theArray[4]:   8   theZoo[4]:   12
theArray[5]:   10   theZoo[5]:   15
theArray[6]:   12   theZoo[6]:   18
theArray[7]:   14   theZoo[7]:   21
theArray[8]:   16   theZoo[8]:   24
theArray[9]:   18   theZoo[9]:   27

ANALYSIS Lines 8–26 provide a stripped-down Animal class, created here so that objects of a user-defined type are available to add to the array.

Line 29 declares that what follows is a template and that the parameter to the template is a type, designated as T. The Array class has two constructors as shown, the first of which takes a size and defaults to the constant integer DefaultSize.

The assignment and offset operators are declared, with the latter declaring both a const and a non-const variant. The only accessor provided is GetSize(), which returns the size of the array.

One can certainly imagine a fuller interface, and, for any serious Array program, what has been supplied here would be inadequate. At a minimum, operators to remove elements, to expand the array, to pack the array, and so forth would be required. All this is supplied by the STL container classes, as discussed toward the end of this lesson.

The private data consists of the size of the array and a pointer to the actual in-memory array of objects.

Template Functions

If you want to pass an array object to a function, you must pass a particular instance of the array, not a template. Therefore, if SomeFunction() takes an integer array as a parameter, you may write

```
void SomeFunction(Array<int>&);     // ok
```

but you may not write

```
void SomeFunction(Array<T>&);    // error!
```

because there is no way to know what a T is. You also may not write

```
void SomeFunction(Array &);      // error!
```

because there is no class Array—only the template and the instances.

To accomplish the more general approach, you must declare a template function.

```
template <class T>
void MyTemplateFunction(Array<T>&);    // ok
```

Here the function `MyTemplateFunction()` is declared to be a template function by the declaration on the top line. Note that like other functions, template functions can have any name.

Template functions can also take instances of the template in addition to the parameterized form. The following is an example:

```
template <class T>
void MyOtherFunction(Array<T>&, Array<int>&);    // ok
```

Note that this function takes two arrays: a parameterized array and an array of integers. The former can be an array of any object, but the latter is always an array of integers.

Templates and Friends

Template classes can declare three types of friends:

- A non-template friend class or function
- A general template friend class or function
- A type-specific template friend class or function

Non-Template Friend Classes and Functions

It is possible to declare any class or function to be a friend to your template class. Each instance of the class will treat the friend properly, as if the declaration of friendship had been made in that particular instance. Listing 19.3 adds a trivial friend function, `Intrude()`, to the template definition of the `Array` class, and the driver program invokes `Intrude()`. Because it is a friend, `Intrude()` can then access the private data of the `Array`. Because this is not a template function, it can only be called on `Arrays` of `int`.

INPUT   **LISTING 19.3** Non-Template Friend Function

```
1:     // Listing 19.3 - Type-specific friend functions in templates
2:
3:     #include <iostream.h>
4:
5:     const int DefaultSize = 10;
6:
7:     // declare a simple Animal class so that we can
8:     // create an array of animals
```

continues

19

LISTING 19.3 CONTINUED

```
9:
10:     class Animal
11:      {
12:    public:
13:       Animal(int);
14:       Animal();
15:       ~Animal() {}
16:       int GetWeight() const { return itsWeight; }
17:       void Display() const { cout << itsWeight; }
18:    private:
19:       int itsWeight;
20:      };
21:
22:    Animal::Animal(int weight):
23:    itsWeight(weight)
24:    {}
25:
26:    Animal::Animal():
27:    itsWeight(0)
28:    {}
29:
30:     template <class T>  // declare the template and the parameter
31:     class Array          // the class being parameterized
32:      {
33:    public:
34:        // constructors
35:        Array(int itsSize = DefaultSize);
36:        Array(const Array &rhs);
37:       ~Array() { delete [] pType; }
38:
39:        // operators
40:        Array& operator=(const Array&);
41:        T& operator[](int offSet) { return pType[offSet]; }
42:        const T& operator[](int offSet) const
43:            { return pType[offSet]; }
44:        // accessors
45:        int GetSize() const { return itsSize; }
46:
47:        // friend function
48:        friend void Intrude(Array<int>);
49:
50:    private:
51:        T *pType;
52:        int  itsSize;
53:      };
54:
55:        // friend function. Not a template, can only be used
56:        // with int arrays! Intrudes into private data.
```

```
57:      void Intrude(Array<int> theArray)
58:      {
59:       cout << "\n*** Intrude ***\n";
60:       for (int i = 0; i < theArray.itsSize; i++)
61:          cout << "i: " <<    theArray.pType[i] << endl;
62:       cout << "\n";
63:      }
64:
65:    // implementations follow...
66:
67:    // implement the Constructor
68:    template <class T>
69:    Array<T>::Array(int size):
70:    itsSize(size)
71:    {
72:       pType = new T[size];
73:       for (int i = 0; i<size; i++)
74:          pType[i] = 0;
75:    }
76:
77:    // copy constructor
78:    template <class T>
79:    Array<T>::Array(const Array &rhs)
80:    {
81:       itsSize = rhs.GetSize();
82:       pType = new T[itsSize];
83:       for (int i = 0; i<itsSize; i++)
84:          pType[i] = rhs[i];
85:    }
86:
87:    // operator=
88:    template <class T>
89:    Array<T>& Array<T>::operator=(const Array &rhs)
90:    {
91:       if (this == &rhs)
92:          return *this;
93:       delete [] pType;
94:       itsSize = rhs.GetSize();
95:       pType = new T[itsSize];
96:       for (int i = 0; i<itsSize; i++)
97:          pType[i] = rhs[i];
98:       return *this;
99:    }
100:
101:    // driver program
102:    int main()
103:    {
104:       Array<int> theArray;        // an array of integers
105:       Array<Animal> theZoo;       // an array of Animals
106:       Animal *pAnimal;
107:
```

19

continues

LISTING **19.3**   CONTINUED

```
108:        // fill the arrays
109:        for (int i = 0; i < theArray.GetSize(); i++)
110:        {
111:            theArray[i] = i*2;
112:            pAnimal = new Animal(i*3);
113:            theZoo[i] = *pAnimal;
114:        }
115:
116:        int j;
117:        for (j = 0; j < theArray.GetSize(); j++)
118:        {
119:            cout << "theZoo[" << j << "]:\t";
120:            theZoo[j].Display();
121:            cout << endl;
122:        }
123:        cout << "Now use the friend function to ";
124:        cout << "find the members of Array<int>";
125:        Intrude(theArray);
126:
127:        cout << "\n\nDone.\n";
128:        return 0;
129:    }
```

OUTPUT
```
theZoo[0]:       0
theZoo[1]:       3
theZoo[2]:       6
theZoo[3]:       9
theZoo[4]:       12
theZoo[5]:       15
theZoo[6]:       18
theZoo[7]:       21
theZoo[8]:       24
theZoo[9]:       27
Now use the friend function to find the members of Array<int>
*** Intrude ***
i: 0
i: 2
i: 4
i: 6
i: 8
i: 10
i: 12
i: 14
i: 16
i: 18

Done.
```

ANALYSIS The declaration of the `Array` template has been extended to include the friend function `Intrude()`. This declares that every instance of an int array will consider `Intrude()` to be a friend function; thus, `Intrude()` will have access to the private member data and functions of the array instance.

On line 60, `Intrude()` accesses `itsSize` directly, and on line 61, it accesses `pType` directly. This trivial use of these members was unnecessary because the `Array` class provides public accessors for this data, but it serves to demonstrate how friend functions can be declared with templates.

General Template Friend Class or Function

It would be helpful to add a display operator to the `Array` class. One approach would be to declare a display operator for each possible type of `Array`, but this would undermine the whole point of making `Array` a template.

What is needed is an insertion operator that works for any possible type of `Array`.

```
ostream& operator<< (ostream&, Array<T>&);
```

To make this work, you need to declare `operator<<` to be a template function.

```
template <class T> ostream& operator<< (ostream&, Array<T>&)
```

Now that `operator<<` is a template function, you only need to provide an implementation. Listing 19.4 shows the `Array` template extended to include this declaration and provides the implementation for the `operator<<`.

INPUT **LISTING 19.4** Using Operator ostream

```
1:     #include <iostream.h>
2: // Listing 19.4: using ostream operator
3:     const int DefaultSize = 10;
4:
5:     class Animal
6:     {
7:     public:
8:       Animal(int);
9:       Animal();
10:      ~Animal() {}
11:       int GetWeight() const { return itsWeight; }
12:       void Display() const { cout << itsWeight; }
13:     private:
14:       int itsWeight;
15:     };
16:
17:     Animal::Animal(int weight):
```

continues

LISTING **19.4**   CONTINUED

```
18:        itsWeight(weight)
19:        {}
20:
21:     Animal::Animal():
22:        itsWeight(0)
23:        {}
24:
25:      template <class T>   // declare the template and the parameter
26:      class Array              // the class being parameterized
27:      {
28:      public:
29:          // constructors
30:        Array(int itsSize = DefaultSize);
31:        Array(const Array &rhs);
32:        ~Array() { delete [] pType; }
33:
34:          // operators
35:        Array& operator=(const Array&);
36:        T& operator[](int offSet) { return pType[offSet]; }
37:        const T& operator[](int offSet) const
38:         { return pType[offSet]; }
39:          // accessors
40:        int GetSize() const { return itsSize; }
41:
42:          friend ostream& operator<< <> (ostream&, Array<T>&);
43:
44:      private:
45:        T *pType;
46:        int  itsSize;
47:      };
48:
49:      template <class T>
50:      ostream& operator<< (ostream& output, Array<T>& theArray)
51:      {
52:          for (int i = 0; i<theArray.GetSize(); i++)
53:             output << "[" << i << "] " << theArray[i] << endl;
     return output;
54:      }
55:
56:      // implementations follow...
57:
58:      // implement the Constructor
59:      template <class T>
60:      Array<T>::Array(int size):
61:        itsSize(size)
62:      {
63:         pType = new T[size];
64:         for (int i = 0; i<size; i++)
65:            pType[i] = 0;
66:      }
67:
```

```
68:    // copy constructor
69:    template <class T>
70:    Array<T>::Array(const Array &rhs)
71:    {
72:        itsSize = rhs.GetSize();
73:        pType = new T[itsSize];
74:        for (int i = 0; i<itsSize; i++)
75:            pType[i] = rhs[i];
76:    }
77:
78:    // operator=
79:    template <class T>
80:    Array<T>& Array<T>::operator=(const Array &rhs)
81:    {
82:        if (this == &rhs)
83:            return *this;
84:        delete [] pType;
85:        itsSize = rhs.GetSize();
86:        pType = new T[itsSize];
87:        for (int i = 0; i<itsSize; i++)
88:            pType[i] = rhs[i];
89:        return *this;
90:    }
91:
92:    int main()
93:    {
94:        bool Stop = false;          // flag for looping
95:        int offset, value;
96:        Array<int> theArray;
97:
98:        while (!Stop)
99:        {
100:           cout << "Enter an offset (0-9) ";
101:           cout << "and a value. (-1 to stop): " ;
102:           cin >> offset >> value;
103:
104:           if (offset < 0)
105:               break;
106:
107:           if (offset > 9)
108:           {
109:               cout << "***Please use values between 0 and 9.***\n";
110:               continue;
111:           }
112:
113:           theArray[offset] = value;
114:        }
115:
116:        cout << "\nHere's the entire array:\n";
117:        cout << theArray << endl;
118:     return 0;
119:    }
```

```
Enter an offset (0-9) and a value. (-1 to stop): 1 10
Enter an offset (0-9) and a value. (-1 to stop): 2 20
Enter an offset (0-9) and a value. (-1 to stop): 3 30
Enter an offset (0-9) and a value. (-1 to stop): 4 40
Enter an offset (0-9) and a value. (-1 to stop): 5 50
Enter an offset (0-9) and a value. (-1 to stop): 6 60
Enter an offset (0-9) and a value. (-1 to stop): 7 70
Enter an offset (0-9) and a value. (-1 to stop): 8 80
Enter an offset (0-9) and a value. (-1 to stop): 9 90
Enter an offset (0-9) and a value. (-1 to stop): 10 10
***Please use values between 0 and 9.***
Enter an offset (0-9) and a value. (-1 to stop): -1 -1

Here's the entire array:
[0] 0
[1] 10
[2] 20
[3] 30
[4] 40
[5] 50
[6] 60
[7] 70
[8] 80
[9] 90
```

Note

You must enter **-1** twice in order for the program to complete. That is because the cin is expecting two integer numbers. If you only enter -1 once, the program will sit and wait for the second input (without providing you a prompt of any kind).

ANALYSIS On line 42, the function template operator<<() is declared to be a friend of the Array class template. Because operator<<() is implemented as a template function, every instance of this parameterized array type will automatically have an operator<<(). The implementation for this operator starts on line 49. Every member of an array is called in turn. This works only if an operator<<() is defined for every type of object stored in the array.

Note

Many compilers do not require the <> shown on line 42 of Listing 19.4; g++ does. If you have the line without it (as shown in the following version of line 42 acceptable by most compilers):

```
42:          friend ostream& operator<< (ostream&, Array<T>&);
```

Version 2.9.5 will give you warnings about this code:

```
./lst19-04.cxx:42: warning: friend declaration `class ostream &
➥operator <<(class ostream &, class Array<T> &)'
./lst19-04.cxx:42: warning:   declares a non-template function
./lst19-04.cxx:42: warning:   (if this is not what you
➥intended, make sure
./lst19-04.cxx:42: warning:   the function template has already
➥ been declared,
./lst19-04.cxx:42: warning:   and add <> after the function
➥ name here)
/tmp/ccqfecaq.o: In function `main':
/tmp/ccqfecaq.o(.text+0x121): undefined reference to
➥`operator<<(ostream &, Array<int> &)'
```

So, if you use examples from other books and get that message, you will
need to make the suggested code change (as shown in line 42 of Listing
19.4).

Using Template Items

You can treat template items as you would any other type. You can pass them as
parameters, either by reference or by value, and you can return them as the return values
of functions, also by value or by reference. Listing 19.5 demonstrates how to pass
template objects.

INPUT **LISTING 19.5** Passing Template Object to and from Functions

19

```
1:     #include <iostream.h>
2: // Listing 19.5: Passing Template Objects
3:     const int DefaultSize = 10;
4:
5:     // A trivial class for adding to arrays
6:     class Animal
7:     {
8:     public:
9:     // constructors
10:        Animal(int);
11:        Animal();
12:        ~Animal();
13:
14:        // accessors
15:        int GetWeight() const { return itsWeight; }
16:        void SetWeight(int theWeight) { itsWeight = theWeight; }
17:
```

continues

LISTING **19.5**   CONTINUED

```
18:           // friend operators
19:           friend ostream& operator<< (ostream&, const Animal&);
20:
21:    private:
22:        int itsWeight;
23:    };
24:
25:    // extraction operator for printing animals
26:    ostream& operator<<
27:        (ostream& theStream, const Animal& theAnimal)
28:    {
29:     theStream << theAnimal.GetWeight();
30:     return theStream;
31:    }
32:
33:    Animal::Animal(int weight):
34:    itsWeight(weight)
35:    {
36:        // cout << "Animal(int)\n";
37:    }
38:
39:    Animal::Animal():
40:    itsWeight(0)
41:    {
42:        // cout << "Animal()\n";
43:    }
44:
45:    Animal::~Animal()
46:    {
47:        // cout << "Destroyed an animal...\n";
48:    }
49:
50:    template <class T>  // declare the template and the parameter
51:    class Array              // the class being parameterized
52:    {
53:    public:
54:        Array(int itsSize = DefaultSize);
55:        Array(const Array &rhs);
56:        ~Array() { delete [] pType; }
57:
58:        Array& operator=(const Array&);
59:        T& operator[](int offSet) { return pType[offSet]; }
60:        const T& operator[](int offSet) const
61:            { return pType[offSet]; }
62:        int GetSize() const { return itsSize; }
63:
64:        // friend function
65:        friend ostream& operator<< <> (ostream&, const Array<T>&);
```

```
66:
67:    private:
68:       T *pType;
69:       int  itsSize;
70:    };
71:
70:    template <class T>
72:    ostream& operator<< (ostream& output, const Array<T>& theArray)
73:    {
74:       for (int i = 0; i<theArray.GetSize(); i++)
75:          output << "[" << i << "] " << theArray[i] << endl;
76:       return output;
77:    }
78:
79:    // implementations follow...
80:
81:    // implement the Constructor
82:    template <class T>
83:    Array<T>::Array(int size):
84:    itsSize(size)
85:    {
86:       pType = new T[size];
87:       for (int i = 0; i<size; i++)
88:          pType[i] = 0;
89:    }
90:
91:    // copy constructor
92:    template <class T>
93:    Array<T>::Array(const Array &rhs)
94:    {
95:       itsSize = rhs.GetSize();
96:       pType = new T[itsSize];
97:       for (int i = 0; i<itsSize; i++)
98:          pType[i] = rhs[i];
99:    }
100:
101:    void IntFillFunction(Array<int>& theArray);
102:    void AnimalFillFunction(Array<Animal>& theArray);
103:
104:    int main()
105:    {
106:       Array<int> intArray;
107:       Array<Animal> animalArray;
108:       IntFillFunction(intArray);
109:       AnimalFillFunction(animalArray);
110:       cout << "intArray...\n" << intArray;
111:       cout << "\nanimalArray...\n" << animalArray << endl;
112:       return 0;
113:    }
114:
115:    void IntFillFunction(Array<int>& theArray)
```

19

continues

LISTING 19.5 CONTINUED

```
116:    {
117:       bool Stop = false;
118:       int offset, value;
119:       while (!Stop)
120:       {
121:          cout << "Enter an offset (0-9) ";
122:          cout << "and a value. (-1 to stop): " ;
123:          cin >> offset >> value;
124:       if (offset < 0)
125:          break;
126:       if (offset > 9)
127:       {
128:          cout << "***Please use values between 0 and 9.***\n";
129:          continue;
130:       }
131:       theArray[offset] = value;
132:       }
133:    }
134:
135:
136:    void AnimalFillFunction(Array<Animal>& theArray)
137:    {
138:       Animal * pAnimal;
139:       for (int i = 0; i<theArray.GetSize(); i++)
140:       {
141:          pAnimal = new Animal;
142:          pAnimal->SetWeight(i*100);
143:          theArray[i] = *pAnimal;
144:          delete pAnimal;  // a copy was put in the array
145:       }
146:    }
```

OUTPUT

```
Enter an offset (0-9) and a value. (-1 to stop): 1 10
Enter an offset (0-9) and a value. (-1 to stop): 2 20
Enter an offset (0-9) and a value. (-1 to stop): 3 30
Enter an offset (0-9) and a value. (-1 to stop): 4 40
Enter an offset (0-9) and a value. (-1 to stop): 5 50
Enter an offset (0-9) and a value. (-1 to stop): 6 60
Enter an offset (0-9) and a value. (-1 to stop): 7 70
Enter an offset (0-9) and a value. (-1 to stop): 8 80
Enter an offset (0-9) and a value. (-1 to stop): 9 90
Enter an offset (0-9) and a value. (-1 to stop): 10 10
***Please use values between 0 and 9.***
Enter an offset (0-9) and a value. (-1 to stop): -1 -1

intArray:...
[0] 0
[1] 10
```

```
[2] 20
[3] 30
[4] 40
[5] 50
[6] 60
[7] 70
[8] 80
[9] 90

animalArray:...
[0] 0
[1] 100
[2] 200
[3] 300
[4] 400
[5] 500
[6] 600
[7] 700
[8] 800
[9] 900
```

ANALYSIS   Most of the `Array` class implementation is left out to save space. The `Animal`
class is declared on lines 6–23. Although this is a stripped-down and
simplified class, it does provide its own insertion operator (`<<`) to allow the printing of
`Animal`s. Printing simply prints the current weight of the `Animal`.

Note that `Animal` has a default constructor. This is necessary because, when you add an
object to an array, the object's default constructor is used to create the object. This creates some difficulties, as you will see.

On line 101, the function `IntFillFunction()` is declared. The prototype indicates that
this function takes an integer array. Note that this is not a template function.
`IntFillFunction()` expects only one type of an array—an integer array. Similarly, on
line 102, `AnimalFillFunction()` is declared to take an `Array` of `Animal`.

The implementations for these functions are different from one another because filling an
array of integers does not have to be accomplished in the same way as filling an array of
`Animal`s.

Specialized Functions

If you uncomment the `cout` statements in `Animal`'s constructors (lines 36 and 42) and
destructor (line 47) in Listing 19.5, you can see the unanticipated extra constructions and
destructions of `Animal`s.

When an object is added to an array, the object's default constructor is called. The `Array`
constructor, however, goes on to assign `0` to the value of each member of the array, as
shown on lines 59 and 60 of Listing 19.2.

19

When you write someAnimal = (Animal) 0;, you call the default operator= for
Animal. This causes a temporary Animal object to be created, using the constructor,
which takes an integer (zero). That temporary object is used as the right-hand side of the
operator= and then is destroyed.

This is an unfortunate waste of time because the Animal object was already properly initialized. However, you cannot remove this line because integers are not automatically initialized to a value of 0. The solution is to teach the template not to use this constructor
for Animals, but to use a special Animal constructor.

You can provide an explicit implementation for the Animal class, as indicated in
Listing 19.6.

INPUT   **LISTING 19.6**   Specializing Template Implementations

```
1:      #include <iostream.h>
2:  // Listing 19.6: Specializing Template Implementations
3:      const int DefaultSize = 3;
4:
5:      // A trivial class for adding to arrays
6:       class Animal
7:       {
8:      public:
9:          // constructors
10:         Animal(int);
11:         Animal();
12:         ~Animal();
13:
14:         // accessors
15:         int GetWeight() const { return itsWeight; }
16:         void SetWeight(int theWeight) { itsWeight = theWeight; }
17:
18:         // friend operators
19:         friend ostream& operator<< (ostream&, const Animal&);
20:
21:      private:
22:          int itsWeight;
23:       };
24:
25:       // extraction operator for printing animals
26:      ostream& operator<<
27:          (ostream& theStream, const Animal& theAnimal)
28:       {
29:        theStream << theAnimal.GetWeight();
30:        return theStream;s
31:       }
32:
33:       Animal::Animal(int weight):
```

```
34:        itsWeight(weight)
35:        {
36:            cout << "animal(int) ";
37:        }
38:
39:        Animal::Animal():
40:        itsWeight(0)
41:        {
42:            cout << "animal() ";
43:        }
44:
45:        Animal::~Animal()
46:        {
47:            cout << "Destroyed an animal...";
48:        }
49:
50:    template <class T>  // declare the template and the parameter
51:    class Array              // the class being parameterized
52:    {
53:    public:
54:        Array(int itsSize = DefaultSize);
55:        Array(const Array &rhs);
56:        ~Array() { delete [] pType; }
57:
58:        // operators
59:        Array& operator=(const Array&);
60:        T& operator[](int offSet) { return pType[offSet]; }s
61:        const T& operator[](int offSet) const
62:            { return pType[offSet]; }
62:
63:        // accessors
64:        int GetSize() const { return itsSize; }
65:
66:        // friend function
67:       friend ostream& operator<< <> (ostream&, const Array<T>&);
68:
69:    private:
70:        T *pType;
71:        int  itsSize;
72:    };
73:
74:    template <class T>
75:    Array<T>::Array(int size = DefaultSize):
76:    itsSize(size)
77:    {
78:        pType = new T[size];
79:        for (int i = 0; i<size; i++)
80:            pType[i] = (T)0;
81:    }
82:
83:    template <class T>
```

continues

LISTING **19.6** CONTINUED

```
84:    Array<T>& Array<T>::operator=(const Array &rhs)
85:    {
86:        if (this == &rhs)
87:            return *this;
88:        delete [] pType;
89:        itsSize = rhs.GetSize();
90:        pType = new T[itsSize];
91:        for (int i = 0; i<itsSize; i++)
92:            pType[i] = rhs[i];
93:        return *this;
94:    }
95:    template <class T>
96:    Array<T>::Array(const Array &rhs)
97:    {
98:        itsSize = rhs.GetSize();
99:        pType = new T[itsSize];
100:        for (int i = 0; i<itsSize; i++)s
101:            pType[i] = rhs[i];
102:    }
103:
104:
105:    template <class T>
106:    ostream& operator<< (ostream& output, const Array<T>& theArray)
107:    {
108:        for (int i = 0; i<theArray.GetSize(); i++)
109:            output << "[" << i << "] " << theArray[i] << endl;
110:        return output;
111:    }
112:
113:
114:    Array<Animal>::Array(int AnimalArraySize):
115:    itsSize(AnimalArraySize)
116:    {
117:        pType = new Animal[AnimalArraySize];
118:    }
119:
120:s
121:    void IntFillFunction(Array<int>& theArray);
122:    void AnimalFillFunction(Array<Animal>& theArray);
123:
124:    int main()
125:    {
126:        Array<int> intArray;
127:        Array<Animal> animalArray;
128:        IntFillFunction(intArray);
129:        AnimalFillFunction(animalArray);
130:        cout << "intArray...\n" << intArray;
131:        cout << "\nanimalArray...\n" << animalArray << endl;
```

```
132:      return 0;
133:    }
134:
135:    void IntFillFunction(Array<int>& theArray)
136:    {
137:      bool Stop = false;
138:      int offset, value;
139:      while (!Stop)
140:      {
141:        cout << "Enter an offset (0-9) and a value. ";
142:        cout << "(-1 to stop): " ;
143:        cin >> offset >> value;
144:        if (offset < 0)
145:          break;
146:        if (offset > 9)
147:        {
148:          cout << "***Please use values between 0 and 9.***\n";
149:          continue;
150:        }
151:        theArray[offset] = value;
152:      }
153:    }
154:
155:
156:    void AnimalFillFunction(Array<Animal>& theArray)
157:    {
158:      Animal * pAnimal;
159:      for (int i = 0; i<theArray.GetSize(); i++)
160:      {
161:        pAnimal = new Animal(i*10);
162:        theArray[i] = *pAnimal;
163:        delete pAnimal;
164:      }
165:    }s
```

19

Note	Line numbers have been added to the output to make analysis easier. Line numbers will not appear in your output.

OUTPUT

```
1:  animal() animal() animal() Enter an offset (0-9) and a value. (-1 to
    ➥stop): 0 0
2:  Enter an offset (0-9) and a value. (-1 to stop): 1 1
3:  Enter an offset (0-9) and a value. (-1 to stop): 2 2
4:  Enter an offset (0-9) and a value. (-1 to stop): 3 3
5:  Enter an offset (0-9) and a value. (-1 to stop): -1 -1
6:  animal(int) Destroyed an animal...animal(int) Destroyed an
    ➥animal...animal(int) Destroyed an animal...initArray...
7: [0] 0
```

```
 8: [1] 1
 9: [2] 2
10:
11: animal array...
12: [0] 0
13: [1] 10
14: [2] 20
15:
16: Destroyed an animal...Destroyed an animal...Destroyed an animal...
17: <<< Second run >>>s
18: animal(int)  Destroyed an animal...
19: animal(int)  Destroyed an animal...
20: animal(int)  Destroyed an animal...
21: Enter an offset (0-9) and a value. (-1 to stop): 0 0
22: Enter an offset (0-9) and a value. (-1 to stop): 1 1
23: Enter an offset (0-9) and a value. (-1 to stop): 2 2
24: Enter an offset (0-9) and a value. (-1 to stop): 3 3
25: animal(int)
26: Destroyed an animal...
27: animal(int)
28: Destroyed an animal...
29: animal(int)
30: Destroyed an animal...
31: initArray...
32: [0] 0
33: [1] 1
34: [2] 2
35:
36: animal array...
37: [0] 0
38: [1] 10
39: [2] 20
40:
41: Destroyed an animal...
42: Destroyed an animal...
43: Destroyed an animal...s
```

ANALYSIS   Listing 19.6 reproduces both classes in their entirety so that you can see the creation and destruction of temporary Animal objects. The value of DefaultSize has been reduced to 3 to simplify the output.

The Animal constructors and destructors on lines 33–48 each print a statement indicating when they are called.

On lines 74–81, the template behavior of an Array constructor is declared. On lines 114–118, the specialized constructor for an Array of Animals is demonstrated. Note that in this special constructor, the default constructor is allowed to set the initial value for each Animal, and no explicit assignment is done.

The first time this program is run, the first set of output is shown. Line 1 of the output shows the three default constructors called by creating the array. The user enters four numbers, and these are entered into the integer array.

Execution jumps to `AnimalFillFunction()`. Here a temporary `Animal` object is created on the heap on line 161, and its value is used to modify the `Animal` object in the array on line 162. On line 163, the temporary `Animal` is destroyed. This is repeated for each member of the array and is reflected in the output on line 6.

At the end of the program, the arrays are destroyed, and when their destructors are called, all their objects are destroyed as well. This is reflected in the output on line 16.

For the second set of output (lines 18 to 43), the special implementation of the array of the character constructor, shown on lines 114–118 of the program, is commented out. When the program is run again, the template constructor, shown on lines 74–81 of the program, is run when the `Animal` array is constructed.

This causes temporary `Animal` objects to be called for each member of the array on lines 79 and 80 of the program, and is reflected in the output on lines 18–20.

In all other respects, the output for the two runs is identical, as you would expect.

Static Members and Templates

A template can declare static data members. Each instantiation of the template then has its own set of static data, one per class type. That is, if you add a static member to the `Array` class (for example, a counter of how many arrays have been created), you will have one such member per type: one for all the arrays of `Animals` and another for all the arrays of integers. Listing 19.7 adds a static member and a static function to the `Array` class.

INPUT   **LISTING 19.7**   Using Static Member Data and Functions with Templates

```
1:     #include <iostream.h>
2: // Listing 19.7: Using Static Member Data and Functions
3:     const int DefaultSize = 3;
4:
5:     // A trivial class for adding to arrays
6:       class Animal
7:       {
8:       public:
9:         // constructors
10:        Animal(int);
11:        Animal();
12:        ~Animal();
```

continues

19

LISTING **19.7**   CONTINUED

```
13:
14:          // accessors
15:          int GetWeight() const { return itsWeight; }
16:          void SetWeight(int theWeight) { itsWeight = theWeight; }
17:
18:          // friend operators
19:          friend ostream& operator<< (ostream&, const Animal&);
20:
21:      private:
22:          int itsWeight;
23:      };
24:
25:       // extraction operator for printing animals
26:      ostream& operator<<
27:          (ostream& theStream, const Animal& theAnimal)
28:      {
29:        theStream << theAnimal.GetWeight();
30:        return theStream;
31:      }
32:
33:      Animal::Animal(int weight):
34:      itsWeight(weight)
35:      {
36:          //cout << "animal(int) ";
37:      }
38:
39:      Animal::Animal():
40:      itsWeight(0)
41:      {
42:          //cout << "animal() ";
43:      }
44:
45:      Animal::~Animal()
46:      {
47:        //cout << "Destroyed an animal...";
48:      }
49:
50:      template <class T>  // declare the template and the parameter
51:      class Array            // the class being parameterized
52:      {
53:      public:
54:          // constructors
55:          Array(int itsSize = DefaultSize);
56:          Array(const Array &rhs);
57:        ~Array() { delete [] pType;   itsNumberArrays−; }
58:
59:          // operators
60:          Array& operator=(const Array&);
```

```
61:        T& operator[](int offSet) { return pType[offSet]; }
62:        const T& operator[](int offSet) const
63:           { return pType[offSet]; }
64:        // accessors
65:        int GetSize() const { return itsSize; }
66:        static int GetNumberArrays() { return itsNumberArrays; }
67:
68:        // friend function
69:      friend ostream& operator<< <> (ostream&, const Array<T>&);
70:
71:     private:
72:        T *pType;
73:        int  itsSize;
74:        static int itsNumberArrays;
75:     };
76:
77:     template <class T>
78:        int Array<T>::itsNumberArrays = 0;
79:
80:     template <class T>
81:     Array<T>::Array(int size = DefaultSize):
82:     itsSize(size)
83:     {
84:        pType = new T[size];
85:        for (int i = 0; i<size; i++)
86:          pType[i] = (T)0;
87:        itsNumberArrays++;
88:     }
89:
90:     template <class T>
91:     Array<T>& Array<T>::operator=(const Array &rhs)
92:     {
93:        if (this == &rhs)
94:           return *this;
95:        delete [] pType;
96:        itsSize = rhs.GetSize();
97:        pType = new T[itsSize];
98:        for (int i = 0; i<itsSize; i++)
99:           pType[i] = rhs[i];
100:    }
101:
102:    template <class T>
103:    Array<T>::Array(const Array &rhs)
104:    {
105:       itsSize = rhs.GetSize();
106:       pType = new T[itsSize];
107:       for (int i = 0; i<itsSize; i++)
108:          pType[i] = rhs[i];
109:       itsNumberArrays++;
110:    }
111:
```

19

continues

LISTING 19.7   CONTINUED

```
112:
113:     template <class T>
114:     ostream& operator<< (ostream& output, const Array<T>& theArray)
115:     {
116:        for (int i = 0; i<theArray.GetSize(); i++)
117:           output << "[" << i << "] " << theArray[i] << endl;
118:        return output;
119:     }
120:
121:
122:
123:     int main()
124:     {
125:
126:        cout << Array<int>::GetNumberArrays() << " integer arrays\n";
127:        cout << Array<Animal>::GetNumberArrays();
128:        cout << " animal arrays\n\n";
129:        Array<int> intArray;
130:        Array<Animal> animalArray;
131:
132:        cout << intArray.GetNumberArrays() << " integer arrays\n";
133:        cout << animalArray.GetNumberArrays();
134:        cout << " animal arrays\n\n";
135:
136:        Array<int> *pIntArray = new Array<int>;
137:
138:        cout << Array<int>::GetNumberArrays() << " integer arrays\n";
139:        cout << Array<Animal>::GetNumberArrays();
140:        cout << " animal arrays\n\n";
141:
142:        delete pIntArray;
143:
144:        cout << Array<int>::GetNumberArrays() << " integer arrays\n";
145:        cout << Array<Animal>::GetNumberArrays();
146:        cout << " animal arrays\n\n";
147:     return 0;
148:     }
```

OUTPUT

```
0 integer arrays
0 animal arrays

1 integer arrays
1 animal arrays

2 integer arrays
1 animal arrays

1 integer arrays
1 animal arrays
```

ANALYSIS The declaration of the `Animal` class has been left out to save space. The `Array` class has added the static variable `itsNumberArrays` on line 74, and because this data is private, the static public accessor `GetNumberArrays()` was added on line 66.

Initialization of the static data is accomplished with a full template qualification, as shown on lines 77 and 78. The constructors of `Array` and the destructor are each modified to keep track of how many arrays exist at any moment.

Accessing the static members is the same as accessing the static members of any class: You can do so with an existing object, as shown on lines 132 and 133, or by using the full class specification, as shown on lines 126 and 127. Note that you must use a specific type of array when accessing the static data. One variable exists for each type.

Note

> Version 2.7.2 cannot compile this code—giving you the following messages:
> ```
> lst19-07.cxx:78: sorry, not implemented: static data member
> templates
> lst19-07.cxx:78: end of file read inside definition
> ```
> Use version 2.9.5 instead for all remaining examples in this lesson. It is the newer compiler and has the more advanced features.

Do	Don't
DO use statics with templates as needed.	
DO specialize template behavior by overriding template functions by type.	
DO use the parameters to template functions to narrow their instances to be type-safe.	

19

The Standard Template Library

A new development in C++ is the adoption of the Standard Template Library (STL). All the major compiler vendors now offer the STL as part of their compilers. Newer versions of the GNU compiler include the STL. STL is a library of template-based container classes, including vectors, lists, queues, and stacks. The STL also includes a number of common algorithms, including sorting and searching.

The goal of the STL is to give you an alternative to reinventing the wheel for these common requirements. The STL is tested and debugged, offers high performance, and is free. Most importantly, the STL is reusable; after you understand how to use an STL container, you can use it in all your programs without reinventing it.

Containers

A *container* is an object that holds other objects. The standard C++ library provides a series of container classes that are powerful tools that help C++ developers handle common programming tasks. Two types of Standard Template Library (STL) container classes are sequence and associative. *Sequence* containers are designed to provide sequential and random access to their members, or *elements*. *Associative* containers are optimized to access their elements by key values. As with other components of the standard C++ library, the STL is portable between various operating systems. All STL container classes are defined in namespace std.

Understanding Sequence Containers

The Standard Template Library sequence containers provide efficient sequential access to a list of objects. The standard C++ library provides three sequence containers: vector, list, and deque.

The Vector Container

You often use arrays to store and access a number of elements. Elements in an array are of the same type and are accessed with an index. The STL provides a container class vector that behaves like an array, but that is more powerful and safer to use than the standard C++ array.

A *vector* is a container optimized to provide fast access to its elements by an index. The container class vector is defined in the header file <vector> in namespace std (see Day 17, "Namespaces," for more information on the use of namespaces). A vector can grow itself as necessary. Suppose that you have created a vector to contain 10 elements. After you have filled the vector with 10 objects, the vector is full. If you then add another object to the vector, the vector automatically increases its capacity so that it can accommodate the eleventh object. Here is how the vector class is defined:

```
template <class T, class A = allocator<T>> class vector
{
    // class members
};
```

The first argument (class T) is the type of elements in the vector. The second argument (class A) is an allocator class. *Allocators* are memory managers responsible for memory allocation and deallocation of elements for the containers. The concept and implementation of allocators are advanced topics that are beyond the scope of this book.

By default, elements are created using the operator `new()` and are freed using the operator `delete()`. That is, the default constructor of class `T` is called to create a new element. This provides another argument in favor of explicitly defining a default constructor for your own classes. If you do not define one explicitly, you cannot use the standard vector container to hold a set of instances of your class.

You can define vectors that hold integers and floats as follows:

```
vector<int>     vInts;     // vector holding int elements
vector<float>   vFloats;   // vector holding float elements
```

Usually, you would have some idea as to how many elements a vector will contain. For instance, suppose that in your school, the maximum number of students is 50. To create a vector of students in a class, you will want the vector to be large enough to contain 50 elements. The standard vector class provides a constructor that accepts the number of elements as its parameter. So you can define a vector of 50 students as follows:

```
vector<Student> MathClass(50);
```

The compiler will allocate enough memory spaces for 50 students; each element is created using the default constructor `Student::Student()`.

You can retrieve the number of elements in a vector using a member function, `size()`. In this example, `vStudent.size()` will return `50`.

Another member function, `capacity()`, tells you exactly how many elements a vector can accommodate before its size needs to be increased. You will see more on this later.

A vector is said to be empty if no element is in a vector; that is, the vector's size is zero. To make it easier to test whether a vector is empty, the vector class provides a member function, `empty()`, that evaluates to `true` if the vector is empty.

To assign a `Student` object `Harry` to the `MathClass`, you can use the subscripting operator `[]`:

```
MathClass[5] = Harry;
```

The subscript starts at `0`. As you may have noticed, the overloaded assignment operator of the `Student` class is used here to assign `Harry` to the sixth element in `MathClass`. Similarly, to find out `Harry`'s age, you can access his record using

```
MathClass[5].GetAge();
```

19

As mentioned earlier, vectors can grow automatically when you add more elements than the vector can handle. For instance, suppose one class in your school has become so popular that the number of students exceeds 50. (Well, it may not happen to this math class, but who knows—strange things do happen.) When the fifty-first student, Sally, is added to the MathClass, the compiler will expand storage to accommodate her.

You can add an element into a vector in several ways; one of them is push_back():

```
MathClass.push_back(Sally);
```

This member function appends the new Student object Sally to the end of the vector MathClass. Now MathClass has 51 elements, and Sally is placed at MathClass[50].

For this function to work, the Student class must define a copy constructor. Otherwise this push_back() function will not be able to make a copy of object Sally.

STL does not specify the maximum number of elements in a vector; the compiler vendors are in better positions to make this decision. The vector class provides a member function that tells you what this magic number is in your compiler: max_size(). For GNU, the maximum number of elements depends on the size of each element. No matter which compiler you are using, the best way to determine this number is still the max_size() member function.

Listing 19.8 demonstrates the members of the vector class discussed so far. You will see that the standard string class is used in this listing to simplify the handling of strings. For more details about the string class, check the GNU compiler documentation.

INPUT   **LISTING 19.8**   Vector Creation and Element Access

```
1:     #include <iostream>
2:     #include <string>
3:     #include <vector>
4:     using namespace std;
5:     // Listing 19.8: Vectors
6:     class Student
7:     {
8:     public:
9:             Student();
10:            Student(const string& name, const int age);
11:            Student(const Student& rhs);
12:            ~Student();
13:
14:            void    SetName(const string& name);
15:            string  GetName()        const;
16:            void    SetAge(const int age);
17:            int            GetAge()        const;
```

```
18:
19:                 Student& operator=(const Student& rhs);
20:
21:     private:
22:             string itsName;
23:             int itsAge;
24:     };
25:
26:     Student::Student()
27:     : itsName("New Student"), itsAge(16)
28:     {}
29:
30:     Student::Student(const string& name, const int age)
31:     : itsName(name), itsAge(age)
32:     {}
33:
34:     Student::Student(const Student& rhs)
35:     : itsName(rhs.GetName()), itsAge(rhs.GetAge())
36:     {}
37:
38:     Student::~Student()
39:     {}
40:
41:     void Student::SetName(const string& name)
42:     {
43:             itsName = name;
44:     }
45:
46:     string Student::GetName() const
47:     {
48:             return itsName;
49:     }
50:
51:     void Student::SetAge(const int age)
52:     {
53:             itsAge = age;
54:     }
55:
56:     int Student::GetAge() const
57:     {
58:             return itsAge;
59:     }
60:
61:     Student& Student::operator=(const Student& rhs)
62:     {
63:             itsName = rhs.GetName();
64:             itsAge = rhs.GetAge();
65:             return *this;
66:     }
67:
68:     ostream& operator<<(ostream& os, const Student& rhs)
```

19

continues

LISTING 19.8   CONTINUED

```
69:    {
70:            os << rhs.GetName() << " is " << rhs.GetAge()
➥ << " years old";
71:            return os;
72:    }
73:
74:    template<class T>
75:    void ShowVector(const vector<T>& v);
➥      // display vector properties
76:
77:    typedef vector<Student>        SchoolClass;
78:
79:    int main()
80:    {
81:            Student Harry;
82:            Student Sally("Sally", 15);
83:            Student Bill("Bill", 17);
84:            Student Peter("Peter", 16);
85:
86:            SchoolClass    EmptyClass;
87:            cout << "EmptyClass:\n";
88:            ShowVector(EmptyClass);
89:
90:            SchoolClass GrowingClass(3);
91:            cout << "GrowingClass(3):\n";
92:            ShowVector(GrowingClass);
93:
94:            GrowingClass[0] = Harry;
95:            GrowingClass[1] = Sally;
96:            GrowingClass[2] = Bill;
97:            cout << "GrowingClass(3) after assigning students:\n";
98:            ShowVector(GrowingClass);
99:
100:           GrowingClass.push_back(Peter);
101:           cout << "GrowingClass() after added 4th student:\n";
102:           ShowVector(GrowingClass);
103:
104:           GrowingClass[0].SetName("Harry");
105:           GrowingClass[0].SetAge(18);
106:           cout << "GrowingClass() after Set\n:";
107:           ShowVector(GrowingClass);
108:
109:           return 0;
110:    }
111:
112:    //
113:    // Display vector properties
114:    //
```

```
115:    template<class T>
116:    void ShowVector(const vector<T>& v)
117:    {
118:            cout << "max_size() = " << v.max_size();
119:            cout << "\tsize() = " << v.size();
120:            cout << "\tcapacity() = " << v.capacity();
121:            cout << "\t" << (v.empty()? "empty": "not empty");
122:            cout << "\n";
123:
124:            for (int i = 0; i < v.size(); ++i)
125:                    cout << v[i] << "\n";
126:
127:            cout << endl;
128:    }
129:
```

OUTPUT

```
EmptyClass:
max_size() = 536870911  size() = 0          capacity() = 0  empty

GrowingClass(3):
max_size() = 536870911  size() = 3          capacity() = 3  not empty
New Student is 16 years old
New Student is 16 years old
New Student is 16 years old

GrowingClass(3) after assigning students:
max_size() = 536870911  size() = 3          capacity() = 3  not empty
New Student is 16 years old
Sally is 15 years old
Bill is 17 years old

GrowingClass() after added 4th student:
max_size() = 536870911  size() = 4          capacity() = 6  not empty
New Student is 16 years old
Sally is 15 years old
Bill is 17 years old
Peter is 16 years old

GrowingClass() after Set:
max_size() = 536870911 size() = 4           capacity() = 6  not empty
Harry is 18 years old
Sally is 15 years old
Bill is 17 years old
Peter is 16 years old
```

19

ANALYSIS The Student class is defined on lines 6–24. Its member function implementations are on lines 26–66. It is simple and vector-container-friendly. For the reasons discussed earlier, we defined a default constructor, a copy constructor, and an overloaded assignment operator. Note that its member variable itsName is defined as an instance of the C++ string class. As you can see here, it is much easier to work with a C++ string than with a C-style string `char*`.

The template function `ShowVector()` is declared on lines 74 and 75 and defined on lines 115–128. It demonstrates the usage of some of the vector member functions: `max_size()`, `size()`, `capacity()`, and `empty()`. As you can see from the output, the maximum number of `Student` objects a vector can accommodate in g++ is 536,870,911 (and only 214,748,364 in Visual C++). This number may be different for other types of elements. For instance, a vector of integers can have a lot more elements. If you are using other compilers, you may have a different value and maximum number of elements.

On lines 124 and 125, the program goes through each element in the vector and displays its value using the overloaded insertion operator <<, which is defined on lines 68–72.

Four students are created on lines 81–84. On line 86, an empty vector, properly named `EmptyClass`, is defined using the default constructor of the vector class. When a vector is created in this way, no space is allocated for it by the compiler. As you can see in the output produced by `ShowVector(EmptyClass)`, its size and capacity are both zero.

On line 90, a vector of three `Student` objects is defined. Its size and capacity are both three, as expected. Elements in the `GrowingClass` are assigned with the `Student` objects on lines 94–96 using the subscripting operator `[ ]`.

The fourth student, `Peter`, is added to the vector on line 100. This increases the size of the vector to four. Interestingly, its capacity is now set to six. This means that the compiler has allocated enough space for up to six `Student` objects. Because vectors must be allocated to a continuous block of memory, expanding them requires a set of operations. First, a new block of memory large enough for all four `Student` objects is allocated. Second, the three elements are copied to this newly allocated memory and the fourth element is appended after the third element. Lastly, the original memory block is returned to the memory. When you have a large number of elements in a vector, this deallocation and reallocation process can be time consuming. Therefore, a compiler employs an optimization strategy to reduce the possibility of such expensive operations. In this example, if we append one or two more objects to the vector, no need exists to deallocate and reallocate memory.

On lines 104 and 105, we again use the subscripting operator `[ ]` to change the member variables for the first object in the `GrowingClass`.

Note	GNU Compiler version 2.7.2 cannot compile this code. Use version 2.9.5 instead for this and the remaining examples.

Do	Don't
DO define a default constructor for a class if its instances are likely to be held in a vector.	
DO define a copy constructor for such a class.	
DO define an overloaded assignment operator for such a class.	

The vector container class has other member functions. The front() function returns a reference to the first element in a list. The back() function returns a reference to the last element. The at() function works like the subscription operator [ ]. It is safer because it checks whether the subscript passed to it is within the range of available elements. If it is out of range, it throws an out_of_range exception. (Exceptions are covered on Day 20, "Exceptions and Error Handling.")

The insert() function inserts one or more nodes into a given position in a vector. Then the pop_back() function removes the last element from a vector. Lastly, a remove() function removes one or more elements from a vector.

The List Container

A *list* is a container designed to provide optimal frequent insertions and deletions of elements.

The list STL container class is defined in the header file <list> in the namespace std. The list class is implemented as a doubly linked list, where each node has links to both the previous node and the next node in the list.

The list class has all the member functions provided by the vector class. As you saw in "Week 2 in Review," you can traverse a list by following the links provided in each node. Typically, the links are implemented using pointers. The standard list container class uses a mechanism called the iterator for the same purpose.

19

An iterator is a generalization of a pointer. You can dereference an iterator to retrieve the node it points to. Listing 19.9 demonstrates the use of iterators in accessing nodes in a list.

INPUT   **LISTING 19.9**   Traverse a List Using an Iterator

```
1:      #include <iostream>
2:      #include <list>
3:      using namespace std;
4:      // Listing 19.9: Traversing a List with an iterator
5:      typedef list<int> IntegerList;
6:
7:      int main()
8:      {
9:              IntegerList    intList;
10:
11:             for (int i = 1; i <= 10; ++i)
12:                     intList.push_back(i * 2);
13:
14:             for (IntegerList::const_iterator ci = intList.begin();
15:                                     ci != intList.end(); ++ci)
16:                     cout << *ci << " ";
17:
18:             return 0;
19:     }
```

OUTPUT   2 4 6 8 10 12 14 16 18 20

ANALYSIS   On line 9, intList is defined as a list of integers. The first 10 positive even numbers are added to the list using the push_back() function on lines 11 and 12.

On lines 14 to 16, we access each node in the list using a constant iterator. This indicates that we do not intend to change the nodes with this iterator. If we want to change a node to an iterator, we need to use a non-const iterator instead:

intList::iterator

The begin() member function returns an iterator pointing to the first node of the list. As you can see here, the increment operator ++ can be used to point an iterator to the next node. The end() member function is kind of strange—it returns an iterator pointing to one-pass-last node of a list. So you must be sure that you do not let your iterator reach end().

The iterator is dereferenced the same as a pointer to return the node pointed to, as shown on line 16.

Although this lesson introduces iterators with the `list` class, iterators are also provided by the vector class. In addition to functions introduced in the vector class, the `list` class also provides the `push_front()` and `pop_front()` functions that work just like `push_back()` and `pop_back()`. Instead of adding and removing elements at the back of the list, they add and remove elements in the front of the list.

The Deque Container

A deque is like a double-ended vector—it inherits the `vector` container class's efficiency in sequential read and write operations. But, in addition, the `deque` container class provides optimized front-end and back-end operations. These operations are implemented similarly to the list container class, where memory allocations are engaged only for new elements. This feature of the `deque` class eliminates the need to reallocate the whole container to a new memory location, as the vector class has to do. Therefore, deques are ideally suited for applications in which insertions and deletions take place at either one or both ends, and for which sequential access of elements is important. An example of such an application is a train assembly simulator, in which carriages can join the train at both ends.

Understanding Associative Containers

Although sequence containers are designed for sequential and random access of elements using the index or an iterator, the associative containers are designed for fast random access of elements using keys. The standard C++ library provides four associative containers: map, multimap, set, and multiset.

19

The Map Container

You have seen that a vector is like an enhanced version of an array. It has all the characteristics of an array and some additional features. Unfortunately, the vector also suffers from one of the significant weaknesses of arrays: It has no provision for the random access of elements using key values other than the index or iterator. Associative containers, on the other hand, provide fast random access based on key values.

The C++ Standard Library provides four associative containers: map, multimap, set, and multiset. In Listing 19.10, a map is used to implement the school class example shown in Listing 19.8.

LISTING 19.10   A Map Container Class

```
1:      #include <iostream>
2:      #include <string>
3:      #include <map>
4:      using namespace std;
5:    // Listing 19.10: Map container class
6:      class Student
7:      {
8:      public:
9:              Student();
10:             Student(const string& name, const int age);
11:             Student(const Student& rhs);
12:             ~Student();
13:
14:             void    SetName(const string& name);
15:             string  GetName()       const;
16:             void    SetAge(const int age);
17:             int             GetAge()        const;
18:
19:             Student& operator=(const Student& rhs);
20:
21:      private:
22:             string itsName;
23:             int itsAge;
24:      };
25:
26:      Student::Student()
27:      : itsName("New Student"), itsAge(16)
28:      {}
29:
30:      Student::Student(const string& name, const int age)
31:      : itsName(name), itsAge(age)
32:      {}
33:
34:      Student::Student(const Student& rhs)
35:      : itsName(rhs.GetName()), itsAge(rhs.GetAge())
36:      {}
37:
38:      Student::~Student()
39:      {}
40:
41:      void Student::SetName(const string& name)
42:      {
43:             itsName = name;
44:      }
45:
46:      string Student::GetName() const
47:      {
48:             return itsName;
```

```
49:      }
50:
51:      void Student::SetAge(const int age)
52:      {
53:            itsAge = age;
54:      }
55:
56:      int Student::GetAge() const
57:      {
58:            return itsAge;
59:      }
60:
61:      Student& Student::operator=(const Student& rhs)
62:      {
63:            itsName = rhs.GetName();
64:            itsAge = rhs.GetAge();
65:            return *this;
66:      }
67:
68:      ostream& operator<<(ostream& os, const Student& rhs)
69:      {
70:            os << rhs.GetName() << " is " << rhs.GetAge()
   << " years old";
71:            return os;
72:      }
73:
74:      template<class T, class A>
75:      void ShowMap(const map<T, A>& v);     // display map properties
76:
77:      typedef map<string, Student>          SchoolClass;
78:
79:      int main()
80:      {
81:            Student Harry("Harry", 18);
82:            Student Sally("Sally", 15);
83:            Student Bill("Bill", 17);
84:            Student Peter("Peter", 16);
85:
86:            SchoolClass MathClass;
87:            MathClass[Harry.GetName()] = Harry;
88:            MathClass[Sally.GetName()] = Sally;
89:            MathClass[Bill.GetName()] = Bill;
90:            MathClass[Peter.GetName()] = Peter;
91:
92:            cout << "MathClass:\n";
93:            ShowMap(MathClass);
94:
95:            cout << "We know that " << MathClass["Bill"].GetName()
96:                  << " is " << MathClass["Bill"].GetAge() << "
                  years old\n";
97:
```

19

continues

LISTING **19.10**   CONTINUED

```
98:              return 0;
99:      }
100:
101:     //
102:     // Display map properties
103:     //
104:     template<class T, class A>
105:     void ShowMap(const map<T, A>& v)
106:     {
107:         for (map<T, A>::const_iterator ci = v.begin();
108:                                   ci != v.end(); ++ci)
109:             cout << ci->first << ": " << ci->second << "\n";
110:
111:         cout << endl;
112:     }
```

OUTPUT

```
MathClass:
Bill: Bill is 17 years old
Harry: Harry is 18 years old
Peter: Peter is 16 years old
Sally: Sally is 15 years old

We know that Bill is 17 years old
```

ANALYSIS   On line 3, we include the header file <map> because we will be using the standard map container class. Consequently, we define the ShowMap template function to display the elements in a map. On line 77, the SchoolClass is defined as a map of elements; each consists of a (key, value) pair. The first value in the pair is the key value. In the SchoolClass, we use students' names as their key values, which are of type string. The key value of elements in the map container must be unique; that is, no two elements can have the same key value. The second value in the pair is the actual object, a Student object in the example. The pair data type is implemented in STL as a struct of two members: first and second. You can use these members to access a node's key and value.

You can skip the main() function and take a look at the ShowMap function first. The ShowMap function uses a constant iterator to access a map object. On line 109, ci->first points to the key, or a student's name. ci->second points to the Student object.

Back on lines 81–84, four Student objects are created. The MathClass is defined as an instance of the SchoolClass on line 86. On lines 87–90, we add the four students to the MathClass using the following syntax:

```
map_object[key_value] = object_value;
```

You could also use the push_back() or insert() functions to add a (key, value) pair to the map; you can check the GNU compiler's documentation for more details.

After all Student objects have been added to the map, we can access any of them using their key values. On lines 95 and 96, we use MathClass["Bill"] to retrieve Bill's record.

The Other Associative Containers

The multimap container class is a map class without the restriction of unique keys. More than one element can have the same key value.

The set container class is also similar to the map class. The only difference is that its elements are not (key, value) pairs. An element is only the key.

Finally, the multiset container class is a set class that allows duplex key values.

Stacks

One of the most commonly used data structures in computer programming is the stack. The stack, however, is not implemented as an independent container class. Instead, it is implemented as a wrapper of a container. The template class stack is defined in the header file <stack> in the namespace std.

A *stack* is a continuously allocated block that can grow or shrink at the back end. Elements in a stack can only be accessed or removed from the back. You have seen similar characteristics in the sequence containers, notably vector and deque. In fact, any sequence container that supports the back(), push_back(), and pop_back() operations can be used to implement a stack. Most of the other container methods are not required for the stack and are, therefore, not exposed by the stack.

The STL stack template class is designed to contain any type of objects. The only restriction is that all elements must be of the same type.

A stack is a *LIFO* (*last in, first out*) structure. It is like an overcrowded elevator: The first person who walks in is pushed toward the wall, and the last person stands right next to the door. When the elevator reaches the destination floor, the last person in is the first to go out. If someone wants to leave the elevator earlier, all those who stand between her and the door must make way for her, probably by going out of the elevator and then coming back in.

By convention, the open end of a stack is often called the *top* of the stack, and operations carried out to a stack are often called *push* and *pop*. The stack class inherits these conventional terms.

19

> **Note** The STL stack class is not the same as the stack mechanism used internally by compilers and operating systems, in which stacks can contain different types of objects. The underlying functionality, however, is very similar.

Understanding Queues

A *queue* is another commonly used data structure in computer programming. Elements are added to the queue at one end and taken out at the other. The classic analogy is this: A stack is like a stack of dishes at a salad bar. You add to the stack by placing a dish on top (pushing the stack down), and you take from the stack by "popping" the top dish (the one most recently added to the stack) off the top.

A queue is like a line at the theater. You enter the queue at the back, and you leave the queue at the front. This is known as a *FIFO* (*first in, first out*) structure; a stack is a *LIFO* (last in, first out) structure. Of course, every once in a while, you are second-to-last in a long line at the supermarket when someone opens a new register and grabs the last person in line—turning what should be a FIFO queue into a LIFO stack, and making you grind your teeth in frustration.

Like the stack, the queue is implemented as a wrapper class to a container. The container must support front(), back(), push_back(), and pop_front() operations.

Algorithm Classes

A container is a useful place to store a sequence of elements. All standard containers define operations that manipulate the containers and their elements. Implementing all these operations in your own sequences, however, can be laborious and prone to error. Because most of those operations are likely to be the same in most sequences, a set of generic algorithms can reduce the need to write your own operations for each new container. The standard library provides approximately 60 standard algorithms that perform the most basic and commonly used operations of containers.

Standard algorithms are defined in <algorithm> in namespace std.

To understand how the standard algorithms work, you need to learn the concept of function objects. A function object is an instance of a class that defines the overloaded operator (). Therefore, it can be called as a function. Listing 19.11 demonstrates a function object.

LISTING 19.11 A Function Object

```
1:     #include <iostream>
2:     using namespace std;
3:  // Listing 19.11: A function object
4:     template<class T>
5:     class Print    {
6:     public:
7:         void operator()(const T& t)
8:         {
9:                 cout << t << " ";
10:            }
11:    };
12:
13:    int main()
14:    {
15:        Print<int> DoPrint;
16:        for (int i = 0; i < 5; ++i)
17:            DoPrint(i);
18:        return 0;
19:    }
```

0 1 2 3 4

On lines 4–11, a template class Print is defined. The overloaded operator () on lines 7–10 takes an object and outputs it to the standard output. On line 15, DoPrint is defined as an instance of the Print class. You can then use DoPrint just like a function to print any integer values, as shown on line 17.

Non-Mutating Sequence Operations

Non-mutating sequence operations perform operations that do not change the elements in a sequence. These include operators such as for_each(), find(), search(), count(), and so forth. Listing 19.12 shows how to use a function object and the for_each algorithm to print elements in a vector:

LISTING 19.12 Using the for_each() Algorithm

```
1:     #include <iostream>
2:     #include <vector>
3:     #include <algorithm>
4:     using namespace std;
5:     // Listing 19.12: Using the for_each
6:     template<class T>
7:     class Print
```

19

continues

LISTING **19.12**   CONTINUED

```
 8:      {
 9:      public:
10:          void operator()(const T& t)
11:          {
12:              cout << t << " ";
13:          }
14:      };
15:
16:      int main()
17:      {
18:          Print<int>    DoPrint;
19:          vector<int>    vInt(5);
20:
21:          for (int i = 0; i < 5; ++i)
22:              vInt[i] = i * 3;
23:
24:          cout << "for_each()\n";
25:          for_each(vInt.begin(), vInt.end(), DoPrint);
26:          cout << "\n";
27:
28:          return 0;
29:      }
```

OUTPUT

```
for_each()
0 3 6 9 12
```

ANALYSIS   Note that all C++ standard algorithms are defined in <algorithm>, so we must include it here. Most of the program should be easy for you. On line 25, the for_each() function is called to go through each element in the vector vInt. For each element, it invokes the DoPrint function object and passes the element to DoPrint.operator(). This results in the value of the element to be printed on the screen.

Mutating Sequence Algorithms

Mutating sequence operations perform operations that change the elements in a sequence, including operations that fill or reorder collections. Listing 19.13 shows the fill() algorithm.

LISTING **19.13**   A Mutating Sequence Algorithm

```
1:      #include <iostream>
2:      #include <vector>
3:      #include <algorithm>
4:      using namespace std;
5:      // Listing 19.13: Mutating Sequence
```

```
6:      template<class T>
7:      class Print
8:      {
9:      public:
10:         void operator()(const T& t)
11:         {
12:             cout << t << " ";
13:         }
14:     };
15:
16:     int main()
17:     {
18:         Print<int>    DoPrint;
19:         vector<int>   vInt(10);
20:
21:         fill(vInt.begin(), vInt.begin() + 5, 1);
22:         fill(vInt.begin() + 5, vInt.end(), 2);
23:
24:         for_each(vInt.begin(), vInt.end(), DoPrint);
25:         cout << "\n\n";
26:
27:         return 0;
28:     }
```

OUTPUT   1 1 1 1 1 2 2 2 2 2

ANALYSIS   The only new content in this listing is on lines 21 and 22, where the `fill()` algorithm is used. The fill algorithm fills the elements in a sequence with a given value. On line 21, it assigns an integer value 1 to the first five elements in vInt. The last five elements of vInt are assigned with integer 2 on line 22.

19

Summary

Today you learned how to create and use templates. Templates are a built-in facility of C++, used to create parameterized types—types that change their behavior based on parameters passed in at creation. They are a way to reuse code safely and effectively.

The definition of the template determines the parameterized type. Each instance of the template is an actual object, which can be used like any other object—as a parameter to a function, as a return value, and so forth.

Template classes can declare three types of friend functions: non-template, general template, and type-specific template. A template can declare static data members, in which case each instance of the template has its own set of static data.

If you need to specialize behavior for some template functions based on the actual type, you can override a template function with a particular type. This works for member functions as well.

Q&A

Q **Why use templates when macros will do?**

A Templates are type-safe and built into the language.

Q **What is the difference between the parameterized type of a template function and the parameters to a normal function?**

A A regular function (non-template) takes parameters on which it may take action. A template function enables you to parameterize the type of a particular parameter to the function. That is, you can pass an Array of Type to a function and then have the Type determined by the template instance.

Q **When do you use templates and when do you use inheritance?**

A Use templates when all the behavior, or virtually all the behavior, is unchanged, except in regard to the type of the item on which your class acts. If you find yourself copying a class and changing only the type of one or more of its members, it may be time to consider using a template.

Q **When do you use general template friend classes?**

A When every instance, regardless of type, should be a friend to this class or function.

Q **When do you use type-specific template friend classes or functions?**

A When you want to establish a one-to-one relationship between two classes. For example, array<int> should match iterator<int>, but not iterator<Animal>.

Q **What are the two types of standard containers?**

A Sequence containers and associative containers. Sequence containers provide optimized sequential and random access to their elements. Associative containers provides optimized element access using key values.

Q **What attributes must your class have to be used with the standard containers?**

A The class must define a default constructor, a copy constructor, and an overloaded assignment operator.

Workshop

The Workshop provides quiz questions to help you solidify your understanding of the material covered and exercises to provide you with experience in using what you learned today. Try to answer the quiz and exercise questions before checking the answers in Appendix D, "Answers to Exercises and Quizzes," and make sure you understand the answers before continuing to tomorrow.

Quiz

1. What is the difference between a template and a macro?

2. What is the difference between the parameter in a template and the parameter in a function?

3. What is the difference between a type-specific template friend class and a general template friend class?

4. Is it possible to provide special behavior for one instance of a template but not for other instances?

5. How many static variables are created if you put one static member into a template class definition?

6. What are iterators in the C++ Standard Library?

7. What is a function object?

Exercises

1. Create a template based on this List class:

```
class List
{
private:

public:
    List():head(0),tail(0),theCount(0) {}
    virtual ~List();
    void insert( int value );
    void append( int value );
    int is_present( int value ) const;
    int is_empty() const { return head == 0; }
    int count() const { return theCount; }
private:
    class ListCell
    {
    public:
        ListCell(int value, ListCell *cell =
```

19

```
):val(value),next(cell){}
            int val;
            ListCell *next;
        };
        ListCell *head;
        ListCell *tail;
        int theCount;
    };
```

2. Write the implementation for the List class (non-template) version.

3. Write the template version of the implementations.

4. Declare three list objects: a list of Strings, a list of Cats, and a list of ints.

5. **BUG BUSTER:** What is wrong with the following code? (Assume the List template is defined and Cat is the class defined earlier in the book.)

```
List<Cat> Cat_List;
Cat Felix;
CatList.append( Felix );
cout << "Felix is " <<
        ( Cat_List.is_present( Felix ) ) ? "" : "not " << "present\n";
```

HINT (this is tough): What makes Cat different from int?

6. Declare friend operator== for List.

7. Implement friend operator== for List.

8. Does operator== have the same problem as in Exercise 5?

9. Implement a template function for a swap that exchanges two variables.

10. Implement the SchoolClass in Listing 19.8 as a list. Use the push_back() function to add four students to the list. Then traverse the resulting list and increase each student's age by one.

11. Modify Exercise 10 to use a function object to display each student's record.

DAY 20

Exceptions and Error Handling

The code you have seen in this book has been created for illustration purposes. It has not dealt with errors so that you would not be distracted from the central issues being presented. Real-world programs must take error conditions into consideration.

Today you will learn:

- What exceptions are
- How exceptions are used, and what issues they raise
- How to build exception hierarchies
- How exceptions fit into an overall error-handling approach
- What a debugger is

Bugs, Errors, Mistakes, and Code Rot

All programs have bugs. The bigger the program, the more bugs, and many of those bugs actually "get out the door" and into final, released software. That this is true does not make it okay, and making robust, bug-free programs is the number-one priority of anyone serious about programming.

The single biggest problem in the software industry is buggy, unstable code. The biggest expense in many major programming efforts is testing and fixing. The person who solves the problem of producing good, solid, bulletproof programs at low cost and on time will revolutionize the software industry.

A number of discrete kinds of bugs can trouble a program. The first is poor logic: The program does just what you asked, but you have not thought through the algorithms properly. The second is syntactic: You used the wrong idiom, function, or structure. These two are the most common, and they are the ones most programmers are on the lookout for.

Research and real-world experience have shown beyond a doubt that the later in the development process you find a problem, the more it costs to fix it. The least expensive problems or bugs to fix are the ones you manage to avoid creating. The next cheapest are those the compiler spots. The C++ standards force compilers to put a lot of energy into making more and more bugs show up at compile time.

Bugs that get compiled but are caught at the first test—those that crash every time—are less expensive to find and fix than those that are flaky and only crash once in a while.

A bigger problem than logic or syntactic bugs is unnecessary fragility: Your program works just fine if the user enters a number when you ask for one, but it crashes if the user enters letters. Other programs crash if they run out of memory, if the floppy disk is left out of the drive, or if the modem drops the line.

To combat this kind of fragility, programmers strive to make their programs bulletproof. A *bulletproof* program is one that can handle anything that comes up at runtime, from bizarre user input to running out of memory. Another term for this process is *defensive* programming, which, much like defensive driving, is preparation for the unexpected.

It is important to distinguish between bugs, which arise because the programmer made a mistake in syntax; logic errors, which arise because the programmer misunderstood the problem or how to solve it; and exceptions, which arise because of unusual but predictable problems such as running out of resources (memory or disk space).

Exceptions

Programmers use powerful compilers and sprinkle their code with asserts, which are discussed in Day 21, "What's Next," to catch programming errors. They use design reviews and exhaustive testing to find logic errors.

Exceptions are different, however. You cannot eliminate exceptional circumstances; you can only prepare for them. Your users will run out of memory from time to time, and the only question is what you will do. Your choices are limited to the following:

- Crash the program.
- Inform the user and exit gracefully.
- Inform the user and allow the user to try to recover and continue.
- Take corrective action and continue without disturbing the user.

Although it is not necessary or even desirable for every program you write to automatically and silently recover from all exceptional circumstances, it is clear that you must do better than crashing.

C++ exception handling provides a type-safe, integrated method for coping with the predictable but unusual conditions that arise while running a program.

A Word About Code Rot

Code rot is a well-proven phenomenon in which software deteriorates due to being neglected. A perfectly well-written, fully debugged program will turn bad on your customer's shelf just weeks after you deliver it. After a few months, your customer will notice that a green mold has covered your logic, and many of your objects have begun to flake apart.

Besides shipping your source code in air-tight containers, your only protection is to write your programs so that when you go back to fix the spoilage, you can quickly and easily identify where the problems are.

20

Note

Code rot is somewhat of a programmer's joke used to explain how supposedly bug-free code suddenly becomes unreliable. It does, however, teach an important lesson. Programs are enormously complex, and bugs, errors, and mistakes can hide for a long time before turning up. Protect yourself by writing easy-to-maintain code.

A similar term has been applied to printed books. No matter how careful the author, tech editors, editors, typesetters, and reviewers are, misteakes appear. But it seems the more the book is read (after the book is on the market), the more frequently these errors appear. Think about it!

This means that your code must be commented even if you do not expect anyone else to ever look at it. Six months after you deliver your code, you will read it with the eyes of a total stranger, bewildered by how anyone could ever have written such convoluted and twisty code and expected anything but disaster.

Exceptions

In C++, an exception is an object that is passed from the area of code where a problem occurs to the part of the code that is going to handle the problem. The type of the exception determines which area of code will handle the problem, and the contents of the object thrown, if any, can be used to provide feedback to the user.

The basic idea behind exceptions is fairly straightforward:

- The actual allocation of resources (for example, the allocation of memory or the locking of a file) is usually done at a very low level in the program.
- The logic of what to do when an operation fails, memory cannot be allocated, or a file cannot be locked is usually high in the program, with the code for interacting with the user.
- Exceptions provide an express path from the code that allocates resources to the code that can handle the error condition. If intervening layers of functions exist, they are given an opportunity to clean up memory allocations but are not required to include code whose only purpose is to pass along the error condition.

How Exceptions Are Used

try blocks are created to surround areas of code that may have a problem. For example:

```
try
{
SomeDangerousFunction();
}
```

catch blocks handle the exceptions thrown in the try block. For example:

```
try
{
SomeDangerousFunction();
}
catch(OutOfMemory)
{
// take some actions
}
catch(FileNotFound)
{
```

```
// take other action
}
```

The basic steps in using exceptions are

1. Identify those areas of the program in which you begin an operation that might raise an exception, and put them in `try` blocks.

2. Create `catch` blocks to catch the exceptions if they are thrown, to clean up allocated memory, and to inform the user as appropriate. Listing 20.1 illustrates the use of both `try` blocks and `catch` blocks.

Exceptions are objects used to transmit information about a problem.

A `try` block is a block surrounded by braces in which an exception may be thrown.

A `catch` block is the block immediately following a `try` block, in which exceptions are handled.

When an exception is thrown (or raised), control transfers to the `catch` block immediately following the current `try` block.

> **Note**
>
> Some very old compilers, like GNU version 2.7.2, do not support exceptions. Exceptions are part of the ANSI C++ standard, however, and every compiler vendor's latest edition fully supports native exceptions. If you have an older compiler, you will not be able to compile and run the exercises in this lesson. It would still be a good idea to read through the entire lesson, however, and return to this material when you upgrade your compiler.
>
> Use the compiler version on the CD-ROM (2.9.5) for these examples.

INPUT   **LISTING 20.1**   Raising an Exception

```
1:      #include <iostream.h>
2:  // listing 20.1: raising an exception
3:      const int DefaultSize = 10;
4:
5:      class Array
6:      {
7:      public:
8:        // constructors
9:        Array(int itsSize = DefaultSize);
10:        Array(const Array &rhs);
11:        ~Array() { delete [] pType;}
12:
13:        // operators
```

continues

20

LISTING 20.1   CONTINUED

```
14:            Array& operator=(const Array&);
15:            int& operator[](int offSet);
16:            const int& operator[](int offSet) const;
17:
18:            // accessors
19:            int GetitsSize() const { return itsSize; }
20:
21:            // friend function
22:          friend ostream& operator<< (ostream&, const Array&);
23:
24:            class xBoundary {};   // define the exception class
25:        private:
26:            int *pType;
27:            int  itsSize;
28:        };
29:
30:
31:        Array::Array(int size):
32:        itsSize(size)
33:        {
34:           pType = new int[size];
35:           for (int i = 0; i<size; i++)
36:             pType[i] = 0;
37:        }
38:
39:
40:        Array& Array::operator=(const Array &rhs)
41:        {
42:           if (this == &rhs)
43:              return *this;
44:           delete [] pType;
45:           itsSize = rhs.GetitsSize();
46:           pType = new int[itsSize];
47:           for (int i = 0; i<itsSize; i++)
48:              pType[i] = rhs[i];
49:           return *this;
50:        }
51:
52:        Array::Array(const Array &rhs)
53:        {
54:           itsSize = rhs.GetitsSize();
55:           pType = new int[itsSize];
56:           for (int i = 0; i<itsSize; i++)
57:              pType[i] = rhs[i];
58:        }
59:
60:
61:        int& Array::operator[](int offSet)
```

```
62:        {
63:            int size = GetitsSize();
64:            if (offSet >= 0 && offSet < GetitsSize())
65:                return pType[offSet];
66:            throw xBoundary();
67:            return pType[0]; // appease MSC
68:        }
69:
70:
71:        const int& Array::operator[](int offSet) const
72:        {
73:            int mysize = GetitsSize();
74:            if (offSet >= 0 && offSet < GetitsSize())
75:                return pType[offSet];
76:            throw xBoundary();
77:            return pType[0]; // appease MSC
78:        }
79:
80:        ostream& operator<< (ostream& output, const Array& theArray)
81:        {
82:            for (int i = 0; i<theArray.GetitsSize(); i++)
83:                output << "[" << i << "] " << theArray[i] << endl;
84:            return output;
85:        }
86:
87:        int main()
88:        {
89:            Array intArray(20);
90:            try
91:            {
92:                for (int j = 0; j< 100; j++)
93:                {
94:                    intArray[j] = j;
95:                    cout << "intArray[" << j << "] okay..." << endl;
96:                }
97:            }
98:            catch (Array::xBoundary)
99:            {
100:                cout << "Unable to process your input!\n";
101:            }
102:            cout << "Done.\n";
103:            return 0;
104:        }
```

20

OUTPUT
```
intArray[0] okay...
intArray[1] okay...
intArray[2] okay...
intArray[3] okay...
intArray[4] okay...
intArray[5] okay...
```

```
intArray[6] okay...
intArray[7] okay...
intArray[8] okay...
intArray[9] okay...
intArray[10] okay...
intArray[11] okay...
intArray[12] okay...
intArray[13] okay...
intArray[14] okay...
intArray[15] okay...
intArray[16] okay...
intArray[17] okay...
intArray[18] okay...
intArray[19] okay...
Unable to process your input!
Done.
```

ANALYSIS Listing 20.1 presents a somewhat stripped-down Array class, based on the template developed on Day 19, "Templates."

On line 24, a new class, xBoundary, is declared within the declaration of the outer class Array.

This new class is not in any way distinguished as an exception class. It is simply a class the same as any other. This particular class is incredibly simple; it has no data and no methods. Nonetheless, it is a valid class in every way.

In fact, it is incorrect to say it has no methods, because the compiler automatically assigns it a default constructor, destructor, copy constructor, and the assignment operator (operator equals); so it actually has four class functions, but no data.

Note that declaring it from within Array serves only to couple the two classes together. As discussed on Day 15, "Advanced Inheritance," Array has no special access to xBoundary, nor does xBoundary have preferential access to the members of Array.

On lines 61–68 and 71–78, the offset operators are modified to examine the offset requested, and if it is out of range, to throw the xBoundary class as an exception. The parentheses are required to distinguish between this call to the xBoundary constructor and the use of an enumerated constant. Note that some Microsoft compilers require that you provide a return statement to match the declaration (in this case, returning an integer reference), even though if an exception is thrown on line 66, the code will never reach line 67. This is a compiler bug, proving only that even Microsoft finds this stuff difficult and confusing!

On line 90, the keyword try begins a try block that ends on line 97. Within that try block, 101 integers are added to the array that was declared on line 89.

On line 98, the catch block to catch xBoundary exceptions is declared.

In the driver program on lines 87 to 104, a `try` block is created in which each member of the array is initialized. When j (line 92) is incremented to 20, the member at offset 20 is accessed. This causes the test on line 64 to fail, and `operator[]` raises an xBoundary exception on line 66.

Program control switches to the `catch` block on line 98, and the exception is caught or handled by the `catch` on the same line, which prints an error message. Program flow drops through to the end of the `catch` block on line 100.

---

try Blocks

A `try` block is a series of statements that begins with the keyword `try`; it is followed by an opening brace and ends with a closing brace.

Here is an example:

```
try
{
Function();
};
```

---

catch Blocks

A `catch` block is a series of statements, each of which begins with the keyword `catch`, followed by an exception type in parentheses, followed by an opening brace, and ending with a closing brace.

Here is an example:

```
try
{
Function();
};
catch (OutOfMemory)
{
// take action
}
```

20

Using try and catch Blocks

Figuring out where to put your `try` blocks is nontrivial: It is not always obvious which actions might raise an exception. The next question is where to catch the exception. It may be that you want to throw all memory exceptions where the memory is allocated, but want to catch the exceptions high in the program where you deal with the user interface.

When trying to determine `try` block locations, look to where you allocate memory or use resources. Other things to look for are out-of-bounds errors, illegal input, and so forth.

Catching Exceptions

Catching an exception works this way: When an exception is thrown, the call stack is examined. The call stack is the list of function calls created when one part of the program invokes another function.

The call stack tracks the execution path. If `main()` calls the function `Animal::GetFavoriteFood()`, and `GetFavoriteFood()` calls `Animal::LookupPreferences()`, which in turn calls `fstream::operator>>()`, all these are on the call stack. A recursive function might be on the call stack many times.

The exception is passed up the call stack to each enclosing block. As the stack is unwound, the destructors for local objects on the stack are invoked, and the objects are destroyed.

One or more `catch` statements follow each `try` block. If the exception matches one of the `catch` statements, it is considered to be handled by having that statement execute. If it does not match any, the unwinding of the stack continues.

If the exception reaches all the way to the beginning of the program (`main()`) and is still not caught, a built-in handler is called that terminates the program.

It is important to note that the exception unwinding of the stack is a one-way street. As it progresses, the stack is unwound and objects on the stack are destroyed. There is no going back: After the exception is handled, the program continues after the `try` block of the `catch` statement that handled the exception.

Thus, in Listing 20.1, execution will continue on line 101, the first line after the `try` block of the `catch` statement that handled the `xBoundary` exception. Remember that when an exception is raised, program flow continues after the `catch` block, not after the point where the exception was thrown.

More Than One `catch` Specification

It is possible for more than one condition to cause an exception. In this case, the `catch` statements can be lined up one after another, much like the conditions in a switch statement. The equivalent to the default statement is the "catch everything" statement, indicated by `catch(...)`. Listing 20.2 illustrates multiple exception conditions.

INPUT **LISTING 20.2** Multiple Exceptions

```
1:      #include <iostream.h>
2:   // Listing 20.2: multiple exceptions
3:      const int DefaultSize = 10;
4:
5:      class Array
6:      {
7:      public:
8:         // constructors
9:         Array(int itsSize = DefaultSize);
10:         Array(const Array &rhs);
11:         ~Array() { delete [] pType;}
12:
13:         // operators
14:         Array& operator=(const Array&);
15:         int& operator[](int offSet);
16:         const int& operator[](int offSet) const;
17:
18:         // accessors
19:         int GetitsSize() const { return itsSize; }
20:
21:         // friend function
22:        friend ostream& operator<< (ostream&, const Array&);
23:
24:      // define the exception classes
25:         class xBoundary {};
26:         class xTooBig {};
27:         class xTooSmall{};
28:         class xZero {};
29:         class xNegative {};
30:      private:
31:         int *pType;
32:         int  itsSize;
33:      };
34:
35:      int& Array::operator[](int offSet)
36:      {
37:          int size = GetitsSize();
38:          if (offSet >= 0 && offSet < GetitsSize())
39:             return pType[offSet];
40:          throw xBoundary();
41:          return pType[0];   // appease MFC
42:      }
43:
44:
45:      const int& Array::operator[](int offSet) const
46:      {
47:          int mysize = GetitsSize();
48:          if (offSet >= 0 && offSet < GetitsSize())
49:             return pType[offSet];
```

continues

20

LISTING 20.2   CONTINUED

```
50:                    throw xBoundary();
51:
52:                    return pType[0];   // appease MFC
53:          }
54:
55:
56:     Array::Array(int size):
57:     itsSize(size)
58:     {
59:        if (size == 0)
60:            throw xZero();
61:        if (size < 10)
62:            throw xTooSmall();
63:        if (size > 30000)
64:            throw xTooBig();
65:        if (size < 1)
66:            throw xNegative();
67:
68:        pType = new int[size];
69:        for (int i = 0; i<size; i++)
70:          pType[i] = 0;
71:     }
72:
73:
74:
75:     int main()
76:     {
77:
78:        try
79:        {
80:            Array intArray(0);
81:            for (int j = 0; j< 100; j++)
82:            {
83:                intArray[j] = j;
84:                cout << "intArray[" << j << "] okay...\n";
85:            }
86:        }
87:        catch (Array::xBoundary)
88:        {
89:            cout << "Unable to process your input!\n";
90:        }
91:        catch (Array::xTooBig)
92:        {
93:            cout << "This array is too big...\n";
94:        }
95:        catch (Array::xTooSmall)
96:        {
97:            cout << "This array is too small...\n";
```

```
 98:        }
 99:        catch (Array::xZero)
100:         {
101:            cout << "You asked for an array";
102:            cout << " of zero objects!\n";
103:         }
104:        catch (...)
105:         {
106:            cout << "Something went wrong!\n";
107:         }
108:          cout << "Done.\n";
109:        return 0;
110:        }
```

OUTPUT
```
You asked for an array of zero objects!
Done.
```

ANALYSIS Four new classes are created in lines 26 to 29: xTooBig, xTooSmall, xZero, and xNegative. In the constructor, on lines 56 to 71, the size passed to the constructor is examined. If it is too big, too small, negative, or zero, an exception is thrown.

The try block is changed to include catch statements for each condition other than negative, which is caught by the "catch everything" statement catch(...), shown on line 104.

Try this with a number of values for the size of the array. Then try putting in –5. You might have expected xNegative to be called, but the order of the tests in the constructor prevented this: size < 10 was evaluated before size < 1. To fix this, swap lines 61 and 62 with lines 65 and 66 and recompile.

Exception Hierarchies

Exceptions are classes, and as such, they can be derived from. It may be advantageous to create a class xSize, and to derive from it xZero, xTooSmall, xTooBig, and xNegative. Thus, some functions might just catch xSize errors, and other functions might catch the specific type of xSize error. Listing 20.3 illustrates this idea.

20

INPUT   **LISTING 20.3**   Class Hierarchies and Exceptions

```
1:        #include <iostream.h>
2:  // Listing 20.3: Class Hierarchies and Exceptions
3:        const int DefaultSize = 10;
4:
5:        class Array
6:        {
```

continues

LISTING 20.3   CONTINUED

```
 7:        public:
 8:           // constructors
 9:           Array(int itsSize = DefaultSize);
10:           Array(const Array &rhs);
11:           ~Array() { delete [] pType;}
12:
13:           // operators
14:           Array& operator=(const Array&);
15:           int& operator[](int offSet);
16:           const int& operator[](int offSet) const;
17:
18:           // accessors
19:           int GetitsSize() const { return itsSize; }
20:
21:           // friend function
22:          friend ostream& operator<< (ostream&, const Array&);
23:
24:         // define the exception classes
25:           class xBoundary {};
26:           class xSize {};
27:           class xTooBig : public xSize {};
28:           class xTooSmall : public xSize {};
29:           class xZero  : public xTooSmall {};
30:           class xNegative  : public xSize {};
31:        private:
32:           int *pType;
33:           int  itsSize;
34:        };
35:
36:
37:        Array::Array(int size):
38:        itsSize(size)
39:        {
40:           if (size == 0)
41:              throw xZero();
42:           if (size > 30000)
43:              throw xTooBig();
44:           if (size <1)
45:              throw xNegative();
46:           if (size < 10)
47:              throw xTooSmall();
48:
49:           pType = new int[size];
50:           for (int i = 0; i<size; i++)
51:             pType[i] = 0;
52:        }
53:
54:            int& Array::operator[](int offSet)
```

```
55:          {
56:                  int size = GetitsSize();
57:                  if (offSet >= 0 && offSet < GetitsSize())
58:                      return pType[offSet];
59:                  throw xBoundary();
60:                  return pType[0];   // appease MFC
61:          }
62:
63:
64:          const int& Array::operator[](int offSet) const
65:          {
66:                  int mysize = GetitsSize();
67:                  if (offSet >= 0 && offSet < GetitsSize())
68:                      return pType[offSet];
69:                  throw xBoundary();
70:
71:                  return pType[0];   // appease MFC
72:          }
73:
74:      int main()
75:      {
76:
77:          try
78:          {
79:              Array intArray(0);
80:              for (int j = 0; j< 100; j++)
81:              {
82:                  intArray[j] = j;
83:                  cout << "intArray[" << j << "] okay...\n";
84:              }
85:          }
86:          catch (Array::xBoundary)
87:          {
88:              cout << "Unable to process your input!\n";
89:          }
90:          catch (Array::xTooBig)
91:          {
92:              cout << "This array is too big...\n";
93:          }
94:
95:          catch (Array::xTooSmall)
96:          {
97:              cout << "This array is too small...\n";
98:          }
99:          catch (Array::xZero)
100:          {
101:              cout << "You asked for an array";
102:              cout << " of zero objects!\n";
103:          }
104:
```

20

continues

LISTING 20.3 CONTINUED

```
105:
106:        catch (...)
107:        {
108:            cout << "Something went wrong!\n";
109:         }
110:          cout << "Done.\n";
111:        return 0;
112:     }
```

OUTPUT

This array is too small...
Done.

ANALYSIS

The significant change is on lines 27 to 30, where the class hierarchy is established. Classes xTooBig, xTooSmall, and xNegative are derived from xSize, and xZero is derived from xTooSmall.

The Array is created with size zero, but what happened? The wrong exception appears to be caught! Examine the catch block carefully, however, and you will find that it looks for an exception of type xTooSmall before it looks for an exception of type xZero. Because an xZero object is thrown and an xZero object is an xTooSmall object, it is caught by the handler for xTooSmall. After the exception has been handled, it is not passed on to the other handlers, so the handler for xZero is never called.

The solution to this problem is to carefully order the handlers so that the most specific handlers come first and the less specific handlers come later. In this particular example, switching the placement of the two handlers xZero and xTooSmall will fix the problem.

Accessing Data in Exceptions by Naming Exception Objects

Often you will want to know more than just what type of exception was thrown so that you can respond properly to the error. Exception classes are the same as any other class. You are free to provide data, initialize that data in the constructor, and read that data at any time. Listing 20.4 illustrates how to do this.

INPUT **LISTING 20.4** Getting Data Out of an Exception Object

```
1:      #include <iostream.h>
2:  // Listing 20.4: Getting exception object data
3:      const int DefaultSize = 10;
4:
```

```
5:     class Array
6:     {
7:     public:
8:        // constructors
9:        Array(int itsSize = DefaultSize);
10:       Array(const Array &rhs);
11:       ~Array() { delete [] pType;}
12:
13:       // operators
14:       Array& operator=(const Array&);
15:       int& operator[](int offSet);
16:       const int& operator[](int offSet) const;
17:
18:       // accessors
19:       int GetitsSize() const { return itsSize; }
20:
21:       // friend function
22:       friend ostream& operator<< (ostream&, const Array&);
23:
24:     // define the exception classes
25:       class xBoundary {};
26:       class xSize
27:       {
28:       public:
29:          xSize(int size):itsSize(size) {}
30:          ~xSize(){}
31:          int GetSize() { return itsSize; }
32:       private:
33:          int itsSize;
34:       };
35:
36:       class xTooBig : public xSize
37:       {
38:       public:
39:          xTooBig(int size):xSize(size){}
40:       };
41:
42:       class xTooSmall : public xSize
43:       {
44:       public:
45:          xTooSmall(int size):xSize(size){}
46:       };
47:
48:       class xZero   : public xTooSmall
49:       {
50:       public:
51:          xZero(int size):xTooSmall(size){}
52:       };
53:
54:       class xNegative : public xSize
55:       {
```

20

continues

LISTING 20.4   CONTINUED

```
56:         public:
57:            xNegative(int size):xSize(size){}
58:         };
59:
60:     private:
61:         int *pType;
62:         int  itsSize;
63:     };
64:
65:
66:     Array::Array(int size):
67:     itsSize(size)
68:     {
69:        if (size == 0)
70:           throw xZero(size);
71:        if (size > 30000)
72:           throw xTooBig(size);
73:        if (size <1)
74:           throw xNegative(size);
75:        if (size < 10)
76:           throw xTooSmall(size);
77:
78:        pType = new int[size];
79:        for (int i = 0; i<size; i++)
80:           pType[i] = 0;
81:     }
82:
83:
84:     int& Array::operator[] (int offSet)
85:     {
86:         int size = GetitsSize();
87:         if (offSet >= 0 && offSet < GetitsSize())
88:           return pType[offSet];
89:         throw xBoundary();
90:         return pType[0];
91:     }
92:
93:     const int& Array::operator[] (int offSet) const
94:     {
95:         int size = GetitsSize();
96:         if (offSet >= 0 && offSet < GetitsSize())
97:           return pType[offSet];
98:         throw xBoundary();
99:         return pType[0];
100:    }
101:
102:      int main()
103:      {
```

```
104:
105:          try
106:          {
107:              Array intArray(9);
108:              for (int j = 0; j< 100; j++)
109:              {
110:                  intArray[j] = j;
111:                  cout << "intArray[" << j << "] okay..." << endl;
112:              }
113:          }
114:          catch (Array::xBoundary)
115:          {
116:              cout << "Unable to process your input!\n";
117:          }
118:          catch (Array::xZero theException)
119:          {
120:              cout << "You asked for an Array of zero objects!" << endl;
121:              cout << "Received " << theException.GetSize() << endl;
122:          }
123:          catch (Array::xTooBig theException)
124:          {
125:              cout << "This Array is too big..." << endl;
126:              cout << "Received " << theException.GetSize() << endl;
127:          }
128:          catch (Array::xTooSmall theException)
129:          {
130:              cout << "This Array is too small..." << endl;
131:              cout << "Received " << theException.GetSize() << endl;
132:          }
133:          catch (...)
134:          {
135:              cout << "Something went wrong, but I've no idea what!\n";
136:          }
137:          cout << "Done.\n";
138:          return 0;
139:      }
```

OUTPUT

```
This array is too small...
Received 9
Done.
```

20

ANALYSIS The declaration of xSize has been modified to include a member variable, itsSize, on line 33 and a member function, GetSize(), on line 31. Additionally, a constructor has been added that takes an integer and initializes the member variable, as shown on line 29.

The derived classes declare a constructor that does nothing but initialize the base class. No other functions were declared, in part to save space in the listing.

The `catch` statements on lines 114 to 136 are modified to name the exception they catch, `theException`, and to use this object to access the data stored in `itsSize`.

 Note

> Keep in mind that if you are constructing an exception, it is because an exception has been raised: Something has gone wrong, and your exception should be careful not to kick off the same problem. Therefore, if you are creating an `OutOfMemory` exception, you probably do not want to allocate memory in its constructor.

It is tedious and error-prone to have each of these `catch` statements individually print the appropriate message. This job belongs to the object, which knows what type of object it is and what value it received. Listing 20.5 takes a more object-oriented approach to this problem, using virtual functions so that each exception "does the right thing."

INPUT   **LISTING 20.5**   Passing by Reference and Using Virtual Functions in Exceptions

```
1:        #include <iostream.h>
2:    // Listing 20.5: Passing by reference in exceptions
3:        const int DefaultSize = 10;
4:
5:        class Array
6:        {
7:        public:
8:            // constructors
9:          Array(int itsSize = DefaultSize);
10:           Array(const Array &rhs);
11:           ~Array() { delete [] pType;}
12:
13:           // operators
14:           Array& operator=(const Array&);
15:           int& operator[](int offSet);
16:           const int& operator[](int offSet) const;
17:
18:           // accessors
19:           int GetitsSize() const { return itsSize; }
20:
21:           // friend function
22:          friend ostream& operator<<
23:              (ostream&, const Array&);
24:
25:       // define the exception classes
26:          class xBoundary {};
27:          class xSize
```

```
28:         {
29:         public:
30:            xSize(int size):itsSize(size) {}
31:            ~xSize(){}
32:            virtual int GetSize() { return itsSize; }
33:            virtual void PrintError()
34:            {
35:                cout << "Size error. Received: ";
36:                cout << itsSize << endl;
37:            }
38:         protected:
39:            int itsSize;
40:         };
41:
42:         class xTooBig : public xSize
43:         {
44:         public:
45:            xTooBig(int size):xSize(size){}
46:            virtual void PrintError()
47:            {
48:                cout << "Too big! Received: ";
49:                cout << xSize::itsSize << endl;
50:            }
51:         };
52:
53:         class xTooSmall : public xSize
54:         {
55:         public:
56:            xTooSmall(int size):xSize(size){}
57:            virtual void PrintError()
58:            {
59:                cout << "Too small! Received: ";
60:                cout << xSize::itsSize << endl;
61:            }
62:         };
63:
64:         class xZero  : public xTooSmall
65:         {
66:         public:
67:            xZero(int size):xTooSmall(size){}
68:            virtual void PrintError()
69:            {
70:                cout << "Zero!!. Received: " ;
71:                cout << xSize::itsSize << endl;
72:            }
73:         };
74:
75:         class xNegative : public xSize
76:         {
77:         public:
78:            xNegative(int size):xSize(size){}
```

20

continues

LISTING 20.5   CONTINUED

```
79:            virtual void PrintError()
80:            {
81:                cout << "Negative! Received: ";
82:                cout << xSize::itsSize << endl;
83:            }
84:        };
85:
86:    private:
87:        int *pType;
88:        int  itsSize;
89:    };
90:
91:    Array::Array(int size):
92:    itsSize(size)
93:    {
94:        if (size == 0)
95:            throw xZero(size);
96:        if (size > 30000)
97:            throw xTooBig(size);
98:        if (size <1)
99:            throw xNegative(size);
100:        if (size < 10)
101:             throw xTooSmall(size);
102:
103:        pType = new int[size];
104:        for (int i = 0; i<size; i++)
105:            pType[i] = 0;
106:    }
107:
108:    int& Array::operator[] (int offSet)
109:    {
110:        int size = GetitsSize();
111:        if (offSet >= 0 && offSet < GetitsSize())
112:          return pType[offSet];
113:        throw xBoundary();
114:        return pType[0];
115:    }
116:
117:    const int& Array::operator[] (int offSet) const
118:    {
119:        int size = GetitsSize();
120:        if (offSet >= 0 && offSet < GetitsSize())
121:          return pType[offSet];
122:        throw xBoundary();
123:        return pType[0];
124:    }
125:
126:     int main()
```

```
127:        {
128:
129:          try
130:          {
131:              Array intArray(9);
132:              for (int j = 0; j< 100; j++)
133:              {
134:                  intArray[j] = j;
135:                  cout << "intArray[" << j << "] okay...\n";
136:              }
137:          }
138:          catch (Array::xBoundary)
139:          {
140:              cout << "Unable to process your input!\n";
141:          }
142:          catch (Array::xSize& theException)
143:          {
144:              theException.PrintError();
145:          }
146:          catch (...)
147:          {
148:              cout << "Something went wrong!\n";
149:          }
150:          cout << "Done.\n";
151:        return 0;
152:        }
```

OUTPUT Too small! Received: 9
Done.

ANALYSIS Listing 20.5 declares a virtual method in the xSize class, PrintError(), that prints an error message and the actual size of the class. This is overridden in each of the derived classes.

On line 142, the exception object is declared to be a reference. When PrintError() is called with a reference to an object, polymorphism causes the correct version of PrintError() to be invoked. The code is cleaner, easier to understand, and easier to maintain.

20

Using Exceptions and Templates

When creating exceptions to work with templates, you have a choice: You can create an exception for each instance of the template, or you can use exception classes declared outside the template declaration. Listing 20.6 illustrates both approaches.

```
1:        #include <iostream.h>
2:   // Listing 20.6: Exceptions with Templates
3:        const int DefaultSize = 10;
4:        class xBoundary {};
5:
6:        template <class T>
7:        class Array
8:        {
9:        public:
10:           // constructors
11:           Array(int itsSize = DefaultSize);
12:           Array(const Array &rhs);
13:           ~Array() { delete [] pType;}
14:
15:           // operators
16:           Array& operator=(const Array<T>&);
17:           T& operator[](int offSet);
18:           const T& operator[](int offSet) const;
19:
20:           // accessors
21:           int GetitsSize() const { return itsSize; }
22:
23:           // friend function
24:          friend ostream& operator<< <> (ostream&, const Array<T>&);
25:
26:         // define the exception classes
27:
28:           class xSize {};
29:
30:        private:
31:           int *pType;
32:           int  itsSize;
33:        };
34:
35:        template <class T>
36:        Array<T>::Array(int size):
37:        itsSize(size)
38:        {
39:           if (size <10 || size > 30000)
40:              throw xSize();
41:           pType = new T[size];
42:           for (int i = 0; i<size; i++)
43:             pType[i] = 0;
44:        }
45:
46:        template <class T>
47:        Array<T>& Array<T>::operator=(const Array<T> &rhs)
48:        {
```

```
49:        if (this == &rhs)
50:            return *this;
51:        delete [] pType;
52:        itsSize = rhs.GetitsSize();
53:        pType = new T[itsSize];
54:        for (int i = 0; i<itsSize; i++)
55:            pType[i] = rhs[i];
56:    }
57:    template <class T>
58:    Array<T>::Array(const Array<T> &rhs)
59:    {
60:        itsSize = rhs.GetitsSize();
61:        pType = new T[itsSize];
62:        for (int i = 0; i<itsSize; i++)
63:            pType[i] = rhs[i];
64:    }
65:
66:    template <class T>
67:    T& Array<T>::operator[](int offSet)
68:    {
69:        int size = GetitsSize();
70:        if (offSet >= 0 && offSet < GetitsSize())
71:            return pType[offSet];
72:        throw xBoundary();
73:        return pType[0];
74:    }
75:
76:    template <class T>
77:    const T& Array<T>::operator[](int offSet) const
78:    {
79:        int mysize = GetitsSize();
80:        if (offSet >= 0 && offSet < GetitsSize())
81:            return pType[offSet];
82:        throw xBoundary();
83:    }
84:
85:    template <class T>
86:    ostream& operator<< (ostream& output, const Array<T>& theArray)
87:    {
88:        for (int i = 0; i<theArray.GetitsSize(); i++)
89:            output << "[" << i << "] " << theArray[i] << endl;
90:        return output;
91:    }
92:
93:
94:    int main()
95:    {
96:
97:        try
98:        {
99:            Array<int> intArray(9);
```

continues

LISTING 20.6   CONTINUED

```
100:            for (int j = 0; j< 100; j++)
101:            {
102:                intArray[j] = j;
103:                cout << "intArray[" << j << "] okay..." << endl;
104:            }
105:        }
106:        catch (xBoundary)
107:        {
108:            cout << "Unable to process your input!\n";
109:        }
110:        catch (Array<int>::xSize)
111:        {
112:            cout << "Bad Size!\n";
113:        }
114:
115:        cout << "Done.\n";
116:        return 0;
117:    }
```

OUTPUT
```
Bad Size!
Done.
```

ANALYSIS
The first exception, xBoundary, is declared outside the template definition on line 4.

The second exception, xSize, is declared from within the definition of the template on line 28.

The exception xBoundary is not tied to the template class, but it can be used the same as any other class. xSize is tied to the template and must be called based on the instantiated Array. You can see the difference in the syntax for the two catch statements. Line 106 shows catch (xBoundary), but line 110 shows catch (Array<int>::xSize). The latter is tied to the instantiation of an integer Array.

Triggering Exceptions Without Errors

When C++ programmers get together for a virtual beer in the cyberspace bar after work, talk often turns to whether exceptions should be used for routine conditions. Some maintain that by their nature, exceptions should be reserved for those predictable but exceptional circumstances (hence the name!) that a programmer must anticipate, but that are not part of the routine processing of the code.

Others point out that exceptions offer a powerful and clean way to return through many layers of function calls without danger of memory leaks. A frequent example is this: The user requests an action in a GUI environment. The part of the code that catches the request must call a member function on a dialog manager, which, in turn, calls code that processes the request, which calls code that decides which dialog box to use, which in turn calls code to put up the dialog box, which finally calls code that processes the user's input. If the user presses Cancel, the code must return to the very first calling method where the original request was handled.

One approach to this problem is to put a `try` block around the original call and catch `CancelDialog` as an exception, which can be raised by the handler for the Cancel button. This is safe and effective, but pressing Cancel is a routine circumstance, not an exceptional one.

This frequently becomes something of a religious argument, but a reasonable way to decide the question is to ask the following: Does use of exceptions in this way make the code easier or harder to understand? Are there fewer risks of errors and memory leaks, or more? Will it be harder or easier to maintain this code? These decisions, like so many others, will require an analysis of the trade-offs; no single, obvious right answer exists.

Dealing with Bugs and Debugging

Nearly all modern development environments include one or more high-powered debuggers. The essential idea of using a debugger is this: You run the debugger, which loads your source code, and then you run your program from within the debugger. This enables you to see each instruction in your program as it executes and to examine your variables as they change during the life of your program.

All compilers will let you compile with or without symbols. Compiling with symbols tells the compiler to create the necessary mapping between your source code and the generated program; the debugger uses this to point to the line of source code that corresponds to the next action in the program.

Symbolic debuggers make this chore easier. The GNU debugger, gdb, is a symbolic debugger running in text mode; some other symbolic debuggers support a windowed, full-screen mode. When you load your debugger, it will read through all your source code. You can step over function calls or direct the debugger to step into the function, line by line.

With most debuggers, you can switch between the source code and the output to see the results of each executed statement. More powerfully, you can examine the current state of each variable, look at complex data structures, examine the value of member data within classes, and look at the actual values in memory of various pointers and other memory locations. You can execute several types of control within a debugger that include setting breakpoints, setting watch points, examining memory, and looking at the assembler code.

20

Using gdb—GNU Debugger

The first step in using the GNU debugger (or just about any other debugger) is to make sure that the compiler has included the required code in the executable file. With this information, the debugger knows where variables are stored, the names of variables and functions, and how to relate the source and binary code.

The first question that might come to mind is: "Why not always include the special debugging code in the executable?" The answer is simple; that code slows the execution of the program and causes it to occupy additional memory. We all want our programs to run quickly and use the fewest system resources possible. So, unless we need it, we do not tell the compiler to include this information.

To tell the GNU compiler to include debugging information in your binary code, you use the -g option:

```
g++ -g yourprog.c++ -o yourprog
```

By default, the debugging information is not included.

After you have compiled all your modules with the -g option and linked them into an executable, you are ready to use gdb to debug your program.

Table 20.1 shows some of the common commands for use within gdb.

TABLE 20.1 Common gdb Commands

Command	Purpose
break *file:function*	Set a breakpoint when *function* in *file* is entered. *file* is optional.
bt	Short form of backtrace; display the program stack.
c	Continue running program after breakpoint.
disassemble	Show binary code as assembler code instead of source language (that is, C++).
display *exp*	Display *exp* whenever program stops.
help	Get general help or help on categories of commands, specific commands, and options for specific commands. Almost the most useful command of all.
list *file:line*	Displays ±5 lines of source code. *file* and *line* specify the source to display and are optional.
next	Run next program step without stepping into called functions.

Command	Purpose
print exp	Print *exp*; *exp* can be a variable, function name, or complex expression like the beginning of an array (array name) plus a value to show a specified element. This allows you to examine memory.
quit	Exit from gdb. If you have a running program, you will be prompted to confirm.
run arglist	Run program from the beginning with optional command-line argument list *arglist*.
set *variable* = *exp*	Set source code *variable* to expression *exp*. As with print, *exp* can be a variable, function name, or complex expression. The variable follows the syntax of the source language and recognizes things like array notation. This allows you to alter memory.
set	Alter environment of gdb.
step	Run next program step—stepping into any called functions.
undisplay	Cancel display.
watch	Create a watchpoint.
whatis exp	Display data type of *exp*.

The GNU debugger also accepts command-line options. When you run gdb, you will typically enter a command like this:

gdb yourprog

You can also use gdb to debug a program that fails while running (when a *core* file is produced). In that case, your command will look like:

gdb yourprog corefile

When debugging a core file, you can examine memory and the call stack, but you cannot execute steps because the program is not running.

Tip

Two quick tips for working with gdb:

You should set a breakpoint before you issue the run command. Otherwise, the program will just run to completion or failure. A good habit is to set a breakpoint on main itself so that the standard runtime library initialization can take place, and then you enter your other breakpoints, watch points, and displays.

20

The other tip involves a confusing error message:

`test1.cc:6: No such file or directory (ENOENT).`

If you get this message, it is either because the source file (`test1.cc`) cannot be found, or your source file has a different extension (`test1.cxx`) but, the compiler confused things. The solution to the first is run in the proper directory or use the `-d` option to specify your source directory. The second is a little weird: copy your source file (`test1.cxx`) to the name gdb is seeking (`test1.cc`), and your problem should go away.

For more information about the command-line options and internal commands of gdb, you should check the man page or info file.

The next sections describe what the terms *breakpoint*, *watch point*, *examining and altering memory*, and *disassembly* mean.

Using Breakpoints

Breakpoints are instructions to the debugger that when a particular line of code is ready to be executed, the program should stop. This allows you to run your program unimpeded until the line in question is reached. Breakpoints help you analyze the current condition of variables just before and after a critical line of code.

Using Watch Points

It is possible to tell the debugger to show you the value of a particular variable or to break when a particular variable is read or written to. Watch points enable you to set these conditions, and at times even to modify the value of a variable while the program is running.

Examining and Altering Memory

At times it is important to see the actual values held in memory. Modern debuggers can show values in the form of the actual variable; that is, strings can be shown as characters, longs as numbers rather than as 4 bytes, and so forth. The sophisticated gdb debugger can even show complete classes and provide the current value of all the member variables, including the `this` pointer. Just as important, gdb allows you to change variables as your program is executing.

Disassembly

Although reading through the source can be all that is required to find a bug, when all else fails, it is possible to instruct the debugger to show you the actual assembly code generated for each line of your source code. You can examine the memory registers and flags, and generally delve as deep into the inner workings of your program as required.

Learn to use your debugger. It can be the most powerful weapon in your holy war against bugs. Runtime bugs are the hardest to find and squash, and a powerful debugger can make it possible, if not easy, to find nearly all of them.

Summary

Today you learned how to create and use exceptions. Exceptions are objects that can be created and thrown at points in the program where the executing code cannot handle the error or other exceptional condition that has arisen. Other parts of the program, higher in the call stack, implement `catch` blocks that catch the exception and take appropriate action.

Exceptions are normal, user-created objects, and as such may be passed by value or by reference. They may contain data and methods, and the `catch` block may use that data to decide how to deal with the exception.

It is possible to create multiple `catch` blocks, but after an exception matches a `catch` block's signature, it is considered to be handled and is not given to the subsequent `catch` blocks. It is important to order the `catch` blocks appropriately so that more specific `catch` blocks have first chance, and more general `catch` blocks handle those not otherwise handled.

This lesson also examined some of the fundamentals of symbolic debuggers, including using watch points, breakpoints, and so forth. These tools can help you zero in on the part of your program that is causing the error and let you see the value of variables as they change during the course of the execution of the program.

Q&A

20

Q Why bother with raising exceptions? Why not handle the error right where it happens?

A Often, the same error can be generated in different parts of the code. Exceptions let you centralize the handling of errors. Additionally, the part of the code that generates the error may not be the best place to determine how to handle the error.

Q Why generate an object? Why not just pass an error code?

A Objects are more flexible and powerful than error codes. They can convey more information, and the constructor/destructor mechanisms can be used for the creation and removal of resources that may be required to properly handle the exceptional condition.

Q Why not use exceptions for non-error conditions? Isn't it convenient to be able to express-train back to previous areas of the code, even when non-exceptional conditions exist?

A Yes, some C++ programmers use exceptions for just that purpose. The danger is that exceptions might create memory leaks as the stack is unwound and some objects are inadvertently left in the free store. With careful programming techniques and a good compiler, this can usually be avoided. Otherwise, it is a matter of personal aesthetic; some programmers feel that by their nature exceptions should not be used for routine conditions.

Q Does an exception have to be caught in the same place where the `try` block created the exception?

A No, it is possible to catch an exception anywhere in the call stack. As the stack is unwound, the exception is passed up the stack until it is handled.

Q Why use a debugger when you can use `cout` with conditional (`#ifdef debug`) compiling?

A The debugger provides a much more powerful mechanism for stepping through your code and watching values change without having to clutter your code with thousands of debugging statements.

Workshop

The Workshop contains quiz questions to help solidify your understanding of the material covered and exercises to provide you with experience in using what you have learned. Try to answer the quiz and exercise questions before checking the answers in Appendix D, "Answers to Exercises and Quizzes," and make sure you understand the answers before continuing tomorrow.

Quiz

1. What is an exception?
2. What is a `try` block?
3. What is a `catch` statement?
4. What information can an exception contain?
5. When are exception objects created?
6. Should you pass exceptions by value or by reference?
7. Will a `catch` statement catch a derived exception if it is looking for the base class?
8. If two `catch` statements are used, one for base and one for derived, which should come first?

9. What does `catch(...)` mean?

10. What is a breakpoint?

Exercises

1. Create a `try` block, a `catch` statement, and a simple exception.

2. Modify the answer from Exercise 1, put data into the exception along with an accessor function, and use it in the `catch` block.

3. Modify the class from Exercise 2 to be a hierarchy of exceptions. Modify the `catch` block to use the derived objects and the base objects.

4. Modify the program from Exercise 3 to have three levels of function calls.

5. **BUG BUSTER:** What is wrong with the following code?

```
class xOutOfMemory
{
public:
        xOutOfMemory(){ theMsg = new char[20];
            strcpy(theMsg,"error in memory");}
        ~xOutOfMemory(){ delete [] theMsg; cout
            << "Memory restored." << endl; }
    char * Message()  { return theMsg; }
private:
        char * theMsg;
};

main()
{
    try
    {
        char * var = new char;
        if ( var == 0 )
        {
            xOutOfMemory * px =
            new xOutOfMemory;
            throw px;
        }
    }

    catch( xOutOfMemory * theException )
    {
        cout << theException->Message() <<endl;
        delete theException;
    }
        return 0;
}
```

20

This exercise shows the intended bug: It is allocating memory to present the error message, but it does so precisely when no memory is available to allocate (after all, that is what this exception manages!). You can test this program by changing the line if (var == 0) to if (1), which will force the exception to be thrown.

DAY 21

What's Next

Congratulations! You are nearly done with a full three-week intensive introduction to C++. By now you should have a solid understanding of C++, but in modern programming, there is always more to learn. This day fills in some missing details and then sets the course for continued study.

Most of what you write in your source code files is C++. This is interpreted by the compiler and turned into your program. Before the compiler runs, however, the preprocessor runs, and this provides an opportunity for conditional compilation. Today you will learn:

- What conditional compilation is and how to manage it
- How to write macros using the preprocessor
- How to use the preprocessor in finding bugs
- How to manipulate individual bits and use them as flags
- What the next steps are in learning to use C++ effectively

The Preprocessor and the Compiler

Every time you run your compiler, your preprocessor runs first. The preprocessor looks for preprocessor instructions, each of which begins with a pound symbol (#). The effect of each of these instructions is a change to the text of the source code. The result is a new source code file—a temporary file that you normally do not see, but that you can instruct the compiler to save so that you can examine it if you want to.

The compiler does not read your original source code file; it reads the output of the pre-processor and compiles that file. You have already seen the effect of this with the #include directive. This instructs the preprocessor to find the file whose name follows the #include directive and to write it into the intermediate file at that location. It is as if you had typed that entire file right into your source code, and by the time the compiler sees the source code, the included file is there.

Seeing the Intermediate Form

Nearly every compiler has a switch that you can set either in the integrated development environment (IDE) or at the command line, which instructs the compiler to save the intermediate file.

For the GNU compiler, that option is -E. For other compilers, check your documentation for the right switches to set if you would like to examine this file.

The #define Preprocessor Directive

The #define command defines a string substitution. If you write

```
#define BIG 512"
```

you have instructed the precompiler to substitute the string 512 wherever it sees the string BIG. This is not a string in the C++ sense. The characters 512 are substituted in your source code wherever the token BIG is seen. A token is a string of characters that can be used wherever a string or constant or other set of letters might be used. Thus, if you write

```
#define BIG 512
int myArray[BIG];
```

The intermediate file produced by the precompiler will look like this:

```
int myArray[512];
```

Note that the #define statement is gone. Precompiler statements are all removed from the intermediate file; they do not appear in the final source code at all.

Using #define for Constants

One way to use #define is as a substitute for constants. This is almost never a good idea, however, because #define merely makes a string substitution and does no type checking. As explained in the section on constants, tremendous advantages exist in using the const keyword rather than #define.

Using #define for Tests

A second way to use #define, however, is simply to declare that a particular character string is defined. Therefore, you could write

```
#define BIG
```

Later, you can test whether BIG has been defined and take action accordingly. The precompiler commands to test whether a string has been defined are #ifdef (if defined) and #ifndef (if not defined). Both must be followed by the command #endif before the block ends (before the next closing brace).

#ifdef evaluates to true if the string it tests has been defined already. So, you can write

```
#ifdef DEBUG
cout << "Debug defined";
#endif
```

When the precompiler reads the #ifdef, it checks a table it has built to see if you already defined DEBUG. If you have, the #ifdef evaluates to true, and everything to the next #else or #endif is written into the intermediate file for compiling. If it evaluates to false, nothing between #ifdef DEBUG and #endif will be written into the intermediate file; it will be as if it were never in the source code in the first place.

Note that #ifndef is the logical reverse of #ifdef. #ifndef evaluates to true if the string has not been defined up to that point in the file.

Using the #else Precompiler Command

As you might imagine, the term #else can be inserted between either #ifdef or #ifndef and the closing #endif. Listing 21.1 illustrates how these terms are used.

INPUT   **LISTING 21.1**   Using #define

```
1:    #define DemoVersion
2:    #define NT_VERSION 5
3:    #include <iostream.h>
4: // Listing 21.1 using #define
```

continues

21

LISTING 21.1   CONTINUED

```
5:
6:      int main()
7:      {
8:
9:      cout << "Checking on the definitions of DemoVersion, NT_VERSION
                   ➥and WINDOWS_VERSION...\n";
10:
11:     #ifdef DemoVersion
12:        cout << "DemoVersion defined.\n";
13:     #else
14:        cout << "DemoVersion not defined.\n";
15:     #endif
16:
17:     #ifndef NT_VERSION
18:        cout << "NT_VERSION not defined!\n";
19:     #else
20:        cout << "NT_VERSION defined as: " << NT_VERSION << endl;
21:     #endif
22:
23:     #ifdef WINDOWS_VERSION
24:        cout << "WINDOWS_VERSION defined!\n";
25:     #else
26:        cout << "WINDOWS_VERSION was not defined.\n";
27:     #endif
28:
29:      cout << "Done.\n";

30:      return 0;
31:     }
```

OUTPUT

```
Checking on the definitions of DemoVersion, NT_VERSION_and
➥WINDOWS_VERSION...
DemoVersion defined.
NT_VERSION defined as: 5
WINDOWS_VERSION was not defined.
Done.
```

ANALYSIS   On lines 1 and 2, DemoVersion and NT_VERSION are defined, with NT_VERSION defined with the string 5. On line 11, the definition of DemoVersion is tested, and because DemoVersion is defined (albeit with no value), the test is true and the string on line 12 is printed.

On line 17 is the test that NT_VERSION is not defined. Because NT_VERSION is defined, this test fails and execution jumps to line 20. Here the string 5 is substituted for the word NT_VERSION; this is seen by the compiler as

```
cout << "NT_VERSION defined as: " << 5 << endl;
```

Note that the first word NT_VERSION is not substituted because it is in a quoted string. The second NT_VERSION is substituted, however, and thus the compiler sees 5 as if you had typed 5 there.

Finally, on line 23, the program tests for WINDOWS_VERSION. Because you did not define WINDOWS_VERSION, the test fails and the message on line 26 is printed.

Inclusion and Inclusion Guards

You will create projects with many different files. You will probably organize your directories so that each class has its own header file (for example, .hpp) with the class declaration and its own implementation file (for example, .cpp) with the source code for the class methods.

Your main() function will be in its own .cpp file, and all the .cpp files will be compiled into .obj files, which will then be linked into a single program by the linker.

Because your programs will use methods from many classes, many header files will be included in each file. Also, header files often need to include one another. For example, the header file for a derived class's declaration must include the header file for its base class.

Imagine that the Animal class is declared in the file ANIMAL.hpp. The Dog class (which derives from Animal) must include the file ANIMAL.hpp in DOG.hpp, or Dog will not be able to derive from Animal. The Cat header also includes ANIMAL.hpp for the same reason.

If you create a method that uses both a Cat and a Dog, you will be in danger of including ANIMAL.hpp twice. This will generate a compile-time error because it is not legal to declare a class (Animal) twice, even though the declarations are identical. You can solve this problem with inclusion guards. At the top of your ANIMAL header file, you write these lines:

```
#ifndef ANIMAL_HPP
#define ANIMAL_HPP
...                     // the whole file goes here
#endif
```

This says, if you have not defined the term ANIMAL_HPP, go ahead and define it now. Between the #define statement and the closing #endif are the entire contents of the file.

The first time your program includes this file, it reads the first line and the test evaluates to true; that is, you have not yet defined ANIMAL_HPP. So, it defines it and then includes the entire file.

21

The second time your program includes the ANIMAL.hpp file, it reads the first line and the test evaluates to false; ANIMAL.hpp has been defined. It therefore skips to the next #else (in this case there is not one) or the next #endif (at the end of the file). Thus, it skips the entire contents of the file, and the class is not declared twice.

The actual name of the defined symbol (ANIMAL_HPP) is not important, although it is customary to use the filename in all uppercase with the dot (.) changed to an underscore. This is purely convention, however.

> **Note**
>
> It never hurts to use inclusion guards. Often they will save you hours of debugging time.

Macro Functions

The #define directive can also be used to create macro functions. A macro function is a symbol created using #define; it takes an argument, in much the same way that a function does. The preprocessor will substitute the substitution string for whatever argument it is given. For example, you can define the macro TWICE as follows:

```
#define TWICE(x) ( (x) * 2 )
```

and then in your code you write

```
TWICE(4)
```

The entire string TWICE(4) will be removed, and the value 8 will be substituted! When the precompiler sees the 4, it will substitute ((4) * 2), which will then evaluate to 4 * 2, or 8.

A macro can have more than one parameter, and each parameter can be used repeatedly in the replacement text. Two common macros are MAX and MIN:

```
#define MAX(x,y) ( (x) > (y) ? (x) : (y) )
#define MIN(x,y) ( (x) < (y) ? (x) : (y) )
```

Note that in a macro function definition, the opening parenthesis for the parameter list must immediately follow the macro name, with no spaces. The preprocessor is not as forgiving of whitespace as is the compiler.

If you were to write

```
#define MAX (x,y) ( (x) > (y) ? (x) : (y) )
```

and then tried to use MAX like this:

```
int x = 5, y = 7, z;
z = MAX(x,y);
```

the intermediate code would be

```
int x = 5, y = 7, z;
z = (x,y) ( (x) > (y) ? (x) : (y) )(x,y)
```

A simple text substitution would be done, rather than invoking the macro function. Thus, the token MAX would have substituted for it (x,y) ((x) > (y) ? (x) : (y)), and then that would be followed by the (x,y), which followed MAX.

If you remove the space between MAX and (x,y), however, the intermediate code becomes

```
int x = 5, y = 7, z;
z =7;
```

Why All the Parentheses?

You may be wondering why so many parentheses are in many of the macros presented so far. The preprocessor does not demand that parentheses be placed around the arguments in the substitution string, but the parentheses help you to avoid unwanted side effects when you pass complicated values to a macro. For example, if you define MAX as

```
#define MAX(x,y) x > y ? x : y
```

and pass in the values 5 and 7, the macro works as intended. But if you pass in a more complicated expression, you will get unintended results, as shown in Listing 21.2.

INPUT   **LISTING 21.2**   Using Parentheses in Macros

```
1:     // Listing 21.2 Macro Expansion
2:     #include <iostream.h>
3:
4:     #define CUBE(a) ( (a) * (a) * (a) )
5:     #define THREE(a) a * a * a
6:
7:     int main()
8:     {
9:         long x = 5;
10:        long y = CUBE(x);
11:        long z = THREE(x);
12:
13:        cout << "y: " << y << endl;
14:        cout << "z: " << z << endl;
15:
16:        long a = 5, b = 7;
```

21

continues

LISTING 21.2   CONTINUED

```
17:        y = CUBE(a+b);
18:        z = THREE(a+b);
19:
20:        cout << "y: " << y << endl;
21:        cout << "z: " << z << endl;
22:     return 0;
23:    }
```

OUTPUT

```
y: 125
z: 125
y: 1728
z: 82
```

ANALYSIS   On line 4, the macro CUBE is defined, with the argument x put into parentheses each time it is used. On line 5, the macro THREE is defined, without the parentheses.

In the first use of these macros, the value 5 is given as the parameter, and both macros work fine. CUBE(5) expands to ((5) * (5) * (5)), which evaluates to 125, and THREE(5) expands to 5 * 5 * 5, which also evaluates to 125.

In the second use, on lines 16–18, the parameter is 5 + 7. In this case, CUBE(5+7) evaluates to

((5+7) * (5+7) * (5+7))

which evaluates to

((12) * (12) * (12))

which, in turn, evaluates to 1728. THREE(5+7), however, evaluates to

5 + 7 * 5 + 7 * 5 + 7

Because multiplication has a higher precedence than addition, this becomes

5 + (7 * 5) + (7 * 5) + 7

which evaluates to

5 + (35) + (35) + 7

which finally evaluates to 82.

Macros Versus Functions and Templates

Macros suffer from four problems in C++. The first is that they can be confusing if they get large, because all macros must be defined on one line. In most compilers, you can extend that line by using the backslash character (\), which is known as *line splicing*.

The preprocessor distributed with the GNU compilers does not handle line splicing properly, so all macros must remain on one line. Large macros quickly become difficult to manage.

The second problem is that macros are expanded inline each time they are used. This means that if a macro is used a dozen times, the substitution will appear 12 times in your program, rather than appearing once as a function call will. On the other hand, they are usually quicker than a function call because the overhead of a function call is avoided.

The fact that they are expanded inline leads to the third problem, which is that the macro does not appear in the intermediate source code used by the compilers; therefore, it is unavailable in most debuggers. This makes debugging macros tricky.

The final problem, however, is the biggest: macros are not type-safe. Although it is convenient that absolutely any argument may be used with a macro, this completely undermines the strong typing of C++ and so is anathema to C++ programmers. Of course, the right way to solve this is with templates, as you saw on Day 19, "Templates."

Inline Functions

It is often possible to declare an inline function rather than a macro. For example, Listing 21.3 creates a CUBE function, which accomplishes the same thing as the CUBE macro in Listing 21.2, but it does so in a type-safe way.

INPUT   **LISTING 21.3**   Using Inline Rather Than a Macro

```
1:    #include <iostream.h>
2:    // Listing 21.3: Using Inline instead of a macro
3:    inline unsigned long Square(unsigned long a) { return a * a; }
4:    inline unsigned long Cube(unsigned long a)
5:        { return a * a * a; }
6:    int main()
7:    {
8:        unsigned long x=1 ;
9:        for (;;)
10:        {
11:            cout << "Enter a number (0 to quit): ";
12:            cin >> x;
13:            if (x == 0)
14:                break;
15:            cout << "You entered: " << x;
16:            cout << ".  Square(" << x << "): ";
17:            cout  << Square(x);
18:            cout<< ". Cube(" << x << "): ";
```

continues

21

LISTING 21.3   CONTINUED

```
19:            cout << Cube(x) << "." << endl;
20:        }
21:     return 0;
22:   }
```

OUTPUT

```
Enter a number (0 to quit): 1
You entered: 1.  Square(1): 1. Cube(1): 1.
Enter a number (0 to quit): 2
You entered: 2.  Square(2): 4. Cube(2): 8.
Enter a number (0 to quit): 3
You entered: 3.  Square(3): 9. Cube(3): 27.
Enter a number (0 to quit): 4
You entered: 4.  Square(4): 16. Cube(4): 64.
Enter a number (0 to quit): 5
You entered: 5.  Square(5): 25. Cube(5): 125.
Enter a number (0 to quit): 6
You entered: 6.  Square(6): 36. Cube(6): 216.
Enter a number (0 to quit): 0
```

ANALYSIS   On lines 3 and 4, two inline functions are defined: Square() and Cube(). Each is
declared to be inline, so like a macro function, these will be expanded in place
for each call, and no function call overhead will occur.

As a reminder, expanded inline means that the content of the function will be placed into
the code wherever the function call would be made (for example, on line 17). Because
the function call is never made, there is no overhead of putting the return address and the
parameters on the stack.

On line 17, the function Square is called, as is the function Cube on line 19. Again,
because these are inline functions, it is exactly as if this line had been written like this:

```
16:          cout << ".  Square(" << x << "): "  << x * x << ".
➥Cube(" << x << "): " << x * x * x <<
```

```
"." << endl;
```

String Manipulation

The preprocessor provides two special operators for manipulating strings in macros. The
stringizing operator (#) substitutes a quoted string for whatever follows the stringizing
operator. The concatenation operator bonds two strings into one.

Stringizing

The stringizing operator puts quotes around any characters following the operator, up to the next whitespace. Thus, if you write

```
#define WRITESTRING(x) cout << #x
```

and then call

```
WRITESTRING(This is a string);
```

the precompiler will turn it into

```
cout << "This is a string";
```

Note that the string This is a string is put into quotes, as required by cout.

Concatenation

The concatenation operator allows you to bond more than one term into a new word. The new word is actually a token that can be used as a class name, a variable name, an offset into an array, or anywhere else a series of letters might appear.

Assume for a moment that you have five functions named fOnePrint, fTwoPrint, fThreePrint, fFourPrint, and fFivePrint. You can then declare

```
#define fPRINT(x) f ## x ## Print
```

and then use it with fPRINT(Two) to generate fTwoPrint and with fPRINT(Three) to generate fThreePrint.

At the conclusion of Week 2, a PartsList class was developed. This list could only handle objects of type List. Suppose that this list works well, and you would like to be able to make lists of animals, cars, computers, and so forth.

One approach would be to create AnimalList, CarList, ComputerList, and so on, by cutting and pasting the code in place. This will quickly become a nightmare because every change to one list must be written to all the others.

An alternative is to use macros and the concatenation operator. For example, in most compilers, you could define

```
#define Listof(Type)  class Type##List \
{ \
public: \
Type##List(){} \
private:           \
int itsLength; \
};
```

21

For GNU, you would define it as follows:

```
#define Listof(Type)  class Type##List { public: Type##List(){}
  ➥private: int itsLength; };
```

Of course, the page is not wide enough to show the entire macro as one line. Most editor windows are not wide enough either, but you should get the idea.

This example is overly sparse, concatenation operatorbut the idea would be to put in all the necessary methods and data. When you were ready to create an AnimalList, you would write

```
Listof(Animal)
```

and this would be turned into the declaration of the AnimalList class. Some problems occur with this approach, all of which are discussed in detail on Day 19, "Templates."

Predefined Macros

Many compilers predefine a number of useful macros, including __DATE__, __TIME__, __LINE__, and __FILE__. Each of these names is surrounded by two underscore characters to reduce the likelihood that the names will conflict with names you are using in your program.

When the precompiler sees one of these macros, it makes the appropriate substitutes. For __DATE__, the current date is substituted. For __TIME__, the current time is substituted. __LINE__ and __FILE__ are replaced with the source code line number and filename, respectively. You should note that this substitution is made when the source is precompiled, not when the program is run. If you ask the program to print __DATE__, you will not get the current date; instead, you will get the date the program was compiled. These defined macros are very useful in debugging.

assert()

GNU and many other compilers offer an assert() macro. The assert() macro returns true if its parameter evaluates true and takes some kind of action if it evaluates false. GNU and many other compilers will abort the program on an assert() that fails; still others will throw an exception (see Day 20, "Exceptions and Error Handling").

One powerful feature of the assert() macro is that the preprocessor collapses it into no code at all if NDEBUG is not defined. It is a great help during development, and when the final product ships, there is no performance penalty nor increase in the size of the executable version of the program.

Rather than depending on the compiler-provided assert(), you are free to write your own assert() macro. Listing 21.4 provides a simple assert() macro and shows its use.

INPUT   **LISTING 21.4**   A Simple assert() Macro

```
1:      // Listing 21.4 ASSERTS
2:      #define DEBUG
3:      #include <iostream.h>
4:
5:      #ifndef DEBUG
6:          #define ASSERT(x)
7:      #else
8:          #define ASSERT(x) if (! (x)) { cout << "ERROR!! Assert
    " << #x << " failed\n"; cout << " on line " << __LINE__
    << "\n"; cout << " in file " << __FILE__ << "\n";  }
9: //
10: //
11: //
12: //
13: //
14: //
15:     #endif
16:
17:
18:     int main()
19:     {
20:        int x = 5;
21:        cout << "First assert: \n";
22:        ASSERT(x==5);
23:        cout << "\nSecond assert: \n";
24:        ASSERT(x != 5);
25:        cout << "\nDone.\n";
26:      return 0;
27:     }
```

OUTPUT

```
First assert:

Second assert:
ERROR!! Assert x !=5 failed
 on line 24
 in file lst21-04.cxx
Done.
```

ANALYSIS   On line 2, the term DEBUG is defined. Typically, this would be done from the command line (with the -D command-line argument for g++) at compile time, so you can turn this on and off at will. On lines 8–14, the ASSERT() macro is defined. Typically, this would be done in a header file, and that header (ASSERT.hpp) would be included in all your implementation files.

21

On line 5, the term DEBUG is tested. If it is not defined, ASSERT() is defined to create no code at all. If DEBUG is defined, the functionality defined on line 8 is applied.

The ASSERT() itself is one long statement because the GNU preprocessor does not support line splitting.

Many other preprocessors do support line splitting—where the ASSERT() is split across seven source code lines as far as the precompiler is concerned. An example of code like that would be replace lines 8–14 in listing 21.4

```
8:   #define ASSERT(x) \
9:   if (! (x)) \
10:  { \
11:     cout << "ERROR!! Assert " << #x << " failed\n"; \
12:     cout << " on line " << __LINE__ << "\n"; \
13:     cout << " in file " << __FILE__ << "\n";  \
14:  }
```

On line 9, the value passed in as a parameter is tested; if it evaluates false, the statements on lines 11–13 are invoked, printing an error message. If the value passed in evaluates true, no action is taken.

Debugging with assert()

When writing your program, you will often know deep down in your soul that something is true: a function has a certain value, a pointer is valid, and so forth. It is the nature of bugs that what you know to be true might not be so, under some conditions. For example, you know that a pointer is valid, yet the program crashes. assert() can help you find this type of bug, but only if you make it a regular practice to use assert() liberally in your code. Every time you assign or are passed a pointer as a parameter or function return value, be sure to assert that the pointer is valid. Any time your code depends on a particular value being in a variable, assert() that that is true.

No penalty is assessed for frequent use of assert(); it is removed from the code when you undefine debugging. It also provides good internal documentation, reminding the reader of what you believe is true at any given moment in the flow of the code.

assert() Versus Exceptions

Yesterday, you saw how to work with exceptions to handle error conditions. It is important to note that assert() is not intended to handle runtime error conditions such as bad data, out-of-memory conditions, unable to open a file, and so forth. assert() is created to catch programming errors only. That is, if an assert() "fires," you know you have a bug in your code.

This is critical because when you ship your code to your customers, instances of assert() will be removed. You cannot depend on an assert() to handle a runtime problem because the assert() will not be there.

It is a common mistake to use assert() to test the return value from a memory assignment:

```
Animal *pCat = new Cat;
assert(pCat);    // bad use of assert
pCat->SomeFunction();
```

This is a classic programming error; every time the programmer runs the program, enough memory is available and the assert() never fires. After all, the programmer is running with lots of extra RAM to speed up the compiler, debugger, and so forth. The programmer then ships the executable, and the poor user, who has less memory, reaches this part of the program and the call to new fails and returns NULL. The assert(), however, is no longer in the code and nothing indicates that the pointer points to NULL. As soon as the statement pCat->SomeFunction() is reached, the program crashes.

Getting NULL back from a memory assignment is not a programming error, although it is an exceptional situation. Your program must be able to recover from this condition, if only by throwing an exception. Remember: The entire assert() statement is gone when NDEBUG is undefined. Exceptions were covered in detail on Day 20.

Side Effects

It is not uncommon to find that a bug appears only after the instances of assert() are removed. This is almost always due to the program unintentionally depending on side effects of things done in assert() and other debug-only code. For example, if you write

```
assert (x = 5)
```

when you mean to test whether x == 5, you will create a particularly nasty bug.

Suppose that just prior to this assert(), you called a function that set x equal to 0. With this assert(), you think you are testing whether x is equal to 5; in fact, you are setting x equal to 5. The test returns true because x = 5 not only sets x to 5, but returns the value 5, and because 5 is non-zero, it evaluates as true.

When you pass the assert() statement, x really is equal to 5 (you just set it!). Your program runs just fine. You are ready to ship it, so you turn off debugging. Now the assert() disappears, and you are no longer setting x to 5. Because x was set to 0 just before this, it remains at 0 and your program breaks.

21

In frustration, you turn debugging back on, but—presto! The bug is gone. Again, this is rather funny to watch, but not to live through, so be very careful about side effects in debugging code. If you see a bug that appears only when debugging is turned off, take a look at your debugging code with an eye out for nasty side effects.

Class Invariants

Most classes have some conditions that should always be true whenever you are finished with a class member function. These class invariants are the *sine qua non* of your class. For example, it may be true that your CIRCLE object should never have a radius of zero or that your ANIMAL should always have an age greater than zero and less than 100.

It can be very helpful to declare an Invariants() method that returns true only if each of these conditions are still true. You can then ASSERT(Invariants()) at the start and at the completion of every class method. The exception would be that your Invariants() would not expect to return true before your constructor runs or after your destructor ends. Listing 21.5 demonstrates the use of the Invariants() method in a trivial class.

INPUT   **LISTING 21.5**   Using Invariants()

```
1:     #define DEBUG
2:     #define SHOW_INVARIANTS
3:     #include <iostream.h>
4:     #include <string.h>
5:     // Listing 21.5: Using invariants()
6:     #ifndef DEBUG
7:     #define ASSERT(x)
8:     #else
9:         #define ASSERT(x) if (! (x)) { cout << "ERROR!! Assert
    " << #x << " failed\n"; cout << " on line " << __LINE__
    << "\n"; cout << " in file " << __FILE__ << "\n";   }
10: //
11: //
12: //
13: //
14: //
15: //
16:    #endif
17:
18:
19:    const int FALSE = 0;
20:    const int TRUE = 1;
21:    // typedef int bool;
22:
23:
24:    class String
25:    {
```

```
26:        public:
27:            // constructors
28:            String();
29:            String(const char *const);
30:            String(const String &);
31:            ~String();
32:
33:            char & operator[](int offset);
34:            char operator[](int offset) const;
35:
36:            String & operator= (const String &);
37:            int GetLen()const { return itsLen; }
38:            const char * GetString() const { return itsString; }
39:            bool Invariants() const;
40:
41:        private:
42:            String (int);           // private constructor
43:            char * itsString;
44:           // unsigned short itsLen;
45:            int itsLen;
46:        };
47:
48:    // default constructor creates string of 0 bytes
49:    String::String()
50:    {
51:        itsString = new char[1];
52:        itsString[0] = '\0';
53:        itsLen=0;
54:        ASSERT(Invariants());
55:    }
56:
57:    // private (helper) constructor, used only by
58:    // class methods for creating a new string of
59:    // required size.  Null filled.
60:    String::String(int len)
61:    {
62:        itsString = new char[len+1];
63:        for (int i = 0; i<=len; i++)
64:            itsString[i] = '\0';
65:        itsLen=len;
66:        ASSERT(Invariants());
67:    }
68:
69:    // Converts a character array to a String
70:    String::String(const char * const cString)
71:    {
72:        itsLen = strlen(cString);
73:        itsString = new char[itsLen+1];
74:        for (int i = 0; i<itsLen; i++)
```

continues

21

LISTING 21.5   CONTINUED

```
75:            itsString[i] = cString[i];
76:        itsString[itsLen]='\0';
77:        ASSERT(Invariants());
78:    }
79:
80:    // copy constructor
81:    String::String (const String & rhs)
82:    {
83:        itsLen=rhs.GetLen();
84:        itsString = new char[itsLen+1];
85:        for (int i = 0; i<itsLen;i++)
86:            itsString[i] = rhs[i];
87:        itsString[itsLen] = '\0';
88:        ASSERT(Invariants());
89:    }
90:
91:    // destructor, frees allocated memory
92:    String::~String ()
93:    {
94:        ASSERT(Invariants());
95:        delete [] itsString;
96:        itsLen = 0;
97:    }
98:
99:    // operator equals, frees existing memory
100:   // then copies string and size
101:   String& String::operator=(const String & rhs)
102:   {
103:       ASSERT(Invariants());
104:       if (this == &rhs)
105:          return *this;
106:       delete [] itsString;
107:       itsLen=rhs.GetLen();
108:       itsString = new char[itsLen+1];
109:       for (int i = 0; i<itsLen;i++)
110:           itsString[i] = rhs[i];
111:       itsString[itsLen] = '\0';
112:       ASSERT(Invariants());
113:       return *this;
114:    }
115:
116: //non constant offset operator
117:   char & String::operator[](int offset)
118: {
119:     ASSERT(Invariants());
120:     if (offset > itsLen)
121:     {
122:       ASSERT(Invariants());
123:       return itsString[itsLen-1];
```

```
124:      }
125:       else
126:      {
127:         ASSERT(Invariants());
128:         return itsString[offset];
129:      }
130:  }
131:      // constant offset operator
132:      char String::operator[](int offset) const
133:      {
134:         ASSERT(Invariants());
135:         char retVal;
136:         if (offset > itsLen)
137:             retVal = itsString[itsLen-1];
138:         else
139:             retVal = itsString[offset];
140:         ASSERT(Invariants());
141:         return retVal;
142:      }
143:      bool String::Invariants() const
144:      {
145:  #ifdef SHOW_INVARIANTS
146:         cout << "Invariants Tested";
147:  #endif
148:          return ( (itsLen && itsString) ||
149:             (!itsLen && !itsString) );
150:       }
151:      class Animal
152:      {
153:      public:
154:         Animal():itsAge(1),itsName("John Q. Animal")
155:             {ASSERT(Invariants());}
156:          Animal(int, const String&);
157:         ~Animal(){}
158:         int GetAge() {  ASSERT(Invariants()); return itsAge;}
159:         void SetAge(int Age)
160:         {
161:             ASSERT(Invariants());
162:             itsAge = Age;
163:             ASSERT(Invariants());
164:         }
165:         String& GetName()
166:         {
167:             ASSERT(Invariants());
168:             return itsName;
169:         }
170:         void SetName(const String& name)
171:             {
172:             ASSERT(Invariants());
```

continues

21

LISTING 21.5   CONTINUED

```
173:                  itsName = name;
174:                  ASSERT(Invariants());
175:            }
176:         bool Invariants();
177:     private:
178:         int itsAge;
179:         String itsName;
180:     };
181:
182:     Animal::Animal(int age, const String& name):
183:     itsAge(age),
184:     itsName(name)
185:     {
186:         ASSERT(Invariants());
187:     }
188:
189:     bool Animal::Invariants()
190:     {
191:     #ifdef SHOW_INVARIANTS
192:         cout << "Invariants Tested";
193:     #endif
194:         return (itsAge > 0 && itsName.GetLen());
195:     }
196:
197:     int main()
198:     {
199:         Animal sparky(5,"Sparky");
200:         cout << "\n" << sparky.GetName().GetString() << " is ";
201:         cout << sparky.GetAge() << " years old.";
202:         sparky.SetAge(8);
203:         cout << "\n" << sparky.GetName().GetString() << " is ";
204:         cout << sparky.GetAge() << " years old.";
205:         return 0;
206:     }
```

OUTPUT

```
SHOW_INVARIANTS defined

Invariants TestedInvariants TestedInvariants TestedInvariants
➥TestedInvariants
➥TestedInvariants TestedInvariants TestedInvariants TestedInvariants
➥TestedInvariants TestedInvariants TestedInvariants TestedInvariants
➥TestedInvariants TestedInvariants TestedInvariants TestedInvariants
➥Tested
Sparky is Invariants Tested5 years old.Invariants TestedInvariants
➥TestedInvariants Tested
Sparky is Invariants Tested8 years old.Invariants Tested

SHOW_INVARIANTS undefined

    Sparky is 5 years old.
Sparky is 8 years old.
```

ANALYSIS On line 9, the ASSERT() macro is defined. If DEBUG is defined, this will write out an error message when the ASSERT() macro evaluates false.

On line 39, the String class member function Invariants() is declared; it is defined on lines 143–150. The constructor is declared on lines 49–55; on line 54, after the object is fully constructed, Invariants() is called to confirm proper construction.

This pattern is repeated for the other constructors, and the destructor calls Invariants() only before it sets out to destroy the object. The remaining class functions call Invariants() before taking any action and then again before returning. This both affirms and validates a fundamental principal of C++: Member functions other than constructors and destructors should work on valid objects and should leave them in a valid state.

On line 176, class Animal declares its own Invariants() method, implemented on lines 189–195. Note on lines 155, 158, 161, and 163 that inline functions can call the Invariants() method.

Printing Interim Values

In addition to asserting that something is true using the assert() macro, you may want to print the current value of pointers, variables, and strings. This can be helpful in checking your assumptions about the progress of your program and in locating off-by-one bugs in loops. Listing 21.6 illustrates this idea.

INPUT **LISTING 21.6** Printing Values in DEBUG Mode

```
1:      // Listing 21.6 - Printing values in DEBUG mode
2:      #include <iostream.h>
3:      #define DEBUG
4:
5:      #ifndef DEBUG
6:      #define PRINT(x)
7:      #else
8:      #define PRINT(x)  cout << #x << ":\t" << x << endl;
9: //
10:     #endif
11:
12:     // enum bool { FALSE, TRUE } ;
13:
14:     int main()
15:     {
16:         int x = 5;
17:         long y = 738981;
18:         PRINT(x);
```

continues

21

LISTING 21.6 CONTINUED

```
19:        for (int i = 0; i < x; i++)
20:        {
21:            PRINT(i);
22:        }
23:
24:        PRINT (y);
25:        PRINT("Hi.");
26:        int *px = &x;
27:        PRINT(px);
28:        PRINT (*px);
29:     return 0;
30:    }
```

OUTPUT

```
x:      5
i:      0
i:      1
i:      2
i:      3
i:      4
y:      73898
"Hi.":  Hi.
px:         0x7fffc64
*px:    5
```

ANALYSIS The macro on lines 5–10 provides printing of the current value of the supplied parameter. Note that the first thing fed to cout is the stringized version of the parameter; that is, if you pass in x, cout receives "x".

Next, cout receives the quoted string ":\t", which prints a colon and then a tab. Third, cout receives the value of the parameter (x), and then finally, endl, which writes a new line and flushes the buffer.

Note that you may receive a value other than 0x2100.

Debugging Levels

In large, complex projects, you may want more control than simply turning DEBUG on and off. You can define debug levels and test for these levels when deciding which macros to use and which to strip out.

To define a level, simply follow the #define DEBUG statement with a number. Although you can have any number of levels, a common system to have is four levels: HIGH, MEDIUM, LOW, and NONE. Listing 21.7 illustrates how this might be done, using the String and Animal classes from Listing 21.5.

INPUT **LISTING 21.7** Levels of Debugging

```
1:     #define HIGH 3
2:     #define MED 2
3:     #define LOW 1
4:     #define NONE 0
5:  // Listing 21.7: Levels of Debugging
6:     #define DEBUGLEVEL HIGH
7:
8:     #include <iostream.h>
9:     #include <string.h>
10:
11:    #if DEBUGLEVEL < LOW  // must be medium or high
12:    #define ASSERT(x)
13:    #else
14:       #define ASSERT(x) if (! (x)) { cout << "ERROR!! Assert
   ➥" << #x << " failed\n"; cout << " on line " << __LINE__
   ➥<< "\n"; cout << " in file " << __FILE__ << "\n";  }
15: //
16: //
17: //
18: //
19: //
20: //
21:    #endif
22:
23:    #if DEBUGLEVEL < MEDIUM
24:    #define EVAL(x)
25:    #else
26:    #define EVAL(x) cout << #x << ":\t" << x << endl;
27:    //
28:    #endif
29:
30:   #if DEBUGLEVEL < HIGH
31:    #define PRINT(x)
32:    #else
33:    #define PRINT(x) cout << x << endl;
34:    //
35:    #endif
36:
37:
38:    class String
39:    {
40:      public:
41:         // constructors
42:         String();
43:         String(const char *const);
44:         String(const String &);
45:         ~String();
```

21

continues

LISTING 21.7   CONTINUED

```
46:
47:            char & operator[](int offset);
48:            char operator[](int offset) const;
49:
50:            String & operator= (const String &);
51:            int GetLen()const { return itsLen; }
52:            const char * GetString() const
53:              { return itsString; }
54:            bool Invariants() const;
55:
56:        private:
57:            String (int);          // private constructor
58:            char * itsString;
59:            unsigned short itsLen;
60:        };
61:
62:    // default constructor creates string of 0 bytes
63:    String::String()
64:    {
65:        itsString = new char[1];
66:        itsString[0] = '\0';
67:        itsLen=0;
68:        ASSERT(Invariants());
69:    }
70:
71:    // private (helper) constructor, used only by
72:    // class methods for creating a new string of
73:    // required size.  Null filled.
74:    String::String(int len)
75:    {
76:        itsString = new char[len+1];
77:        for (int i = 0; i<=len; i++)
78:            itsString[i] = '\0';
79:        itsLen=len;
80:        ASSERT(Invariants());
81:    }
82:
83:    // Converts a character array to a String
84:    String::String(const char * const cString)
85:    {
86:        itsLen = strlen(cString);
87:        itsString = new char[itsLen+1];
88:        for (int i = 0; i<itsLen; i++)
89:            itsString[i] = cString[i];
90:        itsString[itsLen]='\0';
91:        ASSERT(Invariants());
92:    }
93:
94:    // copy constructor
```

```
95:     String::String (const String & rhs)
96:     {
97:        itsLen=rhs.GetLen();
98:        itsString = new char[itsLen+1];
99:        for (int i = 0; i<itsLen;i++)
100:           itsString[i] = rhs[i];
101:       itsString[itsLen] = '\0';
102:       ASSERT(Invariants());
103:    }
104:
105:    // destructor, frees allocated memory
106:    String::~String ()
107:    {
108:       ASSERT(Invariants());
109:       delete [] itsString;
110:       itsLen = 0;
111:    }
112:
113:    // operator equals, frees existing memory
114:    // then copies string and size
115:    String& String::operator=(const String & rhs)
116:    {
117:       ASSERT(Invariants());
118:       if (this == &rhs)
119:          return *this;
120:       delete [] itsString;
121:       itsLen=rhs.GetLen();
122:       itsString = new char[itsLen+1];
123:       for (int i = 0; i<itsLen;i++)
124:           itsString[i] = rhs[i];
125:       itsString[itsLen] = '\0';
126:       ASSERT(Invariants());
127:       return *this;
128:    }
129:
130: //non constant offset operator
131:   char & String::operator[](int offset)
132:  {
133:     ASSERT(Invariants());
134:     if (offset > itsLen)
135:     {
136:       ASSERT(Invariants());
137:       return itsString[itsLen-1];
138:     }
139:     else
140:     {
141:        ASSERT(Invariants());
142:       return itsString[offset];
143:     }
```

21

continues

LISTING 21.7   CONTINUED

```
144:    }
145:    // constant offset operator
146:    char String::operator[](int offset) const
147:    {
148:        ASSERT(Invariants());
149:        char retVal;
150:        if (offset > itsLen)
151:            retVal = itsString[itsLen-1];
152:        else
153:            retVal = itsString[offset];
154:        ASSERT(Invariants());
155:        return retVal;
156:    }
157:
158:    bool String::Invariants() const
159:    {
160:        PRINT("(String Invariants Checked)");
161:        return ( (bool) (itsLen && itsString) ||
162:            (!itsLen && !itsString) );
163:    }
164:
165:    class Animal
166:    {
167:    public:
168:        Animal():itsAge(1),itsName("John Q. Animal")
169:            {ASSERT(Invariants());}
170:
171:        Animal(int, const String&);
172:        ~Animal(){}
173:
174:        int GetAge()
175:            {
176:                ASSERT(Invariants());
177:                return itsAge;
178:            }
179:
180:        void SetAge(int Age)
181:            {
182:                ASSERT(Invariants());
183:                itsAge = Age;
184:                ASSERT(Invariants());
185:            }
186:        String& GetName()
187:            {
188:                ASSERT(Invariants());
189:                return itsName;
190:            }
191:
192:        void SetName(const String& name)
```

```
193:            {
194:                ASSERT(Invariants());
195:                itsName = name;
196:                ASSERT(Invariants());
197:            }
198:
199:      bool Invariants();
200:    private:
201:      int itsAge;
202:      String itsName;
203:    };
204:
205:    Animal::Animal(int age, const String& name):
206:    itsAge(age),
207:    itsName(name)
208:    {
209:        ASSERT(Invariants());
210:    }
211:
212:    bool Animal::Invariants()
213:    {
214:        PRINT("(Animal Invariants Checked)");
215:        return (itsAge > 0 && itsName.GetLen());
216:    }
217:
218:    int main()
219:    {
220:        const int AGE = 5;
221:        EVAL(AGE);
222:        Animal sparky(AGE,"Sparky");
223:        cout << "\n" << sparky.GetName().GetString();
224:        cout << " is ";
225:        cout << sparky.GetAge() << " years old.";
226:        sparky.SetAge(8);
227:        cout << "\n" << sparky.GetName().GetString();
228:        cout << " is ";
229:        cout << sparky.GetAge() << " years old.";
230:        return 0;
231:    }
```

OUTPUT

```
AGE:      5
(String Invariants Checked)
(String Invariants Checked)
(String Invariants Checked)
(String Invariants Checked)
(String Invariants Checked)
(String Invariants Checked)
(String Invariants Checked)
(String Invariants Checked)
(String Invariants Checked)
```

21

```
                (String Invariants Checked)
                (String Invariants Checked)
                (String Invariants Checked)
                (String Invariants Checked)
                (String Invariants Checked)
                (Animal Invariants Checked)
                (String Invariants Checked)
                (Animal Invariants Checked)

                Sparky is (Animal Invariants Checked)
                5 years old. (Animal Invariants Checked)
                 (Animal Invariants Checked)
                 (Animal Invariants Checked)

                Sparky is (Animal Invariants Checked)
                8 years old. (String Invariants Checked)
                 (String Invariants Checked)
```

Run again with DEBUG = MEDIUM

```
AGE:        5
Sparky is 5 years old.
Sparky is 8 years old.
```

ANALYSIS On lines 11–21, the assert() macro is defined to be stripped if DEBUGLEVEL is less than LOW (that is, DEBUGLEVEL is NONE). If any debugging is enabled, the assert() macro will work. On line 24, EVAL is declared to be stripped if DEBUG is less than MEDIUM; if DEBUGLEVEL is NONE or LOW, EVAL is stripped.

Finally, on lines 30–35, the PRINT macro is declared to be stripped if DEBUGLEVEL is less than HIGH. PRINT is used only when DEBUGLEVEL is HIGH; you can eliminate this macro by setting DEBUGLEVEL to MEDIUM and still maintain your use of EVAL and assert().

PRINT is used within the Invariants() methods to print an informative message. EVAL is used on line 221 to evaluate the current value of the constantinteger AGE.

Do	**Don't**
DO use CAPITALS for your macro names. This is a pervasive convention, and other programmers will be confused if you don't.	**DON'T** allow your macros to have side effects. Don't increment variables or assign values from within a macro.
DO surround all arguments with parentheses in macro functions.	

Bit Twiddling

Often you will want to set flags in your objects to keep track of the state of your object. (Is it in AlarmState? Has this been initialized yet? Are you coming or going?)

You can do this with user-defined Booleans, but when you have many flags, and when storage size is an issue, it is convenient to be able to use the individual bits as flags.

Each byte has eight bits, so in a 4-byte long you can hold 32 separate flags. A bit is said to be "set" if its value is 1 and clear if its value is 0. When you set a bit, you make its value 1, and when you clear it, you make its value 0. (Set and clear are both adjectives and verbs.) You can set and clear bits by changing the value of the long, but that can be tedious and confusing.

 Note

> Appendix C, "Binary, Octal, and Hexadecimal Numbers and an ASCII Chart," provides valuable additional information about binary, octal, and hexadecimal manipulation.

C++ provides bitwise operators that act upon the individual bits. These look like, but are different from, the logical operators, so many novice programmers confuse them. The bitwise operators are presented in Table 21.1.

TABLE 21.1   The Bitwise Operators

Symbol	Operator
&	AND
		OR
^	Exclusive OR
~	Complement

Operator AND

The AND operator (&) is a single ampersand, in contrast to the logical AND, which is two ampersands. When you AND two bits, the result is 1 if both bits are 1, but 0 if either or both bits are 0. The way to think of this is the following: The result is 1 if bit 1 is set and if bit 2 is set.

21

Operator OR

The second bitwise operator is OR (|). Again, this is a single vertical bar, in contrast to the logical OR, which is two vertical bars. When you OR two bits, the result is 1 if either bit is set or if both are.

Operator Exclusive OR

The third bitwise operator is exclusive OR (^). When you exclusive OR two bits, the result is 1 if the two bits are different.

The Complement Operator

The complement operator (~) clears every bit in a number that is set and sets every bit that is clear. If the current value of the number is 1010 0011, the complement of that number is 0101 1100.

Setting Bits

When you want to set or clear a particular bit, you use masking operations. If you have a 4-byte flag and you want to set bit 8 true, you need to OR the flag with the value 128. Why? The value 128 is 1000 0000 in binary; thus the value of the eighth bit is 128. Whatever the current value of that bit (set or clear), if you OR it with the value 128, you will set that bit and not change any of the other bits. Assume that the current value of the eight bits is 1010 0110 0010 0110. ORing 128 to it looks like this:

```
9 8765 4321
1010 0110 0010 0110   // bit 8 is clear
|    0000 0000 1000 0000   // 128
_ _ _ _ _ _ _ _ _ _
1010 0110 1010 0110   // bit 8 is set
```

There are a few things to note. First, as usual, bits are counted from right to left. Second, the value 128 is all zeros except for bit 8, the bit you want to set. Third, the starting number 1010 0110 0010 0110 is left unchanged by the OR operation, except that bit 8 was set. Had bit 8 already been set, it would have remained set, which is what you want.

Clearing Bits

If you want to clear bit 8, you can AND the bit with the complement of 128. The complement of 128 is the number you get when you take the bit pattern of 128 (1000 0000), set every bit that is clear, and clear every bit that is set (0111 1111). When you AND these numbers, the original number is unchanged, except for the eighth bit, which is forced to zero.

```
1010 0110 1010 0110  // bit 8 is set
& 1111 1111 0111 1111  // ~128
_ _ _ _ _ _ _ _ _ _ _
1010 0110 0010 0110  // bit 8 cleared
```

To fully understand this solution, do the math yourself. Each time both bits are 1, write 1 in the answer. If either bit is 0, write 0 in the answer. Compare the answer with the original number. It should be the same except that bit 8 was cleared.

Flipping Bits

Finally, if you want to flip bit 8, no matter what its state, you exclusive OR the number with 128. Thus:

```
1010 0110 1010 0110  // number
^ 0000 0000 1000 0000  // 128
_ _ _ _ _ _ _ _ _ _ _
1010 0110 0010 0110  // bit flipped
^ 0000 0000 1000 0000  // 128
_ _ _ _ _ _ _ _ _ _ _
1010 0110 1010 0110  // flipped back
```

Do	Don't
DO set bits by using masks and the OR operator. **DO** clear bits by using masks and the AND operator. **DO** flip bits using masks and the exclusive OR operator.	

Bit Fields

Under some circumstances, every byte counts, and saving 6 or 8 bytes in a class can make all the difference. If your class or structure has a series of Boolean variables or variables that can have only a very small number of possible values, you may save some room using bit fields.

Using the standard C++ data types, the smallest type you can use in your class is a type char, which is 1 byte. You will usually end up using an int, which is 2, or more often 4, bytes. By using bit fields, you can store 8 binary values in a char and 32 such values in a long.

Bit fields work like this: Bit fields are named and accessed the same as any class member. Their type is always declared to be unsigned int. After the bit field name, write a colon followed by a number. The number is an instruction to the compiler as to how many bits to assign to this variable. If you write 1, the bit will represent either the value

21

0 or 1. If you write 2, the bit can represent 0, 1, 2, or 3, a total of four values. A three-bit field can represent eight values, and so forth. Appendix C reviews binary numbers. Listing 21.8 illustrates the use of bit fields.

INPUT   **LISTING 21.8**   Using Bit Fields

```
1:        #include <iostream.h>
2:        #include <string.h>
3:     // Listing 21.8: Using Bit Fields
4:        enum STATUS { FullTime, PartTime } ;
5:        enum GRADLEVEL { UnderGrad, Grad } ;
6:        enum HOUSING { Dorm, OffCampus };
7:        enum FOODPLAN { OneMeal, AllMeals, WeekEnds, NoMeals };
8:
9:        class student
10:        {
11:        public:
12:        student():
13:            myStatus(FullTime),
14:            myGradLevel(UnderGrad),
15:            myHousing(Dorm),
16:            myFoodPlan(NoMeals)
17:            {}
18:            ~student(){}
19:            STATUS GetStatus();
20:            void SetStatus(STATUS);
21:            unsigned GetPlan() { return myFoodPlan; }
22:
23:        private:
24:            unsigned myStatus : 1;
25:            unsigned myGradLevel: 1;
26:            unsigned myHousing : 1;
27:            unsigned myFoodPlan : 2;
28:        };
29:
30:        STATUS student::GetStatus()
31:        {
32:            if (myStatus)
33:                return FullTime;
34:            else
35:                return PartTime;
36:        }
37:        void student::SetStatus(STATUS theStatus)
38:        {
39:            myStatus = theStatus;
40:        }
41:
42:
43:        int main()
```

```
44:        {
45:            student Jim;
46:
47:            if (Jim.GetStatus()== PartTime)
48:                cout << "Jim is part time" << endl;
49:            else
50:                cout << "Jim is full time" << endl;
51:
52:            Jim.SetStatus(PartTime);
53:
54:            if (Jim.GetStatus())
55:                cout << "Jim is part time" << endl;
56:            else
57:                cout << "Jim is full time" << endl;
58:
59:            cout << "Jim is on the " ;
60:
61:            char Plan[80];
62:            switch (Jim.GetPlan())
63:            {
64:                case  OneMeal: strcpy(Plan,"One meal"); break;
65:                case  AllMeals: strcpy(Plan,"All meals"); break;
66:                case WeekEnds: strcpy(Plan,"Weekend meals"); break;
67:                case NoMeals: strcpy(Plan,"No Meals");break;
68:                default : cout << "Something bad went wrong!\n"; break;
69:            }
70:            cout << Plan << " food plan." << endl;
71:          return 0;
72:        }
```

OUTPUT
```
Jim is part time
Jim is full time
Jim is on the No Meals food plan.
```

ANALYSIS On lines 4–7, several enumerated types are defined. These serve to define the possible values for the bit fields within the student class.

In lines 9–28, student is declared. Although this is a trivial class, it is interesting because all the data is packed into five bits. The first bit represents the student's status, full-time or part-time. The second bit represents whether this is an undergraduate. The third bit represents whether the student lives in a dorm. The final two bits represent the four possible food plans.

The class methods are written as for any other class and are in no way affected by the fact that these are bit fields and not integers or enumerated types.

The member function GetStatus() reads the Boolean bit and returns an enumerated type, but this is not necessary. It could just as easily have been written to return the value of the bit field directly. The compiler would have done the translation.

21

To prove that to yourself, replace the `GetStatus()` implementation with this code:

```
STATUS student::GetStatus()
{
return myStatus;
}
```

No change whatsoever should occur in the functioning of the program. It is a matter of clarity when reading the code; the compiler is not particular.

Note that the code on line 47 must check the status and then print the meaningful message. It is tempting to write this:

```
cout << "Jim is " << Jim.GetStatus() << endl;
```

That will simply print this:

```
Jim is 0
```

The compiler has no way to translate the enumerated constant `PartTime` into meaningful text.

On line 62, the program switches on the food plan, and for each possible value, it puts a reasonable message into the buffer, which is then printed on line 70. Note again that the switch statement could have been written as follows:

```
case  0: strcpy(Plan,"One meal"); break;
case  1: strcpy(Plan,"All meals"); break;
case  2: strcpy(Plan,"Weekend meals"); break;
case  3: strcpy(Plan,"No Meals");break;
```

The most important thing about using bit fields is that the client of the class need not worry about the data storage implementation. Because the bit fields are private, you can feel free to change them later and the interface will not need to change.

Coding Style

As stated elsewhere in this book, it is important to adopt a consistent coding style, although in many ways it does not matter which style you adopt. A consistent style makes it easier to guess what you meant by a particular part of the code, and you avoid having to look up whether you spelled the function with an initial cap the last time you invoked it.

The following style guidelines are arbitrary; they are based on the guidelines used in my prior projects, and they seem to work well. You can just as easily make up your own, but these will get you started.

As Emerson said, "Foolish consistency is the hobgoblin of small minds," but having some consistency in your code is a good thing. Make up your own, but then treat it as if it were dispensed by the programming gods.

Indenting

Tab size should be three or four spaces. Make sure your editor converts each tab to three or four spaces.

Braces

How to align braces can be the most controversial topic among C and C++ programmers. Here are the tips I suggest:

- Matching braces should be aligned vertically.

- The outermost set of braces in a definition or declaration should be at the left margin. Statements within should be indented. All other sets of braces should be in line with their leading statements.

- No code should appear on the same line as a brace. For example:

```
if (condition==true)
{
    j = k;
    SomeFunction();
}
m++;
```

Long Lines

Keep lines to the width displayable on a single screen. Code that is off to the right is easily overlooked, and scrolling horizontally is annoying. When a line is broken, indent the following lines. Try to break the line at a reasonable place, and try to leave the intervening operator at the end of the previous line (instead of at the beginning of the following line) so that it is clear that the line does not stand alone and that more is coming.

In C++, functions tend to be much shorter than they were in C, but the old, sound advice still applies. Try to keep your functions short enough to print the entire function on one page.

`switch` Statements

Indent switches as follows to conserve horizontal space:

```
switch(variable)
{
    case ValueOne:
        ActionOne();
```

21

```
        break;
    case ValueTwo:
        ActionTwo();
        break;
    default:
        assert("bad Action");
        break;
}
```

Program Text

You can use several tips to create code that is easy to read. Code that is easy to read is easy to maintain.

- Use whitespace to help readability.
- Objects and arrays are really referring to one thing. Do not use spaces within object references (., ->, [ ]).
- Unary operators are associated with their operands, so do not put a space between them. Do put a space on the side away from the operand. Unary operators include !, ~, ++, --, -, * (for pointers), & (casts), and sizeof.
- Binary operators should have spaces on both sides: +, =, *, /, %, >>, <<, <, >, ==, !=, &, |, &&, ||, ?:, =, +=, and so on.
- Do not use lack of spaces to indicate precedence (4+ 3*2).
- Put a space after commas and semicolons, not before.
- Parentheses should not have spaces on either side.
- Keywords, such as if, should be set off by a space: if (a == b).
- The body of a comment should be set off from the // with a space.
- Place the pointer or reference indicator next to the type name, not the variable name:

```
char* foo;
int& theInt;
```

rather than

```
char *foo;
int &theInt;
```

- Do not declare more than one variable on the same line unless it is closely related to the others on that line.

Identifier Names

The following are guidelines for working with identifiers:

- Identifier names should be long enough to be descriptive.

- Avoid cryptic abbreviations.

- Take the time and energy to spell things out.

- I do not use Hungarian notation. C++ is strongly typed and there is no reason to put the type into the variable name. With user-defined types (classes), Hungarian notation quickly breaks down. The exceptions to this may be to use a prefix for pointers (p) and references (r), as well as for class member variables (ints). On the other hand, some people swear by Hungarian notation.

- Short names (i, p, x, and so on) should be used only where their brevity makes the code more readable and where the usage is so obvious that a descriptive name is not needed.

- The length of a variable's name should be proportional to its scope.

- Make sure identifiers look and sound different from one another to minimize confusion.

- Function (or method) names are usually verbs or verb-noun phrases: Search(), Reset(), FindParagraph(), ShowCursor(). Variable names are usually abstract nouns, possibly with an additional noun: count, state, windSpeed, windowHeight. Boolean variables should be named appropriately: windowIconized, fileIsOpen.

Spelling and Capitalization of Names

Spelling and capitalization should not be overlooked when creating your own style. Some tips for these areas include the following:

- Use all uppercase and underscore to separate the logical words of names, such as SOURCE_FILE_TEMPLATE. Note, however, that these are rare in C++. Consider using constants and templates in most cases.

- Macro names should be all uppercase.

- All other identifiers should either be mixed case without underscores or single case (usually lower) with underscores. When using mixed case, function names, methods, class, typedef, and struct names should begin with a capitalized letter; elements such as data members or locals should begin with a lowercase letter.

21

- Enumerated constants should begin with a few lowercase letters as an abbreviation for the enum. For example:

```
enum TextStyle
{
    tsPlain,
    tsBold,
    tsItalic,
    tsUnderscore,
};
```

Comments

Comments can make it much easier to understand a program. Sometimes you will not work on a program for several days or even months. During that time you can forget what certain code does or why it has been included. Problems in understanding code can also occur when someone else reads your code. Comments that are applied in a consistent, well-thought-out style can be well worth the effort. Several tips to remember concerning comments include the following:

- Wherever possible, use C++ `//` comments rather than the `/* */` style.
- Higher-level comments are infinitely more important than process details. Add value; do not merely restate the code.

```
n++; // n is incremented by one
```

This comment is not worth the time it takes to type it in. Concentrate on the semantics of functions and blocks of code. Say what a function does and indicate side effects, types of parameters, and return values. Describe all assumptions that are made (or not made), such as "assumes n is non-negative" or "will return –1 if x is invalid." Within complex logic, use comments to indicate the conditions that exist at that point in the code.

- Use complete English sentences with appropriate punctuation and capitalization. The extra typing is worth it. Do not be overly cryptic and do not abbreviate. What seems exceedingly clear to you as you write code will be amazingly obtuse in a few months.
- Use blank lines freely to help the reader understand what is going on. Separate statements into logical groups.

Access

The way you access portions of your program should also be consistent. Some tips for access include the following:

- Always use `public:`, `private:`, and `protected:` labels; do not rely on the defaults.

- List the public members first, then protected, then private. List the data members in a group after the methods.

- Put the constructor(s) first in the appropriate section, followed by the destructor. List overloaded methods with the same name adjacent to each other. Group accessor functions together whenever possible.

- Consider alphabetizing the method names within each group and alphabetizing the member variables. Be sure to alphabetize the filenames in `include` statements.

- Even though the use of the `virtual` keyword is optional when overriding, use it anyway; it helps to remind you that it is virtual, and it also keeps the declaration consistent.

Class Definitions

Try to keep the definitions of methods in the same order as the declarations. It makes things easier to find.

When defining a function, place the return type and all other modifiers on a previous line so that the class name and function name begin at the left margin. This makes it much easier to find functions.

include Files

Try as hard as you can to keep from including files into header files. The ideal minimum is the header file for the class this one derives from. Other mandatory `includes` will be those for objects that are members of the class being declared. Classes that are merely pointed to or referenced only need forward references of the form.

Do not leave out an `include` file in a header just because you assume that whatever .cpp file includes this one will also have the needed `include`.

Tip

All header files should use inclusion guards.

21

assert()

Use `assert()` freely. It helps find errors, but it also greatly helps a reader by making it clear what the assumptions are. It also helps to focus the writer's thoughts around what is and what is not valid.

const

Use const wherever appropriate: for parameters, variables, and methods. Often there is a need for both a const and a non-const version of a method; do not use this as an excuse to leave one out. Be very careful when explicitly casting from const to non-const and vice versa (at times, this is the only way to do something), but be certain that it makes sense, and include a comment.

Next Steps

You just spent three long, hard weeks working at C++, and you are now a competent C++ programmer, but you are by no means finished. There is much more to learn, and you can get valuable information from many more sources as you move from novice C++ programmer to expert.

The following sections recommend a number of specific sources of information, and these recommendations reflect only my personal experience and opinions. However dozens of books are available on each of these topics, so be sure to get other opinions before purchasing.

Where to Get Help and Advice

The very first thing you will want to do as a C++ programmer will be to tap into one of the C++ conferences on an online service. These groups supply immediate contact with hundreds or thousands of C++ programmers who can answer your questions, offer advice, and provide a sounding board for your ideas.

Many programmers participate in the C++ Internet newsgroups (comp.lang.c++ and comp.lang.c++.moderated), and I recommend them as excellent sources of information and support.

Also, you may want to look for local user groups. Many cities have C++ interest groups where you can meet other programmers and exchange ideas.

Magazines

You can also strengthen your skills by subscribing to a good magazine on C++ programming. Some of the best magazines on this topic are: *C++ Report* from SIGS Publications and *C/C++ Users Journal* from Miller Freeman. Every issue is packed with useful articles. Save them; what you do not care about today will become critically important tomorrow.

Staying in Touch

If you have comments, suggestions, or ideas about this book or other books, feel free to contact the authors. Jesse Liberty can be reached at jliberty@libertyassociates.com (Web page http://www.libertyassociates.com). David Horvath can be reached at cpplinux@cobs.com (Web page http://www.cobs.com/~dhorvath).

Do	Don't
DO look at other books. There's plenty to learn and no single book can teach you everything you need to know.	**DON'T** just read code! The best way to learn C++ is to write C++ programs.
DO subscribe to a good C++ magazine and join a good C++ user group.	

Your Very Next Step

Your very next step, after you catch your breath, is to learn more of the gory details of C++ and Linux. The bonus week of this book takes you there!

Summary

Today you learned more details about working with the preprocessor. Each time you run the compiler, the preprocessor runs first and translates your preprocessor directives such as #define and #ifdef.

The preprocessor does text substitution, although with the use of macros these can be somewhat complex. By using #ifdef, #else, and #ifndef, you can accomplish conditional compilation, compiling in some statements under one set of conditions and in another set of statements under other conditions. This can assist in writing programs for more than one platform and is often used to conditionally include debugging information.

Macro functions provide complex text substitution based on arguments passed at compile time to the macro. It is important to put parentheses around every argument in the macro to ensure that the correct substitution takes place.

Macro functions, and the preprocessor in general, are less important in C++ than they were in C. C++ provides a number of language features, such as const variables and templates, that offer superior alternatives to use of the preprocessor.

21

You also learned how to set and test individual bits and how to allocate a limited number of bits to class members.

Finally, C++ style issues were addressed, and resources were provided for further study.

Q&A

Q If C++ offers better alternatives than the preprocessor, why is this option still available?

A First, C++ is backward-compatible with C, and all significant parts of C must be supported in C++. Second, some uses of the preprocessor are still used frequently in C++, such as inclusion guards.

Q Why use macro functions when you can use a regular function?

A Macro functions are expanded inline and are used as a substitute for repeatedly typing the same commands with minor variations. Again, however, templates offer a better alternative.

Q How do you know when to use a macro versus an inline function?

A Often, it doesn't matter much; use whichever is simpler. However, macros offer character substitution, stringizing, and concatenation. None of these is available with functions.

Q What is the alternative to using the preprocessor to print interim values during debugging?

A The best alternative is to use watch statements within a debugger. For information on watch statements, consult the g++ and gdb manual pages and info file (or whatever documentation is provided for your compiler or debugger if you are using something besides the GNU tools).

Q How do you decide when to use an assert() and when to throw an exception?

A If the situation you're testing can be true without your having committed a programming error, use an exception. If the only reason for this situation to ever be true is a bug in your program, use an assert().

Q When would you use bit structures rather than simply using integers?

A When the size of the object is crucial. If you are working with limited memory or with communications software, you may find that the savings offered by these structures is essential to the success of your product.

Q Why do style wars generate so much emotion?

A Programmers become very attached to their habits. If you are accustomed to the following indentation:

```
if (SomeCondition){
    // statements
}    // closing brace
```

it is a difficult transition to give it up. New styles look wrong and create confusion. If you get bored, try logging on to a popular online service and asking which indentation style works best, which editor is best for C++, or which product is the best word processor. Then sit back and watch as ten thousand messages are generated, all contradicting one another.

Q What is the very next thing to read?

A Here are some books I've written to provide a course of study, although there are many other books of great value. *C++ Unleashed*, *Beginning Object-Oriented Analysis and Design*, and *Career Change C++* are good starting points.

Q Is that it?

A Yes! You've learned C++, but...no, you are not done! Ten years ago it was possible for one person to learn all there was to know about computers and programming, or at least to feel pretty confident that she was close. Today it is out of the question. You can't possibly catch up, and even as you try, the industry is changing. Be sure to keep reading, and stay in touch with the resources—magazines and online services—that will keep you current with the latest changes.

Workshop

The Workshop provides quiz questions to help solidify your understanding of the material covered and exercises to provide you with experience in using what you have learned. Try to answer the quiz and exercise questions before checking the answers in Appendix D, "Answers to Exercises and Quizzes," and make sure you understand the answers before continuing tomorrow.

Quiz

1. What is an inclusion guard?

2. How do you instruct your compiler to print the contents of the intermediate file showing the effects of the preprocessor?

3. What is the difference between #define debug 0 and #undef debug?

21

4. What does the complement operator do?

5. What is the difference between OR and exclusive OR?

6. What is the difference between & and &&?

7. What is the difference between I and II?

Exercises

1. Write the inclusion guard statements for the header file STRING.H.

2. Write an assert() macro that prints an error message and the file and line number if the debug level is 2, that prints a message (without file and line number) if the level is 1, and that does nothing if the level is 0.

3. Write a macro DPrint that tests whether DEBUG is defined and, if it is, print the value passed in as a parameter.

4. Write a program that adds two numbers without using the addition operator (+). Hint: Use the bit operators!

WEEK 3

In Review

The Week 3 in Review program, shown in Listing R3.1,
brings together many of the advanced techniques you learned
during the past three weeks of hard work. Week 3 in Review
provides a template-based linked list with exception handling.
Examine it in detail; if you understand it fully, you are a C++
programmer.

Caution

You need to be using a newer version of the
GNU compilers (2.9.5 or newer) for this example to work.

If your compiler does not support templates, or
if your compiler does not support `try` and
`catch`, you will not be able to compile or run
this listing.

INPUT **LISTING R3.1** Week 3 in Review Listing

```
1:  //
****************************************************
2:  //
3:  // Title:     Week 3 in Review
4:  //
5:  // File:      Week3
6:  //
7:  // Description:  Provide a template-based linked
→list
8:  //                demonstration program with
→exception handling
9:  //
10:  // Classes:   PART - holds part numbers and
→potentially other
11:  //                information about parts.
→This will be the
```

continues

LISTING R3.1 CONTINUED

```
12:   //                        example class for the list to hold
13:   //                        Note use of operator<< to print the
14:   //                        information about a part based on its
15:   //                        runtime type.
16:   //
17:   //             Node - acts as a node in a List
18:   //
19:   //             List - template-based list which provides the
20:   //                        mechanisms for a linked list
21:   //
22:   //
23:   // Author:    Jesse Liberty (jl)
24:   //
25:   // Developed:  Pentium 200 Pro. 128MB RAM MVC 5.0
26:   //
27:   // Target:    Platform independent
28:   //
29:   //
30:   //
31:   // ***************************************************
32:
33:   #include <iostream.h>
34:
35:   // exception classes
36:   class Exception {};
37:   class OutOfMemory :   public Exception{};
38:   class NullNode :    public Exception{};
39:   class EmptyList :    public Exception {};
40:   class BoundsError :   public Exception {};
41:
42:
43:   // *************** Part ***********
44:   // Abstract base class of parts
45:   class Part
46:   {
47:   public:
48:    Part():itsObjectNumber(1) {}
49:    Part(int ObjectNumber):itsObjectNumber(ObjectNumber){}
50:    virtual ~Part(){};
51:    int GetObjectNumber() const { return itsObjectNumber; }
52:    virtual void Display() const =0;  // must be overridden
53:
54:   private:
55:    int itsObjectNumber;
56:   };
57:
58:   // implementation of pure virtual function so that
59:   // derived classes can chain up
```

```
60:   void Part::Display() const
61:   {
62:     cout << "\nPart Number: " << itsObjectNumber << endl;
63:   }
64:
65:   // this one operator<< will be called for all part objects.
66:   // It need not be a friend as it does not access private data
67:   // It calls Display() which uses the required polymorphism
68:   // We'd like to be able to override this based on the real type
69:   // of thePart, but C++ does not support contravariance
70:   ostream& operator<<( ostream& theStream,Part& thePart)
71:   {
72:    thePart.Display();  // virtual contravariance!
73:    return theStream;
74:   }
75:
76:   // *************** Car Part ***********
77:   class CarPart : public Part
78:   {
79:   public:
80:    CarPart():itsModelYear(94){}
81:    CarPart(int year, int partNumber);
82:    int GetModelYear() const { return itsModelYear; }
83:    virtual void Display() const;
84:   private:
85:    int itsModelYear;
86:   };
87:
88:   CarPart::CarPart(int year, int partNumber):
89:    itsModelYear(year),
90:    Part(partNumber)
91:   {}
92:
93:   void CarPart::Display() const
94:   {
95:       Part::Display();
96:       cout << "Model Year: " << itsModelYear << endl;
97:   }
98:
99:   // *************** AirPlane Part ***********
100:   class AirPlanePart : public Part
101:   {
102:   public:
103:    AirPlanePart():itsEngineNumber(1){};
104:    AirPlanePart(int EngineNumber, int PartNumber);
105:    virtual void Display() const;
106:    int GetEngineNumber()const { return itsEngineNumber; }
107:   private:
108:    int itsEngineNumber;
109:   };
```

continues

LISTING R3.1   CONTINUED

```
110:
111:    AirPlanePart::AirPlanePart(int EngineNumber, int PartNumber):
112:     itsEngineNumber(EngineNumber),
113:     Part(PartNumber)
114:    {}
115:
116:    void AirPlanePart::Display() const
117:    {
118:     Part::Display();
119:     cout << "Engine No.: " << itsEngineNumber << endl;
120:    }
121:
122:    // forward declaration of class List
123:    template <class T>
124:    class List;
125:
126:    // ***************  Node ***********
127:    // Generic node, can be added to a list
128:    // **********************************
129:
130:    template <class T>
131:    class Node
132:    {
133:    public:
134:     friend class List<T>;
135:     Node (T*);
136:     ~Node();
137:     void SetNext(Node * node) { itsNext = node; }
138:     Node * GetNext() const;
139:     T * GetObject() const;
140:    private:
141:     T* itsObject;
142:     Node * itsNext;
143:    };
144:
145:    // Node Implementations...
146:
147:    template <class T>
148:    Node<T>::Node(T* pOjbect):
149:    itsObject(pOjbect),
150:    itsNext(0)
151:    {}
152:
153:    template <class T>
154:    Node<T>::~Node()
155:    {
156:     delete itsObject;
157:     itsObject = 0;
```

```
158:    delete itsNext;
159:    itsNext = 0;
160:   }
161:
162:   // Returns NULL if no next Node
163:   template <class T>
164:   Node<T> * Node<T>::GetNext() const
165:   {
166:        return itsNext;
167:   }
168:
169:   template <class T>
170:   T * Node<T>::GetObject() const
171:   {
172:    if (itsObject)
173:        return itsObject;
174:    else
175:        throw NullNode();
176:   }
177:
178:   // *************** List ***********
179:   // Generic list template
180:   // Works with any numbered object
181:   // ********************************
182:   template <class T>
183:   class List
184:   {
185:   public:
186:    List();
187:    ~List();
188:
189:    T*       Find(int & position, int ObjectNumber)  const;
190:    T*       GetFirst() const;
191:    void     Insert(T *);
192:    T*       operator[](int) const;
193:    int      GetCount() const { return itsCount; }
194:   private:
195:    Node<T> * pHead;
196:    int      itsCount;
197:   };
198:
199:   // Implementations for Lists...
200:   template <class T>
201:   List<T>::List():
202:    pHead(0),
203:    itsCount(0)
204:    {}
205:
206:   template <class T>
207:   List<T>::~List()
```

continues

LISTING R3.1　CONTINUED

```
208:    {
209:     delete pHead;
210:    }
211:
212:    template <class T>
213:    T*    List<T>::GetFirst() const
214:    {
215:     if (pHead)
216:        return pHead->itsObject;
217:     else
218:        throw EmptyList();
219:    }
220:
221:    template <class T>
222:    T *  List<T>::operator[](int offSet) const
223:    {
224:     Node<T>* pNode = pHead;
225:
226:     if (!pHead)
227:        throw EmptyList();
228:
229:     if (offSet > itsCount)
230:        throw BoundsError();
231:
232:     for (int i=0;i<offSet; i++)
233:        pNode = pNode->itsNext;
234:
235:    return   pNode->itsObject;
236:    }
237:
238:    // find a given object in list based on its unique number (id)
239:    template <class T>
240:    T*    List<T>::Find(int & position, int ObjectNumber)   const
241:    {
242:     Node<T> * pNode = NULL;
243:     for (pNode = pHead, position = 0;
244:          pNode!=NULL;
245:          pNode = pNode->itsNext, position++)
246:     {
247:        if (pNode->itsObject->GetObjectNumber() == ObjectNumber)
248:          break;
249:     }
250:     if (pNode == NULL)
251:        return NULL;
252:     else
253:        return pNode->itsObject;
254:    }
255:
```

```
256:    // insert if the number of the object is unique
257:    template <class T>
258:    void List<T>::Insert(T* pObject)
259:    {
260:     Node<T> * pNode = new Node<T>(pObject);
261:     Node<T> * pCurrent = pHead;
262:     Node<T> * pNext = NULL;
263:
264:     int New =  pObject->GetObjectNumber();
265:     int Next = 0;
266:     itsCount++;
267:
268:     if (!pHead)
269:     {
270:        pHead = pNode;
271:        return;
272:     }
273:
274:     // if this one is smaller than head
275:     // this one is the new head
276:     if (pHead->itsObject->GetObjectNumber() > New)
277:     {
278:        pNode->itsNext = pHead;
279:        pHead = pNode;
280:        return;
281:     }
282:
283:     for (;;)
284:     {
285:        // if there is no next, append this new one
286:        if (!pCurrent->itsNext)
287:        {
288:           pCurrent->itsNext = pNode;
289:           return;
290:        }
291:
292:        // if this goes after this one and before the next
293:        // then insert it here, otherwise get the next
294:        pNext = pCurrent->itsNext;
295:        Next = pNext->itsObject->GetObjectNumber();
296:        if (Next > New)
297:        {
298:           pCurrent->itsNext = pNode;
299:           pNode->itsNext = pNext;
300:           return;
301:        }
302:        pCurrent = pNext;
303:     }
304:    }
305:
```

continues

```
306:
307:   int main()
308:   {
309:    List<Part> theList;
310:    int choice;
311:    int ObjectNumber;
312:    int value;
313:    Part * pPart;
314:    while (1)
315:    {
316:       cout << "(0)Quit (1)Car (2)Plane: ";
317:       cin >> choice;
318:
319:       if (!choice)
320:          break;
321:
322:       cout << "New PartNumber?: ";
323:       cin >>  ObjectNumber;
324:
325:       if (choice == 1)
326:       {
327:          cout << "Model Year?: ";
328:          cin >> value;
329:          try
330:          {
331:             pPart = new CarPart(value,ObjectNumber);
332:          }
333:          catch (OutOfMemory)
334:          {
335:             cout << "Not enough memory; Exiting..." << endl;
336:             return 1;
337:          }
338:       }
339:       else
340:       {
341:          cout << "Engine Number?: ";
342:          cin >> value;
343:          try
344:          {
345:             pPart = new AirPlanePart(value,ObjectNumber);
346:          }
347:          catch (OutOfMemory)
348:          {
349:             cout << "Not enough memory; Exiting..." << endl;
350:             return 1;
351:          }
352:       }
353:       try
```

```
354:       {
355:           theList.Insert(pPart);
356:       }
357:       catch (NullNode)
358:       {
359:          cout << "The list is broken, and the node is null!" << endl;
360:          return 1;
361:       }
362:       catch (EmptyList)
363:       {
364:          cout << "The list is empty!" << endl;
365:          return 1;
366:       }
367:    }
368:    try
369:    {
370:       for (int i = 0; i < theList.GetCount(); i++ )
371:          cout << *(theList[i]);
372:    }
373:       catch (NullNode)
374:       {
375:          cout << "The list is broken, and the node is null!" << endl;
376:          return 1;
377:       }
378:       catch (EmptyList)
379:       {
380:          cout << "The list is empty!" << endl;
381:          return 1;
382:       }
383:       catch (BoundsError)
384:       {
385:          cout << "Tried to read beyond the end of the list!" << endl;
386:          return 1;
387:       }
388:    return 0;
389:    }
```

OUTPUT

```
(0)Quit (1)Car (2)Plane: 1
New PartNumber?: 2837
Model Year? 90

(0)Quit (1)Car (2)Plane: 2
New PartNumber?: 378
Engine Number?: 4938

(0)Quit (1)Car (2)Plane: 1
New PartNumber?: 4499
Model Year? 94

(0)Quit (1)Car (2)Plane: 1
```

```
New PartNumber?: 3000
Model Year? 93

 (0)Quit (1)Car (2)Plane: 0

Part Number: 378
Engine No. 4938

Part Number: 2837
Model Year: 90

Part Number: 3000
Model Year: 93

Part Number 4499
Model Year: 94
```

ANALYSIS Listing R3.1 modifies the program provided in Week 2 to add templates, ostream processing, and exception handling. The output is identical.

On lines 36–40, a number of exception classes are declared. In the somewhat primitive exception handling provided by this program, no data or methods are required of these exceptions; they serve as flags to the catch statements, which print out a simple warning and then exit. A more robust program might pass these exceptions by reference and then extract context or other data from the exception objects in an attempt to recover from the problem.

On line 45, the abstract base class Part is declared exactly as it was in Week 2. The only interesting change here is in the non-class member operator<<(), which is declared on lines 70–74. Note that this is neither a member of Part nor a friend of Part; it simply takes a Part reference as one of its arguments.

You might want to have operator<< take a CarPart and an AirPlanePart in the hopes that the correct operator<< would be called, based on whether a car part or an airplane part is passed. Because the program passes a pointer to a part, however, and not a pointer to a car part or an airplane part, C++ would have to call the right function based on the real type of one of the arguments to the function. This is called contravariance and is not supported in C++.

There are only two ways to achieve polymorphism in C++: function polymorphism and virtual functions. Function polymorphism will not work here because in every case you are matching the same signature: the one taking a reference to a Part.

Virtual functions will not work here because `operator<<` is not a member function of `Part`. You cannot make `operator<<` a member function of `Part` because you want to invoke

`cout << thePart`

and that means that the actual call would be to `cout.operator<<(Part&)`, and `cout` does not have a version of `operator<<` that takes a `Part` reference!

To get around this limitation, the Week 3 program uses just one `operator<<`, taking a reference to a `Part`. This then calls `Display()`, which is a virtual member function, and thus the right version is called.

On lines 130–143, `Node` is defined as a template. It serves the same function as `Node` did in the Week 2 Review program, but this version of `Node` is not tied to a `Part` object. It can, in fact, be the node for any type of object.

Note that if you try to get the object from `Node`, and there is no object, this is considered an exception, and the exception is thrown on line 175.

On lines 182–183, a generic `List` class template is defined. This `List` class can hold nodes of any objects that have unique identification numbers, and it keeps them sorted in ascending order. Each of the list functions checks for exceptional circumstances and throws the appropriate exceptions as required.

On lines 307–308, the driver program creates a list of two types of `Part` objects and then prints out the values of the objects in the list by using the standard streams mechanism.

Frequently Asked Questions

FAQ: In the comment above line 70 in Listing R3.1 you mention that C++ does not support contravariance. What is contravariance?

Answer: Contravariance is the ability to assign a pointer to a base class to a pointer to a derived.

If C++ did support contravariance, we could override the function based on the real type of the object, at runtime. Listing R3.2 will not compile in C++, but if it supported contravariance, it would. This file will not compile!

Warning: This listing will not compile!

LISTING R3.2   A Demonstration of Contravariance

```cpp
#include<iostream.h>
class Animal
{
public:
        virtual void Speak() { cout << "Animal
                    Speaks\n"; }
};

class Dog : public Animal
{
public:
        void Speak() { cout << "Dog Speaks\n"; }
};


class Cat : public Animal
{
public:
        void Speak() { cout << "Cat Speaks\n"; }
};

void DoIt(Cat*);
void DoIt(Dog*);

int main()
{

        Animal * pA = new Dog;
        DoIt(pA);
        return 0;
}

void DoIt(Cat * c)
{
        cout << "They passed a cat!\n" << endl;
        c->Speak();
}

void DoIt(Dog * d)
{
        cout << "They passed a dog!\n" << endl;
        d->Speak();
}
```

What you can do, of course, is use a virtual function, which partially solves the problem. Listing R3.3 shows how this is done.

Listing R3.3 A Demonstration of Virtual Functions#include<iostream.h>

```cpp
class Animal
{
public:
   virtual void Speak() { cout << "Animal Speaks\n"; }
};

class Dog : public Animal
{
public:
      void Speak() { cout << "Dog Speaks\n"; }
};


class Cat : public Animal
{
public:
      void Speak() { cout << "Cat Speaks\n"; }
};

void DoIt(Animal*);

int main()
{

      Animal * pA = new Dog;
      DoIt(pA);
      return 0;
}

void DoIt(Animal * c)
{
      cout << "They passed some kind of
                  animal\n" << endl;
      c->Speak();
}
```

WEEK 4

At a Glance

You have finished the third and final regular week of learning C++ for Linux. By now you should feel comfortable with the advanced aspects of object-oriented programming.

Where You Are Going

At last, you have reached the bonus week, which covers the more specific and advanced topics of developing C++ programs with Linux. On Day 22, "Linux Programming Environment," you will learn about some of the advanced programming tools under Linux, and on Day 23, "Shell Programming," you will learn how to use the command shells under Linux and create simple shell scripts. Day 24, "System Programming," focuses on operating system interface and C++ runtime library functions and objects that you can use. On Day 25, "Interprocess Communication," you will learn how to use system functions to communicate between processes. Finally, on Day 26, "GUI Programming," you will learn how to create applications that take advantage of the Graphical User Interface (GUI) tools available under Linux.

## 24

DAY 22

The Linux Programming Environment

In the days so far, you have been learning about the C++ programming language. By now, you know about the syntax of the language and how to design and write object-oriented programs. Today's lesson discusses the environment that Linux provides to write programs. What are the tools available? How do you create a program, compile it, debug it, and track its history as you modify it over time?

This lesson touches on the following basics:

- Editors
- Compilers
- Building executables with make
- Libraries and linking
- Debugging with gdb
- Version control with RCS
- Documentation

Philosophy and History

In its early days, Linux was popular almost exclusively with developers—people who wanted to study or write pieces of the kernel, or people who wanted to write tools and other utilities. If you are going to develop software, the first thing you need is development tools. After you have an editor, you need a compiler. As a result, among the first things ported to Linux were compilers, assemblers, and linkers.

A compiler is a difficult thing to write, and you certainly would not want to create one from scratch if you did not have to. It was natural, therefore, for the Linux developers to look for a free compiler, with source code available so that it could be ported. The obvious choice (perhaps the only choice) at the time was the GNU C compiler. The GNU tools adhered to a similar philosophy of open source, and they were widely available and of known high quality.

Unlike many commercial operating systems today, the tools available for Linux are not limited to those that the vendor provides or that you can buy. Linux is open source software, and open source tools available on the Internet generally work with it.

If there is an open source tool that your distribution does not include and you can find it on the Internet, you can probably download a version already built for Linux. On the other hand, almost all Linux distributions come with a very complete set of GNU program development tools.

POSIX

In the 1980s the Institute of Electrical and Electronics Engineers (IEEE) began developing a standard programming environment to promote the portability of applications between different UNIX environments. The name given to this effort and the resulting standard was the "Portable Operating System Interface," and it is commonly known as POSIX. The POSIX standard does not dictate how an operating system should behave, but it does define the programming interface ("API") that should be provided by the operating system to the application program writer. This may seem a bit confusing. Suffice it to say that Linux is "POSIX-compliant." In other words, it provides a standard set of system calls and services as defined by the POSIX standard.

The X Window System

If you have used Macintosh computers or computers running any version of Microsoft Windows, then you are familiar with what is known as the "graphical user interface" (or GUI). In these systems the GUI is an integral part of the operating system. Not so with

Linux. In Linux the GUI is layered on top of windowing system software, which is essentially an accessory to the operating system. There are many advantages to this approach in performance, reliability and flexibility. The name "X Window System" is loosely applied to all of the components of this windowing software, often including the GUI itself. Development of "X", as it is commonly known, began at MIT in the mid-1980's. The X Window System provided with Linux comes from the XFree86 project.

Using the Linux Editors

If you are going to write code, clearly you need some way of entering it into a file. One of the first results of the GNU project was the emacs editor, and editors were among the early ports to Linux.

ed, ex, vi, and the Variants of vi

ed and ex are very early line-based editors historically available with UNIX systems. ed is generally used as a filter to modify text that is passed through it. ex is a serviceable but primitive line-based text editor. One of the earliest screen based editors in UNIX was vi, which is basically a screen-based front end written around ex.

On most Linux systems, the open-source reimplementation of vi named vim is available. Many people consider vi (and vim too) to be cryptic and difficult to use. It does have many advantages over other editors, however:

- It is very powerful.
- It is available on practically all UNIX and Linux systems.
- It requires fewer system resources than emacs, and so will run even if the system is not completely functioning.
- It is not as highly customizable as emacs, which means that all implementations will behave in pretty much the same way.

You may choose to use another editor for daily use, but you should master the basics of vi. UNIX systems always come with vi, and because vim is the implementation of vi provided with Linux, vim is usually linked to vi so that you can invoke it with the name vi. For the rest of this lesson, we use the terms vi and vim interchangeably. We are really referring to vim.

Starting vi

Before you run any of the full-screen editors (including vi), you must have the TERM environment variable set to indicate your terminal type. This variable is normally set automatically to xterm when you start an xterm window.

You may want to view the online manual page for vi with the command: `man vi`. Note that the command `man vim` gives you exactly the same man page.

Extensive help is available within the editor as well.

Start the editor with the command: `vi filename`

vim has a graphical mode, which vi did not provide. It includes mouse support and pull-down menus. You invoke this with the command: `gvim filename` or `vi -g filename`. Note that for graphical mode to work, the editor must have been compiled with that option specifically enabled. Your version may not have been compiled this way. Figure 22.1 shows a file being edited in vi.

FIGURE 22.1

A file being edited in vi.

```
# inittab          This file describes how the INIT process should set up
#                  the system in a certain run-level.
#
# Author:          Miquel van Smoorenburg, <miquels@drinkel.nl.mugnet.org>
#                  Modified for RHS Linux by Marc Ewing and Donnie Barnes
#

# Default runlevel. The runlevels used by RHS are:
#   0 - halt (Do NOT set initdefault to this)
#   1 - Single user mode
#   2 - Multiuser, without NFS (The same as 3, if you do not have networking)
#   3 - Full multiuser mode
#   4 - unused
#   5 - X11
#   6 - reboot (Do NOT set initdefault to this)
#
id:5:initdefault:

# System initialization.
si::sysinit:/etc/rc.d/rc.sysinit

l0:0:wait:/etc/rc.d/rc 0
l1:1:wait:/etc/rc.d/rc 1
l2:2:wait:/etc/rc.d/rc 2
l3:3:wait:/etc/rc.d/rc 3
"inittab" [readonly] line 1 of 57 --1%-- col 1
```

vi Concepts

vi is a screen-based "mode editor" with three modes: command, insert, and ex. By default you are in command mode. This means that keys that you type are commands to the editor rather than input into the file you are working on.

Most vi commands are a single letter, some with a scope modifier. Most can be preceded with a number, which is the "repeat factor" (causing the subsequent command to be repeated that many times).

In insert mode, keystrokes are captured and entered into the file being edited. In this mode, the word *INSERT* is displayed at the bottom of the screen.

The original vi was really a screen-based front end to the ex line editor, and vim emulates this behavior. The third mode available in vim is ex mode. In this mode, a ":" prompt appears at the bottom of the screen. You can enter any ex command at this prompt. The ex commands are useful for switching files without leaving the editor, and offer filename completion to make this easier. Most any other task that can be done with an ex command can also be done from the vi command mode.

To return to command mode from any other mode, press the Esc key. If you are already in command mode, this key has no effect, so if you are ever unsure of what mode you are in, just press Esc a couple of times to return to command mode.

To access the online help as shown in Figure 22.2 with vi, type **:help** from command mode.

FIGURE 22.2

vi help.

Using vi

Now try a sample vi session. You will create a simple C++ program named hello.cc.

1. Type **vi hello.cc** to begin editing the new file.

2. Type **i** to enter insert mode.

3. Enter the following text:
```
#include <stream.h>
main( int argc, char * argv[] ) {
```

```
    cout << "hello world"
        << endl;
}
```

4. Press Esc to end insert mode.

Now that you are back in command mode, note that the h, j, k, and l keys allow you to move the cursor left, down, up, and right respectively.

At any time, you can re-enter insert mode. The i key begins inserting before the cursor and the a key begins inserting after that. Note that while you are in insert mode, the word *INSERT* is displayed at the bottom of the screen. Pressing the Esc key exits insert mode.

5. Type **ZZ** to write the file and exit.

GNU emacs

Religious wars abound. Many Linux users swear that vi is too old-fashioned and the only editor worth using is emacs. You have to decide for yourself which editor is easier to use. Certainly emacs has more features, and there are several substantial books written on it. It is far too complex to discuss in detail here, so this section just covers the basics.

Starting GNU emacs

emacs can run within a terminal window or in a window of its own under X Windows. If you are running X, the command emacs & will open a new window with the editor. To run within the current window, use the command emacs -nw.

If you start emacs without a target filename, it will create a "scratch" buffer for you and will show you a brief help display as shown in Figure 22.3.

If you are running the X version of emacs, you can use the mouse to navigate the pull-down menus at the top of the screen. As you become proficient, you will find that there are keyboard shortcuts for all these pull-down commands.

Table 22.1 shows emac conventional notations.

 Note

> It is common in emacs documentation to refer to key sequences in an abbreviated notation. Table X below describes the conventional emacs notation. The *Meta* key may be assigned differently on different computers. On some it is a key labeled "Meta". If your computer has no such key (most typical PC's do not) then in place of the Meta key press and release the Esc key. So if the emacs documentation says "M-v" then you would press and release Esc, and then press "v".

FIGURE 22.3

Introductory GNU emacs window.

TABLE 22.1 emacs Conventional Notation

Command	emacs notation
Enter	RET
Backspace	DEL
Escape	ESC
Control	C-
Meta	M-
Space	SPC
Tab	TAB

To go directly to the online tutorial press *C-h t* (press Control and *h* simultaneously, and then release both and press *t*).

The `info` system (described later) provides online help for all GNU software. To view info, press *C-h i*.

Other kinds of help are available within emacs. You can press *C-h ?* to find what sorts of help there are. For example, try this:

1. *C-h* (displays help options)
2. *c* (selects "describe key briefly")
3. *C-x C-c* (selects the key to describe)

This will reveal that the sequence *C-x C-c* is a shortcut to the "save-buffers-Kill-emacs" command.

GNU emacs Concepts

Unlike vi, emacs is known as a "modeless" editor. Typing in the emacs window causes characters to be entered into the buffer being edited. Commands in emacs must always be signaled ("escaped") with some sequence of control keys.

emacs has many commands, most of which have very long descriptive names. Many of these commands are "bound" to shorter control key sequences. Use the control sequence *C-h c [Control key]* to discover the bindings for a control key or sequence.

One of the nice things about emacs is the wealth of commands available. One of the difficult things about it is learning the control sequences that these keys are bound to.

You can skip the command shorthand and use the long command name. Press Esc and type **x** to display the prompt M-x at the bottom of the window. Now begin to type a command, for example, save-buffer. Type **sa** and press the spacebar, and emacs will complete the word *save*. Now press the spacebar again and emacs will show you possible completions for the command. Type **b** and press the spacebar, and the word *buffers* is completed. Now press Enter and the command is executed.

At any point, you can press *C-g* to abort any partial command you may have started to type.

Using emacs

Use the following steps to modify the file that you entered earlier in vi.

1. Type **emacs** to start an edit session with no file.

2. Press *C-x C-f* to get a prompt that will let you select a file.

3. Type **hello.cc** to open the file you created earlier. At any point in typing the name, you can press the spacebar. If emacs can unambiguously complete the filename, it will.

4. Press Enter and the file hello.cc will be displayed.

5. Use the arrow keys to move around the file. You can also use *C-n* to move down a line, *C-p* to move up, *C-f* to move forward one character, and *C-b* to move back. Move to the "w" in the word "world."

6. Type **again** and observe that the text is inserted in place at the cursor.

7. Press *C-x C-s* to write the file.

8. Press *C-x C-c* to exit the editor.

Many people use emacs exclusively. You can use it not only to edit files, but also to run commands, compile programs, debug, and run them. If you have compile-time errors, emacs can automatically jump to the line containing the error. It is definitely worth your time to investigate emacs further.

ctags and etags

When you are writing a large C++ program, chances are that you will want to break the source code up into several files. Each file will define the methods for a class or classes.

Later when you are debugging the file, it can become difficult to navigate those sources. You may be editing file A and there is a method invoked that is defined elsewhere, perhaps in file B. The ctags and etags programs create index or "tag" files, which vi and emacs can use to help you navigate your sources.

ctags is the older program, which generates vi tags by default. You can tell it to generate emacs tags. etags generates emacs tags by default, but can also be told to generate vi tags.

ctags Example with vi

Enter the following code into a file named `helloMain.cc`:

```
#include <stream.h>
void doHello(int i);
main( int argc, char * argv[] )
{
  for( int i = 0; i < 5; i++ ) {
    doHello(i);
    cout << endl;
  }
}
```

Now enter the following code into a file named `doHello.cc`:

```
#include <stream.h>
void doHello( int i )
{
  cout << "[" << i
       << "] Hello World";
  return;
}
```

Enter the command: **ctags *.cc**

The new file `tags` has been created.

Begin an edit session with the command **vi helloMain.cc**. Now, using the h, j, k and l keys, line the cursor up over the word doHello. Press *C-]*, and you can see that the editor automatically opens the file that contains the definition of that function (doHello.cc) and sets the cursor at the start of the function.

There is similar functionality in emacs. Use the online help to help exercise it.

Languages

Linux provides all the languages available with traditional UNIX systems, and then some. Many nontraditional languages are available on the Internet. Most distributions come with C and C++ and often a Java implementation. Scripting languages including perl, sed, and awk also are part of most distributions.

gcc and g++

The GNU C compiler is named ;gcc and can compile C, C++, and Objective-C. The C compiler is ANSI standard, and so it should be simple to port most any ANSI C program to Linux. If you are familiar with the C compiler on any other UNIX system, you will find that gcc is quite similar. Because gcc is high quality and free, many commercial sites use it as their C compiler of choice.

Compiling with gcc

You invoke the GNU compiler with the command gcc. By default this will preprocess, compile, and link a C program. There are many options to gcc, and among them are controls that allow you to run any particular phase of the preprocess/compile/link sequence.

The following simple example will roll a die *n* times, and then print out the number of times that each face came up.

Listing 22.1 shows the main program named dice.c.

INPUT   **LISTING 22.1**   Main Program dice.c

```
1: #include <stdio.h>
2: int doRoll(void);
3: main(int argc, char *argv[])
4: {
5:    int i;
6:    int iIter;
7:    int Die[6];
8:      if( argc < 2 ) {
9:        printf("Usage: %s n\n", argv[0]);
10:       exit(1);
```

```
11:     }
12:     iIter = atoi(argv[1]);
13:     memset( Die, 0, sizeof(Die) );
14:     for( i = 0; i < iIter; i++ ) {
15:       Die[doRoll() - 1]++;
16:     }
17:     printf("%d rolls\n", iIter);
18:     printf("\tFace\tRolls\n");
19:     for( i = 0; i < 6; i++ ) {
20:       printf("\t%d :\t%d\n", i + 1, Die[i]);
21:     }
22: }
```

The function doRoll() is implemented in the file doRoll.c:

```
#include <stdio.h>
int doRoll(void)
{
  return( (rand() % 6) + 1 );
}
```

You could use a single command to build this program:

```
gcc -o roll dice.c doRoll.c
```

You can see that -o indicates the name of the output file. gcc is smart enough to see that the files ending with .c are C sources, and so compiles them as such. If you do not specify an output filename, the default output program will be named a.out.

We are trying to demonstrate a slightly more complex concept, so let's do this same thing again, only this time we will compile the modules separately:

```
gcc -c dice.c
gcc -c doRoll.c
gcc -o dice dice.o doRoll.o
```

Compiling with g++

The command gcc is really a compiler "front end." By looking at the files it is given, it knows whether linking or compiling is required. It also knows whether the source is C or C++. If you are compiling C++, you can alternatively invoke the g++ compiler directly with the command g++ *filename*.

Although gcc can compile C++ programs, it does not automatically link with the class libraries required. You will need to use g++ for this. As a result, it's generally simpler to compile and link C++ programs with g++.

For instance, to build the `hello` program that you created with vi earlier, you would use the following g++ commands:

```
g++ -c helloMain.cc
g++ -c doHello.cc
g++ -o hello helloMain.o doHello.o
```

As with gcc, you can accomplish the same thing with the single invocation:

```
g++ -o hello helloMain.cc doHello.cc
```

Scripting Languages (perl, sed, awk)

As a complete UNIX-like environment, Linux also provides the typical scripting languages. perl, sed, and awk are three important languages provided by default with most Linux distributions. Other scripting languages (Tcl/Tk, Python, and Expect among others) are available for Linux, but they are beyond the scope of this discussion.

ELF

When a program is compiled, an object file is generated, and when the program is linked, an executable binary is created. The linker must understand the format of the object files, and because the operating system must load and run the executable, it must understand the format as well.

You learned earlier that the default executable is named a.out. Until not too long ago, the format of object and executable files was known as the `a.out` format. The `a.out` format is fairly old and has several shortcomings. The more modern format used by most UNIX systems and Linux is known as ELF (Executable and Linking Format). ELF is much more versatile than `a.out` was, and lends itself well to creating shared libraries.

You can tell the format of a file by using the `file` command:

```
file roll /usr/bin/file doRoll.o
```

OUTPUT
```
roll:           ELF 32-bit LSB executable, Intel 80386, ...
/usr/bin/file:  ELF 32-bit LSB executable, Intel 80386, ...
doRoll.o:       ELF 32-bit LSB relocatable, Intel 80386, ...
```

Shared Libraries

Often several programs need to do some of the same things, I/O for instance. A long time ago the concept of libraries was developed to accommodate this. The common functions could be put into a file, and then whenever a program is built, it extracts those functions that it needs from the library.

22

This was a breakthrough at the time, but it has several drawbacks. Executables become larger because they each embed code copied from the libraries. If a bug is found in the library or a feature is added, the executable does not make use of it unless it is rebuilt.

The solution to this is the shared (or dynamic) library. The mechanism of how shared libraries work is beyond the scope of this discussion. We will just look at how to make and use them.

Let's return to the earlier dice-rolling program. This program has two source files. We compiled them both and linked them to create an executable.

There seems to be a market for dice-rolling programs, and we think we can use the doRoll() function in a number of products our new company will create. It makes sense to put the function into a library so that all our programs can use it.

First, we need to create the shared library. Compile the module with the following command:

```
gcc -fPIC -c doRoll.c
```

Now turn it into a shared library named libroll.so.1.0:

```
gcc -shared -Wl,-soname,libroll.so.1 -o libroll.so.1.0 doRoll.o
```

Finally, create a link to libroll.so, so that the running program does not need to keep track of the version information in the name of the shared library:

```
ln -s libroll.so.1.0 libroll.so.1
ln -s libroll.so.1 libroll.so
```

Now that we have the library, we must rebuild the main program so that it links with that library at runtime rather than incorporating the code within the executable:

```
gcc -o roll diceMain.c -L. -lroll
```

The -L. option tells the linker to look in the current directory for libraries, and the -lroll option tells it to look for a library named libroll.so.

When you run the program, the operating system will dynamically load the correct library, but it has to know where to find it. If the library is not in a standard place (/usr/lib), you can set an environment variable to tell it where to locate additional libraries:

```
setenv LD_LIBRARY_PATH /home/myname/mylibs
```

Finally, to see what libraries are used by a program, use the ldd command:

```
ldd roll
```

```
libroll.so.1 => /home/Dice/libroll.so.1 (0x40014000)
libc.so.6 => /lib/libc.so.6 (0x4001b000)
/lib/ld-linux.so.2 => /lib/ld-linux.so.2 (0x40000000)
```

Building

You certainly do not want to be typing in all these gcc commands when building your program. With small programs like those demonstrated in this lesson, it's just slightly annoying. With larger programs involving several files and perhaps several libraries, it becomes virtually impossible.

Linux comes with the GNU make utility. make reads a file known as the makefile for the information it needs to build your program. The utility is so important and widespread that it has been specified as a POSIX standard. The GNU version of make is POSIX-compliant.

make

GNU make automatically looks for a makefile named GNUmakefile. If it does not find that, it looks for makefile, and failing that it looks for Makefile. These are the default names. You can name your makefile anything you like and explicitly direct make to use it. A makefile is an ordinary text file with a very specific syntax that the make utility can understand.

make has a great number of built-in rules. For instance, it knows that files ending with .c are C sources, and it knows how to compile those into .o object files. You can override any of these rules if you choose. In the simplest case, all that you need to specify in your makefile is the name your executable is to have and the .o files that are needed to construct it.

Here is a simple makefile that will build the dice-rolling program:

```
    roll:  diceMain.o doRoll.o
$(CC) -o $@ diceMain.o doRoll.o
```

You can now build the program with a single command:

```
make
```

```
gcc    -c diceMain.c -o diceMain.o
gcc    -c doRoll.c -o doRoll.o
gcc -o roll diceMain.o doRoll.o
```

Note: the line in the makefile that begins with "roll" is known as the *target*. It defines the "dependencies" of the program. The next line is the build rule. make requires that the first character on that line be a tab, and not spaces. With spaces instead of a tab, the error make generates is this:

```
make
```

OUTPUT BadMake:2: *** missing separator. Stop.

Here is a slightly more complete makefile:

```
# Makefile to build the dice rolling program
CFLAGS = -O

OBJS   = diceMain.o doRoll.o

all:   roll

roll:  $(OBJS)
        $(CC) $(CFLAGS) -o $@ $(OBJS)

clean:
        - $(RM) roll *.o
```

This makefile defines a rule named clean, which you can use to delete all temporary files and start with a clean directory.

Listing 22.2 shows what the makefile would look like if we want to use shared libraries.

INPUT **LISTING 22.2** Makefile with Shared Libraries

```
 1: # Makefile to build the dice rolling program
 2: # using shared libraries
 3: CFLAGS = -O
 4: OBJS   = diceMain.o
 5: LIBS   = libroll.so
 6:
 7: all:   roll
 8:
 9: roll:  $(OBJS) $(LIBS)
10:        $(CC) $(CFLAGS) -o $@ $(OBJS) -L. -lroll
11:
12: doRoll.o: doRoll.c
13:        $(CC) -fPIC -c $<
14:
15: libroll.so: doRoll.o
16:    -$(RM) libroll*
17:        $(CC) -shared -Wl,-soname,libroll.so.1 \
18:    -o libroll.so.1.0 $<
19:        ln -s libroll.so.1.0 libroll.so.1
20:        ln -s libroll.so.1 libroll.so
21:
22: clean:
23:        - $(RM) roll *.o libroll*
```

make **Command-Line Options**

make has several useful command-line options.

If you want to specify an alternate makefile rather than one of the defaults mentioned earlier, invoke make as follows:

```
make -f filename
```

make is a very sophisticated program. One of the things it does is understand dependencies. For example, it knows that .o files are built from .c files. Your program may consist of several .c source files. If you change one, it is not necessary to recompile them all every time that you build. You only need to recompile the one source file that has changed. make understands this and will compile only those files that are not "current." Sometimes you may want to check first to see what make thinks it needs to build. You can do this with the following command:

```
make -n
```

This tells make to analyze the makefile and report what commands it will issue to build your program. make will stop short of executing any commands.

Another useful facility in make is the use of variables. Notice that we defined a variable named CFLAGS. make automatically passes this variable to the gcc when it compiles your program. You may want to change the value of this variable one time without changing the makefile. You can specify a new value on the command line that will override the one in the file:

```
make CFLAGS="-g -O"
```

Debugging

Any good development environment has to provide some debugging capability, and Linux includes the GNU debugger gdb. This is an excellent source debugger with a command- line interface. Your distribution should also include xxgdb, a version of the same debugger with a graphical interface that runs under X Windows. If you do not have an executable for xxgdb, it is certainly worth building.

gdb

gdb allows you to single-step through a program, set breakpoints, and examine and modify variables by name. You can use it with both C and C++ programs.

In order to prepare a program for debugging, simply supply the -g option to gcc when the program is built. You can do this on the gcc command line (if you are building the program this way). If you are using make, you can put this option into the makefile. Alternatively, if you are using make, you can do this as described earlier, overriding the value of CFLAGS on the make command line:

```
make CFLAGS=-g
```

After your program is built, start gdb with the command:

```
% gdb roll
```

OUTPUT
```
GNU gdb 4.17.0.11 with Linux support
Copyright 1998 Free Software Foundation, Inc.
GDB is free software, covered by the GNU General Public License, and you
➥are welcome to change it and/or distribute copies of it under certain
➥conditions.
Type "show copying" to see the conditions.
There is absolutely no warranty for GDB.  Type "show warranty" for
➥details.
This GDB was configured as "i386-redhat-linux"...
```

gdb has a great many commands available. To see them, type **help**.

```
(gdb) help
```

OUTPUT
```
List of classes of commands:

aliases -- Aliases of other commands
breakpoints -- Making program stop at certain points
data -- Examining data
files -- Specifying and examining files
internals -- Maintenance commands
obscure -- Obscure features
running -- Running the program
stack -- Examining the stack
status -- Status inquiries
support -- Support facilities
tracepoints -- Tracing of program execution without stopping the program
user-defined -- User-defined commands

Type "help" followed by a class name for a list of commands in that
class.
Type "help" followed by command name for full documentation.
Command name abbreviations are allowed if unambiguous.
```

The help command by itself shows you the classes of commands that gdb provides. To find out more about the commandswithin a particular class, use help again:

```
(gdb) help breakpoints
```

```
Making program stop at certain points.

List of commands:

awatch -- Set a watchpoint for an expression
break -- Set breakpoint at specified line or function
catch -- Set breakpoints to catch exceptions that are raised
clear -- Clear breakpoint at specified line or function
commands -- Set commands to be executed when a breakpoint is hit
condition -- Specify breakpoint number N to break only if COND is true
delete -- Delete some breakpoints or auto-display expressions
disable -- Disable some breakpoints
enable -- Enable some breakpoints
hbreak -- Set a hardware assisted  breakpoint
ignore -- Set ignore-count of breakpoint number N to COUNT
rbreak -- Set a breakpoint for all functions matching REGEXP
rwatch -- Set a read watchpoint for an expression
tbreak -- Set a temporary breakpoint
thbreak -- Set a temporary hardware assisted breakpoint
watch -- Set a watchpoint for an expression

Type "help" followed by command name for full documentation.
Command name abbreviations are allowed if unambiguous.
```

Finally, to exit gdb, type **q**.

Table 22.2 shows some of the most useful *gdb* commands.

TABLE 22.2 Useful gdb Commands

Command	Function
break [file:]function	Set a breakpoint at the entrance to function in the file named file.
run [arglist]	Start the program and pass it to the arglist if any.
bt	Display the program stack.
print expr	Evaluate the expression and print the result.
c	Continue execution from the current point.
next	Execute the next program line. If the next line is a function call, then this will call the function and stop at the next line after the call.
step	Execute the next program line, and step into the function if that line is a function call.
help [name]	Show the general help name, or help on the specified topic if one is given.
q	Exit gdb.

xxgdb

xxgdb is a graphical interface built around gdb. Be sure that your DISPLAY environment variable is defined, and type:

```
xxgdb program_name
```

Figure 22.4 shows the xxgdb graphical interface.

FIGURE 22.4

xxgdb.

There are three panes in the xxgdb display. The top pane shows you the source code for the currently running module. The middle pane contains buttons that are shortcuts to various xxgdb commands. The bottom pane is a command window. This shows you program and gdb output. If your program or gdb requires keyboard input, move your mouse into this pane and type.

You can display the value of a variable or expression by highlighting it with the mouse and then pressing the Display button. In this case, another pane will open with a continuously updating display of the value of the variable that you've selected.

Sample gdb Debugging Session

Here is a sample session running the roll program in gdb:

```
% gdb roll
```

OUTPUT

```
GNU gdb 4.17.0.11 with Linux support
Copyright 1998 Free Software Foundation, Inc.
GDB is free software, covered by the GNU General Public License, and you
are welcome to change it and/or distribute copies of it under certain
➥conditions.
Type "show copying" to see the conditions.
There is absolutely no warranty for GDB.  Type "show warranty" for
➥details.
This GDB was configuredas "i386-redhat-linux"...
 (gdb) list 1,20
1        #include <stdio.h>
2
3        int doRoll(void);
4
5        main( int argc, char * argv[] )
6        {
7        int    i;
8        int    iIter;
9        int    Die[6];
10
11         if( argc < 2 ) {
12           printf("Usage: %s n\n", argv[0]);
13           exit(1);
14         }
15
16         iIter = atoi(argv[1]);
17
18         memset( Die, 0, sizeof(Die) );
19
20         for( i = 0; i < iIter; i++ ) {
(gdb) break 16
Breakpoint 1 at 0x80484d0: file diceMain.c, line 16.
(gdb) run 5
Starting program: /home/hal/work/jnk/Dice/roll 5

Breakpoint 1, main (argc=2, argv=0xbffffa44) at diceMain.c:16
16         iIter = atoi(argv[1]);
(gdb) print iIter
$1 = 134518380
(gdb) next
18         memset( Die, 0, sizeof(Die) );
(gdb) print iIter
$2 = 5
(gdb) next
20         for( i = 0; i < iIter; i++ ) {
(gdb) next
21           Die[doRoll() - 1]++;
(gdb) print doRoll()
$3 = 2
(gdb) next
20         for( i = 0; i < iIter; i++ ) {
```

22

```
(gdb) cont
Continuing.
5 rolls
        Number  Rolls
           1 :      0
           2 :      2
           3 :      0
           4 :      1
           5 :      1
           6 :      1

Program exited with code 07.
(gdb)
```

Version Control

Programs are never as simple as you think they will be at the outset. Any good program lives on way beyond your original intentions. Over time there are changes, additions, bug fixes, and enhancements.

Comments are a fine way of keeping some information regarding changes, but for any serious work you need some form of version control. Suppose that you change doRoll.c, adding numerous features. A year later your biggest customer calls and says he does not want all those features; he just wants the original version from last year, with one bug fixed.

Linux comes with *RCS (Revision Control System)*. RCS is a collection of commands that let you track changes to files, retrieve any previous versions, and compare current versions to earlier ones.

RCS

The main commands in the RCS suite are listed in Table 22.3.

TABLE 22.3   RCS Commands

Command	Description
ci	Check a new revision of a file into the repository
co	Check out a version of a file
ident	Search for RCS identifiers in files
merge	Create a version of a file that incorporates changes from two other versions of that file
rcsdiff	Compare two versions of a file
rlog	View the history log of a file

RCS maintains the history of revisions to files in a repository. Generally that repository is a directory named RCS, under your current directory.

In the following example, we initiate the RCS history of one file in our dice-rolling project:

```
% mkdir RCS
% ci Makefile
```

```
RCS/Makefile,v  <--  Makefile
enter description, terminated with single '.' or end of file:
NOTE: This is NOT the log message!
>> Makefile for dice rolling program
>> .
initial revision: 1.1
done
```

We've now checked the Makefile into the RCS repository, and RCS has created a file in the RCS directory named Makefile,v. As we modify the Makefile and check in later versions, RCS will keep track of those changes in its Makefile,v copy.

> **Note**
>
> After you check a file in to RCS, you will see that your original file is gone. Do not panic—it is not lost. RCS has tracked your changes in its copy and deleted your original. You can still check your file out with the co command.

Check in all the source files needed to build the dice program.

Think of RCS as a library that holds your files. You can check out read-only copies with the co filename command. When you want to modify a file, you can check out a writable (locked) copy with co -l. Any number of read-only (unlocked) copies can be checked out at a time. Only one locked copy can be checked out at a time.

There are several identifying keywords that you can place into your file that are recognized by RCS. These keywords all start and end with $. I might modify our diceMain.c program as follows in Listing 22.3:

INPUT   **LISTING 22.3**   Modified diceMain.c Program

```
1: #include <stdio.h>
2: int doRoll(void);
3: main( int argc, char * argv[] )
4: {
5: int    i;
6: int    iIter;
```

```
 7: int    Die[6];
 8:
 9:    if( argc < 2 ) {
10:      printf("Usage: %s n\n", argv[0]);
11:      exit(1);
12:    }
13:
14:    iIter = atoi(argv[1]);
15:    memset( Die, 0, sizeof(Die) );
16:    printf("$Header$\n");
17:    for( i = 0; i < iIter; i++ ) {
18:      Die[doRoll() - 1]++;
19:    }
20:    printf("%d rolls\n", iIter);
21:    printf("\tNumber\tRolls\n");
22:    for( i = 0; i < 6; i++ ) {
23:      printf("\t%d :\t%d\n", i + 1, Die[i]);
24:    }
25: }
```

When I check the file out unlocked (read-only), RCS replaces the $Header$ with information about the name and version of the file. When I check it out locked, RCS does not replace the header. Now I check out a locked copy, build the program, and run it:

```
% roll 10
```

OUTPUT

```
$Header: /tmp/RCS/diceMain.c,v 1.1 1999/12/20 08:37:38 usr Exp $
10 rolls
        Number  Rolls
        1 :     1
        2 :     4
        3 :     0
        4 :     2
        5 :     2
        6 :     1
```

Documentation

A great deal of documentation is available with Linux, and most of it is shipped with the distributions. You have access to man, info, and the Linux HOWTOs and FAQs. Because the documentation can be extensive, many of the distributions make installing the full set optional.

man Pages

Like any UNIX-like operating system, Linux includes man and man pages for all the commands.

Sometimes you will encounter a command with a man page in more than one manual section. Normally when you use man, it displays the first entry that it finds. Using man with the -a option will cause it to display manual pages for the selected command in all manual sections that have one.

The command xman provides a graphical interface to the basic man command. Type

```
xman -notopbox -bothshown
```

You can click the left mouse button on the Sections panel to select another manual section. Left-click any command in the top panel to view the corresponding manual page in the bottom panel. Left-click the Options button and choose the last entry (quit) to exit xman. Figure 22.5 shows the graphical interface to the manual page.

FIGURE 22.5

xman.

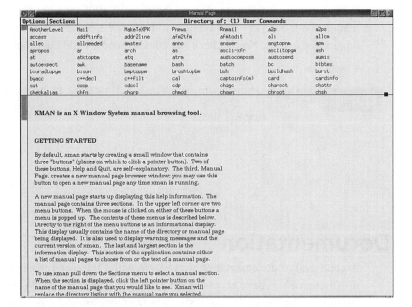

info

Online documentation in the form of man pages has been in UNIX almost from the start. A more recent contribution has been the info system. Navigating info will seem natural to you if you are familiar with emacs. If you are not, it can be a little tough to learn.

You can invoke info from the command line with the command info. If you are already in emacs, press Esc, and then type **-x info**. Figure 22.6 shows info.

FIGURE 22.6

info.

The info command is organized in nodes, where each node represents a major topic. As you read the information in info, you can follow links to other topics or to more information. There are several single-character commands in info. The best way to start to learn it is to access the tutorial with the h command (from the initial info directory window). Use the m command to follow some menu item. Type **m gcc** to follow the link into information on gcc. You can also move the cursor to a menu item and press Enter. At any time you can type **d** to return to the main info directory.

To exit info, type **q**. If you entered info through emacs, use the normal emacs exit sequence *C-c C-h*.

HOWTOs and FAQs

There is a wealth of documentation contributed to Linux by users who have figured out how to do things and then written up their experiences. These write-ups are known as HOWTOs. There is also a long history in Linux of various user groups and organizations providing help to users online. Often the questions and corresponding answers will be collected into documents known as FAQs (Frequently Asked Questions). Most Linux distributions ship with both the HOWTOs and FAQs. They can typically be found in the directory /usr/doc/HOWTO and /usr/doc/FAQ. Your installation may place them elsewhere.

The most recent FAQs and HOWTOs are available online at the Web site of the Linux Documentation Project: `http://www.linuxdoc.org`.

Summary

Today's lesson discussed the programming and debugging environment provided by Linux. This included quick introductions to:

- Editors (vi and emacs)
- Compilers (gcc and g++)
- Building executables with `make`
- Libraries and linking
- Debugging with `gdb`
- Version control with RCS
- Online documentation including `man` and `info`

This is a feature rich environment equivalent to that available on most professional work-stations. It offers all the basic tools necessary for program development.

Q&A

Q I compiled and built my C++ program with gcc. It compiles fine but I have lots of link errors.

A gcc by default links with the standard C libraries, and not the libraries required by C++. You can specify these explicitly; however, it is simpler to use g++ for the link phase of your build.

Q I've created a program using shared libraries, and I've created the libraries. Now when I run the program I get an error indicating: "cannot open shared object file: No such file or directory".

A You have not told the loader where to find the libraries. The environment variable `LD_LIBRARY_PATH` is a list of colon-separated paths to directories where the shared libraries can be found.

Q When I type `make`, it says "make: nothing to be done for ...".

A `make` attempts to look at all the objects and their corresponding source files. It examines the time stamps on these files. If the object is newer than the source, `make` concludes that that object does not need to be recompiled. If your target exists and all the component objects are newer than their sources, `make` believes that there is nothing to be done.

Q **When I run gdb, I cannot see my sources. When I run xxgdb, the top pane does not show any source, and the bottom pane shows the message "No default source file yet."**

A In order for the compiler to preserve symbols and sources so that the debugger can read them, you must compile and link all modules of your program with the -g flag.

Q **I've created an RCS directory and checked in all my sources and header files. Now they are gone.**

A When you check in with the ci command, RCS updates a history file in the RCS directory. Your files probably are not gone; you simply have not checked out versions to work on yet. Use the co command to check out locked or unlocked copies.

Workshop

The Workshop provides quiz questions to help solidify your understanding of the material covered and exercises to provide you with experience in using what you have learned. Try to answer the quiz and exercise questions before checking the answers in Appendix D, "Answers to Exercises and Quizzes," and make sure you understand the answers before continuing tomorrow.

Quiz

1. What is POSIX?
2. What is X Windows?
3. What are the two primary text editors available with Linux?
4. What is a primary distinction between vi and GNU emacs?
5. What is an advantage of shared libraries over static libraries? Static libraries over shared libraries?
6. What is the utility used to compile and build programs? What is it's default input file?

Exercises

1. Create an additional function for the dice program presented in today's lesson. The function should take as input a pointer to the Die array. For each face of the die, this function should print out the percentage of times that this face came up. The function should be in a file separate from main and do Roll.
2. Modify the makefile to link in the new function.
3. Step through the program with gdb.

WEEK 4

DAY 23

Shell Programming

Although you have been studying primarily the C++ language, you have also learned about the specifics and implications of this language in the Linux environment. Continuing in this vein, today's lesson addresses the Linux shell and shell programming.

Even though the shell is independent of the programming language you will be using, you should understand what the shell is and how to use it in order to accomplish anything useful. At the very basic level, you must interact with the shell to do anything. If you understand the basic mechanisms of the shell, you will find it a powerful tool that can help you in your work.

This lesson touches on the following basics:

- What the shell is
- What shells are available
- Shell principles (redirection and backgrounding)
- Shell commands construction (substitution and aliasing)
- Environment variables
- Shell scripts

What Is a Shell?

Many people think the prompt you see when you sit at a computer is the operating system, or identifies it. This is not the case.

The operating system is the software that runs the computer, talks to the hardware, loads and runs programs, and so on. The operating system is something that, basically, you never see.

When you see the computer prompt and enter commands in response, what you are dealing with is the shell. In times past, the shell was known as a command-line interpreter. In fact, in the old DOS world, this software was often known as the CLI, and was named COMMAND.COM.

An interesting feature of UNIX and its derivatives including Linux is that shells are completely independent. A user is free to choose any one of a number of widely available shells. As you will see later in this lesson, a user can choose to interact with one shell but write scripts in another.

Shells Available with Linux

You can think of the shell as a program that sits in between the user and the operating system. It implements the language that the user utilizes to control the operating system. The shell is started automatically when you log in to the system.

The original shell available in UNIX systems was the Bourne shell ("sh"). Two later shells that became popular were the C-shell ("csh") and the Korn shell ("ksh"). Each had unique and very useful features.

The Bourne shell was rewritten, and in a slight play on words the new version became known as the "Bourne again shell", or "bash." The C-Shell was rewritten and named theT-shell ("tcsh"). All three shells are available with Linux: bash, tcsh, and ksh. bash is probably the most frequently used shell, and in many installations it is the default shell.

Shell Operation and Syntax Basics

The shell performs a number of important functions.

First of all, it is the program that enables you to interact with the operating system. The "command line" is the user input to the shell. The shell examines the command line, determines if what you have typed is the name of a program, and if so then the shell starts that program. If the command is the name of a shell script then the appropriate shell is started and the script is fed to it as input.

All shell commands use the following general format:

```
command option1 option2 option3 ... optionN
```

This single line is known as the command line. A *command line* consists of a command name and one or more options (or *arguments*). Whitespace on the command line is generally ignored. Command names and arguments are generally case-sensitive. You end the command by pressing the Enter (or Return) key. You can continue a command on a new line with the backslash (\) key:

```
very-long-command-name long_option_1 long_option_2 \
long_option_3 ... optionN
```

You can concatenate more than one command on a line with a semicolon (;), like this:

```
command_1 option; command_2 option; command_3 option
```

> **Tip**
>
> You might often find the following sequence useful:
>
> ```
> clear; pwd; ls
> ```
>
> This will clear the terminal window, and then in the clean window, it will print the name of the current directory and a list of all the files in that directory.

Shell Features

Shells have far too many features to discuss in great detail here. This section touches on the fundamentals behind shells in general. These features are present in almost all shells. The exact syntax may differ from one shell to another, and so specific examples are limited to the Bourne shell. Be aware that each of the popular shells does add some feature that may not be available in the others.

All the shells have complete and concise man page entries. In addition, the info file for bash is over 3,000 lines long. For more specific or advanced information, you should refer to this online documentation.

I/O Redirection

When Linux programs are run, they have three I/O ports opened for them automatically. These are the *standard input*, the *standard output*, and the *standard error*.

By default, the standard input is usually connected to the keyboard, and the standard output and standard error are usually connected to the screen. Because the shell starts the program you specify, it can reassign these default assignments in a process known as input redirection, output redirection, or more generically as I/O redirection, before the program is started.

Suppose that you want to create a list of files in the /usr/include directory that includes other files. One way to do this might be as follows:

```
grep -l #include /usr/include/*.h > IncludeList
```

The "*" is a "wildcard" character. Wildcards are discussed in more detail later in this lesson. For now, just assume that grep will check every file in /usr/include whose name ends with ".h". It will print the name of every file in which it finds the string #include.

The ">" is the output redirect character. It causes the shell to redirect the output of the grep command to a file named IncludeList. The grep command itself is unaware of the redirection. The names in the IncludeList file will look like this:

```
/usr/include/FlexLexer.h
/usr/include/Fnlib.h
/usr/include/Fnlib_types.h
/usr/include/Imlib.h
/usr/include/Imlib_private.h
/usr/include/Imlib_types.h
/usr/include/QwCluster.h
/usr/include/QwPublicList.h
/usr/include/QwSpriteField.h
```

To replace the /usr/include/ at the beginning of each filename, you can use the sed command:

```
sed 's#^/usr/include/#+  #' < IncludeList > ListIncludes
```

The command sed operates on data from the standard input. Using the "<" input redirection character, you redirect the standard input. Instead of reading from the keyboard, sed will read from the file IncludeList. As with output redirection, the sed command is unaware that its standard input has been redirected (unless it explicitly checks for this). The output of the sed command is redirected to the file ListIncludes.

Note that the ">" character does not redirect the standard error output, but only the standard output. Use >& to redirect the standard error as follows:

```
sed 's#^/usr/include/#+  #' < IncludeList >& SedErr > SedOut
```

The following command redirects both standard error and standard output to the file named Output:

```
sed 's#^/usr/include/#+  #' < IncludeList >& Output
```

This is somewhat confusing and is rarely used. Most often only the standard output is redirected, and standard error is allowed to go to the screen.

Pipes

A related form of redirection is known as a *pipe*.

Perhaps you want a list of files that contain #include, and you want the list to be sorted.

You can use redirection as follows:

```
grep -l #include /usr/include/*.h > IncludeList
sort IncludeList > SortedList
```

Certainly there must be a better way than using two commands and a temporary file. The following is better:

```
grep -l #include /usr/include/*.h ¦ sort > SortedList
```

The pipe character (¦) strings two commands together, and connects (redirects) the standard output of the first one to the standard input of the second. A single command line can contain any number of pipes:

```
grep -l #include /usr/include/*.h ¦ sort ¦ sed  \ 's#^/usr/include/#+  #' >
SortedModifiedList
```

Variables

Very often a program needs some specific information in order to work properly. For instance, the screen editors vi and emacs both need to know what type of terminal you are using.

This information could be provided as a command-line option; however, it would be unnecessarily tedious to require that you add this information every time you start the editor. In addition, there is more information that does not change from one invocation to another beyond just the terminal type the editor requires.

Shells address this problem with environment variables. An *environment variable* is nothing more than a name/string pair. The shell keeps a list of these variables and makes them available to any program.

There are in fact two types of variables: normal shell variables and environment variables. The distinction between these is subtle. Environment variables are also called "global" variables, while shell variables are also known as "local" variables. Global variables are passed on at the start of a new command or shell. To set a shell variable in bash, use this syntax:

23

```
NAME=value
```

To set an environment variable, the syntax is

```
export NAME=value
```

If the variable includes whitespace or other special characters, the value can be enclosed in single or double quotes. Often it is useful to append to an already existing variable. You can do this as follows:

```
export NAME="$NAME new_string"
```

This appends "new_string" to the environment variable NAME.

Variables Used by the Shell

Several environment variables have special significance and are used by the shell. This is a partial list of some of the more notable variables.

- DISPLAY—This variable is read by X programs to know where to display their output. This is typically set to ":0.0", meaning that output will be displayed on the host computer monitor.

- PATH—A colon-separated list of directory names where the shell should search for programs. When you type any command name, the shell will look in these directories for a program by that name.

- TERM—The type of terminal or terminal emulation. Programs such as editors must know the terminal type so that they can send the proper commands to manipulate the screen and cursor.

- PS1—The prompt displayed by the shell to indicate to the user that it is ready for input.

- HOME—The user's home directory.

Variables Set by the Shell

Several variables are set by the shell and may be referenced by programs started from the shell. A partial list of important variables set by the shell includes the following:

- SHELL—This is set by the shell and contains the full pathname of the current shell (that is, /bin/bash).

- PWD—The current directory as set by the most recent cd command.

Backgrounding, Suspension, and Job Control

Normally you type a command name on the command line and then wait for that command to finish. Suppose that the command you run will take a long time. Rather than wait, you could certainly open another xterm window and continue working there. Instead, however, you can make use of the multitasking nature of Linux. You can run the command in the background with the special character "&" as follows:

```
bash# find . -name '*.c' -print ¦ sort > SortedList &
[1] 142
bash#
```

23

This command will create a list of all files whose names end with ".c". It will sort this list and place the output into a file named SortedList. The shell prints "[1] 142" and returns immediately, ready for another command. The output indicates that there is one task running in the background, and that the process I.D. (PID) of this job is 142. You can run more than one job in the background. In this case, this job is number 1 in the background queue.

If you run a program from the command line and do not use the & character, the shell waits for the job to finish before prompting you for a new command. This job is said to be running in the foreground.

If you run a job in the background, and then decide that you want to wait for it, you can "bring it to the foreground" with the command fg.

If a job is running in the foreground and you want to pause it without killing it permanently, press Ctrl+Z (the Control key and "z" at the same time). The job is now suspended. You can resume the job in the foreground with fg, or in the background with bg.

Finally, if you want to kill the job permanently, you can use the kill command. Either kill it by its PID number (kill 142), or else by its place in your background queue (kill %1).

To find out what jobs you are running in the background, use the jobs command.

Figure 23.1 demonstrates job control. The first "find" command is run in the background, and the "jobs" command indicates that it is running there. The next "find" command is run in the foreground and then suspended with Ctrl+Z. Again, jobs shows this. Next, the suspended find command is resumed in the background, and this is verified with jobs. The fg command is used to bring the first background job into the foreground, and it is then suspended with Ctrl+Z.

FIGURE 23.1

Backgrounding, suspension, and job control.

Command Completion

bash includes many shortcuts to reduce the amount of typing that you need to do. This is accomplished through command completion and command substitution. The next section covers substitution and the wildcard mechanism.

Command completion refers to the ability of bash to "guess" what command or filename you are typing. Type the first few characters of a command, and instead of finishing the command, press the Tab key. If bash can uniquely identify the command, it will complete it for you. If it cannot, it will beep. Press the Tab key a second time, and the candidate completions will be displayed.

The same mechanism works if you are specifying a filename as an argument to a command.

For instance, type **mo**, press Tab, and the shell should beep. Press Tab again and you should see a list of commands that start with "mo." Type **r** and press Tab again. The shell should complete the command name more. Now press the spacebar, and then type **/etc/in** and press Tab. The shell beeps. Press Tab again and a list of files in /etc that start with "in" is displayed. Type **e** and then Tab. The filename inetd.conf is completed.

Command Substitution

The shell includes other mechanisms to save typing. These involve substituting strings. Several kinds of substitutions are allowed.

Wildcard Substitution

In many games of cards, a wildcard can be used to replace any other card. Similarly, in the shell, a wildcard can be used as a placeholder that the shell can replace with any other character or characters.

There are two important wildcard characters: the asterisk (*) is matched by the shell by any sequence of zero or more characters in a filename. The question mark (?) matches any single character.

What does this mean? Perhaps you want to run the ls command on the current directory to see a list of all filenames ending with ".h". You can simply enter ls *.h. The shell expands the wildcard character to a list of all filenames ending with ".h" before it invokes the ls command. The full list of filenames is passed to the command.

Perhaps you want to see all filenames containing exactly three characters before the ".h". Then you would type: ls ???.h.

Wildcard substitution in bash is much more sophisticated than in DOS. bash has no trouble expanding "a??def*.xyz" to a list of filenames that start with "a" followed by any two characters, followed by "def," followed by zero or more characters and ending with ".xyz".

Note

> It is important to remember that wildcards (and all other substitutions described in the rest of this lesson) are expanded by the shell *before* the command is started.

String Substitution

bash allows substitution of specific character sequences. There are two styles of substitution.

You can specify a comma-separated list of strings in curly braces, and each one will be used in turn. For example:

```
bash# ls a{b,c,de,fgh}z
abz  acz  adez  afghz
bash#
```

The leading "a" and trailing "z" are combined with the "b" and then the "c" and then the "de" and then the "fgh," which appear in curly braces.

You can specify ranges of characters with square braces:

```
bash# ls a[b-h]z
abz  acz  adz  aez  afz  agz  ahz
bash#
```

The square braces can also specify specific characters:

```
bash# ls a[bcde]z
abz  acz  adz  aez
bash#
```

Finally, you can mix wildcards, curly braces, and square braces.

Command Output Substitution

Another form of substitution is command output substitution. The output of a command can be specified as an argument to another command:

```
bash# ls -l `find /usr/src -name Makefile -print`
```

This example will run the find command to locate all Makefiles in the /usr/src directory tree. The list of files will be presented on the command line to ls, which will display the directory entries of these files.

Variable Substitution

A final useful form of substitution is variable substitution. The shell can replace a variable with its value on the command line.

For example, suppose that your home directory is /home/username:

```
bash# echo  ${HOME}

/home/username
```

The value of the environment variable named "HOME" replaces the string ${HOME} in the command line argument.

Command History and Editing

bash maintains a list of the commands you have typed in what's known as a history list. The length of the list depends on the environment, but is generally no longer than 500 commands. `bash` will preserve this list from one session to the next. If you type the command `history`, the list of commands you have typed will be displayed. So for example consider the following sequence of commands:

```
bash# cd /
bash# cd /tmp
bash# cd
bash# cat .bashrc > /dev/null
bash# history
1  cd /
2  cd /tmp
3  cd
4  cat .bashrc > /dev/null
5  history
```

To invoke any previous command, type an exclamation mark and the command number. To repeat the `cd /tmp` in the preceding sequence, type `!2`.

You can repeat the last command with `!!`, two commands back with `!-2`, and so on.

You can also edit a previous command line before repeating it. Suppose that you type the command `ls -l /TMp`. To correct this command and repeat it, you could type `^TMp^tmp^`. `bash` assumes that you want to edit the preceding command and proceeds with the substitution if possible. Emacs-style editing is also supported. Press Ctrl+P and the previous command will be displayed. Use the arrow keys or Ctrl+B (to move back a character) and Ctrl+F (to move forward a character) and fix the command line. Press Enter to execute the edited command.

Aliases

You probably use certain commands or command sequences quite often. You can create your own shorthand for these, known as aliases. An alias is replaced by the shell with its definition.

For instance, the `ls` command shows you the names of files. With the command-line option `-F`, the type of the file is also indicated ("*" for executable, "/" for directory, and so on). You can create an alias to substitute commands as follows:

```
bash# ls -F
a  b*  c*  d  e  f/  g/
bash# ls
a  b  c  d  e  f  g
bash# alias ls="ls -F"
bash# ls
a  b*  c*  d  e  f/  g/
bash#
```

The ls command with and without the -F argument display their results differently. When ls is aliased, then when you enter the command ls, the shell automatically substitutes the alias: ls -F.

The command rm removes a file. With the -i option, it will first ask for confirmation. Many people find it useful to substitute the rm command to prevent accidentally removing a file: alias rm="rm -i". The quote marks in this alias command are significant, because they group the whole right side of the equal sign as a single argument to the alias command. Without the quote marks, the alias command will try to interpret the -i as an option.

Shell Scripts

Complex sequences of shell commands can be put into a file so that they can be repeated at any time. This is very much like writing a program, except that it does not require compilation. The shell has many of the features of standard languages including variables and control statements (which we have not yet discussed).

All shell scripts begin with #!/bin/sh. The first two characters tell the system that this is a script file, and the /bin/sh starts the bash shell. After the shell is started, the remaining lines in the file are fed to it one at a time.

Shell scripts can be simple one-line programs or complex and hundreds of lines. They are not as fast and efficient as compiled language programs.

Shell scripts must have their "execute" permission bit set. You can set this with the command: chmod a+x *filename*.

Variables

We've already discussed variables in shells. When you are running a script, some useful variables are already defined:

- $$—The process ID of the shell program
- $0—The name of the script
- $1 through $9—The first nine command-line arguments passed to the script
- $#—The number of command-line parameters passed to the script

Control Structures

bash supports control statements analogous to many of those in the C and C++ languages, although the syntax is different. These include statements such as if-then-else, for, case, and while.

The script in Listing 23.1 provides a simple illustration of the major control statements available with a bash script.

LISTING 23.1 Major Control Statements in bash

```
 1: #!/bin/bash
 2:
 3: MAX=9
 4: #
 5: # illustrate the 'if-endif' control
 6: if [ $# -gt $MAX ]; then
 7:   echo "$0 : $MAX or less arguments required"
 8:   exit 1
 9:fi
10: #
11: # echo the first 2 arguments
12: echo "$0 : Parameter 2 : $2"
13: echo "$0 : Parameter 1 : $1"
14: echo ""
15: #
16: # illustrate the 'for-done' control
17: for i in $1 $2; do
18:   ls -l $i;
19: done
20: echo ""
21:
22: #
23: # illustrate the 'case' control
24: echo "case example"
25: for i do
26:   case "$i" in
27:     a ) echo "case a";;
28:     b ) echo "case b";;
29:     * ) echo "default case $i";;
30:   esac
31: done
32: echo ""
33:
34: #
35: # illustrate the 'while-done' control
36: echo "while example"
37: i=1;
38: while [ $i -le $# ]; do
39:    echo $i;
40:    i=$[$i+1];
41: done
42: echo ""
43:
```

continues

LISTING 23.1　CONTINUED

```
44: #
45: # illustrate the 'until-done' control
46: echo "until example"
47: i=1;
48: until [ $i -gt $# ]; do
49:   echo "argument $i";
50:   i=$[$i+1];
51: done
52: echo ""
53:
54: exit 0
```

OUTPUT　The "MAX=9" line sets the shell variable named MAX equal to 9. The "if-fi" group of lines that follows checks the number of command line arguments. If there are more than 9 then a message is printed and the script exits.

The "echo" statements illustrate how command line arguments can be referenced. The shell substitutes all of the arguments on the command line (including the command name) for the variables $0, $1, $2 and so on.

The next several command groupings illustrate the main control statements available in the shell. These include the 'for-done' (similar to a 'for' loop in C), the 'case-esac' (similar to the 'switch' statement in C), the 'while-done' (similar to the 'while' loop in C), and the 'until-done' (similar to 'do-while' in C). More details on the syntax and use of these and other control statements can be found in the bash 'man' page.

The 'ls' command below shows that there are 2 files (named a and b) in the current directory in addition to the shell script named 'simple'. The script is then invoked with 7 arguments. The first 2 arguments are the names of the 2 files.

```
bash# ls -F
a  b simple*
bash# simple a b the quick brown fox jumps
./simple : Parameter 2 : b
./simple : Parameter 1 : a

-rw-r—r—   1 hal      hal           0 Jan 19 22:33 a
-rw-r—r—   1 hal      hal           0 Jan 19 22:33 b

case example
case a
case b
default case the
default case quick
default case brown
```

```
default case fox
default case jumps

while example
1
2
3
4
5
6
7

until example
argument 1
argument 2
argument 3
argument 4
argument 5
argument 6
argument 7
bash#
```

Shell Startup File(s)

An interactive shell (as opposed to a non-interactive shell like the one started for a script) is one in which the standard input is connected to the keyboard and the standard output to the display. If bash is the default shell for the user, upon login an interactive bash shell is started. If a bash shell script is run, a non-interactive shell is started and the script is fed to it a line at a time.

Upon login, the shell looks for a script named /etc/profile. If that script is found, it is executed. If the file .bash_profile exists in the user's home directory, it is executed. If not, .bash_login is checked. If that is not found, .profile is executed.

Upon logout, the file .bash_logout in the home directory is executed if it exists.

These startup files are used to set the path, prompt, and other environment variables that the user wants set upon each login.

Summary

This lesson has been an overview of shells in general and bash in particular. The lesson has covered

- Redirection
- Backgrounding

- History
- Command-line editing, wildcards, and substitution

We've also touched briefly on shell scripts.

The shell is a program that allows the user to interact with the operating system. It provides features that make this interaction easier (such as history, command completion and job control), as well as many of the features of a simple programming language (including variables and variable substitution, and control statements). There are several shells available for Linux, although bash is perhaps the most widely used. The online 'man' pages provide an excellent reference for the syntax and features of the shell.

Q&A

Q I type a common Linux command but I get the error message "command not found."

A This is a common problem. You may have typed the command wrong, or it may not exist. More likely there is an error in your path. bash (and other shells as well) will only execute a file if it can find it in your execution path. The path is set by the PATH environment variable. With the command echo ${PATH} you can determine what your path is. With man you can find out what directory the missing command is in. If that directory is not in your path list, add it with: export PATH="${PATH}:new_directory.

Q I've created a shell script, set its execute permission, and typed its name. I get the error "command not found."

A Check to be certain that "." is in your PATH environment list. The "." means "the current directory."

Workshop

The Workshop provides quiz questions to help solidify your understanding of the material covered and exercises to provide you with experience in using what you have learned. Try to answer the quiz and exercise questions before checking the answers in Appendix D, "Answers to Exercises and Quizzes," and make sure you understand the answers before continuing to tomorrow's lesson.

Quiz

1. What is a shell?

2. What is the general syntax of a shell command line?

3. What are the 3 standard I/O ports available to programs?

4. What are the 3 forms of I/O redirection, and what characters are used to represent them on the command line?

5. Are environment variables "local" or "global"? What about shell variables?

6. What bash environment variable sets the command search path? Which one sets the command prompt?

7. Name 2 command line wildcard substitution characters.

8. What needs to be in a shell script file so that the shell knows what command to feed the script to?

Exercises

1. Write a bash script to print out all of the command line arguments passed to it, as well as the total number of arguments.

23

DAY 24

System Programming

Today's lesson covers Linux system programming using the C++ programming language. Linux system programming is the process of writing programs using the system calls provided by the Linux operating system. System calls are the primary programming interface that interact with the various operating system components. System programming is a vast topic. The lesson today focuses on developing programs using processes and threads.

Processes

A *process* is an executing program. A program is a binary image on disk or other peripheral storage media, for example, ps. ps is a Linux utility that displays process state. When a program is run, it is read from the peripheral storage area, where it resides, into memory, and then executed.

Using ps again as an example, when a user types ps at the command prompt, the ps program is read from peripheral storage into memory and executed.

Each Linux process consists of multiple program segments, system resources and run state information. The segments are stack, heap, data and text. The organization of the segments in memory are illustrated in Figure 24.1. The information about process run state is called *process context*. Process context consists of address space, stack space, register contents, kernel data structures and process state.

Each Linux process runs in its own environment, and every process contains its own virtual memory and address space. In Linux it is not possible to indirectly affect the execution of another process.

FIGURE 24.1

Diagram of a Linux process.

| stack |
| heap |
| data |
| text |

Creation and Termination

A new process is created when a running program calls the fork() system call. fork() creates a new process and then copies the parent's environment to the newly created child process.

Tip

> The program that calls fork() is called the *parent*. The newly created process is called the *child*.

In Linux when a new process is created, the parent process data sections are not copied by the fork() system call. Initially the parent process's sections access permissions are set as read-only and are shared by the parent and child processes. As a child process accesses the parent's section, the specific section being accessed is copied into the child process's environment. The process of delaying the copy of the parent process's sections until they are accessed by the child is called *Copy On Write*. Copy On Write optimizes the fork() system call by minimizing the amount of information copied from the parent process's environment during a fork() call.

When fork() is called, it returns twice. The return from fork in the parent returns the child process ID, and the return from fork in the child returns 0. In both the parent and the child, program execution returns right after the return from fork. The process is a unique identifier in the system; every process is assigned a process ID.

Listing 24.1 shows an example of an interface that creates a process and is able to determine whether it is the parent or child process.

INPUT   **LISTING 24.1**   Listing for the Process Class

```
1:   // Listing 24.1 Process class
2:
3:   #if !defined(c_process_h)
4:   #define c_process_h
5:
6:   class Process
7:   {
8:   public:
9:   Process();
10:  ~Process();
11:
12:  void Create();
13:
14:  bool isParent() { return (pid != 0); }
15:  bool isChild() { return (pid == 0); }
16:
17:  private:
18:  Process& operator=(const Process&);     // disallow copy
19:
20:  int pid;
21:  };
22:
23:  #endif
```

ANALYSIS   The member function `Process::Create()` in line 12 calls `fork()` to create a new process. Two getter functions, `Process::isParent()` line 14, and `Process::isChild()`, line 15, are provided to determine which process is being run, parent or child. Because a process contains system information and kernel data, this class wants to explicitly inhibit a user from copying the class. This is done by making the copy constructor private.

Tip

It is not unusual in system programs to use resources that belong to the kernel. Because the copy of kernel resources may result in undesirable effects, all classes define the copy constructor as a private member function without an implementation. By doing this, you guarantee that users of the class cannot access the copy constructor, and member functions could compile the code but would be unable to link the code.

24

When a child process is created, there is never a guarantee which process, parent or child, will run first. In the preceding example, the parent process waits, via the `sleep()` call, and lets the child run first. This method is insufficient for real applications. A condition in which it is not possible to determine which process will execute next is called a *race condition*.

A process calls the `exit()` system call to terminate. `exit()` takes a parameter, status code, and returns that value to the parent process.

Process Control

A number of Linux system calls are used for process control. This section focuses on the basic routines for process control.

exec

The family of `exec()` system calls replaces the current process image, or program, with the image specified in the argument to `exec()`. Remember from the definition of a process that a process is a program in execution. `fork()` creates a new process that is a copy of the current process, effectively giving you two running instances of the same program. `exec()` gives you the capability to run a different program in an already executing process.

The `exec()` family of functions is used by a child process to run another program. After the child process is created, the child process overlays itself with another program and then continues its execution.

wait

The `wait()` system call causes the parent process to suspend itself until the child process terminates or a signal is received. A typical use of `wait()` would be for the parent to call `wait()` immediately following a `fork()` to wait for the child process to complete.

In Listing 24.2, the `Process` class defined in Listing 24.1 is extended with two new member functions implementing `exec()` and `wait()`.

INPUT **LISTING 24.2** Process Class With Added Process Control Member Functions

```
1:    Listing 24.2 Process class
2:    #include <wait.h>
3:    #include <unistd.h>
4:
5:    #if !defined(c_process1_h)
6:    #define c_process1_h
7:
8:    class Process
```

```
 9:   {
10:   public:
11:   Process();
12:   ~Process();
13:
14:   void Create();
15:
16:   int WaitForChild();
17:   int RunProgram(char *program);
18:
19:   bool isParent() { return (pid != 0); }
20:   bool isChild() { return (pid == 0); }
21:
22:   private:
23:   Process& operator= (const Process&);      // disallow copy
24:
25:   int pid;
26:   int wait_status;
27:   int exec_status;
28: };
29:
30: #endif
```

24

ANALYSIS The added member functions allow a parent process to wait for a child by calling the `Process::WaitForChild()` member function, line 16. The child process can overlay itself with another program image using the `Process::RunProgram()` member function, shown in Listing 24.3.

INPUT   **LISTING 24.3**   Example Code Using Process Control Member Functions

```
 1:   // Listing 24.3 Process control example
 2:   int main(int argc, char** argv)
 3:   {
 4:   Process p;
 5:   char* program = "ls";
 6:
 7:   p.Create();
 8:
 9:   if (p.isParent())
10:   {
11:   p.WaitForChild();
12:   }
13:   else if (p.isChild())
14:   {
15:   p.RunProgram(program);
16:   }
17:
18:   exit(0);
19:   }
```

ANALYSIS In Listing 24.3, line 7 creates a child process. Line 9 determines whether the currently running process is the parent or the child. If the process is the parent, it waits; otherwise, the command `ls` runs and the program exits.

ptrace

`ptrace()` is a system call that allows a parent process to control a running child process by reading or writing to the child process's memory. The primary use for `ptrace` is for debugging a child process. The primary interface primitive for `ptrace()` is signals.

A *signal* is a software interrupt. Signals are generally used to terminate a process, stop process execution, or invoke some other action.

There are two types of signals, synchronous and asynchronous. Synchronous signals result from executing an instruction that causes a problem, for example dereferencing an uninitialized pointer. An asynchronous signal is delivered to a process irrespective of the current instruction it is executing.

`gdb` is an example of a process using `ptrace()` to control a child process for debugging. In this case, `gdb` is the parent process, and the program being debugged is the child process. The child process runs until a signal occurs. When the signal occurs, control is returned to `gdb`. `gdb` blocks on the child via the `wait()` system call. When `gdb` regains control, it performs the operation on the child using `ptrace()`.

The usage of `ptrace()` has largely been superseded by the `/proc` file system.

The `/proc` File System

Linux provides a `/proc` file system, which allows users to query information about the system and individual running processes. `/proc` is not a traditional file system but a memory structure maintained by the kernel that provides system statistics. A user or process may obtain system and process information by issuing read and write calls to the `/proc` file system.

`/proc` is represented as a hierarchical file directory. The `/proc` directory contains a file entry for each running process, and each process has its own subdirectory named by its process ID. In addition to individual processes, `/proc` contains system parameters and resource information. A program or system command may read the directories and files corresponding to a process to query information from the kernel.

You can query `/proc` at any given time to get information about the system.

Tip

> The format of the data presented in the /proc file system may change from kernel release to kernel release. Familiarity with kernel data structures is highly recommended before reading about the /proc file system.

Process State and Priority

Before a discussion of process scheduling, you need to have a basic understanding of process state and process priority.

During the lifetime of a process, it goes through many state transitions. The *process state* is the state, or mode, of the process at a given time. Process states can be found in the linux kernel header file sched.h and are defined following.

- TASK_RUNNING—Process is waiting to run.
- TASK_INTERRUPTIBLE —Task is running and interruptible.
- TASK_UNINTERRUPTIBLE—Task is running and is not interruptible.
- TASK_ZOMBIE—Task has stopped, but the system still considers it running.
- TASK_STOPPED—The process is stopped, typically from receiving a signal.
- TASK_SWAPPING—The task is swapping.

Process priority is an integer assigned to a process or thread in which value is in a given range defined by the scheduling policy. When a process is created, a static priority value is assigned. The value of the process priority is the amount of time (in jiffies) that the scheduler gives this process to run when it is allowed to run. A jiffy is the duration of one clock tick on your system. The amount of time a process is allowed to run is called the *quantum*.

There are two types of Linux processes, normal and real-time. *Normal processes* have a priority of 0. A *real-time process* has priorities in the range of 1-99. Real-time processes are scheduled to have a higher priority than all the other non-real-time processes in the system. The priority of a process can only be altered using system calls such as nice(). If there is a real-time process ready to run, it will always run first. The nice system call changes a process priority. nice takes as an argument a non-negative integer which is added to the current process priority.

Scheduling Algorithms

The most precious resource in an operating system is CPU time. To efficiently use CPU time, operating systems use a concept called *multiprocessing*. Multiprocessing gives the user the impression that many processes are running simultaneously. The object of multi-processing is to have a process running at all times so that the CPU is always busy. This guarantees that the CPU is being used in the most efficient manner.

The implementation of multiprocessing in an operating system consists of dividing its CPU time among many processes. The *scheduler* is the kernel process that determines which process to run next. The scheduler decides which process, of all the processes in the TASK_RUNNING state, to run. The critera, or rules, that determine which process to run next is called the *scheduling algorithm*.

The Linux scheduler uses process priority and process policy to determine which process to run next.

There are three types of process policies: other, first in first out (FIFO), and round robin (RR). A normal process has one type of policy, other. Real-time processes have two types of policies, round robin and first in first out.

Other is implemented as a standard time-sharing scheduling algorithm. That is a policy where each process is given an equal quantum.

First in, first out schedules each runable process in the order that it is in on the run queue, and that order is never changed. A FIFO process will run until it blocks on I/O or is pre-empted by a higher priority process.

Round robin scheduling runs real-time processes in turn. The difference between a FIFO process and a round robin process is that a round robin process will run for a specified time (quantum) and then be swapped out and placed at the end of the priority list.

 Tip | A user must have root privilege to run real-time processes.

Do	Don't
DO run as root when running real-time processes.	DON'T forget to have an intimate understanding of kernel data structures when reading about the /proc file system.

Threads

A *thread* is defined as a sequence of instructions executed within the context of a process. Threads allow a process to do multiple operations in parallel. This is accomplished when an application is written to use multiple threads.

Threads reduce overhead by sharing fundamental sections of a process. Remember that the environment of a process consists of stack, data, and text.

The POSIX thread library package, called LinuxThreads, is an implementation of the POSIX 1003.1c thread package for Linux. POSIX 1003.1c is an API for multi-threaded programming standardized by IEEE as part of the POSIX standards. Most UNIX vendors have endorsed the POSIX 1003.1c standard. POSIX threads are commonly referred to as pthreads. Pthreads and LinuxThreads are terms used interchangeably throughout today's lesson. LinuxThreads run on any Linux system with kernel 2.0.0 or more recent and the glibc 2 library.

> **Note**
>
> To compile with pthreads, you must include the pthread header file, `#include`, and must link to the pthread library. For example:
>
> `cc hello_world.c -o hello_world -lpthreads.`

24

The thread API is the same as the pthreads, but the implementation is different from other operating systems. Other multithreaded operating systems, such as Windows 2000, define a thread to be separate from a process. LinuxThreads defines a thread as a context of execution.

In other operating systems, threads are defined as the CPU context, whereas the process owns the stack, data, and heap. When a new process is created, the thread is created as part of the process context. This implementation of threads has the advantage of very efficient context switching. However, this definition of a thread does not fit the Linux process module. For example, if a process owns the stack, data, and heap resources of a process, how would the `fork()` system call be implemented when called from a thread? LinuxThreads have the advantage of the fast context switch of a traditional thread with the added advantage that it can define which process resources can be shared.

Threads are implemented using the `__clone` system call. `__clone()` takes as an argument flags that specify which section will be shared between the process and the thread. The shareable options are defined in Linux kernel header file `schedbits.h` and are listed following:

- `CLONE_VM`—Share data and stack
- `CLONE_FS`—Share file system
- `CLONE_FILES`—Share open files
- `CLONE_SIGHAND`—Share signals
- `CLONE_PID`—Share PID of the parent (not fully implemented)

Single-Threaded

Single threading is defined as a single context of execution. When a process is created with the fork(), it has a single context of execution.

Multithreaded

Multithreading is defined as multiple contexts of execution. Multithreading separates a process into many context of execution threads, thus allowing the process execution to be distributed over many threads.

Re-entrancy is a characteristic of multithreaded programming where multiple contexts of execution can access shared data or resources and guarantee that the integrity of the shared resources is maintained. When multiple threads share resources, those resources must be protected by thread synchronization primitives. Synchronization is covered in the next section.

Creation and Termination

A thread is created using the pthread_create() system call and destroyed using the pthread_exit() system call. These system calls are encapsulated in the Thread class defined in Listing 24.4.

INPUT   **LISTING 24.4**   Thread Object

```
1:    // Listing 24.4 Thread class
2:    #if !defined(c_tcreate_h)
3:    #define c_tcreate_h
4:
5:    #include <pthread.h>
6:
7:    class Thread
8:    {
9:    public:
10:   Thread(void* r, void* a);        //ctor/dtor
11:   virtual ~Thread();
12:
13:   int Create();   // creates the thread
14:   int Destroy();  // exits thread
15:
16:   private:
17:   Thread& operator=(const Thread&);        // disallow copy
18:
19:   pthread_t       thread;
20:   pthread_attr_t attr;
21:   void*           fn;
22:   void*           fn_args;
```

```
23:  bool            init;
24:  };
25:
26:  #endif
```

ANALYSIS The code in Listing 24.4 presents a `Thread` object that encapsulates basic LinuxThread calls that create and destroy a thread. The constructor on Line 10 takes as arguments a pointer to a function and an argument to be passed to the function. A `Thread` is created by calling the `Thread::Create` member function. `Create` calls `pthread_create` using the parameters passed to the `Thread` constructor. The `Thread::Destroy` member function calls `pthread_exit` to terminate the thread. Listing 24.5 shows a sample program using the Thread class.

INPUT **LISTING 24.5** Producer/Consumer Example

```
1:   // Listing 24.5 Producer/Consumer example
2:   #include <iostream.h>
3:
4:   #include "tcreate.h"
5:
6:   int data = 0;
7:
8:   void read_thread(void* param)
9:   {
10:  while (1)
11:  cout << "read: " << data << endl;
12:  }
13:
14:  void write_thread(void* param)
15:  {
16:  while (1)
17:  cout << "write: " << data++ << endl;
18:  }
19:
20:  int main(int argc, char** argv)
21:  {
22:  Thread thread1((void*)&write_thread, NULL);
23:  Thread thread2((void*)&read_thread, NULL);
24:
25:  thread1.Create();
26:  thread2.Create();
27:
28:  for (int i = 0; i < 10000; i++)
29:  ;
30:
31:  thread1.Destroy();
32:  thread2.Destroy();
33:  }
```

ANALYSIS Listing 24.5 demonstrates the `Thread` object using the classic producer/consumer example in action. Two `Thread` objects are created, `thread1` and `thread2`. `thread1` uses the `write_thread` function defined in lines 9-13, this is the producer. `thread2` uses the `read_thread` function defined in lines 4-8, this is the consumer. The threads begin execution when the `Thread::Create()` member functions are called. `read_thread`, the consumer, reads from the global variable data, and `write_thread`, the producer, writes to the global variable data.

> **Tip**
>
> As with processes, there is never a guarantee which thread will run first, `thread1` or `thread2`.

Do you see the potential disaster in this example? Both `read_thread` and `write_thread` access the global data at any time . This is a potential problem because the `read_data` function could begin execution become suspended , the `write_data` function begin execution and modify global data then become suspended then `read_thread` would continue execution with a different value for global data. This is an example of code that is NOT re-entrant.

Scheduling

Thread scheduling concepts are exactly the same as process scheduling concepts. In fact, the scheduler for threads and processes is the same in Linux. Please refer to the "Scheduling Algorithms" section earlier today for details.

Synchronization

Thread synchronization is a technique to guarantee the integrity of resources shared among threads. LinuxThreads provides the following synchronization primitives: mutexes, semaphores, condition variables, and joining.

Mutexes

A *mutex* is an synchronization primitive used to guarantee mutual exclusive access to a resource, typically data.

A mutex is in one of two states: locked or unlocked. Only one thread can lock a mutex at a time. If another thread attempts to acquire a mutex already held by another thread, the lock fails.

The lock/unlock paradigm can be implemented using multiple synchronization primitives; therefore, we will define a virtual base class for this interface. Listing 24.6 defines a class which represents synchronous locks.

INPUT **LISTING 24.6** Synchronous Lock Class

```
1:   // Listing 24.6 SyncLock pure virtual class
2:   #if !defined c_synclock_h
3:   #define c_synclock_h
4:
5:   class SyncLock
6:   {
7:    public:
8:   SyncLock() {} ;
9:   ~SyncLock() {};
10:
11:  virtual int Acquire() = 0;
12:  virtual int Release() = 0;
13:
14:  private:
15:  SyncLock& operator=(const SyncLock&);      // disallow copy
16:  };
17:
18:  #endif
```

ANALYSIS The SyncLock virtual base class defines an interface for a synchronization primitive that locks a resource for mutual exclusive access and then unlocks that resource, allowing another thread to obtain the lock.

Given the definition of SyncLock, Listing 24.7 shows the implementation of a mutex using the SyncLock interface.

INPUT **LISTING 24.7** Mutex Class

```
1:   // Listing 24.7 Mutex class
2:   #if !defined(c_mutex_h)
3:   #define c_mutex_h
4:
5:   #include <pthread.h>
6:   #include "synclock.h"
7:
8:   class Mutex: public SyncLock
9:   {
10:  public:
11:  Mutex();        // ctor/dtor
12:  ~Mutex();
13:
14:  int  Create();
15:  int  Destroy();
16:
```

continues

LISTING 24.7   CONTINUED

```
17:  int  Acquire();   // obtain the lock
18:  int  Release(); // release the lock
19:
20:  private:
21:  Mutex& operator=(const Mutex&);       // disallow copy
22:
23:  bool                 init;
24:  pthread_mutex_t      mutex;
25:  pthread_mutexattr_t  attr;
26:  };
27
28:  #endif
```

ANALYSIS This mutex class has four major member functions, `Mutex::Create()`, `Mutex::Destroy()`, `Mutex::Acquire()`, and `Mutex::Release()`. After the `Mutex` is created and initialized, a thread acquires the `Mutex` to gain exclusive access to a resource and releases the `Mutex` when it is done.

Using Listing 24.8, let's revisit the producer/consumer example from Listing 24.5 in the previous section, using mutexes.

INPUT   **LISTING 24.8**   Producer/Consumer Example Using Mutex

```
0:  // Listing 24.8 Mutex Producer/Consumer example
1:  #include <iostream.h>
2:
3:  #include "tcreate.h"
4:  #include "mutex.h"
5:
6:  int data;
7:
8:  void read_thread(void* param)
9:  {
10:  Mutex* pMutex = static_cast<Mutex*>(param);
11:
12:  while (1)
13:  {
14:  pMutex->Acquire();
15:  cout << "read: " << data << endl;
16:  pMutex->Release();
17:  }
18:  }
19:
20:  void write_thread(void* param)
21:  {
```

```
22:   Mutex* pMutex = static_cast<Mutex*>(param);
23:
24:   while(1)
25:   {
26:   pMutex->Acquire();
27:   cout << "write: " << data++ << endl;
28:   pMutex->Release();
29:   }
30:   }
31:
32:   int main(int argc, char** argv)
33:   {
34:   Mutex lock;
35:   Thread thread1((void*)&write_thread, &lock);
36:   Thread thread2((void*)&read_thread, &lock);
37:
38:   lock.Create();
39:
40:   thread1.Create();
50:   thread2.Create();
51:
52:   for (int i = 0; i < 100000; i++)
53:   ;
54:
55:   lock.Destroy();
56:
57:   thread1.Destroy();
58:   thread2.Destroy();
60:
61:   return 0;
62:   }
```

ANALYSIS Listing 24.8 once again demonstrates the two threads read_thread and
write_thread. However, the threads receive a parameter, a mutex that allows
each thread to safely access global data. Both read_thread and write_thread now
attempt to acquire the shared mutex using the Mutex::Acquire() member function.
When the threads' access is complete, the mutex is released using the Mutex::Release()
member function.

This is an example of re-entrant code.

Semaphores

A *semaphore* is a counter for a resource shared between threads. Semaphores are
counters that must be accessed atomically. *Atomically* means that when one thread is
modifying the value of the semaphore, another thread cannot simultaneously modify that
semaphore value.

Conceptually there are two basic types of semaphores: *binary semaphores* and *counting semaphores.* A binary semaphore never takes on values other than zero or one, and is logically just like a mutex. A counting semaphore can take on arbitrary non-negative values.

A binary semaphore could be used to implement a `SyncLock` object defined in the previous section. The semaphore interface is defined in the header file `semaphore.h`. Listing 24.9 is a brief listing of the interface.

```
int sem_init(sem_t *sem, int pshared, unsigned int value);

int sem_wait(sem_t * sem);

int sem_trywait(sem_t * sem);

int sem_post(sem_t * sem);

int sem_getvalue(sem_t * sem, int * sval);

int sem_destroy(sem_t * sem);
```

Condition Variables

A *condition variable* is a synchronization primitive that allows a thread to wait for some event to occur while allowing another thread to notify the thread when a condition occurs.

The wait/notify paradigm can be implemented using LinuxThread synchronization primitives; therefore, in Listing 24.10, we define a virtual base class for this interface.

INPUT   **LISTING 24.9**   Event Object Definition

```
1:   // Listing 24.9 Event pure virtual class
2:   #if !defined(c_event_h)
3:   #define c_event_h
4:
5:   class Event
6:   {
7:   public:
8:   Event() {};
9:   virtual ~Event() {};
10:
11:  virtual int Wait() = 0;
12:  virtual int Signal() = 0;
13:  };
14:
15:  #endif
```

The pure virtual Event class defined in listing 24.10 contains an interface for an object that either waits for an event or signals an event.

LISTING 24.10 Condition Variable Object

```
1:    // Listing 24.10 Condition variable class
2:    #if !defined(c_cond_h)
3:    #define c_cond_h
4:
5:    #include <pthread.h>
6:
7:    #include "event.h"
8:
9:    class CondVar : public Event
10:   {
11:   public:
12:   CondVar();
13:   virtual ~CondVar();
14:
15:   void Create();
16:   void Destroy();
17:
18:   int Wait();
19:   int Signal();
20:
21:   private:
22:   CondVar& operator=(const CondVar&);       // disallow copy
23:
24:   pthread_cond_t       cond;
25:   pthread_condattr_t   attr;
26:
27:   pthread_mutex_t       mutex;
28:   pthread_mutexattr_t mattr;
29:   };
30:
31:   #endif
```

Listing 24.10 defines the CondVar object using the Event interface defined earlier. A thread would use the CondVar variable as a synchronization primitive in a similar scheme as Mutex. When the thread accessed data, it would call the CondVar::Wait() member function. When it completed its update, it would release the CondVar by calling Signal.

24

Tip

> It is important that the condition variable be initialized as signaled, or you would have a deadlock condition. This implementation of CondVar *always* initializes the condition variable as signaled.

Joining

Joining is a synchronization primitive that causes a thread to wait for another thread to complete. Joining would not be considered a synchronization primitive because the purpose of joining is to wait for another thread to finish and not run simultaneously.

Deadlock

When you are programming in a multithreaded environment, multiple threads are competing for limited resources. If a thread requests a resource that is not available, that thread enters a waiting state.

A thread could conceivably be waiting indefinitely because the resource it is waiting for is held by another waiting thread; this is called deadlock. *Deadlock* is defined as a thread blocked indefinitely competing for the same limited set of resources as another thread.

Four conditions must exist to characterize a deadlock condition:

1. *Mutual exclusion*—At least one lock is non-shareable.
2. *Hold and wait*—One thread is holding a resource and waiting for a resource held by another thread.
3. *Non-pre-emption*—A held resource can only be released by the thread that has ownership.
4. *Circular wait*—There must be a set of waiting threads, {t0, t1, t2, ... t(n)} where t0 is waiting for a lock held by t1, t1 is waiting for a lock held by t2, ... t(n-1) and t(n) is waiting for a lock held by t0.

Recursive deadlock is a condition in which a thread attempts to acquire a resource that it already owns.

Mutual deadlock occurs when two threads acquire separate locks and are blocked waiting for the other thread to release the lock. This is also defined as a *deadly embrace*.

Do	Don't
DO protect data shared among multiple threads so your code is re-entrant. **DO** properly initialize `LinuxThread` synchronization primitives.	**DON'T** forget to release a mutex after it has been acquired.

Summary

The `LinuxThread` library does not completely implement POSIX 1003.1c, but it's almost complete. The major non-compliant feature is using signals.

In the first half of today's lesson we covered processes and process control techniques as well as some basic C++ classes that use the process system calls that were discussed.

The second half of today's lesson focussed on the creation and destruction of threads and thread synchronization primitives.

Q&A

Q How might the acquisition of a mutex be changed to avoid a deadlock?

A When acquiring a mutex, use a timeout value. If the mutex cannot be acquired, the call to timeout will allow the process or thread to continue.

Q How could a deadly embrace be avoided?

A When acquiring multiple mutexes, always acquire the mutexes in the same order and release them in reverse order of acquisition.

Workshop

The Workshop provides quiz questions to help you solidify your understanding of the material covered and exercises to provide you with experience in using what you have learned. Try to answer the quiz and exercise questions before checking the answers in Appendix D, "Answers to Exercises and Quizzes," and make sure you understand the answers before continuing tomorrow.

Quiz

1. List and define the states of a process.
2. Describe the difference between the FIFO and round robin scheduling policies.

3. What is the difference between a binary semaphore and counting semaphore?

4. List and define the four requisites for a deadlock.

Exercises

1. Using a counting semaphore, how could you resolve the race condition when starting threads?

2. Implement the re-entrant example in Listing 24.8 using the condition variable object CondVar.

DAY 25

Interprocess Communication

Interprocess communication (IPC) is the means by which two processes communicate with one another. Today's lesson discusses some of the methods available for processes to communicate with one another.

Linux offers numerous methods for processes on the same system to communicate with one another. The methods include, but are not limited to pipes, named pipes, and System V interprocess communication. Linux also provides other methods for processes on separate systems to communicate as well, such as sockets. This lesson focuses on interprocess communication for processes on the same system.

Background

Before discussing today's topic, we will begin with the definition of an interface that is used for all today's classes. The Object class defined in Listing 25.1 implements a common interface for object creation and deletion.

In order to implement a common interface for object creation and destruction, a pure virtual interface is defined, Object. All IPC objects defined in today's lesson are derived from the Object class.

Each of our objects inherits this interface for creation and destruction. This interface is defined in object.h in the sample code in Listing 25.1.

INPUT **LISTING 25.1** Object Interface

```
1:   //  Listing 25.1 Object classs
2:
3:   #if !defined(c_object_h)
4:   #define c_object_h
5:
6:   class Object
7:   {
8:   public:
9:   virtual int Create() = 0;
10:  virtual int Destroy() = 0;
11:  };
12:
13:  #endif
```

Additionally, all our IPC methods use kernel data structures, resources, and handles. As such, it is not applicable to copy these objects. For example, if a user copies a pipe, one instance of the pipe object is closed, and then the other instance's pipe handle is no longer valid. For this reason, all the objects in today's lesson define the copy constructor as a private member function. Additionally, the copy constructor is not implemented. By not implementing the copy constructor, other member functions cannot unintentionally call the copy constructor; any attempt to call the copy constructor will result in a linker error.

Pipes

A *pipe* is a simple method that allows one process to attach its standard input to the standard output of another process. A pipe is a half-duplex communication channel between a parent process and child process.

Linux provides the pipe() system call. pipe returns two file descriptors as an array of file descriptors; file descriptor 0 is the read end of the pipe, and file descriptor 1 is the write end of the pipe. The pipe function prototype is shown following:

```
int pipe( int fd[2] );
```

A *file descriptor* is an integer used to refer to an open file by the kernel. When a process wants to read or write from a file, the file is identified by the file descriptor.

Note	As you learned in Day 24, "System Programming," a child process inherits the open handles of the parent processes. This includes handles used for pipes.

Typical usage of a pipe is for a parent process to create a pipe and call `fork()` to create a child process. Because a child process inherits all the parent processes' file descriptors, both the parent and child now contain file descriptors that reference to one another. To complete the setup for a half-duplex pipe for the child to write to the parent, the child process closes `fd[0]`, the read file descriptor, and the parent closes `fd[1]`, the write file descriptor. What remains is the write file descriptor for the child and the read file descriptor for the parent. This sequence of events creates a half-duplex pipe for the child to write to the parent. Figure 25.1 shows a diagram of a pipe between two processes.

FIGURE 25.1

Pipe between two processes.

25

After the pipe is created and the necessary setup has been completed, communication is accomplished by using standard read and write calls.

Pipes, by default, use blocking IO. That is, if a pipe performs a read and there is no data to read, the pipe *blocks* until data is available. If a user does not want to block, the pipe can be opened with the O NONBLOCK flag to disable IO blocking.

Listing 25.2 defines the `Pipe` class. This class encapsulates the pipe system calls.

INPUT **LISTING 25.2** Pipe Class Definition

```
1:   // Listing 25.2 Pipe class
2:   #if !defined(c_pipe_h)
3:   #define c_pipe_h
4:
5:   #include <unistd.h>
```

continues

LISTING 25.2   CONTINUED

```
6:   #include <object.h>
7:
8:   class Pipe : public Object
9:   {
10:  public:
11:  Pipe();
12:  ~Pipe();
13:
14:  int Create();
15:  int Destroy();
16:
17:  void SetToRead();
18:  void SetToWrite();
19:
20:  int ReadFromPipe(char*);
21:  int WriteToPipe(char*);
22:
23:  private:
24:  Pipe& operator=(const Pipe&);     // disallow copy
25:
26:  bool init_;
27:  bool read_;
28:  int pipe_[2];
29:  };
30:
31:  #endif
```

ANALYSIS   The `Pipe` class defined in Listing 25.2 implements the routines discussed in this lesson related to pipes. The parent and the child decide which process reads and which process writes, each process calls either the `SetToRead` or `SetToWrite` member function. After each process initializes its pipe for read or write, it calls either the `ReadFromPipe` or `WriteToPipe` member functions to transfer data.

Pipes are limited to parent/child processes.

The half-duplex pipe must be created and set up by both processes. If either process is not ready, that is, a process writes to a pipe which the other process has not opened for reading, or reads from a pipe which the other process has not opened for writing, the signal `SIGPIPE` is returned.

Half-duplex pipes are implemented using process file descriptors. Because file descriptors are process resources, the file descriptors are returned to the system when the process exits.

Do	**Don't**
DO use a pipe for processes that share the parent child relationship	**DON'T** write to a pipe unless both processes have set up their respective ends of the pipe.

popen and `pclose`

Alternatively, Linux provides another way to create a half-duplex pipe, `popen()`.

```
FILE *popen ( char *command, char *type);
```

The popen system call creates a pipe, performs a `fork`, and then calls `execs` to run the requested command. Read or write access to the pipe created by popen is determined by the `type` argument. The return value from popen is an iostream and must be closed with `pclose`.

To close the stream created by popen, a user should call `pclose`. `pclose` terminates the pipe and returns and process resources to the system.

```
FILE* popen(ls, "r");
```

Named Pipes (FIFOs)

A *named pipe* is a method that allows independent processes to communicate. Named pipes are traditionally called FIFOs (first in first out) in the UNIX world. A named pipe is similar to a pipe; it is a half-duplex pipe between two processes. The difference between a pipe and a named pipe is that when processes are done using the named pipe, the named pipe remains in the system.

Another difference between pipes and named pipes is that because a named pipe is a part of the file system, the named pipe must be opened and closed like a file.

The procedure for using a named pipe is similar to using the `pipe` system call. One process opens the named pipe for writing and another process opens the named pipe for reading. Once the named pipe is open by both the processes, the processes communicate with one another via the named pipe. A named pipe can be created in multiple ways. The shell commands `mknod` and `mkfifo` can be used to create a named pipe. Also a process can use the `mknod()` system call.

```
int mknod( char *pathname, mode_t mode, dev_t dev);
```

25

Note   The mknod shell command is typically reserved for root; however, any user can create a named pipe using mknod.

After the pipe is created, data is passed between the two processes using standard read and write system calls: fopen, fclose, fread, and fwrite.

Listing 25.3 shows our implementation of a named pipe object.

INPUT   **LISTING 25.3**   NamedPipe Class Definition

```
1:   // Listing 25.3 NamedPipe class
2:   #if !defined(c_np_h)
3:   #define c_np_h
4:
5:   #include <sys/types.h>
6:   #include <sys/stat.h>
7:   #include <stdio.h>
8:   #include <object.h>
9:
10:  class NamedPipe : public Object
11:  {
12:  public:
13:  NamedPipe();
14:  ~NamedPipe();
15:
16:  int Create();
17:  int Create(char* name);
18:  int Destroy();
19:
20:  int Open();
21:  int Close();
22:
23:  int Read(char* buf, int len);
24:  int Write(char* buf, int len);
25:
26:  private:
27:  NamedPipe& operator=(const NamedPipe&);      // disallow copy
28:
29:  bool    init_;
30:  FILE*   fp_;
31:  char*   name_;
32:  };
33:
34:  #endif
```

ANALYSIS The Create function is overloaded to either take the name of a named pipe or use a default. After the named pipe is created, it must be opened. After the NamedPipe object is opened, the object can be read from or written to using the Read and Write member functions.

When you are done using the NamedPipe, you should call Close to close the pipe handle and the Destroy function to clean up the kernel data structures related to this connection.

Do	**DON'T**
DO use a named pipe to communicate between any two unrelated processes.	DON'T write to a pipe unless both processes have completed initialization.

System V IPC

AT&T UNIX System V presented three added forms of interprocess communication for processes on the same system: messages, semaphores, and shared memory.

Each of these methods of interprocess communication—messages, semaphores, and shared memory—are described in this section along with a class demonstrating their usage.

25

Key Creation

Each of the mentioned IPC methods uses a key to identify itself. Before delving into the details of System V IPC, we will briefly discuss keys and develop a class to manage keys for the IPC methods.

Creation of a key is the first step in using System V interprocess communication. A key is a non-negative integer. In order for processes to access an IPC method, the method must use a key. A key is of type key_t.

Processes using System V interprocess communication must agree on the key. There are multiple ways for processes to agree on the same key value. In this section, we will call our processes client and server.

- A server can create a new key by specifying IPC_PRIVATE as a key in the appropriate msgget(), semget(), or smget() system call. After creating the key, the server must write the key to a location to be retrieved by the client, a file for example. msgget, semget, and smget are system V IPC routines that create instances of the IPC methods.

- The client and server can agree on a key and share the key in a common header file.
- The client and server can agree on a pathname and an ID and call the system function ftok() to generate a key. ftok is a system call that creates a key based on the input filename and process ID.

In Listing 25.4, we develop a C++ class that manages System V IPC keys. Each of the IPC objects must have a key object to function properly.

INPUT   **LISTING 25.4**   Key Class Definition

```
1:    // Listing 25.4 Key class
2:    #if !defined(c_key_h)
3:    #define c_key_h
4:
5:    #include <object.h>
6:    #include <sys/types.h>
7:    #include <sys/ipc.h>
8:
9:    class Key
10:   {
11:   public:
12:   Key();
13:   ~Key();
14:
15:   int Create(char* name, char id);
16:   int Create(key_t key);
17:   void Destroy();
18:
19:   key_t Get(void);
20:
21:   private:
22:   Key& operator=(const Key&);      // disallow copy
23:
24:   bool  init_;
25:   key_t key_;
26:   };
27:
28:   #endif
```

ANALYSIS   The first step in obtaining a key is creating a key object and calling the Create member function. Create is overloaded, so you can pass a predefined key or have a key created by passing in a filename and an ID. After the key is created, you can obtain the key value by calling the Get member function.

IPC Permission Structure

Each method for IPC contains an `ipc_perm` structure. The `ipc_perm` structure contains the permissions and owner for the IPC object. Listing 25.5 Shows the Linux `ipc_perm` structure.

INPUT **LISTING 25.5** Linux `ipc_perm` Structure

```
 1:    struct ipc_perm
 2:    {
 3:    __kernel_key_t      key;
 4:    __kernel_uid_t      uid;
 5:    __kernel_gid_t      gid;
 6:    __kernel_uid_t      cuid;
 7:    __kernel_gid_t      cgid;
 8:    __kernel_mode_t      mode;
 9:    unsigned short      seq;
10:    };
```

ANALYSIS When an interprocess communication method is created, the `ipc_perm` structure is automatically filled in. During the life of an IPC object, the user may modify the uid, gid, and mode fields via the `msgctl`, `semctl`, or `shmctl` functions. In order to change these fields, the user must have been the creator of the IPC object or superuser. Each of the interprocess communication system calls that create an interprocess communication method takes a flags argument that defines the permissions for that object. Those flags are used to fill in the `ipc_perm` structure.

25

`ipcs` and `ipcrm` Commands

System V interprocess communication methods are implemented in the kernel. If a process exits without cleaning up its IPC methods, the method will remain in the kernel. The `ipcs` and `ipcrm` commands are used to display the status of IPC methods and clean up any residual IPC resources.

The `ipcs` command is used to obtain the status of all IPC objects. Following is the result of using the `ipcs` command—two shared memory segments on my system, IDs 78592 and 78593.

```
------ Shared Memory Segments --------
key         shmid   owner     perms   bytes   nattch    status
0x00bc614e 78592    paul      666     1024    0
0x0000162e 78593    paul      666     64      0

------ Semaphore Arrays --------
```

```
key        semid      owner      perms      nsems      status

------ Message Queues --------
key        msqid      owner      perms      used-bytes messages
```

The `ipcrm` command is used to remove an IPC object from the system. Using the example in the preceding section, we will use the `iprm` command to remove one of the shared memory sections. The following demonstrates the removal of shared memory id 78593.

```
resource deleted
```

Now that we have removed shared memory id 78593, we will rerun the `ipcs` command to verify that the shared memory method has been removed. Following is the results of rerunning the ipcs command.

```
------ Shared Memory Segments --------
key        shmid      owner      perms      bytes      nattch     status
0x0000162e 78593      paul       666        64         0

------ Semaphore Arrays --------
key        semid      owner      perms      nsems      status

------ Message Queues --------
key        msqid      owner      perms      used-bytes messages
```

As you can see the shared memory segment is removed. You may also note that there are no message queues or semaphores on the system.

Message Queues

Message queues are a method for processes to send messages (data) to one another. A message queue is a linked list of messages maintained by the kernel. Messages are added and removed from a FIFO queue by processes. Each message consists of a message ID, message data, and the number of bytes in the message data. Figure 25.2 shows a message queue.

For each message queue, the kernel maintains `msqid_ds` structure defined in the standard kernel header `<linux/msg.h>`. Listing 25.6 shows the Linux `msqid_ds` structure. The `msqid_ds` structure maintains pointers to the messages, number of messages on the queue and other related information about the message queue such as process id of the last process that sent a message and last process that received a message.

FIGURE 25.2

The message queue.

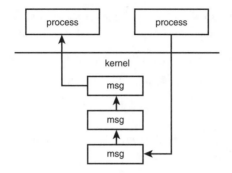

FIFO Message Queue

INPUT   **LISTING 25.6**   Linux msqid_ds Structure

```
1:    /* one msqid structure for each queue on the system */
2:    struct msqid_ds {
3:    struct ipc_perm msg_perm;
4:    struct msg *msg_first;        /* first message on queue */
5:    struct msg *msg_last;         /* last message in queue */
6:    __kernel_time_t msg_stime;    /* last msgsnd time */
7:    __kernel_time_t msg_rtime;    /* last msgrcv time */
8:    __kernel_time_t msg_ctime;    /* last change time */
9:    struct wait_queue *wwait;
10:   struct wait_queue *rwait;
11:   unsigned short msg_cbytes;    /* current number of bytes on queue */
12:   unsigned short msg_qnum;    /* number of messages in queue */
13:   unsigned short msg_qbytes;    /* max number of bytes on queue */
14:   __kernel_ipc_pid_t msg_lspid;    /* pid of last msgsnd */
15:   __kernel_ipc_pid_t msg_lrpid;    /* last receive pid */
16:   };
```

ANALYSIS   Pointers to the actual message queue are the *first and *last members of the
msqid_ds structure shown in Listing 25.6.

Before a message queue can be used, it must be created. The msgget() system call creates a new message queue. msgget() returns the message queue identifer. The message
queue identifer is an int. This identifer is used for the remaining message functions.
Msgget() returns an integer msgqid value, and this msgqid value is passed into the other
msg* functions.

```
/* Get messages queue.  */
extern int msgget __P ((key_t __key, int __msgflg));
```

The key parameter is the key discussed in the previous section. The msgflg parameter is access permissions for the message queue bitwise ORed with the following flags:

- IPC CREAT   Create the queue if it does not exist.
- IPC EXCL   If used with IPC CREAT, fail if queue already exists.

Messages are posted to the message queue using the msgsnd() system call.

```
/* Send message to message queue.  */
extern int msgsnd __P ((int __msqid, void *__msgp, size_t __msgsz,
         int __msgflg));
```

msgsnd() takes as arguments a type struct msgbuf. msgbuf is defined in <linux/msg.h>, size, and msgflag. The msgbuf type is a model definition for the actual message passed to msgbuf. Listing 25.7 shows the Linux msgbuf structure. The size parameter is the size of the message in bytes.

INPUT   **LISTING 25.7**   Linux msgbuf Structure

```
1:    /* message buffer for msgsnd and msgrcv calls */
2:    struct msgbuf {
3:    long mtype;        /* type of message */
4:    char mtext[1];     /* message text */
5:    };
```

An IPC programmer typically redefines the message to conform to the standard msgbuf definition in msh.h. For example, a message could be defined as shown in Listing 25.8.

INPUT   **LISTING 25.8**   Sample User ipc_message msgbuf Structure

```
1:    typedef struct ipc_message
2:    {
3:    long    mtype;
4:    long    header
5:    char    payload[8];
6:    } ipc_message;
```

This message is defined as a message header, mtype. The message type must be a non-negative integer, a header, and payload that is application-specific. The kernel does not modify the message data in any way. The header may be used as a flag to denote how the payload data should be interpreted.

Messages are read from a message queue by calling the msgrcv() system call. The parameter msgtype allows you to exercise some granularity when reading messages. Msgtype values and definitions are as follows.

```
/* Receive message from message queue.  */
extern int msgrcv __P ((int __msqid, void *__msgp, size_t __msgsz,
           long int __msgtyp, int __msgflg));
```

The values for `msgflg` are defined as follows:

- If `msgtype` is zero, the first message on the queue is returned.

- If `msgtype` is greater than zero, the message with an equal message type is returned.

- If `msgtype` is less than zero, the first message with the lowest type that is less than or equal to the absolute value of message is returned.

When an application is done using the message queue, the message queue should be removed from the system. The system call `msgctl` is used to remove a message queue from the system.

```
/* Message queue control operation.  */
extern int msgctl __P ((int __msqid, int __cmd, struct msqid_ds *__buf));
```

Listing 25.9 defines a `Message` object. The `Message` object encapsulates all the message system calls defined in this section.

25

INPUT   **LISTING 25.9**   Message Object

```
1:    // Listing 25.9 Message class
2:    #if !defined(c_message_h)
3:
4:    #define c_message_h
5:
6:    #include <sys/types.h>
7:    #include <sys/ipc.h>
8:    #include <sys/msg.h>
9:    #include <object.h>
10:   #include <key.h>
11:
12:   class Message : public Object
13:   {
14:   public:
15:   Message(Key k);
16:   ~Message(void);
17:
18:   int Create(void);
19:   int Create(int flags);
20:   int Destroy(void);
21:
22:   virtual int Read(char* buf, int len, long type);
```

continues

LISTING 25.9 CONTINUED

```
23:  virtual int Write(char* buf, int len, long type);
24:
25:  private:
26:  Message& operator=(const Message&);      // disallow copy
27:
28:  typedef struct
29:  {
30:  long type;
31:  char *payload;
32:  } TheMessage;
33:
34:  bool  init_;
35:  Key   key_;
36:  int   msgqid_;
37:  };
38:
39:  #endif
```

ANALYSIS The Message object defined in Listing 25.9 contains the standard Create and Destroy member functions defined for all our objects. Note that the constructor takes a Key object. The client and server processes create a Key object by either passing in the same key value or using the same filename and ID; this way they will create a Message object that references the same message queue. After the Message object has been created, the client and server processes send and receive messages using the Read and Write member functions.

The Message object encapsulates the message system calls described in this section. Sample code for this section contains a demonstration of the Message object; the program msgtest uses the Message object to send and receive messages.

Semaphores

Semaphores are a method used to synchronize operations between two processes. Semaphores are not a method to pass data between processes, like messages, but rather a means for two processes to synchronize access to some shared resource.

For a process to obtain access to a resource, the process will test the value of the semaphore. If the value is greater than zero, the process decrements the value by one. If the value is zero, the process blocks until the value is greater than one. When the process is done accessing the resource, it releases it by incrementing the semaphore value by one.

25

> **Note**
>
> A semaphore whose values are limited to zero and one is called a *binary semaphore*. System V semaphores are not limited to zero and one but can be any non-negative integer.

As described in the preceding section, the process of acquiring a semaphore requires two steps; first test the value, and then decrement the value. For this method to work properly among multiple processes, the test and decrement operations must be atomic. In order to make the test and decrement operations atomic, the implementation of these operations is done in the kernel.

For each semaphore in the kernel, the kernel maintains a `semid_ds` structure. `semid_ds` is defined in `<linux/sem.h>`. Listing 25.10 shows the Linux `semid_ds` structure.

INPUT   **LISTING 25.10**   Linux `semid_ds` Structure Definition

```
 1:   /* One semid data structure for each set of semaphores in the system. */
 2:   struct semid_ds {
 3:     struct ipc_perm     sem_perm;        /* permissions .. see ipc.h */
 4:     __kernel_time_t     sem_otime;        /* last semop time */
 5:     __kernel_time_t     sem_ctime;        /* last change time */
 6:     struct sem     *sem_base;          /* ptr to first semaphore in array */
 7:     struct sem_queue *sem_pending;/* pending operations to be processed */
 8:     struct sem_queue **sem_pending_last;     /* last pending operation */
 9:     struct sem_undo     *undo;            /* undo requests on this array */
10:     unsigned short     sem_nsems;        /* no. of semaphores in array */
11:   };
```

ANALYSIS   Before a semaphore can be used, it must be created. The `semget()` `system call` creates a new semaphore. `semget()` returns a semaphore identifier or `-1` if a semaphore cannot be created. The semaphore identifier is an `int`. This identifer is used for the remaining semaphore functions. The function prototype for `semget` is shown in the following lines:

```
/* Get semaphore.  */
extern int semget __P ((key_t __key, int __nsems, int __semflg));
```

Note the value of `nsems`. `semget` can create multiple semaphores in a single call. If `semget` is used to create multiple semaphores, the semaphores are numbered beginning with 0.

After a semaphore is created with `semget()`, a semaphore is accessed using the `semop()` system call.

```
/* Operate on semaphore.  */
extern int semop __P ((int __semid, struct sembuf *__sops,
                unsigned int __nsops));
```

`semop` takes as an argument a `sembuf` structure, which is defined in Listing 25.11.

```
1:  /* semop system calls takes an array of these. */
2:   struct sembuf {
3:     unsigned short  sem_num;     /* semaphore index in array */
4:     short           sem_op;      /* semaphore operation */
5:     short           sem_flg;    /* operation flags */
6:  };
```

`sembuf` uses the `sem_num element` to denote the semaphore being accessed, `sem_op` for the operation, and `sem_flag` for the value of the operation. Valid operations are defined in `sem.h`. The `semid` is used in case you are dealing with multiple semaphores. Using the `semop` structure, you can perform multiple operations in a single call to `semop`.

For example, a member function that acquires the semaphore is implemented this way using the `sembuf` and `semop` system calls. Listing 25.12 shows the implementation of the `Acquire` member function, which is implemented using the `semop` system call.

```
1:int Semaphore::Acquire()
2:{
3:// test the semaphore and decrement
4:static struct sembuf lock[1] =
5:{
6:{0, 1, IPC_NOWAIT}
7:};
8:
9:int len = sizeof(lock) / sizeof(struct sembuf);
10:
11:int stat = semop(semid_, lock, len);
12:
13:return stat;
14:}
```

Semaphores have one more system call, semctl(). semctl() is used to remove a semaphore from the system.

```
/* Semaphore control operation.  */
extern int semctl __P ((int __semid, int __semnum, int __cmd, ...));
```

Listing 25.13 defines a semaphore class that illustrates the uses of the semaphore system calls defined in this section.

INPUT **LISTING 25.13** Semaphore Class Definition

```
1:   // Listing 25-13 Semaphore class
2: #if !defined(c_semap_h)
3: #define c_semap_h
4:
5: #include <sys/sem.h>
6: #include <key.h>
7: #include "object.h"
8:
9: class Semaphore : public Object
10: {
11: public:
12:   Semaphore(Key);
13:   ~Semaphore(void);
14:
15:   int Create(void);
16:   int Create(int flags);
17:   int Destroy(void);
18:
19:   int QueryValue();
20:
21:   int Acquire(void);
22:   int Release(void);
23:
24: private:
25:   Semaphore& operator=(const Semaphore&);     // disallow copy
26:
27:   bool  init_;
28:   Key   key_;
29:   int   semid_;
30:};
31:
32:#endif
```

ANALYSIS The Semaphore object defined in Listing 25.13 contains the standard Create and Destroy member functions defined for all our objects. Once again, note that the constructor takes a Key object; the client and server processes create a Key object by

25

either passing in the same key value or using the same filename and ID. This way they will create a `Semaphore` object that references the same semaphore. After the semaphore has been created, the client and server processes access the semaphore by calling the `Acquire` and `Release` member functions.

The `Semaphore` object encapsulates the semaphore system calls described in this section. The `semtest` program contained on the CD-ROM demonstrates the use of the `Semaphore` object.

Shared Memory

Shared memory is a method that allows two processes to share data directly. Refer back to the earlier discussion of message queues, pipes, and named pipes. Each of these inter-process communication methods allows multiple processes to pass data between each other. A performance issue with these methods of interprocess communication is that the data copied between the processes is copied from the source process into the kernel, and then from the kernel into the destination process. These copies are expensive.

Shared memory allows multiple processes to get a pointer to an area of memory that is shared between the processes. Having a pointer to a segment of memory eliminates the expensive copies in and out of the kernel.

Shared memory is not without its own drawbacks. Even though each of the processes have access to a segment of memory, the accesses to that memory must be synchronized.

Process synchronization to shared memory is typically implemented using semaphores, as described in the previous section.

Before shared memory can be used, it must be created, the `shmget()` creates a shared memory section.

```
/* Get shared memory segment.  */
extern int shmget __P ((key_t __key, int __size, int __shmflg));
```

Each shared memory segment is maintained in the kernel by a `shmid_ds` structure. `shmid_ds` is defined in `<kernel/shm.h>`. Listing 25.14 shows the Linux `shmid_ds` structure.

INPUT **LISTING 25.14** Linux `shmid_ds` Structure Definition

```
1: struct shmid_ds {
2:     struct ipc_perm      shm_perm;    /* operation perms */
3:     int            shm_segsz;    /* size of segment (bytes) */
4:     __kernel_time_t      shm_atime;    /* last attach time */
5:     __kernel_time_t      shm_dtime;    /* last detach time */
```

```
6:      __kernel_time_t        shm_ctime;    /* last change time */
7:      __kernel_ipc_pid_t     shm_cpid;    /* pid of creator */
8:      __kernel_ipc_pid_t     shm_lpid;    /* pid of last operator */
9:      unsigned short         shm_nattch;    /* no. of current attaches */
10:     unsigned short          shm_unused;     /* compatibility */
11:     void               *shm_unused2;     /* ditto - used by DIPC */
12:     void               *shm_unused3;    /* unused */
13:};
```

The shmget() system call opens or creates a shared memory segment but does not provide access to the shared memory. In order for a process to access shared memory, the process must attach to shared memory. The shmat() system call returns a pointer to the shared memory segment:

```
/* Attach shared memory segment.  */
extern void *shmat __P ((int __shmid, __const void *__shmaddr,
[ic:ccc] int __shmflg));
```

When a process is finished with shared memory, it must detach the shared memory segment from the process. This is done by calling shmdt().

```
/* Detach shared memory segment.  */
extern int shmdt __P ((__const void *__shmaddr));
```

After all processes detach the shared memory, the shared memory segment must still be deleted. This is accomplished by calling the shmctl() system call.

```
/* Shared memory control operation.  */
extern int shmctl __P ((int __shmid, int __cmd, struct shmid_ds *__buf));
```

Listing 25.15 defines a SharedMemory object that encapsulates all the shared memory system calls defined in this section.

INPUT   **LISTING 25.15**   SharedMemory Class Definition

```
1:   // Listing 25.15 Shared memory classs
2:   #if !defined(c_smem_h)
3:
4:   #define c_smem_h
5:
6:
7:
8:   #include <sys/shm.h>
9:   #include <string.h>
10:  #include <key.h>
11:  #include <object.h>
```

continues

25

LISTING 25.15   CONTINUED

```
12:
13: class SharedMemory : public Object
14: {
15:  public:
16:
17:    SharedMemory(Key k);
18:    ~SharedMemory(void);
19:
20:    int Create(void);
21:    int Create(int flags, int size);
22:    int Destroy(void);
23:
24:    char* Attach(void);
25:    void Detach(void);
26:
27:    int Read(char* buf, int len, int offset);
28:    int Write(char* buf, int len, int offset);
29:
30:  private:
31:  SharedMemory& operator=(const SharedMemory&);      // disallow copy
32:
33:  bool    init_;
34:  Key     key_;
35:  int     shmid_;
36:  char*   shmaddr_;
37: };
38:
39: #endif
```

ANALYSIS   The SharedMemory object defined in Listing 25.15 contains the standard Create
and Destroy member functions defined for all our objects. Note that the constructor takes a Key object. The client and server processes create a Key object by either passing in the same key value or using the same filename and ID. This way they will create a SharedMemory object that references the same shared memory segment. After the shared memory object has been created, the client and server processes can read and write to shared memory directly using the pointer returned by the shmat system call. It is important to note that access to shared memory should be synchronized using a semaphore.

IPC

Linux also supports the ipc() system call. ipc is a centralized system call that is used to implement the System V IPC calls under Linux. ipc() is only implemented under Linux and is not portable across other UNIX systems. Any of the System V IPC system calls mentioned today can be called using the `ipc` system call. Following is the `ipc` function prototype:

```
int  ipc(unsigned  int  call,  int  first, int second, int
         third, void *ptr, long fifth);
```

Summary

Today we have defined various methods available to the Linux programmer for inter-process communication. Each of the sections of this lesson discusses the use of the methods as well as the details for using the methods.

In the first half of this lesson, we discussed some of the first methods available to UNIX programs for interprocess communication, pipes and named pipes.

In the next half of the lesson, we discussed System V interprocess communication, messages, semaphores and shared memory and developed some C++ object to use these IPC methods.

Q&A

Q What advantage is there for using message queues over a pipe? A named pipe?

A Message queues are a full-duplex channel. Pipes and named pipes are half-duplex.

Q Why is it important to synchronize access to shared memory?

A Because processes are running independently of one another, each of the processes could write to shared memory and corrupt the data read, or written, by the other process.

Workshop

The Workshop provides quiz questions to help you solidify your understanding of the material covered and exercises to provide you with experience in using what you've learned. Try to answer the quiz and exercise questions before checking the answers in Appendix D, "Answers to Exercises and Quizzes," and make sure that you understand the answers before continuing to tomorrow's lesson.

Quiz

1. List the three routines used to create System V interprocess communication methods.

25

2. What signal is thrown if the read and write ends of a pipe are set up?

3. Why is shared memory faster than messages?

4. What is a binary semaphore?

Exercises

1. Implement a client/server program where the client and server share data using the SharedMemory class and synchronize access to shared memory using the Semaphore class.

2. Using pipes, set up a full-duplex communication between a parent and child process.

3. Extend the NamedPipe class to be able to open non-blocking pipes and a Read member function that does not block if there is no data available.

WEEK 4

DAY 26

GUI Programming

In the previous lessons, you have seen how the C++ language is constructed, its syntax and data types, and how you can create objects in it that can interact to produce useful and working programs on the Linux Operating System.

In this lesson, you will take these concepts further and see how you can use classes and objects to represent *real* objects graphically so you can interact with them and your program with a mouse or other graphical input device.

Today you will learn:

- What a Graphical User Interface (GUI) is, and why it is so important for Linux
- How GUIs represent familiar objects as *widgets* with which you can interact
- The history of GUIs on UNIX
- Two new and *free* GUIs or *desktops* for Linux
- How to write basic Linux GUI applications using the development toolkits that come with the GUI distributions
- How to write simple cross-platform C++ GUI applications using the wxWindows toolkit

The Linux Desktop

Until recently, one of the most often heard complaints against Linux (as well as all other UNIXes) as an operating system was that it had only a command-line interface in the form of a "shell" or simple text on the screen. This means that you interact with the computer by typing commands as text and you get the output in the same way: as text. Not even pretty text either: awful chunky single-spaced typewriter text with no formatting, as likely as not.

This is fine for computer freaks and developers, and it is also fine for server systems that connect to other more user-friendly client applications that the real users sit at, but it is a massive obstacle in getting Linux where it belongs: onto the desktop, literally. Your average computer user wants results from the thing, not seemingly endless argument and complaints about bad inputs.

Things began to pick up in the early to mid-1980s when many applications appeared with an intermediate step in user interfaces between the command-line interface and the Graphical User Interface (GUI, usually pronounced "gooey").sThis was the non-graphical menu-based interface, which let you interact by using a mouse rather than by having to type in keyboard commands. Even so, the interface was still chunky and ugly because pictures and boxes were drawn using the line-characters in the extended ASCII character set. Not as nice as the GUIs of today.

Nowadays, of course, most important operating systems, such as all flavors of Windows, the Macintosh, and OS/2, provide a true GUI where the objects with which the user interacts are drawn cleanly and precisely pixel-by-pixel.

Applications typically use the elements of the GUI that come with the operating system and add their own GUI elements and ideas. A GUI sometimes uses one or more metaphors for objects familiar in real life: desktops, windows, or the physical layout of a building.

Note

> When this lesson uses the word "window" or "windows" with a lower case "w," we are talking about the generic bounded object on a screen in which we view data; if we are talking specifically about Microsoft's family of operating systems, we use the capitalized "Windows."

Elements of a GUI include such things as windows, menus, buttons, check boxes, sliders, gauges, scroll bars, icons, emotional-icons that change their nature in real time as you traverse the file system, wizards, mice, joysticks, and dozens of other things. Multimedia devices now form part of most GUIs, and sound, voice, motion video, and virtual reality interfaces seem likely to become a standard part of the GUI for many applications.

A system's graphical user interface along with its input devices is sometimes referred to as its "look and feel." Another thing that tends to characterize GUI application is that they are typically *event driven* rather than *procedural*. This means that a GUI application typically sits and waits for you to ask it to do something rather than starting at the beginning and following a logical path to some end point, and then terminating. Note that an event driven program can still have procedural things happening inside it. An example of this is a GUI Integrated Development Environment which will wait for you to ask it to build the program (an event) and will then run make for you to do the build (procedural).

The GUIs familiar to most people in these modern operating systems and their applications originated at the Xerox Palo Alto Research Laboratory in the late 1970s. Apple used it in their first Macintosh computers; later, Microsoft used many of the same ideas in their first version of the Windows operating system for IBM-compatible PCs. Yet this is not true of Linux: Linux does not have a native GUI, unlike operating systems like Windows NT and the Apple Macintosh where the GUI *is* the operating system, at least in part.

So the thing that really sets Linux apart from other modern operating systems is that even though you can create a GUI for it, using a graphics card, the capabilities of the monitor, and software to drive the whole thing, the GUI is not actually part of the operating system itself. Rather, it is layered on top of it and disguises much of the operating system's command-line complexity from the user. This is generally reckoned to be A Good Thing by most users.

Although this may seem like a trivial and even pedantic difference between it and the operating systems that do have native GUI functionality, it is a difference that provides Linux—and you—with enormous scope for flexibility.

26

Linux is new, but its antecedents, the multifarious flavors of UNIX too numerous to mention, have been around for decades, and people have indeed attempted in the past to use the standard graphics capabilities of UNIX in the form of the X Windowing system to provide GUI functionality. But X programming is complex and difficult (see the sidebar "The X Protocol and More Recent Developments"), and even toolkits like Motif and its free clone LessTif, which are designed to hide much of the awful detail of X programming, barely succeed in making a bad job any better.

The X Protocol and More Recent Developments

You have probably noticed in this lesson that we often mention "X" in connection with graphics on UNIX.

The X Org, a non-profit consortium made up of members, developed the X Protocol in the mid-1980s to answer the need for a network-transparent graphical user interface primarily for the UNIX operating system.

X provides for the display and management of graphical information, in much in the same way as Microsoft's Windows Graphics Device Interface (GDI) and IBM's Presentation Manager.

The chief difference is in the design of the X Protocol itself. Microsoft Windows and IBM's Presentation Manager simply display graphical information on the PC on which they are running, whereas the X Protocol distributes the processing of applications by specifying a client-server relationship at the application level.

The *what to do* part of the application is called an X client and is logically and often physically separated from the *how to do* part, the display, called the X server. X clients typically run on a remote machine that has excess computing power and displays on an X server. This is a true client-server relationship between an application and its display, and has all the attendant advantages of this relationship.

To achieve this separation, the application (X client) is divorced from the display (X server), and the two communicate using a socket-based asynchronous protocol that operates transparently over a network.

X further provides a common windowing system by specifying both a device-dependent and an independent layer. Essentially, the X Protocol hides the quirks of the operating system and the underlying hardware from the applications that use them. In theory, different hardware sets will present a common software interface and still have very different internals.

This is all very well in theory, but the reality of it is that the Xlib API, written in C, incidentally, is extremely complicated, and X programming is considered to be something of a black art.

People have written various layers on top of Xlib in recent times to try to simplify X programming, but these attempts, most notably Motif and its free clone, LessTif, are only partly successful (the API is still hideous) and, in any case, the "look and feel" is now starting to look dated.

Much more recently we have seen developments like GTK++ (a C API layered on top of GLib and GDK, which itself is a layer on top of Xlib), wxWindows (a C++ layer on top of GTK++) and TrollTech's Qt library (a C++ layer on top of Xlib on UNIX and on top of the GDI on Windows).

All this layering might begin to give you a headache, but it really is no cause for concern: Even the more familiar C++ graphics libraries like Microsoft's MFC and Borland's C++ Builder classes are little more than C++ layers on top of the native Windows C API, and the Graphics Device Interface (GDI). Indeed, GDK++, wxWindows, and Qt in particular

> seem to have at last got it right. The two latter libraries provide for platform-independent source trees; that is, you write it once, compile it for your platform using the native library toolkit, and run it. This is somewhat like Java, except that the compilation is done before you send the code out and not when the user runs it.
>
> The Qt and wxWindows examples later in this lesson will compile and run on both Linux and Windows platforms.

But here is a dilemma: we have a first-class, powerful, robust, and *free* operating system that your average user won't want to use because its GUI looks like what it is: tired, dated, and thoroughly unpleasant.

Fortunately for Linux and for us, the programmers who will be called upon to write the new applications, two new projects have put Linux firmly on the desktop with their incredibly successful attempts to turn the Linux GUI into a superb and eminently usable interface.

These two projects are the GNOME project (GNU Network Object Model Environment) from GNU, and the K Desktop Environment (KDE) from the KDE Project. Both of these are free software and released under the GPL. KDE does have one or two licensing issues to do with its underlying TrollTech Qt graphics library, but these seem to have been resolved in the main; however, this does appear to deter hard-core GNU aficionados from embracing the KDE as genuinely free software.

This lesson examines the GNOME and the KDE and creates some basic applications to show how simple writing GUI-driven software for these environments can be.

26

What Is the GNOME?

The GNOME is the GNU Network Object Model Environment, and, of course, the GUI desktop from the GNU Project.

To quote from the original announcement from usenet newsgroup `comp.os.linux.announce`, GNOME is intended to be

> "a free and complete set of user-friendly applications and desktop tools, similar to CDE and KDE but based entirely on free software."

And indeed, the GNOME is everything you would expect from a modern programming environment.In this respect, it is roughly the same as Common Desktop Environment (CDE), Win32, NextStep, and KDE.

The big difference is that, in contrast to the examples just mentioned, every single component of GNOME is free and released under either the GPL or the LGPL. Not only that, but the GNOME is extremely flexible compared to most desktop environments. As an added bonus for the user, you can easily customize it to suit your particular needs.

The GNOME uses the Object Management Group's Common Object Request Broker Architecture (CORBA) to allow software components to interoperate seamlessly, regardless of the language in which they are implemented, or even on what machine they are running. Not only this, but the GNOME developers are working hard on developing an object model called Bonobo, based on CORBA, which is similar to Microsoft's Object Linking and Embedding, v2 (OLE2).

Bonobo will allow programmers to export and import resources as components and will, for example, allow users to use whatever editor they like in their development environment, provided that their editor is supported via a CORBA standardized editor interface.

The GNOME uses the Gimp Tool Kit (GTK+++) as the graphics toolkit for all graphical applications. GTK+++ has a lot of excellent features and sprang from the development of the GNU Image Processing Program (GIMP), which deserves a book all by itself. Because GTK++ underpins GNOME, they both use Imlib, an image library for the X Window System, which supports multiple image formats, from XPM to PNG, and multiple bit-depths, from 24-bit True Color down to 1-bit Black and White, all transparently to the programmer.

GNOME applications are session-aware: If you shut down, say, the GNOME word processor and then start it back up again, it will open up the document that you had open before, and put your cursor back at the same place. This is made possible by the X Session Management system, as implemented in the GNOME Session Manager.

The GNOME also supports the *Uniforum* standard internationalization and localization methods, allowing support for new languages to be added without even requiring a recompile of the application.

In truth the GNOME can be a bit of a pain to install owing to its many dependencies and so on, but Linux vendors now put it in the standard distribution. Red Hat Linux 6.1, for example, comes with GNOME, and you can install it as your default desktop at installation time.

Getting the GNOME and Other GNOME Resources

The GNOME home page is at http://www.gnome.org/. If you are impatient about getting the software, you can go directly to the Linux download page at http://www.gnome.org/start. You will find the GNOME FAQ at http://www.gnome.org/gnomefaq/ and a whole load of other useful information at http://www.gnome.org/gdp, and http://www.gnome.org/mailing-lists/index.shtml has a comprehensive list of GNOME-related mailing lists.

If you are interested in developing GNOME itself or applications that use GNOME, it will be worth your time to look at http://developer.gnome.org/ where you will find lots of extra information and resources.

The current release of GNOME is 1.0.53.

Getting GTK++ and Other GTK++ Resources

The GTK++ home page is at http://www.gtk.org/ and you can download the latest release from ftp://ftp.gtk.org/pub/gtk/v1.2/. The GTK++ home page has a lot of links to other useful sites and essential documentation.

You can get GTK—, a free C++ wrapper library around GTK++, from http://gtkmm.sourceforge.net/. The distribution also includes gnome— a C++ wrapper for the GNOME libraries. At the time of writing, January 2000, gnome— seemed to be undocumented, and GTK— somewhat unstable. It may be worth your while checking out these projects again.

For GTK++ 1.1.7 (current version) and higher, you will need LibSigc++ 0.8.5 or higher. You can get this from http://www.ece.ucdavis.edu/~kenelson/libsigc++/.

What Is the KDE?

The KDE used to be "the Kool Desktop Environment", but, thankfully they have dropped the "Kool" from the name.

The KDE is a network-transparent modern desktop environment for UNIX workstations. It admirably fulfills the need for an easy-to-use desktop for UNIX workstations, similar to the desktop environments found under the MacOS and Windows.

With the advent of KDE, an easy-to-use modern desktop environment is now available for UNIX that rivals anything out there in the commercial market. Like the GNOME, KDE can be a real pain to install, but it too comes with several vendors' releases of Linux. Red Hat Linux 6.1 also comes with KDE 1.1.2, and you can install it as your default desktop instead of the GNOME. In fact, you can configure your machine to switch you into either a GNOME session or KDE session each time you log on.

26

Note | Although installing the standard distributions of GNOME and KDE from the CD is an easy and tempting way to get it up and running, one drawback you may find is that some of the latest releases of useful software, like KDevelop, KOffice, and GNOME Office, require more recent versions of the core libraries than are available on the CD. This is inevitable, as the CD releases have to be frozen at some point.

In combination with Linux, KDE provides a completely free and open computing platform available to anyone free of charge including its source code for anyone to modify to suit their own ends.

Although this is generally true, there are some issues surrounding the Qt libraries that interface the KDE to the depths of the Xlib interface, and for many purists this means that KDE is not free software. Certainly you do not have to pay to use it or modify it or distribute it, but you cannot *sell* software you write using the KDE libraries unless you buy a professional license from TrollTech.

Whatever the purists' objections, and although there will always be room for improvement, the KDE developers, a loosely coupled group of programmers linked together by the Internet, have delivered a viable alternative to some of the more commonly found and commercial operating systems/desktop combinations you can get.

To the user, KDE offers, among other things

- An integrated help system allowing for convenient, consistent access to help on the use of the KDE desktop and its applications.
- Consistent look and feel of all KDE applications.
- Standardized menu and toolbars, key-bindings, color-schemes, and so on.
- Internationalization: KDE is available in more than 25 languages.
- A vast number of useful KDE applications.

In truth the default look and feel of KDE is remarkably like the Window 95 UI, something I believe not to be entirely coincidental.

Getting KDE and Other KDE Resources

The KDE home page is at http://www.kde.org/, and you can download it from any one of the mirror sites listed at http://www.kde.org/mirrors.html/. Links from this page cover topics ranging from the KDE mailing list archives, to KDE documentation, to KDE T-shirts and cuddly toys (I am not making this up).

If you are thinking of developing KDE applications, you will need the free release of TrollTech's Qt libraries; you can get this from their Web site at http://www.troll.no/. The latest version of Qt is 2.0.2. Note that the free version covers you only for X-applications. If you want to compile and link your code on Windows platforms, or you want to sell your programs, you need to buy their Professional package.

KDE is currently running at version 1.1.2, but version 2.0 is promised for spring 2000.

You can read about and download KDevelop by visiting http://www.kdevelop.org/. It is currently at version 1.1beta1, but this number seems to be changing almost daily. By the time you are reading this book, it will have been upgraded several times, so it will be worth checking the home page for the latest release.

Programming in C++ on the Linux Desktop

To help programmers use the services provided by the GNOME and the KDE, each exports an API that programmers can write to and thus ensure compatibility between and consistency across other programs written for the desktop. Applications conform to a set format, or *application framework*; this is a term that will be familiar to anyone who has programmed using Microsoft's MFC or Borland's C++ Builder.

In the KDE the Qt library provides the framework and the mechanism the Qt objects use to communicate with one another; in the GNOME, the GNOME API provides similar services. We call the objects on the UNIX GUI *widgets*. See the sidebar "Widgets."

We will see a third framework in the wxGTK library. This library is similar to the Qt framework, and, indeed, the Microsoft and Borland frameworks in that it implements a Document/View framework where the Document conceptually represents data objects and the View conceptually represents the user's view of those data.

26

Widgets

In computing terms, a *widget* is an element of a graphical user interface (GUI) that displays information or provides a specific way for a user to interact with the operating system and application programs. Widgets include icons, pull-down menus, buttons, selection boxes, progress indicators, on-off checkmarks, scroll bars, windows, window edges (that let you resize the window), toggle buttons, forms, and many other devices for displaying information and for inviting, accepting, and responding to user actions.

In programming, a widget also means the small program that is written in order to describe what a particular widget looks like, how it behaves, and how it interacts with the user. Most operating systems include a set of predefined widgets that a programmer can incorporate in an application, specifying how it is to behave. You can create new widgets by extending existing ones, or you can write your own from scratch.

> The term was apparently applied first in UNIX-based operating systems and the X Window System. In object-oriented programming (OOP), each type of widget is defined as a class (or a subclass under a broad generic widget class) and is always associated with a particular window. In the AIX Enhanced X-Window Toolkit, for instance, a widget is the fundamental data type.

Fundamentals of GNOME Programming

The GNOME is the GNU desktop and unlike the KDE is written entirely in C.

It is based upon the excellent GTK++ library, which is itself a C wrapper library around the GDK, which is a wrapper around the native Xlib libraries (see the sidebar "The X Protocol and More Recent Developments").

Although this is a book on how to learn C++, it is worth taking a brief look at the GTK++ and GNOME C APIs to illustrate some useful programming concepts that follow the more relevant C++ wrapper libraries examined later in this lesson.

First, because the GNOME uses GTK++ as its graphics engine, we will take a brief look at GTK++. GTK++ is a library for creating graphical user interfaces. It is licensed using the LGPL license, so you can develop open software, free software, or even commercial software using GTK++ without having to spend anything for licenses or royalties.

It is called the GIMP Toolkit because it was originally written for developing the General Image Manipulation Program (GIMP, another truly excellent free-software application), but GTK++ has now been used in a large number of software projects, including the GNU Network Object Model Environment (GNOME) project.

GTK++ is built on top of GDK (GIMP Drawing Kit), which is basically a wrapper around the low-level functions for accessing the underlying windowing functions (Xlib in the case of the X windows system). GTK++ is essentially an object-oriented API. Although written completely in C, it is implemented using the idea of classes and callback functions (pointers to functions).

There is a thin-layered C++ binding to GTK++ called GTK—, which provides a more C++-like interface to GTK++. In the current release, GDK++ 1.2, there is also a library called gnome—, which is a C++ wrapper around the GNOME's C API. But gnome— seems to be immature at the moment, a fledgling thing at best. This may have changed, of course, by the time you read this.

If you are determined to use C++, you have three choices:

- First, you can always use one of the specialized wrapper libraries that wraps the GDK++ C API in C++ classes in much the same way as GTK— does. In today's lesson, this is what we actually do because it ties in neatly with the KDE programming environment and thus makes meaningful comparisons easier.

- Secondly, if you don't want to trust your applications to gnome— or yet another C++ wrapper library for whatever reason, you can use only the C subset of C++ when interfacing with GTK++ and then use the C interface. Remember that C is a valid subset of C++ and a valid C program is a valid C++ program, broadly speaking.

- Finally, you can use GTK++ and C++ together by declaring all callbacks as static functions in C++ classes, and again calling GTK++ using its C interface. The buttons example shown in Listing 26.1 does this.

If you choose this third approach, you can include as the callback's data value a pointer to the object to be manipulated (the this pointer).

Selecting between these choices is largely a matter of preference, because in both approaches you get C++ and GTK++. Personally I find the second solution rather ugly and inelegant, and I prefer to use a C++ wrapper library, but your mileage may vary.

None of these approaches requires the use of a specialized preprocessor, so no matter what you choose, you can use standard C++ with GTK++.

Now let us look at the GNOME itself, where it sits above GTK.

A true GNOME program is a GTK+++ GUI application that also uses the GNOME libraries. The GNOME libraries make it possible to have a similar look and feel among applications, and to make simple things simple to program. Not only that, but the GNOME libraries add a lot of widgets that do not properly belong in GTK++.

Unfortunately for budding C++ programmers, the GNOME, like its supporting graphics library, GTK++, has a C API. To be sure, the API is strongly object-oriented and uses opaque structures and accessor functions and so on, but it is nevertheless a C API. You do, of course, have the same three options to choose from for GNOME programming as you do for GTK++ programming.

It is worth your while to look at a small GNOME program (see Listing 26.1) and see how it fits in with the GNOME desktop. You will also see how you can declare a simple class with static member functions that act as callbacks. You could, of course, make the class as complicated and functionally rich as you liked.

26

INPUT **LISTING 26.1** A Basic Gnome Program: `buttons.cc`

```
01: /*
02:  * A basic Gnome program: buttons.cc
03:  */
04:
05: #include <gnome.h>
06:
07: class callback {
08:   public:
09:     static void clicked(GtkWidget *button, gpointer data);
10:
11:     static gint quit(GtkWidget *widget, GdkEvent *event, gpointer data);
12: };
13:
14: void
15: callback::clicked(GtkWidget *button, gpointer data)
16: {
17:   char string = (char*)data;
18:   g_print(string);
19:   g_print(""using C++ callback\n""));
20: }
21:
22: gint
23: callback::quit(GtkWidget *widget, GdkEvent *event, gpointer data)
24: {
25:   gtk_main_quit();
26:   return FALSE;
27: }
28:
29: int
30: main(int argc, char *argv[])
31: {
32:   GtkWidget *app;
33:   GtkWidget *button;
34:   GtkWidget *hbox;
35:
36:   /* Initialize GNOME, this is very similar to gtk_init */
37:   gnome_init ("buttons-basic-example", "0.1", argc, argv);
38:   app = gnome_app_new ("buttons-basic-example","Buttons");
39:
40:   hbox = gtk_hbox_new (FALSE,5);
41:
42:   gnome_app_set_contents (GNOME_APP (app), hbox);
43:
44: /* bind "quit_event to gtk_main_quit */
45:   gtk_signal_connect (GTK++_OBJECT (app), "quit_event",
46:                       GTK++_SIGNAL_FUNC (callback::quit), NULL);
47:
48:   button = gtk_button_new_with_label("Button 1");
```

```
49:     gtk_box_pack_start (GTK++_BOX(hbox), button, FALSE, FALSE, 0);
50:     gtk_signal_connect (GTK++_OBJECT (button), "clicked",
51:                         GTK++_SIGNAL_FUNC (callback::clicked),"Button 1\n");
52:
53:     button = gtk_button_new_with_label("Button 2");
54:     gtk_box_pack_start (GTK++_BOX(hbox), button, FALSE, FALSE, 0);
55:     gtk_signal_connect (GTK++_OBJECT (button), "clicked",
56:                         GTK++_SIGNAL_FUNC (callback::clicked),"Button 2\n");
57:
58:     gtk_widget_show_all(app);
59:     gtk_main ();
60:
61:     return 0;
62: }
```

ANALYSIS The first portion of the code, lines 7–27, contain the declaration of the `class`
`callback` and its `static` callback functions that we created to respond to events
that the GUI detects when we click the displayed buttons:

As you can see, the functions are simple and straightforward, with
`callback::clicked()` merely printing some text to `stdout` at `line 19` (compare to
`cout` in C++) and `callback::quit()` exiting the main program at line 25.

The first call we make in `main()` is to `gnome_init()` at line 37.

This is very similar to a pure GTK++ application where we would call `gtk_init()`; similarly we use a call to `gnome_app_new()` at line 38 to give us an instance of a new
GNOME application. In a pure GTK++ application, the corresponding call would be to
`gtk_window_new()`.

Although `gnome_app_new()` returns a `GtkWindow`, we later verify that to a `GnomeApp` with
the `GNOME_APP` macro. The `GnomeApp` is the principal widget behind each application. It is
the main window of the application containing the document being worked on, the applications menus, toolbars and status bars, and so on. It also remembers the docked positions of menu bars and toolbars and such, so that the user gets the window the way the
application left it when it last shut down.

Creating a new `GnomeApp` widget is as easy as calling `gnome_app_new()` with the name of
the application name and the title of the main window. You can then create the content of
the main window and add it to the `GnomeApp` widget by calling `gnome_app_set_`
`contents()` with your contents as the argument.

In this case, we create a horizontal box to hold the buttons we will shortly be creating
and add it to the application widget at lines 40 and 42.

26

The GnomeApp application framework is part of the libgnomeui library, and it is the part that truly makes a GNOME application a GNOME application. It also makes programming GNOME applications reasonably simple and straightforward, and makes the applications comprehensive and consistent across the desktop. With plain GTK+++ you have to do a lot of things by yourself, but GnomeApp takes care of the standard GNOME UI setup for you and still allows the user to configure the behavior and have it be consistent over different applications.

Lines 45–56 link the callback::quit()event handler to its callback function and then create two buttons and link them to the callback::clicked() event handler, before adding them to the horizontal box.

This means that when we click one of the buttons, the event will be routed to and processed by the callback::clicked() callback function.

Finally, at lines 58 and 59, we tell the main application widget to show itself and all its contents, and then enter the main event loop and await the clicking mouse.

To build this program, you can use the following command:

```
gcc -g -Wall `gnome-config --cflags gnome gnomeui`LDFLAGS=`gnome-config \
--libs gnome gnomeui` buttons.cc -o buttons
```

The Figure 26.1 shows you what your buttons program ought to look like.

OUTPUT

FIGURE 26.1

The output of the buttons *program.*

Wrapping GTK++ with wxWindows

In the last section, you saw how you can use C++ with the GNOME libraries to create GNOME applications.

As far back as 1992 a group of programmers at Edinburgh University in Scotland created version 1.0 of the wxWindows toolkit. The *wxWindows toolkit* is a set of pure C++ libraries that make GUI development much easier. It allows C++ applications to compile and run on several different types of computers, with few if any source code changes.

During 1997 an effort to produce a standard Linux desktop environment was underway— GNOME. Its widget set was GTK++, built on top of X, and it looked as though GTK++ based apps were to become the standard in the Linux universe. This led the wxWindows development team to reaffirm their commitment and release wxWindows 2.0.

Strictly speaking, wxWindows is not a GNOME development environment because wxWindows does not itself use the GNOME libraries. However, it may be that this capability will be included in future releases because, on Linux, wxWindows is aimed explicitly at the GTK++ and GNOME environments. Even so, a wxWindows program will run quite happily under KDE and the GNOME and will take on the look and feel of whatever desktop it is under at the time; but, and this may be important to some users, it will not have access to the desktop functions that GNOME and KDE provide.

> **Note**
>
> Each supported GUI has its own library (such as GTK++, Motif, or Windows); the name wxWindows is the generic name for the whole suite of libraries. The one we are most interested in is wxGTK, which is the specific library that wraps GTK++. However, like the wxWindows documentation, we will use the terms wxWindows and wxGTK synonymously except where the difference is important.

26

In addition to providing a common API for GUI functionality on a wide range of platforms, wxWindows provides functionality for accessing some commonly used operating system facilities, such as copying or deleting files, and will soon include a set of classes to provide cryptographic services.

Hence wxWindows is a "framework" in the sense that it provides a lot of built-in functionality, which the application can use or replace as required, thus saving a great deal of coding effort. It also supports a set of basic data structures, such as strings, linked lists, and hash tables.

But wxWindows is not a translator from one GUI to another: It cannot take a Motif application and generate a Windows application, for example. To program using a *native* GUI interface, you need to learn a *new* API. However, the wxWindows API has been praised for its intuitiveness and simplicity, and can be far easier to learn and use than a native GUI API such as Motif or Windows. The message is simple: if you know wxWindows (or Qt for that matter), you don't need to know the native GUI APIs.

Such a toolkit is not unique—there are several to choose from—but wxWindows is *completely* free under the GPL, well-established, well-documented, and quite broad in its coverage of GUI functionality.

The weight thrown behind GNOME and GTK++, by Red Hat Labs and others, could thrust wxWindows into a fairly important position, as the only tool that can be used to eventually produce GNOME-compatible products as well as Windows, Motif, Mac, and maybe BeOS versions. Linux is becoming an increasingly important and respected variant of UNIX, and this will result in some mainstream wxGTK applications.

Now that you know what wxWindows is, let's see how you can use it.

Creating Your First wxWindows Application—"Hello World"

Listing 26.2 shows the source code for the simplest wxWindows application you can get.

INPUT   **LISTING 26.2**   The wxWindows GNOMEHelloWorld Program

```
01: /*
02:  * GNOMEHelloWorld.cpp
03:  */
04:
05: #ifdef __GNUG__
06: // #pragma implementation
07: #endif
08:
09: // For compilers that support precompilation,
10: #include "wx/wxprec.h"
11:
12: #ifdef __BORLANDC__
13: #pragma hdrstop
14: #endif
15:
16: #ifndef WX_PRECOMP
17: #include "wx/wx.h"
18: #endif
19:
20: class MyApp: public wxApp
```

```
21: {
22:     virtual bool OnInit();
23: };
24:
25: class MyFrame: public wxFrame
26: {
27: public:
28:
29:     MyFrame(const wxString& title,
30:             const wxPoint& pos,
31:             const wxSize& size);
32:
33: };
34:
35: IMPLEMENT_APP(MyApp)
36:
37: bool MyApp::OnInit()
38: {
39:     MyFrame *frame = new MyFrame( "Hello World",
40:                                   wxPoint(50,50),
41:                                   wxSize(200,100) );
42:     frame->Show(TRUE);
43:     SetTopWindow(frame);
44:     return TRUE;
45: }
46:
47: MyFrame::MyFrame(const wxString& title,
48:                  const wxPoint& pos,
49:                  const wxSize& size)
50:        : wxFrame((wxFrame *)NULL, -1, title, pos, size)
51: {
52: }
```

26

ANALYSIS The first thingwe do is include the wxWindows header files in lines 5–18 of the code listing. You will notice some pragmas and #ifdef conditionals: these are normal and help make the source truly portable. Elsewhere in the wxWindows toolkit there are some other macros we can include to help with different compilers and so on, but for clarity we will be assuming a Linux environment only. Thus you can safely ignore these macros from now.

You can include the headers individually, of course, for example `#include "wx/window.h"` or using one global include, that is `#include "wx/wx.h"`. This is especially useful on platforms that support precompiled headers, such as all major compilers on the Windows platform.

The code proper starts at line 20 of the listing where we declare our own application class, deriving it from the standard wxApp class. Practically every wxWindows

application should define a new class derived from wxApp. We can then override
wxApp::OnInit() to initialize the program as we do at line 22.

In lines 25–33 we derive the main window from wxFrame; we name the frame by passing
it a string ("Hello World") as a parameter to its constructor, as you will see later in the
code.

The next line of code, line 35, may seem a little strange, but it becomes clear what it is
when you consider that *all* C++ programs must have a main() function as the program
entry point. The IMPLMENT_APP() macro implements main and instantiates an application
object, as well as beginning the main event loop of the program.

The member function wxApp::OnInit(), implemented in lines 37–45, executes at startup
and initializes the program by creating the main window and showing splash screens and
so on. You'll see here that the frame is given the title in the call to its constructor on
MyApp::OnInit() at line 39.

To compile the program, use the following command:

```
g++ GNOMEHelloWorld.cpp `wx-config —libs` `wx-config —cflags` \
-o GNOMEHelloWorld
```

OUTPUT When you run the program, you should see a single window with the title "Hello
World" running across the top of the pane (see Figure 26.2).

FIGURE 26.2

*The first
GNOMEHelloWorld
program.*

Adding Buttons to Your Own wxWindows Window Class

The first application, as you saw in Listing 26.2, is a fully functioning GNOME program, but is quintessentially boring. It allows no user interaction other than to terminate it.

To make it more interesting, you can add a few lines to it and put in some buttons that will allow you to interact with it. In wxWindows, the framework you usually put buttons and other widgets inside a wxPanel object; a wxPanel is essentially a wxWindow with a bit of extra functionality. These panels usually reside in dialog boxes, but, as you will see in the following example, they can appear almost anywhere.

First, let us take a look at the complete source listing for the new code in Listing 26.3.

INPUT **LISTING 26.3** The wxWindows GNOMEHelloWorld Program with Buttons

```
01: /*
02:  * GNOMEHelloWorld.cpp
03:  */
04:
05:
06: #ifdef __GNUG__
07: // #pragma implementation
08: #endif
09:
10: // For compilers that support precompilation,
11: #include "wx/wxprec.h"
12:
13: #ifdef __BORLANDC__
14: #pragma hdrstop
15: #endif
16:
17: #ifndef WX_PRECOMP
18: #include "wx/wx.h"
19: #endif
20:
21:
22: class MyApp: public wxApp
23: {
24:     virtual bool OnInit();
25: };
26:
27: class MyFrame: public wxFrame
28: {
29: public:
30:
31:     MyFrame(const wxString& title,
```

continues

LISTING 26.3 CONTINUED

```
32:                 const wxPoint& pos,
33:                 const wxSize& size);
34:
35:     void OnQuit(wxCommandEvent& event);
36:     void OnGreet(wxCommandEvent& event);
37:
38:     DECLARE_EVENT_TABLE()
39:
40: private :
41:             wxPanel *m_panel;
42:             wxButton *m_btnGreet;
43:             wxButton *m_btnQuit;
44: };
45:
46:
47: enum
48: {
49:     ID_Quit = 1,
50:     ID_Greet,
51: };
52:
53: BEGIN_EVENT_TABLE(MyFrame, wxFrame)
54:     EVT_BUTTON(ID_Greet, MyFrame::OnGreet)
55:     EVT_BUTTON(ID_Quit, MyFrame::OnQuit)
56: END_EVENT_TABLE()
57:
58: IMPLEMENT_APP(MyApp)
59:
60: bool MyApp::OnInit()
61: {
62:     MyFrame *frame = new MyFrame( "Hello World",
63:                                   wxPoint(50,50),
64:                                   wxSize(200,100) );
65:     frame->Show(TRUE);
66:     SetTopWindow(frame);
67:     return TRUE;
68: }
69:
70:
71: MyFrame::MyFrame(const wxString& title,
72:                  const wxPoint& pos,
73:                  const wxSize& size)
74:         : wxFrame((wxFrame *)NULL, -1, title, pos, size)
75: {
76:     wxSize panelSize = GetClientSize();
77:     m_panel = new wxPanel(this, -1, wxPoint(0, 0), panelSize);
78:
79:     int h = panelSize.GetHeight();
```

```
80:      int w = panelSize.GetWidth();
81:
82:      m_btnGreet = new wxButton(m_panel, ID_Greet,_T("Greet"),
83:                                wxPoint(w/2-70,h/2-10),
84:                                wxSize(50,20));
85:      m_btnQuit = new wxButton(m_panel, ID_Quit,_T("Quit"),
86:                                wxPoint(w/2+20,h/2-10),
87:                                wxSize(50,20));
88: }
89:
90: void MyFrame::OnQuit(wxCommandEvent& WXUNUSED(event))
91: {
92:      Close(TRUE);
93: }
94:
95: void MyFrame::OnGreet(wxCommandEvent& WXUNUSED(event))
96: {
97:      wxMessageBox("This is a wxWindows Hello world sample",
98:                   "Greet Hello World",
99:                   wxOK | wxICON_INFORMATION,
100:                   this);
101: }
```

ANALYSIS Probably the first differences you will notice are in the declaration of the class MyFrame. In lines 35–43 we have now added some extra functions and member variables to the MyFrame class.

The lines 35 and 36 declare two ordinary public member functions, OnQuit() and OnGreet(). You will see that they both take a wxCommandEvent pointer as their sole argument; astute readers will deduce from this that these member functions are intended to respond to events in some way. Indeed, their very names are a clue in themselves.

Next you will see the macro DECLARE_EVENT_TABLE() at line 38. What this does is insert code that will act as a framework in the class to enable us to map events to the functions that should handle them. You will see more of this in a moment.

Finally, the extra code in this declaration includes three member variables, a wxPanel and two wxButtons to put on it.

Immediately under the changed class declaration, you will see some more new code in lines 47–56.

This new code first declares two new enumerated identifiers for identifying events, and then attaches these event identifiers to the new member functions you saw declared earlier. It uses the EVENT_TABLE() macros to associate the event identifiers with the functions that will handle the event objects created. The table defined in lines 53–57 is telling us

26

that the `MyFrame::OnQuit()` member function will handle events occurring with the `ID_Quit` identifier, and that the `MyFrame::OnGreet()` member function will handle events with the `ID_Greet` identifier.

Next you will notice that we have filled out the body of the `MyFrame` constructor with code to initialize, position, and then display the buttons we promised would be included in the application.

The first line of the constructor at line 76 merely gets us the size of the client area of the `MyFrame` object; a `wxSize` object represents the x (length) and y (height) dimensions of the client area. We use this `wxSize` object at line 77 to create a new `wxPanel` that completely fills the client area of the `MyFrame` object.

Note that the first parameter to the `wxPanel` constructor, a pointer to the panel's parent wxWindows object, is `this`, meaning that it belongs to the `MyFrame` object. The default constructor for the `wxPanel` class takes several parameters that determine where it is placed, how large it is, and so on. In line 77, we give it a default ID of –1, set its origin in the topmost left corner of the `MyFrame` object (`wxPoint(0,0)`), and give it the dimensions established in `panelSize`.

We also use panel Size for calculating the positions of the buttons. In this sense it is "frivolous" code as it serves a merely cosmetic function. We reduce the size to its component values, the `int`s `h` and `w` in lines 79 and 80.

Finally we create the buttons you have been waiting for so patiently. We create two of them and make them both belong to the panel we just created. If you look at the constructor arguments we are passing, it is pretty much self-evident what is going on. For instance, on line 82, the button `m_btnGreet` is being given the event identifier `ID_Greet`. From the earlier code, it is evident that this button will generate `ID_Greet` events when used.

You will also note that we set the text of the button in the constructor arguments. The remaining arguments to the constructor that we see specify its position (determined by the height and width of the panel) and its size. Note that we have hard-coded constant values here: This is bad programming practice in general, but we use it here to keep the code more readable.

We create the `m_btnQuit` button in much the same way.

The very last section of the code implements the two event handlers, `OnGreet()` and `OnQuit()`, in lines 90–101.

The only matter of interest here is the `wxMessageBox()` function, beginning on line 97, that displays a message in a box on the screen.

To compile the program, use the following command:

```
g++ GNOMEHelloWorld.cpp `wx-config —libs` `wx-config —cflags` \
-o GNOMEHelloWorld
```

OUTPUT When you run the program, you should see a single window (see Figure 26.3) with the title "Hello World" running across the top of the pane and two buttons marked "Greet" and "Quit" centered in the client area. Clicking the Greet button wins you a salutation, and clicking Quit does the obvious.

FIGURE 26.3

The second GNOMEHelloWorld program, with buttons.

Object Interaction Using Events

Before adding more functionality to GNOMEHelloWorld, we need to look at how the different objects in a wxWindows program communicate. Like most GUI applications, wxWindows programs tend to be event-driven.

26

Event Handling

Generally speaking, the user has two ways to interact with a GUI program: the mouse and the keyboard. For both ways, a graphical user interface has to provide methods that detect actions and methods that do something as a reaction to these actions.

> When a user moves the mouse, or hits a key, or clicks a mouse button, we describe this as an *event*: It is something that *happens* and conveys information to the system, information that must be identified, routed to the object that is interested in receiving it, and then acted upon.
>
> The window system therefore sends all interaction events to the GUI application that has the screen focus.
>
> We use the word *focus* to describe the application that is currently in the foreground, or the one that will take the current input. In most systems, you typically change the settings so that the application that has focus has a different color border or frame, making it easy to tell which application you are currently using.

Because wxGTK is based upon the GTK++ library, it uses the underlying GTK++ mechanism for handling events: signals and callbacks.

GTK++ is an event-driven toolkit, which means it will wait in gtk_main() until an event occurs and control is passed to the appropriate function.

This passing of control is done using the idea of "signals." When an event occurs, such as the click of a mouse button, the appropriate signal will be "emitted" by the widget that was clicked. This is how GTK++ does most of its useful work. There are signals that all widgets inherit, such as destroy(), and there are signals that are widget-specific, such as toggled() on a toggle button.

Note

Note that *signals* in the context of these discussions on GUI development in GNOME and KDE have nothing to do with traditional UNIX signals such as SIGHUP and so on; it is merely a possibly unfortunate coincidence of nomenclature.

To make a button perform an action, we set up a signal handler to catch these signals and call the appropriate function. This is done by using a function such as the following:

```
gint gtk_signal_connect( GtkObject *object,
                         gchar *name,
                         GtkSignalFunc func,
                         gpointer func_data );
```

The first argument is the widget that will be emitting the signal, and the second is the name of the signal you want to catch. The third is the function you want to be called when it is caught, and the fourth, the data you want to have passed to this function.

The function specified in the third argument is called a "callback function," and should generally be of the form

```
void callback_func( GtkWidget *widget, gpointer    callback_data );
```

where the first argument is a pointer to the widget that emitted the signal, and the second a pointer to the data given as the last argument to the gtk_signal_connect() function as shown earlier.

wxWindows extends this idea of signals and callbacks into its own namespace and uses *event tables* to map events to actions.

You place an event table in an implementation file to tell wxWindows how to map events to member functions. These member functions are not virtual functions, but they are all similar in form: They take a single wxEvent-derived argument, and have a void return type.

You may notice that wxWindows' event processing system implements something very close to virtual methods in normal C++; that is, you can alter the behavior of a class by overriding its event-handling functions.

In many cases this works even for changing the behavior of native controls. You can, for example, also filter out a number of key-press events sent by the system to a native text control by overriding wxTextCtrl and defining a handler for key events using EVT_KEY_DOWN. This would indeed prevent any key-press events from being sent to the native control—which might not be what you want. In this case the event handler function calls Skip() to indicate that the search for the event handler should continue.

In summary, instead of explicitly calling the base class version as you would have done with C++ virtual functions (that is, wxTextCtrl::OnChar()), you should instead call Skip().

In practice, that would look like this if the derived text control only accepts "a" to "z" and "A" to "Z":

```
01: void MyTextCtrl::OnChar(wxKeyEvent& event)
02: {
03:   if ( isalpha( event.KeyCode() ) )
04:   {
05:     // key code is within legal range. we call event.Skip() so the
06:     // event can be processed either in the base wxWindows class
07:     // or the native control.
08:     event.Skip();
09:   }
10:   else
11:   {
12:     // illegal key hit. we don't call event.Skip() so the
```

26

```
13:      // event is not processed anywhere else.
14:      wxBell();
15:   }
16: }
```

You will see that line 3 checks to see if the key code was representing a letter, and calls Skip() at line 8 to continue the search for a handler.

The normal order of event table searching by ProcessEvent is as follows:

1. If the object is disabled, usually with a call to wxEvtHandler::SetEvtHandlerEnabled(), the function skips to step (6).

2. If the object is a wxWindow, call ProcessEvent recursively on the window's wxValidator. Exit the function if this returns true.

3. Call SearchEventTable() for an event handler for this event. If this fails, try the base class, and so on until you run out of tables or find an appropriate function, in which case the function exits.

4. Apply the search down the entire chain of event handlers (usually the chain has a length of one). Exit the function if this step succeeds.

5. If the object is a wxWindow and the event is a wxCommandEvent, recursively apply ProcessEvent to the parent window's event handler. Exit if this step returns true.

6. Call ProcessEvent on the wxApp object.

Adding a Menu to Your Own wxWindows Window Class

Finally, we will add a menu to the simple application we have just developed. We won't be adding any more functionality so much as providing a second way of invoking the functionality we already have.

The code change we have to make is very small, so we do not have to include the entire source file: All we need to do is add some extra code (see Listing 26.4) into the MyFrame constructor.

INPUT   **LISTING 26.4**   The wxWindows GNOMEHelloWorld Program with a Menu

```
01: MyFrame::MyFrame(const wxString& title,
02:                  const wxPoint& pos,
03:                  const wxSize& size)
04:         : wxFrame((wxFrame *)NULL, -1, title, pos, size)
05: {
06:     wxSize panelSize = GetClientSize();
07:     int height = panelSize.GetHeight();
```

```
08:        int width = panelSize.GetWidth();
09:        m_panel = new wxPanel(this, -1, wxPoint(0, 0), panelSize);
10:
11:        m_btnGreet  = new wxButton(m_panel, ID_Greet, _T("Greet"),
12:                                   wxPoint(width/2-70, height/2-10),
13:                                   wxSize(50,20));
14:        m_btnQuit   = new wxButton(m_panel, ID_Quit, _T("Quit"),
15:                                   wxPoint(width/2+20, height/2-10),
16:                                   wxSize(50,20));
17:
18:        wxMenu *menuApp = new wxMenu;
19:
20:        menuApp ->Append( ID_Greet, "&Greet..." );
21:        menuApp ->AppendSeparator();
22:        menuApp ->Append( ID_Quit, "&Quit" );
23:
24:        wxMenuBar *menuBar = new wxMenuBar;
25:        menuBar->Append(menuApp, "&Application" );
26:
27:        SetMenuBar( menuBar );
28: }
```

ANALYSIS We have exactly the same code to begin with, and then simply append the code to create the menu and associate the menu events with the event handlers we already have.

At line 18 we create a new menu header on the main menu bar, and lines 20–22 populate the menu header and determine what you will see when you select the menu header and the menu items drop into view.

We then create on line 24 a menu bar, the actual object you see across the top of the client area, and attach the menu header and its appended items to it on line 25.

Finally, we can set the application's main menu to be the menu bar we have just created on line 27.

To compile the program, use the following command:

```
g++ GNOMEHelloWorld.cpp `wx-config --libs` `wx-config --cflags` \
-o GNOMEHelloWorld
```

OUTPUT When you run the program, you should see the same window as in Figure 26.3, but now with a menu across the top of the client area of the window as in Figure 26.4.

26

Figure 26.4

*The third
GNOMEHelloWorld
program, with menu
and buttons.*

Building More Complex wxWindows Applications— wxStudio

So far we have just created a simple application with a single source file. Larger applications with many source files that require close management would obviously need some form of formal development environment.

The wxWindows project has therefore suggested the wxStudio, their very own Integrated Development Environment. Work on wxStudio is still in the early stages, but it is on release and is available by Concurrent Versions System (CVS) download. Interestingly enough, at least on Windows platforms, the MS DevStudio works reasonably well as an IDE and a debugger for the wxWindows library; how other IDEs compare, I do not know.

Because wxStudio is in such an early stage, it is difficult to pass comment on it other than to say that the plan is for a fully-featured platform-independent IDE with debuggers, resource editors, version control, and much, much more. One of the fundamental tenets of the design is that as many functional modules as possible will be provided as plug-ins to allow the user to configure the IDE with the editor, compiler, whatever-you-like of choice.

Getting wxWindows and Other wxWindows Resources

The wxWindows home page is at `http://www.wxwindows.org/`. wxWindows comes in several flavors, so to speak, and provides the widest range of supported platforms I have ever seen for a package of this type. The one you are primarily interested in for this book is wxGTK, and the download page for that is at `http://www.wxwindows.org/dl_gtk.htm`.

The latest version of wxWindows is 2.1.11 and is a substantial upgrade from version 1. I believe version 1 is now considered to be obsolescent if not obsolete. You will need GTK++ 1.2 for wxGTK 2.1.11.

There is also a set of wxWindows mailing lists at `http://www.wxwindows.org/maillst2.htm`. Some of these are quite high-volume, so watch your inbox.

Fundamentals of KDE Programming

The Qt library is the graphics library that underpins the entire KDE. It is a C++ toolkit developed by TrollTech in Norway, and offers graphical elements you can use for creating X GUI applications.

Additionally, the toolkit offers a complete set of classes and methods ready to use even for non-graphical programming code, a solid framework of user interaction using virtual methods and the unique Qt signal and slot mechanism, and a library of predefined GUI elements, GUI widgets, that you can use to create the visible elements. It also offers predefined dialogs that are often used in applications, such as progress indicators and file dialogs.

26

Thus it is highly desirable that you know how to use the Qt classes, even if you want only to program KDE applications using the KDE application framework. It is well worth a visit to the TrollTech site at `http://www.troll.no/` to browse their excellent documentation and tutorials.

But for now, to understand the basic concepts of how to build Qt/KDE GUI-applications, take a look at a sample KDE program.

Creating Your First KDE Application—"Hello World"

In keeping with tradition, we'll have a look (see Listing 26.5) at the "Hello World" program a la KDE and explain how it works.

LISTING 26.5 The KDEHelloWorld Program

```
01: /*
02:  *KDEHelloWorld.cpp
03: */
04:
05: #include <kapp.h>
06: #include <ktmainwindow.h>
07:
08: int main( int argc, char **argv )
09: {
10:   KApplication MyApp( argc, argv );
11:   KTMainWindow *MyWindow = new KTMainWindow();
12:   MyWindow->setGeometry(50,50,200,100);
13:
14:   MyApp.setMainWidget( MyWindow );
15:   MyWindow->show();
16:   return MyApp.exec();
17: }
```

This basic application simply draws an empty KDE-style window with "Hello world" as its title.

Compile these files with the following commands at the prompt:

```
g++ -c -I$KDEDIR/include -I$QTDIR -fno-rtti KDEHelloWorld.cpp
g++ -L$KDEDIR/lib -lkdecore -lkdeui -lqt -o \
KDEHelloWorld KDEHelloWorld.o
```

ANALYSIS In this application, as with all KDE applications, you first have to instantiate a KApplication object, in this case represented by MyApp at line 10.

We pass the program arguments, argv and argc , to the constructor, too, and it uses these before returning them to main() unaltered.

Following this, we instantiate a KTMainWindow object and call it MyWindow on line 11; as the name suggests, this will be the window you will eventually see displayed on the screen. We size and place the window on the screen with the call to setGeometry() on line 12. We move it to coordinates (50, 50), and change the size to 200×100 pixels (width×height).

Finally, we call the setMainWidget() member function on MyApp, followed by the show() method on MyWindow, on lines 14 and 15 respectively. This tells the Kapplication that its main widget or display object is the window we just created; by calling show() we tell the window to make itself visible.

To run the code in KApplication and to draw the main window, we call the exec() member function on MyApp at line 16.

Calling exec() causes the program to enter the main event loop and wait until it returns an integer to the operating system, thereby signaling that the application has exited.

The chief thing here is that the application enters a so-called "main event loop." This means that the program has to wait for user actions and then react to them; moreover, with a KDE application, the program has to be in the main event loop to start the event handling.

OUTPUT Figure 26.5 shows you what the KDEHelloWorld application should look like when you run it. Note that you may see some cosmetic differences because you may have chosen a different desktop "theme" or color scheme from mine.

FIGURE 26.5

The first KDEHelloWorld program.

Creating Your Own KDE Window Class

The example you have just seen was probably the simplest possible KDE program you can write; let us now extend it a little and derive our own window class from the KTMainWindow class.

We can now change the project source files so they contain the code shown in Listing 26.6. Note that we cannot reasonably use a single source file because we have to run the *Qt Meta Object Compiler* (MOC) on the header file.

26

```
01: /*
02: * KDEHelloWorld.h
03: */
04: #include <kapp.h>
05: #include <ktmainwindow.h>
06:
07: class KDEHelloWorld : public KTMainWindow
08: {
09:   Q_OBJECT
10: public:
12:    void closeEvent(QCloseEvent *);
13: };
14:
15: /*
16:  *KDEHelloWorld.cpp
17: */
18:
19: #include " KDEHelloWorld.moc"
20: #include "KDEHelloWorld.h"
21:
22: void KDEHelloWorld::closeEvent(QCloseEvent *)
23: {
24:   kapp->quit();
25: }
26:
27: int main( int argc, char **argv )
28: {
29:    KApplication MyApp( argc, argv, "Hello World!" );
30:    KDEHelloWorld *MyWindow = new KDEHelloWorld();
31:    MyWindow ->setGeometry(50,100,200,100);
32:
33:    MyApp.setMainWidget( MyWindow );
34:    MyWindow ->show();
35:    return MyApp.exec();
36: }
```

Compile these files with the following commands at the prompt:

```
moc KDEHelloWorld.h -o KDEHelloWorld.moc
g++ -c -I$KDEDIR/include -I$QTDIR -fno-rtti KDEHelloWorld.cpp
g++ -L$KDEDIR/lib -lkdecore -lkdeui -lqt -o KDEHelloWorld main.o \
KDEHelloWorld.o
```

ANALYSIS   You will see in the preceding code that the most marked change from the original simple program is the strange Q_OBJECT macro on line 9, in the class declaration of KDEHelloWorld in KDEHelloWorld.h, and the unfamiliar #include directive on line 19.

You will see exactly what these are for later on in this lesson. For now, it is enough to know that you must include the Q_OBJECT in *all* your KDE derived classes. The reason for this is that the Q_OBJECT is used by the Meta Object Compiler (MOC) to create a .moc file that, when #included, enables communications between KDE widgets using Qt's signals and slots mechanism.

You will also note lines 22–25 that implement the event handler for the QCloseEvent object. Events and event-handlers are what the KDE Application uses to determine how the user is interacting with it. In the preceding case, the QCloseEvent* causes the application to quit. If we wanted to, we could add extra code to ask the user if this was really the desired action, and so on. See the sidebar "Events as QEvent Objects."

The main difference you will see when you run the application is that the window title has now changed from "KDEHelloWorld" to "Hello World!" because in this second example, we specified the title for the application title in the KApplication constructor.

Events as QEvent Objects

The KApplication sends events to the active window as QEvent objects, and the widgets themselves then have to decide what to do with them.

A widget receives the QEvent and calls QWidget::event(QEvent*), which then decides which event has been detected and how to react; event() is therefore the main event handler.

The event() function passes the QEvent object to *event filters*, which determine what happened and what to do with the event. If no filter is responsible for handling a given event, the specialized event handlers are called.

You will see from the Qt documentation that all event handlers are virtual functions and are declared as protected; therefore, you can override the events that you need in your own widgets and specify how your widget has to react. QWidget also contains some other virtual methods that can be useful in your programs.

26

Adding Buttons to Your Own KDE Window Class

So far these KDE applications have been pretty dull, to say the least; we may have a GUI but we are not using it to much effect.

In this third example, we will expand upon the code we have and add a couple of buttons to the application. At the same time we will also introduce an important concept that underpins the whole of the Qt (and hence KDE) application framework: signals and slots.

We will first modify our "Hello World" application to use the signals and slots mechanism before we delve more deeply into the mechanics of it.

You can see the modified source and header files in Listing 26.7.

INPUT   **LISTING 26.7**   The KDEHelloWorld Program with Buttons

```
01: /*
02:  *KDEHelloWorld.h
03:  */
04: #include <kapp.h>
05: #include <ktmainwindow.h>
06: #include <qpushbutton.h>
07:
08: class KDEHelloWorld : public KTMainWindow
09: {
10:   Q_OBJECT
11: public:
12:   KDEHelloWorld();
13:   void closeEvent(QCloseEvent *);
14: public slots:
15:   void SlotGreet();
16:   void SlotQuit();
17: private:
18:   QPushButton *m_btnGreet;
19:   QPushButton *m_btnQuit;
20: };
21:
22:
23: /*
24:  * KDEHelloWorld.cpp
25:  */
26:
27: #include "KDEHelloWorld.moc"
28: #include <kmsgbox.h>
29:
30: KDEHelloWorld::KDEHelloWorld() : KTMainWindow()
31: {
32:   m_btnGreet = new QPushButton("Greet", this);
33:   m_btnGreet->setGeometry(45,30,50,20);
34:   m_btnGreet->show();
35:   connect(m_btnGreet,SIGNAL(clicked()),this,SLOT(SlotGreet()));
36:
37:   m_btnQuit = new QPushButton("Quit", this);
38:   m_btnQuit->setGeometry(105,30,50,20);
39:   m_btnQuit->show();
40:   connect(m_btnQuit,SIGNAL(clicked()),this,SLOT(SlotQuit()));
41: }
42:
```

```
43: void KDEHelloWorld::closeEvent(QCloseEvent *)
44: {
45:   kapp->quit();
46: }
47:
48: void KDEHelloWorld::SlotGreet()
49: {
50:   KMsgBox::message(0," KDEHelloWorld","Hello World!");
51: }
52:
53: void KDEHelloWorld::SlotQuit()
54: {
55:   close();
56: }
```

Compile these files with the following commands at the prompt:

```
moc khello.h -o khello.moc
g++ -c -I$KDEDIR/include -I$QTDIR -fno-rtti KDEHelloWorld.cpp
g++ -L$KDEDIR/lib -lkdecore -lkdeui -lqt -o \
KDEHelloWorld KDEHelloWorld.o
```

ANALYSIS Now you can see that things are *really* starting to move. We have several new elements in the code that deserve some explanation.

First, and most simply, you will notice a call to KMsgBox::message() at line 50.

This puts a simple predefined dialog box on the screen giving the user some information; in this case it doesn't say much other than "Hello World," but you can set it to give any message you like. The first string parameter, "KDEHelloWorld", sets the title for the box, and the second, "Hello World", is the message itself.

The second, more important, thing you should notice is the odd keyword combination public slots: in KDEHelloWorld.h. This is not a standard C++ declaration but is part of the signals and slots mechanism of the Qt library; it essentially tells the Meta Object Compiler that these functions can be called in response to signals being emitted. If you look at the implementation of the KDEHelloWorld constructor, KDEHelloWorld::KDEHelloWorld(), you will see that the calls to connect() on lines 35 and 40 act to associate the clicked() signal with the SlotGreet() and SlotQuit() members of the KDEHelloWorld class (see Figure 26.6).

What all this means, essentially, is that by clicking the m_btnGreet widget you will send a clicked() signal and the Qt library will invoke the KDEHelloWorld::SlotGreet() member function for you and display a message. Similarly, by clicking the m_btnQuit widget, you will send a clicked() signal and the Qt library will invoke the KDEHelloWorld::SlotQuit() member function for you and close the window.

26

FIGURE 26.6

The second KDEHelloWorld program, with buttons.

Signals and slots are core elements of the KDE programming framework and so deserve a more detailed explanation.

Object Interaction Using Signals and Slots

The signal and slot mechanism offers a very powerful and useful solution to the problem of object interaction, which is typically solved by callback functions for most X Window toolkits.

Using callbacks is error-prone and frequently leads to the dreaded segmentation fault if misused, and so it requires a strict programming protocol and sometimes makes user interface creation very difficult. TrollTech devised a new system where objects can emit signals that can be connected to methods declared as slots.

The signal and slot mechanism is a central feature of Qt and probably the element that sets the Qt toolkit apart most from the others.

In most GUI toolkits widgets have a callback for each action they can trigger. This callback is a pointer to a function. In Qt, signals and slots have taken over from these error-prone function pointers.

Signals and slots can take any number of arguments of any type. They are completely *typesafe*: at last, deliverance from callback core dumps!

All classes that inherit from `QObject` or one of its subclasses (for example `QWidget`) can contain signals and slots. Objects emit signals when they change their state in a way that may be interesting to the outside world. This is all the object does to communicate. It does not know if anything is receiving the Signal at the other end; moreover, it does not necessarily care, either. This is true data encapsulation, and ensures that the object can be used as a software component.

Slots can receive signals, but they are otherwise normal member functions. A slot does not know or care if it has one or more Signals connected to it; that is, the object does not know about the communication mechanism and can be used as a true software component. You can connect as many signals as you want to a single slot, and a signal can be connected to as many slots as you want.

An object will emit a signal when its internal state has changed in some way that might be relevant to the object's client or owner. Only the class that defines a signal and its subclasses can emit the signal.

A list-box widget, for example, emits both `highlighted()` and `activated()` signals. Most objects will probably be interested only in `activated()`, but some may want to know about which item in the list box is currently highlighted. If the signal is relevant for two different objects, you can connect the signal to slots in both objects.

When an object emits a signal, the slots connected to it execute just like a normal function call. The signal and slot mechanism is totally independent of any GUI event loop. The emit will return when all slots have returned; if several slots are connected to one signal, the slots will be executed one after the other, in an arbitrary order, when the signal is emitted.

The MOC automatically generates the code that emits signals and you must not implement them in the .cpp file yourself. All signals have return type `void`. You, the application programmer, have the job of implementing the slots all by yourself.

Because slots are normal member functions that can be invoked in mysterious ways that we don't have to worry about here, they have access rights like any other class member. Not surprisingly, a slot's access right determines who can connect to it:

- A `public slots:` section contains slots to which anyone can connect signals. You create objects that know nothing about each other, connect their signals and slots, and pass information between them.

26

- A protected slots: section contains slots to which this class and its subclasses may connect signals. This is intended for Slots that are part of the class's implementation rather than its external public interface.

- A private slots: section contains slots to which only instantiated objects of that class itself may connect signals. This is intended for very tightly connected classes, where even subclasses aren't trusted to get the connections right.

Of course, you can also define Slots to be virtual. This is a very useful feature.

As an example of a typical signal and slots implementation, consider the following minimal C++ class declaration:

```
01: class MyClass
02: {
03:   public:
04:     MyClass();
05:     char Letter() const { return m_cVal; }
06:     void SetValue( char cVal );
07:   private:
08:     char m_cVal;
09:};
```

A small Qt class might be declared thus:

```
01: class MyQtClass : public QObject
02: {
03:   Q_OBJECT // note there is no semi-colon after this macro
04:   public:
05:     MyQtClass();
06:     char Letter() const { return m_cVal; }
07:   public slots:
08:     void SetLetter ( char cVal );
09:   signals:
10:     void LetterChanged( char  cVal );
11:   private:
12:     char  m_cVal;
13: };
```

This class is essentially the same, but in addition to the basic functionality of the simple class, it also has support for component programming using signals and slots: This class can tell the world that it has changed state by emitting a signal, LetterChanged(), and it has a slot to which other objects may send signals. We have told the MOC to provide the code to do this by using the Q_OBJECT macro on line 3 and the signals specifier on line 9.

All classes that contain signals, slots, or both *must* also contain the Q_OBJECT macro in their declaration.

Here is one possible implementation of `MyQtClass::SetLetter()`:

```
01: void MyQtClass::SetLetter( char cVal )
02: {
03:    if ( cVal != m_cVal ) {
04:      m_cVal = cVal;
05:      emit LetterChanged(cVal);
06:    }
07:}
```

Line 7 emits the signal `LetterChanged` from the object. As you can see, you emit a signal by using the call emit signal(args).

If we wanted to connect two instances of the `MyClass` object together, we might write this:

```
01: int main(int argc, char** argv)
02: {
03:    MyQtClass Alice, Bob;
04:    connect(&Alice,SIGNAL(LetterChanged(char)),&Bob,SLOT(SetLetter (char)));
05:    Bob. SetLetter( 'a' );
06:    Alice. SetLetter( 'b' );
07:    Bob.Letter();          // this would now be what? 'b', of course
08:    return(0);
09: }
```

Calling `Alice.SetLetter('b')` will make `Alice` emit a signal, which `Bob` will receive; that is, it invokes `Bob.SetLetter('b')`. `Bob` will in turn emit the same signal, which nobody receives or cares about because we have not connected a slot to it. The signal emitted by `Bob` therefore vanishes into the ether never to be seen again.

A close analogy in the world of callbacks might be a NULL pointer to a callback (which would usually lead to a core dump and a depressed programmer).

Note that the `SetLetter()` function sets the value and emits the signal only if `cVal !=` `m_cVal`. This prevents infinite loops in the program where, for instance `Bob.LetterChanged()` was connected to `Alice.SetLetter()`).

Signals and slots are reasonably efficient, but they are nominally slower than "real" callbacks owing to the layered and flexible nature of the call; however, the loss is acceptably small for all but the most time-critical applications.

To implement the Qt signal and slot mechanism, you have to compile the source code with the Meta Object Compiler (MOC), which comes as part of the Qt library. The MOC parses the class declaration in a C++ file and generates C++ code that initializes the meta object. The meta object contains names of all signal and slot members, as well as pointers to these functions. The preprocessor transparently deals with the signals, slots, and emit keywords so the C++ compiler proper won't see anything it can't digest.

26

Adding a Menu to Your own KDE Window Class

Finally, we will give our simple KDE application a final gloss of respectability by adding a menu to the window.

First we need to modify the source code so it looks like Listing 26.8.

INPUT   LISTING 26.8   The KDEHelloWorld Program with Buttons and Menu

```
01: /*
02:  * KDEHelloWorld.h
03:  */
04:
05: #include <kapp.h>
06: #include <ktmainwindow.h>
07: #include <qpushbutton.h>
08: #include <kmenubar.h>
09: #include <qpopupmenu.h>
10:
11: class KDEHelloWorld : public KTMainWindow
12: {
13:   Q_OBJECT
14: public:
15:   KDEHelloWorld();
16:   void closeEvent(QCloseEvent *);
17: public slots:
18:   void SlotGreet();
19:   void SlotQuit();
20: private:
21:   QPushButton *m_btnGreet;
22:   QPushButton *m_btnQuit;
23:   KMenuBar *m_Menu;
24:   QPopupMenu *m_MenuApp;
25: };
26:
27:
28: /*
29:  * KDEHelloWorld.cpp
30:  */
31:
32: #include "KDEHelloWorld.moc"
33: #include <kmsgbox.h>
34:
35: KDEHelloWorld::KDEHelloWorld() : KTMainWindow()
36: {
37:   m_btnGreet = new QPushButton("Greet", this);
38:   m_btnGreet->setGeometry(45,30,50,20);
39:   m_btnGreet->show();
40:   connect(m_btnGreet,SIGNAL(clicked()),this,SLOT(SlotGreet()));
```

```
41:
42:    m_btnQuit = new QPushButton("Exit", this);
43:    m_btnQuit->setGeometry(105,30,50,20);
44:    m_btnQuit->show();
45:    connect(m_btnQuit,SIGNAL(clicked()),this,SLOT(SlotQuit()));
46:
47:    m_MenuApp = new QPopupMenu();
48:    m_MenuApp->insertItem("&Greet",this,SLOT(SlotGreet()));
49:    m_MenuApp->insertItem("&Quit",this,SLOT(SlotQuit()));
50:    m_Menu = new KMenuBar(this);
51:    m_Menu->insertItem("&Application", m_MenuApp);
52: }
53:
54: void KDEHelloWorld::closeEvent(QCloseEvent *)
55: {
56:    kapp->quit();
57: }
58:
59: void KDEHelloWorld::SlotGreet()
60: {
61:    KMsgBox::message(0,"KDEHelloWorld","Hello World!");
62: }
63:
64: void KDEHelloWorld::SlotQuit()
65: {
66:    close();
67: }
```

Compile these files with the following commands at the prompt:

```
g++ -c -I$KDEDIR/include -I$QTDIR -fno-rtti main.cpp
moc KDEHelloWorld.h -o KDEHelloWorld.moc
g++ -c -I$KDEDIR/include -I$QTDIR -fno-rtti KDEHelloWorld.cpp
g++ -L$KDEDIR/lib -lkdecore -lkdeui -lqt -o KDEHelloWorld main.o \
KDEHelloWorld.o
```

ANALYSIS The first things to notice are the extra member variables to represent the menu objects we have added to the KDEHelloWorld class on lines 23 and 24.

The class-names are self-explanatory, as is the initialization code in the KDEHelloWorld constructor that spans lines 47–51.

OUTPUT When you run this program, you should see something like the screen in Figure 26.7.

26

FIGURE 26.7

The third KDEHelloWorld program, with menu and buttons.

Building More Complex KDE Applications—KDevelop

The sample applications you have seen so far are simple and serve only to illustrate the essentials of the KDE application framework. But for more complicated applications, switching between many source files and navigating the classes and so on is a chore; in any case, no self-respecting GUI desktop would be without a GUI Integrated Development Environment, and the KDE is no exception.

The KDevelop Integrated Development Environment provides many features that developers need. In addition, it wraps the functionality of third-party projects such as make and the GNU C++ compilers and makes them an invisible, integrated part of the development process. KDevelop offers the following features:

- All development tools needed for C++ programming, such as the compiler, the linker, automake, and autoconf
- KAppWizard, which generates complete sample applications
- ClassGenerator, which creates new classes and integrates them into the current project
- File management for source files, header files, project documentation, and so on
- The creation of user handbooks written with SGML and the automatic generation of HTML output with the KDE look and feel

- Automatic HTML-based API-documentation for your project's classes with cross-references to the used libraries

- International support for your application, allowing you easily to add their new languages to a project

- WYSIWYG creation of user interfaces with a built-in dialog editor

- Project management using CVS and providing an easy-to-use interface for the most needed functions

- Program debugging using KDbg

- Icon editing using KIconEdit

- The inclusion of any other program you need for development by adding it to the Tools menu according to your individual needs

KDevelop makes it easy to work with all programs in one place and saves time by automating standard development processes as well as giving you direct and transparent access to all information you need to control your project. The integrated browsing mechanisms are designed to support documentation requests that developers have in conjunction with their project.

The class viewer and error finder bring you anywhere in the project code with a mouse click without needing to search for files. File trees give direct access to the project files, and the integrated help system offers superb access to online documentation from anywhere within the IDE.

In short, KDevelop is a fully featured and powerful IDE. Did I mention that it is free?

26

At the time of writing, because KDevelop uses KDE 1.1, I'm referring to the state of the KDE libraries at that release. The main KDE libraries you'll be using for creating your own KDE applications are

- The KDE Core library, containing all classes that are non-visible elements and provide functionality your application may use

- The KDE UI library, containing user interface elements like menu bars, toolbars and the like

- The KFile library, containing the file selection dialogs

Additionally, for specific solutions KDE offers the following libraries:

- The KHTMLW library, offering a complete HTML-interpreting widget that is used by various programs like KDEHelp, KFM, and Kdevelop

- The KFM library, enabling you to use the KDE file manager from within your application

- The KAb library, the KAddressBook. Provides address-book access, for example, for email applications

- The KSpell library, offering widgets and functionality to integrate the use of Ispell, the common spell checker, in applications like editors; used for the KEdit application

Summary

Linux has finally come of age. The two new desktops you have seen today, the GNOME and the KDE, as well as their supporting libraries and applications, provide a choice of modern, intuitive, robust, and free GUIs for the Linux operating system. They also provide a set of powerful development frameworks, environments, and tools that take the drudgery out of writing GUI applications in X and enable you to concentrate on what your application ought to be doing rather than dragging you into a fight you can only lose with an intractable API.

With the new Linux GUI interfaces, you have a genuine choice, and that can only be good for everyone as it will see a marked improvement in quality and price (especially as the Linux desktops are free) in the whole operating system marketplace.

All the packages and libraries I have described in this lesson are being extended and improved almost daily by volunteers, and new ones are appearing almost as frequently.

Their efforts and skill have firmly placed Linux where it belongs: on the desktop.

Q&A

Q Why do we need the KDE and the GNOME?

A The reason is that Linux, unlike Windows and MacOS, doesn't have a native GUI: You interact with it using textual commands. The computer itself has graphics capability (usually), but Linux alone doesn't know how to drive it. The GNOME and the KDE provide a framework for you to interact with the computer graphically and to have your commands routed transparently to the operating system. In truth we don't *need* them both: They are different enough for them to coexist, and time will tell which one, if either, becomes more widespread.

Q Why can't I just use the Common Desktop Environment or Motif as my GUI?

A You can if you want to. The beauty of Linux is that it is free, and if you use GNU software or KDE software, that is also free. You *can* get versions of the CDE and Motif for Linux, but they are proprietary software and you have to pay for them. Not only that, but to many people, the GUIs these provide are now starting to look a little old-fashioned.

Q If I am writing a GUI Application for GNOME, will it still run under KDE, and vice versa?

A Maybe. If you write applications for one desktop, they will still run under the other if and only if you have the correct runtime libraries present on your machine. Moreover, if they run they will not behave as you might expect and want them to behave because the persistent session information from a GNOME application will be ignored by the KDE desktop (and similarly the other way around). More important, on some installations, GNOME applications, like the GIMP, upset the KDE color scheme when they have the focus. On my machine, when running Red Hat Linux 6.1, if I run the GIMP under KDE, the entire screen turns blue when the GIMP has the focus. If you just want a generic application, you can always use wxWindows, which uses the GTK++ but doesn't use GNOME.

Q What is cross-platform source code? Why might it be important?

A This is source code that you write once and compile using the correct toolkit on your target machine. The Qt library and wxWindows are both "platform-independent," meaning that the source code for a given application is the same no matter what platform you compile it on; obviously, the toolkit libraries are significantly different, but that isn't your concern. This is the area where some people think KDE falls down: The Qt libraries have a free license only for Linux and other UNIX builds. If you want to create software for Windows with the Qt libraries, you have to buy a license.

Q I want to use C++ but I don't want to use wxWindows or GTK— or any other wrapper. Can I use C++ direct on the GNOME/GTK++ libraries?

A Yes. Although it will probably lead to messier code, you can declare your callback functions as static members of your classes. You can then implement the classes that have the static callback members however you please and get them to do what you want.

26

Workshop

The Workshop provides quiz questions to help solidify your understanding of the material covered and exercises to provide you with experience in using what you have learned. Try to answer the quiz and exercise questions before checking the answers in Appendix D, "Answers to Exercises and Quizzes," and make sure you understand the answers before continuing tomorrow.

Quiz

1. What is the difference between event-driven programs and procedural ones?

2. What is a widget, in computing terms?

3. What is a callback function, and why are these prone to errors?

4. What is a Qt slot, and how does it react to Qt signals?

5. Signals and slots are typesafe. What does this mean and why is it a good thing?

6. How would you tie the following wxWindows event handler handler to a EVT_MENU event from a menu item with an ID of ID_MY_HELP? Assume OnHelp() is a member of the class MyFrame, and MyFrame is derived from wxFrame.

   ```
   void OnHelp(wxCommandEvent& WXUNUSED(event));
   ```

7. What does the IMPLEMENT_APP() macro do?

8. What does the Q_OBJECT macro do?

Exercises

1. Using the buttons.cc source file as a base, extend the program so that the callback class puts up a dialog box when you click the buttons rather than writing directly to stdout.

2. Taking either the final wxWindows or KDE example as a basis, extend the code to display a file-browse button that will enable you to select a file using a standard file-selection dialog.

3. Extend the code from Exercise 2 so that when you click OK and select the file, the program displays it in a text control on the main window.

4. Look at your results from Exercise 1 and consider how you might wrap the entire application into one class. Consider why you might want to implement the callback functions as private static members of the class and expose only "wrappers" that call them when the user triggers events. See the function do_message() in file ex26-01.cxx for example. Think how you might extend the idea to create a generic wrapper for the application and use virtual functions for setting the main window and connecting signals.

WEEK 4

In Review

You should be proud of yourself! You not only completed the 21 days to learn C++ for Linux, but you also completed the extra five days of the bonus week. That week covered the following topics:

- The Linux Programming Environment
- Shell Programming
- System Programming

- Interprocess Communication
- GUI Programming

Of course, these lessons just introduced you to the topic. There is much more for you to learn about all these topics and the C++ language. The best way to learn is by doing. Write programs, try tools, and work with various libraries of functions and objects.

Good luck!

APPENDIX **A**

Operator Precedence

It is important to understand that operators have a precedence, but it is not essential to memorize the precedence.

Precedence is the order in which a program performs the operations in a formula. If one operator has precedence over another operator, it is evaluated first.

Higher precedence operators "bind tighter" than lower precedence operators; thus, higher precedence operators are evaluated first. The lower the rank in Table A.1, the lower the precedence.

TABLE A.1   Operator Precedence

Rank	Name	Operator
1	Scope resolution (binary, unary)	`::`
2	Function calls, parentheses, subscripting, member selection, postfix increment and decrement	`() []` `. ->` `++ --`
3	`sizeof`, C++ casting, prefix increment and decrement, unary plus and minus, negation, complement, C casting, `sizeof()`, address of, dereference `new`, `new[]`, `delete`, `delete[]`	`++ --` `+ -` `! ~ ( cast )` `& *`
4	Member selection for pointer	`.* ->*`
5	Multiply, divide, modulus	`* / %`
6	Add, subtract	`+ -`
7	Bitwise shift	`<< >>`
8	Inequality relational	`< <= > >=`
9	Equality, inequality	`== !=`
10	Bitwise AND	`&`
11	Bitwise exclusive OR	`^`
12	Bitwise OR	`|`
13	Logical AND	`&&`
14	Logical OR	`||`
15	Conditional	`?:`
16	Assignment operators= `*= /= %=`	`+= -= <<=` `>>=` `&= |= ^=`
17	Comma	`,`

APPENDIX B

C++ Keywords

Keywords are reserved to the compiler for use by the language. You cannot define classes, variables, or functions that have these keywords as their names. The list is a bit arbitrary, as it contains the standard keywords as well as some of the keywords that are specific to g++. Some of the keywords are not available with all compilers or with older versions of the g++ compiler. Your mileage may vary slightly.

asm	float	static
auto	for	static_cast
bool	friend	struct
break	goto	switch
case	if	template
catch	inline	this
char	int	throw
class	long	true
const	mutable	try
const_cast	namespace	typedef
continue	new	typeof
default	operator	typeid
delete	private	typename
do	protected	union
double	public	unsigned
dynamic_cast	register	using
else	reinterpret_cast	virtual
enum	return	void
explicit	short	volatile
extern	signed	while
false	sizeof	

APPENDIX C

Binary, Octal, and Hexadecimal Numbers and an ASCII Chart

You learned the fundamentals of arithmetic so long ago that it is hard to imagine what it would be like without that knowledge. When you look at the number 145, you instantly see "one hundred forty-five" without much reflection.

Understanding different systems of numeric notation requires that you re-examine the number 145 and see it not as a number, but as a code for (or *representation* of) a number.

Start small: Examine the relationship between the number three and "3." The numeral 3 is a squiggle on a piece of paper; the number three is an idea. The numeral is used to represent the idea of a number.

The distinction can be made clear by realizing that three, 3, |||, III, and *** all can be used to represent the same idea of three.

In base 10 (decimal) math, you use the numerals 0, 1, 2, 3, 4, 5, 6, 7, 8, 9 to represent all numbers. How is the number ten represented?

One can imagine that we might have evolved a strategy of using the letter A to represent ten; or we might have used IIIIIIIII to represent that idea. The Romans used X. The Arabic system, which we use, makes use of position in conjunction with numerals to represent values. The first (right-most) column is used for "ones," and the next column (to the left) is used for "tens." Thus, the number fifteen is represented as 15 (read "one, five"); that is, one 10 and five 1s.

Certain rules emerge, from which some generalizations can be made:

1. Base 10 uses the digits 0–9.
2. The columns are powers of ten: 1s, 10s, 100s, and so on.
3. If the third column is 100, the largest number you can make with two columns is 99. More generally, with n columns you can represent 0 to (10^n-1). Thus, with three columns you can represent 0 to (10^3-1) or 0–999.

Beyond Base 10

It is not a coincidence that we use base 10; we have 10 fingers. One can imagine a different base, however. Using the rules found in base 10, you can describe base 8:

1. The digits used in base 8 are 0–7.
2. The columns are powers of 8: 1s, 8s, 64s, and so on.
3. With n columns, you can represent 0 to 8^n-1.

To distinguish numbers written in each base, write the base as a subscript next to the number. The number fifteen in base 10 would be written as 15_{10} and read as "one, five, base ten."

Thus, to represent the number 15_{10} in base 8, you would write 17_8. This is read "one, seven, base eight." Note that it can also be read "fifteen" as that is the number it continues to represent.

Why 17? The 1 means one 8, and the 7 means seven 1s. One 8 plus seven 1s equals 15. Consider 15 asterisks:

```
*****     *****
*****
```

The natural tendency is to make two groups, a group of ten asterisks and another of five. This would be represented in decimal as 15 (one 10 and five 1s). You can also group the asterisks as

```
****          *******
****
```

That is, a group of eight asterisks and another of seven. That would be represented in base 8 as 17_8. That is, one 8 and seven 1s.

Around the Bases

You can represent the number fifteen in base 10 as 15, in base 9 as 16_9, in base 8 as 17_8, in base 7 as 21_7. Why 21_7? In base 7, there is no numeral 8. In order to represent fifteen, you will need two 7s and one 1.

How do you generalize the process? To convert a base 10 number to base 7, think about the columns: in base 7 they are ones, sevens, forty-nines, three-hundred forty-threes, and so on. Why these columns? They represent 7^0, 7^1, 7^2, 7^4, and so forth. Create a table for yourself:

4	3	2	1
7^3	7^2	7^1	7^0
343	49	7	1

The first row represents the column number. The second row represents the power of 7. The third row represents the decimal value of each number in that row.

To convert from a decimal value to base 7, here is the procedure: Examine the number and decide which column to use first. If the number is 200, for example, you know that column 4 (343) is 0, and you don't have to worry about it.

To find out how many 49s there are, divide 200 by 49. The answer is 4, so put 4 in column 3 and examine the remainder: 4. There are no 7s in 4, so put a zero in the 7s column. There are four 1s in 4, so put a 4 in the 1s column. The answer is 404_7.

To convert the number 968 to base 6:

5	4	3	2	1
6^4	6^3	6^2	6^1	6^0
1296	216	36	6	1

There are no 1296s in 968, so column 5 has 0. Dividing 968 by 216 yields 4 with a remainder of 104. Column 4 is 4. Dividing 104 by 36 yields 2 with a remainder of 32. Column 3 is 2. Dividing 32 by 6 yields 5 with a remainder of 2. The answer therefore is 4252_6.

5	4	3	2	1
6^4	6^3	6^2	6^1	6^0
1296	216	36	6	1
0	4	2	5	2

There is a shortcut when converting from one base to another base (such as 6) to base 10. You can multiply:

$4 * 216 = 864$

$2 * 36 = 72$

$5 * 6 = 30$

$2 * 1 = 2$

968

Binary

Base 2 is the ultimate extension of this idea. There are only two digits: 0 and 1. The columns are:

Col:	8	7	6	5	4	3	2	1
Power:	2^7	2^6	2^5	2^4	2^3	2^2	2^1	2^0
Value:	128	64	32	16	8	4	2	1

To convert the number 88 to base 2, you follow the same procedure: There are no 128s, so column 8 is 0.

There is one 64 in 88, so column 7 is 1 and 24 is the remainder. There are no 32s in 24, so column 6 is 0.

There is one 16 in 24, so column 5 is 1. The remainder is 8. There is one 8 in 8, and so column 4 is 1. There is no remainder, so the rest of the columns are 0.

0	1	0	1	1	0	0	0

To test this answer, convert it back:

```
1 * 64 =  64
0 * 32 =   0
1 * 16 =  16
1 *  8 =   8
0 *  4 =   0
0 *  2 =   0
0 *  1 =   0
              88
```

To convert from binary to decimal, you just follow the method used in double-checking our decimal to binary conversion—multiply the binary result by the value of the respective columns.

Why Base 2?

The power of base 2 is that it corresponds so cleanly to what a computer needs to represent. Computers do not really know anything at all about letters, numerals, instructions, or programs. At their core they are just circuitry, and at a given juncture there either is a lot of power or there is very little.

To keep the logic clean, engineers do not treat this as a relative scale (a little power, some power, more power, lots of power, or tons of power), but rather as a binary scale ("enough power" or "not enough power"). Rather than saying "enough" or "not enough," they simplify it to "yes" or "no." Yes or no, or true or false, can be represented as 1 or 0. By convention, 1 means true or yes, but that is just a convention; it could just as easily have meant false or no.

When you make this great leap of intuition, the power of binary becomes clear: With 1s and 0s you can represent the fundamental truth of every circuit (there is power or there isn't). All a computer ever knows is, "Is you is, or is you ain't?" Is you is = 1; is you ain't = 0.

Bits, Bytes, and Nybbles

When the decision is made to represent truth and falsehood with 1s and 0s, binary digits (or bits) become very important. Because early computers could send 8 bits at a time, it was natural to start writing code using 8-bit numbers—called *bytes*.

Note

Half a byte (4 bits) is called a nybble!

With 8 binary digits, you can represent up to 256 different values. Why? Examine the columns: If all 8 bits are set (1), the value is 255. If none is set (all the bits are clear or zero), the value is 0. The range 0–255 gives you 256 possible states.

What's a KB?

It turns out that 2^{10} (1,024) is roughly equal to 10^3 (1,000). This coincidence was too good to miss, so computer scientists started referring to 2^{10} bytes as 1KB or 1 kilobyte, based on the scientific prefix of kilo for thousand.

Similarly, 1024 * 1024 (1,048,576) is close enough to one million to receive the designation 1MB or 1 megabyte, and 1,024 megabytes is called 1 gigabyte (*giga* implies thousand-million or billion).

Binary Numbers

Computers use patterns of 1s and 0s to encode everything they do. Machine instructions are encoded as a series of 1s and 0s and interpreted by the fundamental circuitry. Arbitrary sets of 1s and 0s can be translated back into numbers by computer scientists, but it would be a mistake to think that these numbers have intrinsic meaning.

For example, the Intel 80×6 chipset interprets the bit pattern 1001 0101 as an instruction. You certainly can translate this into decimal (149), but that number per se has no meaning.

Sometimes the numbers are instructions, sometimes they are values, and sometimes they are codes. One important standardized code set is ASCII (which stands for American Standard Code for Information Interchange). In ASCII every letter and punctuation character is given a 7-digit binary representation. For example, the lowercase letter "a" is represented by 0110 0001. This is not a number, although you can translate it to the number 97 (64 + 32 + 1). It is in this sense that people say that the letter "a" is represented by 97 in ASCII; but the truth is that the binary representation of 97, 01100001, is the encoding of the letter "a," and the decimal value 97 is a human convenience.

Octal

Because binary numbers are difficult to read, we seek a simpler way to represent the same values. Translating from binary to base 10 involves a fair bit of manipulation of numbers; it is simpler translating to base 10 from octal.

To understand this, you must first understand base 8, which is known as *octal*. In base 8, there are eight numerals: 0, 1, 2, 3, 4, 5, 6, and 7. The columns in octal are

Col:	5	4	3	2	1
Power:	8^4	8^3	8^2	8^1	8^0
Value:	4096	512	64	8	1

To convert the number 88 to octal, you follow the same procedures with binary: There are no 4096s or 512s, so columns 5 and 4 respectively are 0.

There is one 64 in 88, so column 3 is 1 with 24 as the remainder. There are three 8s in 24, so column 2 is 3 with a remainder of zero (so the remaining column is 0).

   0   0   1   3   0

To test this answer, convert it back:

```
1 * 64 =  64
3 * 8  =  24
0 * 1  =   0
             88
```

To convert from octal to decimal, you just follow the method used in double-checking our decimal to octal conversion—multiply the octal result by the value of the respective columns.

Why Octal?

The power of octal (base 8) is that it is at a higher level than binary. Each octal digit represents 3 binary digits. Historically, the original computer systems that UNIX and C were developed on were 12-bit machines. It required 4 octal digits to describe one memory word.

Each octal digit is 3 binary digits. It becomes very easy to line up the octal digits and convert them, one at a time, into binary. And the inverse conversion is easy too.

Hexadecimal

Because binary numbers are difficult to read, we need a simpler way to represent the same values. Translating from binary to base 10 involves a fair bit of manipulation of numbers; but it turns out that translating from base 2 to base 16 is very simple, because there is a very good shortcut.

To understand this, you must first understand base 16, which is known as hexadecimal. In base 16, there are sixteen numerals: 0, 1, 2, 3, 4, 5, 6, 7, 8, 9, A, B, C, D, E, and F. The last six are arbitrary; the letters A–F were chosen because they are easy to represent on a keyboard. The columns in hexadecimal are

4	3	2	1
163	162	161	160
4096	256	16	1

To translate from hexadecimal to decimal, you can multiply. Thus, the number F8C represents:

```
F * 256 = 15 * 256 = 3840
8 * 16 =            128
C * 1 = 12 * 1 =     12
3980
```

Translating the number FC to binary can be done by translating first to base 10, and then to binary:

```
F * 16 = 15 * 16 =  240
C * 1 = 12 * 1 =     12
252
```

Converting 252_{10} to binary requires the chart:

```
Col:       9    8    7   6    5    4    3    2    1
Power:      28   27   26   25   24   23   22   21   20
Value:    256  128   64  32   16   8    4    2    1
```

```
There are no 256s.
1 128 leaves 124
1 64 leaves 60
1 32 leaves 28
1 16 leaves 12
1 8 leaves 4
1 4 leaves 0
0
0
1   1   1   1   1   1   0   0
```

Thus, the answer in binary is 1111 1100.

Now, it turns out that if you treat this binary number as two sets of 4 digits, you can do a magical transformation.

The right set is 1100. In decimal that is 12, or in hexadecimal it is C.

The left set is 1111, which in base 10 is 15, or in hex is F.

Thus, you have:

```
1111 1100
F    C
```

Putting the two hex numbers together is FC, which is the real value of 1111 1100. This shortcut always works. You can take any binary number of any length, and reduce it to sets of 4, translate each set of 4 to hex, and put the hex numbers together to get the result in hex. Here's a much larger number:

```
1011 0001 1101 0111
```

The columns are 1, 2, 4, 8, 16, 32, 64, 128, 256, 512, 1024, 2048, 4096, 8192, 16384, and 32768.

```
1 x 1 =          1
1 x 2=           2
1 x 4 =          4
0 x 8 =          0

1 x 16 =         16
0 x 32 =         0
1 x 64 =         64
1 x 128 =        128

1 x 256 =        256
0 x 512 =        0
0 x 1024 =       0
0 x 2048 =       0

1 x 4096 =       4,096
1 x 8192 =       8,192
0 x 16384 =      0
1 x 32768 =      32,768
Total:           45,527
```

Converting this to hexadecimal requires a chart with the hexadecimal values.

```
65535    4096    256    16    1
```

There are no 65,536s in 45,527, so the first column is 4096. There are eleven 4096s (45,056), with a remainder of 471. There is one 256 in 471 with a remainder of 215. There are thirteen 16s (208) in 215 with a remainder of 7. Thus, the hexadecimal number is B1D7.

Checking the math:

```
B (11) * 4096 =    45,056
1 * 256 =          256
D (13) * 16 =      208
7 * 1 =            7
Total          45,527
```

The shortcut version would be to take the original binary number, 1011000111010111, and break it into groups of 4: 1011 0001 1101 0111. Each of the four then is evaluated as a hexadecimal number:

```
1011 =
1 x 1 =     1
1 x 2 =     2
0 x 4 =     0
1 x 8 =     8
Total      11
Hex:        B

0001 =
1 x 1 =     1
0 x 2 =     0
0 x 4 =     0
0 * 8 =     0
Total       1
Hex:        1

1101 =
1 x 1 =     1
0 x 2 =     0
1 x 4 =     4
1 x 8 =     8
Total      13
Hex =       D

0111 =
1 x 1 =     1
1 x 2 =     2
1 x 4 =     4
0 x 8 =     0
Total       7
Hex:        7

Total Hex:  B1D7
```

Hexadecimal is very popular with systems that are even multiples of 4 bits. These days most systems fall into this category: 16, 32, and 64. By the time this book is printed, there will probably be 128-bit systems on the market.

ASCII

ASCII is the most common character representation in use today. Table C.1 shows binary, octal, decimal, hexadecimal, and ASCII equivalents.

TABLE C.1   Numeric and ASCII Equivalents

Binary	Octal	Hex	Decimal	ASCII
00000000	0	0	0	<nul>
00000001	1	1	1	<soh>
00000010	2	2	2	<stx>
00000011	3	3	3	<etx>
00000100	4	4	4	<eot>
00000101	5	5	5	<enq>
00000110	6	6	6	<ack>
00000111	7	7	7	<bel>
00001000	10	8	8	<bs>
00001001	11	9	9	<tab>
00001010	12	a	10	<newline>
00001011	13	b	11	<vt>
00001100	14	c	12	<ff>
00001101	15	d	13	<cr>
00001110	16	e	14	<so>
00001111	17	f	15	<si>
00010000	20	10	16	<dle>
00010001	21	11	17	<dc1>
00010010	22	12	18	<dc2>
00010011	23	13	19	<dc3>
00010100	24	14	20	<dc4>
00010101	25	15	21	<nak>
00010110	26	16	22	<syn>
00010111	27	17	23	<etb>
00011000	30	18	24	<can>
00011001	31	19	25	<em>
00011010	32	1a	26	<sub>
00011011	33	1b	27	<esc>
00011100	34	1c	28	<fs>
00011101	35	1d	29	<gs>
00011110	36	1e	30	<rs>

C

continues

TABLE C.1 CONTINUED

Binary	Octal	Hex	Decimal	ASCII
00011111	37	1f	31	\<us\>
00100000	40	20	32	\<space\>
00100001	41	21	33	!
00100010	42	22	34	"
00100011	43	23	35	#
00100100	44	24	36	$
00100101	45	25	37	%
00100110	46	26	38	&
00100111	47	27	39	'
00101000	50	28	40	(
00101001	51	29	41	)
00101010	52	2a	42	*
00101011	53	2b	43	+
00101100	54	2c	44	,
00101101	55	2d	45	-
00101110	56	2e	46	.
00101111	57	2f	47	/
00110000	60	30	48	0
00110001	61	31	49	1
00110010	62	32	50	2
00110011	63	33	51	3
00110100	64	34	52	4
00110101	65	35	53	5
00110110	66	36	54	6
00110111	67	37	55	7
00111000	70	38	56	8
00111001	71	39	57	9
00111010	72	3a	58	:
00111011	73	3b	59	;
00111100	74	3c	60	<
00111101	75	3d	61	=
00111110	76	3e	62	>

Binary	Octal	Hex	Decimal	ASCII
00111111	77	3f	63	?
01000000	100	40	64	@
01000001	101	41	65	A
01000010	102	42	66	B
01000011	103	43	67	C
01000100	104	44	68	D
01000101	105	45	69	E
01000110	106	46	70	F
01000111	107	47	71	G
01001000	110	48	72	H
01001001	111	49	73	I
01001010	112	4a	74	J
01001011	113	4b	75	K
01001100	114	4c	76	L
01001101	115	4d	77	M
01001110	116	4e	78	N
01001111	117	4f	79	O
01010000	120	50	80	P
01010001	121	51	81	Q
01010010	122	52	82	R
01010011	123	53	83	S
01010100	124	54	84	T
01010101	125	55	85	U
01010110	126	56	86	V
01010111	127	57	87	W
01011000	130	58	88	X
01011001	131	59	89	Y
01011010	132	5a	90	Z
01011011	133	5b	91	[
01011100	134	5c	92	\
01011101	135	5d	93	]
01011110	136	5e	94	^

continues

TABLE C.1 CONTINUED

Binary	Octal	Hex	Decimal	ASCII
01011111	137	5f	95	_
01100000	140	60	96	`
01100001	141	61	97	a
01100010	142	62	98	b
01100011	143	63	99	c
01100100	144	64	100	d
01100101	145	65	101	e
01100110	146	66	102	f
01100111	147	67	103	g
01101000	150	68	104	h
01101001	151	69	105	i
01101010	152	6a	106	j
01101011	153	6b	107	k
01101100	154	6c	108	l
01101101	155	6d	109	m
01101110	156	6e	110	n
01101111	157	6f	111	o
01110000	160	70	112	p
01110001	161	71	113	q
01110010	162	72	114	r
01110011	163	73	115	s
01110100	164	74	116	t
01110101	165	75	117	u
01110110	166	76	118	v
01110111	167	77	119	w
01111000	170	78	120	x
01111001	171	79	121	y
01111010	172	7a	122	z
01111011	173	7b	123	{
01111100	174	7c	124		
01111101	175	7d	125	}
01111110	176	7e	126	~
01111111	177	7f	127	<del>

The values 0–127 (decimal) are part of the ASCII standard. Some systems support what is known as "high ASCII" (128–255) for special printable characters. Any ASCII entries in Table C.1 shown between angle brackets (like <space>) are special characters or are difficult to represent in print.

There are other character sets besides ASCII: EBCDIC and Unicode are the two most common. EBCDIC (Extended Binary Coded Decimal Interchange Code) is the character set you will find on IBM mainframes. Unicode is a new standard allowing representation of characters in most languages in the world; ASCII is a subset of Unicode.

Listing C.1 demonstrates the program that produced Table C.1 (except for the special characters in angle brackets like <space>—I had to edit those by hand).

INPUT   **LISTING C.1**   Table C.1 Creation Program

C

```
1: // listing C.1 (lstxc-01.cxx) - Create Table C.1.
2: #include <iostream.h>
3: #include <iomanip.h>
4: #include <math.h>
5:
6: void bin(int in, char results[]);
7:
8: int main()
9: {
10:     int loop;
11:     char binresult[9];
12:
13:     for (loop = 0; loop < 128; loop++)
14:     {
15:         bin(loop, binresult);
16:         cout << binresult << "\t" << oct << loop << "\t" <<
17:         hex << loop << "\t" << dec << loop << "\t" << (char) loop;
18:         cout << endl;
19:     }
20:
21:     return 0;
22: }
23:
24: void bin(int in, char results[])
25: {
26:     int loop;
27:     for (loop = 0; loop < 8; loop++)
28:     {
29:         results[loop] = in / (int) pow(2, 7-loop);
30:         in %= (int) pow(2, 7-loop);
31:         results[loop] += '0';
```

continues

LISTING C.1   CONTINUED

```
32:     }
33:     results[8] = '\0';
34:
35:     return;
36: }
```

OUTPUT   The output of this program is shown in Table C.1.

ANALYSIS   C++ allows me to specify the format for my output—octal, hexadecimal, and decimal. But it will not allow me to specify binary as an output format. So I had to code a conversion function, the prototype of which is on line 6 with the function itself on lines 24 through 36.

The main program is very simple: one `for` loop. Within that loop is a call to `bin()` and my output statement. On line 17, for `cout` to show the final copy of the loop variable as a character, I had to cast it as a character and not an integer.

The function `bin()` implements the decimal-to-binary conversion described in the "Binary" section of this appendix. Lines 29 and 30 use the `pow()` function to determine the decimal value of a specific power of 2. The `pow()` function is defined in `math.h` (line 4) and returns a type `double`; because integer division and modulus is required, the result of `pow()` is cast to be type `int`.

The only real trick of this function is line 31, which converts integer ones and zeros to printable characters (by adding the value of an ASCII zero). An ASCII one is one number higher (61 versus 60) than ASCII zero, so this works correctly.

Line 33 adds in a null terminator so that the results array can be treated like a string.

In this case, I chose to have an 8-position (8-bit) number with the highest value position being first.

This is a good example of some of the tricks that C and C++ will let you do. The example in Listing C.1 is complex to read, but number conversion itself can be complex.

APPENDIX D

Answers to Exercises and Quizzes

Day 1

Quiz

1. What is the difference between interpreters and compilers?

   Interpreters read through source code and translate a program, turning the programmer's code, or program instructions, directly into actions. Compilers translate source code into an executable program that can be run at a later time.

2. How do you compile the source code with your compiler?

   Every compiler is different. Be sure to check the documentation that came with your compiler. With GNU you can use the `man` (manual) or `info` commands.

3. What does the linker do?

The linker's job is to tie together your compiled code with the libraries supplied with your GNU compiler and other sources. The linker lets you build your program in pieces and then link together the pieces into one big program.

4. What are the steps in the development cycle?

Edit source code, compile, link, test, repeat.

Exercises

1. Initialize two integer variables and then print out their sum and their product.

2. See the GNU compiler documentation (or Day 2, "The Parts of a C++ Program").

3. You must put a # symbol before the word `include` on the first line.

4. This program prints the words `Hello World` to the screen, followed by a newline (carriage return).

Day 2

Quiz

1. What is the difference between the compiler and the preprocessor?

Each time you run your compiler, the preprocessor runs first. It reads through your source code and includes the files you asked for, and performs other housekeeping chores. The preprocessor is discussed in detail on Day 18, "Object-Oriented Analysis and Design."

2. Why is the function `main()` special?

`main()` is called automatically each time your program is executed.

3. What are the two types of comments, and how do they differ?

C++-style comments are two slashes (`//`), and they comment out any text until the end of the line. C-style comments come in pairs (`/* */`), and everything between the matching pairs is commented out. You must be careful to ensure you have matched pairs.

4. Can comments be nested?

Yes, C++-style comments can be nested within C-style comments. You can, in fact, nest C-style comments within C++-style comments, as long as you remember that the C++-style comments end at the end of the line.

5. Can comments be longer than one line?

C-style comments can. If you want to extend C++-style comments to a second line, you must put another set of double slashes (//).

Exercises

1. Write a program that writes I love C++ to the screen.

```
1: #include <iostream.h>
2:
3: int main()
4: {
5:    cout << "I love C++\n";
6:    return 0;
7: }
```

2. Write the smallest program that can be compiled, linked, and run.

```
int main(){ return 0; }
```

3. **BUG BUSTER**: Enter this program and compile it. Why does it fail? How can you fix it?

```
1: #include <iostream.h>
2: int main()
3: {
4:      cout << Is there a bug here?";
5:   return 0;
6: }
```

Line 4 is missing an opening quote for the string.

4. Fix the bug in Exercise 3 and recompile, link, and run it.

```
1: #include <iostream.h>
2: main()
3: {
4:      cout << "Is there a bug here?";
5: }
```

Day 3

Quiz

1. What is the difference between an integral variable and a floating-point variable?

Integer variables are whole numbers; floating-point variables are "reals" and have a "floating" decimal point. Floating-point numbers can be represented using a mantissa and an exponent.

2. What are the differences between an `unsigned short int` and a `long int`?

   The keyword `unsigned` means that the integer will hold only positive numbers. On most computers, short integers are 2 bytes and long integers are 4.

3. What are the advantages of using a symbolic constant rather than a literal?

   A symbolic constant explains itself; the name of the constant tells what it is for. Also, symbolic constants can be redefined at one location in the source code, rather than the programmer having to edit the code everywhere the literal is used.

4. What are the advantages of using the `const` keyword rather than `#define`?

   `const` variables are "typed"; thus, the compiler can check for errors in how they are used. Also, they survive the preprocessor; thus the name is available in the debugger.

5. What makes for a good or bad variable name?

   A good variable name tells you what the variable is for; a bad variable name gives no information. `myAge` and `PeopleOnTheBus` are good variable names, but `xjk` and `prndl` are probably less useful.

6. Given this enum, what is the value of `Blue`?
   ```
   enum COLOR { WHITE, BLACK = 100, RED, BLUE, GREEN = 300 };
   BLUE = 102
   ```

7. Which of the following variable names are good, which are bad, and which are invalid?

   a. `Age`

      Good

   b. `!ex`

      Not legal

   c. `R79J`

      Legal, but a bad choice

   d. `TotalIncome`

      Good

   e. `__Invalid`

      Legal, but a bad choice

Exercises

1. What would be the correct variable type in which to store the following information?

    a. Your age.

        `Unsigned short integer`

    b. The area of your back yard.

        `Unsigned long integer or unsigned float`

    c. The number of stars in the galaxy.

        `Unsigned double`

    d. The average rainfall for the month of January.

        `Unsigned short integer`

2. Create good variable names for this information.

    a. `myAge`

    b. `backYardArea`

    c. `StarsInGalaxy`

    d. `averageRainFall`

3. Declare a constant for *pi* as 3.14159.

   `const float PI = 3.14159;`

4. Declare a `float` variable and initialize it using your *pi* constant.

   `float myPi = PI;`

Day 4

Quiz

1. What is an expression?

   Any statement that returns a value.

2. Is `x = 5 + 7` an expression? What is its value?

   Yes. `12`

3. What is the value of `201 / 4`?

   `50`

4. What is the value of `201 % 4`?

   `1`

5. If `myAge`, `a`, and `b` are all `int` variables, what are their values after:

```
myAge = 39;
a = myAge++;
b = ++myAge;
```

   `myAge: 41, a: 39, b: 41`

D

6. What is the value of `8+2*3`?

   `14`

7. What is the difference between `if(x = 3)` and `if(x == 3)`?

   The first one assigns 3 to x and returns `true`. The second one tests whether x is equal to 3; it returns `true` if the value of x is equal to 3 and `false` if it is not.

8. Do the following values evaluate to `true` or `false`?

   a. `0`

      `false`

   b. `1`

      `true`

   c. `-1`

      `true`

   d. `x = 0`

      `false`

   e. `x == 0 // assume that x has the value of 0`

      `true`

Exercises

1. Write a single `if` statement that examines two integer variables and changes the larger to the smaller, using only one `else` clause.

   ```
   if (x > y)
       x = y;
   else            // y > x || y == x
       y = x;
   ```

2. Examine the following program. Imagine entering three numbers, and write what output you expect.

   ```
   1:    #include <iostream.h>
   2:    int main()
   3:    {
   4:        int a, b, c;
   5:        cout << "Please enter three numbers\n";
   6:        cout << "a: ";
   7:        cin >> a;
   8:        cout << "\nb: ";
   9:        cin >> b;
   10:       cout << "\nc: ";
   11:       cin >> c;
   12:
   13:       if (c = (a-b))
   ```

```
14          {
15:             cout << "a: " << a << " minus b: ";
16:             cout << b << " _equals c: " << c;
17:         }
15:         else
16:             cout << "a-b does not equal c: ";
17:     return 0;
18: }
```

3. Enter the program from Exercise 2; compile, link, and run it. Enter the numbers 20, 10, and 50. Did you get the output you expected? Why not?

Enter 20, 10, 50.

Get back a: 20 b: 10 c: 10.

Line 13 is assigning, not testing for equality.

4. Examine this program and anticipate the output:

```
1:      #include <iostream.h>
2:      int main()
3:      {
4:              int a = 1, b = 1, c;
5:              if (c = (a-b))
6:                  cout << "The value of c is: " << c;
7:      return 0;
8:      }
```

5. Enter, compile, link, and run the program from Exercise 4. What was the output? Why?

Because line 5 is assigning the value of a-b to c, the value of the assignment is a (1) minus b (1), or 0. Because 0 is evaluated as false, the if fails and nothing is printed.

Day 5

Quiz

1. What are the differences between the function prototype and the function definition?

The function prototype declares the function; the definition defines it. The prototype ends with a semicolon; the definition need not. The declaration can include the keyword inline and default values for the parameters; the definition cannot. The declaration need not include names for the parameters; the definition must.

2. Do the names of parameters have to agree in the prototype, definition, and call to the function?

No. All parameters are identified by position, not name.

3. If a function doesn't return a value, how do you declare the function?

Declare the function to return void.

4. If you don't declare a return value, what type of return value is assumed?

Any function that does not explicitly declare a return type returns int.

5. What is a local variable?

A local variable is a variable passed into or declared within a block, typically a function. It is visible only within the block.

6. What is scope?

Scope refers to the visibility and lifetime of local and global variables. Scope is usually established by a set of braces.

7. What is recursion?

Recursion generally refers to the ability of a function to call itself.

8. When should you use global variables?

Global variables are typically used when many functions need access to the same data. Global variables are very rare in C++; when you know how to create static class variables, you will almost never create global variables.

9. What is function overloading?

Function overloading is the ability to write more than one function with the same name, distinguished by the number or type of the parameters.

10. What is polymorphism?

Polymorphism is the ability to treat many objects of differing but related types without regard to their differences. In C++, polymorphism is accomplished by using class derivation and virtual functions.

Exercises

1. Write the prototype for a function named Perimeter, which returns an unsigned long int and which takes two parameters, both unsigned short ints.

   ```
   unsigned long int Perimeter(unsigned short int, unsigned short int);
   ```

2. Write the definition of the function Perimeter as described in Exercise 1. The two parameters represent the length and width of a rectangle and have the function return the perimeter (twice the length plus twice the width).

   ```
   unsigned long int Perimeter(unsigned short int length, unsigned short
   int width)
   {
     return 2*length + 2*width;
   }
   ```

3. **BUG BUSTER**: What is wrong with the following function?

```
#include <iostream.h>
void myFunc(unsigned short int x);
int main()
{
    unsigned short int x, y;
    y = myFunc(int);
    cout << "x: " << x << " y: " << y << "\n";
return 0;
}

void myFunc(unsigned short int x)
{
    return (4*x);
}
```

The function is declared to return void and it cannot return a value. Pass x to myFunc rather than int.

4. **BUG BUSTER**: What is wrong with the following function?

```
#include <iostream.h>;
int myFunc(unsigned short int x);
int main()
{
    unsigned short int x, y;
    y = myFunc(x);
    cout << "x: " << x << " y: " << y << "\n";
return 0;
}

int myFunc(unsigned short int x)
{
    return (4*x);
}
```

This function would be fine, but there is a semicolon at the end of the function definition's header.

5. Write a function that takes two unsigned short int arguments and returns the result of dividing the first by the second. Do not do the division if the second number is 0, but do return -1.

```
short int Divider(unsigned short int valOne, unsigned short int
valTwo)
{
    if (valTwo == 0)
        return -1;
    else
        return valOne / valTwo;
}
```

6. Write a program that asks the user for two numbers and calls the function you wrote in Exercise 5. Print the answer, or print an error message if you get -1.

```cpp
#include <iostream.h>
typedef unsigned short int USHORT;
typedef unsigned long int ULONG;
short int Divider(
unsigned short int valone,
unsigned short int valtwo);
int main()
{
    USHORT one, two;
    short int answer;
    cout << "Enter two numbers.\n Number one: ";
    cin >> one;
    cout << "Number two: ";
    cin >> two;
    answer = Divider(one, two);
    if (answer > -1)
        cout << "Answer: " << answer;
    else
        cout << "Error, can't divide by zero!";
return 0;
}
```

7. Write a program that asks for a number and a power. Write a recursive function that takes the number to the power. Thus, if the number is 2 and the power is 4, the function will return 16.

```cpp
#include <iostream.h>
typedef unsigned short USHORT;
typedef unsigned long ULONG;
ULONG GetPower(USHORT n, USHORT power);
int main()
{
    USHORT number, power;
    ULONG answer;
    cout << "Enter a number: ";
    cin >> number;
    cout << "To what power? ";
    cin >> power;
    answer = GetPower(number,power);
    cout << number << " to the " << power << "th power is " <<
answer << endl;
return 0;
}

ULONG GetPower(USHORT n, USHORT power)
{
    if(power == 1)
      return n;
```

```
            else
                return (n * GetPower(n,power-1));
        }
```

Day 6

Quiz

1. What is the dot operator, and what is it used for?

   The dot operator is the period (.). It is used to access the members of the class.

2. Which sets aside memory—declaration or creation?

   Definitions of variables set aside memory. Declarations of classes do not set aside memory (you have to create the object).

3. Is the declaration of a class its interface or its implementation?

   The declaration of a class is its interface; it tells clients of the class how to interact with the class. The implementation of the class is the set of member functions stored—usually in a related CPP file.

4. What is the difference between public and private data members?

   Public data members can be accessed by clients of the class. Private data members can be accessed only by member functions of the class.

5. Can member functions be private?

   Yes. Both member functions and member data can be private.

6. Can member data be public?

   Although member data can be public, it is good programming practice to make it private and to provide public accessor functions to the data.

7. If you declare two Cat objects, can they have different values in their itsAge member data?

   Yes. Each object of a class has its own data members.

8. Do class declarations end with a semicolon? Do class method definitions?

   Declarations end with a semicolon after the closing brace; function definitions do not.

9. What would the header for a Cat function, Meow, that takes no parameters and returns void look like?

   The header for a Cat function, Meow(), that takes no parameters and returns void looks like this:

   ```
   void Cat::Meow()
   ```

D

10. What function is called to initialize a class?

The constructor is called to initialize a class.

Exercises

1. Write the code that declares a class called `Employee` with these data members: `age`, `yearsOfService`, and `Salary`.

```cpp
class Employee
{
    int Age;
    int YearsOfService;
    int Salary;
};
```

2. Rewrite the `Employee` class to make the data members private, and provide public accessor methods to get and set each of the data members.

```cpp
class Employee
{
public:
    int GetAge() const;
    void SetAge(int age);
    int GetYearsOfService()const;
    void SetYearsOfService(int years);
    int GetSalary()const;
    void SetSalary(int salary);

private:
    int Age;
    int YearsOfService;
    int Salary;
};
```

3. Write a program with the `Employee` class that makes two `Employees`; sets their age, `YearsOfService`, and `Salary`; and prints their values.

```cpp
int main()
{
    Employee John;
    Employee Sally;
    John.SetAge(30);
    John.SetYearsOfService(5);
    John.SetSalary(50000);

    Sally.SetAge(32);
    Sally.SetYearsOfService(8);
    Sally.SetSalary(40000);

    cout << "At AcmeSexist company, John and Sally have the same
job.\n";
```

```
        cout << "John is " << John.GetAge() << " years old and he has
    been with";
        cout << "the firm for " << John.GetYearsOfService << "
    years.\n";
        cout << "John earns $" << John.GetSalary << " dollars per
    year.\n\n";
        cout << "Sally, on the other hand is " << Sally.GetAge() << "
    years old and has";
        cout << "been with the company " << Sally.GetYearsOfService;
        cout << " years. Yet Sally only makes $" << Sally.GetSalary();
        cout << " dollars per year!  Something here is unfair.";
        return 0;
    }
```

4. Continuing from Exercise 3, provide a method of `Employee` that reports how many thousands of dollars the employee earns, rounded to the nearest 1,000.

```
float Employee:GetRoundedThousands()const
{
    return (Salary+500) / 1000;
}
```

5. Change the `Employee` class so that you can initialize age, `YearsOfService`, and `Salary` when you create the employee.

```
class Employee
{
public:

    Employee(int Age, int yearsOfService, int salary);
    int GetAge()const;
    void SetAge(int Age);
    int GetYearsOfService()const;
    void SetYearsOfService(int years);
    int GetSalary()const;
    void SetSalary(int salary);

private:
    int Age;
    int YearsOfService;
    int Salary;
};
```

6. **BUG BUSTER**: What is wrong with the following declaration?

```
class Square
{
public:
    int Side;
}
```

Class declarations must end with a semicolon.

7. **BUG BUSTER**: Why isn't the following class declaration very useful?

```
class Cat
{
    int GetAge()const;
private:
    int itsAge;
};
```

The accessor `GetAge()` is private. Remember: All class members are private unless you say otherwise.

8. **BUG BUSTER**: What three bugs will the compiler find in this code?

```
class  TV
{
public:
    void SetStation(int Station);
    int GetStation() const;
private:
    int itsStation;
};

main()
{
    TV myTV;
    myTV.itsStation = 9;
    TV.SetStation(10);
    TV myOtherTv(2);
}
```

You can't access `itsStation` directly. It is private.

You can't call `SetStation()` on the class. You can call `SetStation()` only on objects.

You can't initialize `itsStation` because there is no matching constructor.

Day 7

Quiz

1. How do I initialize more than one variable in a `for` loop?

   Separate the initializations with commas, such as

   `for (x = 0, y = 10; x < 100; x++, y++)`

2. Why is `goto` avoided?

   `goto` jumps in any direction to any arbitrary line of code. This makes for source code that is difficult to understand and therefore difficult to maintain.

3. Is it possible to write a `for` loop with a body that is never executed?

   Yes. If the condition is `false` after the initialization, the body of the `for` loop will never execute. Here's an example:

   ```
   for (int x = 100; x < 100; x++)
   ```

4. Is it possible to nest `while` loops within `for` loops?

   Yes. Any loop can be nested within any other loop.

5. Is it possible to create a loop that never ends? Give an example.

   Yes. Following are examples for both a `for` loop and a `while` loop:

   ```
   for(;;)
   {
       // This for loop never ends!
   }
   while(1)
   {
       // This while loop never ends!
   }
   ```

6. What happens if you create a loop that never ends?

   Your program hangs, and you usually must reboot the computer.

Exercises

1. What is the value of x when the `for` loop completes?

   ```
   for (int x = 0; x < 100; x++)
   100
   ```

2. Write a nested `for` loop that prints a 10×10 pattern of 0s.

   ```
   for (int i = 0; i< 10; i++)
   {
       for ( int j = 0; j< 10; j++)
           cout << "0";
       cout << "\n";
   }
   ```

3. Write a `for` statement to count from 100 to 200 by 2s.

   ```
   for (int x = 100; x<=200; x+=2)
   ```

4. Write a `while` loop to count from 100 to 200 by 2s.

   ```
   int x = 100;
   while (x <= 200)
       x+= 2;
   ```

5. Write a do...while loop to count from 100 to 200 by 2s.

   ```
   int x = 100;
   do
   ```

D

```
{
    x+=2;
} while (x <= 200);
```

6. **BUG BUSTER**: What is wrong with this code?

```
int counter = 0
while (counter < 10)
{
    cout << "counter: " << counter;
}
```

counter is never incremented and the while loop will never terminate.

7. **BUG BUSTER**: What is wrong with this code?

```
for (int counter = 0; counter < 10; counter++);
    cout << counter << "\n";
```

There is a semicolon after the loop, and the loop does nothing. The programmer may have intended this, but if counter was supposed to print each value, it won't.

8. **BUG BUSTER**: What is wrong with this code?

```
int counter = 100;
while (counter < 10)
{
    cout << "counter now: " << counter;
    counter—;
}
```

counter is initialized to 100, but the test condition is that if it is less than 10, the test will fail and the body will never be executed. If line 1 was changed to int counter = 5;, the loop would not terminate until it had counted down past the smallest possible int. Because int is signed by default, this would not be what was intended.

9. **BUG BUSTER**: What is wrong with this code?

```
cout << "Enter a number between 0 and 5: ";
cin >> theNumber;
switch (theNumber)
{
    case 0:
        doZero();
    case 1:                 // fall through
    case 2:                 // fall through
    case 3:                 // fall through
    case 4:                 // fall through
    case 5:
        doOneToFive();
        break;
    default:
```

```
            doDefault();
            break;
    }
```

Case 0 probably needs a break statement. If it does not, it should be documented with a comment.

Day 8

Quiz

1. What operator is used to determine the address of a variable?

   The address of operator (&) is used to determine the address of any variable.

2. What operator is used to find the value stored at an address held in a pointer?

   The dereference operator (*) is used to access the value at an address in a pointer.

3. What is a pointer?

   A pointer is a variable that holds the address of another variable.

4. What is the difference between the address stored in a pointer and the value at that address?

   The address stored in the pointer is the address of another variable. The value stored at that address is any value stored in any variable. The indirection operator (*) returns the value stored at the address, which itself is stored in the pointer.

5. What is the difference between the indirection operator and the address of operator?

   The indirection operator returns the value at the address stored in a pointer. The address of operator (&) returns the memory address of the variable.

6. What is the difference between const int * ptrOne and int * const ptrTwo?

   The const int * ptrOne declares that ptrOne is a pointer to a constant integer. The integer itself cannot be changed using this pointer.

   The int * const ptrTwo declares that ptrTwo is a constant pointer to an integer. After it is initialized, this pointer cannot be reassigned.

Exercises

1. What do these declarations do?

   a. int * pOne;

   b. int vTwo;

   c. int * pThree = &vTwo;

a. `int * pOne;` declares a pointer to an integer.

b. `int vTwo;` declares an integer variable.

c. `int * pThree = &vTwo;` declares a pointer to an integer and initializes it with the address of another variable.

2. If you have an `unsigned short` variable named `yourAge`, how would you declare a pointer to manipulate `yourAge`?

```
unsigned short *pAge = &yourAge;
```

3. Assign the value `50` to the variable `yourAge` by using the pointer that you declared in Exercise 2.

```
*pAge = 50;
```

4. Write a small program that declares an integer and a pointer to integer. Assign the address of the integer to the pointer. Use the pointer to set a value in the integer variable.

```
int theInteger;
int *pInteger = &theInteger;
*pInteger = 5;
```

5. **BUG BUSTER**: What is wrong with this code?

```
#include <iostream.h>
int main()
{
    int *pInt;
    *pInt = 9;
    cout << "The value at pInt: " << *pInt;
return 0;
}
```

`pInt` should have been initialized. More importantly, because it was not initialized and was not assigned the address of any memory, it points to a random place in memory. Assigning `9` to that random place is a dangerous bug.

6. **BUG BUSTER**: What is wrong with this code?

```
int main()
{
    int SomeVariable = 5;
    cout << "SomeVariable: " << SomeVariable << "\n";
    int *pVar = & SomeVariable;
    pVar = 9;
    cout << "SomeVariable: " << *pVar << "\n";
return 0;
}
```

Presumably, the programmer meant to assign `9` to the value at `pVar`. Unfortunately, `9` was assigned to be the value of `pVar` because the indirection operator (`*`) was left off. This will lead to disaster if `pVar` is used to assign a value.

Day 9

Quiz

1. What is the difference between a reference and a pointer?

   A reference is an alias, and a pointer is a variable that holds an address. References cannot be null and cannot be assigned to.

2. When must you use a pointer rather than a reference?

   When you may need to reassign what is pointed to, or when the pointer may be null.

3. What does new return if there is insufficient memory to make your new object?

   A null pointer (0).

4. What is a constant reference?

   This is a shorthand way of saying "a reference to a constant object."

5. What is the difference between passing by reference and passing a reference?

   Passing by reference means not making a local copy. It can be accomplished by passing a reference or by passing a pointer.

Exercises

1. Write a program that declares an int, a reference to an int, and a pointer to an int. Use the pointer and the reference to manipulate the value in the int.

```
int main()
{
int varOne;
int& rVar = varOne;
int* pVar = &varOne;
rVar = 5;
*pVar = 7;
return 0;
}
```

2. Write a program that declares a constant pointer to a constant integer. Initialize the pointer to an integer variable, varOne. Assign 6 to varOne. Use the pointer to assign 7 to varOne. Create a second integer variable, varTwo. Reassign the pointer to varTwo.

```
int main()
{
    int varOne;
    const int * const pVar = &varOne;
    *pVar = 7;
    int varTwo;
```

```
    pVar = &varTwo;
return 0;
}
```

3. Compile the program in Exercise 2. What produces errors? What produces warnings?

    You can't assign a value to a constant object, and you can't reassign a constant pointer.

4. Write a program that produces a stray pointer.

```
int main()
{
int * pVar;
*pVar = 9;
return 0;
}
```

5. Fix the program from Exercise 4.

```
int main()
{
int VarOne;
int * pVar = &varOne;
*pVar = 9;
return 0;
}
```

6. Write a program that produces a memory leak.

```
#include <iostream.h>

int * FuncOne();
int main()
{
    int * pInt = FuncOne();
    cout << "the value of pInt back in main is: " << *pInt << endl;
    return 0;
}

int * FuncOne()
{
    int * pInt = new int (5);
    cout << "the value of pInt in FuncOne is: " << *pInt << endl;
    return pInt;
}
```

7. Fix the program from Exercise 6.

```
#include <iostream.h>

int FuncOne();
int main()
```

```
{
    int theInt = FuncOne();
    cout << "the value of pInt back in main is: " << theInt << endl;
    return 0;
}

int FuncOne()
{
    int * pInt = new int (5);
    cout << "the value of pInt in FuncOne is: " << *pInt << endl;
    delete pInt;
    return temp;
}
```

8. **BUG BUSTER**: What is wrong with this program?

```
1:      #include <iostream.h>
2:
3:      class CAT
4:      {
5:          public:
6:              CAT(int age) { itsAge = age; }
7:              ~CAT(){}
8:              int GetAge() const { return itsAge;}
9:          private:
10:             int itsAge;
11:     };
12:
13:     CAT & MakeCat(int age);
14:     int main()
15:     {
16:         int age = 7;
17:         CAT Boots = MakeCat(age);
18:         cout << "Boots is " << Boots.GetAge() <<
    " years old\n";
19:         return 0;
20:     }
21:
22:     CAT & MakeCat(int age)
23:     {
24:         CAT * pCat = new CAT(age);
25:         return *pCat;
26:     }
```

MakeCat returns a reference to the CAT created on the free store. There is no way to free that memory, and this produces a memory leak.

9. Fix the program from Exercise 8.

```
1:      #include <iostream.h>
2:
3:      class CAT
```

```
4:      {
5:          public:
6:              CAT(int age) { itsAge = age; }
7:              ~CAT(){}
8:              int GetAge() const { return itsAge;}
9:          private:
10:             int itsAge;
11:     };
12:
13:     CAT * MakeCat(int age);
14:     int main()
15:     {
16:         int age = 7;
17:         CAT * Boots = MakeCat(age);
18:         cout << "Boots is " << Boots->GetAge() << " years old\n";
19:         delete Boots;
20:       return 0;
21:     }
22:
23:     CAT * MakeCat(int age)
24:     {
25:         return new CAT(age);
26:     }
```

Day 10

Quiz

1. When you overload member functions, in what ways must they differ?

   Overloaded member functions are functions in a class that share a name but differ in the number or type of their parameters.

2. What is the difference between a declaration and a definition?

   A definition sets aside memory, but a declaration does not. Almost all declarations are definitions; the major exceptions are class declarations, function prototypes, and typedef statements.

3. When is the copy constructor called?

   Whenever a temporary copy of an object is created. This happens every time an object is passed by value.

4. When is the destructor called?

   The destructor is called each time an object is destroyed, either because it goes out of scope or because you call delete on a pointer pointing to it.

5. How does the copy constructor differ from the assignment operator (=)?

The assignment operator acts on an existing object; the copy constructor creates a new one.

6. What is the `this` pointer?

The `this` pointer is a hidden parameter in every member function that points to the object itself.

D

7. How do you differentiate between overloading the prefix and postfix increments?

The prefix operator takes no parameters. The postfix operator takes a single `int` parameter, which is used as a signal to the compiler that this is the postfix variant.

8. Can you overload the `operator+` for `short` integers?

No, you cannot overload any operator for built-in types.

9. Is it legal in C++ to overload `operator++` so that it decrements a value in your class?

It is legal, but it is a bad idea. Operators should be overloaded in a way that is likely to be readily understood by anyone reading your code.

10. What return value must conversion operators have in their declaration?

None. Like constructors and destructors, they have no return values.

Exercises

1. Write a `SimpleCircle` class declaration (only) with one member variable: `itsRadius`. Include a default constructor, a destructor, and accessor methods for `itsRadius`.

```
class SimpleCircle
{
public:
    SimpleCircle();
    ~SimpleCircle();
    void SetRadius(int);
    int GetRadius();
private:
    int itsRadius;
};
```

2. Using the class you created in Exercise 1, write the implementation of the default constructor, initializing `itsRadius` with the value 5.

```
SimpleCircle::SimpleCircle():
itsRadius(5)
{}
```

3. Using the same class, add a second constructor that takes a value as its parameter and assigns that value to itsRadius.

```
SimpleCircle::SimpleCircle(int radius):
itsRadius(radius)
{}
```

4. Create a prefix and postfix increment operator for your SimpleCircle class that increments itsRadius.

```
const SimpleCircle& SimpleCircle::operator++()
{
    ++(itsRadius);
    return *this;
}


// Operator ++(int) postfix.
// Fetch then increment
const SimpleCircle SimpleCircle::operator++ (int)
{
// declare local SimpleCircle and initialize to value of *this
    SimpleCircle temp(*this);
    ++(itsRadius);
    return temp;
}
```

5. Change SimpleCircle to store itsRadius on the free store, and fix the existing methods.

```
class SimpleCircle
{
public:
    SimpleCircle();
    SimpleCircle(int);
    ~SimpleCircle();
    void SetRadius(int);
    int GetRadius();
    const SimpleCircle& operator++();
    const SimpleCircle operator++(int);
private:
    int *itsRadius;
};


SimpleCircle::SimpleCircle()
{itsRadius = new int(5);}

SimpleCircle::SimpleCircle(int radius)
{itsRadius = new int(radius);}

SimpleCircle::~SimpleCircle()
{
```

```
        delete itsRadius;
}

const SimpleCircle& SimpleCircle::operator++()
{
    ++(*itsRadius);
    return *this;
}

// Operator ++(int) postfix.
// Fetch then increment
const SimpleCircle SimpleCircle::operator++ (int)
{
// declare local SimpleCircle and initialize to value of *this
    SimpleCircle temp(*this);
    ++(*itsRadius);
    return temp;
}
```

6. Provide a copy constructor for SimpleCircle.

```
SimpleCircle::SimpleCircle(const SimpleCircle & rhs)
{
    int val = rhs.GetRadius();
    itsRadius = new int(val);
}
```

7. Provide an operator= for SimpleCircle.

```
SimpleCircle& SimpleCircle::operator=(const SimpleCircle & rhs)
{
    if (this == &rhs)
        return *this;
    delete itsRadius;
    itsRadius = new int;
    *itsRadius = rhs.GetRadius();
    return *this;
}
```

8. Write a program that creates two SimpleCircle objects. Use the default constructor on one and instantiate the other with the value 9. Call increment on each and
   then print their values. Finally, assign the second to the first and print its values.

```
#include <iostream.h>

class SimpleCircle
{
public:
    // constructors
    SimpleCircle();
    SimpleCircle(int);
    SimpleCircle(const SimpleCircle &);
```

D

```
    ~SimpleCircle() {}

// accessor functions
    void SetRadius(int);
    int GetRadius()const;

// operators
    const SimpleCircle& operator++();
    const SimpleCircle operator++(int);
    SimpleCircle& operator=(const SimpleCircle &);

private:
    int *itsRadius;
};


SimpleCircle::SimpleCircle()
{itsRadius = new int(5);}

SimpleCircle::SimpleCircle(int radius)
{itsRadius = new int(radius);}

SimpleCircle::SimpleCircle(const SimpleCircle & rhs)
{
    int val = rhs.GetRadius();
    itsRadius = new int(val);
}
SimpleCircle::~SimpleCircle()
{
        delete itsRadius;
}
SimpleCircle& SimpleCircle::operator=(const SimpleCircle & rhs)
{
    if (this == &rhs)
        return *this;
    *itsRadius = rhs.GetRadius();
    return *this;
}

const SimpleCircle& SimpleCircle::operator++()
{
    ++(*itsRadius);
    return *this;
}

// Operator ++(int) postfix.
// Fetch then increment
const SimpleCircle SimpleCircle::operator++ (int)
{
// declare local SimpleCircle and initialize to value of *this
    SimpleCircle temp(*this);
```

```
    ++(*itsRadius);
    return temp;
}
int SimpleCircle::GetRadius() const
{
    return *itsRadius;
}
int main()
{
    SimpleCircle CircleOne, CircleTwo(9);
    CircleOne++;
    ++CircleTwo;
    cout << "CircleOne: " << CircleOne.GetRadius() << endl;
    cout << "CircleTwo: " << CircleTwo.GetRadius() << endl;
    CircleOne = CircleTwo;
    cout << "CircleOne: " << CircleOne.GetRadius() << endl;
    cout << "CircleTwo: " << CircleTwo.GetRadius() << endl;
return 0;
}
```

9. **BUG BUSTER**: What is wrong with this implementation of the assignment operator?

```
SQUARE SQUARE ::operator=(const SQUARE & rhs)
{
    itsSide = new int;
    *itsSide = rhs.GetSide();
    return *this;
}
```

You must check to see whether rhs equals this, or the call to a = a will crash your program.

10. **BUG BUSTER**: What is wrong with this implementation of operator+?

```
VeryShort  VeryShort::operator+ (const VeryShort& rhs)
{
    itsVal += rhs.GetItsVal();
    return *this;
}
```

This operator+ is changing the value in one of the operands, rather than creating a new VeryShort object with the sum. The right way to do this is as follows:

```
VeryShort  VeryShort::operator+ (const VeryShort& rhs)
{
    return VeryShort(itsVal + rhs.GetItsVal());
}
```

Day 11

Quiz

1. What is a v-table?

   A v-table, or virtual function table, is a common way for compilers to manage virtual functions in C++. The table keeps a list of the addresses of all the virtual functions and, depending on the runtime type of the object pointed to, invokes the right function.

2. What is a virtual destructor?

   A destructor of any class can be declared to be virtual. When the pointer is deleted, the runtime type of the object will be assessed and the correct derived destructor invoked.

3. How do you show the declaration of a virtual constructor?

   There are no virtual constructors.

4. How can you create a virtual copy constructor?

   By creating a virtual method in your class, which itself calls the copy constructor.

5. How do you invoke a base member function from a derived class in which you've overridden that function?

   `Base::FunctionName();`

6. How do you invoke a base member function from a derived class in which you have not overridden that function?

   `FunctionName();`

7. If a base class declares a function to be virtual, and a derived class does not use the term `virtual` when overriding that class, is it still virtual when inherited by a third-generation class?

   Yes, the virtuality is inherited and cannot be turned off.

8. What is the `protected` keyword used for?

   `protected` members are accessible to the member functions of derived objects.

Exercises

1. Show the declaration of a virtual function taking an integer parameter and returning `void`.

   `virtual void SomeFunction(int);`

2. Show the declaration of a class `Square`, which derives from `Rectangle`, which in turn derives from `Shape`.

```
class Square : public Rectangle
{};
```

3. If, in Exercise 2, `Shape` takes no parameters, `Rectangle` takes two (`length` and `width`), and `Square` takes only one (`length`), show the constructor initialization for `Square`.

```
Square::Square(int length):
    Rectangle(length, length){}
```

4. Write a virtual copy constructor for the class `Square` (from the preceding question).

```
class Square
    {
        public:
        // …
        virtual Square * clone() const { return new Square(*this); }
        // …
    };
```

5. **BUG BUSTER**: What is wrong with this code snippet?

```
void SomeFunction (Shape);
Shape * pRect = new Rectangle;
SomeFunction(*pRect);
```

Perhaps nothing. `SomeFunction` expects a `Shape` object. You've passed it a `Rectangle` "sliced" down to a `Shape`. As long as you don't need any of the `Rectangle` parts, this will be fine. If you do need the `Rectangle` parts, you'll need to change `SomeFunction` to take a pointer or a reference to a `Shape`.

6. **BUG BUSTER**: What is wrong with this code snippet?

```
class Shape()
{
public:
    Shape();
    virtual ~Shape();
    virtual Shape(const Shape&);
};
```

You can't declare a copy constructor to be virtual.

Day 12

Quiz

1. What are the first and last elements in `SomeArray[25]`?

   `SomeArray[0]`, `SomeArray[24]`

2. How do you declare a multidimensional array?

   Write a set of subscripts for each dimension. For example, `SomeArray[2][3][2]` is a three-dimensional array. The first dimension has two elements, the second has three, and the third has two.

3. Initialize the members of the array in Question 2.

   ```
   SomeArray[2][3][2] = { { {1,2},{3,4},{5,6} } ,
   { {7,8},{9,10},{11,12} } };
   ```

4. How many elements are in the array `SomeArray[10][5][20]`?

   $10 \times 5 \times 20 = 1,000$

5. What is the maximum number of elements that you can add to a linked list?

   There is no fixed maximum. It depends on how much memory you have available.

6. Can you use subscript notation on a linked list?

   You can use subscript notation on a linked list only by writing your own class to contain the linked list and overloading the subscript operator.

7. What is the last character in the string "Brad is a nice guy"?

   The null character.

Exercises

1. Declare a two-dimensional array that represents a tic-tac-toe game board.

   ```
   int GameBoard[3][3];
   ```

2. Write the code that initializes all the elements in the array you created in Exercise 1 to the value 0.

   ```
   int GameBoard[3][3] = { {0,0,0},{0,0,0},{0,0,0} }
   ```

3. Write the declaration for a `Node` class that holds integers.

   ```
   class Node
   {
   public:
       Node ();
       Node (int);
       ~Node();
       void SetNext(Node * node) { itsNext = node; }
   ```

```
      Node * GetNext() const { return itsNext; }
      int GetVal() const { return itsVal; }
      void Insert(Node *);
      void Display();
   private:
      int itsVal;
      Node * itsNext;
   };
```

4. **BUG BUSTER**: What is wrong with this code fragment?

```
unsigned short SomeArray[5][4];
for (int i = 0; i<4; i++)
     for (int j = 0; j<5; j++)
          SomeArray[i][j] = i+j;
```

The array is 5 elements by 4 elements, but the code initializes 4×5.

5. **BUG BUSTER**: What is wrong with this code fragment?

```
unsigned short SomeArray[5][4];
for (int i = 0; i<=5; i++)
     for (int j = 0; j<=4; j++)
          SomeArray[i][j] = 0;
```

You wanted to write i<5, but you wrote i<=5 instead. The code will run when i ==
5 and j == 4, but there is no such element as SomeArray[5][4].

Day 13

Quiz

1. What is a down cast?

   A down cast (also called "casting down") is a declaration that a pointer to a base
   class is to be treated as a pointer to a derived class.

2. What is the v-ptr?

   The v-ptr, or virtual-function pointer, is an implementation detail of virtual functions. Each object in a class with virtual functions has a v-ptr, which points to the
   virtual function table for that class.

3. If a round rectangle has straight edges and rounded corners, your RoundRect class
   inherits both from Rectangle and from Circle, and they in turn both inherit from
   Shape, how many Shapes are created when you create a RoundRect?

   If neither class inherits using the keyword virtual, two Shapes are created: one
   for Rectangle and one for Shape. If the keyword virtual is used for both classes,
   only one shared Shape is created.

4. If `Horse` and `Bird` inherit `virtual public` from `Animal`, do their constructors initialize the Ánimal constructor? If `Pegasus` inherits from both `Horse` and `Bird`, how does it initialize `Animal`'s constructor?

Both `Horse` and `Bird` initialize their base class, `Animal`, in their constructors. `Pegasus` does as well, and when a `Pegasus` is created, the `Horse` and `Bird` initializations of `Animal` are ignored.

5. Declare a class `Vehicle` and make it an abstract data type.

```
class Vehicle
{
    virtual void Move() = 0;
}
```

6. If a base class is an ADT, and it has three pure virtual functions, how many of these functions must be overridden in its derived classes?

None must be overridden unless you want to make the class non-abstract, in which case all three must be overridden.

Exercises

1. Show the declaration for a class `JetPlane`, which inherits from `Rocket` and `Airplane`.

```
class JetPlane : public Rocket, public Airplane
```

2. Show the declaration for 777, which inherits from the `JetPlane` class described in Exercise 1.

```
class 777 : public JetPlane
```

3. Show the declarations for the classes `Car` and `Bus`, which each derive from the class `Vehicle`. Make `Vehicle` an ADT with two pure virtual functions. Make `Car` and `Bus` not be ADTs.

```
class Vehicle
{
    virtual void Move() = 0;
    virtual void Haul() = 0;
};

class Car : public Vehicle
{
    virtual void Move();
    virtual void Haul();
};

class Bus : public Vehicle
{
    virtual void Move();
    virtual void Haul();
};
```

4. Modify the program in Exercise 3 so that Car is an ADT, and derive SportsCar and Coupe from Car. In the Car class, provide an implementation for one of the pure virtual functions in Vehicle and make it non-pure.

```
class Vehicle
{
    virtual void Move() = 0;
    virtual void Haul() = 0;
};

class Car : public Vehicle
{
    virtual void Move();
};

class Bus : public Vehicle
{
    virtual void Move();
    virtual void Haul();
};

class SportsCar : public Car
{
    virtual void Haul();
};

class Coupe : public Car
{
    virtual void Haul();
};
```

Day 14

Quiz

1. Can static member variables be private?

   Yes. They are member variables, and their access can be controlled like any other. If they are private, they can be accessed only by using member functions or, more commonly, static member functions.

2. Show the declaration for a static member variable.

   ```
   static int itsStatic;
   ```

3. Show the declaration for a static function.

   ```
   static int SomeFunction();
   ```

4. Show the declaration for a pointer to function returning `long` and taking an integer parameter.

```
long (* function)(int);
```

5. Modify the pointer in Exercise 4 to be a pointer to member function of class `Car`.

```
long ( Car::*function)(int);
```

6. Show the declaration for an array of 10 pointers as defined in Exercise 5.

```
typedef long (Car::*Function)(int);
Function theArray[10];
```

Other (non-GNU) compilers may prefer the following:

```
long ( Car::*function)(int) theArray [10];
```

Exercises

1. Write a short program declaring a class with one member variable and one static member variable. Have the constructor initialize the member variable and increment the static member variable. Have the destructor decrement the member variable.

```
1:     class myClass
2:     {
3:     public:
4:         myClass();
5:         ~myClass();
6:     private:
7:         int itsMember;
8:         static int itsStatic;
9:     };
10:
11:    myClass::myClass():
12:     itsMember(1)
13:    {
14:        itsStatic++;
15:    }
16:
17:    myClass::~myClass()
18:    {
19:        itsStatic—;
20:    }
21:
22:    int myClass::itsStatic = 0;
23:
24:    int main()
25:    {}
```

2. Using the program from Exercise 1, write a short driver program that makes three objects and then displays their member variables and the static member variable.

Then destroy each object and show the effect on the static member variable.

```
1:     #include <iostream.h>
2:
3:     class myClass
4:     {
5:     public:
6:         myClass();
7:         ~myClass();
8:         void ShowMember();
9:         void ShowStatic();
10:    private:
11:        int itsMember;
12:        static int itsStatic;
13:    };
14:
15:    myClass::myClass():
16:     itsMember(1)
17:    {
18:        itsStatic++;
19:    }
20:
21:    myClass::~myClass()
22:    {
23:        itsStatic-;
24:        cout << "In destructor. ItsStatic: " << itsStatic << endl;
25:    }
26:
27:    void myClass::ShowMember()
28:    {
29:        cout << "itsMember: " << itsMember << endl;
30:    }
31:
32:    void myClass::ShowStatic()
33:    {
34:        cout << "itsStatic: " << itsStatic << endl;
35:    }
36:    int myClass::itsStatic = 0;
37:
38:    int main()
39:    {
40:        myClass obj1;
41:        obj1.ShowMember();
42:        obj1.ShowStatic();
43:
44:        myClass obj2;
45:        obj2.ShowMember();
46:        obj2.ShowStatic();
47:
48:        myClass obj3;
49:        obj3.ShowMember();
```

D

```
50:        obj3.ShowStatic();
51:     return 0;
52:     }
```

3. Modify the program from Exercise 2 to use a static member function to access the static member variable. Make the static member variable private.

```
1:      #include <iostream.h>
2:
3:      class myClass
4:      {
5:      public:
6:          myClass();
7:          ~myClass();
8:          void ShowMember();
9:          static int GetStatic();
10:     private:
11:         int itsMember;
12:         static int itsStatic;
13:     };
14:
15:     myClass::myClass():
16:      itsMember(1)
17:     {
18:         itsStatic++;
19:     }
20:
21:     myClass::~myClass()
22:     {
23:         itsStatic—;
24:         cout << "In destructor. ItsStatic: " << itsStatic << endl;
25:     }
26:
27:     void myClass::ShowMember()
28:     {
29:         cout << "itsMember: " << itsMember << endl;
30:     }
31:
32:     int myClass::itsStatic = 0;
33:
34:     void myClass::GetStatic()
35:     {
36:         return itsStatic;
37:     }
38:
39:     int main()
40:     {
41:         myClass obj1;
42:         obj1.ShowMember();
43:         cout << "Static: " << myClass::GetStatic() << endl;
44:
```

```
45:          myClass obj2;
46:          obj2.ShowMember();
47:          cout << "Static: " << myClass::GetStatic() << endl;
48:
49:          myClass obj3;
50:          obj3.ShowMember();
51:          cout << "Static: " << myClass::GetStatic() << endl;
52:       return 0;
53:       }
```

4. Write a pointer to a member function to access the non-static member data in the program in Exercise 3, and use that pointer to print the value of that data.

```
1:       #include <iostream.h>
2:
3:       class myClass
4:       {
5:       public:
6:           myClass();
7:           ~myClass();
8:           void ShowMember();
9:           static int GetStatic();
10:      private:
11:          int itsMember;
12:          static int itsStatic;
13:      };
14:
15:      myClass::myClass():
16:       itsMember(1)
17:      {
18:          itsStatic++;
19:      }
20:
21:      myClass::~myClass()
22:      {
23:          itsStatic—;
24:          cout << "In destructor. ItsStatic: " << itsStatic << endl;
25:      }
26:
27:      void myClass::ShowMember()
28:      {
29:          cout << "itsMember: " << itsMember << endl;
30:      }
31:
32:      int myClass::itsStatic = 0;
33:
34:      int myClass::GetStatic()
35:      {
36:          return itsStatic;
37:      }
38:
```

D

```
39:    int main()
40:    {
41:        void (myClass::*PMF) ();
42:
43:        PMF=myClass::ShowMember;
44:
45:        myClass obj1;
46:        (obj1.*PMF)();
47:        cout << "Static: " << myClass::GetStatic() << endl;
48:
49:        myClass obj2;
50:        (obj2.*PMF)();
51:        cout << "Static: " << myClass::GetStatic() << endl;
52:
53:        myClass obj3;
54:        (obj3.*PMF)();
55:        cout << "Static: " << myClass::GetStatic() << endl;
56:     return 0;
57:    }
```

5. Add two more member variables to the class from the previous question. Add accessor functions that get the value of this data and give all the member functions the same return values and signatures. Use the pointer to the member function to access these functions.

```
1:     #include <iostream.h>
2:
3:     class myClass
4:     {
5:     public:
6:         myClass();
7:         ~myClass();
8:         void ShowMember();
9:         void ShowSecond();
10:        void ShowThird();
11:        static int GetStatic();
12:     private:
13:        int itsMember;
14:        int itsSecond;
15:        int itsThird;
16:        static int itsStatic;
17:     };
18:
19:     myClass::myClass():
20:      itsMember(1),
21:      itsSecond(2),
22:      itsThird(3)
23:     {
24:         itsStatic++;
25:     }
```

```
26:
27:     myClass::~myClass()
28:     {
29:         itsStatic—;
30:         cout << "In destructor. ItsStatic: " << itsStatic << endl;
31:     }
32:
33:     void myClass::ShowMember()
34:     {
35:         cout << "itsMember: " << itsMember << endl;
36:     }
37:
38:     void myClass::ShowSecond()
39:     {
40:         cout << "itsSecond: " << itsSecond << endl;
41:     }
42:
43:     void myClass::ShowThird()
44:     {
45:         cout << "itsThird: " << itsThird << endl;
46:     }
47:     int myClass::itsStatic = 0;
48:
49:     int myClass::GetStatic()
50:     {
51:         return itsStatic;
52:     }
53:
54:     int main()
55:     {
56:         void (myClass::*PMF) ();
57:
58:         myClass obj1;
59:         PMF=myClass::ShowMember;
60:         (obj1.*PMF)();
61:         PMF=myClass::ShowSecond;
62:         (obj1.*PMF)();
63:         PMF=myClass::ShowThird;
64:         (obj1.*PMF)();
65:         cout << "Static: " << myClass::GetStatic() << endl;
66:
67:         myClass obj2;
68:         PMF=myClass::ShowMember;
69:         (obj2.*PMF)();
70:         PMF=myClass::ShowSecond;
71:         (obj2.*PMF)();
72:         PMF=myClass::ShowThird;
73:         (obj2.*PMF)();
74:         cout << "Static: " << myClass::GetStatic() << endl;
75:
76:         myClass obj3;
```

```
77:        PMF=myClass::ShowMember;
78:        (obj3.*PMF)();
79:        PMF=myClass::ShowSecond;
80:        (obj3.*PMF)();
81:        PMF=myClass::ShowThird;
82:        (obj3.*PMF)();
83:        cout << "Static: " << myClass::GetStatic() << endl;
84:     return 0;
85:     }
```

Day 15

Quiz

1. How do you establish an *is-a* relationship?

   With public inheritance.

2. How do you establish a *has-a* relationship?

   With containment; that is, one class has a member that is an object of another type.

3. What is the difference between containment and delegation?

   Containment describes the idea of one class having a data member that is an object of another type. Delegation expresses the idea that one class uses another class to accomplish a task or goal. Delegation is usually accomplished by containment.

4. What is the difference between delegation and implemented-in-terms-of?

   Delegation expresses the idea that one class uses another class to accomplish a task or goal. Implemented-in-terms-of expresses the idea of inheriting implementation from another class.

5. What is a friend function?

   A friend function is a function declared to have access to the protected and private members of your class.

6. What is a friend class?

   A friend class is a class declared so that all its member functions are friend functions of your class.

7. If Dog is a friend of Boy, is Boy a friend of Dog?

   No, friendship is not commutative.

8. If Dog is a friend of Boy, and Terrier derives from Dog, is Terrier a friend of Boy?

   No, friendship is not inherited.

9. If Dog is a friend of Boy and Boy is a friend of House, is Dog a friend of House?

   No, friendship is not associative.

10. Where must the declaration of a friend function appear?

Anywhere within the class declaration. It makes no difference whether you put the declaration within the `public:`, `protected:`, or `private:` access areas.

Exercises

1. Show the declaration of a class `Animal` that contains a data member that is a `String` object.

```
class Animal:
{
private:
    String itsName;
};
```

2. Show the declaration of a class `BoundedArray` that is an array.

```
class boundedArray : public Array
{
//...
}
```

3. Show the declaration of a class `Set` that is declared in terms of an array.

```
class Set : private Array
{
// ...
}
```

4. Modify Listing 15.1 to provide the `String` class with an extraction operator (>>).

```
1:          #include <iostream.h>
2:          #include <string.h>
3:
4:          class String
5:          {
6:              public:
7:                  // constructors
8:                  String();
9:                   String(const char *const);
10:                  String(const String &);
11:                  ~String();
12:
13:                  // overloaded operators
14:                  char & operator[](int offset);
15:                  char operator[](int offset) const;
16:                  String operator+(const String&);
17:                  void operator+=(const String&);
18:                  String & operator= (const String &);
19:                  friend ostream& operator<<
20:                      ( ostream&  _theStream,String& theString);
21:                  friend istream& operator>>
```

```
22:                    ( istream& _theStream,String& theString);
23:              // General accessors
24:              int GetLen()const { return itsLen; }
25:              const char * GetString() const { return itsString; }
26:              // static int ConstructorCount;
27:
28:          private:
29:              String (int);          // private constructor
30:              char * itsString;
31:              unsigned short itsLen;
32:
33:      };
34:
35:      ostream& operator<<( ostream& theStream,String& theString)
36:      {
37:          theStream << theString.GetString();
38:          return theStream;
39:      }
40:
41:      istream& operator>>( istream& theStream,String& theString)
42:      {
43:          theStream >> theString.GetString();
44:          return theStream;
45:      }
46:
47:      int main()
48:      {
49:          String theString("Hello world.");
50:          cout << theString;
51:      return 0;
52:      }
```

5. **BUG BUSTER**: What is wrong with this program?

```
1:      #include <iostream.h>
2:
3:      class Animal;
4:
5:      void setValue(Animal& , int);
6:
7:
8:      class Animal
9:      {
10:     public:
11:         int GetWeight()const { return itsWeight; }
12:         int GetAge() const { return itsAge; }
13:     private:
14:         int itsWeight;
15:         int itsAge;
16:     };
17:
```

```
18:     void setValue(Animal& theAnimal, int theWeight)
19:     {
20:         friend class Animal;
21:         theAnimal.itsWeight = theWeight;
22:     }
23:
24:     int main()
25:     {
26:         Animal peppy;
27:         setValue(peppy,5);
28:       return 0;
29:     }
```

D

You can't put the friend declaration into the function. You must declare the function to be a friend in the class.

6. Fix the listing in Exercise 5 so that it will compile.

```
1:      #include <iostream.h>
2:
3:      class Animal;
4:
5:      void setValue(Animal& , int);
6:
7:
8:      class Animal
9:      {
10:     public:
11:         friend void setValue(Animal&, int);
12:         int GetWeight()const { return itsWeight; }
13:         int GetAge() const { return itsAge; }
14:     private:
15:         int itsWeight;
16:         int itsAge;
17:     };
18:
19:     void setValue(Animal& theAnimal, int theWeight)
20:     {
21:         theAnimal.itsWeight = theWeight;
22:     }
23:
24:     int main()
25:     {
26:         Animal peppy;
27:         setValue(peppy,5);
28:       return 0;
29:     }
```

7. **BUG BUSTER**: What is wrong with this code?

```
1:      #include <iostream.h>
2:
3:      class Animal;
```

```
4:
5:        void setValue(Animal& , int);
6:        void setValue(Animal& ,int,int);
7:
8:        class Animal
9:        {
10:       friend void setValue(Animal& ,int); // here's the change!
11:       private:
12:          int itsWeight;
13:          int itsAge;
14:       };
15:
16:       void setValue(Animal& theAnimal, int theWeight)
17:       {
18:           theAnimal.itsWeight = theWeight;
19:       }
20:
21:
22:       void setValue(Animal& theAnimal, int theWeight, int theAge)
23:       {
24:          theAnimal.itsWeight = theWeight;
25:          theAnimal.itsAge = theAge;
26:       }
27:
28:       int main()
29:       {
30:          Animal peppy;
31:          setValue(peppy,5);
32:          setValue(peppy,7,9);
33:        return 0;
34:       }
```

The function setValue(Animal&,int) was declared to be a friend, but the over-loaded function setValue(Animal&,int,int) was not declared to be a friend.

8. Fix Exercise 7 so it compiles.

```
1:        #include <iostream.h>
2:
3:        class Animal;
4:
5:        void setValue(Animal& , int);
6:        void setValue(Animal& ,int,int); // here's the change!
7:
8:        class Animal
9:        {
10:       friend void setValue(Animal& ,int);
11:       friend void setValue(Animal& ,int,int);
12:       private:
13:          int itsWeight;
14:          int itsAge;
```

```
15:    };
16:
17:    void setValue(Animal& theAnimal, int theWeight)
18:    {
19:        theAnimal.itsWeight = theWeight;
20:    }
21:
22:
23:    void setValue(Animal& theAnimal, int theWeight, int theAge)
24:    {
25:        theAnimal.itsWeight = theWeight;
26:        theAnimal.itsAge = theAge;
27:    }
28:
29:    int main()
30:    {
31:        Animal peppy;
32:        setValue(peppy,5);
33:        setValue(peppy,7,9);
34:      return 0;
35:    }
```

D

Day 16

Quiz

1. What is the insertion operator and what does it do?

   The insertion operator (<<) is a member operator of the ostream object and is used for writing to the output device.

2. What is the extraction operator and what does it do?

   The extraction operator (>>) is a member operator of the istream object and is used for writing to your program's variables.

3. What are the three forms of cin.get() and what are their differences?

   The first form of get() is without parameters. This returns the value of the character found, and will return EOF (end of file) if the end of the file is reached.

   The second form of cin.get() takes a character reference as its parameter; that character is filled with the next character in the input stream. The return value is an iostream object.

   The final form of get() takes three parameters. The first parameter is a pointer to a character array, the second parameter is the maximum number of characters to read plus one, and the third parameter is the termination character. The return value is the iostream object.

4. What is the difference between `cin.read()` and `cin.getline()`?

   `cin.read()` is used for reading binary data structures.

   `getline()` is used to read from the `istream`'s buffer.

5. What is the default width for outputting a `long` integer using the insertion operator?

   Wide enough to display the entire number.

6. What is the return value of the insertion operator?

   A reference to an `istream` object.

7. What parameter does the constructor to an `ofstream` object take?

   The filename to be opened.

8. What does the `ios::ate` argument do?

   `ios::ate` places you at the end of the file, but you can write data anywhere in the file.

Exercises

1. Write a program that writes to the four standard `iostream` objects: `cin`, `cout`, `cerr`, and `clog`.

```
1:     #include <iostream.h>
2:     int main()
3:     {
4:         int x;
5:         cout << "Enter a number: ";
6:         cin >> x;
7:         cout << "You entered: " << x << endl;
8:         cerr << "Uh oh, this to cerr!" << endl;
9:         clog << "Uh oh, this to clog!" << endl;
10:    return 0;
11:    }
```

2. Write a program that prompts the user to enter her full name and then displays it on the screen.

```
1:     #include <iostream.h>
2:     int main()
3:     {
4:         char name[80];
5:         cout << "Enter your full name: ";
6:         cin.getline(name,80);
7:         cout << "\nYou entered: " << name << endl;
8:     return 0;
9:     }
```

3. Rewrite Listing 16.9 to do the same thing, but without using `putback()` or `ignore()`.

```
1:      // Listing
2:      #include <iostream.h>
3:
4:      int main()
5:      {
6:          char ch;
7:          cout << "enter a phrase: ";
8:          while ( cin.get(ch) )
9:          {
10:             switch (ch)
11:             {
12:               case '!':
13:                   cout << '$';
14:                   break;
15:               case '#':
16:                   break;
17:               default:
18:                   cout << ch;
19:                   break;
20:             }
21:         }
22:         return 0;
23:     }
```

4. Write a program that takes a filename as a parameter and opens the file for reading. Read every character of the file and display only the letters and punctuation to the screen. (Ignore all non-printing characters.) Then close the file and exit.

```
1:      #include <fstream.h>
2:      enum BOOL { FALSE, TRUE };
3:
4:      int main(int argc, char**argv)    // returns 1 on error
5:      {
6:
7:          if (argc != 2)
8:          {
9:              cout << "Usage: argv[0] <infile>\n";
10:             return(1);
11:         }
12:
13:     // open the input stream
14:         ifstream fin (argv[1],ios::binary);
15:         if (!fin)
16:         {
17:             cout << "Unable to open " << argv[1] <<
➥" for reading.\n";
18:             return(1);
19:         }
```

```
20:
21:        char ch;
22:        while ( fin.get(ch))
23:            if ((ch > 32 && ch < 127) ¦¦ ch == '\n' ¦¦ ch == '\t')
24:                cout << ch;
25:        fin.close();
26:    }
```

5. Write a program that displays its command-line arguments in reverse order and does not display the program name.

```
1:     #include <fstream.h>
2:
3:     int main(int argc, char**argv)    // returns 1 on error
4:     {
5:         for (int ctr = argc-1; ctr ; ctr—)
6:             cout << argv[ctr] << " ";
7:       return 0;
8:     }
```

Day 17

Quiz

1. Can I use names defined in a namespace without using the using keyword?

   Yes, you can use names defined in a namespace by prefixing them with the namespace qualifier.

2. What are the major differences between normal and unnamed namespaces?

   Compilers add an implied using directive to an unnamed namespace. Therefore, names in an unnamed namespace can be used without a namespace qualifier. Normal namespaces do not have implied using directives. To use names in normal namespaces, you must either apply the using directives or using declarations, or qualify the names with the namespace qualifier.

   Names in a normal namespace can be used outside of the translation unit where the namespace is declared. Names in an unnamed namespace can only be used within the translation unit where the namespace is declared.

3. What is the standard namespace?

   The standard namespace std is defined by the C++ Standard Library. It includes declarations of all names in the Standard Library.

Exercises

1. **BUG BUSTER**: What is wrong in this program?

```
#include <iostream>

int main()
{
    cout << "Hello world!" << end;
    return 0;
}
```

The C++ standard iostream header file declares cout and endl in namespace std. They cannot be used outside of the standard namespace std without a namespace qualifier.

2. List three ways to fix the problem found in Exercise 5.

```
1.    using namespace std;
2.    using std::cout;
      using std::endl;
3.    std::cout << "Hello world!" << std::endl;
```

Day 18

Quiz

1. What is the difference between object-oriented programming and procedural programming?

   Procedural programming focuses on functions separate from data. Object-oriented programming ties data and functionality together into objects, and focuses on the interaction among the objects.

2. To what does "event-driven" refer?

   Event-driven programs are distinguished by the fact that action is taken only in response to some form of (usually external) event, such as a user's keyboard or mouse input.

3. What are the stages in the development cycle?

   Typically, the development cycle includes analysis, design, coding, testing, programming, and interaction and feedback among these stages.

4. What is a rooted hierarchy?

   A rooted hierarchy is one in which all the classes in the program derive directly or indirectly from a single base class.

D

5. What is a driver program?

A driver program is simply a function that is designed to exercise whatever objects and functions you are currently programming.

6. What is encapsulation?

Encapsulation refers to the (desirable) trait of bringing together in one class all the data and functionality of one discrete entity.

Exercises

1. Suppose you had to simulate the intersection of Massachusetts Avenue and Vassar Street—two typical two-lane roads with traffic lights and crosswalks. The purpose of the simulation is to determine whether the timing of the traffic signal allows for a smooth flow of traffic.

What kinds of objects should be modeled in the simulation? What should be the classes defined for the simulation?

Cars, motorcycles, trucks, bicycles, pedestrians, and emergency vehicles all use the intersection. In addition, there is a traffic signal with Walk/Don't Walk lights.

Should the road surface be included in the simulation?

Certainly, road quality can have an effect on the traffic, but for a first design, it may be simpler to leave this consideration aside.

The first object is probably the intersection itself. Perhaps the intersection object maintains lists of cars waiting to pass through the signal in each direction, as well as lists of people waiting to cross at the crosswalks. It will need methods to choose which and how many cars and people go through the intersection.

There will be only one intersection, so you may want to consider how you will ensure that only one object is instantiated (hint: think about static methods and protected access).

People and cars are both clients of the intersection. They share a number of characteristics: they can appear at any time, there can be any number of them, and they both wait at the signal (although in different lines). This suggests that you will want to consider a common base class for pedestrians and cars.

The classes would therefore include

```
class Entity;    // a client of the intersection

// the root of all cars, trucks, bicycles and emergency vehicles.
class Vehicle : Entity ...;

// the root of all People
class Pedestrian : Entity...;
```

```
class Car : public Vehicle...;
class Truck : public Vehicle...;
class Motorcycle : public Vehicle...;
class Bicycle : public Vehicle...;
class Emergency_Vehicle : public Vehicle...;

// contains lists of cars and people waiting to pass
class Intersection;
```

2. Suppose the intersections from Exercise 1 were in a suburb of Boston, which has arguably the most unfriendly streets in the United States. At any time, there are three kinds of Boston drivers:

Locals, who continue to drive through intersections after the light turns red; tourists, who drive slowly and cautiously (in a rental car, typically); and taxis, which have a wide variation of driving patterns, depending on the kinds of passengers in the cabs.

Also, Boston has two kinds of pedestrians: locals, who cross the street whenever they feel like it and seldom use the crosswalk buttons; and tourists, who always use the crosswalk buttons and cross only when the Walk/Don't Walk light permits. Finally, Boston has bicyclists, who never pay attention to stoplights.

How do these considerations change the model?

A reasonable start on this would be to create derived objects that model the refinements suggested by the problem:

```
class Local_Car : public Car...;
        class Tourist_Car : public Car...;
        class Taxi : public Car...;
        class Local_Pedestrian : public
Pedestrian...;
        class Tourist_Pedestrian : public
Pedestrian...;
        class Boston_Bicycle : public Bicycle...;
```

By using virtual methods, each class can modify the generic behavior to meet its own specifications. For example, the Boston driver can react to a red light differently than a tourist does, while still inheriting the generic behaviors that continue to apply.

3. You are asked to design a group scheduler. The software allows you to arrange meetings among individuals or groups, and to reserve a limited number of conference rooms. Identify the principal subsystems.

Two discrete programs need to be written for this project: the client, which the users run; and the server, which would run on a separate machine. In addition, the client machine would have an administrative component to enable a system administrator to add new people and rooms.

If you decide to implement this as a client/server model, the client would accept input from users and generate a request to the server. The server would service the request and send back the results to the client. With this model, many people can schedule meetings at the same time.

On the client's side, there are two major subsystems in addition to the administrative module: the user interface and the communications subsystem. The server's side consists of three main subsystems: communications, scheduling, and a mail interface that would announce to the user when changes have occurred in the schedule.

4. Design and show the interfaces to the classes in the room-reservation portion of the program discussed in Exercise 3.

A meeting is defined as a group of people reserving a room for a certain amount of time. The person making the schedule might want a specific room, or a specified time; but the scheduler must always be told how long the meeting will last and who is required to attend.

The objects will probably include the users of the system as well as the conference rooms. Don't forget to include classes for the calendar, and perhaps a Meeting class that encapsulates all that is known about a particular event.

The prototypes for the classes might include:

```
class Calendar_Class;          // forward reference
class Meeting;                 // forward reference
class Configuration
{
public:
     Configuration();
     ~Configuration();
     Meeting Schedule( ListOfPerson&, Delta Time
duration );
     Meeting Schedule( ListOfPerson&, Delta Time
duration, Time );
     Meeting Schedule( ListOfPerson&, Delta Time
duration, Room );
     ListOfPerson&     People();      // public
accessors
     ListOfRoom&      Rooms();      // public accessors
protected:
     ListOfRoom      rooms;
     ListOfPerson     people;
};
typedef long       Room_ID;
class Room
{
public:
```

```
      Room( String name, Room_ID id, int capacity,
String directions = "", String description = "" );
      ~Room();
      Calendar_Class Calendar();

protected:
      Calendar_Class     calendar;
      int                capacity;
      Room_ID     id;
      String             name;
      String             directions;         // where is
this room?
      String             description;
};
typedef long Person_ID;
class Person
{
public:
      Person( String name, Person_ID id );
      ~Person();
      Calendar_Class Calendar();          // the access
point to add meetings
protected:
      Calendar_Class     calendar;
      Person_ID     id;
      String             name;
};
class Calendar_Class
{
public:
      Calendar_Class();
      ~Calendar_Class();

      void Add( const Meeting& );               // add a
meeting to the calendar
      void Delete( const Meeting& );
      Meeting* Lookup( Time );               // see if
there is a meeting at the
                                        // given time

      Block( Time, Duration, String reason = "" );
// allocate time to yourself...

protected:
      OrderedListOfMeeting meetings;
};
class Meeting
{
public:
      Meeting( ListOfPerson&, Room room,
```

```
              Time when, Duration duration, String purpose
    = "" );
        ~Meeting();
protected:
    ListOfPerson      people;
    Room              room;
    Time              when;
    Duration          duration;
    String            purpose;
};
```

Day 19

Quiz

1. What is the difference between a template and a macro?

   Templates are built into the C++ language and are type-safe. Macros are implemented by the preprocessor and are not type-safe.

2. What is the difference between the parameter to a template and the parameter to a function?

   The parameter to the template creates an instance of the template for each type. If you create six template instances, six different classes or functions are created. The parameters to the function change the behavior or data of the function, but only one function is created.

3. What is the difference between a type-specific template friend class and a general template friend class?

   The general template friend function creates one function for every type of the parameterized class; the type-specific function creates a type-specific instance for each instance of the parameterized class.

4. Is it possible to provide special behavior for one instance of a template but not for other instances?

   Yes, create a specialized function for the particular instance. In addition to creating `Array<t>::SomeFunction()`, also create `Array<int>::SomeFunction()` to change the behavior for integer arrays.

5. How many static variables are created if you put one static member into a template class definition?

   One for each instance of the class.

6. What are iterators in the C++ Standard Library?

Iterators are generalized pointers. An iterator can be incremented to point to the next node in a sequence. It can also be dereferenced to retrieve the node it points to.

7. What is a function object?

A function object is an instance of a class where the overloaded operator () is defined. It can be used just like a normal function.

D

Exercises

1. Create a template based on this List class:

```
class List
{
private:

public:
    List():head(0),tail(0),theCount(0) {}
    virtual ~List();

    void insert( int value );
    void append( int value );
    int is_present( int value ) const;
    int is_empty() const { return head == 0; }
    int count() const { return theCount; }
private:
    class ListCell
    {
    public:
        ListCell(int value, ListCell *cell = 0):val(value),
next(cell){}
        int val;
        ListCell *next;
    };
    ListCell *head;
    ListCell *tail;
    int theCount;
};
```

Here is one way to implement this template:

```
template <class Type>
class List
{

public:
    List():head(0),tail(0),theCount(0) { }
    virtual ~List();

    void insert( Type value );
    void append( Type value );
```

```
          int is_present( Type value ) const;
          int is_empty() const { return head == 0; }
          int count() const { return theCount; }

    private:
          class ListCell
          {
          public:
              ListCell(Type value, ListCell *cell = 0):val(value),
    ⮠next(cell){}
              Type val;
              ListCell *next;
          };

          ListCell *head;
          ListCell *tail;
          int theCount;
    };
```

2. Write the implementation for the List class (non-template) version.

```
    void List::insert(int value)
    {
          ListCell *pt = new ListCell( value, head );
          assert (pt != 0);

          // this line added to handle tail
          if ( head == 0 ) tail = pt;

          head = pt;
          theCount++;
    }

    void List::append( int value )
    {
          ListCell *pt = new ListCell( value );
          if ( head == 0 )
                head = pt;
          else
                tail->next = pt;

          tail = pt;
          theCount++;
    }

    int List::is_present( int value ) const
    {
          if ( head == 0 ) return 0;
          if ( head->val == value || tail->val == value )
                return 1;
```

```
        ListCell *pt = head->next;
        for (; pt != tail; pt = pt->next)
            if ( pt->val == value )
                    return 1;

        return 0;
}
```

3. Write the template version of the implementations.

```
template <class Type>
List<Type>::~List()
{
        ListCell *pt = head;

        while ( pt )
        {
            ListCell *tmp = pt;
            pt = pt->next;
            delete tmp;
        }
        head = tail = 0;
}

template <class Type>
void List<Type>::insert(Type value)
{
        ListCell *pt = new ListCell( value, head );
        assert (pt != 0);

        // this line added to handle tail
        if ( head == 0 ) tail = pt;

        head = pt;
        theCount++;
}

template <class Type>
void List<Type>::append( Type value )
{
        ListCell *pt = new ListCell( value );
        if ( head == 0 )
                head = pt;
        else
                tail->next = pt;

        tail = pt;
        theCount++;
}

template <class Type>
```

D

```
int List<Type>::is_present( Type value ) const
{
    if ( head == 0 ) return 0;
    if ( head->val == value || tail->val == value )
        return 1;

    ListCell *pt = head->next;
    for (; pt != tail; pt = pt->next)
        if ( pt->val == value )
            return 1;

    return 0;
}
```

4. Declare three `List` objects: a list of strings, a list of `Cats`, and a list of ints.

```
List<String> string_list;
List<Cat> Cat_List;
List<int> int_List;
```

5. **BUG BUSTER**: What is wrong with the following code? (Assume the `List` template is defined, and `Cat` is the class defined earlier in the book.)

```
List<Cat> Cat_List;
Cat Felix;
CatList.append( Felix );
cout << "Felix is " <<
    ( Cat_List.is_present( Felix ) ) ? "" : "not " << "present\n";
```

Hint: (this is tough) What makes `Cat` different from `int`?

`Cat` doesn't have operator `==` defined; all operations that compare the values in the `List` cells, such as `is_present`, will result in compiler errors. To reduce the chance of this, put copious comments before the template definition stating what operations must be defined for the instantiation to compile.

6. Declare friend operator `==` for `List`.

```
friend int operator==( const Type& lhs, const Type& rhs );
```

7. Implement friend operator `==` for `List`.

```
template <class Type>
int List<Type>::operator==( const Type& lhs, const Type& rhs )
{
    // compare lengths first
    if ( lhs.theCount != rhs.theCount )
        return 0;       // lengths differ

    ListCell *lh = lhs.head;
    ListCell *rh = rhs.head;

    for(; lh != 0; lh = lh.next, rh = rh.next )
```

```
        if ( lh.value != rh.value )
            return 0;

    return 1;          // if they don't differ, they must match
}
```

8. Does operator== have the same problem as in Exercise 4?

Yes, because comparing the array involves comparing the elements, operator!= must be defined for the elements as well.

9. Implement a template function for swap, which exchanges two variables.

```
// template swap:
// must have assignment and the copy constructor
// defined for the Type.
template <class Type>
void swap( Type& lhs, Type& rhs)
{
    Type temp( lhs );
    lhs = rhs;
    rhs = temp;
}
```

10. Implement the SchoolClass in Listing 19.8 as a list. Use the push_back() function to add four students to the list. Then traverse the resulting list and increase each student's age by one.

```
#include <list>

template<class T, class A>
void ShowList(const list<T, A>& aList); // display vector properties

typedef list<Student>    SchoolClass;

int main()
{
        Student Harry("Harry", 18);
        Student Sally("Sally", 15);
        Student Bill("Bill", 17);
        Student Peter("Peter", 16);

        SchoolClass GrowingClass;
        GrowingClass.push_back(Harry);
        GrowingClass.push_back(Sally);
        GrowingClass.push_back(Bill);
        GrowingClass.push_back(Peter);
        ShowList(GrowingClass);

        cout << "One year later;\n";

        for (SchoolClass::iterator i = GrowingClass.begin();
```

D

```
                             i != GrowingClass.end(); ++i)
                    i->SetAge(i->GetAge() + 1);

            ShowList(GrowingClass);

        return 0;
}

//
// Display list properties
//
template<class T, class A>
void ShowList(const list<T, A>& aList)
{
        for (list<T, A>::const_iterator ci = aList.begin();
                         ci != aList.end(); ++ci)
            cout << *ci << "\n";

        cout << endl;
}
```

11. Modify Exercise 10 to use a function object to display each student's record.

```
#include <algorithm>

template<class T>
class Print
{
public:
void operator()(const T& t)
{
cout << t << "\n";
}
};

template<class T, class A>
void ShowList(const list<T, A>& aList)
{
        Print<Student>        PrintStudent;

        for_each(aList.begin(), aList.end(), PrintStudent);

        cout << endl;
}
```

Day 20

Quiz

1. What is an exception?

   An exception is an object that is created as a result of invoking the keyword throw. It is used to signal an exceptional condition, and is passed up the call stack to the first catch statement that handles its type.

2. What is a try block?

   A try block is a set of statements that might generate an exception.

3. What is a catch statement?

   A catch statement has a signature of the type of exception it handles. It follows a try block and acts as the receiver of exceptions raised within the try block.

4. What information can an exception contain?

   An exception is an object and can contain any information that can be defined within a user-created class.

5. When are exception objects created?

   Exception objects are created when you invoke the keyword throw.

6. Should you pass exceptions by value or by reference?

   In general, exceptions should be passed by reference. If you don't intend to modify the contents of the exception object, you should pass a const reference.

7. Will a catch statement catch a derived exception if it is looking for the base class?

   Yes, if you pass the exception by reference.

8. If there are two catch statements, one for base and one for derived, which should come first?

   catch statements are examined in the order they appear in the source code. The first catch statement whose signature matches the exception is used.

9. What does catch(...) mean?

   catch(...) will catch any exception of any type.

10. What is a breakpoint?

    A breakpoint is a place in the code where the debugger will stop execution.

D

Exercises

1. Create a try block, a catch statement, and a simple exception.

```cpp
#include <iostream.h>
class OutOfMemory {};
int main()
{

    try
    {
        int *myInt = new int;
        if (myInt == 0)
            throw OutOfMemory();
    }
    catch (OutOfMemory)
    {
        cout << "Unable to allocate memory!\n";
    }
 return 0;
 }
```

2. Modify the answer from Exercise 1, put data into the exception along with an accessor function, and use it in the catch block.

```cpp
#include <iostream.h>
#include <stdio.h>
#include <string.h>
class OutOfMemory
{
public:
    OutOfMemory(char *);
    char* GetString() { return itsString; }
private:
    char* itsString;
};

OutOfMemory::OutOfMemory(char * theType)
{
    itsString = new char[80];
    char warning[] = "Out Of Memory! Can't allocate room for: ";
    strncpy(itsString,warning,60);
    strncat(itsString,theType,19);
}

int main()
{

    try
    {
        int *myInt = new int;
        if (myInt == 0)
```

```
                throw OutOfMemory("int");
        }
        catch (OutOfMemory& theException)
        {
            cout << theException.GetString();
        }
    return 0;
     }
```

3. Modify the class from Exercise 2 to be a hierarchy of exceptions. Modify the
   catch block to use the derived objects and the base objects.

```
1:      #include <iostream.h>
2:
3:      // Abstract exception data type
4:      class Exception
5:      {
6:      public:
7:          Exception(){}
8:          virtual ~Exception(){}
9:          virtual void PrintError() = 0;
10:     };
11:
12:     // Derived class to handle memory problems.
13:     // Note no allocation of memory in this class!
14:     class OutOfMemory : public Exception
15:     {
16:     public:
17:         OutOfMemory(){}
18:         ~OutOfMemory(){}
19:         virtual void PrintError();
20:     private:
21:     };
22:
23:     void OutOfMemory::PrintError()
24:     {
25:         cout << "Out of Memory!!\n";
26:     }
27:
28:     // Derived class to handle bad numbers
29:     class RangeError : public Exception
30:     {
31:     public:
32:         RangeError(unsigned long number){badNumber = number;}
33:         ~RangeError(){}
34:         virtual void PrintError();
35:         virtual unsigned long GetNumber() { return badNumber; }
36:         virtual void SetNumber(unsigned long number) {badNumber =
                        ?number;}
37:     private:
38:         unsigned long badNumber;
```

```
39:    };
40:
41:    void RangeError::PrintError()
42:    {
43:        cout << "Number out of range. You used " << GetNumber() <<
➡                                    ?"!!\n";
44:    }
45:
46:    void MyFunction();   // func. prototype
47:
48:    int main()
49:    {
50:        try
51:        {
52:            MyFunction();
53:        }
54:        // Only one catch required, use virtual functions to do the
55:        // right thing.
56:        catch (Exception& theException)
57:        {
58:            theException.PrintError();
59:        }
60:        return 0;
61:    }
62:
63:    void MyFunction()
64:    {
65:        unsigned int *myInt = new unsigned int;
66:        long testNumber;
67:        if (myInt == 0)
68:            throw OutOfMemory();
69:        cout << "Enter an int: ";
70:        cin >> testNumber;
71:        // this weird test should be replaced by a series
72:        // of tests to complain about bad user input
73:        if (testNumber > 3768 || testNumber < 0)
74:            throw RangeError(testNumber);
75:
76:        *myInt = testNumber;
77:        cout << "Ok. myInt: " << *myInt;
78:        delete myInt;
79:    }
```

4. Modify the program from Exercise 3 to have three levels of function calls.

```
1:    #include <iostream.h>
2:
3:    // Abstract exception data type
4:    class Exception
5:    {
6:    public:
```

```
 7:        Exception(){}
 8:        virtual ~Exception(){}
 9:        virtual void PrintError() = 0;
10:     };
11:
12:     // Derived class to handle memory problems.
13:     // Note no allocation of memory in this class!
14:     class OutOfMemory : public Exception
15:     {
16:     public:
17:        OutOfMemory(){}
18:        ~OutOfMemory(){}
19:        virtual void PrintError();
20:     private:
21:     };
22:
23:     void OutOfMemory::PrintError()
24:     {
25:        cout << "Out of Memory!!\n";
26:     }
27:
28:     // Derived class to handle bad numbers
29:     class RangeError : public Exception
30:     {
31:     public:
32:        RangeError(unsigned long number){badNumber = number;}
33:        ~RangeError(){}
34:        virtual void PrintError();
35:        virtual unsigned long GetNumber() { return badNumber; }
36:        virtual void SetNumber(unsigned long number) {badNumber =
➡                       ?number;}
37:     private:
38:        unsigned long badNumber;
39:     };
40:
41:     void RangeError::PrintError()
42:     {
43:        cout << "Number out of range. You used " << GetNumber() <<
➡                       ?"!!\n";
44:     }
45:
46:     // func. prototypes
47:     void MyFunction();
48:     unsigned int * FunctionTwo();
49:     void FunctionThree(unsigned int *);
50:
51:     int main()
52:     {
53:        try
54:        {
55:           MyFunction();
```

```
56:        }
57:        // Only one catch required, use virtual functions to do the
58:        // right thing.
59:        catch (Exception& theException)
60:        {
61:            theException.PrintError();
62:        }
63:        return 0;
64:    }
65:
66:    unsigned int * FunctionTwo()
67:    {
68:        unsigned int *myInt = new unsigned int;
69:      if (myInt == 0)
70:        throw OutOfMemory();
71:      return myInt;
72:    }
73:
74:    void MyFunction()
75:    {
76:        unsigned int *myInt = FunctionTwo();
77:
78:        FunctionThree(myInt);
79:        cout << "Ok. myInt: " << *myInt;
80:        delete myInt;
81:    }
82:
83:    void FunctionThree(unsigned int *ptr)
84:    {
85:        long testNumber;
86:        cout << "Enter an int: ";
87:        cin >> testNumber;
88:        // this weird test should be replaced by a series
89:        // of tests to complain about bad user input
90:        if (testNumber > 3768 || testNumber < 0)
91:            throw RangeError(testNumber);
92:        *ptr = testNumber;
93:    }
```

5. **BUG BUSTER**: What is wrong with the following code?

```
#include "stringc.h"          // our string class

class xOutOfMemory
{
public:
        xOutOfMemory( const String& where ) : location( where ){}
        ~xOutOfMemory(){}
        virtual String where(){ return location };
```

```
private:
    String location;
}

main()
{
    try {
        char *var = new char;
        if ( var == 0 )
            throw xOutOfMemory();
    }
    catch( xOutOfMemory& theException )
    {
        cout << "Out of memory at " <<
➥theException.location() << "\n";
    }
}
```

In the process of handling an "out of memory" condition, a string object is created by the constructor of xOutOfMemory. This exception can only be raised when the program is out of memory, so this allocation must fail.

It is possible that trying to create this string will raise the same exception, creating an infinite loop until the program crashes. If this string is really required, you can allocate the space in a static buffer before beginning the program, and then use it as needed when the exception is thrown.

Day 21

Quiz

1. What is an inclusion guard?

   Inclusion guards are used to protect a header file from being included into a program more than once.

2. How do you instruct your compiler to print the contents of the intermediate file showing the effects of the preprocessor?

   For the GNU compiler, the option is -E. If you are using a different compiler, the answer to this quiz question must be discovered by you (by looking at the appropriate documentation).

3. What is the difference between #define debug 0 and #undef debug?

   #define debug 0 defines the term debug to equal 0 (zero). Everywhere the word debug is found, the character 0 will be substituted. #undef debug removes any definition of debug; when the word debug is found in the file, it will be left unchanged.

4. What does the complement operator do?

   It flips every bit in a number.

5. What is the difference between OR and exclusive OR?

   OR returns true if either or both bits are set; exclusive OR returns true only if one, but not both, is set.

6. What is the difference between & and &&?

   & is the bitwise AND operator, and && is the logical AND operator.

7. What is the difference between ¦ and ¦¦?

   ¦ is the bitwise OR operator, and ¦¦ is the logical OR operator.

Exercises

1. Write the inclusion guard statements for the header file STRING.H.

```
#ifndef STRING_H
#define STRING_H
...
#endif
```

2. Write an assert() macro that prints an error message and the file and line number if debug level is 2, prints just a message (without file and line number) if the level is 1, and does nothing if the level is 0.

```
1:      #include <iostream.h>
2:
3:      #ifndef DEBUG
4:      #define ASSERT(x)
5:      #elif DEBUG == 1
6:      #define ASSERT(x) \
7:        if (! (x))\
8:        { \
9:           cout << "ERROR!! Assert " << #x << " failed\n"; \
10:                                      }
11:     #elif DEBUG == 2
12:     #define ASSERT(x) \
13:       if (! (x) ) \
14:       { \
15:        cout << "ERROR!! Assert " << #x << " failed\n"; \
16:        cout << " on line " << __LINE __ << "\n'; \
17:          cout << " in file " << __LINE __ << "\n'; \
18:       }
19:     #endif
```

3. Write a macro DPrint that tests whether DEBUG is defined and, if it is, make the macro print the value passed in as a parameter.

```
#ifndef DEBUG
```

```
#define DPRINT(string)
#else
#define DPRINT(STRING) cout << #STRING ;
#endif
```

4. Write a program that adds two numbers without using the addition operator (+), subtraction operator (-), increment (++), or decrement (−). Hint: Use the bit operators!

If you take a look at the addition of two bits, you'll notice the answer will contain two bits: the result bit and the carry bit. Thus, adding 1 and 1 in binary results in 1 with a carry of 1. If we add 101 to 001, here are the results:

```
101  // 5
001  //1
110  //6
```

If you add two "set" bits (each is valued as one), the result is that the result bit is 0 but the carry bit is 1. If you add two clear bits, both the result and the carry are 0. If you add two bits with one set and the other clear, the result bit is 1, but the carry bit is 0. Here is a table that summarizes these rules:

```
lhs   rhs  ¦   carry   result
-- -- --+-- -- -- --
0     0    ¦   0       0
0     1    ¦   0       1
1     0    ¦   0       1
1     1    ¦   1       0
```

Examine the logic of the carry bit. If both bits to be added (lhs and rhs) are 0 or either side is 0, the answer is 0. Only if both bits are 1 is the answer 1. This is exactly the same as the AND operator (&).

In the same way, the result is an XOR (^) operation: if either bit is 1 (but not both), the answer is 1; otherwise, the answer is 0.

When you get a carry, it is added to the next most significant (leftmost) bit. This implies either iterating through each bit or recursion.

```
#include <iostream.h>

unsigned int add( unsigned int lhs, unsigned int rhs )
{
    unsigned int result, carry;

    while ( 1 )
    {
        result = lhs ^ rhs;
        carry = lhs & rhs;

        if ( carry == 0 )
```

```
                break;

            lhs = carry << 1;
            rhs = result;
        };

        return result;
}

int main()
{
        unsigned long a, b;
        for (;;)
        {
                cout << "Enter two numbers. (0 0 to stop): ";
                cin >> a >> b;
                if (!a && !b)
                        break;
                cout <<a << " + " << b << " =  " << add(a,b) << endl;
        }
        return 0;
}
```

Alternatively, you can solve this problem with recursion:

```
#include <iostream.h>

unsigned int add( unsigned int lhs, unsigned int rhs )
{
        unsigned int carry = lhs & rhs;
        unsigned int result = lhs ^ rhs;

        if ( carry )
                return add( result, carry << 1 );
        else
                return result;
}

int main()
{
        unsigned long a, b;
        for (;;)
        {
                cout << "Enter two numbers. (0 0 to stop): ";
                cin >> a >> b;
                if (!a && !b)
                        break;
                cout <<a << " + " << b << " =  " << add(a,b) << endl;
        }
        return 0;
}
```

Day 22

Quiz

1. What is POSIX?

   POSIX is the result of an attempt in the 1980s to create a standardized programming interface for operating systems. The word POSIX is derived from "Portable Operating System Interface."

2. What is X Windows?

   X Windows is the windowing system developed at MIT in the mid-1980s. It is a complex standard based on a client/server model.

3. What are the two primary text editors available with Linux?

   The primary text editors that come with Linux are vim and GNU emacs. vim is an open-source implementation of the vi editor. GNU emacs is an open-source implementation of the original emacs editor.

4. What is a primary distinction between vi and GNU emacs?

   vi and vim are "mode" editors because they have distinct modes. In "insert" mode, all typed characters are inserted into the file being edited. In "command" mode, typed characters are interpreted as commands to the editor. GNU emacs is a "modeless" editor because it does not have these distinct modes. At any time, typed characters may be commands to the editor or inserted into the file, depending on the character sequence.

5. What is an advantage of shared libraries over static libraries? Static libraries over shared libraries?

   Shared libraries result in smaller executable programs. Furthermore, they allow for program upgrade or enhancement without requiring rebuilding of the program. Static libraries simplify installation because program loaders do not need to know the whereabouts of separate libraries at load time.

6. What is the utility used to compile and build programs? What is its default input file?

   The `make` utility is used to compile and build programs. The default input command file is named `GNUmakefile`. If that is not found, `make` will look for `makefile`, and if that is not found, it will look for `Makefile`.

Exercises

1. Create an additional function for the `dice` program presented in today's lesson. The function should take as input a pointer to the `Die` array. For each face of the die,

this function should print out the percentage of times that this face came up. The function should be in a file separate from `main` and `doRoll`.

```
/*
** Listing chapter 22 workshop exercise: "doAverage.c"
*/

#include <stdio.h>

void
doAverage( int * Die )
{
int     i;
int     TotRolls = 0;
double Pct;
double TotPct = 0.0;

  printf("\n\n");
  for( i = -0; i < 6; i++ ) {
    TotRolls += Die[i];
  }

  printf("%d total rolls.\n", TotRolls);

  for( i = 0; i < 6; i++ ) {
    Pct = ((float)Die[i] / (float)TotRolls) * 100.0;
    printf("\t%2d\t%5.2f%%\n", i, Pct);
    TotPct += Pct;
  }
  printf("\t\t=====\n\t\t%5.2f%%\n", TotPct);
}
```

2. Modify the makefile to link in the new function.

```
#
# Makefile for chapter 22 workshop exercise
# no shared libraries
#
#
# $Header$
# $Id$
#
# Makefile to build the dice rolling program
# without shared libraries.

CFLAGS = -O
OBJS   = dice_ex.o doRoll_ex.o doAverage_ex.o

all:    dice
```

```
dice:  $(OBJS)
    $(CC) $(CFLAGS) -o $@ $(OBJS)

clean:
    - $(RM) dice *.o
```

3. Step through the program with gdb.

Day 23

Quiz

1. What is a shell?

   A shell is the program that is the user interface to the operating system. It reads user commands and executes the necessary commands.

2. What is the general syntax of a shell command line?

   Shell command lines are case sensitive, and whitespace is generally ignored. The general syntax of a command line is as follows:

   ```
   command option1 option2 option3 ... optionN
   ```

3. What are the three standard I/O ports available to programs?

   The three ports available to a program are the "standard input" (usually the keyboard), the "standard output" (usually the display), and the "standard error" (also usually the display).

4. What are the three forms of I/O redirection, and what characters are used to represent them on the command line?

   The three main forms of I/O redirection are input redirection (invoked with the "<" character), output redirection (invoked with the ">" character) and pipes (invoked with the "|" character).

5. Are environment variables "local" or "global"? What about shell variables?

   Environment variables are global and are passed to any program or shell initiated by the current shell. Shell variables are local to the current shell.

6. What bash environment variable sets the command search path? Which one sets the command prompt?

   In the bash shell, the PATH variable sets the command search path, and the variable PS1 sets the command prompt.

7. Name two command-line wildcard substitution characters.

   The asterisk (*) is a wildcard character that matches any sequence of 0 or more characters. The question mark (?) matches any single character.

8. What needs to be in a shell script file so that the shell knows what command to feed the script to?

The first line of any shell script should contain #! followed by the complete path to the name of the shell that should be used to process the script. For example, line 1 of a bash script would contain #!/bin/sh.

Exercises

1. Write a bash script to print out all the command-line arguments passed to it, as well as the total number of arguments.

```
#!/bin/bash
#
echo "$# arguments"

for i do
  echo "argument <$i>"
done
```

Day 24

Quiz

1. List and define the states of a process.

- TASK_RUNNING—Process is waiting to run.

- TASK_INTERRUPTIBLE—Task is running and is interruptible.

- TASK_UNINTERRUPTIBLE—Task is running and is not interruptible.

- TASK_ZOMBIE—Task has stopped, but the system still considers it running.

- TASK_STOPPED—The process is stopped, typically from receiving a signal.

- TASK_SWAPPING—The task is swapping.

2. Describe the difference between the FIFO and Round Robin scheduling policy.

First in, first out schedules each runnable process in the order that it is in on the run queue, and that order is never changed. A FIFO process will run until it blocks on I/O or is pre-empted by a higher priority process.

Round robin scheduling runs real-time processes in turn. The difference between a FIFO process and a round-robin process is that a round-robin process will run for a specified time (quantum) and then be swapped out and placed at the end of the priority list.

3. What is the difference between a binary semaphore and counting semaphore?

   Conceptually there are two basic types of semaphores: *binary semaphores* and *counting semaphores*. A binary semaphore never takes on values other than zero or one, and is logically just like a mutex. A counting semaphore can take on arbitrary nonnegative values.

4. List and define the four requisites for a deadlock.

   Four conditions must exist to characterize a deadlock condition:

   1. Mutual exclusion—At least one lock is non-shareable.
   2. Hold and wait—One thread is holding a resource and waiting for a resource held by another thread.
   3. Non-pre-emption—A held resource can only be released by the thread that has ownership.
   4. Circular wait—There must be a set of waiting threads, {t0, t1, t2, ... t(n)}.

Exercises

1. Using a counting semaphore, how could you resolve the race condition when starting threads?

   - Create a semaphore and decrement its value to the number of threads being started; that is, if there are three threads, decrement the semaphore three times.
   - At the beginning of each thread, acquire the semaphore.
   - The threads will block until all the threads are started.

2. Implement the re-entrant example in Listing 24.8 using the condition variable object, CondVar.

```
#include <iostream.h>

#include "tcreate.h"
#include "mutex.h"

int data;

void read_thread(void* param)
{
    CondVar* pCond = static_cast<CondVar*>(param);

    while (1)
    {
```

```cpp
            pCond->Wait();
            cout << "read: " << data << endl;
            pCond->Signal();
        }
    }

    void write_thread(void* param)
    {
        CondVar* pCond = static_cast<CondVar*>(param);

        while(1)
        {
            pCond->Wait();
            cout << "write: " << data++ << endl;
            pCond->Signal();
        }
    }

    int main(int argc, char** argv)
    {
        CondVar lock;
        Thread thread1((void*)&write_thread, &lock);
        Thread thread2((void*)&read_thread, &lock);

        lock.Create();

        thread1.Create();
        thread2.Create();

        for (int i = 0; i < 100000; i++)
        ;   // Null Statement

        lock.Destroy();

        thread1.Destroy();
        thread2.Destroy();

        return 0;
    }
```

Day 25

Quiz

1. List the three routines used to create System V interprocess communication mechanisms.

   msgget, semget, and shmget

2. What signal is thrown if the read and write ends of a pipe are set up?

SIGPIPE

3. Why is shared memory faster than messages?

Copies of data are not performed via the kernel; they are to/from shared memory directly.

4. What is a binary semaphore?

A semaphore whose value is limited to zero and one.

D

Exercises

1. Implement a client/server program where the client and server share data using the SharedMemory class and synchronize access to shared memory using the Semaphore class.

The first listing is ex25-01.cxx—the client; the second listing is ex25-02.cxx—the server; the third listing is ex25-03.mak—the makefile; and the final listing is ex25-04.h—file ex1.h. You will have to rename the files for the make command and #include directives to work properly.

```
#include <lst25-13.h>#include <lst25-15.h>#include "ex1.h"int main(int
argc, char** argv){  char Buffer[BUFFER_SIZE];  // create semaphore  Key*
semkey = new Key();
  semkey->Create(SEM_KEY);
  Semaphore* sem = new Semaphore(*semkey);
  sem->Create(SEM_PERM);


  // create shared memory
  Key *smkey = new Key();
  smkey->Create(SMEM_KEY);
  SharedMemory *smem = new SharedMemory(*smkey);
  smem->Create(SMEM_PERM, BUFFER_SIZE);
  smem->Attach();

  while (1)
  {
    sem->Acquire();

    memcpy(Buffer, smem, BUFFER_SIZE);

    sem->Release();
  }

  // cleanup
  sem->Destroy();
  smem->Destroy();
```

```
  delete sem;
  delete semkey;
  delete smem;
  delete smkey;

  return (0);
}
```

```
#include <lst25-13.h>#include <lst25-15.h>#include "ex1.h"int main(int
argc, char** argv){  // create semaphore  Key* semkey = new Key();   semkey-
>Create(SEM_KEY);  Semaphore* sem = new Semaphore(*semkey);
  sem->Create(SEM_PERM);


  // create shared memory
  Key *smkey = new Key();
  smkey->Create(SMEM_KEY);
  SharedMemory *smem = new SharedMemory(*smkey);
  smem->Create(SMEM_PERM, BUFFER_SIZE);
  smem->Attach();

  while (1)
  {
    int i = 0;

    sem->Acquire();

    memset(smem, i, BUFFER_SIZE);

    sem->Release();
  }

  // cleanup
  sem->Destroy();
  smem->Destroy();

  delete sem;
  delete semkey;
  delete smem;
  delete smkey;

  return (0);
}
```

```
INCLUDES= -I../inc -I../SharedMemory -I../Semaphores -I../KeyCFLAGS= -
WallOBJS=../obj/key.o ../obj/semap.o ../obj/smem.o all: client
serverclient: client.cxx    gcc -o client client.cxx $(OBJS) -lstdc++
$(INCLUDES)server: server.cxx
   gcc -o server server.cxx $(OBJS) -lstdc++ $(INCLUDES)
```

```
#define SEM_KEY   1122#define SEM_PERM  0666#define SMEM_KEY  5678#define
SMEM_PERM 0666#define BUFFER_SIZE 4096
```

2. Using pipes, set up full duplex communication between a parent process and a child process.

The first listing is ex25-05.cxx—the main program; the second listing is ex25-06.mak—the makefile; and the final listing is ex25-07.cxx—the pipe (which is the same as 1st25-02.cxx from that day). You will have to rename the files for the make command and #include directives to work properly.

```cpp
#include <iostream>
#include "1st25-02.h"

using namespace std;

int main(int argc, char** argv)
{
  Pipe* rp = new Pipe;
  Pipe* wp = new Pipe;

  char msg[] = "hello world\n";
  char buf[128];

  rp->Create();
  wp->Create();

  if (fork() > 0)
  {
    rp->SetToRead();
    rp->ReadFromPipe(static_cast<char*>(buf));

    wp->SetToWrite();
    wp->WriteToPipe(static_cast<char*>(msg));

    cout << buf << endl;
  }
  else
  {
    rp->SetToWrite();
    rp->WriteToPipe(static_cast<char*>(msg));

    wp->SetToRead();
    wp->ReadFromPipe(static_cast<char*>(buf));
  }

  delete rp;
  delete wp;

  exit (0);
}
INCLUDES=-I../inc -I../Key -I../Pipes
CFLAGS=-c
```

D

```
OBJS=pipe.o

all: pipetest

main.o : main.cxx
    gcc $(CFLAGS) -o main.o main.cxx $(INCLUDES)

pipetest: pipe.o main.o
    gcc -o pipetest main.o $(OBJS) -lstdc++
```

```cpp
#include <iostream>#include "lst25-02.h"
Pipe::Pipe() :
  init_(false),
  read_(false)
{
}

Pipe::~Pipe()
{
  if (init_)
    Destroy();
}

int Pipe::Create()
{
  if (pipe(pipe_) >= 0)
    init_ = true;
}

int Pipe::Destroy()
{
  if (read_)
    close(pipe_[0]);
  else
    close(pipe_[1]);
}

void Pipe::SetToRead()
{
  read_ = true;
  close(pipe_[1]);
}

void Pipe::SetToWrite()
{
  read_ = false;
  close(pipe_[0]);
}

int Pipe::ReadFromPipe(char* buf)
{
```

```
    if (!read_)
      return -1;

    read(pipe_[0], buf, strlen(buf));
  }

  int Pipe::WriteToPipe(char* buf)
  {
    if (read_)
      return -1;

    write(pipe_[1], buf, strlen(buf));
  }
```

3. Extend the NamedPipe class in order to open nonblocking pipes and create read and write routines that reflect that there was no data available. Do this so that the NamedPipe object can detect that there is no data and therefore perform other actions.

The first listing is ex25-08.cxx—the client; the second listing is ex25-09.cxx— the server; the third listing is ex25-10.cxx—the named pipe implementation; the fourth listing is ex25-11.h—file np.h; and the final listing is ex25-12.mak—the makefile. You will have to rename the files for the make command and #include directives to work properly.

```
#include <iostream>
#include "np.h"

int main(int argc, char**argv)
{
  NamedPipe* pipe = new NamedPipe;

  pipe->Create();
  pipe->Open();

  int i = 0;
  do
  {
    const int len = 32;
    char buf[len];

    sprintf(buf, "%d", i++);

    pipe->Write(&buf[0], static_cast<int>(strlen(buf)));

    cout << "client" << buf << endl;
  } while (i < 10);

  pipe->Close();
```

```
    pipe->Destroy();

    delete pipe;
}
#include <iostream>
#include "np.h"

int main(int argc, char**argv)
{
  NamedPipe* pipe = new NamedPipe;

  pipe->Create();
  pipe->Open();

  int i = 0;
  do
  {
    const int len = 32;

    char buf[len];

    if (pipe->Read(buf, len) > 0)
      cout << "server" << buf << endl;

  } while (i < 10);

  pipe->Close();
  pipe->Destroy();

  delete pipe;
}
#include <stdio.h>
#include <string.h>
#include <unistd.h>
#include <sys/types.h>
#include <sys/stat.h>
#include <fcntl.h>
#include "np.h"

NamedPipe::NamedPipe() :
  init_(false),
  fp_(static_cast<int>(0)),
  name_(static_cast<char*>(0))
{
}

NamedPipe::~NamedPipe()
{
  if (init_)
```

```
    Destroy();
}

int NamedPipe::Create()
{
  char name[] = "NP";

  umask(0);

  int stat = mknod(name, S_IFIFO | 0666, 0);

  name_ = new char[strlen(name)];
  strcpy(name_, name);
  init_ = true;
}

int NamedPipe::Open()
{
  // the key to non b,locking IO is the O_NONBLOCK flag
  fp_ = open(name_, O_RDWR | O_NONBLOCK);
}

int NamedPipe::Close()
{
  close(fp_);
  fp_ = static_cast<int>(0);
}

int NamedPipe::Create(char* name)
{
  mknod(name, S_IFIFO|0666, 0);

  name_ = new char[strlen(name)];
  strcpy(name_, name);
  init_ = true;
}

int NamedPipe::Destroy()
{
  if (fp_ != 0)
    close(fp_);

  delete []name_;
  init_ = false;
}

int NamedPipe::Read(char* buf, int len)
{
  len = read(fp_, buf, len);

  return len;
```

D

```
}

int NamedPipe::Write(char* buf, int len)
{
  write(fp_, buf, len);

  return len;
}
// Listing 25.3 Named pipe class
#if !defined(c_np_h)
#define c_np_h

#include <sys/types.h>
#include <sys/stat.h>
#include <stdio.h>
#include <lst25-01.h>

class NamedPipe : public Object
{
 public:
  NamedPipe();
  ~NamedPipe();

  int Create();
  int Create(char* name);
  int Destroy();

  int Open();
  int Close();

  int Read(char* buf, int len);
  int Write(char* buf, int len);

 private:
  NamedPipe& operator=(const NamedPipe&);      // disallow copy

  bool    init_;
  int     fp_;
  char*   name_;
};

#endif

INCLUDES=-I../inc -I../Key
CFLAGS=-c
OBJS= ../obj/key.o ../obj/np.o

all: client server

np.o : np.cxx np.h
```

```
        gcc $(CFLAGS) -o np.o np.cxx $(INCLUDES)
        cp np.o ../obj

client.o : client.cxx
        gcc $(CFLAGS) -o client.o client.cxx $(INCLUDES)

server.o : server.cxx
        gcc $(CFLAGS) -o server.o server.cxx $(INCLUDES)

client: np.o client.o
        gcc -o client client.o $(OBJS) -lstdc++

server: np.o server.o
        gcc -o server server.o $(OBJS) -lstdc++
```

D

Day 26

Quiz

1. What is the difference between event-driven programs and procedural ones?

   A procedural program starts at the beginning and works its way through to the end, following its control paths depending upon inputs. An event-driven program waits in a loop for events to impinge upon it from the outside world and then acts in response to those events.

2. What is a widget, in computing terms?

   In computing terms, a *widget* is an element of a graphical user interface (GUI) that displays information or provides a specific way for a user to interact with the operating system and application programs.

3. What is a callback function, and why are these prone to errors?

   A callback function is a function call that is passed by *reference* to another function. Callbacks are often defined with type (void)(*func)(), which means that the compiler cannot know at compile time whether the function being passed is of a suitable type. Even if the type declaration is safe, unscrupulous programmers can use type-casting to dire effect. Worse than this, the pointer can also be NULL or invalid, both of which usually lead to the dreaded core dump.

4. What is a Qt slot, and how does it react to Qt signals?

   A Qt slot is a normal member function, which you have linked to a signal using the connect() function. Slots connected to signals in this way will be invoked when the connected signal is emitted by the specified object.

5. Signals and slots are typesafe. What does this mean and why is it a good thing?

   Slots and signals are always of the correct types, which means a slot never receives the wrong type of signal and you don't get core dumps from them. In fact, slots and signals are loosely coupled in that an object emitting a signal doesn't know or care if its signal has been caught by a slot or completely ignored.

6. How would you tie the following wxWindows event handler to a EVT_MENU event from a menu item with an ID of ID_MY_HELP? Assume OnHelp() is a member of the class MyFrame, and MyFrame is derived from wxFrame.

   ```
   void OnHelp (wxCommandEvent& WXUNUSED(event));
   ```

   With this event table declaration:

   ```
   BEGIN_EVENT_TABLE(MyFrame, wxFrame)
        EVT_MENU(ID_MY_HELP, MyFrame::OnHelp)
   END_EVENT_TABLE()
   ```

7. What does the IMPLEMENT_APP() macro do?

   The IMPLEMENT_APP() macro implements the main() function of a wxWindows application and hides the detail of the main event loop from the programmer.

8. What does the Q_OBJECT macro do?

   The Q_OBJECT macro is used by the Meta Object Compiler to turn the Qt-specific signals: and slots: sections in KDE class declarations into the form that the standard C++ compiler can understand.

Exercises

1. Using the buttons.cc source file as a base, extend the program so that the callback class puts up a dialog box when you click the buttons rather than writing directly to stdout.

   Here you will see that we create a new static member function callback::do_message() as our callback function. In it, we create a dialog box with a call to gnome_message_box_new() and display it with gnome_dialog_run(). We then call do_message() from the callback functions we connected with gtk_signal_connect() in main().

   ```
   /* the very basic gnome include */
   #include <gnome.h>

   class callback {
     public:
       static void button_clicked(GtkWidget *button, gpointer data);
       static gint delete_event(GtkWidget *widget,
   ⮥GdkEvent *event, gpointer data);
     private:
   ```

```
    static void do_message(const char*);
};

void
callback::do_message(const char * msg)
{
  GtkWidget *dialogue;
  int ret;
  dialogue = gnome_message_box_new (
                   msg,
                   "",
                   "OK",
                   NULL);
  ret = gnome_dialog_run (GNOME_DIALOG (dialogue));

}

void
callback::button_clicked(GtkWidget *button, gpointer data)
{
  do_message((char*)data);
}

/* called when the user closes the window */
gint
callback::delete_event(GtkWidget *widget, GdkEvent *event,
➥gpointer data)
{
        /* signal the main loop to quit */
        g_print("using C++ callback to quit\n");
        gtk_main_quit();
        /* return FALSE to continue closing the window */
        return FALSE;
}

int
main(int argc, char *argv[])
{
        GtkWidget *app;
        GtkWidget *button;
        GtkWidget *hbox;

        /* Initialize GNOME, this is very similar to gtk_init */
        gnome_init ("buttons-basic-example", "0.1", argc, argv);

        /* Create a Gnome app widget, which sets up a basic window
           for your application */
        app = gnome_app_new ("buttons-basic-example",
                                "Buttons");

        /* bind "delete_event", which is the event we get when
```

```
        the user closes the window with the window manager,
        to gtk_main_quit, which is a function that causes
        the gtk_main loop to exit, and consequently to quit
        the application */
    gtk_signal_connect (GTK_OBJECT (app), "delete_event",
                        GTK_SIGNAL_FUNC (callback::delete_event),
                        NULL);

    /* create a horizontal box for the buttons and add it
       into the app widget */
    hbox = gtk_hbox_new (FALSE,5);
    gnome_app_set_contents (GNOME_APP (app), hbox);

    /* make a button and add it into the horizontal box,
       and bind the clicked event to call button_clicked */
    button = gtk_button_new_with_label("Button 1");
    gtk_box_pack_start (GTK_BOX(hbox), button, FALSE, FALSE, 0);
    gtk_signal_connect (GTK_OBJECT (button), "clicked",
             GTK_SIGNAL_FUNC (callback::button_clicked),
                        "Button 1\n");

    /* and another button */
    button = gtk_button_new_with_label("Button 2");
    gtk_box_pack_start (GTK_BOX(hbox), button, FALSE, FALSE, 0);
    gtk_signal_connect (GTK_OBJECT (button), "clicked",
             GTK_SIGNAL_FUNC (callback::button_clicked),
                        "Button 2\n");

    /* show everything inside this app widget and the app
       widget itself */
    gtk_widget_show_all(app);

    /* enter the main loop */
    gtk_main ();

    return 0;
}
```

2. Taking either the final wxWindows or KDE example as a basis, extend the code to display a file-browse button that will enable you to select a file using a standard file-selection dialog.

You will see in ex26-02KDE.h that we have added an extra button member variable, m_btnBrowse. We initialize this by creating a new button in ex26-02KDE.cxx and use the signal/slot mechanism to connect it to the SlotBrowse() handler of the application. In the handler itself we use the static member function QFileDialog::getOpenFileName() to open a standard file-browsing dialog. Note that we #include "ex26KDE-01.moc" even though we do not have this file in our listings. This is normal because the MOC creates the .moc file for us when it processes the header files.

D

```
/*
 * ex26-01KDE.h
 */

#include <kapp.h>
#include <ktmainwindow.h>
#include <qpushbutton.h>
#include <kmenubar.h>
#include <qpopupmenu.h>

class KDEHelloWorld : public KTMainWindow
{
  Q_OBJECT
public:
  KDEHelloWorld();
  void closeEvent(QCloseEvent *);
public slots:
  void SlotGreet();
  void SlotQuit();
  void SlotBrowse();
private:
  QPushButton *m_btnGreet;
  QPushButton *m_btnQuit;
  QPushButton *m_btnBrowse;
  KMenuBar *m_Menu;
  QPopupMenu *m_MenuApp;
};

/*
 * ex26-01KDE.cxx
 */

#include "ex26KDE-01.moc"
#include <kapp.h>
#include <ktmainwindow.h>
#include <kmsgbox.h>

KDEHelloWorld::KDEHelloWorld() : KTMainWindow()
{
  m_btnGreet = new QPushButton("Greet", this);
  m_btnGreet->setGeometry(45,30,50,20);
  m_btnGreet->show();
  connect(m_btnGreet, SIGNAL(clicked()), this, SLOT(SlotGreet()));

  m_btnQuit = new QPushButton("Exit", this);
  m_btnQuit->setGeometry(105,30,50,20);
  m_btnQuit->show();
  connect(m_btnQuit, SIGNAL(clicked()), this, SLOT(SlotQuit()));

  m_btnQuit = new QPushButton("Browse", this);
  m_btnQuit->setGeometry(155,30,50,20);
```

```
  m_btnQuit->show();
  connect(m_btnQuit, SIGNAL(clicked()), this, SLOT(SlotBrowse()));

  m_MenuApp = new QPopupMenu();
  m_MenuApp->insertItem("&Greet", this, SLOT(SlotGreet()));
  m_MenuApp->insertItem("&Quit", this, SLOT(SlotQuit()));
  m_MenuApp->insertItem("&Browse", this, SLOT(SlotBrowse()));
  m_Menu = new KMenuBar(this);
  m_Menu->insertItem("&Application", m_MenuApp);
}

void KDEHelloWorld::closeEvent(QCloseEvent *)
{
  kapp->quit();
}

void KDEHelloWorld::SlotGreet()
{
  KMsgBox::message(0,"KDEHelloWorld","Hello World!");
}

void KDEHelloWorld::SlotBrowse()
{
    QString fileName = QFileDialog::getOpenFileName(
➥QString::null, QString::null, this );
}

void KDEHelloWorld::SlotQuit()
{
  close();
}


int main( int argc, char **argv )
{
  KApplication MyApp( argc, argv );
  KTMainWindow *MyWindow = new KTMainWindow();
  MyWindow->setGeometry(50,50,200,100);

  MyApp.setMainWidget( MyWindow );
  MyWindow->show();
  return MyApp.exec();
}


//compile these files with the commands:
//moc ex26-01KDE.h -o ex26-01KDE.moc
//g++ -c -I$KDEDIR/include -I$QTDIR -fno-rtti ex26-01KDE.cxx
//g++ -L$KDEDIR/lib -lkdecore -lkdeui -lqt -o ex26-01KDE ex26-01KDE.o
```

In ex26-02wxWin.cxx, we have added an extra button member variable, m_btnBrowse in the MyFrame class declaration. We initialize the member and create our button in the MyFrame() constructor and connect the event ID, ID_Browse, to the handler MyFrame::OnBrowse() in the EVENT_TABLE() declaration. When you click the button, the handler invokes wxFileSelector() to display a standard file-browse dialog.

```
/*
 * ex26-02wxWin.cxx
 */


#ifdef __GNUG__
// #pragma implementation
#endif

// For compilers that support precompilation, includes "wx/wx.h".
#include "wx/wxprec.h"

#ifdef __BORLANDC__
#pragma hdrstop
#endif

#ifndef WX_PRECOMP
#include "wx/wx.h"
#endif


class MyApp: public wxApp
{
    virtual bool OnInit();
};

class MyFrame: public wxFrame
{
public:

    MyFrame(const wxString& title, const wxPoint& pos,
➥const wxSize& size);
    void OnQuit(wxCommandEvent& event);
    void OnGreet(wxCommandEvent& event);
    void OnBrowse(wxCommandEvent& event);
    DECLARE_EVENT_TABLE()
private :
    wxPanel *m_panel;
    wxButton *m_btnGreet;
    wxButton *m_btnQuit;
    wxButton *m_btnBrowse;
};
```

D

```
enum
{
    ID_Quit = 1,
    ID_Greet,
    ID_Browse,
};

BEGIN_EVENT_TABLE(MyFrame, wxFrame)
    EVT_MENU(ID_Quit, MyFrame::OnQuit)
    EVT_MENU(ID_Greet, MyFrame::OnGreet)
    EVT_BUTTON(ID_Greet, MyFrame::OnGreet)
    EVT_BUTTON(ID_Quit, MyFrame::OnQuit)
    EVT_BUTTON(ID_Browse, MyFrame::OnBrowse)
END_EVENT_TABLE()

IMPLEMENT_APP(MyApp)

bool MyApp::OnInit()
{
    MyFrame *frame = new MyFrame( "Hello World",
➥wxPoint(50,50), wxSize(200,100) );
    frame->Show(TRUE);
    SetTopWindow(frame);
    return TRUE;
}


MyFrame::MyFrame(const wxString& title,
➥const wxPoint& pos, const wxSize& size)
: wxFrame((wxFrame *)NULL, -1, title, pos, size)
{

    wxSize panelSize = GetClientSize();
    const int buttonWidth=50;
    const int buttonHeight=25;
    const int buttonSpacing=10;
    const wxSize buttonSize(buttonWidth, buttonHeight);



    int height = panelSize.GetHeight();
    int width = panelSize.GetWidth();
    m_panel = new wxPanel(this, -1, wxPoint(0, 0), panelSize);

    m_btnGreet  = new wxButton(m_panel, ID_Greet,
                            _T("Greet..."),
                            wxPoint((width/2)-
➥(buttonWidth/2+buttonWidth+buttonSpacing), 10), buttonSize);
    m_btnQuit  = new wxButton(m_panel, ID_Quit,
```

```
                              _T("Quit"),
                              wxPoint((width/2)-(buttonWidth/2),
➡10), buttonSize);

    m_btnBrowse  = new wxButton(m_panel, ID_Browse,
                              _T("Browse..."),
                              wxPoint((width/2)+
➡(buttonWidth/2+buttonSpacing), 10), buttonSize);

    wxMenu *menuApp = new wxMenu;

    menuApp->Append( ID_Greet, "&Greet..." );
    menuApp->Append( ID_Browse, "&Browse..." );
    menuApp->AppendSeparator();
    menuApp->Append( ID_Quit, "&Quit" );

    wxMenuBar *menuBar = new wxMenuBar;
    menuBar->Append( menuApp , "&Application" );

    SetMenuBar( menuBar );

}


void MyFrame::OnQuit(wxCommandEvent& WXUNUSED(event))
{
    Close(TRUE);
}

void MyFrame::OnBrowse(wxCommandEvent& WXUNUSED(event))
{
    const wxString& file = ::wxFileSelector("Select a file");
}

void MyFrame::OnGreet(wxCommandEvent& WXUNUSED(event))
{
    wxMessageBox("This is a wxWindows Hello world sample",
        "Greet: Hello World", wxOK ¦ wxICON_INFORMATION, this);
}


// compile this file with the command
// gcc -g -Wall `gnome-config —cflags gnome gnomeui \
//`LDFLAGS=`gnome-config \
// —libs gnome gnomeui` ex26-02wxWin.cxx -o ex26-02wxWin
```

3. Extend the code from Exercise 2 so that when you click OK and select the file, the program displays it in a text control on the main window.

We further extend the `KDEHelloWorld` class declaration in `ex26-03KDE.h` to include a `QString` member variable to hold the name of the file we selected, and a `QTextView` control that displays text in its client area. We create the text view in the constructor and position it arbitrarily on the main window.

We then extend the `SlotBrowse()` slot function to take the filename from the file-browse dialog, and then use it to initialize a `QFile` object. We open the file with the `open()` member of `QFile`, and loop around reading a line at a time until we have read the entire file into a temporary string object. We then set this string as the text to be displayed in the text-view object. This is a very simplistic approach and deals only with text files: if you read in a binary file, you may see some odd results.

```
/*
 * ex26-03KDE.h
 */

#include <kapp.h>
#include <ktmainwindow.h>
#include <qpushbutton.h>
#include <kmenubar.h>
#include <qpopupmenu.h>

class KDEHelloWorld : public KTMainWindow
{
  Q_OBJECT
public:
  KDEHelloWorld();
  void closeEvent(QCloseEvent *);
public slots:
  void SlotGreet();
  void SlotQuit();
  void SlotBrowse();
private:
  QPushButton *m_btnGreet;
  QPushButton *m_btnQuit;
  QPushButton *m_btnBrowse;
  QTextView   *m_textView;
  QString *m_fileName;

  KMenuBar *m_Menu;
  QPopupMenu *m_MenuApp;
};
/*
 * ex26-03KDE.cxx
 */

#include "ex26KDE-03.moc"
#include <kapp.h>
#include <ktmainwindow.h>
```

D

```
#include <kmsgbox.h>

KDEHelloWorld::KDEHelloWorld() : KTMainWindow()
{
  m_btnGreet = new QPushButton("Greet", this);
  m_btnGreet->setGeometry(45,30,50,20);
  m_btnGreet->show();
  connect(m_btnGreet, SIGNAL(clicked()), this, SLOT(SlotGreet()));

  m_btnQuit = new QPushButton("Exit", this);
  m_btnQuit->setGeometry(105,30,50,20);
  m_btnQuit->show();
  connect(m_btnQuit, SIGNAL(clicked()), this, SLOT(SlotQuit()));

  m_btnQuit = new QPushButton("Browse", this);
  m_btnQuit->setGeometry(155,30,50,20);
  m_btnQuit->show();
  connect(m_btnQuit, SIGNAL(clicked()), this, SLOT(SlotBrowse()));

  m_textView = new QTextView( this );
  m_textView->setMinimumSize( 450, 250 );
  m_textView->show();

  m_MenuApp = new QPopupMenu();
  m_MenuApp->insertItem("&Greet", this, SLOT(SlotGreet()));
  m_MenuApp->insertItem("&Quit", this, SLOT(SlotQuit()));
  m_MenuApp->insertItem("&Browse", this, SLOT(SlotBrowse()));
  m_Menu = new KMenuBar(this);
  m_Menu->insertItem("&Application", m_MenuApp);
}

void KDEHelloWorld::closeEvent(QCloseEvent *)
{
  kapp->quit();
}

void KDEHelloWorld::SlotGreet()
{
  KMsgBox::message(0,"KDEHelloWorld","Hello World!");
}

void KDEHelloWorld::SlotBrowse()
{
    m_fileName = QFileDialog::getOpenFileName( QString::null,
➥QString::null, this );

    if(!fileName.IsEmpty()) {
    // we need to read the file

      QFile theFile(m_fileName);
```

```
        if ( theFile.open(IO_ReadOnly) ) {// file opened successfully
            QTextStream theStream( &theFile );   // use a text stream
            QString text;
            int n = 1;
            while ( !theStream.eof() ) {          // until end of file...
                text += theStream.readLine();
➡ // line of text excluding '\n'
            }
        theFile.close();
        m_textView.setText(text);
      }
    }
}

void KDEHelloWorld::SlotQuit()
{
  close();
}


int main( int argc, char **argv )
{
  KApplication MyApp( argc, argv );
  KTMainWindow *MyWindow = new KTMainWindow();
  MyWindow->setGeometry(100,100,500,500);

  MyApp.setMainWidget( MyWindow );
  MyWindow->show();
  return MyApp.exec();
}


//compile these files with the commands:
//moc ex26-03KDE.h -o ex26-03KDE.moc
//g++ -c -I$KDEDIR/include -I$QTDIR -fno-rtti ex26-03KDE.cxx
//g++ -L$KDEDIR/lib -lkdecore -lkdeui -lqt -o ex26-03KDE ex26-03KDE.o
```

This is simpler than the KDE version. We add a wxTextCtrl to the MyFrame class declared in ex26-03wxWin.cxx, as well as a wxString to hold the filename. This is almost identical to what we did for the KDE example. We initialize the text control in the MyFrame constructor. In the event handler, MyFrame::OnBrowse(), opening and displaying the file is as simple as retrieving its filename and then instructing the text control to load its data from that file by calling LoadFile() on the text control object.

```
/*
 * ex26-03wxWin.cxx
 */
```

D

```
#ifdef __GNUG__
// #pragma implementation
#endif

// For compilers that support precompilation, includes "wx/wx.h".
#include "wx/wxprec.h"

#ifdef __BORLANDC__
#pragma hdrstop
#endif

#ifndef WX_PRECOMP
#include "wx/wx.h"
#endif


class MyApp: public wxApp
{
    virtual bool OnInit();
};

class MyFrame: public wxFrame
{
public:

    MyFrame(const wxString& title, const wxPoint& pos,
const wxSize& size);
    void OnQuit(wxCommandEvent& event);
    void OnGreet(wxCommandEvent& event);
    void OnBrowse(wxCommandEvent& event);
    DECLARE_EVENT_TABLE()
private :
    wxPanel *m_panel;
    wxButton *m_btnGreet;
    wxButton *m_btnQuit;
    wxButton *m_btnBrowse;
    wxString m_fileName;
    wxTextCtrl *m_textViewer;
};


enum
{
    ID_Quit = 1,
ID_Greet,
ID_Browse,
};

BEGIN_EVENT_TABLE(MyFrame, wxFrame)
    EVT_MENU(ID_Quit, MyFrame::OnQuit)
    EVT_MENU(ID_Greet, MyFrame::OnGreet)
```

```
        EVT_BUTTON(ID_Greet, MyFrame::OnGreet)
        EVT_BUTTON(ID_Quit, MyFrame::OnQuit)
        EVT_BUTTON(ID_Browse, MyFrame::OnBrowse)
END_EVENT_TABLE()

IMPLEMENT_APP(MyApp)

bool MyApp::OnInit()
{
    MyFrame *frame = new MyFrame( "Hello World",
➥wxPoint(50,50), wxSize(500,500) );
    frame->Show(TRUE);
    SetTopWindow(frame);
    return TRUE;
}


MyFrame::MyFrame(const wxString& title, const wxPoint& pos,
➥const wxSize& size)
: wxFrame((wxFrame *)NULL, -1, title, pos, size)
{

    wxSize panelSize = GetClientSize();
    const int buttonWidth=50;
    const int buttonHeight=25;
    const int buttonSpacing=10;
    const wxSize buttonSize(buttonWidth, buttonHeight);


    int height = panelSize.GetHeight();
    int width = panelSize.GetWidth();
    m_panel = new wxPanel(this, -1, wxPoint(0, 0), panelSize);

    m_btnGreet  = new wxButton(m_panel, ID_Greet,
                        _T("Greet..."),
                        wxPoint((width/2)-
(buttonWidth/2+buttonWidth+buttonSpacing), 10), buttonSize);
    m_btnQuit  = new wxButton(m_panel, ID_Quit,
                        _T("Quit"),
                        wxPoint((width/2)-(buttonWidth/2),
➥10), buttonSize);

    m_btnBrowse = new wxButton(m_panel, ID_Browse,
                        _T("Browse..."),
                        wxPoint((width/2)+
➥(buttonWidth/2+buttonSpacing), 10), buttonSize);

    m_textViewer = new wxTextCtrl(m_panel, ID_Browse,
                        _T(""),
                        wxPoint(10,40),
```

```
➥wxSize(width-20,height-100),
                              wxHSCROLL¦wxTE_MULTILINE¦wxTE_READONLY);

    wxMenu *menuApp = new wxMenu;

    menuApp->Append( ID_Greet, "&Greet..." );
    menuApp->Append( ID_Browse, "&Browse..." );
    menuApp->AppendSeparator();
    menuApp->Append( ID_Quit, "&Quit" );

    wxMenuBar *menuBar = new wxMenuBar;
    menuBar->Append( menuApp , "&Application" );

    SetMenuBar( menuBar );

}


void MyFrame::OnQuit(wxCommandEvent& WXUNUSED(event))
{
    Close(TRUE);
}

void MyFrame::OnBrowse(wxCommandEvent& WXUNUSED(event))
{
    m_fileName = ::wxFileSelector("Select a file");
    if(!m_fileName.IsEmpty()) {
      m_textViewer->LoadFile(m_fileName);
      }
}

void MyFrame::OnGreet(wxCommandEvent& WXUNUSED(event))
{
    wxMessageBox("This is a wxWindows Hello world sample",
        "Greet: Hello World", wxOK ¦ wxICON_INFORMATION, this);
}


// compile this file with the command
// gcc -g -Wall `gnome-config —cflags gnome gnomeui\
//`LDFLAGS=`gnome-config \
// —libs gnome gnomeui` ex26-03wxWin.cxx -o ex26-03wxWin
```

4. Look at your results from Exercise 1 and consider how you might wrap the entire application into one class. Consider why you might want to implement the callback functions as private static members of the class and expose only "wrappers" that call them when the user triggers events. See the function do_message() in file ex26-01.cxx for example. Think how you might extend the idea to create a generic wrapper for the application and use virtual functions for setting the main window and connecting signals.

You can see that in `ex26-04.cxx` we have created a new class, `TheAppClass`, and in it we declare the Gtk widgets that represent the application and the box that contains the buttons as member variables.

We create the buttons themselves in `CreateWidgets()` and pack them into the box. Note that the new class encapsulates all the widgets we are using, and static member functions of this same class will handle the events that arise when you click the buttons.

This means that all we need to do in `main()` is instantiate the application object, tell it to create its own widgets, and then tell it to run itself.

```
/*
  ex26-04.cxx - wrapping the app as a class. You can expand this
  to any degree of abstraction you like
*/

#include <gnome.h>

class TheAppClass {
  public:
    TheAppClass(int argc, char* argv[]);
    virtual gint CreateWidgets();
    void Run();
  private:
    static void button_clicked(GtkWidget *button, gpointer data);
    static gint delete_event(GtkWidget *widget, GdkEvent *event,
➥gpointer data);
    static void do_message(const char*);

    GtkWidget *app;
    GtkWidget *hbox;

};

gint
TheAppClass::CreateWidgets()
{
  GtkWidget *button=0;

  button = gtk_button_new_with_label("Button 1");
  gtk_box_pack_start (GTK_BOX(hbox), button, FALSE, FALSE, 0);

  gtk_signal_connect (GTK_OBJECT (button), "clicked",
                      GTK_SIGNAL_FUNC (TheAppClass::button_clicked),
                      "Button 1");

  button = gtk_button_new_with_label("Button 2");
  gtk_box_pack_start (GTK_BOX(hbox), button, FALSE, FALSE, 0);
  gtk_signal_connect (GTK_OBJECT (button), "clicked",
```

```
                                GTK_SIGNAL_FUNC (TheAppClass::button_clicked),
                                "Button 2");
    return 0;
}

TheAppClass::TheAppClass(int argc, char* argv[])
{

    gnome_init ("buttons-basic-example", "0.1", argc, argv);

    app = gnome_app_new ("buttons-basic-example",
➥"Class-Wrapped Buttons");

    gtk_signal_connect (GTK_OBJECT (app), "delete_event",
                        GTK_SIGNAL_FUNC (TheAppClass::delete_event),
                        NULL);

    hbox = gtk_hbox_new (FALSE,5);

    gnome_app_set_contents (GNOME_APP (app), hbox);

}

void
TheAppClass::do_message(const char * msg)
{
    GtkWidget *dialogue;
    int ret;
    dialogue = gnome_message_box_new (
                    msg,
                    "",
                    "OK",
                    NULL);
    ret = gnome_dialog_run (GNOME_DIALOG (dialogue));

}

void
TheAppClass::button_clicked(GtkWidget *button, gpointer data)
{
    do_message((char*)data);
}

/* called when the user closes the window */
gint
TheAppClass::delete_event(GtkWidget *widget, GdkEvent *event,
➥gpointer data)
{
    gtk_main_quit();
    return FALSE;
}
```

```
void
TheAppClass::Run()
{
  gtk_widget_show_all(app);
  gtk_main ();
}

int
main(int argc, char *argv[])
{
  TheAppClass MyApp(argc, argv);
  MyApp.CreateWidgets();
  MyApp.Run();
  return 0;
}

// compile this file with the command
/*
  gcc -g -Wall `gnome-config —cflags gnome gnomeui\
`LDFLAGS=`gnome-config \
 —libs gnome gnomeui` ex26-04.cxx -o ex26-04.cxx
*/
```

INDEX

SYMBOLS

! (logical NOT operator), 92

!= (not equal operator), 80

" " (quotation marks), placing around strings, 757

(pound symbol), 30, 748

#define statement
constant substitutions, 749
listing, 749-750
string substitutions, 748
tests, 749

#else precompiler command, 749-751

#ifdef precompiler command, 749

#ifndef precompiler command, 749

#include directive, 101-102, 748

% (modulus operator), 72-73

& (AND operator), 775

& (reference operator), 260-262, 284-285

&& (logical AND operator), 91-92

( ) (parentheses), 78
grouping, 93
macro syntax, 753-754
nesting, 78-79

> (greater than) operator, 81

> (output redirect character), 838

>= (greater than or equals) operator, 81

; (semicolon), 68

~ (tilde), 159

* (indirection operator), 229-230, 284-285

+ (addition operator), 317-320

++ (increment operator), 75-77

++ (prefix operator), 308-310

+= (self-assigned addition operator), 74

- (decrement operator), 75
postfix, 75-77
prefix, 77

- (subtraction operator), 71-72

. (dot operator), 155, 241

/< comments, 34, 41

// comments, 34, 41

/proc file system, 858

:: (scope resolution operator), 601

< (less than) operator, 32, 81

<< (insertion operator), 549, 553, 698

<< (redirection operator), 21, 31

<= (less than or equals) operator, 81

= (assignment operator), 51, 68, 71, 321-322, 324
confused with equals (= =) operator, 80
listing, 322-323
precedence, 78

= 0 notation, 441

== (equals operator), 80

Read This Before Opening the Software

By opening this package, you are agreeing to be bound by the following agreement:

You may not copy or redistribute the entire CD-ROM as a whole. Copying and redistribution of individual software programs on the CD-ROM is governed by terms set by individual copyright holders.

The installer and code from the author(s) are copyrighted by the publisher and author(s). Individual programs and other items on the CD-ROM are copyrighted by their various authors or other copyright holders. Some of the programs included with this product may be governed by the GNU General Public License, which allows redistribution; see the license information for each product for more information.

Other programs are included on the CD-ROM by special permission from their authors.

This software is provided as-is without warranty of any kind, either expressed or implied, including but not limited to the implied warranties of merchantability and fitness for a particular purpose. Neither the publisher nor its dealers or distributors assume any liability for any alleged or actual damages arising from the use of this program. (Some states do not allow for the exclusion of implied warranties, so the exclusion may not apply to you.)

CD-ROM Installation

Windows 95/98/NT/2000 Installation Instructions

1. Insert the CD-ROM disc into your CD-ROM drive.
2. From the Windows 95 desktop, double-click on the My Computer icon.
3. Double-click on the icon representing your CD-ROM drive.
4. Open the README.txt file for descriptions of Third Party products.

Linux and UNIX Installation Instructions

These installation instructions assume that you have a passing familiarity with UNIX commands and the basic setup of your machine. As UNIX has many flavors, only generic commands are used. If you have any problems with these commands, please consult the appropriate man page or your system administrator.

Insert CD-ROM in CD drive.

If you have a volume manager, mounting of the CD-ROM will be automatic. If you don't have a volume manager, you can mount the CD-ROM by typing the following:

Mount -tiso9660 /dev/cdrom /mnt/cdrom

 Note

/mnt/cdrom is just a mount point, but it must exist when you issue the mount command. You may also use any empty directory for a mount point if you don't want to use /mnt/cdrom.

Open the readme.txt file for descriptions of Third Party products.

Operator Precedence and Associativity

Level	Description	Operators	Evaluation Order
1	Scope resolution (binary, unary)	: :	left to right
2	Function calls, parentheses, subscripting, member selection, postfix increment and decrement	() [] . -> ++ —	left to right
3	sizeof, C++ casting, prefix increment and decrement, unary plus and minus, negation, complement, C casting, sizeof(), address of, dereference new, new[], delete, delete[]	++ — + - ! ~ (cast) & *	right to left
4	Member selection for pointer.	* ->*	left to right
5	Multiply, divide, modulus	* / %	left to right
6	Add, subtract	+ -	left to right
7	Bitwise shift	<< >>	left to right
8	Inequality relational	< <= > >=	left to right
9	Equality, inequality	== !=	left to right
10	Bitwise AND	&	left to right
11	Bitwise exclusive OR	^	left to right
12	Bitwise OR	|	left to right
13	Logical AND	&&	left to right
14	Logical OR	||	left to right
15	Conditional	?:	right to left
16	Assignment operators	= *= /= %= += -= <<= >>= &= | = ^=	right to left
17	Comma	,	

Operators at the top of the table have higher precedence than operators below. In expressions beginning with arguments in the innermost set of parentheses (if any), programs evaluate operators of higher precedence before evaluating operators of lower precedence.

In the absence of clarifying parentheses, operators on the same level are evaluated according to their left-to-right or right-to-left evaluation order.

Operators That May Be Overloaded

*	/	+	-	%	^	&	|	~	!	,
=	<	>	<=	>=	++	—	<<	>>	==	!=
&&	||	*=	/=	%=	^=	&=	| =	+=	-=	<<=
>>=	->	->*	[]	()	new	delete				

Operators +, -, *, and & may be overloaded for binary and unary expressions. Operators ., .*, ::, ?:, and sizeof may not be overloaded. In addition, =, (), [], and -> must be implemented as nonstatic member functions.

Standard Container Class Templates

Class Template	Description
vector	Linear sequence, similar to a C++ array.
list	Double-linked list.
deque	Double-ended queue.
set	Associative array of unique keys. A special form of a set capable of holding binary values is called a bit set.

continues